PASTOR AND LAITY IN
THE THEOLOGY OF
JEAN GERSON

PASTOR AND LAITY IN THE THEOLOGY OF JEAN GERSON

D. CATHERINE BROWN

Assistant Professor of History
Queen's University
Kingston, Ontario

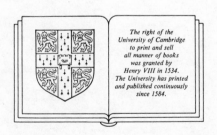

The right of the
University of Cambridge
to print and sell
all manner of books
was granted by
Henry VIII in 1534.
The University has printed
and published continuously
since 1584.

CAMBRIDGE UNIVERSITY PRESS

Cambridge
London   New York   New Rochelle
Melbourne   Sydney

Published by the Press Syndicate of the University of Cambridge
The Pitt Building, Trumpington Street, Cambridge CB2 1RP
32 East 57th Street, New York, NY 10022, USA
10 Stamford Road, Oakleigh, Melbourne 3166, Australia

First published 1987

Printed in Great Britain by
the University Press, Cambridge

British Library cataloguing in publication data
Brown, D. Catherine
Pastor and laity in the theology of Jean
Gerson.
1. Gerson, Jean
I. Title
230′.092′4   BX4705.G45

Library of Congress cataloguing in publication data
Brown, D. Catherine (Dorothy Catherine), 1928–
Pastor and laity in the theology of Jean Gerson.
Bibliography.
1. Pastoral theology – History of doctrines – Middle
Ages, 600–1500. 2. Preaching – History – Middle Ages,
600–1500. 3. Mysticism – History – Middle Ages, 600–1500.
4. Gerson, Jean, 1363–1429. I. Title.
BV4006.B76   1987   253.092′4   86-17092

ISBN 0 521 33029 7

For Norman, Paul, Hilary and Clare

CONTENTS

vii

PREFACE

Throughout the period during which this book has taken shape, I have received encouragement, support and help from many people. I should like to thank especially a number of my colleagues at Queen's University. Professor Christopher Crowder (my former supervisor) suggested Gerson to me as a subject of study, gently directed my research, and read, with an eagle eye, every version of the typescript. Dr James Stayer's graduate seminar on the Reformation introduced me to the historiography of late medieval theology, and Dr Stayer's friendly and patient criticism of my work has proved invaluable. Dr W. D. McCready and Dr P. Rogers both read an early version of the study and offered valuable suggestions and criticisms. Beyond the Queen's community, I received much encouragement and sound advice from Father Leonard Boyle, O.P. I should like to thank him and also the advisers to and the editor and sub-editor at Cambridge University Press for their helpful suggestions and assistance. Above all, I should like to thank my family for their patient tolerance and support during the years I have been engaged on this study, and especially my husband, whose willingness to discuss problems at length, to make suggestions and to proof-read has been of inestimable value.

D. CATHERINE BROWN

Queen's University, Kingston, Ontario
October 1986

ABBREVIATIONS

AHDLMA	*Archives d'Histoire doctrinale et littéraire du moyen âge*
Annales : E.S.C.	*Annales : economies, sociétés, civilisations*
CCSL	*Corpus Christianorum. Series Latina*
CH	Church History
CSEL	*Corpus scriptorum ecclesiasticorum Latinorum*
DTC	*Dictionnaire de théologie catholique*
EETS	Early English Text Society publications
FC	*The Fathers of the Church*
G	*Jean Gerson : Ouevres complètes*, ed. P. Glorieux, 10 vols. (Paris, 1960–73)
HTR	*Harvard Theological Review*
JEH	*Journal of Ecclesiastical History*
MPG	Migne, *Patrologia Graeca*
MPL	Migne, *Patrologia Latina*
MS	*Medieval Studies*
NCE	*The New Catholic Encyclopedia*
NPNF	*A Select Library of Nicene and Post-Nicene Fathers of the Christian Church*
P	*Jean Gerson : Opera omnia*, ed. L. Ellies du Pin, 4 vols. (Antwerp, 1706)
RHE	*Revue d'histoire ecclésiastique*
RMAL	*Revue du moyen âge latin*
RSR	*Revue des sciences religieuses*
RTAM	*Recherches de théologie ancienne et médiévale*
TRHS	*Transactions of the Royal Historical Society*
WA	*D. Martin Luthers Werke : Kritische Gesamtausgabe*

INTRODUCTION

Late medieval religion was generally depicted by historians of the first half of the twentieth century as decadent; its theology sterile and played out, its practice superficial and superstitious. For this 'waning' culture, it was sometimes argued, the sixteenth-century Reformation came as a just desert. In the last few decades, however, the fourteenth and fifteenth centuries have come under increasing scrutiny and it is now becoming apparent that the theology of the period, far from being 'worn out', was of a wide and rich variety, while its piety often displayed a genuine spirituality.[1] Yet there is still considerable obscurity and this is likely to remain until the sermons, tracts and other works, many still in manuscript, of more theologians of the period are edited and examined.

The purpose of the present study is to add another piece to the variegated picture of late medieval religion that is emerging. Its chief focus is on that part of Jean Gerson's teaching intended for the laity, either directly as it appears in his vernacular sermons and tracts, or indirectly as in his Latin works for pastors. This approach will shed light not only on Gerson's own thought and theological positions, but also to some degree on popular mentality. If we cannot often hear 'the voice of the people' in the medieval period, we can at least hear the ideas, attitudes and assumptions they were exposed to from the pulpit and the confessional. We may also discover – though here the ground is rather treacherous, for preachers and moralists frequently work with traditional commonplaces – something about the particular vices, virtues and practices of the day.

With Jean Gerson we are working, not with an obscure cleric, but with one of Europe's most influential churchmen of the early fifteenth century, and no mean theologian, especially in the area of pastoral theology. Despite his very wide interests and the prominent role he played in public life, he was above all a pastor. Concern for the spiritual welfare of the people lies at the centre of almost all his writings and activities. Even his university lectures reveal his preoccupation with *les simples gens*.[2] In these he never treats reflection on dogmas as a purely theoretical activity but constantly keeps before his students' minds their future role as spiritual guides of the people. He himself was a very popular preacher, both in court circles and in parish churches in Paris. In fact, crowds used to follow him from church to church because of his ability to captivate his hearers.[3] An examination

of Gerson's sermons is, then, an examination of material heard by a
comparatively large number of people. The same is true of a fair number
of Gerson's vernacular tracts, which are extant in a large number of
manuscripts.[4] But Gerson's influence stretched well beyond his own
lifetime. On the eve of the Reformation many local French councils and
synods gave directions to the clergy to use some of Gerson's writings to
help them in the pastorate.[5] Even before the end of the fifteenth century
there had been six printed editions of his complete works[6] apart from the
numerous manuscripts and printed editions of single works or selected
groups of his writings that were produced during the century. The stream
continued into the sixteenth century and included three more complete
editions. Gerson's influence seems to have been particularly strong in
German-speaking areas, for the first printed editions were produced in
Cologne (1483), Strasburg (1488–9 and 1494), Nuremberg (1489), and
Basle (1489).[7] The Strasburg pastor Geiler was strongly influenced by
Gerson and translated a number of his works into German and adapted
them for preaching to the people. In fact it was Geiler who collected the
Gerson manuscripts that formed the material for the 1488–9 Strasburg
edition.[8] Biel of Tübingen, too, used Gerson as one of his major authorities,[9]
and the chancellor was an important source for John Pupper of Goch in
the mid fifteenth century and for Staupitz, Luther's mentor, in the early
sixteenth century,[10] while in France Gerson's influence was quite marked
in the sermons of Michel Menot.[11] Biel, Geiler and Menot were famous
preachers of their day, and so Gerson's influence would thus have spread
through them beyond the clergy to the laity. There must have been many
other preachers also who used the works of the *doctor Christianissimus* to
aid them in the cure of souls, and many pastors who relied on Gerson's
opinions in matters relating to sin and confession, judging from the number
of extant manuscripts of his works on this topic, and the number of times
his name was invoked by later moral theologians.[12] Thus an analysis of
Gerson's pastoral teaching is an analysis of what a fair number of the laity,
in France and Germany at least, were hearing and reading in the fifteenth
and early sixteenth centuries. Certainly it is not only the members of the
French court, the parishioners of a few Parisian churches and Gerson's
sisters, for whom some of the vernacular tracts were originally written, who
are involved here.

With Gerson, too, we are working with a theologian whose complete
works have recently been re-edited.[13] Most of the studies of Gerson done
before the 1960s were based on the 1706 edition by Ellies du Pin, now
known to be defective in numerous ways.[14] The new edition by Glorieux
is much better, but is not, unfortunately, a fully critical edition. Nevertheless, in so far as it has taken account of the recent critical editing done
by Gersonian scholars,[15] it can be used with confidence for the most part.[16]

Gerson's writings cover a wide variety of topics. In this century the topics that have so far attracted most attention are his ecclesiology and mysticism. In both areas major studies have been produced.[17] His pastoral theology as a whole has been less explored. Of the older works, J. L. Connolly's *Jean Gerson: Reformer and Mystic*[18] deals with some aspects of his pastoral teaching, but, as the title suggests, its focus is on Gerson's proposals for reform. Connolly's work, moreover, though still valuable, bears traces of the confessional bias that can be detected in many of the older studies on Gerson, as scholars tried to claim this attractive pastor and theologian for their side, by trying to show either that he was a Reformation Protestant manqué or that he was not a thoroughgoing nominalist or conciliarist,[19] and hence a more presentable Catholic.

Of the more recent works, L. Mourin's two books, *Six sermons français inédits de Jean Gerson* and *Jean Gerson, prédicateur français*, are the most valuable. In the former and in several articles,[20] Mourin has produced critical editions of a number of Gerson's sermons. The major contribution of the second book is its attempt to date all the vernacular sermons. Aside from this, Mourin's major focus is on the literary rather than the doctrinal aspects of the sermons, and he does not look at all at the vernacular tracts or pertinent Latin works. L. B. Pascoe's book *Jean Gerson: Principles of Church Reform*[21] is also valuable in that it contains discussions of Gerson's pastoral efforts. However, as it is primarily – and usefully – concerned with disclosing the ideological basis for Gerson's reform programme, its focus is entirely different from that presented here.

Even within the corpus of those writings that are of a direct pastoral importance, that is, sermons and tracts written in French for the laity, and Latin opuscules, sermons, lectures and treatises directed to the clergy on various aspects of pastoral work, Gerson touches on a wide variety of subjects. He writes not only on theological and ethical questions and spirituality, but also about ecclesiastical and secular politics and about numerous social and economic matters. By developing a number of these topics I hope to enable the reader to acquire the flavour of the sort of views being presented to the laity by one late medieval authority on the pastorate.

I

GERSON'S LIFE

Jean Gerson had a very humble beginning. Born on 14 December 1363, in the village of Gerson-lès-Barbey from which he later took his name, he was the eldest of the twelve children of Arnould le Charlier and his wife, Elizabeth.[1] The village lay in Champagne about two miles from the town of Rethel and in the diocese of Rheims. Although the village was ultimately within the overlordship of the Duke of Burgundy, Gerson's father was a tenant on the land of the Benedictine priory of Rethel. He supported his large family of five boys and seven girls by farming. One of the boys, Pierre, died while still a child, but the Charliers were able, though with some financial difficulty, to send the other four sons, all named Jean except for Nicholas, the youngest, to school, where they studied for the priesthood. All but Gerson himself eventually became monks.[2] Only one of Gerson's sisters married. One died as a child and the others remained at home forming for a time an informal pious community under the spiritual direction of their eldest brother, who guided them from afar by means of letters and tracts. Gerson's early formation was clearly in an atmosphere of fervent Christian piety. He makes several references in his letters and other works to the spiritual guidance and instruction afforded his siblings and himself by both his parents,[3] and there is abundant evidence of his mother's piety, spirituality and loving concern for her children in her letter to two of Gerson's brothers.[4] Whatever may have been the general level of Christian formation among the rural and urban populations of France, the Charlier family is an example of profound piety in a peasant milieu. Perhaps their residence in the ambience of a Benedictine priory had a notable effect on their lives.

Gerson probably began his formal education at that priory and then moved to the school attached to the mother house, the Abbey of Saint-Rémy, in Rheims.[5] From there, at the age of fourteen, he went to Paris to study at the university and was enrolled as a member of the College of Navarre, becoming at this time a centre of French humanism and enjoying a prestige equal to that of the Sorbonne.[6] One of his fellow students there was Nicholas de Clamanges, who, together with one of his teachers, Pierre d'Ailly, was to remain on terms of close friendship with Gerson for many years.

In 1381 Gerson received the degree of bachelor of arts and began his theological instruction. He followed the normal course of studies, attending lectures on the Bible for four years and on the *Sentences* for a further two. In 1387, now a bachelor of theology, Gerson lectured on the Bible for two years and on the *Sentences* for nine months. After this period of apprenticeship he became a *baccalarius formatus* and thereafter was expected to take a leading part in the public activities of the university, for example in disputations and preaching. In 1392, after the usual disputations, he was awarded the licentiate in theology and two years later the doctorate.

While still a young theology student, Gerson served as proctor of the French nation during the academic year 1383–4. In 1388, aged only twenty-four, he rose to prominence when he became a member of the university's embassy that went to Avignon to present to the pope the university's case in favour of the condemnation of the Dominican Jean de Monzon, who had argued against the doctrine of the Immaculate Conception. The embassy won its case and the Dominicans were expelled from the university, not to return until 1403. D'Ailly, by now rector of the College of Navarre and chaplain to the king and ambitious for even higher office, was also a member of the delegation. It was almost certainly through d'Ailly's influence that Gerson went to Avignon. Gerson was not only the pupil but the protégé of the rector, and his being a representative of the university in the defence of a doctrine traditionally dear to the hearts of the Parisian masters could only further his career.[7] It was in connection with this affair that Gerson wrote, in 1389, his treatise against Jean de Monzon.[8] Apart from this, no academic writings remain from these early years, but some of the sermons Gerson delivered are extant, of which the earliest is *Quaerite dominum*, preached in French on Ash Wednesday 1389 to the king and court.[9] It was again, no doubt, through the influence of d'Ailly, chancellor of the university by the fall of 1389, that Gerson began to preach at court so early in his career. But he soon established his own reputation as a preacher. Of the twelve or so vernacular sermons that remain from the 1390s almost all were preached before the court.[10] Meanwhile Gerson had acquired a powerful patron in the person of Philip, Duke of Burgundy, whose almoner he had become by 1393. In the same year he was provided by the duke to the deanery of the collegiate church of Saint-Donatien at Bruges, but he visited his benefice only rarely and for the most part his duties were carried out by deputy.[11]

In 1395 Gerson succeeded d'Ailly, now a bishop, as chancellor of the university. He held this office until his death and raised its formerly modest prestige to an entirely new level by his activities and strong personality. Its stature grew with Gerson's.[12] As chancellor, Gerson inevitably became more heavily involved in the initiatives of the university to end the schism, now almost twenty years old. Although a partisan of the *via cessionis* (way of resignation), Gerson opposed the growing movement in the university for withdrawal of obedience, because he feared that such action would

merely enlarge the schism.[13] His efforts proved unavailing and in 1398 a
synod of bishops, clergy and university officials voted in favour of withdrawal of obedience. This policy was adopted by the French government
but proved a failure as a means of ending the schism. It was not till 1403
and the replacement of Burgundian by Orleanist influence at court that
Benedict XIII was again recognised by France.

Gerson seems to have suffered from a crisis of discouragement during
this period. He became depressed, and dissatisfied with his public work.
He left Paris in June 1399 and went to Bruges, where he remained for a
comparatively lengthy period, not returning to Paris until September 1400.
The turmoil of mind and despair he felt at this time come across vividly
in the letter he sent to Paris in February 1400, giving reasons why he should
resign the chancellorship.[14] Each sentence of the first half of the letter
begins with 'Cogor' ('I am driven' or 'forced'). He complains of the
situation at court, where he feels buffeted by the rival factions and where
his words and actions are misconstrued and criticised. 'I am driven by these
and similar things to forget to say or to say absentmindedly my masses and
prayers.' His university duties are distasteful, for he is forced to confer
degrees on ignorant and incapable students and to listen to scandalous
doctrines. 'I have to overlook the false doctrines others teach, or with great
personal danger protest against them, if indeed one were allowed to
protest.' His own sermons are no good, for he has to preach to people who
listen only out of vain curiosity. His duties at court and the university force
him to neglect the cure of souls and his own spiritual progress. What he
wants to do, he says, is to take up a life of quiet contemplation, even if
people accuse him of fickleness because he now wants to resign the position
he once so assiduously sought. It is a sad – even pathetic – letter.

Somehow Gerson pulled himself out of this depression. His friends from
the College of Navarre and the Duke of Burgundy were able to persuade
him to return to Paris, though his departure from Bruges was delayed for
some months because of physical illness. But he had a burst of mental
energy during this time and drew up proposals for the reform of theological
studies at Paris. These he presented in a series of letters, the first, dated
1 April, to d'Ailly and the others, written later, to the members of the
College of Navarre.[15] His general aim in this quite detailed scheme was to
reduce the amount of 'vain' theological speculation that went on in the
faculty of theology and to promote the study of the Bible and the 'safe'
authors, such as Aquinas, Bonaventure, Richard of St Victor, Bernard and
Anselm. He also wanted more attention paid to the moral and spiritual
formation of the students and to their training for the tasks of the
pastorate.[16] This post-depression period in Bruges proved also very productive in another area that was of concern to Gerson – the religious
instruction of ordinary people. It was at Bruges that he wrote, initially for
his sisters, the *Montaigne de contemplation*, to be followed, after his return

to Paris, by the *Mendicité spirituelle*, both long treatises on the spiritual life, and extant in numerous manuscripts.[17] The years 1400–1 saw, in fact, the production of a whole series of vernacular tracts aimed at the Christian formation of the *simples gens*. Among these are works on the ten commandments, on temptations, on blasphemy, on scrupulosity, and on mortal and venial sin.[18]

Back in Paris, Gerson began lecturing to the theology students again, attempting in these lectures, which had as their texts verses from St Mark's Gospel, to carry out his plans for theological renewal.[19] This series of lectures continued, with many interruptions, until 1414. He also resumed preaching in the vernacular, but this time his audiences were composed of the people of the parishes of Paris rather than the court, for the bulk of the forty or so extant French sermons that probably date from the first four years of the fifteenth century was delivered to popular rather than courtly congregations.[20] Many of these sermons were preached in the parish of Saint-Jean-en-Grève, to which Gerson was granted the expectation in 1403.[21] He preached in other Parisian churches too, for example in Saint-Severin, Saint-Paul, and Saint-Germain.[22] The population of the parish of Saint-Jean-en-Grève was not composed only of poor people, for the tax rolls show that it contained numbers of officials and business men.[23] Moreover, certain remarks in some of Gerson's sermons preached here indicate an audience that included members of the middle and upper classes.

For the period after 1404 until he left Paris for good in 1415 there are virtually no popular sermons extant and Gerson seems to have returned to his earlier task of preaching before the king and court on special occasions.[24] This does not necessarily mean that he gave up popular preaching altogether, for sermons of this period could well be lost, or perhaps have been delivered only from brief notes that were not thought worth preserving. For the period after 1414 there are no further vernacular sermons of any kind, and after the Council of Constance, where Gerson preached at least ten sermons, there are only two further extant Latin sermons.[25] Nevertheless, Gerson had not fallen silent, as will be seen. The years of his popular preaching also saw the production of some more vernacular tracts, including the *Science de bien mourir*, which proved to be a very popular work, being extant in both French and Latin versions in numerous manuscripts.[26] After 1403 vernacular treatises become sparse.

One of the reasons for the slackening of Gerson's vigorous programme of popular preaching after 1403 was the fact that he became more involved in the movement to end the schism. After the restoration of obedience to Benedict XIII Gerson, with six other masters, left Paris in October 1403, to present a series of requests to the pope at Avignon. This visit to Avignon seems to have disillusioned the chancellor about Benedict's intentions to bring the schism to an end. However, the election of the apparently well-intentioned Gregory XII as Roman pope in 1406 gave Gerson – and others – new hope that the *via cessionis* would succeed. In March of 1407 a commission, including Gerson and d'Ailly, was sent by the French government to negotiate with both popes. Although absent for over a year the commission failed to achieve the abdication of either. The obvious bankruptcy of the *via cessionis* turned Gerson into a committed supporter of the *via concilii*. In 1409 the dissident cardinals of both papal courts convoked the Council of Pisa, and Gerson wrote several treatises defending this action.[27] Although he did not attend the council himself, he at once adhered to the new pope, Alexander V (1409–10), elected there. This did not, however, end the schism as neither of the other two popes would resign. Eventually the Pisan pope, now John XXIII (1410–15), had to yield to the pressure exerted by the Emperor Sigismund, and convoke the Council of Constance to resolve the situation. In February of 1415 Gerson left Paris for Constance as a delegate of the king, the university and the ecclesiastical province of Sens. His leading role in the council is well known. It was his sermon, *Ambulate*,[28] that was instrumental in calming the anxiety and confusion caused by John XXIII's sudden departure from the council in March 1415. Gerson urged the members to remain in session and produced arguments to justify the legitimacy of the council despite the absence of the pope. His arguments were accepted and eventually the council succeeded in getting rid of the three popes and elected Martin V. Gerson also played an important role in the condemnation of Wyclif and Hus, serving as a member of the commission that interrogated the latter. He also spent a good deal of time at the council working for the condemnation of Jean Petit's justification of tyrannicide, and he became involved in the case against the Dominican Matthew Grabon, who had attacked the Brethren of the Common Life. Grabon held that the practice of Christian perfection should be restricted to members of established orders who professed the traditional vows of poverty, chastity and obedience. Gerson, by contrast, argued that the practice of Christian perfection was open to all Christians, and not necessarily tied to a life under vows.

Although Gerson played a major part in the resolution of the schism by his sermons and writings at Constance and no doubt by work behind the scenes, his role in the formulation of the reform decrees was minimal. This may have been because of his preoccupation with the Petit affair, as Morrall argues, or because he saw reform more in terms of personal, spiritual conversion on the part of clergy and laity than in terms of institutional change, and reduction of papal taxation and control of appointment to benefices, as Pascoe suggests.[29]

It was not, however, only high ecclesiastical affairs that occupied Gerson's attention in the period after 1403. The political situation in France was disturbing and no doubt played its part in reducing the amount of time he could devote to popular preaching and writing. His acceptance of the patronage of Philip of Burgundy inevitably drew Gerson into the factionalism of French politics and, after the death of Philip in 1404 and the succession of John the Fearless, the rivalry between the Orleanist and Burgundian parties for control of the government of the unfortunate Charles VI was intensified. In 1407 the Duke of Orleans was murdered by agents of Burgundy, and the Parisian theologian Jean Petit was called upon to justify this action on the basis of legitimate tyrannicide. This put Gerson in a difficult position, for he did not approve of the murder but was beholden to the Burgundian house, and above all was anxious for the situation not to deteriorate further. It did, of course, deteriorate and Gerson is found in 1408, in the name of the university, making a fervent plea for reconciliation to the pro-Orleanist court in his discourse *Veniat pax*.[30] He helped organise numerous processions for civil peace in Paris during these years, and he approved the truces, albeit temporary, concluded between the rivals, for example, the peace of Auxerre of 1412. In the pro-Burgundian Cabochien revolt of 1413, however, Gerson's own house in Paris was pillaged. By this time he seems to have abandoned entirely any pro-Burgundian leanings. He had lost his benefice at Bruges in 1411, the Burgundians were expelled from Paris in 1413 and Gerson now made a frontal attack on Petit's doctrine. In September 1413, as university spokesman, he delivered a discourse before the king condemning nine assertions of Petit.[31]

During this decade before the Council of Constance Gerson was also busy with university affairs. A number of graduation addresses delivered by him remain from these years,[32] and two vernacular discourses that indicate the lead which he had to take on occasions when the university's privileges were at stake and the masters suspended their lectures in protest.[33] He was involved, too, in the affairs of the Hôtel-Dieu, whose provisor he became in 1404 and for whom he pleaded financial assistance from the king in a discourse of 1406.[34] In 1404 also he was charged with responsibilities for the choir school of Notre-Dame. He was now involved with seven Parisian schools and he took his responsibilities seriously, as is shown by his numerous Latin writings of this period on the education and confessing of children. Many other writings remain from this decade which reveal Gerson's concern with a wide variety of problems and topics: the role of the Mendicants in parish work, the need for episcopal and parochial reform, the reunion of the Greeks to the Roman church, the cult of St Joseph, mystical theology and the case of the Flemish mystic Ruysbroeck, and numerous doctrinal and moral questions.

After the Council of Constance Gerson still had over ten years of fruitful work ahead of him, though in rather a different milieu. It was not safe for him to return to France after the end of the council, for the Duke of Burgundy was now in charge, following English successes in the war. There was no love lost between the chancellor and the duke after Gerson's

repeated attacks against Petit's justification of the 1407 Burgundian murder
of the Duke of Orleans. Instead of returning home Gerson travelled
through Bavaria and then went on to Austria, where he stayed with the
Abbot of Melk for a while and then went to the University of Vienna at
the invitation of Archduke Albert V. In 1419 the situation in France
changed dramatically with the murder of the Duke of Burgundy. Gerson
now felt he could return to France, if not to Paris. In November 1419, he
arrived in Lyons, in territory controlled by the dauphin, and took up
residence in the Celestine convent where one of his brothers was prior. He
remained here until 1425, when the Archbishop of Lyons asked him to take
charge of the choir school of the collegiate church of Saint-Paul. Gerson
remained in Lyons until his death in 1429, and this last decade proved to
be another very productive literary period. He was by now a recognised
authority in pastoral theology and numerous clerics wrote to him, seeking
his advice. In his replies to them and in the treatises he wrote during this
period Gerson showed his continued interest in theological, mystical and
moral questions and in diocesan reform.[35] A particular interest of these
years was in astrology and superstition of all kinds, which Gerson strove
to combat in a number of treatises,[36] while one of his last writings was in
defence of Joan of Arc, whose revelations he was prepared to accept as
genuine.[37] He died on 12 July 1429, in his sixty-sixth year, and was buried
in a chapel near the church of Saint-Paul.

It had been an exceedingly full life, and a very productive one. Gerson's
prodigious literary output – well over 500 extant works – is witness to his
energy and dedication.

2

THE ART OF THE PREACHER

THE LATE MEDIEVAL PREACHING TRADITION

'There are almost as many different modes of preaching as there are capable preachers.' So wrote Robert of Basevorn in 1322 in his treatise *Forma praedicandi*.[1] Basevorn confined himself to describing in detail only what he called the 'modern' method, but it is obvious from his discussion that the modern method itself could yield great variety. If one adds to this variety those sermons of the late medieval period that do not conform to the modern method at all, then the mixture is even richer. The gamut runs from the homely to the eloquent, the simple to the complex, the intellectual to the emotional.

There are, of course, some common features, which is not surprising when one takes into account the number and variety of preaching aids available by the fourteenth century: biblical concordances, collections of *exempla*, collections of model sermons, *florilegia*, and treatises like Basevorn's on the art of preaching.[2] Use of these aids certainly leads to homogeneity in certain areas. A biblical text, for example, used by one preacher as a theme for a particular feast reappears as another preacher's theme. 'Mansionem apud eum faciemus' is a favourite for Pentecost, 'Ave gracia plena' for the Annunciation, and 'Puer natus est' for the Nativity. Gerson uses all these, but they can be found elsewhere. 'Mansionem', for instance, is used by Pierre d'Ailly for his Pentecost sermon and also, later in the century, by Olivier Maillard.[3] Within sermons the same commonplaces keep turning up, and certain images and metaphors and certain *exempla* become very familiar. Yet the traditional material is used in a variety of ways and each preacher puts his own imprint on his sermons, though some much more than others. Gerson's sermons certainly bear his imprint. Although he and d'Ailly use the same theme for their Pentecost sermons and employ the same metaphor of house-cleaning and setting a table in their admonitions about preparing one's soul for the coming of the Holy Spirit, the overall flavour of the two sermons is quite different. Yet d'Ailly may well have been one of those who taught Gerson how to preach.[4]

If one is to bring some order into the rich variety of late medieval sermons, the primary division should be between ancient and modern. The ancient method, so called by some of the authors of treatises on preaching because it was that used by the Fathers,[5] consisted simply in a commentary on the gospel or epistle for the day. This could be either a running commentary or an overall explication of the text as a whole, with doctrinal or moral lessons drawn for the edification of the congregation. Fewer vernacular sermons of this type appear to have been preserved than of the modern type for the late medieval period, but this does not necessarily mean that fewer were preached. It may be only that the means or the intention of preservation was lacking. About one-third of the Middle English sermons found in one manuscript are written in the ancient mode.[6] These sermons are usually brief, simple in construction and homely in tone. They usually contain, near the beginning, a sentence like the following: 'The gospel of this day tells us that...'. Then the preacher proceeds to expound the text. A sermon for Easter Sunday, for instance, is a running commentary on Mark 16:1–7, the story of the three Marys going to the sepulchre to anoint the body of Christ, finding the body gone, but being comforted by the angel in white. The lesson drawn is that we too must earnestly seek Christ with prayer, which is likened to the ointment, and live clean lives, represented by the white clothing of the angel, if we are to have the comfort and joy of heaven.[7]

The 294 vernacular sermons formerly attributed to Wyclif generally follow the ancient style of preaching.[8] Sermon XI in the Sunday Gospel series comments on Christ's parable about the Pharisee and the publican. The whole gospel text is first translated into English. The preacher then underlines the chief point of the text, that is, the warning against hypocrisy, 'the first kind of pride'. He then goes on to draw a parallel between the pharisee and the 'new sects' (monks, canons, friars) of his own day, applying the charges made by Christ against the pharisee to the 'sects'.[9] The sermon on the parable of the prodigal son from the same collection follows a similar pattern. The gospel text is translated and then a moral lesson drawn about conversion from sin.[10]

These sermons in the ancient mode are by no means devoid of similitudes, allegorical interpretations or illustrative narratives (*exempla*). The robe, the ring, the shoes and the fatted calf in the above-mentioned sermon on the prodigal son are all interpreted by the preacher as representing spiritual things; the fatted calf, for instance, is the Eucharist. A sermon on the gospel text (Matt. 25:21–8) about the miraculous healing of the daughter of the Canaanite woman contains, as well as gospel commentary, a fairly long story about a knight who put off repentance till it was too late.[11] But in basic construction all these sermons can be said to be simple.

This is not the case with sermons in the modern mode. If one looked only at the treatises on the art of preaching, one would be left with the impression that modern sermons were structured in a very complicated, even convoluted, manner, and would be very difficult to follow. But in fact, many late medieval sermons that are unmistakably based on the modern mode are comparatively easy to follow, though their construction is certainly more complex than that of 'ancient' sermons. They are by no means all the bizarre or dry productions that some critics have thought them to be.[12] Further, they tend to be much richer in content, more eloquent in style, more moving, than those written in the older form. The best of them – including Gerson's – should perhaps be described as 'modified modern', in that they do not always keep strictly to the rules laid down in the manuals on the art of preaching. About 300 of these manuals are known, most of them composed between the thirteenth and fifteenth centuries. Of these, about thirty are now in print.[13] Although they differ in length, stress and content, the basic structure recommended for the modern or 'artistic' sermon in these works is roughly the same.

In the first place, the sermon has to be grounded in Scripture. The *theme* must be a scriptural text, normally from the gospel or epistle of the day; for example, 'Gloria in altissimis est' for Christmas Day. The preacher must be careful to choose a theme that will yield sufficient material, because the whole sermon has to flow from it. Having pronounced his theme, and, in the case of a vernacular sermon, translated it, the preacher has to move on to what is referred to as either the *protheme* or antetheme. Some authors state that the purpose of this part of the sermon is to introduce a prayer. The preacher should choose another biblical text, a protheme, related to his principal theme in words or sense (hence the need for biblical concordances), which lends itself to a brief discussion leading adroitly to the *prayer*.[14] Then comes the *introduction* to the theme, a restatement of the chief scriptural text and an explanation of the purposes of the sermon, with an indication of the ideas the preacher is going to extract from the text. There are numerous suggestions and rules about composing introductions. Robert of Basevorn, for instance, suggests using an authority, a passage from a philosopher, a poet or someone with reputation. Or, he says, one could proceed by one of eight types of argument, for example, induction, syllogism or *exemplum*.[15]

After the introduction comes the *division*, the statement of the parts into which the theme and hence the body of the sermon will be divided. The rules for division are often quite elaborate, for the parts (usually three) have genuinely to come out of the theme. The preacher must beware of making any false interpretations and so he must confirm each member of his division by biblical authorities. He must justify his interpretation by the Word of God, so that he teaches nothing that is not founded on Scripture. The author of a fourteenth- or fifteenth-century treatise attributed to Aquinas gives us an example. The theme is 'O death, how bitter is the remembrance of thee' (Eccles. 41:1). It is divided into two parts: 'Death is twofold, spiritual and corporeal.' Both parts are subdivided: 'Of things spiritual, some are virtuous, some vicious...of deaths corporeal, some are natural, some violent.' All parts are confirmed, the last two as follows: 'On the former... "We all die, and are as water spilt on the ground" (II Sam. 14:14). On the latter... "Let us condemn him to a most shameful death" (Wisdom, 2:20).'[16]

This may not sound very enlightening, but the body – the meat – of the sermon is yet to come. The preacher must now proceed to the *amplification* of each of the parts – the divisions and subdivisions. And he must not be too long or too brief in doing so. A sermon, says Basevorn, should not be shorter than a low mass or longer than a solemn mass with music.[17] Again there are numerous suggestions about how to amplify. Some treatises, in fact, more or less confine themselves to this aspect of preaching, as *On the Mode of Dividing a Theme for Dilating Sermon Material* by Simon of Alcock (d. 1459).[18] Fourteen methods are suggested by Jean de Chalons (*fl.* 1370), but it was more usual to describe fewer than this. Richard of Thetford (*fl.* 1245), in his *Art of Amplifying Sermons*, sets out eight modes, as does Basevorn, while the 'Aquinas'-tract has nine.[19] There is a good deal of overlap. A preacher, the theorists tell us, could make use of one or more of the four senses of Scripture and speak of the literal, moral, allegorical or anagogical meanings of the biblical phrases he is discussing. He could concentrate on explicating a word; its derivation, its definition, its opposite. Or he could multiply concordant authorities, biblical and otherwise. He could proceed by various types of argument; by logical demonstration, by the use of *exempla* (usually reckoned as a type of inductive argument), by exploring causes and effects (of a vice or a virtue, for example), or he could consider the natural qualities of things and draw useful analogies from them. This is where most theorists leave the discussion of sermon structure, but some of them think that there should be a *peroration*, or epilogue, consisting of a summary of the sermon and a final exhortation to the congregation.[20]

This all sounds very complex. One can imagine the beginner, armed with his concordances, alphabetical lists and Basevorn's *Forma praedicandi*, struggling to produce an 'artistic' sermon. The result may well have been a convoluted work that juggled with words, strained meanings, piled authority on authority and subdivision on subdivision, and got lost in logical disputation and carried away with obscure or inappropriate *exempla*. But in the hands of a master, familiar with all the materials and endowed with spiritual insight, the result could be very different. The theorists were aware of the dangers. Some of them describe infelicitous practices that they have observed in preachers, which is an indication that there were indeed some bad modern sermons. They warn against various types of excess. The preacher must not make so many divisions and subdivisions that he confuses his hearers, writes Thomas Chobham in his early-thirteenth-century *Summa de arte praedicandi*.[21] Later in the century, Humbert of Romans tells preachers that he considers as vicious the habit of multiplying distinctions, authorities, reasons, examples and synonyms. He tells them to avoid all prolixity, repetition and irrelevancy, and to be careful not to be so concerned with the form that they forget the matter.[22] Preaching is not a form of disputation, states Richard of Thetford, warning his readers against becoming too dialectical when amplifying their sermons. The author of the late medieval tract attributed to Henry of Hesse[23] ends his brief treatise on a cautionary note: 'For one sermon, let one correction, one exemplification, one exhortation, one definition, one question suffice.'

Although a number of the theorists take up a considerable part of their treatises in discussing themes, prothemes, introductions and divisions, we should remember that these parts of the sermon are simply preliminaries and are disposed of very quickly by many preachers. The theorists themselves sometimes telescope these parts of the sermon. In the first place, the original purpose of the protheme – to introduce the prayer – seems to have been lost sight of in some quarters. Basevorn, for example, appears to connect it with getting the attention of the audience.[24] The same is true of Thomas Chobham, who states that some preachers set out a brief theme before the principal one in order to make the audience attentive.[25] The author of the 'Aquinas'-tract writes of the protheme as if it were the introduction and does not mention the latter at all.[26] Meanwhile Thomas Waleys says that he does not fully understand why preachers employ introductions. He thinks it may be to catch the attention of the audience.[27] It would seem that the protheme and the introduction are being fused into one, so that eventually one author can write: 'Whatever is said between the theme and its division is the protheme.'[28] These differences of opinion among the theorists clearly reflect variety among preachers in the way they began their sermons, and no doubt theory, in its turn, influenced practice.

There is variety, too, in the way preachers develop the body of their sermons. The *Artes praedicandi* themselves provide many options with their lists, discussions and examples of ways to amplify the divisions and subdivisions of the theme. Moreover preachers, like poets, composers and other artists, sometimes take liberties with the recommended procedures. There are even some sermons that hover uneasily between the ancient and modern modes.

A Middle English sermon for the Epiphany on the theme 'Natus est rex' (Matt. 2:2) is an example of a sermon that has a tendency to ramble but which nevertheless preserves the modern form.[29] Following the statement of the theme, the preacher begins with a prayer to the almighty, wise and benign Lord, asking Him to help preacher and audience receive His doctrine and to strengthen their wills to do good afterwards.[30] Thereafter follows a protheme, based on the biblical text about Moses and the burning bush (Ex. 3:1–6). The preacher links this to his principal theme by comparing the burning, yet unconsumed bush, to the child-bearing, yet virgin Mary. This leads him on to a general discussion about miracles and how we must just accept them on faith, as we must accept all parts of God's and the church's laws. Moreover, all estates of the realm, nobles, priests and lower men, should restrict themselves to their proper spheres. At the end of this relatively long protheme-introduction comes another prayer for preacher and congregation.

The theme is now stated, translated and divided into four parts, based on four questions: Who is this king? What is the manner of his living? What is his authority? Where does he dwell?[31] The four parts of the division are confirmed by the citation of scriptural passages. The preacher is showing that it is reasonable to ask these questions because they are asked in the Bible. He now moves directly to the amplification of the first part, initially by means of authorities. A number of biblical texts are quoted which answer the question of the king's identity. He is the Son of God, He is man and God, He is almighty, wise and good. There is a smooth transition here as the preacher changes his method of amplification to that of argument. The narrative of the gospel of the day, he says, reveals this might, wisdom and goodness. His might is proved by His incarnation, His wisdom by His showing, at His birth, a star to the three kings who were pagans and therefore of 'unreasonable belief', and angels to the shepherds who were Jews and therefore of 'reasonable belief'. His goodness is revealed by His moving the three kings and through them all other men and women to come to Him, and so be saved, if they believe and keep His law. At this point the preacher changes his method of amplification again and asks and answers a series of questions about the three kings: Why are they called 'magi'? Why did they ask for the king of the Jews when they knew that Herod was the king? How were they able to come so quickly? In his replies the preacher includes information about fixed stars, planets, epicycles and comets and about the speed at which dromedaries travel. This concludes the development of the first part of the division. One cannot tell how the preacher amplified the other parts, for the sermon breaks off abruptly twenty lines later. Had he continued at the same place, the sermon would probably have taken between forty-five and sixty minutes to deliver.

This is a sermon that is certainly easy to follow. It flows smoothly, despite the large number of supporting quotations, most of them from the Bible, but some from the Fathers, and one each from Horace, Boethius and Isidore. It holds one's attention but it is not very rich in doctrine; its language is dignified and elegant, but it is not particularly eloquent, and it is not very moving – at least not in the parts that are extant. But of its clarity there can be no doubt. It is an example of a modern sermon where, because the preacher has mastered the form and has something to say, the recommended structure itself is an aid to clarity. And it is certainly a sermon where the form is not allowed to dominate the matter.

By contrast, in the sermon attributed to Hugh Legat (*fl.* 1410), on the theme 'Accipiant repromissionem vocati' (Heb. 9:15), the form does dominate.[32] It is a very clever sermon structurally. The theme is divided into three members, based on its three words. These three members are each subdivided into three parts, and there is complete concordance among these subdivisions. Laws from a king (and therefore from God) can be received (*accipiant*) in three ways: they can be rejected, meekly taken or gladly received. God will do what He has promised (*repromissionem*) to people according to the way they receive His laws: punish them, treat them with mercy, give them the crown of heavenly bliss. People will be named (*vocati*) according to their behaviour and God's treatment of them: enemies, servants, heirs. The trouble with this sermon is that the parts are not amplified sufficiently, while the structure is continually being underlined. One is left with the pattern firmly imprinted on one's mind but little in the way of a message.

Sermons with numerous subdivisions did not have to be form-dominated. Robert of Ciboule, one of Gerson's successors as Chancellor of the University of Paris, preached a vernacular sermon on the Eucharist in 1446 which has two main parts, one on the dogma of the sacrament and the other on its effects.[33] These are subdivided respectively into four and three parts, some of which are themselves further subdivided. But each of the main parts reads as a connected whole, and the sermon is rich in doctrinal and moral teaching. Ciboule uses variety in his methods of amplification and in his tone, so that nothing is used to excess. He asks and answers some questions, he employs some images, he reasons from cause to effect, he argues cases. He sometimes adopts a familiar tone with his audience, but he remains dignified, measured and elegant throughout. It is a fine performance and one is left with solid doctrine and food for thought.

One of the reasons Ciboule's sermon is so well finished and seems so satisfying is that it is a complete sermon, probably revised and polished by the author himself after he had first delivered it. He preached it at least once more, in 1447.[34] Some extant sermons, by contrast, are obviously incomplete, or have been touched up by other, less skilful hands. A number of them have come down to us in note form only, either the preliminary notes of the preacher himself, or those of reporters present at the sermon.[35] These notes are often quite extensive, but it would obviously be unfair to judge such a sermon against Ciboule's.[36] There are, however, more than enough relatively complete vernacular sermons surviving from the late medieval period to form a quarry from which one can extract some to serve as a basis for comparison with Gerson's.

GERSON'S THEORY OF PREACHING

About sixty of Gerson's French sermons are extant[37] and they can be roughly divided, according to their ostensible topics, into sermons on morality, sermons for liturgical occasions, including saints' days, and sermons of circumstance. There are seventeen sermons in the first category, all preached between 3 December 1402 and 18 March 1403, to the people of Paris. They form a series, with the theme 'Poenitemini et credite evangelio', on the subject of the seven capital sins, one each on avarice, anger and envy, two on gluttony and sloth, three on pride and seven on lust and its opposing virtue, chastity.[38] Of the twenty-six liturgical sermons, some of which were preached before the court, there are two each for Christmas, Ash Wednesday, Easter Sunday, Palm Sunday and Pentecost, three for Trinity Sunday and All Souls and one each for other liturgical occasions including Epiphany, Good Friday and All Saints.[39] Three sermons are devoted to St Anthony, the patron saint of Philip of Burgundy, one to St Peter and St Paul, one each to St Michael and John the Baptist, and three to the Virgin.[40] The sermons and discourses of circumstance all fall in the period 1405–13 and were delivered generally before the court on the subjects noted in the last chapter.

Not all of these sermons have come down to us in as complete and polished a form as Ciboule's *Qui manducat me*, though very few are mere notes. In some cases the first part of a sermon is fully developed, but then it tails off into very brief statements, as *Obsecro*. In this sermon Gerson says he is going to talk about the seven virtues needed by pilgrims, that is by all of us on our journey to our goal in heaven. He discussed the first two, but the treatment of each of the other five is very summary, consisting of not much more than a scriptural quotation for confirmation and one or two sentences or headings.[41] Sometimes, sermons that are otherwise complete have one or two passages of notes in the body of the text, often about an *exemplum* Gerson wants to use. Nevertheless there are enough complete sermons and enough fully written up passages to provide a general picture of Gerson's sermon style.

Although none of the manuscript sermons is in Gerson's own hand, it seems probable that most were taken from his own initial or revised versions. Some may have been written up from reporters' notes.[42] But even if what we have does come from Gerson's own version, this is no guarantee that what we are reading is exactly what his congregations heard. He may well have changed, added or left out bits when he was preaching, even if he had written out his sermon fully beforehand. But this is true of any medieval preacher, and with Gerson we at least have a large number of sermons on which to base our discussion.

What is the nature of these sermons as a group? In the first place, like many medieval sermons, they are above all sermons on morality. Whatever their major topic, be it the Trinity, St Anthony or gluttony, all Gerson's sermons have an ethical thrust; they all draw some moral lesson. This is what Gerson thought sermons should do. More than once he affirms his belief that a preacher should not only teach people about the good, as some think, but should also aim to move their hearts and affections to love, desire and accomplish the good.[43] Here Gerson is echoing the theorists. A number of them define the aim of preaching in a way similar to Gerson's. The author of the tract attributed to Aquinas says that preaching recalls men from error to truth, from vices to virtues; it inculcates faith, raises hope and enkindles charity.[44] More prosaically, Basevorn defines preaching as the persuasion of many to meritorious conduct.[45] Gerson had no doubt read one or more of these treatises, and he had certainly reflected on the problem of preaching, on what the tasks of the preacher are and how they should be carried out. He makes a number of statements on the subject in his vernacular sermons and elsewhere. He does not discuss the technicalities of sermon structure but confines himself to those questions the theorists often deal with rather summarily under such headings as the value of preaching, the qualities of a good preacher, delivery, or precautions.[46]

Gerson views the task of preaching as very important. By preaching, prelates, both major (bishops) and minor (parish clergy), carry out their essential hierarchical function of illuminating those in their care. The kingdom of Christianity, he tells a lay congregation, is instituted in a hierarchical order of prelacies, because God wished prelates to govern others and lead them to Him by means of the three activities that belong to prelacy: purifying, illuminating and perfecting.[47] Preaching, in fact, argues Gerson against those who are always wanting contact with God by means of revelations or miracles, is the natural means chosen by God to illuminate us and to make His will known to us.[48] Its purpose is to provide the nourishment necessary for the maintenance of spiritual life. As the body needs earthly bread, so the soul needs the celestial bread brought by preaching.[49] Hearing the word of God preached can cleanse the soul and bring 'vivificacion, fortificacion, consolacion'.[50] Thus the preacher plays a major role in opening the way to salvation, in freeing the soul of the sinner from eternal death by turning him from the error of his ways. In other words, the major purpose of preaching is the conversion of sinners.[51] The author of the 'Aquinas'-tract agrees: 'The hearing of God's Word is the way of conversion from sin.'[52]

Other preachers of the period underlined the importance of preaching. Gerson does not go so far as Bernardine of Siena who tells his lay audience that preaching is really more important than the sacraments, because it is only the person who has heard and responded to the living Word who can participate in the reality of the mass and the sacraments. Therefore, if you have to choose between hearing mass and hearing the preaching, it is better to hear the latter.[53] Gerson would have approved much that the Wycliffites said about preaching, despite their heretical beliefs in other areas. In a Lollard sermon in the Sunday Epistle cycle, preaching is described as bearing the liquid of the wisdom of God, a liquid that should be valued more highly than the oil of tombs, because it heals men's souls more than the oil heals men's bodies. It raises up man's soul, brings belief and is a means of salvation.[54]

Since Gerson views preaching as above all concerned with the conversion of sinners, it is not surprising that he thinks that the preacher must aim above all to move his hearers, to enflame them by his ardour. He must not speak in a cold, dead way, but rather be like John the Baptist, who was 'ardent and shining', and Elijah, 'whose words burned like fire'.[55] Not all preachers apparently agreed with Gerson about this. There are a number of rather lifeless sermons remaining from the period. Michel Menot (1450–1518), though, has the same precept as Gerson. The first requirement of preaching, he says, is that the preacher must speak, not only from his mouth, but also from his heart; he must be ardent in his exhortation.[56]

If the aim of preaching is the moral renewal of the faithful then, says Gerson, the preacher must not make his sermon simply a story-telling session. People like to hear all sorts of tales, and they applaud the story-telling preacher much more than one who preaches the truth. But a true preacher does not seek applause. He does not try to delight his audience with useless things but to improve them with wholesome things.[57] Nor should a preacher enter into discussions of strange and abstruse questions, for these merely titillate the curiosity of a congregation and are a hindrance rather than a help to conversion and salvation.[58] The preacher should also avoid trying to please his hearers by making attacks on secular and ecclesiastical authorities. Much as the laity enjoys such criticism, it can produce only harm.[59] Having avoided all these snares, the preacher must make sure that he adapts his oratory to his audience. Giving Gregory as his reference, Gerson tells his clerical audience that different styles of preaching are needed for the learned and the unlearned, for the laity and the clergy.[60]

Although all sermons must aim at the moral reformation of the hearers, Gerson insists that they must be firmly built on the basic tenets of Christianity. The people must be instructed by preachers about the ten commandments, the important articles of faith, the seven mortal sins and the works of charity.[61] In fact, Gerson holds that parish priests without a university education can still do an effective preaching job by concentrating on these things, even by just dealing with the commandments, for the ten commandments contain the essentials of Christian perfection and therefore are of major importance in the moral renewal of sinners.[62]

Gerson is aware that preaching is a difficult task; it is not easy to strike just the right note, to avoid implicitly encouraging one vice when castigating its opposite. It is often difficult to get across one's message to dull-witted hearers or to those who hear only what they want to hear.[63] Thus the preaching office demands:

a quick, shrewd and versatile mind. It demands an eloquence that is fluid, vehement, pleasing and that persuades. It demands a knowledge of the Scriptures and of everything else concerning morality. It demands a wide experience of human behaviour and of the condition of those who are to be taught. It demands an exemplary life and irreproachable behaviour, free from all sin, especially from avarice and lust, which are particularly ruinous of reputation;...It demands the spiritual experience of contemplation, for how can one enkindle in others the desire for eternal things if one remains totally cold and frigid oneself?[64]

Gerson is setting a very high standard, though his reflections on preaching do not constitute any radical new departure in religious oratory. He perhaps stresses the need for vibrancy and eloquence to a greater extent than do some of the theorists. He certainly seems to think them more important than do a number of the practitioners. Some of the theorists, in fact, warn against too embellished a sermon. William of Auvergne (1191–1249) thinks that a simple sermon, unpolished and unadorned, is best for edifying the audience,[65] while Alain de Lille (fl. 1200) condemns what he describes as theatrical preaching, though he does not want 'bloodless words' either. Rather, a middle course should be followed.[66] Both these authors, however, emphasise the importance of the preacher's moving the hearts of his audience. Alain even writes about moving the congregation to tears of repentance, though not for too long.[67]

Gerson is following the medieval tradition in insisting that sermons aim above all at the moral reform of the audience, a tradition that was brought to a climax by the popular itinerant preachers of the fifteenth century, such as St Vincent Ferrier (1350–1419), St Bernardine of Siena (1380–1444), and later Olivier Maillard (1430–1502) and Michel Menot (c. 1450–1518). Their preaching is far more moral than dogmatic in content and is centred around the basic themes of penitence and conversion.[68] The Franciscan Maillard, for instance, preached a series of seventy Lenten sermons in 1498 at Saint-Jean-en-Grève in Paris, one of the churches in which Gerson had preached earlier in the century, and another series of fifty-seven at Nantes during Lent 1507. The topics of the latter series are the commandments, penitence and restitution.[69]

There is no new departure in Gerson's requirements that the preacher be well grounded in the teaching of the church and that he be a man of upright life. These are commonplaces among the theorists from Gregory onwards. Basevorn states that the first necessity in a preacher is purity of life, and the second is that he have competent knowledge, at least of the articles of faith, the ten commandments and the differences between sin and non-sin.[70] Humbert of Romans is more demanding. He thinks that the preacher's knowledge should be very extensive, including knowledge of the Scriptures, creatures, history and the laws of the church. Like Gerson, he also thinks that a wide experience of people is valuable, especially that gained in the cure of souls.[71] The theorists, unlike Gerson, do not appear to think that the spiritual experience of contemplation is a requirement for good preaching. By the time Gerson said this (1408) he had already written treatises on mysticism. Perhaps he had had some mystical experiences) which he found helpful to him in his preaching.

Gerson's strictures against story-telling preachers reflect an aspect of

contemporary practice rather than the treatises on preaching. Most of the
latter encourage the use of *exempla*, illustrative stories, as a means of
conveying a point effectively. Stories could be drawn from the Bible or
from history or from the collections of *exempla* that were available.[72] The
stories in these collections were usually designed to make a moral point, and
the characters involved range from saints and the devil to ordinary people
and animals. A number of the stories are humorous; many are full of
superstition. What Gerson has in mind in his criticism is not so much the
restrained use of respectable *exempla*, as the unrestrained use of undignified
exempla, those that encouraged superstition or were designed to raise a
coarse laugh.[73] That such sermons were preached is evidenced by the
criticism of them found in this period.[74] In the sixteenth century a council
at Sens decreed that preachers who told ridiculous and scurrilous tales from
the pulpit were to be suspended from office. A similar decree was
promulgated in Milan.[75] If the sermons collected in Mirk's *Festial*[76] were
ever preached in the form presented in the text, they would certainly have
fallen under Gerson's censure. They are structured neither in the ancient
nor in the modern mode; there is no scriptural commentary, no formal
division. Some of them are simply a collection of stories linked together,
some of them improving, some funny and some that now seem obscene.
The sermon on the death of Nero must be one of the most ridiculous and
coarse for any period.[77]

Gerson's warning against the discussion of abstruse theological questions
in vernacular sermons is echoed by a few of the theorists.[78] But it seems
to have been difficult for preachers who were well versed in the university
method of disputation to avoid altogether raising theological problems and
even becoming dialectical. The technique of raising questions seems, in
fact, to be used deliberately by some preachers. Gerson raises questions
himself. So does Ciboule. Towards the end of each part of his sermon *Qui
manducat me*, Ciboule asks and answers a series of questions, among them
the following: Do angels partake of the Eucharist? If someone is in mortal
sin without knowing it, does he sin if he takes the sacrament? The answers
are not a simple positive or negative. Ciboule argues his case clearly,
without becoming long-winded, over-subtle or patronising, and his discussions add to the interest of the sermon.[79] Olivier Maillard, too, likes to
discuss doctrinal or moral problems in his sermons, usually near the
beginning. But he deals with them in a much more chatty, though not less
effective way than Ciboule, bringing his hearers into the debate by putting
words into their mouths.[80] Michel Menot is perhaps less successful. In a
sermon for Sexagesima he introduces the problem of whether God is
responsible for evil. The ensuing discussion reads like someone's commentary on Lombard's *Sentences*. Numerous authorities are cited and
subtle distinctions made, but then, at the point when the reader (and
presumably the hearer) has become thoroughly confused, Menot turns to

the crowd. 'Women, you can understand. You have a young son who has the stone. You have to agree that he be cut. You weep to see your son suffer, as God weeps when he sends us tribulations.'[81] Even so, the preceding dialectical exercise seems inappropriate for a sermon *ad populum*.[82] There were clearly effective and less effective ways of dealing with puzzling theological questions in sermons. Perhaps Gerson was warning only against the inappropriate handling of such questions, and perhaps his stress was on abstruse (*estrangez et curieuses*) questions.[83]

GERSON'S FRENCH SERMONS

In his statements about the qualities needed in a preacher and the ways in which he should carry out his task, Gerson has set a high, if not particularly novel standard. Does he live up to it?

In his own day he was recognised as one of the best preachers in Paris. Jean De Montreuil, in a letter of 1400 to Nicholas de Clamanges, wrote of Gerson and Jean Courtecuisse (1353–1423) as the two stars of sacred eloquence in the Parisian church.[84] In a letter to Guillaume Fillastre, Montreuil went further, calling Gerson's sermons incomparable, because of the way they gripped and moved the audience. Montreuil declared that he would go to Rheims to hear Gerson preach rather than hear any other orator of renown who happened to be preaching in a church nearby.[85] Gerson was praised by a chronicler who wrote of his always preaching 'elegantly and eloquently'.[86] Another chronicler commented on his vernacular funeral oration of January 1415, in honour of Duke Louis of Orleans: the Chancellor preached 'si parfondement et haultement que plusieurs docteurs en theologie et autres s'en esmerveillerent'.[87]

Not all Gerson's sermons, in their written form, live up to this praise. But some do, and the qualities that impressed his contemporaries are qualities that impress the reader. He can be eloquent, moving and elegant. He can preach in a 'grand' style, which puts his sermons at the other end of the spectrum from the homely, simple, undramatic homilies that one can find among sermons written in the ancient mode. Some of Gerson's) sermons might be called theatrical. One can imagine his congregations leaving the church feeling that they had been present at a great occasion, as well as having had a moving experience. This is not to say that Gerson maintains a high emotional level throughout an entire sermon. Like any good orator he varies his tone and his methods of amplification.[88]

Another outstanding quality of Gerson's vernacular sermons is their richness in doctrinal content. In this they are unusual, though not unique. Ciboule's *Qui manducat me* has the same quality and so, to a lesser extent, do some of the sermons of the other 'star' of the Parisian scene, Jean Courtecuisse. The latter's sermon of December 1406 on the theme 'Bonus est prestolari cum silentio salutare Dei', for instance, discusses the reasons for the Incarnation, though not, of course, to the length and depth of such a discussion in a theological *Summa*.[89] But few late medieval vernacular sermons contain the richness in dogmatic and ethical teaching that Gerson's do.[90]

How does Gerson organise his sermons and achieve his effects? Basically his sermons follow the modern mode, though he is no slave to the technique. There are a few occasions, indeed, where he all but abandons the recommended structure, for example in his 1403 sermon on the Passion, *Ad deum vadit*.[91] What Gerson does here is to expound, in twenty-four sections, the gospel story. It is not a simple explication, however. Gerson uses his imagination, painting very vivid pictures – the street scenes are especially good – and putting speeches into the mouths of the characters so that they become alive. The lamentation of the Virgin, for example, is very moving. Throughout his exposition Gerson draws moral lessons and sometimes he stops to raise and answer questions: Why should Judas be blamed? Why did God allow Peter to deny Christ? Sermons on the Passion, however, were often constructed differently from ordinary sermons, precisely because they were meant, as one anonymous preacher says, to imprint the memory of the Passion in the hearts of the faithful.[92] Courtecuisse's Passion sermon, *O vos*, follows a similar pattern to Gerson's.[93] In fact there is one passage in the Virgin's lamentation that is almost word for word the same as Gerson's.[94] The Passion sermon preached by Vincent Ferrier in 1416 is of the same type. Vincent's sermon is not as dramatic as Gerson's, but its lyrical beauty and its stress on the *mater dolorosa* render it even more moving.[95]

Generally, though, Gerson uses the modern method. Following the rules, he takes his theme from the gospel or the epistle of the day, though occasionally, if it is a feast-day sermon, from the Introit of the mass. He then, though not in all cases, translates the theme into French, sometimes into a rhymed couplet. *Beati qui lugent*, for example, yields

> Ceulz yci sont beinheureux
> Qui les cuers ont doloreux.[96]

Occasionally Gerson passes immediately from the statement of his text to a prayer,[97] but usually he develops a protheme, not, however, based on a second scriptural text. Gerson's prothemes seem to be chiefly designed to catch the attention of his audience, because he nearly always speaks of something concrete. He may recall some specific circumstance, as in one of his sermons for the feast of St Anthony, where he refers to the birthday of the Duke of Burgundy,[98] or he may develop an image or an allegory suggested by the text, as in the sermon *Multi in nativitate eius gaudebunt*, where the theme of the nativity of John the Baptist leads him to draw a picture of the rejoicing of nature.[99] Sometimes he tells a short story: such is the case in *Puer natus est*, where he tells of the conversion of a sinner as a result of reflection on the Nativity.[100] Perhaps most commonly he presents the subject, or part of the subject of the gospel of the day, sometimes at length.[101] Whatever method he chooses, he then moves smoothly to a brief statement on the need for grace both for himself and for his hearers and so on to the *Ave Maria*, with the Virgin presented, for example, as the treasurer of grace, or as having practised the virtue Gerson is going to speak of.[102]

It is rare for Gerson to move directly from the protheme to the division.[103] There is almost always an introduction of the theme, often quite lengthy. One of the ways in which Gerson forms his introductions is to raise and refute objections that might arise out of the theme. In a sermon on the Eucharist he draws a picture of a hideous beast, Unbelief, who raises six objections to the dogma of the sacrament. These objections are answered at length.[104] In *Quomodo* he replies to Impatience, who is tired of the new difficulties that menace the church.[105] Alternatively, Gerson might make a general commentary on the theme, as in a sermon for All Souls where he discusses in turn the attitudes of the souls in purgatory, the living and the blessed to the theme 'It is holy to pray for the dead.'[106] One of his favourite methods of forming an introduction is to place the chief subject of the sermon in a larger context. For instance, the topic of a sermon for the feast of St Anthony is self-knowledge. Gerson discusses the various branches of human knowledge from the seven liberal arts through medicine and physical science to the mechanical arts, showing that self-knowledge is more important than all these.[107]

Gerson, then, is not one of those who rush over the preliminary parts of their sermons. He appears to take particular care in composing his prothemes and introductions, always with the intention of making a good beginning that will make his audience attentive. Citations from authorities are used sparingly, and even the introductions that proceed by some form of argumentation often contain a striking image or an *exemplum* to make a point concrete.[108]

To move from the introduction to the division the preacher had to find a 'key' by means of which he could 'open' the theme and take out of it the two, three or four ideas that he wished to develop. Occasionally, Gerson uses what was technically known as an 'intrinsic' key. In this case the division had to be based, in some way, directly on the words of the text, for instance, by following the order of the words or the logical order of the ideas the words represented.[109] Gerson's sermon on the text 'Glory to God in the highest and on earth peace to men of goodwill' is divided into two parts, one on peace and the other making the point that peace is accorded only to men of goodwill.[110] With the text 'We have thought of your mercy, O God, in the midst of thy temple', Gerson proposes a four-fold division based on the four senses of *templum*. He will speak, he says, of God's mercy as it is shown to the visible church in the Purification, following the literal meaning, and to the church within us, following the moral meaning. He also proposes allegorical and anagogical interpretations, but the sermon is incomplete.[111]

Far more frequently Gerson uses an extrinsic key: that is, he uses ideas that are extrinsic to his text and applies them to it.[112] In his sermon for Palm Sunday, whose theme is 'Ecce rex tuus venit tibi mansuetus',[113] Gerson takes the factious situation in France where there is murmuring against and opposition to the king, and where there is crime and vice, and applies it to his text by contrasting it to the welcome accorded to Christ in Jerusalem on Palm Sunday. The cause of the difference, he states, lies in 'delit terrein', which drives out the three theological virtues, and the three major parts of the division and subsequent amplification consist of a commentary on these virtues and what happens when they are abandoned. The theme 'Omne regnum in seipsum divisum desolabitur'[114] has applied to it an extrinsic key taken from the gospel story of the healing of the man possessed by a devil and who was dumb, blind and deaf. Gerson makes his three-fold division by describing the kingdom of the soul when it is divided against itself because its three powers – reason, will and sensuality – are corrupted by sin and so become, figuratively, feeble, dumb, blind and deaf.

Often Gerson produces a rhymed version of his division to fix it in his hearers' minds. The three parts of his sermon for All Souls on the theme 'Beati qui lugent' are based on the benefits of 'cuer doloreux' or penitence.

> Cuer doloreux delivre ses amis de dur emprisonnement,
> Delivre soy meismes de rigoreux jugement,
> Recort yci joyeux sentement.[115]

This device was in accord with the advice of the theorists,[116] and was frequently used by Gerson's contemporaries. In the case of d'Ailly, the device is, to my mind, over-used. He rhymes not only his themes and divisions but frequently his subdivisions also, and often in a complex way. This would seem to defeat the original purpose of helping the unlettered to remember the preacher's points. There would be too many complex verses to remember. Gerson uses rhymes moderately, as do Courtecuisse and Ciboule, and all three keep the verses simple, not to say banal.

So far we have seen Gerson following the recommendations of the *Artes praedicandi*, and doing so effectively. His prothemes and introductions are good, and his divisions rarely seem strained or artificial. However, there are some sermons that do not have proper divisions at all. The sermon on the Trinity with the theme 'Videmus nunc per speculum in enigmate' is an example. Here Gerson, by examining the human soul (the mirror), provides evidence for the existence of God, for His unity, His nature, the three persons of the Trinity and their attributes, and of the mystical knowledge of God. The sermon develops progressively without any formal division.[117] The same is true of the sermon on the Eucharist. After the protheme and introduction, the sermon is centred on one main point: the wonders of the Eucharist. Through the mouth of 'Theology' Gerson shows that the sacrament manifests the divine attributes; he exalts its benefits and explores the causes which prevent those benefits from being realised.[118] Two of the sermons on lust in the *Poenitemini* series are also devoid of divisions; Gerson simply discusses the various forms of this vice.[119] These are cases where Gerson really breaks with one of the most fundamental aspects of the modern sermon. There are other cases where, although a division is stated, the sermon follows a simple and progressive development so that the division almost seems irrelevant. This is true, for instance, of a Palm Sunday sermon, where Gerson preaches about sin and penitence, moving in straightforward fashion through the causes, effects and gravity of sin to the reasons for the lack of penitence.[120] In other words, Gerson does not let form dominate content. In some cases, at least, it seems clear that he starts with the subject he wants to preach about and then fits it into the form. If the subject cannot be accommodated within the recommended form, then he abandons that form. His primary aim is to expound his material in a clear, interesting and moving fashion, not to be 'artistic'.

Some of d'Ailly's vernacular sermons, by contrast, leave the impression that the concern to be artistic comes first. D'Ailly underlines his subdivisions and the concordances among them, and usually summarises as he goes along. If the actual discussion of the point is relatively brief, as it not infrequently is, then it is the pattern that stands out.[121] In Courtecuisse's sermons, however, it is the content that appears to dominate. This is particularly the case with a sermon for the Resurrection on the theme 'Quis revolvet nobis lapidem'. After the introduction, which centres on the Resurrection as opening the way to our salvation, the sermon develops one chief subject: the need to roll away the stone of sin from our conscience.[122]

Another of the rules is broken by Gerson. He does not always confirm the parts of his division with scriptural authorities.[123] This, however, was quite a common infraction. There is no confirmation of parts in a number of the modern sermons in the English collection edited by Ross, and both d'Ailly and Courtecuisse sometimes offend in this way. Perhaps it was done deliberately, to avoid cluttering up sermons *ad populum*. This may well be true of Gerson, whose vernacular sermons in general avoid the multiplication of short quotations from authorities characteristic of some preachers.[124]

Of the many ways of amplification open to the 'modern' preacher Gerson most frequently proceeds by some form of analysis. He might discuss the ways in which something is done: the six ways in which the devil tempts us; the four ways in which bad will takes away from the glory of God; the three ways of avoiding purgatory.[125] Sometimes he concentrates on effects: the contrasting effects of 'cuer douloureux' to those of 'plaisir mondain'; the twelve effects of peace.[126] In a number of the sermons in the *Poenitemini* series he examines different types of a particular vice. Frequently he explores causes or motives. Like other preachers of the period he is particularly fond of the numbers three and four and their multiples, not only in his amplifications, but also in his divisions. Frequently there are three or four main parts in the division, and each of these will be subdivided into three or four sections. The sermon on St Anthony of 1402, for instance, is divided into four main parts; within the first and second there are four considerations, and within the third and fourth, there are three.[127] Twelve to sixteen subdivisions do not seem to hold out much promise for a unified, flowing sermon. Yet Gerson can achieve it. When he has one major topic he wants to preach about, he creates a unity, however many the subdivisions. This is true of many of the sermons for feasts; for example, the single subject of *Tota pulchra es* is the Immaculate Conception.[128] In the discourses of circumstance there is normally only one topic; for example, in *Miserere* he centres on a plea for financial assistance for the Hôtel-Dieu.[129] Not all sixty sermons live up to this standard. In the sermons in the *Poenitemini* series, for instance, Gerson is doing two things: commenting on the gospel of the day (from which the theme is *not* taken) and attacking the capital sins. In most cases the result is not a unified sermon. This is probably by design, though, rather than through ineptitude. There are, however, a few cases where Gerson lets a topic that is of concern to him lead to a lengthy digression from the main subject which breaks the unity of the sermon. In *Nimis*, for example, Gerson's principal aim is to lead his congregation towards the ideal of holiness achieved by Peter and Paul, but he is sidetracked into a discussion of the foolish and unhealthy attitude of people who are always wanting miracles.[130] In *Mansionem* the discussions and castigations of the sins of impurity (in this case, rape, incest and masturbation) seem to have too prominent a place and distract from the chief topic of the sermon: the preparation for and reception of the Holy Spirit in the soul.[131]

These digressions and intrusions make the sermons concerned less elegant, but not necessarily less interesting. Perhaps it is again a case of content taking precedence over style. When Gerson digresses it is usually on a subject of particular concern to him, either in general or at that time or before that audience. Before the royal court, for instance, Gerson sometimes interrupts his chief subject with a digression on the particular vices he associates with courts: flattery, lust, sorcery, rapacity, 'estat pompeux'.[132] Even in sermons where there are interruptions Gerson cannot be accused of lack of clarity. One would just come away from the sermon with an extra lesson or two.

Gerson's sermons generally end quite abruptly. There is sometimes no peroration at all, at least in the written version. Where there is one, it generally consists simply of an exhortation and a prayer, sometimes preceded by a very brief summary of the sermon.

Within this largely traditional framework Gerson preached his message of moral renewal, by attacking the evils and sins of his day and pointing out to the people, whatever their station, how they could amend their lives. In the course of his sermons he also gets across a fair amount of explication of basic dogma, about the nature and attributes of God,[133] the Incarnation, Passion and Resurrection,[134] the Eucharist,[135] and the Trinity.[136] If his sermons never consist only of an explanation of the gospel of the day, nevertheless they can be described as essentially scriptural. He frequently does narrate and explicate the gospel as part of his discourse and, whatever his topic, his sermons have many references to the Bible, especially to the New Testament, to the story of Christ's life and love. He also, of course, uses the authority of the Fathers and here it is Augustine who plays the largest role, with Jerome and Gregory the Great also having important places. Ambrose and the Greek Fathers, Origen and Chrysostom, follow some way behind, but Gerson frequently quotes from Pseudo-Dionysius, far more frequently than is usual in vernacular sermons of the period.[137] This no doubt reflects his concern with hierarchical order and mysticism.[138] The medieval theologians, apart from Bernard, are cited only rarely.[139] Here Gerson follows the general practice; the 'ancients', having more authority, were always given a more prominent place than the 'moderns'. Pagan antiquity, however, is often made use of by Gerson. Aristotle, for instance, is employed fairly frequently, especially for ideas about war, kingship and the duties of kings, tyrants, the law, the populace, justice and natural phenomena. Of the Latin authors Cicero is the most frequently cited, especially for his moral doctrine, but there are also quotations from Seneca, Sallust, Cato, Scipio, Terence, Horace, Virgil, Juvenal, Ovid and Livy, though more often in the sermons to the court than in those to the people.[140] From his own contemporaries or near contemporaries there are almost no citations at all, though he does quote twice from Petrarch.[141]

Gerson, in accord with his precept that a preacher should aim both to teach his hearers about the good and to enflame them with desire to accomplish it, uses a variety of techniques to make his sermons clear, lively and moving. The *exemplum* is one of his favourite devices. He uses it chiefly to persuade his audience to behave in a certain way, the way the character in the story behaved or did not behave. Again it is chiefly from Scripture that Gerson culls his *exempla* of people representative of a particular virtue or vice. Zacharius and Elizabeth are proffered as models of husband and wife,[142] Mary Magdalene as an example of contrition,[143] Anne as a model of the good widow who practised the three types of chastity,[144] and Pilate as an evil official.[145] Gerson uses stories connected with the princes of the Old Testament as *exempla* of pride, disobedience, sorcery, envy, the evils of flattery and so on. Adam and Eve figure frequently as models of pride, weakness of spirit and deception, while the destruction of Sodom and

Gomorrah is often described to show the dangers of lust. In his court sermons especially Gerson draws *exempla* from pagan antiquity, probably via Augustine, Gregory and Valerius Maximus, and usually to illustrate the perils of particular vices. More than once he uses Anthony and Cleopatra as examples of lust,[146] Xerxes of pride[147] and Sulla of tyranny.[148] He also takes *exempla* from church history, the lives of the Fathers, from mythology and from French history. Hence Clotilde is a model of the virtuous woman,[149] and Charlemagne and St Louis of the Christian king.[150] Perhaps the most interesting and striking of Gerson's *exempla* are taken from everyday contemporary life. Before the court he draws a picture of poverty.

Notez se une povre femme grosse malade,
honteuse a vi enfans, estoit en la froidure
et n'eust pain pour donner a ses enfans qui
cririoent a la rage de fain...[151]

Frequently he produces a picture of the relationship between children and parents, or between schoolchildren and masters. In *Veniat pax*, for example, in order to stress the paramount need for peace between the princes, Gerson describes the mischief the pupils get up to when the schoolmasters quarrel among themselves.[152] Other *exempla* are taken from contemporary professions, occupations and sports.

Many of Gerson's *exempla* are familiar. The wicked princes of the Old Testament appear in Legrand's vehement sermon before the French court; Mary Magdalene, Pilate, Xerxes and Charlemagne are subjects of *exempla* in Courtecuisse's sermons. And of course the *exempla* about Adam and Eve, about the lives of the Fathers and the saints keep turning up elsewhere. But even if he did not invent them – and from the pedagogical point of view there is a lot to be said for oft-told tales – Gerson makes very effective use of his *exempla*, particularly those drawn from everyday life. They always make the lessons he wishes to get across concrete and thus easily understandable. They do not provide comic relief. Gerson's *exempla* are never funny.

Another device used frequently by Gerson, and by most medieval preachers, was imagery, especially personification and allegory. To the modern reader, this zest for allegory is somewhat tedious, but late medieval audiences and readers had a taste for it and no doubt enjoyed Gerson's theatrical passages. For the court Gerson produced allegories drawn from chivalry. In *Adorabunt*[153] the soul is presented as a kingdom with its queen, *franche voulente*, sitting on the throne of reason and surrounded by the different virtues, who represent councillors. The knights are clothed in the armour of prayer and fasting. The kingdom has to withstand the assaults of the tyrant pride and his band of followers, the other capital sins. Sometimes the life of the soul is presented as a pilgrimage, or man as a church, the doors and windows of which represent his five senses, the altar his will, the priest the Holy Spirit, the bells inspirations, the lamp his faith and so on.[154] Sometimes Gerson pictures the world as a vast ocean disturbed by tempestuous winds on which the ship laden with precious gifts – representing either the church or man's soul – has to struggle to keep afloat.[155] Occasionally almost the whole of a sermon is constructed around a vast allegory. An example is *Tota pulchra es*, where the reasons in favour of belief in the Immaculate Conception are presented by means of an imagined discussion in the court of heaven among Dame Nature, Chastity, Wisdom, Obedience, Mercy, Virginity, Prudence and God.[156]

Personification is also rampant in Gerson's sermons: the virtues and vices are frequently treated in this way. 'Orgueil le dedaigneux, flatterie la traiteuse, desloyal bruit mondaine, curiosite presumpteuse' are some of the characters recurrent in his writings.[157] And similes are everywhere. Sin is like sickness that needs the medicine of penitence or devotion or holy thoughts to cure it, or it is like the ice that destroys the fruit. The sinner is like a leper; the glutton and lecher like a pig. Grace is like the gentle rain that refreshes; virginity like a beautiful flower. Demons are like fierce dogs, hypocrites like serpents, and the flatterer is like a cloud that hides the clear light of truth. The whole realm of nature is used by Gerson as a source for similes. All late medieval preachers used similitudes, but Gerson's sermons seem particularly rich in them.[158]

A third way of keeping interest alive that Gerson uses is the raising of questions and the discussion of particular moral cases. These questions and answers do break the flow of sermons, but, to my mind, the price is worth paying. Gerson is attempting to teach his congregations and this is an effective way of covering minor or puzzling points. It also enables him to adopt from time to time a more familiar tone with his congregation. 'You might ask (or wonder) if...' is a phrase he sometimes uses to begin his question period.

Most of the sermons on the seven capital sins have sections where problems are raised. One of the sermons on gluttony, for instance, ends with a long series of questions and answers about various occasions when one may or may not have committed this sin. Some deal with problems connected with abstinence: If one eats meat on Friday, without knowing it, is this a mortal sin? If one has made a vow never to eat meat or fish, but is fainting with hunger, and these are the only foods available, would one sin by eating? The answer is negative on both counts.[159] The sermons on lust, sloth and anger end in a similar way. Apart from this series, other sermons too – sermons to the court as well as sermons to the people – use this technique. The sermon for All Souls, for instance, poses numerous questions about prayers for the dead and indulgences.[160] Dogmatic as well as moral topics are sometimes treated in this way. Why, Gerson asks, did Our Lady marry? Why did God want to become incarnate as a man and not as a woman?[161] Occasionally he poses a series of questions and then seems to wish he had desisted, as in the middle of an Advent sermon of 1402 when the questions are about the day of judgement. When will the day of judgement come? Will the antichrist be a man or a devil in human form? Will the fire that destroys the world be like the fire that we see about us? Will the trumpets of the angels be material? At this point his own strictures against speculative questions seem to come to his mind, for he says, 'Devout people, let us leave other abstruse [*curieuse*] questions, for they should not concern the people, nor for that matter the majority of theologians. These things are as God ordains, and we know only what it pleases Him to reveal.'[162]

Gerson never becomes as familiar with his audiences in these question periods – or indeed in any part of his sermons – as Bernardine, Maillard and Menot do. Bernardine in particular engages in dialogue – one might say repartee – with his hearers, though it is he who is doing all the talking.[163] Maillard even introduces quotations in a familiar way: 'Listen. Saint James tells us about that in his epistle. Come and speak, Saint James, my friend,...' The text follows.[164] In addition, Bernardine, Maillard and Menot all tell funny stories from time to time. Gerson is not a popular preacher in the way that these three missionary Franciscans are. He always remains dignified.

Yet one can see why he would have been a more effective preacher *ad populum* than, for example, d'Ailly. The latter's sermons are in general more artistic literary productions than Gerson's. But d'Ailly, though he employs imagery and allegory, makes little use of *exempla* or questions. And there is less food for the mind in d'Ailly's sermons. This is one of the things that makes the difference between d'Ailly's Pentecost sermon and Gerson's, both with the same theme – 'Mansionem apud eum faciemus' – and the same central allegory. On an intellectual level, many of Gerson's sermons come close to the level reached by Ciboule in his *Qui manducat me*. Neither preacher is afraid of tackling difficult dogmatic questions. Ciboule scores on polish but his sermon is not very rich in imagery or allegory, and he is a less vibrant and moving preacher than his predecessor. Courtecuisse's sermons are perhaps nearest to Gerson's in style. Courtecuisse uses imagery, allegory, *exempla* and questions. He can be more vehement than Gerson, but he can also be gentle and moving. In his Nativity sermon there is a beautiful passage on love and friendship, beginning with the story of Piramus and Thisbe, and leading up to the great love shown to us by Christ.[165] One is tempted to say that these French contemporaries of Gerson's did not have as much of the common touch as he did. But the temptation must be resisted for, almost without exception, the extant vernacular sermons of d'Ailly and Courtecuisse are all for special occasions, the great majority for feast-days, and the remainder, sermons before the court on political or ecclesiastical matters.[166] There is nothing comparable to Gerson's *Poenitemini* series. One simply does not know how d'Ailly or Courtecuisse tackled or would have tackled a series like that.

The vernacular sermons of d'Ailly and Courtecuisse are so far known to survive in only one manuscript copy each, with no early printed editions. Some of Gerson's survive in many manuscripts. Apart from his sermon on the Passion, which is exceptional in being extant in about twenty manuscripts, about thirty sermons survive in five to twelve copies, and only about a dozen in one copy only. And there were early printed editions (in Latin) of many of the sermons. This difference in survival-rate can hardly be completely accidental, or solely because of Gerson's reputation in other spheres.

GERSON AND CLASSICAL RHETORIC

Jean de Montreuil, we have seen, couples Courtecuisse and Gerson together as the two stars of the preaching scene in Paris because of their skill in oratory. He links this skill, as far as Gerson goes, with obedience to the rules of rhetoric and eloquence, without which, he says, discourse (*sermocinatio*) is rendered useless, empty and unprofitable, as the supreme orator Cicero declares.[167] Jean de Montreuil was a member of that group of French humanists, or pre-humanists as they have sometimes been called, which flourished around the turn of the fourteenth century in Paris and, to some extent, at the papal court in Avignon. Gerson was linked to this group, a number of whose members had been students at the College of Navarre. Some of them were churchmen, as Nicholas de Clamanges, Courtecuisse and Gerson, others had secular rather than religious responsibilities; Montreuil himself and Gontier Col, for instance, were secretaries in the royal chancellery.[168]

Gerson, like the others, wished to encourage the study of the classics. In a Latin university sermon of 1392 he argues the legitimacy of using classical material in theological writing, and vigorously defends the right to read classical authors, against those theologians opposed to the infiltration of such literature into theology. One can combine poetry, rhetoric and philosophy with sacred letters, he says, as Paul, Augustine, Jerome and the rest of the great did and still do to this day.[169] The classical disciplines, however, he adds, should play the role of handmaiden to the mistress, theology. Gerson's arguments here are reminiscent of some of those used by the contemporary Italian humanist, Coluccio Salutati (1331–1406), a few years earlier in his letters to the chancellor of Bologna.[170] Gerson's treatise of 1389 against Jean de Monzon had already taken up the same topic.[171] Though it is largely concerned with the latter's attack on the doctrine of the Immaculate Conception, the treatise contains a lengthy opening section on the glories of the University of Paris. Gerson complains, however, that the study of rhetoric is sadly neglected there. He bitterly criticises the results of this neglect in a lecture to his theology students – potential preachers – in 1401. 'Sophists' is the name he gives to those preachers of the day who use only bare logic or metaphysics in their sermons and ignore the rules and ornaments of rhetoric. Rhetoric, he argues, is a branch of logic and is absolutely necessary in a sermon, where the aim is to incite people to good moral behaviour.[172]

The classical art of rhetoric, although it was not the only root of medieval preaching theory, had not by any means been ignored by the authors of the *Artes praedicandi*.[173] Augustine had laid a foundation in his *De doctrina christiana*, where he stresses the value of Ciceronian rhetoric for theology and urges preachers to study it and so learn how to express their thoughts.[174] In the medieval period, Thomas of Chobham is a good example of a theorist who makes wide use of classical rhetoric. He sees the goal of the orator and that of the preacher as exactly the same: persuasion. Therefore, he argues, rhetorical doctrine is absolutely necessary to fulfil the task of preaching.[175] Thomas attempts to demonstrate how the parts of a modern sermon compare with the parts of a classical oration, and he is concerned, as the classical theorists were, that the speaker should keep his hearers in mind and not overburden them with too many details. Some of the theorists copy the classical writers in paying attention to delivery.[176] The author of the 'Aquinas'-tract tells his reader to vary the tone of his voice according to the subject matter. Sometimes he must speak vigorously, sometimes with wonder, or with grief, horror, derision or impatience, sometimes with gracious countenance or with joy. And he must always speak intelligibly and never drop his voice at the end of a sentence.[177]

There is no point, then, in drawing too sharp a line between medieval preaching theory and humanist theory, as it was expressed by Gerson and his circle. There was clearly a gap, however, between humanist theory and some preaching practice of the period. Despite the warnings issued by the *Artes praedicandi*, some preachers, according to Gerson at least, were letting themselves be over-influenced by logic and dialectical reasoning and under-influenced by rhetoric. Gerson did not let this happen to him. His sermons are never dry, pedantic or abstruse. He does not, of course, abandon the modern mode; the medieval sermon does not become the classical oration in his hands, any more than it does in the hands of Courtecuisse.[178] It was not, after all, until 1416 that Poggio discovered a complete text of Quintilian's *Institutio oratoria* in a monastery in St Gall, and not until 1421 that Cicero's *De oratore* came to light in Lodi Cathedral in Italy.[179]

By the sixteenth century Erasmus and others had fully explored the classical texts on rhetoric and were writing treatises which not only advise preachers to adopt classical forms but also show them how to do it.[180] Theory was reflected in practice. Some sixteenth-century preachers have so modified the modern form that their sermons do bear a strong resemblance to the classical oration, in that they pursue a fairly straightforward development more or less on the basis of the standard parts of the classical oration.[181] Not all sixteenth-century sermons adopted this form. As in Gerson's day there were still sermons in the ancient mode and still some with a modern or modified modern form. In addition some preachers, chiefly Protestant, used yet another method in which there was no formal symmetry. A passage from Scripture was read out and expounded by gathering 'Doctrines' or lessons and 'Uses' or moral applications from it, sometimes verse by verse.[182] There was, then, still rich variety in preaching after the Renaissance.

Gerson's sermons show that their author had not drunk as deeply at the fountain of classical rhetoric as later humanists were to do. But he had done more than sip. And this is one of the reasons why most – not all – of his vernacular sermons are so effective and so eloquent. If it had occurred to him to do so he could have made his sermons more like classical orations. That he had the necessary knowledge and skill is shown in a vernacular speech that he delivered before the Parlement of Paris on 19 July 1404. This speech was made on behalf of the university against Charles, Duke of Savoisy and some of his retainers because of an incident that had occurred five days earlier. During an official university mass, the duke's troops had attacked and wounded some members of the congregation. Gerson's plea, despite his text, *Estote misericordes* – and he makes play with this – is that justice be done.[183] The speech is a masterpiece of persuasive oratory. It has most of the parts of the classical oration including an exposition of the arguments for leniency put forward by the opposition, a narration of the circumstances of the crime and a refutation of the opposition's case.[184] It is clever, and it is gripping. One is reminded of Cicero's speeches for the prosecution. Not surprisingly Gerson's plea was successful and the duke was punished.[185]

That Gerson did not go further in modifying the modern form is not surprising at this early humanist stage. No theorist was suggesting that he should and Jean de Montreuil thought Gerson's sermon style incomparable as it was. We may not agree with this opinion of Montreuil's when reading some of the less impressive of Gerson's sermons, but at his best Gerson lived up to the high standard of preaching he had set himself.

3
THE ROLE OF THE PASTOR

THE ECCLESIASTICAL HIERARCHY

The young Luther has recently been described as an anti-clerical tribune standing in the great reforming tradition leading from Gerson through Geiler.[1] Certainly Gerson criticised contemporary clerics, and he criticised them for some of the same vices that Luther did.[2] But Gerson is not anti-clerical in the sense of attacking the power and position of the priesthood. On the contrary, he stands out, even among his contemporaries, as a very vocal and firm upholder of the clerical estate, and in particular of one segment of that estate: the pastors. We have already seen the vital importance which Gerson attaches to preaching in the life of the church. But pastors, that is bishops and parish priests, or major and minor prelates as he usually calls them, had additional tasks, and these tasks together Gerson saw as making the role of the pastor absolutely essential in leading the laity to a life of Christian perfection. For Gerson 'No salvation outside the church' might well have been rendered 'No salvation without the pastor.' He would have been in full agreement with an anonymous English preacher's remark that without priests 'there is no help to any Christian man'.[3]

Gerson's general view of the role of the pastor vis-à-vis the laity can be characterised broadly as paternalistic. Certainly his own attitude to the laity, as it comes across in his vernacular sermons and in many of the tracts and sermons he wrote for the instruction of the clergy, bears this characteristic. He gives the impression that he had little faith in the laity's ability to keep on the right track without close clerical supervision, and he was fond of quoting the passage from Ecclesiastes ($1:15$): 'stultorum infinitus est numerus'. It occurs, for instance, in his tract against the Flagellants, where he seems to envisage chaos resulting if there is any departure from the authority of the hierarchy. No sort of cult ought to be introduced by the people, he writes, but everything must be ordained by the mandates of superiors so that in no way is the hierarchical order brought into confusion. But there will be confusion if anybody thinks that he can institute a new rite without a proper leader, without a stable law, without order, where there are mixed up together youths and girls, old and young, rich and poor and all that great crowd of the stupid whose number is infinite, as Ecclesiastes says.[4]

He frequently stressed the importance of following the advice of one's superior, be he parish priest, bishop or abbot, or of an expert in the field, for example a doctor of theology or a discerner of spirits. He was not alone among his contemporaries in emphasising the need for guidance. Thomas à Kempis in his *Imitation of Christ* advises his readers not to be too confident in their own opinion as they seek to advance in the spiritual life, but to be willing to hear the judgement of others.[5] Vincent Ferrier gives similar advice, though he bemoans the fact that it is difficult to find good directors nowadays.[6] But the emphasis is stronger and more central in the chancellor's writings, partly perhaps because of his official position. Moreover, there were some things, he thought, which it would be better if the laity did not hear about at all. Not all knowledge was suitable for all people; subtle points of doctrine, for example, which could be digested by theology students, should be forbidden to the laity, whose need was for milk, not solid food.[7] And he was very doubtful about the value of vernacular translations of the Bible. In fact in one of his lectures on the reform of the theology faculty at Paris he recommended that such translations should be prohibited.[8] What he feared was the laity's getting hold of them and, because of lack of proper theological training, being led into error. He expressed this view cogently in a Christmas sermon, probably to the court, when he was discussing errors about the Virgin Birth:

it is a very dangerous thing to put into the hands of *simples gens* who are not learned clerics the books of Holy Scripture translated into French, for by faulty understanding they can quickly fall into error.[9]

Later in the century Geiler, the other so-called 'forerunner' of the anti-clerical Luther, showed himself almost as fearful as Gerson about laymen reading the Bible and substituting their own interpretations for those of the church.[10]

That Gerson should have had this lack of confidence in the laity is not surprising. He was a very well-educated theologian himself and knew the difficulties involved in biblical interpretation and theological speculation. He had seen theology students and faculty at the University of Paris led astray from what he regarded as the true paths,[11] and if these trained men could err, how much more danger there was of the uneducated, *les simples gens*, wandering off in erroneous and even heretical directions. Further, Gerson had had personal experience of religious deviants among the laity,[12] and was perfectly well aware of the considerable amount of superstition and the number of unorthodox beliefs and practices rampant in his day. He expended much energy, especially in his later years, in trying to combat these deviations, producing numerous tracts on such subjects as magic, astrology and the feast of fools. His sermons, too, contain frequent references to superstitious beliefs that he wished to help to eradicate.[13]

There were, however, churchmen of the period who had more confidence in the laity than Gerson did and who approved of and encouraged lay reading of the Bible. Gerard Zerbolt (1367–98), a priest of the Brethren of the Common Life, is an example. He argues that God gave man the Scriptures so that he could learn about his sinful state, experience sorrow for his sins and refrain from sinning in the future. Hence it is essential that all people, cleric and lay, read the Scriptures.[14] Though the orthodoxy of the Brethren was sometimes questioned, Gerson himself was a firm supporter of the movement. Yet in general he remained nervous about lay initiatives and lay Bible reading, and with good reason from his point of view. Geiler mentions the beliefs of the Waldensians, the Hussites and the Brethren of the Free Spirit as examples of heresies resulting from misinterpretation of the Bible by the uneducated. He could with justice have included the Lollards in this list, a prime example in the fifteenth century of a group of Bible-reading laity and clerics who fell into heresy and made the English bishops as nervous as Gerson about vernacular bibles.[15]

Practical experience and actual conditions, then, led Gerson to the conviction that the laity needed very firm guidance in religious matters. But behind this conviction there lay also a theory about the nature of the church, a theory not original to Gerson, but expressed quite clearly in numerous places in his writings and adapted to some extent to fit the conditions of his lifetime. These discussions about ecclesiology occur chiefly in Latin rather than vernacular works. One of the reasons for this is that Gerson saw the pastors of his day as not properly fulfilling their role in the church, as not living up to the ideal. Hence they had to be admonished and shown what this ideal was. But Gerson was adamant in his opinion that clerics should not be criticised in the hearing of lay folk,[16] and in his own popular sermons there is virtually no such criticism, and hence very little of that systematic discussion of the nature of the church for which such criticism was frequently the occasion. Rather, such discussions are found in his Latin sermons to local synods and certain related tracts.[17] He was also moved to write on the subject at various points during the controversy over the relationship between the papacy and a general council, while the conflict between the Mendicants and the secular clergy was the occasion of a number of works by the chancellor on the status of the latter in the church. There is in fact one vernacular sermon, preached in 1410, that belongs to this latter group, and which contains a clear statement and discussion of the nature of the church and the place of prelates in it.[18]

Gerson conceived of the church as essentially hierarchical in nature. In fact, from one point of view, he can be said to have seen the church as made up of ordered ranks of clerics only, with the laity as outsiders, inferiors to be helped towards their spiritual end by the church, but not true members of it. He does, of course, from time to time, along with most medieval theologians, refer to the church as the congregation of the faithful.[19] This definition was a commonplace by the High Middle Ages.[20] But for all practical purposes, the visible church, for Gerson, is hierarchical and clerical. He is very far indeed from holding the radical views of some of his predecessors and contemporaries. He specifically criticises an opinion, mentioned though perhaps not held by Occam in the latter's *Dialogus*, that the church being essentially a spiritual society would still exist if it were reduced to laity or even to only one faithful layman or laywoman.[21] With this state of affairs, Gerson argues, no sacramental life or continuity would be possible; the church must have a hierarchy of clergy.[22] Essentially it *is* a hierarchy of ecclesiastics. For Gerson, if the laity was part of the church, it was merely *ecclesia audiens*. This was a very different notion of the church from that envisaged by the doctrine of the priesthood of all believers, already present in Gerson's lifetime among some of the Lollards and appearing full-blown in Luther a century later.[23] This was a doctrine whereby Gerson's and indeed most medieval theologians' division of Christendom into clergy and laity was rendered meaningless, and all Christians were seen as being of the same estate. Gerson would have been horrified at it, judging by his reaction to the views put forward by a spiritual Franciscan that the prayer of a devout woman or layman is worth as much as many masses of a sinful priest, and that the life of one devout person is more useful to the church than the life of proud preachers or the preaching of the divine Word. Gerson shows a formidable fierceness in his response. He calls the assertions scandalous, erroneous, dangerous and to be utterly repudiated. They derogate from the position of the ecclesiastical hierarchy and will lead to pride and rebellion on the part of the laity. All his distrust of laymen and especially laywomen, and even nuns, pours forth as he defends the status of prelates.[24]

What, then, were the contours of Gerson's hierarchical church? His thought on this subject was strongly influenced, as was that of many other preceding and contemporary theologians, by the writings of Pseudo-Dionysius, still believed by most people in Gerson's day to have been the Areopagite, the disciple of St Paul, and thereby carrying great weight as an authority.[25] The Dionysian universe of living beings was essentially hierarchical in nature, with the terrestrial order reflecting the celestial order, the church here below imitating and made in the image of the heavenly church. At the apex was God, from whom all creatures came and towards whom all creatures, according to their capacity, should strive. The celestial hierarchy was composed of nine ranks of angels, arranged in groups of threes: Seraphim, Cherubim and Thrones; Dominions, Virtues and Powers; Principalities, Archangels and Angels, with each triad also constituting a hierarchy and having within itself distinct gradations.[26] Each rank, with the help of divine grace, engaged in the hierarchical activities of purifying, illuminating and perfecting the rank below it, towards the end of a union of love of each, according to his capacity, with God. For Dionysius, divine grace that leads to this union must be transmitted by mediators; only the highest rank of angels, the Seraphim, can communicate with God directly. They then, by their hierarchical activity, act as transmitters to the rank below them and so on down to the Angels, who are the ultimate mediators between God and man.[27]

Dionysius' ecclesiastical hierarchy is not a perfect image of his celestial hierarchy. The former has only two triads, not three. The first triad is made up of bishops, priests and ministers (lectors, acolytes, deacons), and the second of monks, holy laity and those undergoing purification (catechumens, energumens and penitents). Nor do all ranks engage in all the hierarchical activities towards the rank immediately beneath them, as was the case with the celestial hierarchy. The bishops' task is chiefly to perfect; but to perfect not only the priests but also members of the second triad, especially the monks. The task of illumination falls to the priests, and they illumine primarily the holy people, while purification of the catechumens, energumens and penitents is performed by the ministers. Although the bishop's predominant task is perfecting, Dionysius does acknowledge that he can perform the other two lesser hierarchical activities, while the priest can also purify. The members of the second triad perform no hierarchical activities at all; they are essentially passive. The monks have no role to play vis-à-vis the holy people, nor the holy people towards the catechumens. Moreover the mediation rule is not perfectly applied, for the bishop ordains not only priests but also ministers, and he baptises the catechumens, while the priest teaches and consecrates monks, without the mediation of the ministers.[28] It is clear that the author had to adapt his scheme to the actual situation in the church of his own day and hence a perfect symmetry could not be attained. With the celestial hierarchy, however, there were very few data to go on, and the Neo-Platonic concept of the triadic nature of the divine order, with strict rules of mediation, could be more perfectly preserved. But the basic thrust of Dionysius' thought is clear. Grace comes from the Deity and creatures approach the Deity by means of mediators. There is no direct and immediate contact.

The Dionysian concept that the terrestrial order was a reflection of the celestial order and that the church on earth mirrored the hierarchy of the church in heaven was a commonplace of theological thought long before and during Gerson's time.[29] But there were numerous opinions about the actual form of the terrestrial hierarchy and the activities performed by each rank. The actual institutions of the church had changed since the fifth century, and hence descriptions of the ecclesiastical hierarchy had to change. The variations in opinion occurred because theologians viewed the relative importance of institutions (for example, the papacy, the religious orders, the parish priests) differently.

Gerson's view is in the tradition of the Parisian secular theologians of the thirteenth and fourteenth centuries. The church was founded by Christ and is ordered hierarchically, since 'if all things which are from God are ordered, as the Apostle says, this must certainly be true of the church'.[30] Further the church was founded 'in its orders according to the pattern of the celestial order'.[31] And the celestial hierarchy is made up of the same nine orders of angels, grouped in three triads, as those of Dionysius.[32] But the ecclesiastical hierarchy is rather different from the fifth-century version. In the first place, there are three ranked groups, not two. The pope and cardinals form the first group and correspond to the first angelic triad, while patriarchs, archbishops, bishops and parish priests mirror the second angelic triad. The third group is formed by the religious orders and laity.[33] Although Gerson has adapted the upper ranks of the church, he still has the religious and laity together at the bottom as Dionysius had.

Despite the fact that Gerson had departed in some respects from his mentor, he regards the ecclesiastical hierarchy as he describes it as divinely instituted and not to be altered or disturbed in any way by anyone, even the pope. The status of parish priests and bishops, he writes, was instituted by Christ. This is clear because the apostles, whose successors the bishops are, and the seventy-two disciples, whose successors the parish priests are, were sent directly by Christ and received hierarchical power, not from Peter but from Christ Himself. It follows therefore that the pope cannot abolish or remove the status of bishops or parish priests from the church. Nor can the pope remove or suspend the subjection due from all parishioners to the parish priests.[34] In the same work Gerson argues that the parish clergy do not have the same relationship to their bishops as bailiffs do to kings. Bailiffs have merely delegated jurisdiction, whereas parish priests have ordinary jurisdiction over their subordinates; their jurisdiction is theirs by right, and they cannot be removed from office at the mere wish of their bishop, without due cause, whereas princes can remove bailiffs at will.[35] The same is true of the relationship between bishop and pope.[36] Further, bishops, although they have authority to appoint coadjutor confessors in their dioceses, must take great care if they do this not to disturb the ecclesiastical hierarchy by taking away directly or indirectly the power of the parish clergy.[37] In the same way, the papacy in granting privileges to the Mendicant orders must not interfere with the authority of bishops or of parish priests.[38]

What happens to hierarchical order if the pastor is a sinner? Does he lose his hierarchical power as the Donatists claimed? The church, of course, had had an answer to the Donatist heresy ever since Augustine's times. The answer finds its place with varying degrees of explanation in the writings of Hugh of St Victor, St Thomas and other scholastic theologians.[39] By

Gerson's time the problem had developed a certain urgency with the reappearance of the heresy among Wycliffites and Hussites.[40] Gerson saw the danger and vehemently attacked the heresy. He thought that the denial of hierarchical authority to prelates presumed to be in a state of sin was the most pernicious of all Hus' errors, a threat to the whole conservation of the church.[41] The question of the validity of the sacraments administered by sinful priests seems also to have bothered the *simples gens*, judging from the number of times, even in his vernacular sermons, that Gerson asserted the doctrine that the authority of neither bishops nor priests is dependent on their state of soul; they do not have to be in a state of grace to maintain their hierarchical status. 'And why? Because otherwise the hierarchical order of ecclesiastical power would be unstable, doubtful and uncertain.'[42] The same concern is shown by Geiler, who frequently tells his congregations that the moral state of a priest does not affect the validity of the masses he says or the sacraments he administers.[43]

Donatism was not the only problem threatening to disturb the hierarchical order of Gerson's lifetime. The complex and difficult situation caused by the schism was even more serious and led Gerson to produce a number of writings as he tried to define the exact position and power of the papacy in the ecclesiastical hierarchy and its relationship especially to a general council. His views in fact shifted as the concrete situation changed, and it was by almost reluctant stages that he came to accept not only the necessity of a general council of the church but also its legitimacy.[44] He never, however, any more than the other moderate conciliarists, became anti-papal. In a work of 1409 he explicitly rejects the extreme position of Marsilius of Padua (1290–1345) who exalted councils over popes in principle, not just for situations of emergency, and who considered every bishop a pope within his own diocese.[45] On the contrary, writes Gerson, the church is an immutable monarchy with one head, founded as such by Christ.[46] Gerson never denied the need for a supreme pontiff, and his goal during the whole schism was always the restoration of peace in the church with one pope as head of the hierarchy and an undivided and reformed Christendom.

But how much power should this head have? Gerson was far from being a papal absolutist of the brand of Aegidius Romanus (d. 1316), for whom the power of the pope was 'spiritual, heavenly and divine', and so great that it exceeds 'all weight, number and dimension'.[47] By at least 1402 Gerson was openly rejecting this type of papal absolutism. The power of the pope, he says, is not absolute. On the contrary, it would be lawful to resist the pope if he attempted unlawful aggression against the lives or property of the faithful and thereby offended against justice. The reason for this limitation of authority is that 'the power of a superior cannot enact anything against the truth of natural and divine law, because that power was not given for destruction but for edification'.[48]

His final position on papal power was basically a *via media* between the two extremes. Even though he had not been a conciliarist from the beginning like Conrad of Gelnhausen and Henry of Langenstein,[49] Gerson eventually became a committed one, and committed not only to the doctrine that if there was no true pope or if there were rival claimants, the whole power of the church could be exercised by a general council, but also ultimately to the doctrine that a council had a part to play even when there was a single true pope. His mature doctrine appears in both *Ambulate*, the sermon he preached in March 1415 after John XXIII's flight from Constance, and in *De potestate ecclesiastica*, presented at the Council in February 1417. In both works Gerson gives the pope an exalted place in the church. It is in the pope under Christ, he declares, that the unity of the church consists. He has a plenitude of power granted by Christ, and superior to that of any other ecclesiastical or temporal power, which a general council cannot take away. However, a general council can regulate and limit the pope's use of that power if it is necessary for the edification of the church. And it can do this because it is greater (*major*) than the pope in breadth, in infallible guidance, in the reformation of morals, in coercive power, in decisions about matters of faith, and greater finally because more abundant (*copiosior*), representing as it does the hierarchy of the whole church. Moreover, a general council is so ruled by the Holy Spirit that 'everyone of whatsoever rank, even papal, is obliged to hear and obey it'. When it ordains anything about the regulation of the church, the pope is not superior to those laws and so he cannot, at will, abrogate them. As for its own reformation, the church has no more effective means than to establish a continuous sequence of general councils.[50]

This appears like an attempt to have it both ways. Plenitude of power belongs to the pope, the supreme head of the hierarchy, but he shares power with the council, and in this sharing the council ultimately has the upper hand. Gerson makes this latter point quite clear in his *De examinatione doctrinarum* of 1423. He argues that the authentic examiner and final judge of doctrines pertaining to the faith (he is thinking here of private revelations and true or false prophets) is a general council. The pope is the juridical examiner of doctrine, after the general council. It is true that the pope may deceive or be deceived, yet he is a suitable judge because he is always in session, as it were, whereas a council is not. However, if he does err there always remains the remedy of a general council whose 'final, authoritative and judicial power is founded indestructibly in the words of Christ about fraternal correction: if he refuses to listen to the church let him be to you as a gentile and a publican (Matt. 18:17). Without doubt the pope is under the law.'[51] There were conciliarists, for example the members of the schismatic Council of Basle, who were more radical than Gerson and who would have made the pope hardly more than a figurehead in the government of the church.[52] But the circumstances of the schism had certainly made Gerson go quite far in setting limits to the power of the pope, the peak of the ecclesiastical hierarchy.

If Gerson's view about the top rank of the hierarchy shifted, his views about the middle rank and its relationship to the ranks below it and above it remained consistent. Bishops and parish priests were the successors of the apostles and disciples and had been part of the hierarchical church from the very beginning. Gerson is aware, however, that developments in this hierarchy have taken place since the time of Christ and the primitive church, when numbers were small. Aristotelian teleology helps him to cope with the problem. If numbers have expanded, he says, and further gradations of ranks have appeared, these were present in essence from the beginning and the developments are merely an unfolding and flowering of these elements, just as the oak is the full development of the potentialities in the acorn.[53]

HIERARCHICAL ACTIVITY

Major and minor prelates, then, are an integral part of the divinely instituted ecclesiastical hierarchy. What is their specific role in the church? As in the Dionysian scheme their task is to engage in the hierarchical activities of purgation, illumination and perfection towards the rank beneath them. It is no doubt because of his interest in mysticism that Gerson so often describes the tasks of prelates in Dionysian terms, for it was chiefly the medieval mystics and medieval theologians writing about mysticism who used and developed this particular Dionysian theme.[54] But Gerson alters Dionysius' scheme. Whereas the latter's ministers purified, priests illuminated and bishops perfected the monks and laity, Gerson's bishops and parish priests each perform all these activities, especially in relation to the laity.[55] Parish priests no less than bishops have the right and duty to purify by correction, that is by excommunication and by the sacrament of penance, to illuminate by teaching and preaching, and to perfect by administration of the other sacraments, especially the Eucharist. These tasks were enjoined upon them by Christ and He gave to both orders the power of the keys, the authority to bind and loose.[56] These powers are also enjoyed, of course, by the first order of the hierarchy, the pope and cardinals; but these perform the hierarchical activities principally towards the members of the second order, the prelates. It is the bishops and priests who have the primary duty towards the laity, who themselves, with the other members of the third order, have no hierarchical duties.[57] This is why the church consists chiefly of the first two orders and not the third.[58] The church is essentially a church of prelates, and the laity is less a part of it than popes, cardinals, bishops and priests, precisely because laymen have no divinely ordained hierarchical functions.

The goal of the pastor's hierarchical activity is, as was the case in Dionysius' scheme, to lead those in his charge towards a union of love with God, to sanctify them and to restore the image of God in them, insofar as this is possible on earth. A perfect union of love can generally be realised only in heaven, but steps towards it can be and should be taken within the terrestrial church.[59] Thus the salvation of souls lies in the hands of prelates,[60] for as Gerson expresses it more than once, quoting Dionysius, 'the lowest are led back to the highest by means of the intermediate'.[61] The primary meaning he attaches to this phrase is that the third order of the ecclesiastical hierarchy, the laity and the religious, is led by the two upper orders, especially the pastors, to God. There are occasional exceptions to this rule of mediation, as when God revealed Himself directly to St Paul. But, as Gerson reminds his congregation, this is not the normal method of procedure, any more than it is normal for a king to deliver his own messages to an individual rather than to send an officer.[62] Occasionally, too, people without hierarchical rank and without being commanded by a member of the hierarchy can perform the hierarchical function of preaching, but only if they can show by a miracle or prophecy or some other sign that they are sent directly by God.[63] And clearly this is very rare. The divine ordinance is that in almost all cases members of the two upper orders of the hierarchy, or those to whom they grant such powers, may alone perform hierarchical functions.

Gerson's ecclesiastical hierarchy no more mirrors exactly the celestial hierarchy than that of Dionysius did. Popes do not perform hierarchical activities only towards cardinals, nor bishops only towards priests, and religious as such do not have any part to play in the purifying and illuminating of the laity. Further, Gerson's emphasis, in his works about the education of children, on each person's guardian angel involves several hierarchical jumps. And where do doctors of theology fit in? Gerson places great importance on their role in the church, especially in the problems of reform and the ending of the schism. The University of Paris and especially the faculty of theology he regards as illuminating the entire church.[64] But doctors of theology as such have no place in the ecclesiastical hierarchy, and Gerson becomes involved in subtle reasoning to show that the first two ranks of the hierarchy can be corrected on doctrinal matters by theologians, and that prelates should not authoritatively define anything with respect to the faith unless it has first been discussed and decided by doctors of the church.[65] He has to argue, for instance, that the determining and teaching authority of theologians is in fact granted by the hierarchy, though, having been granted, and this by human and not divine ordinance, it cannot be taken away. Gerson's contemporary, Jean Courtecuisse, had a similar lofty view of the place of doctors of theology in the church. He argues that in the exposition of Scripture they rank above prelates and those who possess jurisdictional powers, and so do not have to recant their assertions at the mere warning of prelates or even of the pope.[66] A century or so earlier St Thomas had ranked doctors of theology above parish clergy. The latter, in his opinion, are like manual workers, whereas the former are like master craftsmen because they study and teach how others should achieve the salvation of souls. For Thomas, however, bishops also are master craftsmen because they order and organise the work of the parish priests.[67] The intervening years would seem to have given doctors of theology an enhanced sense of the importance of their office. Clearly, the establishment and development of universities was causing trouble for those, like Gerson, who wished to preserve the essence of the Dionysian scheme, but who also had a high regard for the teaching office. Luther, who in 1520 defended his opposition to what he regarded as the errors of the papacy on the grounds that he was a doctor of Holy Scripture,[68] did not have the same trouble. He was prepared to abandon the hierarchy.

The Mendicant orders, too, caused trouble for Gerson's theory and he gives them a place which did not really correspond to their actual role in the church. The Dionysian ecclesiastical hierarchy was out-of-date and Gerson failed to bring it completely up-to-date. Others tried in different ways; for example St Bonaventure, in one of his characterisations of the ecclesiastical hierarchy, has the laity alone in the lowest order corresponding to the lowest triad of angels; secular clergy, including popes, in the middle; and religious in the highest order, with the followers of St Francis, as one might expect, corresponding to the Seraphim, the very highest rank in the celestial hierarchy.[69] Bonaventure is ordering the church here according to activities exercised and he sees the purely active life as lowest, and the contemplative as highest, with the mixed life led by secular clerics holding the middle position. Gerson, on the other hand, above all wished to exalt the position of the bishops and the parish clergy, for he placed most of his hopes for reform and for the salvation of souls on them, because they were or ought to have been in close and constant contact with the laity.[70]

In one important way Gerson departed completely from Dionysian principles. For Dionysius, Christ influenced and acted upon the ecclesiastical hierarchy only through the mediacy of the celestial hierarchy, whereas for Gerson Christ could perform hierarchical functions directly towards the ecclesiastical hierarchy. In a synodal sermon Gerson has Christ say to the bishops:

Your office is to purify, illuminate and perfect others so that they bear the celestial image; therefore I have purified, illuminated and perfected you, because what is dirty cannot clean, what is dark cannot illuminate, what is broken cannot perfect.[71]

There is no mention of angelic mediators here. But whatever the relationship was between Christ, the celestial hierarchy and the upper ranks of the church, it remained true for Gerson that normally the laity was led to a life of Christian perfection by its pastors.

All in the church 'without distinction' are called to pursue perfection according to Christ's injunction. This is a thesis endorsed by a twentieth-century general council, Vatican II.[72] Gerson would have fervently endorsed it. The belief that the life of Christian perfection, insofar as it is attainable on earth, is open to all and not just confined to those in religious orders echoes through his writings. It forms the chief topic of three of his works that among them span about thirty years: the disputation *De consiliis evangelicis et statu perfectionis* of the 1390s; the brief tract *Contra conclusiones Mathaei Graben* of 1418; and the *De perfectione cordis* of 1423, while in between are those vernacular tracts that call the *simples gens*, whatever their station, to the perfect Christian life.[73]

The reason that a life of Christian perfection is open to all is that it consists not in severe asceticism, but rather in *caritas*. A person who has given charity the primary place in his life is close to God. Just as the life of the body is more perfect, the closer the union between it and the soul, which activates, informs and vivifies it, so too the life of the soul is more perfect, the closer it is united to God, its vital and perfect principle. And this closeness is achieved through charity, 'since he who abides in charity abides in God and God in him'. Living in charity means obeying the precepts: 'Love God with your whole heart and soul and love your neighbour as yourself.' Only the blessed in heaven can fulfil these commands completely, but even on earth they should and can be fulfilled to the extent that *viatores* can, in varying degrees, live close to God and so live a life of Christian perfection.[74]

This was by no means a new doctrine. It is expressed clearly, for instance, by Aquinas.[75] But it needed restating because opposing it was the view that a life of perfection was open only to an elite group: those who followed not only the precepts but also the evangelical counsels, that is members of religious orders, who made vows of poverty, chastity and obedience. Gerson refers specifically to Matthew Grabon, who had put forward this opinion at Constance. On the contrary, Gerson argues, vows of poverty, chastity and obedience, and all types of ascetic practice, with or without vows, are not of the essence of the life of perfection; they are not even virtues, but merely aids to virtue and to the life of charity.[76] It is no doubt easier for the man who has undertaken poverty voluntarily, the ascetic and the virgin to love God and his neighbour, but this does not mean that the rich, the married, and the sick and old who are unable to fast are thereby incapable of loving God and their neighbour, and are bound therefore to be imperfect.[77]

Gerson finds support for his belief in various examples taken from Scripture. Abraham was rich and married and yet was in close union with God, and the same is true of other Old Testament patriarchs and prophets.[78] Nowhere is it written that Christ Himself made vows of poverty, chastity and obedience, and yet who lived more perfectly than He? Many of the

apostles and disciples and Christians in the primitive church were married
and had possessions and yet lived lives of Christian perfection.[79] The
primitive church as a whole in fact proves for Gerson that the union of love
with God is open to all. Moreover, it is clear, he argues, that there are many
living under vows in the so-called state of perfection who are far from
perfect, while there are others living outside the religious orders who are
much nearer to perfection.[80]

Vatican II declared that even though the way of perfection is open to all,
the observance of the evangelical counsels is 'a singular help' to holiness.[81]
Gerson would have agreed, and even with the word 'singular'.[82] There
were people in his lifetime, however, who thought the profession of vows
a hindrance to holiness. Some of the Lollard preachers are prime examples
here with their attacks on monks and friars, often likened to the Pharisees
and scribes of the New Testament.[83] In the years before and during the
Reformation the debate continued at various levels. One thinks of Erasmus'
colloquy *The Seraphic Funeral*, where the arguments on both sides are put
forward in light and amusing vein, with a number of glimpses of popular
superstitions attaching to the supposed perfection of, in this case, the
Franciscans.[84] Gerson would probably not have approved of Erasmus'
humorous handling of such a serious subject, but he would have agreed
with the chief message of the piece: 'There's room for evangelical perfection
in every walk of life.'[85] Gerson's relegation of the laity to a very lowly
position in the hierarchical church has to be seen in this context: 'In every
status, sex, order, rank holy people [*perfecti viri*] can be found.'[86]

PREACHING AND EDUCATION

If the life of Christian perfection is a possibility for all, then the responsibility
of the pastor, who is the necessary mediator between the laity and God, is
indeed grave. How is he to lead his flock to union with God? Gerson,
especially in his synodal sermons, provides a great deal of guidance for
bishops and parish priests as he elaborates on what he thinks the hierarchical
functions of purifying, illuminating and perfecting actually involve. He was
very much aware that many pastors were falling short of the ideal and at
times he is bitterly critical of their failings. They are wolves who threaten
and devour their flocks, rather than shepherds, he says more than once.[87]
But on the whole his synodal sermons leave an optimistic impression as he
paints his picture of the ideal pastor, and puts forward practical suggestions
for the reform of the existing situation. He distinguishes, of course,
between the role and tasks of the bishop and those of the parish priest.
Though both major and minor prelates are called upon to perform the same
hierarchical functions they are not expected, in all cases, to perform them
in the same way.

In *De potestate ecclesiastica* Gerson defines purgation as correction by excommunication and interdict and by the sacraments of baptism and penance; illumination is to be carried out by teaching and preaching, while perfection is performed by the administration of the other sacraments.[88] In the synodal sermons Gerson deviates somewhat from this characterisation. In *Redde quod debes* teaching and preaching remain the ways in which the illumination of the laity is performed, but purification now is carried out largely by the example of the pastor's own holy life, and the work of perfecting is performed by the administration of all the sacraments.[89] Similarly in *Bonus pastor* Gerson exhorts the clergy to feed their flocks with the word of preaching, the example of a good life, and the aid of charity and grace; and the latter, he says, can be fed to Christ's sheep no more efficaciously than by the administration of the sacraments.[90]

Although for Dionysius purification had to come first, illumination second and perfection last as the culmination of hierarchical activity, Gerson by no means always follows this order when he is preaching or writing on the topic. In some works on the tasks of pastors he does not write explicitly in terms of the hierarchical activities at all. In other words he is no slave to the Dionysian pattern and does not always feel bound to fit the manifold duties of pastors into the three-fold framework.

He generally begins with preaching, which, as we have seen, he along with other medieval theologians regarded as vitally important in the salvation of souls. It was above all on the pastors that the duty of preaching lay.[91] The New Testament, Gerson argues, stresses the need for preaching above all else and it is the prelates, major and minor, to whom this task was specifically assigned by Christ.[92] Though all medieval theologians would have agreed with Gerson here with respect to major prelates, some would have dissented about minor prelates. St Thomas, for instance, sees the bishop as the only one on whom the preaching office primarily devolves.[93] Basevorn adds the pope and cardinals to the category of those who must preach 'by necessity of salvation'.[94] Neither excludes parish priests from preaching; rather it is a question of where the commission comes from, Christ or the bishop. For Gerson it comes from Christ and there is no doubt that he insists more strongly than Thomas or Basevorn on the duty of minor prelates to preach to their parishioners.[95] He does, however, agree with them that major prelates have a greater responsibility in preaching than minor prelates, in the sense that the former need to know more. The bishop must have a more profound knowledge of the law of God, by which Gerson means a knowledge of Scripture and the divine law contained therein, together with a knowledge of those things deduced from Scripture by the church, and those things told directly to the apostles and disciples by Christ and handed down by apostolic succession.[96] Parish priests, by contrast, need only a general and broad knowledge (*cognitio generalis et grossa*). The reason for this is that bishops, unlike parish priests, need to be able to answer all questioners and to argue with subtlety against heretics and the like.[97] Courtecuisse puts it a little differently in a Pentecost sermon: the Holy Spirit gives bishops the gift of wisdom (*sapientia*), that is true knowledge of God and the savour of His goodness so that they can preach it to others; clergy of lesser degree should know the commandments of God and explain them to the *menu peuple*; this is accomplished by the gift of knowledge (*science*).[98] Courtecuisse is being brief here – as suits a vernacular sermon – about the knowledge required of a parish priest. Gerson goes into more detail. He frequently lists the items that he thinks fall under the heading of *cognitio generalis et grossa*. In *Bonus pastor*, for example, the list includes, as well as the commandments, the articles of faith, the sacraments, the distinction of sins and which of them are reserved. The priest should know these 'cum quadam explanatione grossa'.[99] In his letter to the newly appointed bishop of Coutances he suggests various books which the bishop should see that his parish clergy study: Gregory's homilies and *Pastoral Rule*, the lives and collections of sayings of the Fathers, the legends of the saints, the *Manipulus curatorum*, a recent life of Christ and some books of devotion. The bishop himself, in addition to these works, should also read the gospels, especially those of Luke and John, Paul's Epistles, the Decretum, the IIa-IIae of St Thomas, the *Summa de vitiis et virtutibus* and certain recent tracts, published in Paris, on the commandments, mortal sins, instructing the dying, the approach to contemplation and so on.[100] The parish priest, in other words, is not expected to have the breadth and depth of learning of the bishop because he is not expected to preach such learned sermons as the bishop could, if the occasion demanded. In his sermons the parish priest needs to transmit to his congregation – made up for the most part of simple and uneducated people – only the basic message of the gospel, the commandments, the articles of faith, the mortal sins and the works of charity.[101] He can guide his parishioners satisfactorily if he is known as a man of charity and good moral life, even if he lacks learning. Besides he can easily (*cum facili studio*) acquire what he needs to know for governing his parish.[102]

Gerson's standards for the educational level of parish priests seem fairly low, but they are no lower than, for example, St Thomas' a century earlier. The latter too thought that the knowledge required of parish priests could be easily learned (*de facili addiscitur*), for it was very limited in scope. The parish priest must, of course, know how to administer the sacraments. He should also know 'those things which pertain to the teaching of faith and morals', but he does not have to know 'how to prove matters of faith and hope', but simply 'how to show in a general way their probability', a task, Aquinas concludes, 'which does not demand any great learning'.[103] A half-century later William of Pagula, in his *Oculus sacerdotis*, stated that candidates for the priesthood were not to be examined 'too rigidly, but rather in a summary fashion and leniently'. In fact, he argued, as long as the candidate had a reasonable literacy and a public reputation as a man of good character, the examination could be dispensed with.[104]

Perhaps these low standards were the only ones practical for the time. The actual standards reached, with the prevailing 'apprenticeship' method for the training of many of the parish clergy, were in many cases even lower than Gerson recommended. There was no possibility that all parish priests could go to university and there were no seminaries.[105] The 'stupid priest' was indeed a target for popular criticism during the later Middle Ages. The criticism finds its way into sermons too. 'They fish in the night, that is in ignorance', says an anonymous fifteenth-century preacher of northern France.[106] Gerson, with his strong conviction that parish priests had a divinely ordained preaching mission, was aware of the problem and, like a number of other members of the clerical establishment of the period, wanted the situation reformed. He recommends that schools of theology be set up in all dioceses for the theological training of parish clergy,[107] and here he is envisaging something resembling the seminary system established after the Council of Trent. He also thinks that a period of absence for study – presumably at a university – could be valuable for a parish priest, 'if the purpose were sincere, if the permission of the superior were given and if arrangements were made for a good substitute'.[108] His other recommendations are less ambitious: the proper examination of candidates for ordination; the publishing of handbooks on the basic elements of the faith to help the parish clergy; and the teaching of these basic elements to the clergy in diocesan synods and during visitations.[109]

He himself produced a brief vernacular compendium of basic doctrine for parish priests, which lists the twelve articles of faith, the ten commandments, the seven mortal sins, with their various 'branches', the three theological virtues, the seven sacraments with the proper verbal *formulae* for each, and the sins reserved for absolution by bishops and the pope.[110] His *Doctrinal aux simples gens*, a much fuller discussion of the same topics, was meant to be read by parish priests to their congregations.[111] He wrote a number of other tracts for *curés* to help them not only in their work of preaching but also in their other hierarchical activities. Clearly the training and education of parish priests was of great concern to him, precisely because they were the members of the hierarchy in closest touch with the laity. Moreover, perhaps the simple and basic knowledge was enough. If a *curé* could lead the members of his congregation to keep the commandments and avoid sin, he had, on Gerson's premises, succeeded in leading them far along the road to a life of Christian perfection. This was the purpose of all hierarchical activity. Although Gerson stated that preaching was the way in which illumination was carried out, he clearly envisaged sermons as also purifying and perfecting. For the aim was not simply to teach the faithful basic doctrine but to move them to right action, to purge themselves of sin and to perfect their lives.[112]

EXAMPLE

Preaching was not enough on its own to achieve the desired end. Pastors must also so perfect their own lives that they provide an ideal for the faithful to follow. This dictum had echoed down the centuries. It found forcible expression in Gregory's *Pastoral Rule*, a work that was extremely influential throughout the Middle Ages. The pastor must provide a good example, wrote Gregory, for if he 'who has the name and rank of sanctity' sins, the offence spreads as the flock feels free to imitate him.[113] Gerson takes this very seriously and he agrees with his Italian contemporary, Bernadine, that a pastor who gives bad example injures the souls of his parishioners.[114] It is when he is discussing this subject that Gerson is most critical of contemporary pastors, especially the bishops, and it is their misuse of their wealth that disturbs him most.[115] Gerson was far from aligning himself with those who thought that the clergy should divest themselves of all their wealth and pursue lives of evangelical poverty. Although he praised the primitive church as primarily a spiritual institution, because it owned few material possessions, he did not thereby condemn the Donation of Constantine, which he thought had been responsible for the temporal endowment of the church. Rather, whereas it was necessary in the early missionary days for the church to be free of material cares,[116] by the time of Constantine circumstances had changed and it was seen that temporalities would aid the church in spreading the gospel. Now was the time to attract the upper classes, the wealthy and the learned, who brought new honour to the church. The Holy Spirit, he says, does not always call people in the same way. 'Now by adversity, now by prosperity; now by poverty, now by abundance He draws those whom He knows as His own.'[117] It was all part of God's plan that the church should be endowed at that point, and the acceptance of that endowment by the holy Fathers and by others right up to the present day is a sign that it was divinely inspired.[118]

However, Gerson does see that the Donation had some unfortunate consequences. Some of the clergy came to value the temporal above the spiritual, to become absorbed in their material possessions and to neglect their spiritual duties. At times he even seems to hanker after the poverty of the primitive church. 'If all things in prelates were in accord with the status of poverty of Christ and His apostles, the imitation of Christ and the apostles would be more perfect and useful than is the case with the magnificent status maintained by prelates nowadays.'[119] But this was in a private letter to d'Ailly. Gerson would not, in contrast to some, have uttered such words before the laity. In public he always maintained that the endowment of the church was God's plan for this part of the church's history and that what mattered was the spirit in which ecclesiastical wealth was used. After all, poverty itself was not a virtue; it too could be used both properly and improperly. 'To have riches and to use them well can be in

EXAMPLE   53

many cases a greater perfection than to have nothing and to beg...the state of begging can lead to theft and frauds and other evils, when the person is not content with what others give to him voluntarily.'[120]

In his own day, Gerson saw too much improper use of ecclesiastical wealth, too much attention given to temporal possessions and their maintenance and increase. The shepherds have turned into wolves, he writes again, who steal wool, milk, flesh and bones from the sheep, by their heavy tallages, excessive charges for litigation and their own luxurious living.[121] Curbs must be put on these and similar practices. In other words, pastors, and Gerson has bishops especially in mind here, must be, and must be seen to be, free from the sins of avarice and gluttony. In the first place bishops must prohibit their officials from using their authority to inflict unjust charges on the laity. Legal officers, for example, must be stopped from making unjust arrests just so that they can collect fees from the legal procedures necessary to free the innocent. It would be far better if such officers were to receive adequate salaries from the bishop so that they were not tempted to such expedients.[122] Punishments in the form of financial exactions should be avoided in the bishop's courts when other types of punishment would be of more use in reforming the guilty. Where monetary penalties are imposed the money should be used for charitable purposes.[123]

Gerson's second recommendation is about the avoidance of simony. Simony came in for a good deal of criticism in this period. Simoniacal priests, along with tyrannical princes, flattering counsellors and thieving knights were of the school of the devil, according to d'Ailly.[124] For Maillard the church is not so much the perpetrator of simony as the victim of it, for it is by simony that rapacious, ignorant, ambitious and lascivious members of feudal society acquire benefices for themselves.[125] Gerson, too, is concerned about the acquisition of benefices by simony, but he is equally concerned about the practices of pastors in office. They must avoid all taint of simony. And this applies to parish priests as well as to bishops. They must not give the impression that spiritual benefits, such as the sacraments, are up for sale. They must be prepared to administer these freely if necessary – in fact the sacraments themselves should be administered freely if at all possible – but normally pastors may take the customary, moderate payments for burials and so on.[126] This question of simony exercised Gerson greatly and some time after 1416 he wrote a treatise on it, trying to draw the very fine line between the perfectly legal and moral receiving of contributions in return for the conferment of spiritual benefits and the illegal and immoral practice of simony. His conclusion is that pastors are clearly justified in receiving some payment for their work – the labourer is worthy of his hire – but financial reward must not be their primary motive, though it may be a secondary one.[127]

Thirdly, Gerson argues that it is better from all points of view that pastors should live austerely and not luxuriously. In *Bonus pastor* he criticises especially the lavish meals served in bishops' households, the costly clothes worn and the general pomp and size of episcopal *entourages*, made up often of lustful and drunken retainers.[128] In a university lecture of 1402, he points out that such an extravagant style of living does not please God, to whom pious works are much more gratifying. Nor does it please or edify the people, for pomp in clerics scandalises the laity, and makes them envious and ready to murmur against all ecclesiastics. The frugality of the clergy of the primitive church inspired far more devotion and honour than does the 'dispendiousness' of the present generation. Moreover, Gerson continues, luxurious living costs vast sums of money which can be obtained only from unjust exactions from the populace. A prelate is entitled to maintain a decent status, but he should not go beyond this. Gerson acknowledges that 'decent status' is difficult to define, but it is better and safer to err on the side of frugality, to imitate the humility and poverty of Christ, than to try to ape the princes of this world.[129]

On the positive side, Gerson urges prelates to be lavish and open in charitable works. After all, ecclesiastical wealth beyond that which is necessary for the maintenance of a decent standard of living for clerics is the patrimony of the poor, and should be used accordingly.[130] Pastors, therefore, should be 'those who aid schoolboys, widows, prisoners, the sick and afflicted, old husbandmen, the feeble and those burdened with children'. They should maintain and supervise hospitals for the poor and homes for lepers and for 'fallen women'.[131]

Although Gerson does warn the parish clergy against simony and rapacious practices, he is far more concerned about the poverty than the wealth of this group. He urges bishops to see that each cure of souls has an adequate provision so that suitable clerics are attracted to this vital rank of the hierarchy and receive proper reverence and obedience from their parishioners. Bishops should also help the parochial clergy in this respect by reducing the heavy episcopal tallages and dues imposed upon them.[132] It would be far easier for *curés* to avoid the sin of avarice and to be charitable if they knew they had adequate material provision. And pastors, Gerson insists, must be free from all taint of avarice and cupidity, not only because these sins make them hated and despised by the laity, but also so that 'by their bad example they do not corrupt, lead into errors or render imperfect the lower classes, ever-ready to follow the good example of virtue or the bad example of vice'.[133]

Although he tends to concentrate on their misuse of wealth, Gerson does quite frequently refer to other ways in which contemporary clerics fall short of the ideal of holy living. Good bishops, he writes, are those who prohibit all evil habits among their subordinates, especially such scandal-causing practices as 'concubinage, adultery, gambling, drunkenness and the frequenting of bawdy-houses'.[134] The parish clergy particularly, Gerson thinks, do not set a good example in sexual morality, for they frequently live in concubinage. This question of clerical concubinage exercised Gerson. Perhaps he exaggerated the extent of the problem, but he certainly saw it as difficult to deal with.[135] He felt that it was impossible to eradicate the evil altogether and therefore wondered if perhaps concubines should be tolerated lest the offending priests sought to fulfil their lust in worse ways. If, on the other hand, priests were allowed to keep their concubines, parishioners might be led to fear (wrongly) that the sacraments they administered were invalid. If such priests were excommunicated, however, there would be no sacraments administered in their parishes at all. On the whole Gerson leans to the side of leniency here and warns bishops against wholesale excommunication for concubinage.[136] About this particular sin on the part of pastors Gerson remains pessimistic. He does not, of course, expect perfection in other areas either; not all parish priests will provide good examples to the laity all the time and in all ways. But with the help of divine grace they can move along the road to the life of Christian perfection, and restore the image of God within themselves, thereby helping to lead their flocks to the same goal.

ADMINISTRATION OF THE SACRAMENTS

In the administration of the sacraments – the vehicles of perfection *par excellence* – pastors were aided by God even more directly in the carrying out of their hierarchical activity. For here pastors were largely instruments, though absolutely necessary instruments, of God. As long as the minister, whether he was sinful or not, followed the correct forms and had the correct intention – which Gerson says can be rationally assumed – grace was conferred on the recipient.[137] It was conferred by virtue of the performance of the rite (*virtute operis operati*), 'that is beyond or above the merit of the recipient, by virtue of the merits of Christ instituting the sacrament'.[138] This does not mean that the recipients were not able to do or omit things that blocked the reception of grace; for example, someone who lied in confession rendered the absolution invalid.[139] It does not mean either that there was not room for improvement in the administration of the sacraments. But it does mean that less personal skill and sanctity were required on the part of pastors for this hierarchical activity than for the other two, except in the case of the sacrament of penance, and here, as will be seen, Gerson demands a very high level of skill indeed.

When Gerson states that there should be improvements in the administration of the sacraments he has in mind that there should be more decorum attending them and also that the correct forms should be followed. It seems that some priests simply did not know the correct forms, for Gerson in more than one of his sermons urges bishops to examine the parish priests of the dioceses 'in case some of them are ignorant of the correct forms and so confer nothing in their administration of the sacraments'.[140] If such ignorance is found the offending priests must be instructed in synods and visitations.[141] It would be better, of course, if the evil could be remedied at its source by bishops examining candidates for ordination to ensure not only that they were virtuous men but also that they had all the necessary information about the administration of the sacraments. It was important too that midwives and members of the laity who might be called on to baptise should be acquainted with the *formulae* so that the infant did indeed receive baptismal grace. Aside from knowing the correct forms, pastors should see that the sacraments are administered with decency and order. Gerson criticises especially the unseemly behaviour that often accompanied the sacrament of matrimony, and the irreverence shown by many of the laity during mass and the sacrament of the Eucharist. He suggests that it would be better if there were in fact fewer feast-days, for these simply give the populace too much leisure, which they often spend in secular and immoral behaviour and so dishonour God and harm their own souls. As far as the sacrament of confirmation is concerned, Gerson urges bishops to see that it is administered more frequently throughout their dioceses. The sacrament of extreme unction, he advises, should be administered while the sick person still has full control of his senses and is conscious of the sacramental action, otherwise he will not reap the full benefit of the sacrament.[142]

The sacrament of penance

Its importance

It is the sacrament of penance, 'which retrieves the fallen and gives life back to the dead',[143] that concerns Gerson most. He has much to say on a number of aspects of this topic not only in his synodal sermons but also in a series of tracts for the instruction of confessors and in a number of vernacular works. The summas and manuals for confessors formed a flourishing *genre* in the later Middle Ages,[144] but a number of Gerson's thirty or so tracts on the subject, most written for pastors but some for the laity and some for religious, enjoyed more success than many other works of this sort. He in fact became an 'authority' on some aspects of the subject and we find some later authors quoting his opinions with approval.

The sacrament of penance was founded, states Gerson, following what by this time was traditional doctrine, in divine law, not just by ecclesiastical decree, and having been instituted by God it cannot be abandoned by man. Not even the pope can abrogate it.[145] It is like a second baptism by which all sins are washed away, charity is infused and guilt expelled. 'As Bernard says, it causes the angels to rejoice, confounds the devils, reconciles the soul to God, closes hell and opens heaven.'[146] As all men fall into sin after baptism, it is absolutely necessary that there be some means by which they may be reconciled to God, and the sacrament of penance is the divinely appointed way. Further it is the most efficacious way. 'Let another think what he will; I in my simplicity judge confession, if rightly performed, to be the most efficacious way to Christ.'[147] For these reasons it must not be bypassed. Indeed one of Gerson's chief criticisms against the Flagellants was that they ignored the sacrament of penance because they believed that flagellation was more effective for wiping out sin.[148] They were completely wrong, he argued, for sacramental confession was essential in the economy of salvation. This did not imply that it was impossible for God to forgive a person without his going through the process of sacramental confession and absolution. In his *Doctrinal aux simples gens* he writes:

If you do not have a priest to hear your confession and are truly repentant for all your sins, and would confess them freely if there was a priest at hand, if you die in this state, it suffices for God and you are free from the peril of damnation.[149]

Gerson, then, preserves the connection with the sacrament by stating that the intention to confess sacramentally must be present, even though it is not carried out. By his time this was generally accepted doctrine.[150]

The sacrament of penance is thus essential in the life of the *viator*, and further its administration is probably the most important of the pastor's activities, for by no other means 'are the wandering sheep called back, the sick healed and the hungry fed better than in this sacrament'.[151] It is certainly the sacrament that requires the most skill on the part of the pastor. In the others the recipient is largely passive, but in confession he is active and therefore has to be guided carefully so that he fulfils his part correctly. Confession is the time when the pastor comes face to face with his flock and gets to know them personally and discovers their particular difficulties, characteristics and tendencies, and comes to realise that each has to be treated differently. Over and over again Gerson quotes Christ's saying: 'Know the face of thy flock', and explains that it is in the sacrament of penance that this can best be done.[152]

If this sacrament is so vitally important, how often should a person receive it? Is it necessary to confess at once if one has committed a sin? Gerson's answer to this last question is the standard one: one is not bound to rush off to confession at once even if one has committed a mortal sin, and venial sins do not need to be confessed at all, although they may be and 'c'est bien fait et perfection'.[153] One is, however, if one is in a state of mortal sin, bound to confess, according to ecclesiastical ordinance, at least once a year around Easter; before one receives the Eucharist[154] or any other sacrament except baptism; when one is in danger of death and when there is a confessor at hand who can absolve one from any reserved sins one may have committed.[155] These occasions, however, represent only a minimum and Gerson does recommend for most people more frequent confession, perhaps four times a year, or every month or even every week on feast-days.

It is after all much better to be in a state of grace so that one's works bear merit for eternal life.[156] However, it very much depends on the individual. If a person feels that habit is making frequent confession produce less and less devotion he should abstain from it for a while. But if he feels that he profits more and more from it and has greater peace of conscience, he can confess and take communion every day.[157] Gerson does advise people who confess only once a year not to leave it to the last minute, for the pastor will then be very busy and not have time to give them the attention they need, for 'often a good half-day is not sufficient to confess a person well'.[158] This gives some idea of how seriously Gerson expected pastors to undertake their role as confessors.

The decree *Omnis utriusque sexus* of the fourth Lateran council in 1215, which commanded yearly confession, also stated that the confessor should be 'one's own priest'.[159] This latter phrase was sometimes interpreted broadly, but Gerson pushes the case for the local pastor. He thought it much better, *ceteris paribus*, for penitents to confess to their own parish priest than to an outsider. In the first place it is safer, he argues, because there is no doubt about his having the authority to hear confessions and absolve. It is more merit-worthy because of the obedience and honour due to one's pastor, who serves one in many ways. It is also more fruitful because he who knows the penitent can give better counsel. For the same reason ideally he should know and hear the confessions of a whole family.[160] Gerson was well aware, however, that other things were not always equal, that some parish priests were incompetent as confessors and that therefore there was a need for the expertise of the Mendicants. But he insisted that such Mendicant confessors must have licences from the proper hierarchical authorities, and the use of the Mendicants in this capacity always remained a second-best for him. The pastor who knew the face of his flock should be the family confessor.

Some clerics, by contrast, reversed the emphasis. The preachers Bernardine and Maillard both urge penitents to seek above all good and faithful, knowledgeable and thorough confessors.[161] The same is true of some of the authors of manuals.[162] Humbert of Romans in the thirteenth century thought it was useful to go to different confessors on different occasions, just as it is beneficial for a sick person to consult several doctors,[163] while Angelus de Clavasio, who wrote one of the most popular summas for confessors in the late fifteenth century, declares that 'today there are many priests whom we may call our own and to whom we may legitimately confess'.[164] All the above were Mendicants. This is no doubt why they place the emphasis differently from Gerson, who wanted to exalt the role of the parish clergy in the ecclesiastical hierarchy. But there is more to it than this. Penitents told that they must seek a wise confessor in order to be properly confessed might well have had doubts about whether they had indeed found one. Gerson is always concerned to allay doubts, and his advice to penitents to confess to their parish priest removes this cause of anxiety.

Contrition

Almost every time he discusses the sacrament of penance Gerson divides his subject into three parts: repentance (or contrition), confession and satisfaction. These acts of the penitent are, in Thomistic terms, the matter of the sacrament, while the priest's absolution is the form.[165] This was the standard division well before Gerson's time, although the church's doctrine about penance had undergone change since the twelfth century and there were still variations of teaching on some points in the fifteenth century. This change is often described as a change from contritionism to absolutionism, or, more critically, as a development from a doctrine in which the penitent, truly sorry for his sins, is forgiven by God directly, to a doctrine in which the interior disposition of the penitent, it is argued, is of little account and he is forgiven by means of the words of absolution uttered by the priest whose power as an intermediary is therefore vastly increased. Criticism of absolutionism, indeed, occurred among anti-clericals in Gerson's own time. It appears frequently in Lollard writings,[166] and of course later in the Protestant reformers of the sixteenth century.[167] But the story is not all about the exaltation of the power of the priesthood. There is certainly a development away from Abelard's (1079–1142) teaching that in the sigh of true contrition 'we are instantly [statim] reconciled to God', our sins forgiven and their eternal punishment remitted. Abelard does argue that oral confession is usually necessary, but only as a part of satisfaction, that is for remission of the temporal punishment of sin, due in this life or in purgatory. For forgiveness itself priests, according to Abelard, have the power only of declaring a judgement already made by God.[168] Peter Lombard is a contritionist in the same sense as Abelard. He argues that contrition is the principal part of penance and that one can obtain forgiveness of sins without oral confession and even without the purpose of confession. Sacramental confession he sees as useful, however, though the priest in his words of absolution merely declares that God has already forgiven the contrite sinner.[169] By the time we reach St Thomas in the thirteenth century an important change has taken place. Contrition is still essential ('The use of the keys, in order to be effective, always requires a disposition on the part of the penitent'), it is still God alone who forgives and remits guilt, but the role of the priest is now instrumental. The sacrament effects what it signifies, and sacramental confession, either in fact or in desire, is necessary for the forgiveness of sins. Moreover – though Thomas sees this as an unusual situation – a person who comes to the sacrament with an inadequate sorrow (attrition) can become fully contrite 'at the very time of sacramental confession and absolution'. The sacrament itself, provided the penitent does not place any obstacle, can bring about the necessary disposition.[170] What is unusual for Thomas becomes normal for Scotus (1265–1308): attrition is a sufficient disposition for the penitent when he approaches the sacrament. Further, whereas for Thomas attrition is acceptable only when it is a case of the penitent's being mistaken about the nature of his sorrow, for Scotus the penitent can *know* that he is only attrite and that the sacrament itself can and will effect the necessary change in disposition, provided that he place no obstacle.[171] Scotus moves further away from the twelfth-century theologians than Thomas in another way. The essence of the sacrament is for him the absolution of the priest; the traditional three parts – contrition, confession and satisfaction – are merely necessary conditions.[172]

Where does Gerson stand on these issues? He is not a contritionist in the Lombardian sense for, as we have seen, he holds that a penitent cannot achieve forgiveness without at least having the intention to confess. In fact he includes the intention to confess in his definitions of what he understands by contrition – the first part of the sacrament. These definitions occur in a number of Gerson's works; they vary to some extent but the essence is the same: contrition is displeasure at one's sins, with the firm purpose not to sin again and with the intention of confessing one's sins sacramentally.[173]

This definition puts Gerson on the other side of the fence from Scotus in one respect. Scotus argues that it is sufficient if the penitent does not have at that moment the intention of sinning.[174] For Gerson, the penitent must have the purpose of not sinning in the future if the sacrament is to be efficacious. He specifically argues against the 'mild' (*mitis*) opinion in his *Regulae mandatorum*. His own opinion, he says, is more probable and more safe.[175] There were a few authors in the later Middle Ages who held to the 'milder' opinion,[176] but Gerson stands here with the 'rigorists' – the larger group.[177] He makes it quite clear, however, that penitents need not be able to, in fact cannot, guarantee that they will never sin again.[178]

What of the penitent who is not fully contrite? Like both Aquinas and Scotus in the thirteenth century, and Antoninus, Angelus de Clavasio and other writers of the literature for confessors in the later medieval period, Gerson teaches that attrition can become contrition in the sacrament itself.[179] What is the difference between these two types of sorrow? For Thomas they are to be distinguished by the completeness or incompleteness of the break with sin, and by their being informed or not informed by grace. Contrition is perfect sorrow for one's sins, informed by grace; attrition is imperfect sorrow, not informed by grace.[180] Other theologians, following the same line, write about attrition being less of a 'breaking-up' than contrition; the former occurs when the hard heart, like a stone, is broken by imperfect sorrow for sin; the latter occurs when the heart is totally crushed by perfect sorrow, informed by grace.[181] Although he has no lengthy discussions on the subject, Gerson holds to the distinction established in the thirteenth century. Attrition for him is a lesser sorrow, while contrition is 'great sorrow of heart and great repentance of all one's sins';[182] it involves 'detesting one's sins, grieving and groaning with one's whole heart for the evils one has done'.[183] That he sees contrition as formed by charity, as coming from the working of God's grace, is clear from his teaching that the penitent who is only attrite to begin with can become contrite during the sacrament itself. He makes the point explicitly in a treatise for the instruction of confessors, De forma absolvendi a peccatis: a man may be contrite already or 'by virtue of the sacrament contrition is infused in that very absolution'.[184] And in a sermon of 1403 he tells his congregation that the journey up the mountain of contemplation must begin with contrition, 'that is with sorrow informed by grace'.[185]

Gerson does not appear to distinguish between attrition and contrition in terms of psychological motivation. In other words he does not follow what has been termed the nominalist position on this question.[186] Theologians such as Durandus, Occam, Biel and Geiler, who have been said to adhere to this position, are held to teach that if a penitent is attrite for his sins, then he is motivated only by fear of punishment and hell; whereas if he is truly contrite, then he is motivated by the love of God.[187] Gerson does at times distinguish between the motives of fear and love, for instance with respect to resistance to temptation,[188] but he does not do so in the context of attrition and contrition. This is not surprising. Very few of the late medieval authors of summas and manuals for confessors do. The Thomist distinction is far more common.[189] In any case, in his vernacular sermons and tracts Gerson does not belabour the distinction; he is usually content to say that one must have sorrow for one's sins. He almost invariably adds the need to have the intention of amendment and of confessing sacramentally.[190] The latter two conditions are easier for the penitent to identify than the degree of his sorrow. This is no doubt why Gerson, always more the practitioner of the cure of souls than the theorist, stresses them. His desire to help penitents is also evidenced by his frequent references, in sermons especially, to the distinction between sorrow of the emotions (dolor sensualis) and sorrow of the will (dolor voluntatis). It is true that he writes sometimes of grieving and groaning, and of the tears of contrition.[191] But he makes it perfectly clear that contrition is essentially a matter of the will and not of the feelings. In one of the Poenitemini sermons he explains that sorrow of the will occurs when there is accord between the reason, which judges that sin is worse than anything that is not sin, and the will. The result is a detestation of one's sins. But this accord is not always followed by feelings of grief and tears, nor is it necessary that the latter occur. It is only sorrow of the will that is essential.[192] This distinction was a traditional one; it is clearly explained by Aquinas and is repeated by Antoninus and Angelus, among others.[193] However, some preachers and manualists are not as careful as Gerson about bringing it to the attention of their audiences. They write about contrition in terms of sadness, grief and weeping, very often with reference to the tears of the Magdalene.[194] This might well have led some penitents to have doubts and anxiety about the quality of their sorrow, to think they were not contrite when in fact they were. Gerson is wise to underline the distinction, for without contrition, he argues, either already present in the penitent or infused during the sacrament, there can be no forgiveness of sins. Those who do not repent, those who still have the will to sin, who still have hatred of others and the desire for vengeance 'should know that there is no prelate, not even the pope, who can or should absolve them'.[195]

Thomas would not have quarrelled with this. But on the question of the disposition with which the penitent ought to approach the sacrament of penance Gerson stands much closer to Scotus. One does not need to be fully contrite. The mercy of God is so great, he tells one congregation, that if one has only 'une petite desplaisance de son pechie', and the intention to confess sacramentally, God's pardon will follow.[196] He tells another congregation that even if a person feels that he is not repentant after he has made a full confession of his sins, as long as he has the purpose of amendment then the confessor should absolve him, for 'I consider it to be very great repentance to confess one's sins.'[197] The point is that a person may not *feel* contrite; the contrition that is infused during the sacrament 'may remain hidden from him', but this does not prevent the sacrament from being efficacious.[198] The reason Gerson is following a Scotist position here is made clear by the argument he uses in favour of what he considers the best formula for absolution: 'I absolve you from your sins in the name of the Trinity.' This is all that is required and it is positively dangerous, he argues, to qualify it by saying 'from your sins for which you are contrite', for absolution can remit sins for which one was only attrite at first 'by means of grace after one comes to confess'. Further, the addition injects a scruple of despair. Penitents for a variety of reasons sometimes lack feelings of devotion. When such a person hears the words 'from those sins for which you are contrite', he seizes the opportunity 'for brooding and doubting and consequently is in peril'.[199] Gerson goes on to argue that qualifying 'I forgive' with the phrase 'in so far as I can and ought' is also dangerous for the same reason; it can sow seeds of doubt and even despair in the penitent's mind. Gerson's version of pre-Tridentine 'attritionism', then, does exalt the power of the keys, but the motivation behind it is not sinister. What Gerson wants to do is to bring consolation and confidence to penitents, not power to the priesthood. It is, after all, as he consistently argues, only God who forgives, and, what is more, even if the penitent is contrite before he approaches confession, his contrition is the result of God's grace ('informed by grace'), just as much as the contrition infused during the sacrament.

Many of the late medieval authors of the literature for confessors discuss forms of absolution.[200] Most insist that the words 'I absolve you' must occur, but some advise a number of additions.[201] Others say that the simple formula is enough. It is Gerson, however, who forcefully and clearly explains the dangers of qualifiers, and his arguments were adopted by some later authors.[202] This is a case where Gerson is leading the way within a late medieval trend towards absolutionism. There were still versions of the older contritionism in some authors, though characterising the words of absolution as merely declaratory is very rare.[203] Relatively more common is advising confessors to say 'I absolve you from your sins for which you are contrite', together with statements that the penitent must have true contrition and that to confess without contrition is fraudulent.[204] But these authors are in a minority and Gerson clearly repudiates their position.

Confession

Of the remaining two parts of the sacrament of penance it is the second that concerns Gerson more – the confession itself and the techniques the confessor should use to ensure that the penitent fulfils his own role properly. Gerson propounds no new doctrines about confession, but his presentations of various aspects of the topic are very skilful indeed. This is particularly true of what he has to say about the differentiation between mortal and venial sin, the art of questioning penitents and the methods of dealing with over-scrupulosity. His treatises on these – and other – topics fit between the two extremes of the practical literature for confessors. On the one hand are the reference works, the summas, with lengthy and complex discussions, often bristling with different opinions and 'authorities'. On the other are those simplistic handbooks which set out the various points of doctrine without much explanation and which betray little insight. Gerson has the gift of being able to distil the discussions of the theologians in a cogent manner, and his treatises combine brevity and practicality with forcefulness, explanation and insight, which is no doubt why they achieved popularity.

Following the standard doctrine, Gerson holds that the penitent must confess all his mortal sins, for, if any are deliberately left out, the sacrament is not efficacious. The confessor, then, must know what is and what is not mortal sin. Indeed the penitent should know this too, so that he can in the first place try to avoid committing mortal sins, and also so that he can prepare himself for confession by examining his conscience intelligently. This is why Gerson advises pastors to preach on the seven capital sins. He himself set a good example with his *Poenitemini* series concerning these sins in all their manifold forms. But sermons on the sins are common enough. Of more importance here are the treatises and tracts already mentioned, some in the vernacular, which were written primarily to aid penitents in the examination of conscience but which would also be helpful to pastors for both pulpit and confessional, and some in Latin.

The first thing Gerson wishes pastors and penitents to be clear about is the difference between mortal and venial sins, for the former must be confessed while the latter do not need to be. The authors of theological and pastoral summas tend to produce lengthy discussions about why this is so.[205] Gerson goes straight to the main point: mortal sins cut the link between God and man, and lead to a loss of grace and to damnation; venial sins, although they displease God and do some harm, do not break the relationship.[206]

Sin, says Gerson, can be venial in two ways: either *ex genere*, that is, because the matter is not grave, or if there is not perfect consent by the subject.[207] Thus an action which involved grave matter, for example wounding one's innocent neighbour, could nevertheless be a venial sin only because it was not done with deliberation and perfect consent. 'In all of the sins can be found venial sin only.'[208] Gerson is quite insistent on this question of consent. Any thought or feeling that comes to one unbidden from the sensual appetite is not sinful at all; if the will unreflectively takes delight in these feelings, then there is venial sin. It is only when the will freely and deliberately consents to this delight, against the judgement of reason, that there is mortal sin.[209] Gerson has escaped, as indeed most medieval moralists from Abelard onwards had escaped, from the early medieval penitential ethos, where it was the act itself, and not the consent and ultimate intentions of the actor, that was the over-riding criterion in judging sinfulness and criminality.[210] On the difference between mortal and venial sin as regards the matter involved, Gerson has more to say and here he can become quite subtle, revealing the vast amount of thought, discussion and argument that had been expended on this subject by his predecessors, and his own sensibility and psychological expertise.[211]

To help penitents in their examination of conscience Gerson suggests three basic techniques, all of them traditional. Penitents could use the seven capital sins as a guide, and in various of his works he lists the numerous ways in which a person can commit each of these sins. Or penitents could recall their sins on the basis of the ten commandments. For the young, Gerson recommends the senses as a guide. Have you sinned with the mouth, by being gluttonous, saying shameful things, criticising others, lying, not keeping promises or secrets, swearing, boasting? He has similar lists under the headings of eyes, ears, nose and touch.[212] Any one of these methods of classification is enough, notes Gerson. He is being moderate here. Some authors, like Gerson, suggest only a very limited number of classifications,[213] but others produce a veritable catalogue of things against which, or according to which, one can sin.[214] Gerson is careful to underline the fact that an examination of conscience using the seven deadly sins as a guide will also uncover all the sins one may have committed according to the five senses, the works of mercy, the articles of faith and the ten commandments.[215]

One thing that complicates the question of what constitutes sin is the question of conscience. On several occasions Gerson states the traditional doctrine: to act against conscience is a sin.[216] This means, he says, that an action or thought or desire that is not *per se* sinful can become a sin, if in conscience a person thinks it so.[217] This is another reason why pastors, in their role as confessors, must be expert in the knowledge of sin. The individual conscience can err through over-scrupulosity or through ignorance and it is the duty of the pastor to see that the consciences of his penitents are well informed, that is, in line with the laws of God and with the standards set by the ecclesiastical authorities. Gerson is particularly concerned with the over-scrupulous conscience, but he does not neglect the problem of the ignorant conscience. He does not argue that, if a person performs an action which is against the laws of God or the church, but which in conscience he thinks is not sinful, he has therefore not committed a sin – though that would seem to be the corollary to the teaching that whatever is done against conscience is a sin. For Gerson, as for other theologians and moralists of the High and later Middle Ages, to act against conscience is always wrong, but to act according to conscience is not always right.[218] Conscience may be in error through ignorance, and the point is that ignorance by no means always excuses. Ignorance of moral principles is always culpable. The reason for this, according to Gerson, is that ignorance of the divine law 'does not occur in a person doing what is in him [*facientem illud quod in se est*]', because the Holy Spirit teaches such a man either directly or indirectly those things necessary for salvation which he cannot reach by his own natural powers.[219] There *is* an ignorance which excuses – invincible ignorance – but this is always about the factual circumstances of a particular case, never about the moral principles involved. Gerson's example of a situation involving invincible ignorance is that of a person who, on a Friday, thinks he is eating fish when in fact someone has given him meat under the semblance of fish. There is no sin here.[220] Apart from this sort of situation ignorance does not excuse, and the only thing to be done with an errant conscience, if one is to avoid both the sin of acting against conscience and the sin of following an errant conscience, is to set it aside and get oneself properly informed. It is clear from this why Gerson is concerned that penitents should be fully informed about sin, even if this means putting into their minds ideas about sins that they never had before. 'It is more tolerable that some should learn from such teaching, *per accidens*, how to act badly than that vice be cultivated and be left without the remedy of confession.'[221] Mortal sin cuts the sinner off from God, and Gerson does not want to leave people thinking they are in a state of grace when in fact they are in a very perilous situation. Gerson, then, though he

teaches that the individual conscience must be followed, is by no means
teaching freedom of conscience with its twentieth-century connotations.
Nor were other theologians and moralists in the period,[222] but what Gerson
has to say on the subject of conscience, although it is based on the more
subtle argumentation of scholastic writers, is clear, direct and designed for
practical use.[223]

If an expertise in the knowledge of what constitutes sin is the first
demand Gerson makes of the pastor as confessor, the second is that he must
know to what sins particular classes and work-groups are prone.[224] But
there is far more involved than this. The confessor should have certain
spiritual, mental and psychological characteristics. He must be a man of
purity himself, always relying on and praying for divine help and direction
in his task. He must seek no material gain from his work, treating rich and
poor alike and allowing his integrity and sincerity to shine through so that
he can touch even the hardest of hearts. He should treat the shy and weak,
especially young people and women, with tenderness, making sure that
they know that whatever is said in confession is secret and that the aim is
to help, absolve and quiet them; and that the confessor will not upbraid
and hate them, whatever sins they may confess.[225] In fact in all cases, with
all types of people, confessors should see to it 'that they are not harsh in
speaking to those who confess to them; and at least that they do not let
penitents leave without giving them good comfort and good consolation'.[226]
Other authors require the confessor to be kind and charitable with his
penitents,[227] but the stress on gentleness and on the confessor as the bringer
of comfort is quite striking in Gerson and is characteristic of all his tracts
on confession. However, this does not mean that he wants the confessor to
be over-lenient and to let penitents deceive him, for above all he must
ensure that all mortal sins are confessed. Over and over again Gerson
stresses the necessity for a complete confession.[228] If any mortal sin is held
back then the absolution will not be efficacious and all the mortal sins
already confessed will have to be reconfessed together with the one held
back. Gerson explains why. 'The doctors agree that one mortal sin cannot
be wiped out without the others; otherwise it would follow that grace can
be present with mortal sin.'[229] So the confessor must see that the penitent
holds nothing back. Sometimes, however, it is a case of the penitent
forgetting a mortal sin, and here again the confessor has the responsibility
of doing all he can to jog the sinner's memory. Forgotten sins do not, of
course, fall into the same category as sins deliberately held back, but
nevertheless they can have harmful consequences, because absolution from
forgotten sins is conditional on the sinner's confessing them when they
return to his mind.[230] If they are never remembered there is no problem,
but once they are remembered then the sinner is again cut off from God
and His grace.

Gerson has various techniques which he recommends to help the confessor to extract complete confessions. They are explained best in his treatise *De arte audiendi confessiones*, which is one of the most masterly of all the works produced during the late medieval period about how to question penitents. The treatise is quite short and does not become lost in long lists of possible questions. Rather, Gerson confines himself to general principles, with a few examples.[231]

The confessor, he writes, should be affable at first to gain the confidence of the penitent and impress upon him the necessity of hiding nothing. If he suspects someone of lying he should first give the impression that he thinks this is being done out of inadvertence rather than with deliberation, so that a confrontational atmosphere is not created. Penitents should be praised for telling the truth. They may be reprimanded for any very serious sins, but never to such an extent that they start to deny them.

It is advisable, Gerson thinks, for the confessor to begin by asking questions about sins which almost all people commit and which are therefore easy to admit. From there he should move on to rarer and more serious sins. Sometimes it is permissible to trick penitents into admitting a sin, by asking about it in such a way as to give the impression that the action in question is praiseworthy. Sins of the flesh cause most difficulty, Gerson thinks, and the approach here must be very careful and gradual, with the age, intelligence-level and character of the penitent being taken into account, so that each can be led to talk about things that are shameful. Throughout the whole questioning process the penitent must feel that the confessor will not think badly of him because of his sins, but is there to help him to make a good confession and to restore him to God's grace. Too much curiosity must not be shown about the circumstantial details of sins; but, on the other hand, penitents must be encouraged to tell enough so that the confessor can counsel properly and the conscience of the penitent be quieted. If at the end of the confession the pastor thinks the penitent is still hiding something he can either send him away and tell him to return later, or he can point out that the absolution will be invalid if all sins have not been confessed.[232]

Although Gerson's techniques for extracting full confessions involve some elements of trickery and fear, the kindness, sensitivity, gentleness and psychological insight shown are more apparent. After all, as he says himself, those who come to confession are at least half-turned to God already and therefore can and should be treated kindly and inspired with confidence. The pastor can afford to be harsher in his sermons when he is trying to reach the more stubborn of his flock, though Gerson himself remains more gentle than harsh even in his vernacular sermons. As a confessor he must have been very good – thorough yet always empathetic.

Satisfaction

The pastor's final task, in his role as confessor, aside from giving absolution, is to assign penances. He must point out to the penitent, however, that if he has damaged another in any way he must make restitution as well as performing his penance. Gerson is as insistent on the need for restitution as other preachers and authors of the period. Without it there can be no remission of sins, as Gerson frequently tells his congregations.[233] The confessor must inform his penitents that anything stolen must be given back, or the equivalent in money handed over, in instalments if necessary. Anything taken from another unjustly by means of usury, fraud, sharp business or legal practice or by disloyal counsel must also be restored. And amends must be made for any defamation of another's character.[234]

Similarly the penances assigned by the confessor must be performed if the sacrament is to be efficacious. Gerson does not wish to make penance a difficult or insuperable hurdle for the penitent. Thus he insists that penances must be assigned with the consent of the penitent,[235] and that they should be too light rather than too heavy, for 'it is safer to send a penitent to purgatory with a small penance which he fulfils, than to hell with a large one which he does not fulfil, as William of Paris says'.[236]

In opting for light penances Gerson is moving with a late medieval trend. Although there are echoes of the older, more rigorous penitential system (seven years' penance for each mortal sin) in some of the manuals for confessors, most authors advocate light penances imposed with the penitent's consent. Angelus de Clavasio goes so far as to advise confessors to assign a penance that can be done at once, before the penitent leaves the church, and therefore before he can fall into sin again.[237] If he were to commit a mortal sin before he completed the penance then the sacrament would be inefficacious, and the confessor by giving too heavy or long a penance would have 'bound' rather than 'loosed', as Angelus says. It is not at all surprising to find Gerson on the side of mildness here. He wants the sacrament to console as well as cure, and 'binding' would do neither. He does, though, advise confessors to give penances that the penitent has to do himself, such as saying prayers, making pilgrimages and fasting, rather than telling him to have masses said, 'for the body which sinned ought to do the penance and make amends, if possible'.[238] He has not moved as far towards mildness as some.

Scrupulosity

There is a strong psychological basis to Gerson's theology about the sacrament of penance, and this is nowhere more apparent than in the treatises he wrote for the over-scrupulous and anxious. The authors of confessional literature all know about doubt, despair and scrupulosity, and tried to take care of them, but this is one of the areas in which Gerson outshines his colleagues. Even Antoninus, who relies heavily on Gerson in his treatment of pusillanimity, fails to achieve the latter's directness, freshness and vitality.[239]

No one, states Gerson, repeating a traditional doctrine, can have evident or absolute certainty that, for instance, he is sufficiently worthy to celebrate mass. If he could, then he could know that he was in a state of grace.[240] But only God can know this. However, he argues, a priest does not need evident certainty about his worthiness to celebrate mass, nor does a layman need evident certainty that he is worthy to communicate. All that is needed is moral certainty and for this it is sufficient if one is not conscious of having committed any unconfessed mortal sin or of having any intention of sinning mortally.[241] Again Gerson provides criteria that are at least relatively objective. Ciboule, in his sermon on the Eucharist, is not so careful. He agrees with Gerson that no one can know for certain that he is in a state of grace. But, he argues, there are four signs of grace: hearing the Word of God willingly; being prompt in good works; having the purpose to abstain from sin; grieving for one's past sins.[242] There are grounds for doubt here: is one prompt enough? is one grieving sufficiently? Gerson stifles other potential anxieties. Moral certainty, he says, is compatible with a certain amount of doubt and vacillation about one's state of soul.[243] It is 'even compatible with some disorder of the inferior members which are not often within our control'.[244] In all his tracts on over-scrupulousness Gerson reminds his readers that there is not mortal sin if there is no consent of reason and will, that is, the will of the spirit. For man has a double will, of the spirit and of the flesh, often at war with each other. But 'man is not judged according to the will of the flesh, but only according to the will of the spirit'.[245] Some over-scrupulous persons, for instance, who become anxious and fearful about the state of their souls, start to feel despair and then they feel even more anxious because despair can be a mortal sin. But, says Gerson, this feeling of despair in itself is not a sin at all because it comes unbidden, and as long as reason does not consent to it there is no loss of charity and grace. As long as the intention to adhere to God is there, however small, all is well, for charity can grow from even a small spark, just as cinders can be rekindled.[246]

But what of those persons who are not sure if their reason and will are consenting, for example, to lustful thoughts?[247] They should take the advice of their superiors. Here Gerson relates a story of St Bernard, who was faced with an anxious, over-scrupulous monk who felt unworthy to say mass. Bernard told him, 'Go, brother, and celebrate in my faith.' The monk obeyed and all was well. Gerson does not leave the question here. Someone may object, he writes, saying that if he had an abbot such as Bernard, there would be no difficulty about obeying him, but 'when I see the small share of wisdom of my superior I dare not commit my conscience and salvation to his faith'. This would be wrong, argues Gerson, for in committing yourself and your salvation to your superior you are not doing so because he is very learned and devout, but just because he is your prelate and thus in obeying him you are obeying not a man but God. Moreover, often your obedience will be more pleasing to God, and more fruitful, the more unworthy is your prelate.[248] No one can say that Gerson did not try to take care of every eventuality. Equally it is clear that the fears of the anxious neurotic can be endless. The late medieval theology of the sacrament of penance and of justification may have been partly responsible for creating such neurosis, but a man like Gerson did his best to cope with it.

The advice propounded in De praeparatione ad missam was intended primarily for clerics, but Gerson gives similar advice to lay people. They too if they find themselves anxious and fearful should put themselves in the hands of their pastor, and so the weight of responsibility will be removed from them and with it the feeling of anxiety. Again the strong paternalism of Gerson's thought is revealed.

This feeling of anxiety and lack of a sense of devotion and spiritual consolation are not, Gerson states, important in so far as our salvation is concerned, for they are feelings beyond our control. They do not harm a man or separate him from God. In the same way positive feelings of devotion and spiritual consolation do not assure a man that he is in a state of grace and more perfect than others. Both those with and those without spiritual consolation could be equal in charity. Moreover the man who has strong feelings of devotion could become over self-confident, while he who lacks this spiritual sweetness and yet does what is in him could in fact be more acceptable to God because of his humility. And if the consolation is long in coming, if he has to persevere humbly, then he could be in a more meritorious state than if the anxiety were allayed at once.[249] One does not ever need to feel guilty or despairing or outside of God's care because one is over-scrupulous, anxious or depressed.

It would be better, however, for one's own peace of mind if one did not have these unpleasant feelings, though Gerson, in a tract meant for the laity, warns that 'a householder ought not to expect to have such peace and tranquillity of heart and thought as a solitary'.[250] It is painful both for the person concerned and for his superiors when he keeps repeating prayers and psalms because he feels that they were not said with enough attention in the first place, and when he confesses over and over again because he does not think he was sufficiently contrite.[251] Gerson's basic advice here is to put one's whole trust in the mercy of God. It is by divine gift and not by our own work and preparation that we are made worthy to participate in the sacrament of the Eucharist. We could not make ourselves worthy in a thousand years.[252] It is by divine grace that we receive spiritual consolation and have confidence, not by our own merits.[253] All those who are over-scrupulous, fearful and anxious should be counselled 'to put their trust not in their own righteousness but in the mercy of God, and however heavily they weight their own sin, they should weight much more heavily the clemency of the infinite God'.[254] Those who feel that their sorrow and confessions are never adequate should pray to God, saying 'I know well that if I confessed a thousand times I would not be clean; only your mercy will cleanse me.'[255] In short, one should put oneself in the hands of God, who cleanses, feeds, heals, quiets and saves us. 'Hope in God and He will free you, feed you, not confound you.'[256]

There is, however, a rider to this reliance on the mercy of God. One must also do what one can oneself. We may not be made worthy by our own work and preparation, but nevertheless these are required of us.[257] If we lack a sense of spiritual sweetness, as well as putting our trust in the divine mercy, we must also work for that devotion by doing what is in us.[258] There is surely here a basis for further self-doubt. How can one be sure that one has done what one can? There can be no evident certainty, says Gerson, but God does not demand the impossible of us; His demands are reasonable. He does not demand excessive fasting, weeping, doubting and sadness, or constant thinking about one's past sins, or about hell and death.[259] Further, we are not always required to do the better rather than the good, nor are we required to do it in the best way we can.[260] God could demand this, but in fact He is content if we keep His commandments, and even here it should be remembered that not every breaking of a commandment is a sin, for often we do not have perfect consent to our thoughts and actions.

In this way Gerson attempts to allay doubts that might arise from the *facere quod in se est* doctrine. How widely he and pastors who followed his methods were successful in this and in consoling others whose anxieties and scruples had their roots in other aspects of the theology of the sacrament of penance it is impossible to say. But his attempts show a deep psychological sensitivity and insight, and he demands a similar sensitivity from all pastors in their role as confessors.

One can see why Gerson thought it important that a person should make his confession to his parish priest who knew him or at least got to know him as an individual in confession. It was important to be able to distinguish between those people with a tendency to over-confidence and pride and those with a tendency to doubt and anxiety, and to be able to distinguish even further within these categories, for doubts and anxieties, for example, could have different causes and be centred on different topics in different individuals.

For the same reason and others Gerson wanted the number of cases that were taken out of the hands of the parish priest and reserved to bishops or their specially appointed penitentiaries to be reduced. He was, in fact, in the vanguard of the late-medieval movement against the proliferation of reserved cases, and we find other authors citing him as an 'authority' on the subject. Gerson did not advocate the entire abolition of reservations. Very serious sins that had become public knowledge, for instance homicide, arson, heresy, sorcery, perjury, adultery and usury, should be reserved. But he did think – and he expresses this in a number of places – that many sins that were purely private but which were nevertheless reserved in some dioceses should be left to the parish priest.[261] He was especially concerned that such sins committed by women or by boys should not be reserved, for these people needed very careful handling and were often afraid to go to strange and more senior ecclesiastics. Thus their sins remained unconfessed and they themselves often succumbed to despair.[262]

Godescale Rosemondt, a sixteenth-century author, follows Gerson specifically in his *Confessionale*, as he protests against the number of reservations and the problems they cause.[263] So does John Eck, and also Sylvester Mazzolini, the author of the last of the pre-Reformation summas for confessors.[264] But support for reservations can still be found in some of the manuals. A Spanish contemporary of Gerson's, Andreas de Escobar, upholds the system and lists forty cases that are – and should be – reserved for bishops.[265] Antoninus, who follows Gerson on other matters, does not do so in this case, and he too presents a long list of sins reserved for absolution by bishops.[266] Opinions, then, differed on this issue. But there is no doubt where Gerson stands. His position chiefly reflects his concern for penitents, but it is also part of his overall desire to preserve the position and authority of the parish clergy, in this case in their role as confessors.

EPISCOPAL VISITATION

Gerson has described the ways in which pastors should carry out their hierarchical functions of purifying, illuminating and perfecting those in their charge. Major prelates, he says, are responsible for seeing that minor prelates perform these duties properly, and one of the most effective methods to this end is the episcopal visitation. 'This is the hinge on which the whole reformation of the church hangs.'[267] In more than one work he gives detailed instructions about how visitations should be carried out. So thorough are these that it seems likely that Gerson had acted as an official visitor, perhaps in Cambrai, where d'Ailly was bishop, or at Rheims, under the administration of Guy de Roye. It was at the invitation of the latter that Gerson came to Rheims to deliver his sermon *Bonus pastor* to the clergy assembled for the synod of 1408.[268]

In his instructions Gerson shows a very practical spirit. A schedule for the visitors must be drawn up and the parishes to be visited must be advised ahead of time so that everything is ready at the appointed hour. It would be best, in fact, if a vanguard could be sent to see to these preparations and also to advise if any of the clergy are so opposed to the visitation that it would be wise to ignore their parishes for the time being.[269]

The bishop was responsible for the non-exempt monasteries in his diocese, the hospitals, schools and so on, and these ought to be visited. As far as the parish priests were concerned Gerson drew up a comprehensive questionnaire so that the visitors could get information about every relevant aspect of the lives of the *curés*: their knowledge of the basic tenets of the faith and of how to administer the sacraments, especially the sacrament of penance; their preaching; their assiduity in performing their spiritual functions in general; their moral behaviour. Gerson saw nothing wrong in asking parishioners secretly about the morality of their *curé*. The visitors were also to enquire about the lives of the parishioners: about the major vices, sins and superstitions in the parish, the paying of tithes, the attitudes to ecclesiastical officials, the behaviour at mass and so on. By means of these questions the visitors could discover in what ways the parish priest was falling short of the ideal and what needed amendment. Hence they could direct their reforming efforts in a fruitful manner.[270]

Of course bishops, by their visitations, and both bishops and parish priests by their hierarchical activities in general, cannot expect to rescue all men from their depravity. Nevertheless, 'whatever little they do has worth for those who are predestined and preordained to eternal life, either to their correction, or to their consolation and their confirmation in good'.[271] The pastor is the tool of God.

THE PARISH CLERGY AND THE MENDICANTS

The institution of the Mendicant orders in the thirteenth century was bound to cause trouble for a hierarchical theory of the church such as Gerson's. For the Mendicants were founded with a specifically teaching, evangelical mission. One of their more important tasks was to work with and for the laity as preachers and confessors.[272] In other words they were expected to perform some of the hierarchical functions hitherto the preserve of pastors. How were they to be fitted into the scheme of things? In practice trouble occurred for a variety of reasons. For example there was often financial competition between Mendicants and parish priests. What the former were able to extract from the laity for such things as funerals and bequests was lost to the latter. Mendicants were sometimes guilty of criticising and ridiculing parish priests who were less learned and moral than themselves, and so of leading the laity to hold the latter in disrespect. These and other practical problems are all mentioned in Gerson's writings. On the other hand, the expertise of the Mendicants in both preaching and confessing was certainly needed to counterbalance the weakness of many pastors in these areas.

Theoretically the problem was equally difficult. The doctrine of the divine institution of both major and minor prelates was well established in the University of Paris by the thirteenth century, as was the tradition stemming from Dionysius about the relative hierarchical positions of prelates and monks. Thus the coming of the Mendicants was seen by the secular theologians of Paris as a threat to these doctrines and a conflict began that continued with varying degrees of severity into the fifteenth century.[273]

During Gerson's tenure as chancellor the conflict flared up again, reaching a climax in 1408, when a Franciscan theologian, Jean Gorel, put forward in a formal disputation five theses that offended the faculty of theology. The third and fourth are particularly relevant here. In these Gorel argues that parish priests as such do not have competence to preach, confess, administer extreme unction, perform burials, or receive tithes, because their order was not instituted by Christ but rather set up by Pope Dionysius (259–68). Mendicants, by contrast, do have competence to preach and hear confessions because it is of the essence of their order (*regula*).[274] In January of 1409 these theses were condemned by the chancellor and the faculty of theology. Gorel had to retract them and make certain positive statements about the role of parish priests, for example that they were instituted by Christ and do have, from their status, the right to preach and administer the sacraments, and that this right belongs to them 'essentially' and to the Mendicants only 'per accidens ex privilegio' by permission of prelates.[275] However, in June of 1409 Alexander V, a Franciscan, became pope and Gorel appealed his case to him, with the result that in October Alexander issued the bull *Regnans in excelsis*, which rejected these positive statements and affirmed the rights of the Mendicants to preach and hear confessions. The university at once took a stand in opposition to the bull. It was against this background that Gerson produced a series of works that defended the authority and status of parish priests against the Mendicants. Among them are his tract *De statu papae et minorum praelatorum* of October 1409, his sermon *Quomodo stabit* of February 1410 and his official statement against the bull of March 1410. The arguments he uses in these works are not original, but the works themselves were influential and were drawn on by some later theologians for their own attacks on Mendicant pretensions.[276]

While the order of parish priests, Gerson argues, is of divine institution, the order of religious, including the Mendicants, is of human foundation. The latter were given the privilege of preaching and hearing confessions, not in the early church, but in order to help prelates, overburdened as a result of the church's acquisition of temporalities.[277] This does not mean that religious orders should be abolished, any more than that the temporal endowment of the church should be ended, just because it occurred after the period of the primitive church. But it does mean that these 'factitious' orders are not an intrinsic and essential part of the upper ranks of the ecclesiastical hierarchy and therefore they do not have any intrinsic right or duty to perform the hierarchical activities of purifying, illuminating and perfecting the laity.[278] The pope may grant them the right to perform some hierarchical activities, for example preaching and hearing confessions, but only with the permission of the bishops and parish priests involved.[279] Further, religious are subject to the mere will (*purae voluntati*) of the pope. He can, without injustice or sin, restrict or remove their privileges. But this he cannot do with respect to bishops and parish priests. For these reasons, Gerson argues, the estate of parish priests is higher than that of religious.[280]

The Mendicants were prepared to concede that the episcopate was divinely instituted, but they saw the parish clergy differently. St Thomas, for instance, against whose position Gerson argues specifically in *De consiliis evangelicis*, held that whereas bishops had their authority directly from Christ, the order of parish priests was of human institution and therefore *curés* had only a delegated authority from bishops, of the same type as bailiffs had from the king.[281] From this it followed, and so the Mendicant theologians including St Thomas argued, that the Mendicants, having received their evangelical mission from their superiors and from the pope, could preach and hear confessions without the permission of parish priests.[282] Some of them went even further and claimed the right to perform these activities without the licence of the bishop. They were here exalting the power of the papacy and viewing the relationship between popes and bishops in a very different way from that envisaged by Gerson and the secular theologians. For the Franciscan Bonaventure, for example, the pope was the 'fountain, origin and ruler of all ecclesiastical principalities. From him, the highest of all, all ordained power in the church is derived.'[283] For Gerson, by contrast, the hierarchical status and power of both bishops and parish priests were quite independent of the papacy. In *Quomodo stabit* the message comes across very clearly. Although he insists on his reverence for Pope Alexander and his belief that the latter was pressured unwillingly by the Mendicants into issuing the bull *Regnans in excelsis*, Gerson states unequivocally that the pope may not, under any circumstances, interfere with the divinely constituted rights of bishops and parish priests, as he has attempted to do in the offending bull, by granting privileges to the Mendicants.[284] There are seeds of Gallicanism in this position.

Gerson does not, of course, believe that the pope has no authority whatsoever over bishops and parish clergy. The pope has executive authority, that is, he has authority to see that the divinely constituted power of prelates is executed properly. Prelates, as he puts it, are under the rational will of the pope (but not under the 'mere will'), and so they can be removed from office for moral wickedness (*propter malitiam*). But there is a limitation on papal power even here, for Gerson argues that the 'rational will' of the pope is best expressed by the determinations of a general council with the agreement of the pontiff. Further the pope, like the prelates, can be removed from office *propter malitiam*. Both offices, papacy and prelacy, were divinely ordained for the common good of the ecclesiastical community, and evil occupants frustrate this end.[285]

In his campaign to exalt the role of pastors Gerson is not content to use only the doctrine of their divinely instituted hierarchical position. He has additional material. The state of perfection, we have seen him argue, is not confined to religious but is open to all. This gives bishops and parish priests a status equal to that of religious. But in fact, Gerson argues in *De consiliis evangelicis*, the status of pastors is a higher state of perfection than that of religious. He is not here referring to the actual degree of perfection attained by individuals – there were persons who lived very imperfect lives among both religious and pastors – but to the type of perfection concomitant with particular ranks of the hierarchy. A state of perfection, he says, is a mode of life in which there is a definite obligation to acquire perfection and/or to perfect others. The state of acquiring perfection belongs to religious, while that of exercising perfection (that is perfecting others) belongs to prelates.[286] But the state of exercising perfection is higher than the state of merely acquiring it. Apart from anything else the goal is higher, for the primary end is to perfect others, whereas the status of acquiring perfection is directed only to the self. 'The first, from its abundance, flows forth to others, the second remains in itself.' Further, the status of prelacy essentially demands, whatever the actual state of affairs, that a high level of personal perfection has already been reached by the prelate so that he can 'pour out his own good on to others'. In short, self-perfection, which the religious is striving for, is presupposed in the case of prelates, major and minor. Gerson points out that prelates are not, however, presumed to be in a state of the highest self-perfection; there is always room for improvement. Hence their state is also a state of acquiring perfection, but only secondarily. It is essentially and primarily a state of exercising perfection, that is, sanctifying the laity by the performance of the hierarchical activities.[287]

Throughout this treatise – and elsewhere – Gerson insists that not only bishops but also parish priests have the status of exercising perfection. They too are in a higher state of perfection than religious. This had always been one of the chief points of contention in the quarrel between the secular and Mendicant theologians. Thomas, for instance, agrees that 'the state of perfection is more excellent in bishops than in religious', but he explicitly denies that this is the case with parish priests.[288] This does not mean that Thomas in any way despises parish priests, but he has a lower view of their status in the church than Gerson does.[289]

Another reason Gerson adduces for the superiority of pastors to religious is that the former are engaged *ex officio* in both the active and contemplative life. For Gerson everything that concerns the spiritual life, both of the cleric himself and of the laity to whom he ministers, belongs to the contemplative life, for example, prayer, preaching, administration of the sacraments. To the active life belong all those things done by the pastor for the temporal needs of the laity, for instance making material provision for the sick and needy.[290] Because he combines in his life both contemplation and action, the pastor is doubly useful to the church, for he ameliorates the condition of mankind that is weakened not only in soul but also in body because of original sin. Further his life imitates that of Christ, who not only preached but also healed the sick.[291] This same theme of the superiority of prelates because they realise the *vita mixta* is repeated in a Pentecost sermon that Gerson delivered at Constance in 1416, where he stresses the superabundant graces that are given to pastors so that they can fulfil their two-fold task.[292]

Although these two discussions of the 'ambidextrous' life of prelates are not particularly polemical, Gerson's attacks on the Mendicants are, in general, quite severe. The primary cause of this severity is Gerson's belief in the divine and essential role of the pastor in the church. The privileges granted by the papacy to the Mendicants were undermining the position of bishops and especially that of parish clergy, and, as it was the parish priests who were closest to the laity, who were in constant contact with their parishioners, Gerson wanted their position exalted, not undermined. Moreover, that the laity should be brought to perfection by the prelates was Christ's intention, and the privileges granted to the Mendicants were frustrating this intention and disturbing the whole divine plan.[293]

Gerson's works of the 1409–10 period refer frequently to the ways in which the Mendicants and their privileges undermine the position of parish priests. The Mendicants affirm openly and with immunity, he writes, 'that pastors are to be spurned, deserted, hated, and themselves followed'.[294] They do harm, especially in rural areas where the people are simple and the pastors less able to defend themselves than those in Paris who have the aid of learned theologians. The Mendicants are robbers not of gold and silver, but of the 'dignities, offices and honour of others'.[295] Everywhere they are in competition with the parish clergy: in preaching, hearing confessions, burials, and tithes and other fees, and so they destroy the relationship of mutual obligation that should exist between *curé* and parishioners.[296]

Gerson's severity towards the Mendicants also has roots in the fact that he was a secular theologian and spent almost forty years at the University of Paris, where the anti-Mendicant tradition was very strong. But Gerson's attack was not as fundamental as that of some of his predecessors who had gone so far as to question the very existence of the Mendicants.[297] Nor was it as fundamental as that of the contemporary Wycliffites or the later Protestant reformers. Gerson was concerned only about the ways in which he thought the Mendicants undermined the position of the parish clergy. The religious orders, including the Mendicants, had, for Gerson, their place in the church, though it was not in the upper ranks of the hierarchy. Gerson had three brothers who were in religious orders and he had himself

at one time wanted to become a monk.[298] He wrote many letters to the heads
of religious houses, replying to their requests for advice, and in general he
admired the monastic ideal. In one of his vernacular sermons he refers to
it as the better way to attain sanctity and enter paradise.[299]

As far as the Mendicants in particular were concerned Gerson saw their
role as assistants in pastoral work.[300] He had no desire to exclude them from
this field; there was room for them here, provided that they respected the
rights and authority of both bishops and parish clergy, and worked 'with
a spirit of charity, and not for gain, or with a spirit of rivalry and
ambition'.[301] They must not preach or hear confessions in parish churches
except with the permission of the parish priest concerned. They could,
however, preach to the laity in their own churches or in public, when the
bishop himself did not preach or appoint a public preacher. But they must
not criticise the local clergy in their sermons. They could also hear
confessions in their own churches provided they had the licence of the
bishop.[302] But, Gerson tells the laity, 'it is a more perfect thing to confess
to one's own parish priest than to any outsider', and to hear mass on
Sundays and feast-days at one's own parish church and not elsewhere.[303]
Under no circumstances were the Mendicants to administer to the laity the
sacraments of marriage or extreme unction, or the Eucharist, and only in
case of necessity might they baptise. As far as burials were concerned,
Gerson insisted that the Mendicants must not seduce the laity to be buried
in their churches or cemeteries. If a layman did so choose, then a quarter
of any legacy or funeral fee was to go to the parish priest.[304]

One can infer from these statements that a number of unseemly wrangles
must have taken place between the Mendicants and the parish priests.
Gerson wanted to end all these. He begs both parties to strive to share their
burdens without contention and rivalry and not to behave 'like steers, who
bite and consume each other', otherwise evil opinion and bitter words
about the clergy will rise up among the laity.[305] He wanted co-operation,
and the best basis for achieving this, he thought, was for the Mendicants –
and the pope – to accept the superior hierarchical status and perfection of
the pastors. If they did not and if the divinely ordained order was upset
in any way at all, then calamities would occur. Indeed they have already
occurred, bemoans Gerson in a dramatic passage. All the beauty and order
with which the church was founded have been lost; 'the image of heaven
has gone; there is only the image of hell, where there is no order and where
eternal horror dwells'. Gerson urges the pope to banish the confusion by
'ordering each to keep to his proper place, to be content with his rank and
not to step outside the proper boundaries of his office'.[306] Only if this is
done will there be peace and order; and in this order the pastors have their
special and vitally important role of purifying, illuminating and perfecting
the laity of Christendom.

4

THE MEANS OF SALVATION

LATE MEDIEVAL NOMINALIST THEOLOGY: THE STATE OF
THE QUESTION

In past and recent scholarship Gerson has generally been labelled as a
nominalist theologian. He is characterised in this way, for example, by
Oberman and some of his pupils in various works of the last few decades.
It is not, of course, the older view of nominalism that these historians are
working with. The traditional interpretation saw the movement, because
of its anti-realist logic, as characterised by a rejection of metaphysics and
natural theology, and sometimes by a thoroughgoing, almost Humean,
epistemological scepticism. This meant that the realms of faith and reason
were so separated that only a blind fideism and trust in revelation and the
authority of the church could result. Further, the nominalist emphasis on
the divine omnipotence and will, rather than on the divine intellect and
reason, was thought to undermine the thirteenth-century ethical system of
natural law, and to result in a moral order that was unstable and irrational
because it depended only on the arbitrary will of God, who could have
established and indeed still could establish an entirely different moral
economy where present vices became virtues, and present virtues vices.[1]
The movement was held to have been very influential in the English,
French and German universities during the latter Middle Ages, and its
decadence was thought to have contributed to the coming of the Protestant
Reformation. Thus, whatever the confessional position of the historian the
movement was assessed in a negative way.

This interpretation of late medieval nominalism has undergone considerable revision recently as the works of more theologians have been
studied, and the movement is now seen in a more positive light. An
important part of this work of revision has been done by Oberman, whose
views are expressed in numerous articles written in the 1960s and especially
in his study of Gabriel Biel.[2] Oberman's views have undergone some
modification since 1960, but the basic interpretation remains and is still
apparent in more recent articles.[3] Douglass and Steinmetz, two of Oberman's
pupils, have come to conclusions similar to Oberman's as a result of their
studies of individual late medieval theologians.[4] A discussion of the
question outside the Oberman school, though largely in agreement with it,

is Francis Oakley's both in his book on d'Ailly and in his more general works on medieval Europe.[5] From the work of these historians a new picture of late medieval nominalism emerges.

In the first place, the inner core of the movement is seen as not so much its philosophical and logical elements as certain theological concepts, particularly its concept of God and the stress on His omnipotent will.[6] From this stress comes a new emphasis on the distinction, born in the eleventh century, between the absolute and ordained powers of God. *De potentia absoluta* God could have created a very different universe and imposed a different order on it. Thus the actual order He created is contingent.[7] This contingency was emphasised by the nominalists, as it was by Scotus before them, because they were reacting against the necessitarianism of Aristotle and his Moslem interpreters which was condemned in 1277. However, God's freedom to create and do anything, the fact that the present structure of justice rests on the will of God and not vice versa, does not render the present order, God's actual covenant with men, unreliable, unstable and irrational, threatened always by the unpredictable exercise of *potentia absoluta*. Far from it; the established order is reliable; present virtues will not become vices, and God will follow, *de potentia ordinata*, the rules by which He has promised to act.[8] Late medieval nominalists stress the omnipotent will of God, but this does not mean that they deny God's intellect and goodness. Rather, they hold tenaciously to the doctrine of the simplicity of God, arguing that the attributes predicated of God are merely human mental concepts that do not correspond to any objective distinctions in the nature of God Himself. In God, will, intellect and goodness are one with essence, and this fact is a guarantee of 'the unbreakable relation and co-operation of intellect and will in God's *opera ad extra*'.[9]

Following from the doctrine of the contingency of the established order comes the nominalist stress on the authority of revelation and its superiority to philosophy. Connected with this is the view that the authority for determining the faith is not only the Scriptures and the writings of the Fathers, but also the decisions of the church.[10] However, though the nominalists attacked vain theological and metaphysical speculation they did not discard the use of human reason in theology. Revelation is viewed by them as basically reasonable. Some elements of the Christian faith can be grasped by reason alone. If other elements are beyond reason, they are not contrary to reason and thus probable reasons can be adduced.[11]

If agreement is seen to exist among late medieval nominalist theologians on the above doctrines, disagreement is seen on one important topic: the respective roles of God's grace and man's free will in the process of justification. In other words, these theologians agree about the structure of the covenant God makes with men, but disagree about the content of the covenant thus established. For some nominalists, man has a responsibility to do what is in his natural powers (*facere quod in se est*) before he can expect God to help him, either with the grace of illumination in the pursuit of truth, or with justifying grace in the pursuit of holiness and salvation. These nominalists, we are told, believe that man can, unaided by grace, do the will of God, that is, bring forth an act of love for God above all things (*super omnia*). From this doctrine of justification follows a view of predestination that stresses the role of divine foreknowledge, that is, predestination after foreseen merits (*post praevisa merita*). Occam, Biel and Geiler are examples of nominalists said to hold these doctrines.[12] At the other end of the spectrum are nominalists such as Gregory of Rimini, Pupper of Goch and Staupitz who hold an Augustinian view on the justification and predestination questions. For them, man cannot, by his own natural powers (*de puris naturalibis*), earn merits or even act virtuously. Grace is necessary every step of the way and predestination is before foreseen merits (*ante praevisa merita*). The content of the covenant for them is not God's promise to aid those who do their best but rather His promise to preserve the elect.

Such are the basic tenets of late medieval nominalism according to the Oberman school.[13] Not all historians, however, who have published revisionist works in the last fifty years have reached the same conclusions as the Oberman school and Oakley. Some have left the traditional interpretation of nominalism intact but come to the conclusion that the particular theologian under study was not a nominalist.[14] This approach might leave us with an empty category in late medieval theology – a result that would be deplored by some historians but welcomed by others. The more usual approach, though, has been to redefine nominalism, and generally on the lines described in the previous pages. Courtenay, in fact, who has surveyed much of the revisionist work, sees a consensus now developing on these lines at least with regard to the major theologians generally associated with 'moderate nominalism', specifically Occam, d'Ailly and Biel.[15] However, as he acknowledges, the interpretation of the majority of late medieval theologians is still controversial.[16] This is true of the interpretation of Gerson.

Although he has most often been referred to as a nominalist, in both the old and newer senses, Gerson has also been called anti-Occamist, realist, voluntarist, Bonaventurian, Augustinian, Thomistically inclined, and eclectic, while his mysticism has been labelled as Gersonism by one commentator.[17] Connolly, for instance, working with the older, negative assessment of nominalism, and seeing it as a philosophical movement with unfortunate theological overtones, asserts that, though Gerson had been trained as a nominalist in philosophy and could not shake himself entirely free from it, yet he was a realist in his theology and his mysticism. Further, Connolly argues that Gerson was largely responsible for the replacement of nominalism by realism in the philosophy curriculum of the arts faculty at Paris in 1405.[18] Gilson too sees Gerson as a reluctant nominalist, adhering to philosophical nominalism only in so far as it was a safeguard against the sort of realism that 'ran the risk of leading to the doctrine of Scotus, Wyclif and Hus'.[19] Although Oberman has no difficulty in enclosing Gerson and his mysticism within the nominalist fold, Ozment is not so sure. The latter cites with approval Combes' view that Gerson retained 'a qualified realist metaphysics which permits real contact between the soul and God' – realist assumptions which, Ozment argues, were 'too quickly passed over by Oberman'.[20] There is no agreement, then, that Gerson held to a pure, unadulterated nominalism. But how many late medieval 'nominalist' theologians did? If there is one thing that the recent literature reveals it is that the 'nominalist' theologians studied do not belong exclusively in every aspect of their thought to one 'school'. Thus d'Ailly was a 'truly many-sided thinker,...not lacking even in Thomist sympathies', showing Thomist influence especially in the psychological foundations of his epistemology and in his teaching on the relation of truth and knowledge, with its rejection of the Averroist doctrine of the double truth.[21] Mirecourt was a 'cautious, non-radical, somewhat eclectic theologian', whose position on sacramental causality was Thomistic, and not Occamist.[22] Staupitz was a representative of no single school of theological thought. 'His theology is a creative amalgam of insights drawn from many sources and graced with certain unique touches all his own.'[23] Geiler, though a nominalist, showed an eclecticism in his preaching and used widely the writings of Augustinian and Thomistic theologians, as well as those of the nominalist tradition, while Biel drew upon many scholastic sources to form an eclectic and sometimes original synthesis of several traditions.[24] This does not mean that we should abandon all schools and movements and see each theologian as being *sui generis*. But we should bear in mind the plurality of thought within schools and the fact that the lines between schools are often crossed.

But should the 'school' to which Occam, d'Ailly, Gregory of Rimini, Biel, Geiler, Pupper and even Gerson have been said to belong be called nominalist at all? The term, after all, seems to be anachronistic for much of the period in question. It had been used in the twelfth and thirteenth centuries to denote a particular position on the question of universals in the field of logic. In the fourteenth century, however, it seems to have dropped out of usage and Occam, for instance, was never called a nominalist by his contemporaries – nor was he one by twelfth-century criteria. The word was reintroduced in the fifteenth century, probably initially as a term of abuse for their contemporary opponents, by advocates of the revival of a 'realistic' approach to Aristotle, based on Averroes, Albert, Thomas, Bonaventure and Scotus. Again the context was logic and epistemology.[25] Some historians, for example Moody, argue that, if 'nominalist' is to be used for the late Middle Ages, it should be confined to a philosophical position.[26] There is much to be said for this suggestion now that the theological concepts are seen to be prior in the thought of 'nominalist' theologians. There is even more to be said for it when one considers that one of the central tenets of 'nominalist theology', the omnipotence and utter freedom of God and the consequent contingency of everything except God, was also held by theologians who were not philosophical nominalists. The realist Scotus is a prime example here. But he is not the only one, as Leff has demonstrated. Writing of the mid fourteenth century, Leff states that this central tenet was explicitly acknowledged 'by the majority of thinkers. It affected knowledge and belief alike; in neither did it imply an Ockhamist standpoint' – or a nominalist standpoint. To imagine that it did, Leff argues, is 'the greatest single misconception still prevalent about the thought of the fourteenth and indeed fifteenth centuries' – a period whose most notable aspects for Leff were heterogeneity and consequent eclecticism.[27]

There is every reason for adopting Leff's position. It would indeed be logical to abandon altogether the adjective 'nominalist' in discussions of late medieval theology. The term, however, has been used in the wider, theological sense so frequently in the historiography that it has a certain convenience and, if used with inverted commas, perhaps even legitimacy. It will be used in this way here.

If we do adopt Leff's position then there is no problem about Gerson's having a 'qualified realist metaphysics' and yet displaying some of the characteristics attributed to 'nominalist' theologians. Nor will it be incongruous if he also shows some affinity with other theological schools, if he betrays the eclecticism that Leff sees as characteristic of the period, and that other historians have seen in their particular 'nominalist' theologians.

GOD

It is not to be expected that anyone who followed Gerson around and listened to all his French sermons and read all his vernacular tracts would come away with a clear picture of the chancellor's theological doctrine neatly docketed under the chapter headings used by modern historians in their discussions of late medieval theology: the nature of God, faith and reason, the nature of man before and after the fall, justification and predestination and so forth. The message that would have come across – indeed that does come across – is a moral one: repent at once, fight against the assaults of the devil, turn to God, sin no more or else you will go to hell.

A person who sins mortally denies God by his deed and gives himself to the devil, just as one who leaves his rightful seigneur and goes to another repudiates the former without saying a word, and becomes the man of the latter. A sinner is in the hatred of Our Lord; he is deprived of all the blessings of holy church; he is banished from paradise; he is the serf of the devil and of his sin; if he dies in his sin, he will suffer the pains and torments of hell.[28]

On the other hand, if you want salvation, you must keep God's commandments; indeed God makes us His sons and the heirs of His kingdom if we truly love Him. To the good Christ says, 'Come, you who are blessed of God my father, to the kingdom of paradise which is prepared for you.'[29] In other words Gerson's basic message to the faithful is a ringing call to make a great effort to live according to God's law and so gain salvation. This description is, of course, an over-simplification. Complications are added by Gerson's desire to comfort the anxious and despairing, to answer the puzzled and to avoid any form of the Pelagian heresy. But there is no doubt about the major message and here Gerson is in line with most medieval preachers.

Nevertheless amidst this moral sermonising Gerson's views on major theological issues can be discerned. On the relevant feasts, for instance, he stops to comment on the Incarnation, the Trinity, the Immaculate Conception and so forth. But there is more than this. Because he considered it essential for *les simples gens* to be informed about such matters as the creed, the commandments and the sacraments he naturally saw it as his duty to preach about the doctrines contained in or implied by these basic elements of the Christian faith. He does not simply state doctrines baldly. He is very much aware of the scholastic disputes on certain issues and, although on principle he rarely tackles subtle points head on in his popular works, he often tries to explain to his audience difficulties that arise on questions of doctrine. One has the impression indeed that he is often trying to combat perhaps quite widespread misunderstanding and, more rarely, doubt and even unbelief about some basic tenets of the Christian religion.

'I believe in God the Father almighty, maker of heaven and earth', the first article of the creed, elicits from Gerson numerous discussions about the nature of God. For his popular audiences he paints a picture of God as a seigneur, in fact, the seigneur of seigneurs, the omnipotent Lord in whose mercy we all lie. God is, for instance, like a temporal seigneur who founds a city and peoples it. His intention is not to harass or destroy the people; rather he wants them to live well. 'Nevertheless he orders a gibbet to be set up for hanging evil-doers; and this gibbet is held in great honour as a sign of his justice. Similarly it is with hell.'[30] We, on our part, are like serfs, bound to God by the ties of obedience to His commandments, and we must behave as good serfs, using well all His gifts and not committing treachery against Him.[31] Over and over again Gerson uses this simile of God as a seigneur and men as His subjects or serfs, and no doubt in French society of the later Middle Ages the preacher's message would be clear. D'Ailly too makes liberal use of the same imagery, though he most often calls the subjects of the *souverain Seigneur* vassals, not serfs, as befits vernacular sermons to the court.³² God, however, says Gerson is a good seigneur, not a tyrant. This does not mean that He is 'soft', but that He rules justly and, when it pleases Him, mercifully.³³ Gerson also refers to God as the good judge and the good teacher, as the good friend and the good father,³⁴ but it is the seigneur image that predominates.

As God is the seigneur of seigneurs He has no superior; He is totally free. Moreover His will is not constrained by any laws. Even in Gerson's vernacular sermons there is a constant stress on the absolute freedom of God – far more of a stress, for instance, than in the extant vernacular sermons of his contemporaries, d'Ailly and Courtecuisse. If the soul of man, he writes, is free to move and govern at will its little world, that is the body, then so much the more ought God, the most powerful of all, to have freedom and liberty; and on this point Aristotle and almost all the philosophers have fallen into horrible errors, when they deny the free will of God.³⁵

Gerson elaborates this point in one of his university lectures of 1402. The philosophers, he argues, say that God works not so much freely as by a natural necessity. On the basis of experiential knowledge of the fixed nature of the order of the universe they assert that the cause which governs all things is immovable, and here they are correct, but they go on to say that this cause is necessitated to act in a way which cannot be ordered otherwise. When they say that God does not administer all things to us by gratuitous freedom but rather by servile necessity, they destroy all reverence and gratitude to Him.³⁶ Later in the same lecture Gerson blames Plato as being one of the sources of current problems because of his concept of the Ideas, eternal universals outside the soul and outside God. He has led some Christian philosophers into error, and now these 'posit eternal essences [*quidditates*], outside the mind, which are not God, or produced by God, or producible or destructible by God'. And this, Gerson continues, is against the Parisian articles promulgated at the time of William of Paris and Bonaventure.³⁷ Such eternal universals would, of course, limit the creative will of God. Gerson suggests that the solution to the problem might be found in Aquinas. And indeed a solution can be found in Aquinas. In a number of places Thomas does discuss aspects of this question at some length, concluding that God does not act or will by any natural necessity, that God's will has no cause, and that He could have, *de potentia absoluta*, created different things and imposed a different order on them.³⁸

In another lecture Gerson criticises Augustine's doctrine of the immutable and eternal ideas in the mind of God, but this time refers his students to Occam's 'subtle' discussion, noting that the holy doctors in many matters should be 'respectfully glossed rather than amplified' because they did not always pay attention to the propriety of their language. The commentator should therefore not say more but rather 'reduce the language to propriety'.³⁹ Gerson is almost certainly referring here to Occam's discussion, in his commentary on the *Sentences*, of the question 'Whether God understands all things by their ideas'.[40] Here Occam 'respectfully glosses' Augustine, but nevertheless completely demolishes the traditional interpretation, which gave the divine ideas transcendental status and regarded them as part of the divine essence and the source of the being of creatures. For Occam the divine ideas are not universal ideas, but merely the ideas God has of actual or possible individual creatures. They are, in fact, individual creatures as known by God, and, as such, pose no threat to either the freedom of God's act of creation or to His utter simplicity of being. Here Gerson stands with Occam and against Thomas, who, although he rejects Platonic Ideas, affirms the existence of exemplary ideas within the mind of God.[41] But it is not only that Gerson, though he can find many points of agreement with Thomas, specifically rejects some Thomistic doctrines. The ambience of their respective discussions on the omnipotence of God is different. The context has changed. Like Occam, Gerson is writing in the shadow of the 1277 condemnations, and the doctrine of the freedom and omnipotence of God and the contingency of everything else has moved to centre stage. We have already seen Gerson refer to the condemnations. His teacher, d'Ailly, also does so – in the very first pages of his commentary on the *Sentences*.[42] We can, therefore, on the question of divine omnipotence align Gerson with Oberman's 'nominalist theologians' and with Leff's 'majority'.

Gerson places firm emphasis on the fact that it is the *will* of God, His pleasure, that determines His actions. God can do as He wills with His creatures, he tells one congregation, and put obligations on them according to His good pleasure. 'All He need say in explanation is: it pleases me. Can He not retain some sign of His lordship [*seigneurie*] over His creatures?'[43] Another congregation are told that, if they ask why such a difficult ordinance (the need for grief and punishment for sin) is put on Christians, the completely sufficient answer is 'God wishes it.'[44] The will of God, he writes in another sermon, is the first and sovereign law by which all things are regulated, and it is not reasonable to seek the cause of God's will, which is itself first and sovereign cause. We must allow to God greater lordship over all His creatures than the potter has over his clay. God, in fact, has sovereignty and complete domination over all His creatures so that He can, without injustice or cruelty, annihilate or punish them eternally. People who question God's actions, in this case in the area of predestination, are being misled because 'they are considering God as a mortal prince bound by established [*crees*] laws and a debtor to us', and this shows great ignorance of the holy Scripture.[45] God, then, is more than a seigneur or temporal prince, because He is not bound by any laws at all, or so it seems so far. He could, for example, have brought about our salvation in any way He chose, at His good pleasure. In fact He chose the way of the Incarnation and Passion.[46] He could move us towards salvation directly by His own actions but in fact He wishes that a man be saved by the help of others or of angels, that is, He generally wishes to work by means of secondary causes.[47] This is a case where Gerson could have referred his readers to St Thomas, who says that at times God miraculously instructs people by His grace about things that could be known by natural reason, 'even as He sometimes brings about miraculously what nature can do'.[48] Alternatively he could have referred them to Occam who, more boldly, says: 'Whatever God can produce by means of secondary causes, He can directly produce and preserve without them.'[49] Gerson does not speculate here about the other things God could do or could have done. He does not, for instance, say, as Occam does, that God can accept the sinner without grace, dispense with baptism, remit directly all sin and its penalty, including Adam's, or command someone to hate Him so that obedience in this would be a worthy act.[50] His statement about God's annihilating His creatures, though, does come close to Occam's remark that God could annihilate someone who loved Him and all of whose works He accepted[51] – an action that seems to contradict God's goodness and justice. Thomas would not have accepted this.[52]

Behind what Gerson is saying in these vernacular works is the distinction between the *potentia absoluta* and the *potentia ordinata* of God. This distinction also lies behind his statement that God could have created another world than the one He in fact created, and that philosophers are wrong who deny this. They are also wrong, he continues, when they deny that God can create nothing new without using matter already there, when they deny that he can change one thing into another.[53] To show that He governs all by His pure and free will, without any limitations or contradictions, without being bound by the laws of nature, God instituted the miraculous sacrament of the Eucharist.[54] Gerson makes the same point about God's utter freedom in his allegory about the Immaculate Conception, where he has Prudence say

I am amazed that Justice wants the sovereign Emperor and founder of laws to be so bound by them that in no way can He or ought He to change them in a particular case. He would be more of a serf to His laws than temporal princes are to theirs.[55]

Prudence goes on to comment about all the miracles against the ordained laws of nature that God has already performed. Thus there is nothing to prevent Him from bringing about the Immaculate Conception.

For Gerson, then, God, by means of His absolute power, as well as having freely ordained the present system, can and does make incursions into that system from time to time. Gerson is interpreting the *potentia ordinata* in the second of two senses described by d'Ailly.[56] The first interpretation is that God's absolute power refers only to the possibilities initially open to God and so the *potentia ordinata* must denote the complete plan of God for His creation, miracles included. The second interpretation, by contrast, identifies God's ordained power with the laws by which the established order normally operates and thus God's absolute power is seen as an ability to transcend those laws. The second interpretation, favoured by d'Ailly and by Gerson, does seem to leave God even freer and the present order even more contingent than does the first interpretation. Biel too follows d'Ailly here, and in fact cites him, when he argues that, *de potentia absoluta*, God can suspend natural laws so that a created cause can produce effects contrary to those it now produces, *de potentia ordinata*.[57] Occam, by contrast, holds to the first sense of *potentia ordinata*, and in this he shows himself closer than d'Ailly, Gerson and Biel to the thirteenth-century understanding of the distinction of the two powers, though he uses it much more extensively and centrally than his predecessors.[58]

Although Gerson on this question holds what, on the surface, appears to be a more radical position than Occam's and although he presents God to his popular congregations as an absolutely free being, not constrained even by His own laws, he does not leave the impression that God is an arbitrary and capricious tyrant. On the contrary, God is the good friend who never fails; everything He wills and does is for man's benefit.[59] His prohibition of fornication, for instance, is to man's profit, as anyone can see who thinks of the natural evils that follow for men, women and children if this stricture is disregarded.[60] The institution of the sacrament of penance, when God gave power to His apostles and disciples and their successors to pardon sin, is for man's benefit although the acts men must perform to receive absolution may seem burdensome.[61] Although all sins are in their essence an offence against God and therefore deserve the appellation 'mortal' and the punishment of death, the fact that some sins are counted as only venial is entirely due to God's will and grace. Even mortal sin, if remitted, is not punished by death, and here is shown the mercy of God, who charges sins only with temporal punishment, sins 'which in themselves are imputable to death; venial sins *de possibile* and mortal sins *de lege statuta*'.[62] Gerson is not here using the terms *de potentia absoluta* and *de potentia ordinata*, but the terms he uses are not uncommon equivalents.[63] What he is saying is that the order and system which God has freely ordained about sin, as indeed about everything else, including the whole economy of salvation, work to man's benefit. It is true that God does not approve actions because they are good, but rather that they are good because He approves them; in other words that the standards of justice and morality rest on the will of God.[64] But the point is that the actions which God approves are good as we normally understand the term, because God 'is just in all His ways and holy in all His works'.[65]

Gerson is here teaching on the same lines as Occam, d'Ailly and Biel, though there is something of a difference between the tone of the first of his six lectures, *De vita spirituali animae*, and their more academic commentaries on the *Sentences*. His lecture has strong echoes of the preacher and ends with a plea to his students to turn from intellectual to affective theology. It is almost by the way that he mentions the doctrines and discussions he has learned from or read in d'Ailly and Occam. Nevertheless he does endorse their opinion that acts are good or bad not of their own nature but simply because God has commanded or forbidden them, and he does discuss, as they do, in what possible circumstances an evil act could be good.[66] But he is very quick to bring God's wisdom and goodness into the discussion, and later in the lecture, returning to the question, he asks whether divine law and the obligation to obey it are to be attributed to the divine intellect or to the divine will. 'To both' is his reply.[67] In a Latin sermon, probably preached as early as 1391, having stated that divine law can be called the divine wisdom or the divine will or the divine judgement of right reason, he declines on this occasion to answer whether this eternal law should be said to proceed from the divine intellect or the divine will and refers his audience to Thomas for a discussion of the problem.[68] The stress in Thomas is on the connection between the divine law and the divine wisdom rather than the divine will. But generally in Gerson, as in Occam and d'Ailly, the reverse is true, though none of them ignores the divine wisdom.

On numerous occasions in his popular sermons when Gerson refers to the sovereign power and will of God causing something or performing some action he couples God's wisdom, benevolence or justice with God's will. The angels, for example, were created 'from the pure goodness and will of God', while the world was formed by God from His eternity 'according to the order of His wisdom and according to His free will'.[69] Every seigneur, he writes, if he is to govern his subjects well, needs power, wisdom and benevolence, and so it is with God, 'who is in His essence infinite power, infinite wisdom, infinite benevolence', and who shows His power in forming the world, His wisdom in ordering it and His benevolence in conserving and governing it.[70] Everything God does and wishes to do is 'justly done, wisely done, gently done, be it in punishing by justice or pardoning by grace'.[71] Examples could be multiplied[72] but in all cases Gerson is making the same point: God's will is bound up with His wisdom and goodness.

This linking of God's power (or will), wisdom and goodness is a commonplace, going back at least to Augustine.[73] It is prominent in Bonaventure who stresses, like Gerson, that God's works are all directed to man's benefit.[74] The point is, of course, that God is simple, that He is a unity.[75] This emphasis on the simplicity of God's being is typical of the 'nominalist' theologians. For Occam, God's will is merely another word for God's essence. 'In no way is the divine essence distinct from the divine will, but in every way they are identical...therefore if the will is the cause, the essence will be the cause.'[76] For d'Ailly, 'the divine will and the divine intellect or reason are identical, formally and really', and 'for God it is the same to will and to understand'.[77] Similarly Biel argues that 'the divine intellect and the divine essence are identical', and that 'the divine will or essence is the cause of all things'.[78]

Thomas also argues for the unity and simplicity of God. 'In God will, wisdom and goodness are really identical...In Him the will is really identical with the intellect, and for this reason the correctness of His will is really the same as His will itself.'[79] There is, however, a difference between the Thomist position and that of Occam. For neither is there a real distinction among the attributes of God; the distinction is one of reason, but whereas for Occam the distinction of reason is a purely human mental concept, for Thomas there is a foundation in God for our concepts, imperfect though they are, of the divine attributes. The meaning (ratio) of wisdom and goodness, of will and intellect, differ in God and so every added concept of God increases our knowledge of Him.[80] For Thomas the divine attributes are not mere synonyms.[81] But this is precisely what they are for Occam. 'God's divine attributes are merely mental, vocal or written terms designed to stand for Him...They are really distinct from one another as terms, but they mean (ratione) the same in standing for God.'[82] Gerson is with Occam here and against Thomas. God's essence, life, intellect, wisdom, justice and fortitude, he says, all denote the same thing in fact (ex parte rei): namely God Himself.[83]

The general impression that Gerson's congregations would acquire, then, about God is that He is absolutely free, but that what He has created and ordained, and the actions which He sometimes performs against the ordained laws, are all in accord with His wisdom and benevolence and for man's benefit. Why, then, Gerson has Impatience ask in one of his sermons, are there so many miseries in the world? What sweetness can there be, what mercy when all goes ill, when all goes 'from worse to worse, from affliction to affliction, from torment to torment'? If God is king, why does He allow such misery in the church with this execrable schism and division?[84] Not only are there public miseries but there are also private tribulations. In numerous sermons Gerson tackles this question. It was obviously something which people found it difficult to understand, and which led them to despair or to grumble against and even repudiate God.[85] Moreover, tribulations afflict not only the wicked but also the good.[86] And why, in any case, does God allow some men to be wicked?[87] Gerson has, of course, like the many other preachers who took up this topic, a complicated state of affairs to explain here, to which the Manichean answer would probably be the simplest. But no one gives that answer. Courtecuisse, who devotes the whole of his sermon Justum adiutorium, to the problem of tribulations, says some of them come from our sins, from which 'the enemy of hell is often not far distant', while the others come from the justice and providence of God who knows all things and can turn all to good. He elaborates on 'our sins' (pride, ambition and covetousness) and then tries to explain why God sends tribulations, basically arguing that they are good for us.[88] Gerson's answer is similar but he does emphasise, more than Courtecuisse, that nothing is done or occurs without the just ordinance of God.[89] Tribulations of mind and body, miseries and adversities, both public and private, are all sent from God but for a good end: for example, to encourage us to turn to God in our troubles, to humble us, to make us patient, to correct us.[90] They can even be sent to prevent us from sinning, as bodily infirmity, for instance, removes the hunger for lustful delights.[91] Tribulations are the Holy Spirit knocking at our door and asking to come in – prevenient graces, in fact.[92] Just as all tribulations fall within God's ordinance, so too does He suffer all evil that good may come.[93] Thus all is taken care of. The faithful, whatever their present suffering, may be comforted, provided that they *are* faithful and are doing what they can to obey God's will.

THE DEVIL

There is clearly no room in the scheme of things just described for any independent activity on the part of the devil, yet the devil and his countless minions are ever present in Gerson's sermons. The devil and demons, of course, appear in many vernacular sermons of the period, for they are favourite characters in *exempla*. St Bernardine brings them on stage frequently and Courtecuisse spends a large part of one sermon describing the ruses of the devil and how to escape them. But there is hardly a vernacular sermon of Gerson's in which some mention of the devil is not made. It is a very crowded universe that Gerson describes. God is by no means alone in heaven; with Him are the legions of angels grouped in their three-fold ranks, all the saints and the blessed, while in hell are Lucifer and his grim company. In purgatory are numerous souls waiting to be released from their sufferings. On earth are men, the *viatores*. Moreover, all these realms are inter-connected. The angels bring aid and comfort to men and help them to glory,[94] and the saints intercede for men.[95] The *viatores*, for their part, have a job to do in helping to release souls from purgatory.[96] But it is the activity of the demons who bring trouble to men that seems to concern Gerson most. Judging from the number of times Gerson condemns sorcery it would seem that the activity of demons was of wide concern and interest to his congregations also.

Gerson states in one place that it is heretical to deny the existence of devils, and that people who do so are judging falsely and without experience.[97] But in general he assumes the belief, and in himself the belief is very strong and the presence of devils very real. Indeed it seems that he feels that most of the evil and sin in the world is caused by diabolical activity. Occasionally he remarks that, for example, temptations can come from natural causes, from the disposition of the body, from too much eating and drinking or from laziness,[98] that is from the world and the flesh as well as from the devil; but the devil, 'l'ennemi de l'humaine lineage', seems to play by far the greatest role. But there is no Manicheanism in this. The devil has no power beyond what God allows; without God's permission the devil can do nothing.[99] Thus Gerson has the problem which he does not flinch from raising from time to time, of why God allows the devil and his legions to exist in the first place, and to afflict men with miseries and temptations in the second.

In his sermon for the feast of St Michael, Gerson relates to his congregation the familiar story of the creation and fall of Lucifer and his followers.[100] Gerson acknowledges that some difficulties arise about this story. Why did God make the bad angels when He knew very well that they would be damned? His answer is that God gave all the angels free will to use well and so acquire their confirmation in glory. But Lucifer and his companions used their free will badly and hence evil befell them. It was a matter of justice. It was not that God had as his principal intention, when He created them, that they should be damned, any more than kings who kill their own children for the sake of justice have such an intention when they engender those children. The further doubt that might arise from this – that God is not like an ordinary king, because He has foreknowledge and nothing can happen against His will – is not tackled by Gerson. He assumes that that doubt has been settled and moves on to the next. Why did God not annihilate Lucifer after his sin? His answer is not entirely satisfactory, as he again argues that the justice of God demands the punishment of the wicked. Elsewhere he suggests that devils are needed by God to bring trouble to and test men. Why the devils were not redeemed or received into penitence is his third question. His answer is that they sinned without any temptation from outside and used very badly all the time they were given to merit and deserve paradise; and, he adds, so will we be damned if we use badly our time on earth. Gerson's answers, in other words, are based on the existence of free will in Lucifer and his company and he seems to brush over in this sermon the problem of how this can be reconciled with the providence of God. But at least he raises the problem, which is more than d'Ailly, Courtecuisse or Hugh Legat do when they describe or mention the fall of Lucifer.[101]

In what ways do these fallen angels cause trouble for men? Just as the good angels were ordained by divine providence to guard human beings and help them to acquire glory, by contrast the demons 'exert themselves [firent leur effort] to make man sin and prevent him from mounting to the heaven from which they fell'. From this came the temptation of Eve and Adam, all from the envy of the enemy.[102] Gerson is careful here. The good angels were ordained by God to help men, but the fallen angels 'firent leur effort'. In other words God ordains good but not evil. The most that could be said is that He allows the devils to pursue their nefarious activities; He does not compel them, for they have free will, though He could prevent them.[103]

In a number of sermons Gerson relates the various evils brought by devils, in their attempt to prevent men from reaching heaven. They bring tyranny, heresy, superstition and sorcery, schism and lust.[104] They make cruel assaults against men's souls by sending pride, avarice, sloth, envy, anger, lust, gluttony and other countless vices, 'and now by force, now by fraud, by treason, by evil subtlety they want to enter our castle to drive away or put an end to all the chivalric army of virtues'.[105] It is the devil who forges an alliance between ambitious covetousness and men, especially prelates, presidents and governors. And it is he who is responsible, via the covetousness he causes in men, for the present sufferings of the church.[106] He brings adversity and anxiety to men so that they will be impatient, murmur against God and eventually start to fear demons and ask them for mercy and then to honour them. It is the devil who has perverted the Roman pope so that he has turned against the way of resignation, whereas before he supported it.[107] It is clear from all this that 'the office of the enemy is to bring harm to others'.[108]

Gerson only occasionally speaks of the devil causing evils, causing sin, as if he did it directly, unlike Bernardine, who almost always portrays the devil in this way.[109] For Gerson, the devil is most often seen as carrying out his work by tempting men. The chancellor wrote much about temptation and its remedies both in his popular sermons and writings and in Latin works, and it is the devil who is portrayed as the chief, though not the only, source of temptation. Moreover Satan works not only in direct and obvious ways but also in very cunning and subtle ways, and he knows his man, knows what sort of temptation will be most effective against this person and what against that. Once again Gerson's psychological astuteness, his awareness of the ways in which men justify their actions, is very apparent. He impressed Luther, who said of him: 'He is the only one who wrote about spiritual temptation.'[110] Gerson is not the only one, of course. Tauler and Courtecuisse both wrote about it, but neither with the insight of Gerson.[111] The latter's most complete treatment of the topic occurs in a French treatise of 1400–1, perhaps written for his sisters, but extant in a fair number of manuscripts.[112] But many of the points which he makes in this treatise occur scattered throughout his sermons. The devil, for instance, if he cannot prevent a person from performing a good act will attempt to corrupt the intention behind it, so that it is done for vainglory. For example, the almsgiver is tempted to be charitable so that he acquires the praise of others, or some service from the recipient. If this temptation fails, the almsgiver is tempted so that he feels proud for having overcome the previous temptation. Sometimes the devil tempts people to undertake works of virtue that are beyond them, such as excessive fasting so that

'vuideur de teste et melancolie et tristesse' follow.[113] Or he tempts them
to avoid great works of virtue and to concentrate on little ones so that they
become proud because of their success in virtue, or so that they never reach
perfection. He tempts some, under the guise of discretion, not to take vows
against the sins to which they are inclined so that they remain sinful.
Similarly, he tempts others, under the guise of seeking humility, not to do
good works in case they are thought by others to be virtuous and so become
proud. He tempts some to seek great wealth by telling them that they can
then become great almsgivers, and others not to point out the faults of their
fellows so that they can exhibit the virtue of mercy. He tempts some to
murmur against God if their petitions are not answered and others to
over-confidence if their petitions are granted. He sends doubts of conscience
that can lead to despair, and security of conscience that can lead to sin that
is never repented. Sometimes he tempts people to seek counsel from one
whom they know will not advise them to give up their sin, while others are
tempted to rely on themselves and seek no counsel. This is 'la plus
perilleuse tentation'.[114] Then there is the method of making a person feel
full of devotion after he has eaten and drunk well, so that he begins to see
gluttony as a cause of devotion and so indulges in this sin. Whatever a
person's estate in life, the devil can tempt him or her to be discontented
with it and envy others in other estates. He tempts some not to fulfill their
necessary earthly duties by arguing that they ought to be thinking of God,
and others to work too hard so that they never have time to think of God.
He makes people think about whether God has ordained that they be saved
or damned so that they fall into either foolish hope or despair.

And so it goes on at some length.[115] It is clear that one could always be
in a state of doubt about one's motives and actions, always wondering if
one were succumbing to some diabolical temptation. As was the case with
contrition and confession, it seems as if the doctrine taught here could well
lead to neurosis. But, of course, one is not left alone in recognising and
facing these temptations. If one were, then despair would be a real
possibility. But there is God to help.

But why does God allow these temptations in the first place 'since man
is sufficiently inclined in himself to accomplish evil', and since without
God's permission devils can do nothing?[116] As this is a matter of the will
of God, Gerson argues, we can say no more than it pleases Him: 'So I wish,
so I order.' Nevertheless one can give some probable reasons. In the first
place God allows the beings He has created to act according to their nature
or condition. Thus as the devils desire to harm others, God lets them tempt
men. Secondly, just as the good angels, by aiding men, gain glory and
paradise for themselves, so do the demons, by harming men, receive heavy
punishment by the just judgement of God. A third reason why God allows
diabolical temptations is because of their effects on men. He uses the free
will and evil inclinations of devils in order either to punish men or to test

them and help them to turn humbly to their Creator and become more virtuous.[117]

What then should men do to overcome and so get the best out of the temptations that afflict them? What are the remedies against the temptations of the devil? Gerson is adamant when he writes that the remedy is not sorcery. Sorcery is useless, because the devils have free will and cannot be coerced by anyone except God. Indeed they might pretend to be coerced by superstitious practices in order to lure humans into consorting with them, but this is very dangerous, for the devil 'has no loyalty, friendship or love towards men, but hates him to the death'.[118] Basically the remedy against temptation is to turn to God and His grace and to amend one's life. One must have recourse to the mercy of God, put one's hopes in Him, pray to Him and correct one's life. Especially one must chase away the devil by contrition, confession and satisfaction.[119] This latter admonition would have prompted some preachers to relate one of the *exempla* that show how confession – and this sometimes appears to be its chief purpose – almost magically confounds the devil, empties his sack containing all one's sins or instantaneously erases one's sins from his notebook or his memory.[120] Gerson does not relate such *exempla*. It would have been contrary to the whole spirit of his teaching about confession and of his teaching about the devil.

In the *Dialogue spirituel*, written for his sisters, Gerson writes at some length about the remedies against temptations, both in general and in particular. Sometimes he urges a measure of self-help; one should be prepared for all types of temptation, be on the look-out for the snares of the devil. Against the temptation of gluttony, for instance, one should keep oneself busy so that one is not always thinking of food and drink, one should think of the thirst suffered by Christ on the cross, one should avoid the occasions of this sin, refuse dinner invitations, think of the needs of the poor, think of the afflictions suffered by gluttons and drunkards. But Gerson's chief message is the same as that given in his sermons: seek the help of God, for 'without God one can do nothing good'.[121] And in any case temptations, as tribulations, are generally a good sign: they mean God has not given one up for lost.[122]

MAN AND THE FALL

Gerson's discussions of the omnipotent God and of the 'enemy', the devil, form the background for what is his chief concern in his sermons and pastoral writings: man's journey in life towards salvation in heaven or damnation in hell. To the question of why men were created, he gives his audiences 'catechism' answers. They were created, by God, he says, with immortal souls made in His likeness 'to know, love, serve and honour Him, so that by living well in this life they will come hereafter to eternal glory

in paradise with the good angels to fill up the places of the bad angels'. With
the latter will be damned all those 'who live as if they were beasts without
souls, or devils in human flesh'.[123]

Man, then, being created along with the angels and the rest of the
universe out of nothing by the free decision of God, owes everything to his
Creator. As God is the only independent cause, everything is dependent
on Him and so, above all, man owes humility to God. As man was created
in the image of God, his faculties and abilities are a reflection of the
Trinitarian nature of the Creator. Thus man reflects the *potentia* of the
Father when he shows fortitude; he reflects the *sapientia* of the Son by
having faith, and the *bonitas* of the Holy Spirit when he is charitable and
benevolent.[124] These characteristics of power, wisdom and goodness are
associated by Gerson with the faculties of the soul. Fortitude and power
are associated with the *vis irascibilis*, wisdom and faith with the *vis rationalis*
and benevolence and will with the *vis concupiscibilis*.[125] Sometimes Gerson
identifies the Trinitarian image in man with man's faculties of understanding
or intellect, memory and will.[126] Thus man starts off with great natural
advantages and capabilities and these can be seen especially in Adam before
the fall, for his soul reflected very clearly the image of the Trinity.[127]

These psychological characterisations of man have a long history behind
them. The 'spirited, rational and desiring' faculties go back to Plato;
Augustine writes of man's intellect, memory and will as do many writers
in the Augustinian tradition, including Bonaventure, while the latter and
Hugh of St Victor also use the power, wisdom, goodness triad.[128] Aquinas,
on the other hand, prefers the Aristotelian division of the soul into two main
groups of faculties: the intellective and the appetitive.[129] Gerson sometimes
employs this latter division,[130] but generally, and especially in his pastoral
writing, he follows the Augustinian tradition.

In addition to his natural faculties, Gerson tells us, Adam also had
original justice. This Gerson defines as a gift of grace whereby the first man
was given a spiritual heritage. Because of this grace, in Adam and Eve 'the
soul held peacefully in subjection or obedience the flesh, the members and
the corporeal senses. These did not rebel against or disobey what wise
reason wished or commanded.' Moreover, original justice enabled our first
parents always to have 'true judgement without error, good will without
sin, sensuality well governed without any detestable movement or passion
in seeing, hearing, tasting and touching'. Finally it preserved them from
death, and he was able to gain his livelihood without sweat, and she to bring
forth children without pain.[131] With this state of affairs there was no need
for positive laws and a coercive judicial system to make men behave well.
Original justice would be enough to make men render to each his own; to
God, to his body, to his neighbours, to every creature.[132]

In these sermons, where Gerson talks about the well-established doctrine
that prelapsarian man was endowed with supernatural as well as natural

gifts, he is stating that it is the supernatural quality, the grace of original justice, that enabled Adam not only to be free of toil, sickness and death but also to keep his reason free from error, his will following his reason, and his corporeal senses obeying his will. In the sermon *Omne regnum*, however, the stress is a little different. The kingdom of the soul as it was instituted in Adam, Gerson says, was such that all the faculties fulfilled their functions perfectly. But unfortunately the devil entered this kingdom which was 'made in this way by nature and guarded in peace by original justice'.[133] This statement, though rather ambiguous, seems to put the stress on human nature itself as the foundation of the happy state of affairs in the garden of Eden. However, the passage from *Tota pulchra es* is unambiguous in making the grace of original justice the foundation. The most that can be said is that Gerson probably saw human nature as potentially ordered in prelapsarian man and made actually so by the grace of original justice: 'grace supplies what nature lacks', as Thomas puts it.[134]

Unfortunately the happy state of affairs in the garden did not last. Adam and Eve sinned. Their sin was basically one of disobedience and pride; they laid themselves open to God's justice 'by breaking His commandment not to eat the apple and by setting up their will against His by pride and foolish rebellion'. They committed the crime of 'lese majesté'.[135] The results of this sin were dire indeed. Not only did they lose, for themselves and their descendants, their temporal heritage but they also lost their spiritual heritage, that is, original justice. And so there came to rule within them a dreadful tyrant called Original Sin instead of the virtues and the king, Original Justice.[136] They became serfs to tribulation and were delivered over to some very cruel tyrants for torment, to Hunger, Thirst, Anxiety, Misery, Sadness and Sickness.[137] But this is largely metaphor. Where does Gerson stand amidst the various lines of thought on the essence and effects of original sin?

Connolly, defending Gerson from the charge of being a proto-Lutheran, declares categorically that Gerson teaches 'the traditional Catholic doctrine on original sin. There is no mention of concupiscence, but only of disobedience.'[138] If Connolly means that Gerson saw the sin of Adam as chiefly one of disobedience, he is correct, but he is not getting to the heart of the matter. If, on the other hand, he is making some reference to the effects of Adam's actual sin, that is to the essence of original sin, then he is incorrect, for in Gerson's view concupiscence is certainly involved. It is true that, in the passage on which Connolly bases his argument that Gerson's doctrine of original sin is traditional, Gerson states that the effect of original sin is the loss of original justice, and he does not mention concupiscence.[139] But this is not *the* traditional doctrine of original sin; it is only one traditional line of thought, the one stemming from Anselm, and in any case it is not Gerson's only word on the subject.

After the sin of Adam and Eve, Gerson states, 'shameful concupiscence, in rebellion against reason, became entrenched in their members and they were ashamed and covered themselves with leaves'. And that is why, he continues, nudity and talking about the facts of procreation 'arouse more and more this vile and rebellious concupiscence'.[140] Because of the corruption of original sin the flesh is always contrary to the spirit and to reason, and constantly rebels.[141] Because of original sin all is overturned, all is disordered, in contrast to the state of innocence, where all the faculties of man were properly ordered.[142] The body is in schism and rebellion against her proper mistress and queen, reason, and from this come all sins.[143]

That Gerson sees concupiscence as at least part of the essence of original sin and that he regards it as connected – even synonymous – with the loss of original justice is made quite clear by a passage from a Latin work on the definition of terms.

The 'instinct of corrupted nature with respect to sensuality' is the strong inclination of sensuality to its own objects, not waiting on the rule of reason, and it comes to us from the sins of our first parents. 'The law of corrupt nature' means the same. 'The tinder of sin' (fomes peccati) the same. 'The loss of original justice' the same. 'The instinct of corrupt nature with respect to the intellect' is the strong inclination to bend to sensuality, to use God and enjoy creatures and to fornicate spiritually.[144]

It is clear that in this work, probably meant as a handbook for students, and in his French sermons and writing, Gerson does not produce carefully worked out discussions on the nature of original sin. He does not describe and distinguish the positions held by the various schools of thought on this topic as Biel does in his commentary on the *Sentences*, or Aquinas to a lesser extent in his *Summa*,[145] nor does he give any indication as to which school he thinks he belongs to.

Three schools of interpretation concerning the doctrine of original sin have been distinguished by historians, following Biel or Aquinas.[146] The strictly Augustinian school held that the essence of original sin was concupiscence. 'Concupiscence is the guilt [reatus] of original sin', says Augustine.[147] Peter Lombard and Gregory of Rimini agree with him, though Gregory adds that the loss of original justice is also involved.[148] The second school, stemming from Anselm, and defining sin as a deprivation, the absence of good, saw the loss of original justice as the essence of original sin, though resulting in concupiscence as God's punishment of men.[149] Occam follows Anselm here – at least as far as the ordained order is concerned.[150] Aquinas, along with Alexander of Hales and Bonaventure, formed a third school which held a mediating position, in effect combining the two older definitions. For Aquinas, for example, the absence of original justice is the form, and concupiscence the matter of original sin, or, in less technical language, once original justice, by means of which man's will was made subject to God, was lost, the will turned away from God and so disorder (inordinatio) reigned in all the other powers of the soul.[151] In all these interpretations the loss of original justice and concupiscence are involved, but in different ways. It may be that Biel is correct in arguing that there is no decisive difference between including concupiscence in the essence of original sin and seeing it as its automatic accompaniment.[152] In actual fact, however, it was those theologians like Gregory of Rimini and Staupitz who identified original sin with concupiscence who came closest to holding an Augustinian position on justification and predestination.

As for Gerson, all that can be said is that, like Thomas before him and Biel after him, he appears to steer a middle course between the two extremes, seeing both concupiscence and the loss of original justice as essential elements of the original sin inherited by all Adam's descendants. That he does not define his position with exactitude in his pastoral works is not surprising. Nor does d'Ailly in his. D'Ailly's descriptions of the fall and its effects, in his vernacular sermons, refer to the loss of the spiritual gifts with which Adam had been endowed and to the ensuing disasters when 'all falsity, all sin and all vice began to reign'.[153] He is, in fact, much vaguer altogether than Gerson on the subject.

Deprived of original justice and with a nature so wounded and corrupted how can man escape his miserable predicament, how can he be healed and justified? Gerson leaves no doubt in the minds of his hearers and readers that their predicament is miserable. He often describes life on earth as a time of exile. 'Pilgrims we are, banished from our city, from our peace, from our heritage, from our final felicity, in the desert of this world, in the vale of tears, in the region of poverty.'[154] But Gerson is not an advocate of despair. There is a way out so that, despite its miseries, this life can be seen as a journey to security, to man's home in heaven, though the journey is never an easy one.

The way out is, of course, provided by God; by His Incarnation and Passion and grace He has made it possible for men to be redeemed, to be forgiven, healed and sanctified and so accepted into heaven. But Gerson does not leave the impression that it is all up to God. Man has an important role to play. In the first place, despite original sin, despite concupiscence, man still has free will. When he is attempting to give his congregation some conception of the Trinity, Gerson invites them to look into themselves as images of the Trinity. You will see, he writes,

that you have free will so that you can, with the things that are subject to you, discard or keep them at your pleasure, kill or not kill; of the same lump of clay or lead or silver you can make a vessel for a good use, or for a vile use; from the same piece of wood you can make fire and cinders or make a beautiful image. In your flock of sheep, you can take one to kill, and another to keep.[155]

But it is not only over one's possessions that one has free will; one has free will over oneself, so to speak. 'God has given you free will and has shown you the good way and the bad; if you take the bad, you take it by your action, not God's.'[156] God has granted free will to every person so that he can do well or ill. Therefore any who do ill, as Judas did, have only themselves to blame for their damnation. No one, not even Judas, is constrained to do evil. God is not responsible for man's sins, and man is punished on the basis of his own sin for real guilt.[157] So man is free to disobey God's laws, to take the wrong path. That he does so is not surprising considering the corruption of his nature as a result of original sin. Further, man has free will to reject any grace God offers him. But is man able, of his free will alone, to accept grace and to take the right path? In some sense it would seem that he is. 'God has given you free will to accept grace or not; he does not wish to constrain you to one or the other.'[158] Further, a good will, that is one that obeys reason, is in man's power. Man can be full of grace if he wishes it, therefore 'take good will which is in your power, and you will conquer all adversities and patiently bear them'.[159] Man can choose to love God instead of the world, as Peter and Paul did.

We are men as they were. Our soul as theirs was made by God to know and love Him. Let us therefore not despise, deceive or dishonour ourselves, but rather let us be such that we can be numbered among the friends of God.[160]

Gerson is not, of course, denying that God's grace plays the chief role in man's salvation – he is no Pelagian. But he does seem in these passages to be exalting the power of man's free will not only to do evil but also to do good. The concupiscence inherent in man after the fall does not seem to leave man utterly helpless for Gerson. Man's nature is not so wounded and corrupted that he cannot help himself to some extent.

In holding this position, Gerson puts himself outside the camp of the Augustinians with their belief in the radical depravity of human nature. After the fall, says Augustine, the will, if left to itself, inevitably wills sin.[161] The late medieval Augustinians, too, held that man, as a result of original sin, has lost all freedom to serve God and has become incapable of acting virtuously, let alone meritoriously. As Staupitz puts it: 'Without the grace of God it is impossible for man to do anything which is morally good. He is the servant and not the master of his own disobedient members.'[162]

Gerson seems closer to Thomas, for whom the fallenness of man is not as radical as it is for the strict Augustinians. 'Fallen human nature is not altogether corrupted by sin', Thomas writes, arguing that, although original justice was totally lost, the natural inclination to virtue which Adam had before the fall was 'diminished', not destroyed as a result of the first man's sin. As for man's will, like his reason and sensitive appetite (concupiscibilis), it was 'wounded'.[163] This means that it is possible for fallen man with his natural powers to perform morally good works, though not meritorious ones, and that therefore not all acts done outside a state of grace are sins.[164] In a lecture of 1402 Gerson makes the same point. Fallen and corrupted man can, he states, by his natural powers, do morally good works. He then goes on to attack directly the position, later held by Luther and which we have seen was held by the late medieval Augustinians, of those people – unnamed – who hold that because of original sin man is utterly depraved and incapable of morally good works. 'This opinion', he says, 'was long ago rejected as hard and leading more to despair than edification.'[165] Again we see evidence of Gerson's pastoral concern. He foresees, he says, desperation if the faithful think that honouring their parents, almsgiving, keeping the commandments and the rules of the church, if done outside a state of grace, are mortal transgressions. For Gerson, such acts, 'although not meritorious of eternal life, are morally good'.[166] Further – and here Gerson appears to go beyond Thomas and move closer to 'nominalist' theologians like Occam, Geiler and Biel – such acts 'are a preparation congruent for grace [de congruo] because by them man does what is in him; for I understand "to do what is in one" as meaning to do what a man can by the powers which he actually has'.[167] Thomas, by contrast, in reference to the question whether a man by himself can prepare himself for grace, replies by defining 'to do what is in one' as doing what is in one's power 'according as one is moved by God'.[168] Gerson here apparently rejects this definition and follows Occam's assertion that men, by doing their natural moral best, without the infusion of grace can merit de congruo, not salvation, but the grace necessary for salvation.[169] For Biel too man's will remains free after the fall and though man is more inclined to evil than to good deeds, nevertheless he can turn to God and do morally good works by his natural powers alone, and so be worthy de congruo of grace.[170]

So much then for the capabilities of fallen man. He seems, from what we have seen Gerson say so far, to be able to turn to God and to do morally good acts. He cannot, of course, insists Gerson, by his natural powers alone work his own salvation; 'to assert the opposite was the Pelagian error'. The soul's end, after all, is supernatural, therefore it needs something supernatural to reach that end. In other words it needs grace.[171]

JUSTIFICATION

The problem of justification has been called the central theme of late medieval theology. For Oakley there was an 'intense preoccupation with the interrelated questions of sin, grace, freewill, justification and predestination which became the dominant focus of theological discussion'. Similarly for Ozment 'no topic was more hotly argued among scholastic theologians and Protestant reformers than the notions of religious justification and predestination'.[172] The problem was certainly central for Luther, who was trained in the late medieval schools, and Oberman and his followers have argued convincingly that it was central in the theology of Biel, Geiler and Staupitz. In some sense it is a central theme for Gerson also, perhaps even the central theme in that almost all his sermons are concerned with telling people to stop sinning if they wish to gain salvation and avoid damnation. But it is not a central *problem* for Gerson, the pastor and advisor of pastors. He does not expend the major part of his energies in his sermons and popular writings in arguing the cases for and against justification by grace and justification by human effort, in trying to effect a reconciliation between God's omnipotence and man's free will. He is aware that there is a problem and he sometimes raises questions about it, but he is far more concerned, as a good pastor should be, to lead his congregations to perfect their lives than to tease their brains. He seems in general, like other late medieval preachers, to hold in tension the contribution of God's grace and the contribution of man's free will to the process of justification.[173] Sometimes he stresses the work of grace, when he wishes to induce comfort or humility or to exalt the omnipotence of God, and sometimes the work of man's free will, usually when he wants to bestir men to action and repentance. One thing is certain: grace is a necessary condition for justification, hence man's efforts are not sufficient. But man's efforts are also a necessary condition, which means that God's grace is not sufficient either.

Each should do what he ought towards God and His love without resisting His grace and His secret movement, and God will do the rest. For by the law of the ordained order the one without the other cannot bring about the justification of the sinner; neither grace without will, nor will without grace. You see in St Paul that immediately on the call or prevenience of God he opened the door of his consent: Lord what do you will that I should do?[174]

Both grace and free will are necessary for justification, but what is the relation between them? How does the mechanism work and have the ground rules been so laid down that both God's omnipotence and man's free will are truly safeguarded? There are some knotty problems here which had exercised theologians ever since St Augustine had wrestled with the Pelagians and the 'semi-Pelagians' in the fifth century.[175] Gerson does not solve them in his sermons, for one reason because he does not tackle them systematically. But we can see whether he leaves the impression with his congregations that their salvation is chiefly up to God or whether it is chiefly up to them.

There are many passages in his sermons and popular writings where Gerson does leave the impression that the latter is the case. Here the idea seems to be that God is just waiting there to do his part and it is up to man to make the first move. 'God was content to give us a certain number of commandments, and if we fulfil these we have His grace, and that suffices for Him and we gain paradise.'[176] We should repent now and turn our hearts to God, who is the way of all blessings and of all joy and consolation, for if we do not repent now, in this present life, when we can, after death we will not turn to God, for we will not be able to, but 'maintenant les graces sont ouvertes'.[177] The whole theme of this Ash Wednesday sermon, indeed, is a plea to men to turn to God and repent now: 'Return to me with your whole heart, with fasting, weeping and mourning.' And Gerson seems to be saying that it is within man's power to do this. 'Assuredly if we ask for grace we shall not come to judgement... if we ask for mercy, truly we shall receive it.'[178]

Courtecuisse, too, sometimes puts the stress this way. He tells his congregations that whenever we ask God for pardon He gives it and receives us into His grace; that God will not let those perish who with a true heart seek grace; that one need have only a good and firm will or diligence, and grace will be granted.[179] The members of one of Bernardine's congregations are told that they need to dispose themselves for grace and that the more disposed they are the more grace they will receive.[180]

It is not that Gerson thinks that repentance and turning to God are always easy. In a Palm Sunday sermon of 1402 he acknowledges the difficulties. Certain servants of the devil, he writes, try to prevent us from returning to God through penitence; shame, which makes us fearful of speaking of the mire into which we have fallen; despair and obstinacy, which make us sure we will fall again and that therefore it is not worth confessing; presumption, which makes us think we will be all right anyhow, and fear, which makes us dread penances.[181] But against all these there are remedies, most of which could be called measures of self-help: pray to God, get permission to go to a good confessor if one's own *curé* is stupid, think of all those who die suddenly without having time to repent and confess, remember that only penances that are within the penitent's power are assigned.[182] It seems, then, that one can get over the hurdles, or at least take the first steps to get over them by oneself. In any case repentance is what matters, and from this all blessings flow. Those who serve God with their whole heart by doing His commandments, who, as soon as they sin, are repentant and do penance, go straight to paradise when they die. Those who have done nothing or little of what God commands go straight to hell. Those who have not been punished and purged adequately on earth for their sins, but who nevertheless die in grace, go to purgatory for further purging.[183] This sounds indeed like a programme of salvation by works and would seem to lead to a doctrine of predestination *post praevisa merita*.

For those who think that it is very difficult to do God's will, to keep His commandments and so make sure of salvation, Gerson has an answer.

Whoever says that the commandments of God are too hard and burdensome makes God a liar, for He affirms the opposite: my yoke is sweet and my burden light. Is not this a great kindness of this friend who, not weighing any offences committed against Himself, pardons everything if one has contrition?[184]

For those who are not particularly worried by having to keep the commandments but feel that they ought to be doing more, to be doing their very best always, Gerson also has an answer. God knows our fragility, our feeble power, he says, and because of this, He does not require of us all the service

which we ought to do according to His justice, but He has given us a certain
number of commandments, and their accomplishment suffices.[185] A person
is not bound to do all the good to which he feels moved; in fact there are
often perils in this course. It is enough to obey the commandments.[186] So
there is no necessity to set one's goals too high. Seemingly there were
members of Gerson's congregations who did set too high a standard for
themselves, judging from the number of times he makes this point.[187]

So far, then, we have seen Gerson preach and write as if man's salvation
were chiefly in his own hands. He has only to make the right move and God
will grant him grace, and, if he does not resist this grace, salvation will
follow. We seem to be moving in a 'semi-Pelagian' realm, and so had better
turn to what Gerson has to say about grace. He has a lot to say on this
subject. In fact early in nearly every sermon Gerson invokes the assistance
of the Virgin, and asks her to intercede with God to get grace for us. 'Grace
is necessary to us, and where better to find it than from Mary who is the
mother of this grace?'[188] Gerson's congregations would be left in no doubt
about the necessity of grace for salvation. 'But alas, who is there who
without the grace of God can be saved?'[189] There is nothing in this that is
necessarily incompatible with the 'semi-Pelagian' position described
above, for Gerson could simply be saying that everything is sustained by
God's grace. In *De vita spirituali animae* he distinguishes between graces.
If we call everything a grace that God freely gives us without merit, he says,
then our whole being and life – our natural powers – count among His gifts,
and the same is true of beasts. 'According to this manner of speaking it is
clear that we can do nothing without God.'[190] The numerous occasions
when Gerson cites, translates or paraphrases the biblical passage 'without
me you can do nothing' could also be taken to mean that we can do nothing
without the general providence of God.[191] However, there are many
passages where Gerson clearly does not mean the general providence of
God when he writes of grace. Rather he means what he defines as 'an
infused gift, over and above our natural powers and activities'.[192] Moreover
this grace does seem to be interfering in what elsewhere Gerson describes
as man's moral efforts. If we are to climb the mountain of penitence, he
writes, which is hard and bitter, especially at the beginning, grace is
necessary to give us spiritual life, vigour and strength.[193] He makes the
same point in a sermon for the feast of St Anthony: 'we cannot do any work
of penitence or even speak fruitfully without grace'.[194] A Christmas Day
sermon brings forth the plea to God to convert and correct all bad wills into
good ones by true repentance.[195] It begins to look as if God is making the
first move. 'By myself I can neither do nor know anything. You are my sole
hope and refuge. Perfect in me the good You have begun.'[196]

This is confirmed when Gerson tells his congregation that every time
they feel displeasure with their condition, or fear death, or have a horror
of the pains of hell, 'you can know for certain that it is the sound of the

Holy Spirit who is knocking at your door'.[197] Every time they have a good inspiration and will to do what is right, it is God who is approaching them, be it by means of preaching, tribulation, illness or prosperity. If they are at table, for instance, and judge that they are eating too much, it is God's work, though they can of course refuse to take any notice of God's move and so open the door to the devil.[198] It is God who moves us to pray in the first place; without His special inspiration we could not have the heart to pray.[199] In fact just as a father who sees his son falling into the way of perdition tries all means to bring him back to the good path, so does God, the Father of mercy, use all means to bring us back to Him, by gentle persuasion, by promises, if necessary by threats.[200] God often uses preaching to turn our hearts to Him, but not only that, the Holy Spirit must be present in the congregation if the preacher's words are to have any effect.[201] On our journey through life it is God's grace alone that gives us the power to resist the assaults of the devil, and in fact all the power we have comes from the grace of God without consideration of our merits.[202]

Courtecuisse, d'Ailly and Bernardine whom we have seen, on the one hand, urge their congregations to turn their wills to good, or dispose themselves or ask for pardon, also stress the absolute necessity of grace. 'Of yourselves, you can do only evil', says Bernardine, speaking here in Augustinian terms.[203] Courtecuisse makes it clear that it is God who makes the first move: it is God who gives us the will to amend, the Holy Spirit who makes hard hearts humble, who moves us to think of God, who makes us grieve. In fact, 'there is no good work that we do that avails us anything unless the grace of God goes before [previent] and moves us'.[204]

One of the most telling remarks Gerson makes about the moves God takes to turn us to the right path is in a sermon for the feast of St Anthony in 1403. Here he tells us that people should not reject God's inspirations, should not resist the Holy Spirit when he knocks at the door of their thought by inspiring them with good will and purpose to turn from their evil habits and convert to God. For 'if the Holy Spirit ceases to knock, you will lose all purpose to do good'.[205] It seems that it is only by God's actions that men have any good will at all. 'Alas, what can frail human will do without God?'[206] The answer seems to be – nothing. 'It is true that we can do nothing without the special grace of God.'[207]

This line of thought seems to place Gerson closer to thirteenth-century theologians like Thomas and Bonaventure and further away from 'nominalist' theologians like Occam and Biel. The latter, as we have seen, hold that man can, by doing what is in him, prepare himself for the infusion of justifying grace. Both argue that it is possible, if not usual, for man, of his natural powers alone, to love God super omnia. Man can, says Occam, merit grace de congruo by virtuous acts accomplished ex puris naturalibus, such as loving God above all and detesting sin – acts which the will elicits by following right reason.[208] Biel says virtually the same thing: 'The will can

elicit an act of love for God above all from its natural powers even without
the infusion of grace'.[209] But Gerson here is denying that man can have a
good will, can turn to God, can be truly penitent without God's special
grace, just as Thomas denies that man can keep the commandments or love
God above all things without that grace.[210] And yet, as we have seen,
Gerson frequently leaves the impression that man's salvation is up to man.
One feels that his congregations would not have gone home with a very
clear conception of exactly what was involved in the process of salvation.
They would have known that they should not sin, that they should repent
and turn to God, but they would not have been sure if, when they made
an effort to do this, they were to be congratulated, because it was their
effort, or grateful, because it was God's. They were, in fact, less likely to
feel that they should be congratulated, for Gerson so often stresses humility
and so often berates pride and presumption. And if they failed to make the
effort they could have wondered whether they were to be blamed or
commiserated with. But again Gerson so often insists that man's sin is
man's fault that the first alternative is the more likely. If, however, they
were present at one or two key sermons – that is key sermons for this
topic – or read the *Dialogue spirituel*, which Gerson wrote for his sisters,
they would have heard or read their problem discussed.

Unfortunately, neither in these key works, nor in any other vernacular
work, does Gerson make any completely unequivocal and exact statements
about the covenant which God has made with men or about its content.
There are some hints. For instance in his sermon *Gloria*, he says that God
could have redeemed us in another way at His pleasure. But He wished to
ordain this way, primarily to move us to love Him.[211] And what is this way?
In the first place it is the way of the Incarnation and Passion. This is the
foundation on which our salvation basically rests. But beyond that God has
ordained that we must work for heaven. 'You ask why God does not give
us paradise without our labour.' That, Gerson replies, is like asking why
one cannot serve one's knightly overlord without serving him in battle. In
any case 'God, according to the ordinance of His wisdom, wished it to be
so.'[212] This would seem to be the bargain that God has laid down, the
covenant He has made with men, though Gerson does not speak here in
terms of bargains or covenants. The ultimate victory comes from God's aid,
not from our own strength or virtue or good habits or will, 'but each must
always do what he can and God will do the rest'.[213]

Biel's statement about the covenant and its content in his sermon on the
Circumcision is much fuller and clearer. The German preacher relates a
parable about a king who publishes a decree saying that he will embrace
with his favour any of his enemies who desire his friendship, provided they
mend their ways for the present and the future. In addition those received
in this way will be given golden rings set 'with precious and powerful
stones' to help them to do works to the honour of the king, and these works

will be rewarded by the king above and beyond their value. So it is, Biel concludes, that God has established the rule that whoever turns to Him and does what he can will receive forgiveness of sins, and infused grace, with the help of which he can perform meritorious works.[214] The chief subject of the sermon is God's grace and Biel makes liberal use of quotations from Augustine in support of the doctrine of its necessity for salvation. He also warns against the Pelagian error. Despite this the parable and its explanation make it clear that for Biel, God has, *de potentia absoluta*, freely ordained that men can and should do something on their own. If they do then God has promised to give them grace. In his commentary on the *Sentences* Occam affirms the same doctrine. When man, he writes, has striven on his own and succeeded in detesting sin, God immediately gives him grace. In fact God must do so. He has promised this. By His ordained power God cannot not pour forth His grace when the *viator* reaches this stage.[215] Robert Holcot (*c.* 1290–1349) makes the position abundantly clear in a lecture. There is no compulsory or absolute necessity with regard to God, he says. However, 'an unfailing or conditional necessity' is appropriate to God because of His promises, that is, His covenant, or established law. 'According to God's established law the *viator* who does whatever he can to dispose himself for grace always receives grace.' God gives grace by unfailing necessity, by fidelity to His promises.[216]

Passages from some of Gerson's Latin works add a little information about his conception of the covenant. In *Regulae mandatorum* he states: 'In those things necessary for salvation God does not fail anyone doing what is in him, that is, using well the gifts of God he already has.'[217] The sinful soul, he writes elsewhere, by striving to do what is in it, disposes itself to life; not that that disposition suffices, for it has nothing of the spiritual life in it, but the soul can do nothing greater than 'to use well its natural powers and the gifts it is given, which though of grace are not vivifying'. It is only when, 'by the sole omnipotent liberality of the Creator', vivifying grace is infused that the soul's efforts are brought to fruition.[218]

Is the content of the covenant which God makes with men the same for Gerson as it is for Occam, Holcot and Biel? At first sight it might appear so, and in fact this case has been argued.[219] Despite this it is probable that Gerson is following Thomas and Bonaventure rather than Occam on this point. Thomas tackles the problem of the content of the covenant when he asks whether grace is necessarily given to those who prepare themselves for it, who do what is in them. His reply is a qualified one. If the preparation is looked upon as coming from man's free will alone, then grace does not necessarily follow, because the gift of grace exceeds every preparation of human power. But if the preparation is considered as coming from God, then grace does necessarily follow, because God's intention cannot fail.[220] Thomas' point is that man by his own natural powers alone cannot do what is in him, cannot prepare himself adequately. Every preparation in man must be by the help of God.[221] As this is the case, then grace *is* given to those who, with God moving them, do what is in them. And this seems to be close to what Gerson means when he defines 'doing what is in one' as using God's gifts well.[222]

This definition also puts Gerson very close to one of his favourite authors, Bonaventure. In the *Breviloquium* Bonaventure states that we speak of grace in three ways: general, special and proper or sanctifying (*gratia gratum faciens*). The first denotes divine aid freely given to creatures. Without it we would be unable to do anything or to continue in existence. We call grace 'special' when it is given by God as an aid to a person in his preparation for sanctifying grace. Without this special grace which Bonaventure calls *gratia gratis data* 'no one can adequately do what is in him, namely, prepare himself for salvation'.[223]

This brings us to the heart of the problem – the relationship between prevenient graces and the moral efforts of man. Gerson tackles the problem in a Lenten sermon. He has been telling his congregation to repent now, while there is opportunity, and then he raises an objection. If I have fallen into the ditch of sin, I cannot climb out by myself and so cannot worthily turn to God. How then can God command, and even with great threats of punishment, that I turn myself to Him?[224] So far the question looks as if it is just a complaint that it is very difficult for a sinner to repent. But Gerson's reply reveals otherwise. Although, he writes, no one can turn to God worthily without the grace and special help of God – this he holds to be notorious and completely settled by Scripture and by the holy doctors against the Pelagian error – nevertheless God reasonably commands that we, who by evil actions have offended and left Him, should turn ourselves to Him by holy works and penitence. For, and this is witnessed in Scripture and by the holy doctors, God by His infinite grace and mercy and kindness is always ready to help and raise us however much we have offended Him, and to move us to all good. But we must wish to follow, obey and consent to His holy inspirations, movements and eternal exhortations, by which he never stops moving us to all good. Nevertheless if we do not give our consent to His grace and mercy, and if we do not follow it, if we do not give ourselves, if we do not take the hand to help us as He wishes us to do, then certainly He will reasonably and justly punish us.[225]

This is certainly a statement of the problem. No one can turn to God unless God gives special grace. Nevertheless God reasonably tells us to turn to Him. God is always ready to help, but we must wish to follow and obey His inspirations. The burden of Gerson's answer seems to be that the first movements came from God but that we have the independent power to accept or reject them. It also seems in this passage as if God is always assisting us in one manner or another, so that it is always in the last resort up to us, despite the fact that the first movement comes from God.

Gerson discusses the problem more fully in the *Dialogue spirituel*. He is instructing his sisters on the remedies against temptations and one of the twelve things he wishes them to remember in this regard is the need for the grace of God. His sisters agree that without God one can do nothing, but if this is so, they argue, why should they try to accomplish anything? 'Everything is up to God; if He wishes it will be so; if He does not wish, one works for nothing.'[226] Gerson agrees that we cannot resist the least temptation by ourselves, and therefore we should put all our efforts into acquiring God's grace. But how, his sisters object, can we work to acquire grace without the grace of God? 'We would have to say that we have grace and do not have grace at the same time.' And in any case if the grace of God is so necessary that it is grace that works all the good in us, what praise ought those to have who do good? Gerson accepts that these are indeed forceful objections and that they have in times past led some into the Pelagian heresy. It is necessary, he replies, to distinguish between graces. His distinctions here follow Bonaventure's quite closely. In its narrowest sense, Gerson says, grace is the virtue of charity, vivifying grace, and this is the only grace that makes us pleasing to God and worthy of heaven. In a wider sense grace is any gift beyond the natural that God gives to men to comfort them and help them in the means required to come to salvation, though such gifts are not justifying. This sense of grace is clearly the same as Bonaventure's 'special grace', *gratia gratis data*, and both theologians are here indicating prevenient grace.[227] In its widest sense, says Gerson, grace is every gift of God, natural or not. When one says that one can do nothing good without the grace of God, one is taking grace in the second or third sense. And it is by the use of this grace that one seeks justifying grace; and this seeking is what the doctors call 'faire ce que en soy est'.

Gerson goes on to argue that a person does deserve praise if he does good with the aid of grace, just as a horse who obeys his rider in a joust deserves praise as much as if he had taken part in the joust without his master. The grace of God is the rider of our soul and so the soul deserves praise if it follows the commands of grace. But the grace would not come into a soul not properly disposed because of mortal sin, if it had not already done what is in it, 'by means of the help of the other graces'.[228]

Gerson acknowledges the difficulty of all this when he has his sisters say: 'Brother, this matter in our view is too high and subtle for our simplicity.'[229] They then raise another problem about grace and salvation. They have heard people say that there is no point, before the infusion of charity, in doing good when it has no profit towards salvation. Good works, almsgiving, fasting, prayers, virtuous acts and so on do not suffice for salvation, Gerson replies, but they are profitable and do dispose a person for justifying grace, so they are certainly worth doing; in fact they must be done, with of course the help of prevenient graces.

That Gerson's doctrine of justification is more Thomist than Occamist is made quite clear by a Latin sermon he delivered at Constance in 1416.

Here he argues that the Holy Spirit comes spontaneously to the soul without consideration of works or merits. Nevertheless the Scriptures urge the soul to prepare itself, to dispose itself, to do what is in it by prayer, weeping and so on. For we are co-workers with God, and if the will does nothing, where is the merit? It is clear that the will works by spontaneous consent, obeying the movements of the Holy Spirit. But it cannot so work and obey of itself without grace. It must be led by prevenient grace. Thus the merit is given by prevenient grace and not on the basis of purely natural capabilities and achievements. And indeed it is more pleasing to God that He should find in this consent His own gift which He accepts. Further the soul is rendered more humble and grateful to God when it is realised that whatever merit the soul has, prevenient grace gives. It is presumptuous to think that God servilely acts according to the action of men. This is the Pelagian error. Yet this prevenient grace does not take away man's liberty or necessitate him. As Augustine says: God does not administer things so that He does not allow them to use their own motion. In fact the will is freer and more efficacious the more grace goes before (*praevenit*), vivifies, forms, strengthens and heals it.[230]

Gerson, like Thomas and Bonaventure, is here giving God's grace clear priority in the process of justification, yet at the same time trying to safeguard man's free will and moral efforts. Among late medieval theologians Gerson stands closer to Staupitz than to Biel, for Staupitz also taught that prevenient grace must be added to free will before the soul can be disposed for the reception of sanctifying grace. The Augustinian Staupitz, however, differs from Gerson – and Thomas – when he denies that any human act before the infusion of charity can be morally good, let alone meritorious.[231]

For Luther, Gerson, though not as bad as Occam and his followers, who were the worst Pelagians,[232] would be as Pelagian as the earlier scholastics, including Thomas, because he left room for the co-operation of the human will with divine grace. For Gerson not only is grace resistible, but men must work with grace, prevenient as well as justifying, to meet God's requirements, to earn merits and so become acceptable to God.[233] Gerson is *not*, of course, Pelagian, any more than Occam and Biel are. None of them holds that man's nature is innately capable of perfection or that Adam's sin has no inherited effect on the souls of his descendants, which was Pelagius' view.[234] Gerson is not even semi-Pelagian, for he teaches the necessity of prevenient grace, and he certainly does not hold that God has to wait for the first move to come from man before He can grant His grace, which was the core of the fifth-century semi-Pelagian position condemned at the Council of Orange in 529.[235] But if Gerson is no sort of Pelagian, if he insists on the need for grace every step of the way, nevertheless he leaves the definite impression in his sermons that man has a lot to do towards his own salvation. There is no question of sitting back and doing nothing. Man must be active in love and good works, he must co-operate with the grace of God. 'Faith must issue in action and work through love, for, as James says, faith without works is dead.'[236] In short, for Gerson, as for medieval theologians in general, justification includes sanctification.

PREDESTINATION

This view of justification which, though it gives priority to grace, insists on man's freedom to accept or reject that grace, leaves Gerson, as it had left other theologians, with a problem on the question of predestination. In fact Gerson sometimes almost gives up on the problem by simply saying that the judgements of God are incomprehensible; we cannot tell why He saves some and not others, and in any case we should not be asking such questions that lie within the free will of God.[237] Nevertheless he is aware that there is a problem here, a problem that genuinely bothers some people, that causes others to ask 'curious' questions and to deride religion, and that leads some into errors and heresy. And so on several occasions in his sermons he tackles the question.[238]

Like most medieval theologians Gerson wishes to assert three things: that God is omnipotent, that He can do what He wills with creatures; that God is just; and that human free will and moral effort are necessary. In other words he wishes to assert predestination and good works. But if he follows Augustine's doctrine of predestination, that is, that God predestines some to heaven and others to hell, without reference to their foreseen merits (*ante praevis merita*),[239] then there seems to be little room for contingent human activity, or for divine justice. If, on the other hand, he interprets predestination as based on God's foreknowledge of how men will behave (*post praevis merita*), then God's sovereignty is endangered. By the High Middle Ages Augustine's doctrine of predestination had been somewhat tempered. Thomas, for instance, agrees with Augustine that God's decision to choose some for heaven is totally free and not based on His foreknowledge of their merits.[240] But he insists that God's reprobation of the rest works differently from His predestination. The latter is the cause of the grace and glory that the elect receive, but reprobation is not the cause of the sins of the reprobate. God permits the reprobate to sin, by not granting them grace, but they sin from their own free will and receive the punishment of damnation on account of that sin.[241] Thomas also tries to save free will in the predestined. He argues that though predestination is certain since God knows and wills that the elect will attain heaven, this does not do away with liberty of choice. This is because God wills that the elect are directed to the goal according to their free will. Though God's will is the first cause of the salvation of the elect, man's free will is its proximate cause.[242]

This, however, did not safeguard human freedom – or divine justice – enough for some theologians. And indeed the case for the other interpretation of predestination, that is predestination on the basis of foreseen merits, seems a strong one even when put by its opponents, such as Thomas and Bradwardine.[243] Occam is one who prefers the second interpretation. He states firmly that both the cause of reprobation and the cause of predestination lie in the sins of the reprobate and the merits of the predestinate which God foresees. 'For just as God is not a punisher before a man is a sinner, so He is not a rewarder before a man is justified by grace.'[244] For Biel, too, both reprobation and election are based on God's foreknowledge of human behaviour.[245]

There was a reaction against this doctrine of predestination *post praevisa merita* on the part of some theologians in the late medieval period. The most extreme reaction came from Gregory of Rimini (d. 1358), whom Luther singled out as the only non-Pelagian among the 'modern theologians'.[246] To safeguard God's omnipotent will Gregory went back to an Augustinian double predestination: God predestines and reprobates in eternity purely as He pleases, without any consideration of man's future merits or demerits.[247] Bradwardine and Staupitz each in his own way, the former polemically and the latter almost mystically, express the view that God cannot be dependent on anything outside Himself, cannot be man's debtor, and that therefore the cause of predestination is God's sovereign will, not His foreknowledge of man's merits. Neither, though, affirms with Gregory a doctrine of predestination to damnation.[248]

Amidst this variety of opinion where does Gerson stand? In its simplest form Gerson's position is that 'no one is damned without guilt, just as no one is saved without grace'.[249] The first part of this statement is clear and Gerson never moves from it. For him men go to hell because they deserve to, because they have sinned mortally and not repented in time, because God foresees their evil behaviour. 'God does not punish any rational creature except for his sin or demerit.'[250] It is true, he writes, that God allows that many hear the call outwardly, but not inwardly with the ears of their soul, but this in itself is 'in punishment for their faults'.[251] There is, then, no doctrine of double predestination in Gerson.

The second part of his statement – 'without grace no one is saved' – is not so clear, for it could cover a variety of doctrines. Both Gregory of Rimini and Biel would agree with it. In an early sermon, *Puer natus est*, of 1396, Gerson appears to be teaching a doctrine of predestination *post praevisa merita*. It is heretical, he states, to believe that all men will be saved, however they live. On the contrary, if people do not keep God's commandments they will be damned. It is also heretical to argue that, since God knows who will be the damned and who the saved, it does not matter whether a person does more good than evil, because things will, in any case, turn out as God has ordained. On the contrary, Gerson affirms, you must believe that if you accomplish Christ's law, without doubt you will be saved.[252] The teaching in a sermon of 1402 is more nuanced. Gerson is dealing with people who say that God does not want all to be saved, and that He gives grace to some and not to others and so is an acceptor of persons. If He did want to save us all, they argue, He could, so why does He give sufficient grace to some, for example to Peter and Paul, and not to others, for example Judas? Gerson's first reply is that this type of question does not consider the absolute sovereignty of God, who can do what He will with creatures without any injustice. His second reply accords with what he wrote in *Puer natus*: God does not punish any rational creature except for his sin or demerit, nor does He withdraw His grace unless a person does not wish to convert to God. His third response goes back to the tenor of the first: such questions seek to know the cause of the will of God, which is itself the first and sovereign cause. Just as the potter can, from the same piece of clay, make one vessel that is beautiful and one that is not, so God can dignify some people and not others.[253]

Gerson here seems to be holding two interpretations of the doctrine in tandem. Moreover, it is not clear that we can extricate him by arguing that in the first and third responses he is writing in terms of the *potentia absoluta* of God, and in the second in terms of the *potentia ordinata*. The rest of the passage[254] gives no indication that Gerson sees the solution to the problem of safeguarding both the omnipotence of God and man's free will and moral efforts in the way that Occam, Holcot and Biel do, that is by arguing that God by His sovereign will (*de potentia absoluta*) has ordained that people are saved or damned according to their foreseen merits or demerits.

There are similar ambiguities on the subject of predestination in other sermons and writings of this period. The only cause, he writes in *Videmus nunc*, for God's giving grace and salvation to some and not others is His just will. He can give grace to whom He pleases without doing wrong to those whom He leaves in prison. Nevertheless, if you want this grace and freedom, be humble towards God, and wait and devoutly ask for His grace. 'For whoever perseveres in doing this, truly he cannot be damned.'[255] To those asking why, if God saves the few He elects by grace alone, we should work for our salvation, Gerson replies that no good goes unrewarded.[256] Earlier in the same sermon Gerson states that God always calls us; the trouble is that all of us do not respond.[257]

Gerson seems to think that about a quarter of men are saved. He works this out from the parable of the sower, when only one quarter of the seed fell on good ground and bore good fruit.[258] Writing in 1407 to his sisters who wonder, when so few are saved, if they have any chance of gaining heaven, Gerson replies: 'the number is not so small that you could not be among them'.[259] This seems a fair assumption if as many as a quarter are saved, when Gerson's sisters seem, in Gerson's opinion, to have formed an oasis of sanctity amidst a desert of sinners.

There is little discussion of predestination in Gerson's later popular sermons and writings, which in any case start to peter out after 1403. There is, however, a further statement in a later Latin work, *De consolatione theologiae*, written in 1418. Here Gerson's position seems to be more clearly in the Augustinian/Thomist tradition. In one place, for instance, he states that the only reason which can be given for why, among so many possible things that could be, this and not that has been brought to pass, is the fact that it is pleasing to God. So much the more, he argues, should this be said about our regeneration to the spiritual life. Nor must we take refuge in the merits or works of those whom God has predestined from eternity, because if it is from works, it is not from grace. But there is no prior cause for the eternal will of God, who does all things according to Himself, even to the cruel day of judgement.[260]

In this work Gerson again makes reference to the potter and his clay, and to the fact that God is in no way our debtor. These references to the potter and his clay are significant. The Pauline text (Romans 9:20–4, based on Jeremiah 18:6) appears in many discussions of predestination, usually as a powerful authority to support an Augustinian position. Bradwardine, for example, uses it in *The Cause of God against Pelagius* in a particularly uncompromising way, arguing that the reprobate (the vessels made for menial use) have been created for the sake of the elect (the vessels made for beauty), and both for God's own service, praise, glory and honour.[261] Holcot, by contrast, in answer to the objection that man is related to God as clay is to the potter, says that one cannot apply the analogy in every respect to man. In the first place there is no covenant between the potter and the clay, as there is between God and man; secondly the clay, unlike man, can neither partially nor fully merit anything from the potter.[262] In his conflict with Luther over free will, Erasmus, too, repudiates the analogy. He insists that people are not lumps of clay, but thinking, willing beings, created in the image of God. What is the good of man, he asks, 'if God can treat him like the potter his clay, or deal with him like a rock'?[263] Gerson makes no such comments when he uses the text. Rather, in *De consolatione theologiae*, he reinforces the analogy between God and the potter, by pointing to the fact that men themselves can do what they choose with the animals they own. There is no more injustice in their unequal treatment of their sheep when they preserve some and kill others than in God's treatment of us. And if only a few are saved, God's grace is made all the more manifest, just as when among the deaf, dumb, blind and dead there are fewer who are miraculously cured than left in their existing condition. If we come down to individuals and ask why God chose Peter and Paul for salvation and left Judas, 'we must put our fingers to our lips, confessing this only, that the Lord is just in all His ways'.[264]

It is true that this treatise also has passages in which the importance of human effort is stressed, but these can be seen within the overall context of a doctrine of predestination *ante praevisa merita*. For those loving and hoping in God, Gerson writes, quoting St Paul, all things work together for good; first seek the kingdom of God and all these things will be added unto you; nor can any of the predestined ever perish. The contrary is true of the reprobate, for whom all things work together for evil. However, since we do not know which among men will be saved or how they will be saved, 'we should do good to all men, by praying, reminding, encouraging, upbraiding and by striving to lead them away from errors and vices'.[265] What Gerson means here is that, as he says, God has ordained various and innumerable ways by which His eternal decree is to be carried out. Thus our prayers and other good works may be the means God has preordained to help another person or ourselves towards their predestined salvation.[266]

If Gerson in some of his earlier French sermons appears to be teaching, like Biel, a doctrine of predestination *post praevisa merita*, by 1418 he is clearly holding the doctrine of predestination *ante praevisa merita*. If we had his commentary on the *Sentences*, which would have been composed in 1389–90, we might be able to discover whether he did indeed change his mind on this issue. But even if Gerson's views on predestination place him close to Thomas, he cannot be neatly pigeon-holed as a Thomist. Some of his doctrines, as we have seen, are much closer to those of the 'nominalist' theologians, while he also shows an affinity with Bonaventure. It is not surprising that he has had attached to him so many different labels.

In general Gerson's pastoral teaching lays emphasis on man's free will and moral efforts, but without ignoring either the need for God's grace, prevenient and justifying, or God's predestination. His congregations would certainly go away with the impression that they must repent and try not to sin again. And they would be aware of the blessings in store if they were successful, with the help of grace, in their efforts, and of the pains awaiting them in hell if they made no effort. The joys of heaven and the pains of hell, after all, were two of the things Gerson believed every Christian should know about.[267] Although by the standards of the time Gerson does not in his sermons excessively emphasise the horrors of death, judgement and hell, the stress is there. He wants his congregation to know what awaits them and he firmly castigates those who disbelieve in hell and purgatory.[268] His purpose here as elsewhere is to spur the faithful to repentance.

Though he would seem to view most of the members of his congregations as sinners needing a spur, Gerson also bears in mind, as we have seen him do in his works on confession, those with other difficulties. There are those who despair and for them Gerson speaks of the tender mercy of God. There are those who are presumptuous and for them Gerson stresses the justice of God. For both groups he emphasises the grace of God that is necessary for salvation so that the one group do not despair of their own efforts and so that the other are not too confident in their own works.[269] But Gerson's chief concern remains: to turn men from their sins.

5

THE ANALYSIS OF SIN

In every one of his sixty extant vernacular sermons Gerson discusses sin. The same is true of his vernacular treatises. Sin is always in the picture and usually in a fairly central position. This is not, of course, surprising, when one recalls the great importance he attaches to the sacrament of penance – and the need for complete confession within that sacrament – in the life of the *viator*. He is by no means peculiar in giving sin such strong and central emphasis in his pastoral teaching. Sin and the sacrament of penance loom large in the sermons of many other preachers of the period and, of course, in the *Summae confessorum* and manuals for parish priests. Basically Gerson's emphasis is typical of what some historians have seen as a sin-ridden, neurosis-creating late medieval religion, one of whose major purposes was social control.[1] But, whatever the result – and this is not easy to assess – in Gerson's case at least the conscious purpose behind his teaching on sin is not to create neurosis or achieve social control, but rather to console and bring about the reconciliation of the sinner with God.

The chancellor's attitude almost certainly influenced a large number of clergy in the later Middle Ages, for his treatise on the subjects of sin and confession had, even more than his other writings, a very wide readership. The *Opus tripartitum*, for example, a vernacular work chiefly concerned with these subjects, had achieved an almost quasi-official status by the beginning of the sixteenth century. At least sixteen different printings of the work had been made by 1500. It was translated from the original French and printed first in Latin and then in German, Swedish, Flemish, probably for use in the diocese of Liège, Spanish for use in Mexico and back into French. It was explicitly commended by many bishops and there are extant episcopal letters requiring its use throughout the dioceses of Paris (1506), Evreux (1507), Le Mans (1508), and Chartres (1531).[2] Others of Gerson's works on sin and confession were also widely read and influential: *De arte audiendi confessiones*, *De modo vivendi omnium fidelium*, *De remediis contra recidivum peccati*, *De pollutione nocturna*, *Regulae mandatorum*, *De remediis contra pusillanimitatem*, *Le Profit de savoir quel est péchié mortel et venial*.[3] It is, in fact, the judgement of Tentler, who has made a careful study of the late medieval literature on the forgiveness of sins, that because of 'the ubiquity of his opinion and the authority accorded it' Gerson's 'is the greatest voice in the cure of souls'.[4]

Gerson's voice, as one would expect, contains many echoes of the teaching of his predecessors. He had clearly studied and read some of the literature about sin that had proliferated after the conciliar decree of 1215 which made annual confession obligatory. He was particularly influenced by the *Summa de vitiis et virtutibus*, a handbook written perhaps as early as 1236 by the Dominican William Peraldus.[5] He sometimes quotes from this work and he refers to it a number of times as well worth reading, for instance in the *Dialogue spirituel*, written for his sisters, and in his letter of 1417 to the tutor of the dauphin Charles, where the *Summa* is listed among those books essential for the young prince to read.[6] Another book Gerson recommends for the prince is *La Somme le roy*, a vernacular work written in 1279 by the Dominican Lorens of Orleans, and itself relying heavily on Peraldus' handbook as well as on the influential *Summa casuum poenitentiae* (1220–45) of Raymond of Penaforte, another Dominican.[7] Gerson was also familiar with John of Freiburg's *Summa confessorum*, of which he possessed a copy and which he recommends to his brother Nicholas in a letter of 1410.[8] Boyle considers that this work, written at the end of the thirteenth century, was the most widely read of all the medieval *Summa confessorum* in the later Middle Ages and that through it the moral and pastoral teaching of Aquinas and some of his theological contemporaries, as well as that of Raymond of Penaforte and some of the thirteenth-century canonists, was popularised.[9] But Gerson probably knew Thomas' work directly too, for he specifically recommends the IIa-IIae of the latter's *Summa Theologiae* as a work bishops should read.[10] He had also read some of what Albert the Great had to say about sin, as evidenced in the chancellor's comprehensive *Enumeratio peccatorum ab Alberto posita*.[11] Thus Gerson knew the thirteenth-century authorities on his subject, and indeed he knew the chief earlier authorities also. He often says he is following a definition or a categorisation of the branches of a particular sin established by Augustine or, more frequently, by Gregory the Great.[12]

The fact the Gerson was well versed in the established literature on sin does not mean that he consistently merely repeats what he has read. He has his own preferences, nuances and emphases on this subject just as he had on the subject of confession. He has even been signalled by some historians as an innovator in certain aspects of the topic. Wenzel, for example, sees Gerson's treatment of the sin of *acedia* as progressive, while Flandrin views him as taking part in the encouragement of a more severe attitude towards the sin of masturbation.[13] Gerson's overall teaching on sin, however, cannot be called startlingly original. He writes within the tradition, though one needs to remember that the tradition was by no means a monolith; there was room for manoeuvre.

SIN IN GENERAL: EFFECTS, CAUSES, ESSENCE

As well as being assessed as psychologically unhealthy, late medieval religion has been accused of having an ideal of lay piety that was monastic and ascetic without concessions made for people living in the world.[14] Is this true of Gerson's teaching on sin? Does he set the goal too high or is it possible of achievement? Does harshness of tone or gentleness predominate? Does he overstress sin so that the life of the *viator* is made burdensome and joyless? As we shall see, no short, simple or unqualified answers can be given to these questions.

The sin to be dealt with in this chapter is not original sin, but actual sin, the sins committed by human beings in the course of their lives on earth. Original sin is of course the basic reason why it is difficult for men to avoid committing actual sin. But men are born with this defect, this is the given, and Gerson, like other pastoral writers, sees it as his task to define, categorise and classify sins so that *viatores* know what thoughts, words and actions to try to avoid in the first place, and what to confess when they fail, as they all sometimes will, to keep the moral law.[15] And, when they fail, complete confession is essential. Gerson is perfectly clear about the awful effects of sin.

One would not have to have attended many of Gerson's sermons or to read very far in his vernacular treatises to be aware of the evils sin is responsible for. In the first place there are what may be broadly termed the psychological effects. Man was created in the image of God and when he sins he distorts that image. Sin 'obscures and blinds' the reason; it 'depraves, corrupts and enfeebles' the will, and it 'attracts and inclines the senses to evil delights'.[16] On many occasions Gerson writes of this result of sin, stressing particularly the blindness of understanding and the ignorance suffered by the sinful man.[17] Further, the soul that was created upright has, through sin, become *curva*, bent down, and leans towards what is temporal, earthly and pleasing to its lower or animal faculties. Man in a state of sin is like the beasts, like the stupid ox and the pig with its face always turned downward toward the mire and its stomach always close to the earth.[18] And there is no joy in this. Gerson is at pains to disabuse his hearers of the idea that sin can lead to any real pleasure. On the contrary, 'those who have sent away the Holy Spirit by divers sins are almost always sad and have no pure happiness. If they seem to laugh and play it is the laugh and song of the mad.'[19] Sin, indeed, can make men insane, make them hate themselves and sometimes lead them to suicide, as was the case with Judas.[20] Even if sin does not result in this grim fate, it brings anguish, tribulation, misery and affliction to the soul: 'Pride beats it, envy blinds it, anger tears it, avarice pulls it, sloth binds it, gluttony buries it, lust burns it.'[21] And on its deathbed the sinful soul, devoid of earthly pleasures because its five senses are dulled and failing, finds itself totally without consolation.[22] It would be better if the sinner had never been born, for he has put himself into the vile servitude of the devil, his mortal enemy, who will punish him eternally.[23] While on earth the sinner, Gerson says, lives a life of misery, but it is not really a life at all, for mortal sin forges the sword that kills and the chain that strangles the soul. That the sinful, unconfessed soul is a dead soul Gerson makes clear on a number of occasions.[24] It can of course be revived by penitence, and the whole point of these descriptions of the hideous effects of sin is to move Gerson's hearers to repentance.

Sins, however, do not affect only the psychological and ontological state of the sinner. They also affect God and the relationship between man and God, Sin, says Gerson, frustrates God; the Holy Spirit cannot enter the soul of a sinner. Sin saddens God; in fact each mortal sin crucifies God again.[25] However, the 'emotions' Gerson ascribes most frequently to God when He is confronted by mortal sin are anger and hatred. By mortal sin man angers God, his sovereign seigneur; sin is so displeasing to God that it makes Him seem furious. God hates sin; it is insupportable to Him.[26] Moreover it is not just the mortal sin that God hates and is angry about; He hates the sinful soul itself. 'Sin makes souls the enemies of and hateful to God.'[27] Gerson seems to be giving his congregations a picture of a vengeful Jehovah. But he softens the effect, for usually after a particularly grim picture of an angry God he refers to God's mercy. If we repent God will cease to be angry and will pardon us. God hates sin, but by His mercy He delivered His Son to death and His mother to the anguish of the Passion, in order to destroy it.[28] The anger is a righteous anger and the hatred a righteous hatred. God's intentions are good and there is a way out, a way to escape the divine anger and hatred.

Given the psychological effects of sin on both man and God, it is not surprising that the relationship between them is adversely affected when a mortal sin is committed. The unconfessed sinner does not show the love and subjection towards God which is God's due. He is deprived of grace. There is no accord and peace in his relationship with God. The sinner is unable to reach the end for which he was created, that is, to know and love God and praise and glorify Him for ever. Rather, he is headed for eternal damnation, for eternal burning at the hands of the angry God.[29]

Gerson has given his congregations ample reasons for avoiding sin, or at least for repenting of their mortal sins. To round out the picture he frequently points to what might be called the external effects of sin. Generally these are direct external effects, though occasionally Gerson suggests that certain major calamities and disturbances are the indirect effect of the countless sins committed by people in general.[30] The major calamities he has most in mind here are the schism in the church and the civil disturbances in France. There is some trace here of what was called in sixteenth-century England the doctrine of judgements, the doctrine that some calamity, a famine perhaps, was God's punishment on people for their sins.[31] The doctrine was not, of course, invented by English Protestants. It had solid Old Testament foundation and appears frequently in sermons and books of around Gerson's time. The preacher Maillard, for instance, in one of his sermons on the third commandment argues that the wars and famines of his day are punishments sent by God because people are not observing the precepts about Sundays and other holy days. Similarly Bernardine tells the people of Siena that because of their daily blaspheming their land will be laid waste, their city will burn, and their country will fall under the rule of their enemy and be sacked.[32] Antoninus, fifteenth-century Bishop of Florence, devotes half of his chapter on the evil effects of mortal sin to detailing, with appropriate Old Testament examples, the punishments that can be visited on man as a result of his sin: loss of worldly possessions, honour, family, children, health and bodily powers.[33] Gerson's use of this rather frightening doctrine is very moderate indeed. Far more often he traces the natural causal relation between sin and external calamity. Lack of charity, insistence on rights and the breaking of agreements by the dukes have led to civil war.[34] The devil's perversion of the Roman pope has prevented the ending of the schism by the way of resignation.[35] When Gerson writes of particular sins he frequently refers to external evils that result from them. Thus envy can lead to persecutions and subversions,[36] fornication can result in a child with only one parent to care for it.[37] In other words, sin produces victims. Not only does sin harm the sinner himself and ruin his relationship with his Creator, it can cause havoc for his neighbours, and even wreck the civil and social order and split the church.

What causes men to commit sins which have such dire effects? There is some confusion in Gerson's discussions on this topic, or perhaps it would be better to say that he is dealing with a complex question and, sensibly, he does not give a simple answer.[38] The underlying condition for the commission of actual sins is original sin. Because of this and the resulting removal of original justice man is born with a built-in tendency towards sinful behaviour. But man has free will and Gerson, along with all orthodox theologians, insists that there is no sin unless the will freely consents. All sin is voluntary.[39] But, despite the existence of original sin, not all men sin all the time, so there must be other factors involved. The impression left by Gerson in his French sermons and writings about the question is that the chief factors are external forces. He frequently personifies sins and this means that his hearers will tend to see the sins as objective, external entities. Thus we have 'Pride, the false tyrant who wants to rule over us; hard-hearted Avarice, who makes great efforts to turn us to her end; Sloth, the sleeper, Envy, the hater, furious Anger, blind Lust, and Gluttony, the villain'.[40] Sometimes it is sin in general that is personified, for example as 'the disloyal and cursed traitor of God...who makes bitter and mortal war against the whole human race'.[41] Frequently the sins are seen not as autonomous entities but as servants or sons or captives of the devil, sent by him to torment men and destroy the virtues.[42] Sometimes the sins are portrayed as devils themselves, as evil spirits that possess a man.[43] Alternatively, Gerson can write without personifying the sins themselves, but he still has an external force leading men to behave sinfully – the devil, who enters our soul and turns the order that should prevail therein upside down.[44] Generally Gerson sees the devil's role as that of tempter, leaving room for the operation of man's free will. But sometimes the human soul is portrayed almost as a passive ground whereon the devil and his minions fight it out with the good spirits or angels.[45] The human soul is thus almost the mere victim of opposing objective forces. However, more often Gerson tells his congregations that they must and can, with God's help, fight against the devil and the sins. Not only that, they have to fight against two other traditional sources of temptation and sin: the world and the flesh. These again are frequently personified as external forces acting on the soul.[46] Then there is an internal force that can lead man to sin: his own temperament, which, for physiological reasons, may make him prone to a particular sin: to anger, for example.

The strongest impression that one acquires from a reading of Gerson's vernacular sermons is that life on earth is one long battle against sin. And this gives us the other side of the picture. Sin is something that men do, rather than something with which they are simply afflicted. There are many forces working against man, but in the last resort man himself, with his free will, is responsible for the sins he commits. Although at times, especially when he talks about the powerful and wicked tyrants, the devil and his captains, the sins, his hearers might have felt that the odds against them were too great, nevertheless they would have known that their pastor believed that victory, with God's help, was possible and that they must and could fight.[47]

A rather different impression would have been created had Gerson injected more of Aristotle into his pastoral moral teaching, as Thomas before him and Antoninus after him did in their books on moral theology.[48] It is not that Gerson never presents vices as excesses or deficiencies of natural and therefore good human passions or desires, and the goal as the rational control of these internal appetites. He does do this when he is defining some of the sins, as we shall see. But much more of the time in his vernacular works, especially in the sermons, he is personifying and allegorising so that the struggle is seen as one of the will against external forces. Gerson relies more – with regard to this topic – on his non-Aristotelian sources, Gregory, Augustine and Peraldus and his followers, than he does on the IIa-IIae of St Thomas. But then so do most sermons and handbooks of the period.[49]

What does Gerson see as the essence of actual sin? Thomas had defined sin as an inordinate act, contrary to nature and thus, because man is a rational animal, contrary to the order of reason. He combined this quite easily with Augustine's definition of sin as any word, deed or desire contrary to eternal law.[50] Gerson does not disagree with this, but he does not leave it there. When he is writing about sin in general in his vernacular works Gerson leaves the definite impression that the morality underlying his concept of sin is based on a monastic, ascetic ideal with a strong dose of dualism. In the first place, sin for Gerson, as for Augustine, is essentially disobedience to God's will, not loving Him above all else, not being subject to Him, not rendering to Him the honour that is His due. It is lese-majesty towards the Creator, a turning of the will away from God to accomplish one's own will.[51] Sin, then, is self-will, when that will is opposed to God's will. It is the way God's will is conceived that gives this morality its ascetic, even dualistic tone. Loving God above all else, as He demands, involves turning one's back to a large degree on the things of this world. We ought to die to the world to live in Christ, Gerson declares.[52] Like St Paul, we should not seek honour but the cross, not riches but poverty, not delicacies but abstinence, fasts and sobriety, not power and domination but subjection and humility.[53] We should not look for our good, our salvation, in the world. Like St Anthony we should disdain all worldly things, for they are all vain.[54] Worldly love must be rooted out, for it is like glue that prevents us from achieving the end which God wants for us.[55] And so it goes on; there is hardly a sermon in which Gerson does not tell his hearers that they must turn their backs on worldly things. And this involves holding their own bodies in subjection and disdaining the pleasures and comforts of the flesh. Sin is allowing the body to control the soul, allowing the senses to dominate the reason and the will. This is as foolish, he says, as allowing the maidservant to dictate to the mistress, and far more perilous.[56] Rather we must mortify and root out from our hearts the inclinations of the body and the flesh, so that they are obedient to the spirit without any resistance.[57] The morality behind Gerson's concept of sin is a morality of denial of the world and denial of the flesh, and in fact a denial of the self. Not only must the flesh be submissive to the soul, but the soul itself, the whole person, must be submissive to secular and religious superiors and authorities and to God. The great virtue is humility. One must be always mindful of everything that God has commanded and never follow one's own will. One must think oneself worthless and unprofitable for any good work, and truly believe and acknowledge oneself to be 'the vilest and the least of all', worse than all the rest. And one must be humble not only in heart, but also display it in one's demeanour, with downcast eyes in all places and at all times.[58] Gerson is here, in a vernacular work for the laity, paraphrasing, without comment, a passage from the Rule of St Benedict. Cassian, too, had urged the monks for whom he wrote to consider themselves 'inferior to everyone else'.[59] The advice had biblical authority: 'In humility count others better than yourselves' (Phil. 2:3), and it is frequently repeated, particularly in the works of mystical writers. It is expounded at length in *The Book of*

Vices and Virtues, the English translation of *Somme le roi*, one of Gerson's sources. Here lay readers are told that to attain true humility, true poverty of spirit, they must wish to be despised, 'to be held for naught and foul'; they must truly think of themselves without any pretence as nothing and as having nothing.[60] For this author and for Gerson sin is not just self-assertion; it is self-respect. To the twentieth-century reader the picture seems rather bleak. But it is the general impression left by Gerson's sermons, especially by the grand rhetorical passages where he is deliberately trying to instil a sense of sin into his hearers and move them to repentance and a life of virtue. It is only when he comes down to categorising sins and discussing cases that we can discern that he does make concessions to human weaknesses, or rather to legitimate human needs, both individual and social. But that Gerson is working from the base of a monastic morality of self-denial there can be no doubt.

CLASSIFICATION: THE SEVEN CAPITAL SINS

However much Protestants may later have abhorred categorisations and distinctions of sins, it was absolutely essential, if one were working within the medieval theology of the sacrament of penance and largely with uneducated laity, to have some practical scheme to help people search their consciences and confessors examine their penitents. The most popular scheme of classification was that of the seven capital sins, whose history goes back to the monks of the Egyptian desert of the fourth century.[61] However, some historians see a change occurring at the end of the fourteenth century. The ten commandments, they argue, displaced the seven sins as the favourite scheme of classification. Ozment bases his position largely on Johannes Geffken's *Picture Catechisms of the Fifteenth Century* (1855), a book which concentrated especially on confessional manuals. Ozment argues that the ten commandments became the main guideline for oral catechism and confession at the end of the fourteenth century and that this had the important result of complicating confession for the laity by making examinations longer and more involved and by tempting confessors to be overly inquisitive.[62] Lewis Spitz goes so far as to argue that at this time 'the ten commandments became so prominent as to virtually exclude all other parts of the confessional catechism'.[63] If this is so, then Gerson was rather old-fashioned, because the chief scheme of classification he uses is that of the seven capital sins. Apart from the fact that he preached a series of seventeen sermons on these sins, this scheme is the one that springs most readily to his mind when he is discussing sin in other sermons. In the vernacular and Latin treatises that he wrote on sin and confession the ten commandments have by no means replaced the seven sins as the chief scheme of classification. Both occur, but so do other schemes. Gerson's order of preference seems to be the following: the seven capital sins, sins of the heart and the five senses, sins against the ten commandments and sins of various groups of people. Moreover, it does not seem that a scheme based on the ten commandments would necessarily complicate confession. Whatever scheme he is using Gerson manages to include a great variety of sins. There are frequently – and here Gerson, like most medieval preachers and moralists, is following Gregory – branches or daughters of a particular sin and sometimes twigs or grand-daughters as well.[64] As Gerson's favourite scheme of classification is the seven capital sins, we shall discuss what thoughts, words and actions he considers to be sins within this framework.

Throughout their history the seven sins have not always been presented in the same order. Both Bloomfield and Wenzel see significance in these alterations of order and in the changes of emphasis that occurred. The sequence used by the Egyptian monk Cassian in the fifth century was gluttony, lust, avarice, anger, sadness, *acedia*, vainglory and pride. Cassian writes very much in a monastic setting. The temptations to gluttony and lust, he writes, are the first a monk must overcome. The sadness and *acedia* he describes are those suffered by men living an enclosed, contemplative life. He defines avarice as love of money (literally) and sees it, unlike the other sins, as foreign to human nature. He puts pride last, not because it is the least important, but because it is the most dreadful and perilous.[65] In the seventh century Gregory the Great altered the order and emphasis and thereby, according to Bloomfield, broadened 'the application of the sins so that they were no longer considered primarily monastic but became part of the general theological and devotional tradition'.[66] Gregory put vainglory and pride at the beginning of the list, gluttony and lust at the end, added envy and merged sadness and *acedia*. Not long afterwards vainglory merged with pride, and the sequence became pride, anger, envy, avarice, *acedia*, gluttony and lust. This order was not always strictly adhered to, however, as the second, third, fourth and fifth sins often changed places. Bloomfield notes a change in emphasis as well as in order occurring during the course of the Middle Ages. He sees the emphasis on the carnal sins of gluttony and lust giving way to a stress on pride and envy, and then, in the late Middle Ages, avarice, together with *acedia* (which had by now come to mean sloth or laziness instead of spiritual weariness and depression), gained predominance. He goes on to argue: 'The ascetic view of life gave way to the feudal corporate view, which in turn receded before the rising practical bourgeois philosophy.'[67] There may be something in this conclusion. Antoninus, for example, in Renaissance Italy not only puts avarice before pride but also gives it far fuller treatment.[68] Gerson, however, is not part of the trend, if there is a trend, for he does not lay his chief emphasis on avarice and sloth in his works for the laity, though he certainly sees avarice as a besetting sin of the upper ranks of the clergy.

Where does Gerson lay his emphasis? In the first place he does not follow a rigid order in his treatment of the seven sins. The most usual order is pride, envy, anger, avarice, sloth, gluttony, lust; in other words like most of his predecessors he follows a Gregorian order. Pride and envy are almost always in first and second place, respectively, and gluttony and lust at the end, usually in that order, but sometimes reversed. There is some interchange among anger, avarice and sloth, especially between the latter two.[69] The only place where a roughly Cassianic sequence occurs is in the series of sermons on the seven sins and here Gerson has almost certainly simply reversed his usual order to lead up to pride.

The order of the sins, however, does not tell us enough; it could in fact be misleading. It is obvious that sins of the nose, which Gerson puts fourth when he is writing about the sins of the five senses, are trivial to say the least and certainly less important than sins of the sense of touch (sins of lust), which are always placed last. Similarly sins related to gluttony are generally less serious than those related to lust. On the evidence of the amount of space he devotes to each of the seven vices and of the seriousness of the sins he lists and discusses under each of them, one can conclude that for Gerson pride and lust are the worst of the seven capital sins. Although this stress on pride is not at all unusual among moralists of the thirteenth, fourteenth and fifteenth centuries, there are a number who emphasise lust much less than Gerson does. *The Book of Vices and Virtues*, for instance, gives avarice the longest treatment, then pride, while lust is beaten for bottom place only by anger.[70] Antoninus, whom we have seen give far more space to avarice than pride, gives less space to lust than sloth, though more than to the three remaining sins, while in an anonymous Middle English sermon lust received very scant treatment compared with pride, avarice and sloth.[71] Not everyone, then, was as concerned with the sins of the flesh as Gerson was.

It is not that Gerson does not think that homicide, which could fall under anger, or envy, or avarice, or gluttony for that matter, is a serious sin, but he seems, in general, to be less concerned, though by no means unconcerned, with sins that are also crimes and therefore punishable by secular or ecclesiastical laws, and more concerned with 'private' sins. This does not at all mean, however, that he does not pay attention to the social aspects and consequences of sin. He is a socially concerned person, but it is the individual and the individual's state of soul that is his guiding interest, and so there can be sins of thought that are mortal and sins of action that are only venial. Indeed some crimes that are fairly judged as worthy of severe punishment by a civil court may be only venial sins in the eyes of God. This could be true of homicide, committed for example in a flash of anger or in a state of drunkenness. It is the psychological state of the sinner and his intentions that are of prime importance.

Pride

Gerson treats the sin of pride in a number of tracts. It is the chief topic of three of the *Poenitemini* series of sermons, and discussion of it, sometimes detailed, occurs in several other sermons, especially in those to the court. No doubt there was more outward evidence of pride among the ruling classes than elsewhere in fifteenth-century society. Nevertheless Gerson sees pride as a sin that can and does occur in all ranks and conditions of men.

As, for Gerson, the essence of sin is self-assertion, it is not surprising that he should frequently quote the statement from the Bible: 'Pride is the beginning of all sin' (Ecclus. 10:13). Gregory had long ago pin-pointed this statement and it can be guaranteed to appear in almost every medieval discussion of sin. Gerson quotes it in the *Dialogue spirituel*, paraphrases it as 'Every sin is born of pride', and then goes on to show how pride, which he defines as the desire for one's own excellence, the desire to be like God and the desire to fulfil one's own will and pleasure, is present in all sins. Sloth, for example, wishes to live without labour or affliction as God does; gluttony and lust want pleasures without punishment as God has. Even the sin of despair is born of pride, for it is based on the mistaken belief that one's salvation can come about by one's own efforts.[72] Gerson's definition of pride as the desire for one's own excellence is a version of a traditional one stemming from Augustine and appearing in many later works on Christian morality. Gerson has, unfortunately, left out an important qualifier. Augustine had said of pride that it was 'a perverse desire of highness' and in the hands of the scholastics this definition became 'the inordinate desire for one's own excellence', or 'the appetite for excellence in excess of right reason'.[73] Gerson's omission – and it seems to be an omission in his concept of pride as well as in his written definitions – colours the whole tone of his teaching about pride, so that it leaves a different impression from that of, say, Thomas or Antoninus.

Pride, for Gerson as for other moralists, has its most serious manifestations in the relationship between God and man. Here pride is a wrong perception of that relationship. The proud man thinks either that he has graces which he hasn't or that the graces that he has come from his own wisdom and strength, or that he deserves to be given those graces by God, as if God were bound to act as a result of man's actions. Gerson sees the Pharisee as guilty of this sort of pride; although he thanked God for his blessings, it is clear from his attitude to the publican that he thought that his blessings came from his own efforts and not from God alone. In all these three cases a mortal sin is being committed if there is deliberation and full consent to the belief. Gerson admits that in the first case one might sin through ignorance; for example a person could think he was properly repentant and confessed when in fact he was not. Then the sin would be venial only. It is better, though, Gerson argues, not to feel certain of such things, but to have a reasonable fear of the judgements of God and of one's own frailty. Perhaps the temperamentally proud man needs reminding of this, but for the over-scrupulous person, looking frantically for a sense of security, this doctrine could not have been very comforting. Pride in these three manifestations, Gerson continues, is acting against what one often says, namely that all the good one has comes from God and not from oneself. One needs to bring one's understanding and will into line with one's words, and give all the praise and glory to God.[74]

Gerson does not explain how pride, which he has defined in terms of desire, becomes a matter of perception, that is, he does not reconcile Augustine's definition with Gregory's. The latter had said that pride was thinking that the goods one has come from oneself, not from God. Antoninus reconciles the two definitions by arguing that the root of pride lies in the appetite, but that the man with an irrational desire for his own excellence very easily comes to overestimate his abilities and achievements.[75]

Another traditional branch of this form of pride which Gerson explicates is presumption; one presumes that the mercy of God will save one, even while one sins and perseveres in sin. This is a manner of sin, he says, which is called tempting God, when a person could help himself by repenting and going to confession, but does not, expecting God to do everything.[76] One is almost then caught both ways. One is committing the sin of pride if one praises oneself for what God in fact does, but there is pride also in leaving everything to God, presuming on His mercy, and not doing what one can. If pride, in this form, can prevent penitence, it can also have a detrimental effect on confession in another way. It is a sin of pride to lie in confession because of the shame one feels in retailing the details of a particular sin. It is not the feeling of shame that is a sin; it is the desire not to fall in the confessor's estimation and the consequent lying that form the sin.[77]

To desire to have knowledge equal to that of God is a sin of pride, the sin that caused the fall of Lucifer and that of Adam and Eve. It follows then that curiosity is a sin of pride. 'It is prideful curiosity to wish to seek out and understand the judgements of God, just as it is for a subject or a student vis-à-vis his seigneur or schoolmaster.'[78]

Although the most serious sins of pride occur in man's attitude to God, pride also manifests itself, for Gerson as for other moralists, in man's relationship to his fellows. 'Pride is hateful to God and to men.'[79] Here Gerson presents the picture of the man with a high opinion of himself (*elatus in se ipso*): arrogant, boastful, haughty, congratulating himself on his abundance of material or natural goods. He is proud of his youth, his beauty, his strength, his wisdom or his noble lineage, his clothes, wealth, friends, power or kingship. If one has felt proud about any of these things and boasted about them to one's fellows, one must confess one's fault. All these things are gifts of God, and in any case there are problems about all of them: youth and beauty pass away, friends may let one down, riches and kingship bring great cares and responsibilities.[80] It is a more serious sin, however, to be proud of one's spiritual advantages, one's gifts of grace.[81] We must not be proud of our justice, our pity and compassion for others, or of our generosity in almsgiving, our virtues as preachers, pastors, counsellors or governors, nor must we be proud of our humility. The goal *is* humility, but there must be no self-satisfaction when we reach it.[82]

Pride can lead us to be too insistent on our own opinions so that we will not suffer correction from our superiors. This is a sin.[83] Further, such misplaced reliance on one's own ideas can lead to idolatry, apostasy, blasphemy, sorcery, astrology, necromancy and to all sorts of superstitious beliefs and practices. All these activities are *ex genere suo* mortal sins, though circumstances (unspecified here) could make them only venial.[84]

The man who is proud of himself generally seeks the praise and approval of others, and so he is led into the sins associated with vainglory, defined by Gerson as a desire for the praise of the world.[85] It is a sin, he writes in a sermon, to desire great worldly honours or estate, and this can lead to great evils, for example the wars brought about by Julius Caesar and Hannibal. It can also lead to religious hypocrisy, the performing of ascetic and religious works for the wrong reasons.[86] In itself, however, he argues in a vernacular tract, it is only a venial sin, though it can become mortal according to the end for which one seeks praise, or the means one uses.[87] It is not a sin at all if one's aim in seeking praise is to rebut a charge that one is an infamous person, a thief for example. Nor is it a sin if one seeks praise or glory solely for spiritual ends, that is for the glory of God or the edification of one's neighbours, though Gerson points out that it is difficult to do this in public without some sinful desire becoming involved. It is better done in private among one's intimate friends. One may thus speak of the blessings one has received to one's friends for the purpose of advising or consoling them. If, on the other hand, one seeks glory for the sake of avarice or to have greater leeway in doing evil, this is a mortal sin. It is only venial, however, if one's aim is to get 'slight pleasure' from the praise of others, for the end – the seeking of this slight pleasure – is only a venial sin itself.

As far as the means by which one seeks glory go, if they are mortal sins in themselves, for example killing 'un proudhon', committing arson or rape, then seeking glory in these cases is a mortal sin. Today one would tend to regard such actions done for this reason as symptoms of psychological disturbance. Gerson identifies arson and so on as actions sometimes performed for the sake of notoriety, but here, he still regards them as mortal sins. However, on his own definition of mortal sin as sin requiring the full deliberation and consent of reason and will, such actions could be only venial sins. Perhaps he is psychologically wise, though, not to stress this point in the middle of his discussion of the means used to acquire vainglory. If the means, on the contrary, are good in themselves, as for example almsgiving, fasting and prayer, nevertheless one could still commit a mortal sin if one's principal aim were to further one's own reputation. If the principal aim were the doing of the good work then there would be no mortal sin, though there would be venial sin if one were seeking as a secondary end slight pleasure from the praise of others. Gerson points out that it is better to try to get rid of all desire for praise in the performance of good works. If the means by which one seeks praise are indifferent, for example having a new dress, riches or beauty, then there is no mortal sin 'de soy', though evils can follow which one ought to eschew. For example, the new dress or the beauty could lead to sins of lust in others. Clearly it would be a mortal sin if in addition to the desire for praise one had the desire to cause others to sin, but if one's desire is for praise only, there is no mortal sin, though reasonable precautions should be taken to avoid causing sin in others. A woman, however, does not need to go so far as to 'disfigure herself or dress in a sack or never go to church' in order to prevent some fool from coveting her lustfully.[88]

It is interesting, considering his ranting against all worldly things in some of his sermons, that here Gerson states that a new dress, riches and beauty are indifferent, not vain or evil in themselves. His attitude here is more in line with the Aristotelian-influenced scholastics than it is with missionary Mendicant preachers like Bernardine and Maillard, who frequently castigate women for their dress and who sometimes leave the impression that it would be better if women did wear sacks.[89]

Pride in one's own abilities, possessions and virtues generally leads one to despise others not so well endowed. This leads Gerson to the discussion of another traditional set of daughters of pride. First there is despising *per se*; disdaining others because they lack the goods of fortune and grace that one has oneself; being ashamed of one's poor friend.[90] Less straightforward is the question of judging others. In the *Modus brevis confitendi* he suggests that the penitent confess:

By pride I was presumptuous in my correctings and reprehensions...I made very many rash and presumptuous judgements against my neighbours, by despising and deriding them, or thinking badly of them, and by interpreting their words and deeds in a bad rather than a good light.[91]

The question comes up in two other tracts and here the treatment is more complex. 'Judging others comes from pride', Gerson states firmly in his work on mortal and venial sin.[92] But then he distinguishes between types and manners of judging. One can judge a person's actions or the person himself, and one can judge with certainty or with light presumption and suspicion. It is a mortal sin to judge firmly that a person is bad in God's eyes and deserves damnation, because in a moment the Holy Spirit could make him good and the person could repent in time. One should not, in fact, judge persons at all. 'Deeds, therefore, not persons are to be judged by us.'[93] As far as judging actions goes, if the actions are so obviously bad that in no way, whatever the intention, could they be good, then one may judge with certainty that the person has done wrong. But if the actions could be right or wrong, then to judge them wrong is a mortal sin. If, however, in such a case, one were to make only 'aucuns soupecons et jugemens legiers', then there is no mortal sin, though it would be better to say nothing. Moreover, one must be careful in making suggestions about another's guilt that one does not damage the other's reputation or harm him in some way. The second tract adds another point. To judge another as an evil-doer, if it is done in an official capacity and by means of legitimate witness, is not of itself evil, but in fact virtuous, 'even if through confession or otherwise the accused is known by the judge to be innocent, and if the judge is unable to escape from fulfilling the functions of his office'.[94] There is obviously no pride here. The judge is merely doing his job. In this tract Gerson reveals some doubts about what he has stated is sinless in *Le Profit*, namely the case of the ordinary person who makes a judgement where the guilt is obvious and certain. There may, he says, be a venial or even mortal sin of curiosity involved here, or a man 'by this judging may be impeded from doing better things or become puffed up in pride'.[95] In other words, one should mind one's own business, and it is better not to judge other people or their actions at all, unless one is acting in an official capacity.

The last major branch of the sin of pride is disobedience. Disobeying God's commandments is generally a sin of pride, because it is asserting one's own will against God's will.[96] Disobeying one's superiors is, in some but not all cases, a sin of pride. When the disobedience occurs because one despises one's superior and holds him in contempt, there is always mortal sin involved. But if one disobeys the order of a superior because of one's frailty or for some other causes then there is no sin of contempt.[97] What are these other causes? In the first place, one is obliged to obey only those orders of superiors which fall within the legitimate sphere of their authority.[98] Secondly, superiors may not oblige subordinates, under pain of mortal sin, to do things unless those things are found explicitly or implicitly in Divine law.[99] One form of disobedience to the orders of superiors that Gerson regards as a serious sin of pride is that of not observing the rules about excommunication. In fact it is a sin of pride to have been excommunicated in the first place, but it is an additional sin to hear mass when one is excommunicated. Further, it is a sin knowingly to hear mass with excommunicates or to have anything to do with them.[100]

This sin of disobedience to superiors figures largely in Gerson's three sermons on pride. In the first one it is disobedience to the fasting laws of the church that Gerson berates. These laws are reasonable, he argues, and 'you know that it is the worst pride to disobey one's sovereigns, and holy church and her prelates are your sovereigns'.[101] In the second sermon it is disobedience in not doing the ordered penance that comes under criticism. Thus it is that the sin of pride leading to disobedience prevents in various ways repentance and restoration to God's grace.

There is a passage in *La Mendicité spirituelle* where Gerson expresses strongly what seems to be his basic feeling about the sin of pride. This treatise is about the mystical life, but the same tone pervades many of the passages in his sermons where he speaks of pride.

I want to know, presumptuous pride, by what title and right your always wish to reign in me and all my works; humility rather should reign there, for I have nothing in me which is mine except evil; and if any goods have been put there by the liberality of my seigneur, I have lost or corrupted them, as for example the white and pure tunic of innocence or righteousness which has been given to me many times, as in baptism or at the holy sacrament of penance. Alas, what have I done with it? Mortal sin has quickly torn it and thrown it away, or venial sin has covered it with black, foul stains so that I could never show it to my seigneur... What reply have you, pride? Will you boast of such cloth that was once so white and beautiful? I think not.[102]

There is clearly no room here for self-satisfaction, or even for self-respect. No concessions are made to what would seem to be the basic human need to feel oneself worth something. Nor are any concessions made to the human need for the approval of one's fellows. It is still a venial sin to seek even slight pleasure in the praise of others. The only reason for which one may legitimately and without sin speak of one's virtues and blessings are the glorification of God and the edification of one's neighbours; and if there is any desire for praise for oneself as well, then there is venial sin. Gerson clears St Paul of the sin of boasting and seeking vainglory by arguing that he needed to stress his credentials and abilities in order to be able to carry out God's work. But for ordinary people, Gerson counsels in a sermon, 'It is safest to hide all the virtues one thinks one has more carefully than others hide their vices.'[103] As Gerson presents it to the laity there is no sinless aspect to the human tendency to feel pride. The ideal seems too high.

Gerson did not write a *Summa confessorum* or a *Summa moralium*. One cannot in fact imagine him having either the time or inclination to do so. His interests were more practical, pastoral and mystical than legalistic or truly academic. This lack of a summa on morality means that, although he does far more than merely list sins, there is no systematic analysis of sin in Gerson's moral teaching, as there is for instance in the IIa-IIae of St Thomas. Thomas' book is distinctive in that it is not divided up, as most moral summas were (unless they were arranged alphabetically), into separate sections on, say, the virtues, the vices, and the ten commandments.[104] Rather, it is entirely organised within the framework of the seven virtues: faith, hope, love, prudence, justice, fortitude and temperance. As he discusses each virtue Thomas deals with the gifts corresponding to it and the vices opposed to it. In this way, as he says himself in the prologue, everything will be covered and 'nothing in morals will be omitted'. It is indeed a comprehensive treatment. But, more to the point, a systematic discussion within the context of the virtues that makes ample use of Aristotelian psychology and ethics leaves a very different impression from a discussion of the sins by themselves. Pride, for instance, is treated by Thomas in the context of temperance, because it is an excessive as opposed to a rational and measured desire for one's own excellence: 'He who wishes to overstep what he is, is proud. For right reason requires that every man's will should tend to that which is proportionate to him.'[105] Pride is inordinate self-esteem, as opposed to 'true self-esteem'.[106] Thomas treats presumption in the context of fortitude and, following Aristotle, he sees it as opposed by excess to the virtue of magnanimity. Magnanimity, he states, 'denotes the stretching forth of the mind to great things'. A magnanimous man is one who 'is minded to do some great act', and who deems himself worthy of great things, but all in proportion to his own ability. He 'does not tend to anything greater than is becoming to him'. The presumptuous man, by contrast, does 'strive to do what exceeds his ability', does deem himself more worthy of things than he is.[107] Thomas also sees ambition and vainglory as opposed to magnanimity by excess, ambition being defined as an inordinate desire for honour, and vainglory as an inordinate desire for glory.[108]

Antoninus, although he treats the seven sins and their branches separately from the virtues, does borrow and amplify some of Thomas' arguments. As a result, the ideal of moral behaviour for the laity that emerges seems quite far from monastic. At the beginning of his chapter on pride, for instance, Antoninus states firmly that the desire for excellence and honours is natural and, in the form of magnanimity, is virtuous.[109]

Gerson, by contrast, as far as the sin of pride goes, appears to have ignored or discarded the Thomistic line of argument. Had he written an academic summa he might have taken a different approach, but for the laity and for those who were to minister to the laity the doctrine he propounds in his discussion of pride seems uncompromising and hard.[110]

Envy

Gerson defines envy in the traditional way as feeling joy and exultation at the misfortunes of others, either at the evil that afflicts them or at the evil they do, and feeling sadness, displeasure, grief, even hatred at the good fortune and happiness of others. It is wishing that ill should befall someone and that good should not.[111] If the envy is of the spiritual rather than the natural or temporal goods of another, then the sin is a more serious one. In fact, in this case it is one of the sins against the Holy Spirit.[112] Envy *per se* is a mortal sin because it is contrary to charity. This does not mean, however, that every case of envy is a mortal sin; both intentions and consequences must be taken into account. In the first place, the rule about unbidden natural feelings applies. If there is no deliberation and no consent to these feelings, or if someone is of a particularly melancholy disposition (in which case also there would be no consent), there is no sin at all. If there is some deliberation and consent so that one does not banish such feelings as quickly as one could, then there is venial sin. If one's displeasure at the goods of others arises because one fears the evil results which might occur, then the displeasure, consented to, is no sin.[113] One might, for instance, be distressed that a bad person has acquired a great deal of power, because he could thereby cause harm to another, to his own salvation or to the state. Displeasure for a just cause or a good end is no sin. But is such displeasure envy at all? In his sermon on envy, where Gerson attempts an analysis of the status of the various sins of envy, he calls this displeasure 'bonne jalousie ou envie'. But in the two tracts that also analyse the sins of envy, he says that such displeasure is not envy, and this would seem to be a more accurate conclusion.[114] In the sermon Gerson introduces another case, that does not appear in the treatises, of apparent envy that is consented to but which is not de soi a mortal sin. This is the case of the person who is envious because he does not possess the goods that another has, wishes that he had similar goods, but is content that the other retain his.[115] This sort of envy, Gerson writes, could be impatience against God or unjustified displeasure at one's own status. He does not take the opportunity at this point, as some moralists do, to write about the sort of envy that spurs a person on to great deeds, 'invida pro zelo', as Antoninus cells it, or simply 'zeal' or 'emulation'. If the zeal is about spiritual or virtuous goods, Antoninus argues, it is praiseworthy, and even if it is about temporal goods, it may be sinless.[116] Gerson does, in his sermons, often urge his congregations to emulate a saint whose deeds he has just described, but he does not discuss zeal in connection with envy.

Because an envious person frequently tends to cast aspersions on the one he envies, it is natural – and traditional – that the whole topic of criticism and defamation of others should be discussed in connection with the sin of envy. Gerson usually calls this criticism 'detraction'. English writers of the period call it 'backbiting'. In one place, however, Gerson distinguishes between detraction, which is the hidden or private (occulta) diminution of the reputation of another, defamation, which is the same thing done in public, and contumely or upbraiding, which is criticism expressed in front of the one envied.[117] However, if the loss to the other's reputation is only slight or if one criticises only 'par aucune legiereté de parler', then only a venial sin is involved. The levity of speech, though, could lead to serious damage to the other, in which case there is mortal sin. In other words, the consequences must be taken into account in assessing the status of this sin. The intentions are also important, for one could criticise another for a good purpose, for instance to prevent third parties from being harmed, for the good of the state or community, or for fraternal correction. In this case there is no sin. But if any ill will is involved in this criticism for a good end, then there is venial sin, and Gerson points out that for the ordinary run of men it is very difficult to upbraid and criticise others for a good purpose without any ill will entering in.[118]

Reverting to a more rhetorical style in the one sermon specifically on envy, Gerson provides justification for the need to root out envy by describing some of the awful effects of this sin. It was the envy of the Jews about the praise bestowed on Jesus for His wisdom, virtue and goodness that led to the Crucifixion. It is envy that stirs up divisions between and within the three estates of the realm. The bourgeoisie envy and murmur against the clergy because they think the latter have their livelihood without any work. The clergy envy and murmur against the bourgeoisie when the latter try to acquire learning. From this envy of one estate for another arise defamation, accusations of simony, luxury, pride and avarice against the clergy; accusations of pride, pomp and unjust exactions against the nobility; accusations of usury and disobedience against the bourgeoisie, 'without respect for place or time; and not with any desire to improve or correct, but rather to disparage, hate and persecute'.[119]

Further, the person full of envy is harming himself. Apart from the fact that he is in mortal sin, he gives himself a miserable life; he is blinded, for he can see good nowhere, except in evil. In the presence of true good he only grieves. He is very often angry and full of indignation. His envy drives out charity, the only cure for his condition. 'Envy has no share in whatever is good in the world; so it is truly poor; by contrast he who has charity is lord of all...Do you wish that all were yours? Then love your neighbour as yourself...you will be joyful over his goods as well as your own.'[120]

Anger

The sin of anger, like envy, is *per se* mortal because it is contrary to charity. Gerson uses the traditional definition. Anger is the desire for vengeance and the desire to bring harm to another by words or actions. The outward manifestations of anger are, of course, also *per se* mortal sins: murmuring against others, menacing and vilifying them with angry words, striking them. Striking a cleric is worse than striking a lay person and mutilation is worse than striking. Presumably homicide would be the worst of all, though Gerson does not mention this in his discussion of the sin of anger. Taking action through the law to recover one's rights can also involve mortal sin.

In the sermon against anger Gerson sets forth the ideal: forgive everything and everyone, and have compassion on your neighbour, as you wish God to pardon and have compassion on you. Moreover, you will gain in the long run. You may not get your vengeance here and now, and you may be mocked by men for not seeking your rights, but you will have mercy from God hereafter. Leave the vengeance to God: 'he who has wronged you will be more heavily punished than you could ever have wished or thought of'.[121] It is true that this thought of your enemy's punishment hereafter does not seem to fit in with the ideal of compassion, but the point Gerson is making is that one ought to leave the righting of wrongs to the proper authorities, to God if necessary. For he certainly believes that one has a claim to the restoration of one's rights. This is clear in all his writings on anger. Some self-assertion, though by means of the proper processes, is allowed here. The ideal of patience, forgiveness and compassion is there, but it is soft-pedalled. For one thing, by no means all feeling and manifestations of anger are mortal sins, or sins at all, for that matter. *Ira per zelum*, that is, felt and manifested anger against evil is *ex se* praiseworthy, though it could become blameworthy if shown at the wrong time, in the wrong place or in the wrong manner.[122] One ought to be angry against sins, one's own and other people's; one ought to desire that wrong-doing be punished, including wrong-doing against oneself. 'The desire that crime be punished by law and by the duly appointed judges, so that one has one's rights, is good; and there is no sin here.'[123] However, in the case of a wrong done to oneself sin can enter if one does not pursue one's rights by due process, and if one's chief aim is to inflict damage on the other rather than to recover one's own rights.[124] Anger, in other words, though Gerson does not spell this out, if it takes the form of zealous or righteous anger, should be seen in the context of the cardinal virtue of justice, rather than in the context of the theological virtue of charity.[125]

In the second place, writes Gerson, anger can simply be a lack of affection towards another, without the desire that ill befall him. In this case there is only diminution of charity, and there is no mortal sin, unless one fails to come to the aid of the other when he is in dire necessity. Similarly, anger is sometimes mere impatience at the actions of other people without any desire for vengeance. This impatience is not really anger and there is no mortal sin.[126] The rule about unbidden feelings also applies. If there is no deliberation and consent there is no sin. So sudden, uncontrollable flare-ups of anger are not sinful. Moreover, some people, those of a choleric or melancholy disposition and those who are old, are particularly prone to anger and for them even lasting anger can be without mortal sin. Gerson seems to have a fair amount of sympathy for angry persons. He certainly writes as if he had had a good deal of experience of anger in others and perhaps in himself. In the one sermon devoted to this sin, he describes vividly the choleric or melancholic or old person in a fit of anger, becoming red in the face, his eyes inflamed, throwing his hands, feet and body around, banging on the table and making threatening gestures or saying threatening words.[127] There is no mortal sin here, but there could be if the results of the anger were serious: if, for instance, one were to strike someone without cause and whom one ought not to strike, or to say something publicly very injurious about another. If such results ensue, Gerson argues, it is a sign of deliberation and consent.[128] There seems to be something contradictory here. If the anger is uncontrollable there is no sin, but if the results of such anger are serious, there can be mortal sin. Consequences seem to take precedence over intentions in this case. In the tracts the stress is on intentions: no deliberation or consent, no sin. Perhaps it is because he is preaching a sermon that Gerson stresses results. He wishes people to curb their anger before the fact, or at least not to let their anger get out of bounds, whereas in the tracts he is concerned more with anger after the fact, with examination of conscience.

In the sermon Gerson suggests various remedies against quick anger: looking in the glass when one is angry to see how ugly anger looks; considering how badly people will think of one; drinking less strong wines; avoiding lust, which can make people impatient; avoiding occasions of anger, such as arguments; keeping silent; making no signs of contempt and so on. He then distinguishes between this sudden anger, or quick temper, and lasting (*lointaine*) anger. But even lasting anger, he says, is not always mortal sin. Temperament can again excuse, and so can lack of consent, for Gerson recognises that one can have unbidden feelings of anger at actions long since done, and that anger can persist despite efforts to resist it. If there is full consent to the desire for vengeance and the taking of vengeance then the results determine whether a mortal sin is involved or not: if the vengeance one takes or desires is according to law and reason, that is, to recover one's rights or repair one's honour, then there is no sin, though it would be more perfect to pardon all. But, as Gerson so often says, one is not always bound to do the more perfect thing. If, on the other hand, one desires great harm to another by unreasonable means then there is mortal sin.

Gerson's treatise on the examination of conscience and the sermon agree on the question of reconciliation, though this is not discussed in the *Regulae mandatorum* or in the tract on mortal and venial sin. You should, he writes, always be ready to forgive those who ask for pardon and who make reparation, and to apologise to those with whom you have been angry, though seigneurs and masters and fathers need not apologise as subjects should. However, if no voluntary amendment is forthcoming from the offender, you may legitimately continue to seek your rights and break off relations with him until he does make reparation, although this should be done in the spirit of charity, not hatred.[129] One thing you must not do in your anger – permissible or not – and in your seeking of your rights is to curse God, for blasphemy is a very great sin.[130]

Gerson distinguishes, in the sermon, a third type of anger: *ire grevaine*, which under the cover of justice in fact produces many evils. He has in mind here wars, especially civil wars, excessive punishment by superiors of those in subjection to them, and rigorous execution of the law by judges who do not take particular circumstances into account, who do not temper justice with mercy. But, he is quick to point out, mercy without justice is just as dangerous to the state. A prince or prelate ought not to pardon an injury, if the injury prejudices his estate, or if the pardon would be bad for the offender or an encouragement to wrong-doing in others.[131] On this note, apart from a word or two about patience, the sermon ends.

The general impression left, from a reading of this sermon and from the more technical tracts, is that though charity and forgiveness are the ideals, anger is very natural, often sinless, often excusable, often justified and often even perhaps better expressed than bottled up.[132] One may, indeed almost should, for the good of the state, seek to regain one's rights and repair one's honour by legitimate and reasonable means. This is reminiscent of Gerson's arguments in favour of the endowment of the church. Poverty is an ideal and is all right in its time and place, but this is not the time or the place. Forgiving all is an ideal, but fifteenth-century society is not the time or the place. Pragmatic considerations must be taken into account. In his treatment of the sin of anger, then, Gerson does make concessions in both the social and individual spheres to the needs and weaknesses of human nature. His teaching here is much more in line than is his teaching on pride with that of the Aristotelian theologians, who regard anger, the 'rising up' against anything harmful or hurtful as natural, a necessary and useful part of human nature. It is only when this passion is not controlled by reason, when it is 'inordinate' with regard to degree or means, that it is sinful. One is not always bound to turn the other cheek.[133] Like these theologians and like some other medieval preachers and manualists who write – though often only briefly – about 'good anger',[134] Gerson has moved far from Cassian, who told his monks that the only permissible anger was anger against oneself.[135]

Avarice

The fourth capital sin, avarice, involves Gerson in more technical discussions than have been encountered so far, for it is under this heading that he deals with the question of usury and trading practices in general. It would be by no means true to say that there were no ecclesiastical or secular laws about any of the sins related to pride, envy, anger, sloth, gluttony or lust. But the economic practices that are classed as sins of avarice were subject to more actual legislation and juristic discussion than were practices classed as sins of pride, envy and so on. Moreover, the question of usury was a very complex one and the opinions of canonists and theologians varied considerably about what business practices came under the usury prohibition.[136] Further, views changed as new economic practices came into being and accommodations were made. Usury and trade, however, are not the only topics Gerson discusses under the heading of avarice.

He defines avarice in the traditional manner as the immoderate love of having and keeping.[137] It is not that any desire to have things or any action taken to acquire things is sinful. On the contrary, the desire and acquisition of the things necessary for one's livelihood or to keep up one's estate in life are perfectly legitimate. There is nothing wrong with private property.[138] It is only the desire of having which is immoderate, disordered, beyond reason which is avaricious and therefore sinful. In the sermon on avarice Gerson paints a picture of the evil results, personal and social, of 'ceste vielle dampnee avarice convoiteuse'. He calls it a hideous beast which is to be found in all classes, among merchants especially, but also among craftsmen, clergy, lawyers and seigneurs. It keeps a man glued to the things of the world. He can think of nothing but having earthly goods and so he has no time for spiritual concerns, no time for God. He is disliked and cursed by others, especially by the poor. Avarice promises him sufficiency and security, power and liberty, repose and pleasure. But in fact it brings him none of these. The avaricious man never thinks he has sufficient; the more he has the more he wants. Nor does he have security, for the more he has the more he fears the loss of his goods. 'A poor man sings in the woods, without fear of robbers; a rich man fears them; he fears seigneurs; he fears his friends and his enemies.'[139] Avarice, says Gerson, using the well-worn biblical quotation, is the root of all evil (I Tim. 6:10), the mother of all the vices. It is accompanied by flattery, pride, carnality, anger, envy and the impoverishment of those who are the miser's victims. Avarice destroys friendship and brotherhood. And all for nothing, for man's true riches lie in God.[140]

At the end of the sermon Gerson discusses, but only in a very general way, remedies against avarice: avoid the occasions, turn to Christ and Mary, repent. In between these two rhetorical passages comes a technical section on usury and sins in trade – a section that stylistically does not fit in very well with the tone of the rest of the sermon.[141] It reflects, however, the tone of his treatment of avarice in the tracts. Here he proceeds analytically. The disordered love of having, when it is manifested in thought alone, may or may not be a mortal sin. You may desire something to the extent that you would take it if you could; this, he says, is theft in thought and is a mortal sin. It is also a mortal sin if you desire with knowledge and full deliberation, that is, consenting to the desire, something for which you are not qualified or worthy, for example, a judicial or political office. If, however, you desired something conditionally, that is, if you wished to have it only if you were worthy, or could have it without angering God or harming someone else, then there is no sin or only venial sin. But Gerson points out the danger of encouraging this sort of desire, for it might come to absorb one and prevent one from fulfilling one's other obligations, in which case one would be moving into the realm of mortal sin. It is certainly a mortal sin to desire unnecessary or superfluous things so ardently that one forgets to think of one's salvation. If, however, the desire does not prevent one from thinking of God and one's salvation, then the sin is only venial.[142]

Avarice in acquiring, again, may or may not be a mortal sin. It depends on the end and the means. If the end is immoderate possessions – and of course what is immoderate for an artisan will not be immoderate for a bishop or seigneur – there is clearly some sin involved. As far as the means go, the general rule is that if the means are only venial sins in themselves then only venial sin is involved provided the end is honest. But if the means are mortal sins then the acquisition is a mortal sin. Gerson's example of a venial sin of avarice is that of a minstrel or court fool, who, to make a living, sings, jokes and makes pleasantries to amuse a seigneur. As seigneurs often need such distractions to take away the melancholy caused by their great responsibilities, Gerson thinks such performers cannot be outside a state of salvation. One would indeed hope not. Gerson attaches venial sin to the activities of comedians because of the traditional view that frivolities of all sorts are unseemly.[143] But what, one might ask, has this venial sin to do with avarice? The aim was to make a living. This is the trouble with some of the sins listed under avarice. They are sins for other reasons, because, for example, they are against the commandment 'Thou shalt not steal', or against the disciplinary rules of the church, or against canon law, and logically are sins of avarice only if the end is avaricious. But if a writer is working with the scheme of the seven capital sins, the only place to put such sins would be under avarice, especially as much of the sin involved in acquisition was perpetrated by people seeking immoderate gain, or so it would appear from Gerson's writings. The scheme of the seven sins may be pragmatically useful, but it is not always logically sound.

The means used to acquire goods or money are manifold and cover a multitude of sins. Gerson lists many of the illicit means, but discusses in detail only those connected with trade in general and usury in particular, because this is where the legal difficulties lay. In general it is sins against justice that Gerson is concerned with rather than sins against charity. He does occasionally write about uncharitable behaviour: avarice leads to hardness of heart towards one's neighbour; it can cause suffering to the poor and reduce them to indigence; it can prevent a man from coming to the aid of his neighbours when they are in distress.[144] But far more often it is justice, giving to each that to which he is entitled, that Gerson is interested in.[145] Straight theft falls under this heading, and stealing something in a church or belonging to a church is the worst kind of theft because it involves sacrilege also. Keeping something found is also theft. There is, however, one kind of 'theft' that is not sinful. If you take and keep something belonging to another without the knowledge of the owner, but know that the owner would not mind your having it and is not suffering loss by not having it himself, or ought not to mind because you are in extreme need, then there is no mortal sin, especially if you mean to return it when you can.[146] Then there is a whole group of practices that are related to theft in one way or another: not paying one's tithes or offerings to the church; not paying one's debts to a seigneur; hiding the fact that you owe someone something; not carrying out the requests of a testator about alms; keeping bequests of money or property that you know to have been sinfully acquired; wasting your relations' or seigneur's goods or foolishly spending your own or another's money. It is a sin not to pay lawfully instituted taxes, but, Gerson points out, it is equally sinful for a prince to demand unjust subsidies.[147] It is sinful for a seigneur or master not to pay the wages of his servants and workers, or even to pay them late. Seigneurs, judges, lawyers and legal officials who, for their own gain, deliberately pervert the cause of justice in a law case, by taking bribes (*dons contre raison*) or by acting to produce what they know is a wrong verdict, will end up in hell unless they make restitution. Similarly flattering someone to get something out of him is sinful, as is rejoicing at the misfortune of another because it leads to your gain, and wishing for someone's death so that you may inherit. Gambling is another illicit practice, and any gains acquired in this way ought to be given for pious uses in whatever way one's confessor suggests.

In the *Regulae mandatorum* Gerson discusses a number of ecclesiastical practices that are sins of avarice. Simony is a prime example. Another is the misuse of ecclesiastical revenues instituted for the poor. Any cleric who takes these for his own use is obliged to make restitution. If, however, the terms of the foundation are such that no revenues are specifically set aside for the poor, the cleric who does not use some of the general revenues for this purpose, though he sins gravely (against charity), is not bound to make restitution.[148] Similarly a cleric is not bound to make restitution for the revenues he has received by being a pluralist without dispensation, although he sins gravely. Pluralism with permission, however, is, Gerson argues, perfectly all right if more than one benefice is required to enable the occupant to keep up a decent status and if scandal is avoided and the cure of souls not neglected.[149]

To increase one's wealth by any form of usury is a mortal sin. Usury, for Gerson as for his predecessors and contemporaries, is the lending of money, not just for a high rate of interest, but for any interest or gain whatsoever, and it is against divine, natural and positive law.[150] Gerson gives one of the traditional reasons for usury's being contrary to natural law. To take profit and cause loss to another from what is not one's own is a sin against justice for, in the case of money as in the case of grain and other consumables, use cannot be separated from ownership. You cannot use the money or grain lent except by 'consuming' them, so in effect ownership is transferred in the loan, and what the lender is doing if he extracts interest is to force the borrower to pay in return for what is now his.[151] Such a usurer ought to be excommunicated until he is penitent and makes restitution. And the same applies to notaries, seigneurs and others who aid and abet usurers, and to those who work in a company that lends at usury.

There is, however, an exception to this prohibition of usury. This is the case of the man who comes to the help of his indigent neighbour by lending him money for a certain term. The contract specifies that if the money is not paid back by the due date then interest is to be paid in compensation for the loss caused to the lender by not having his money when he expected and needed it. As long as the lender would prefer to have his money on the due date rather than later with the interest, then the whole transaction, argues Gerson, could be a work of piety.[152] This sort of contract with interest allowed for delay was fairly generally accepted by the canonists and theologians of Gerson's period. But like Gerson they underline the importance of intention. If the intention is obviously fraudulent then the loan falls under the usury prohibition, as in the case of a loan granted for such a short time that the borrower could hardly be expected to meet his obligation.[153] Gerson does not go as far as two later fifteenth-century theologians, Bernardine and Antoninus, who argue – though in a rather qualified way – that in the case of a private charitable loan interest might accrue from the beginning of the loan, if the lender is a merchant who suffers a loss of the profits he could have made, had he kept his money and employed it fruitfully in his business.[154] This opinion, however, was a minority one.

What is the moral status of the borrower in a usurious loan? Gerson is no exception here when he argues that the borrower, if he is compelled by necessity, does not commit a mortal sin by agreeing to pay interest, because he is not, properly speaking, a participant in the usurer's crime.[155] As Thomas puts it, the borrower does not consent to the usurer's sin, but makes use of it for a good purpose.[156]

In the sermon Gerson then moves on from this manifest usury (*usure desnuee*) to what he calls hidden usury (*usure cachee*), and under this heading he examines various practices in buying and selling and leasing commodities that might or might not involve disguised usurious loans.[157] Whether buying futures cheaply is usury is his first question. If it is done to relieve the indigence of the seller, and if the seller has a sufficient price, and if the purpose is to provide for the household of the buyer, then there is no sin. It is the intention that matters. Presumably, then, Gerson holds that the buying of futures with the intention of making a profit by later sale is usurious. This was the general opinion of the period.[158] Are credit sales at a price higher than the cash price allowable? Again it is the intention that counts. If the seller is bound to gain by the contract and to lose nothing by not having his money now, then the contract is sinful, for it is really a disguised loan with interest. But if he would truly prefer to have his money now rather than more later, then to compensate him the contract may lawfully be carried through. Buying new grain to hold back in order to sell when it is dearer is sinful, says Gerson, unless the intention excuses. He does not say what sort of intention would excuse such action.[159] Joint ownership of livestock with shared profit and risk is allowable. However, any contract which 'limps' (cloche) is prohibited, that is a contract in which one party is sure of gaining whatever happens, while the other is at risk. Gerson's example of a limping contract is similar to the one used in *The Book of Vices and Virtues*:[160] one leases a cow to someone and he has to continue to pay even if the cow dies. The merchant partnership (*societas*), however, where one partner furnishes the money and the other the labour, and where the profits and losses are shared, is perfectly valid. There is nothing new in all this. Gerson's views on credit sales, limping contracts, the *societas* and shared-risk partnerships were fairly generally accepted opinions by his time.[161] To discuss these topics in a vernacular sermon, however, as Gerson does, is rather unusual.

Gerson now moves on to what he calls *usure enmatelee*, but what he discusses under this heading is not usury or even cloaked usury, as he admits in the *Regulae mandatorum*. What he does examine are trading practices that would more properly fall under the doctrine and legislation about the just price. All fraud in trade is wrong. This fraud could take the form of selling one thing and saying it is another, for example selling brass and saying it is gold.[162] Or one could lie about the quality of the goods; for instance, you sell a horse saying it is healthy when in fact it is broken-winded; or you show an example of good writing for producing a book and then copy it in a bad hand.[163] If the fault in the goods can be easily seen then you do not need to point it out, but you must charge less than you would if the goods were faultless, and you must not indulge in any tricks to conceal the visible faults. In general, Gerson says, every time you sell above the just price you sin and must make restitution.

What is the just price for Gerson? A common view among scholastics is that the just price is what we would now call the market price, that is, it reflects supply and demand. Antoninus, for instance, says that the value and therefore the just price of a good depends on its usefulness for satisfying human needs, its scarcity and its desirability.[164] Gerson, by contrast, although he says nothing against the utility theory of value and price, stresses in this sermon and elsewhere a different determinant. That good servant, Just Price, he says, 'holds the balance' between the needs, expenses, risks and labour of the seller, and the price.[165] It would be going too far to argue from this that Gerson has a labour theory of value, that he sees labour as the chief determinant of price. He is preaching a sermon, not giving a lecture on economics, and he is only concerned to tell the traders in his congregation which business practices are licit and which illicit. A merchant may sell goods at a higher price than he paid for them to compensate for his costs, risks and labour. But if he has expended no labour, has not improved the condition of the goods themselves, or not brought them from a place where they are abundant to where they are scarce, then he should adjust the price accordingly. In no circumstances must merchants form monopolies, buying up all the iron or books or grain in a city or province, in order to fix a high selling price.

Fraud in trade, continues Gerson, can also involve deception about the quantity of goods sold. No trickery with weights and measures should be indulged in, no dampening of wool, for example, to make it heavier.[166]

For all these acts of injustice, from simple theft to the non-payment of taxes, usury and fraudulent trading practices, restitution must be made before the sinner can be absolved. Further, it is better for those in trade to avoid swearing oaths when they bargain, for they may commit perjury, which is a very serious sin. As far as breaking the Sabbath and holy days is concerned, Gerson is less rigorous than many preachers. Mass at least must be heard, but with regard to working or trading on these days, the custom of the area should be observed and this may vary from place to place.[167]

Amidst the variety of economic opinion prevalent in the later Middle Ages, Gerson's teaching does not stand out as particularly original or radical. Yet he is no conservative. He has moved well beyond the earlier medieval intense dislike of merchants and the view that 'in buying and selling it is almost impossible to avoid sin'.[168] There is still a trace of this older view in Aquinas,[169] but it is only a trace and it is balanced by some positive statements, for instance that 'buying and selling seem to be established for the common advantage of both parties'.[170] Gerson would agree. He has no eulogistic passages about merchants such as occur in Maillard, who in one sermon declares that merchants are indispensable to the state for importing and exporting, for wholesale and retail selling, and for manufacture.[171] Nevertheless Gerson's economic thought is respectably up-to-date.

The last manifestation of avarice that Gerson discusses is retaining possessions. One is perfectly entitled, he states, to keep all that one needs for oneself and one's family. This does not mean only the bare necessities, but also whatever is needed to maintain one's estate and dignity. However, if one retains superfluous things, there can be mortal sin, especially when one's desire to keep them is so ardent that one prefers that the goods rot or spoil in one's own possession rather than be put to good use elsewhere. But if the love of one's superfluous possessions is only slight, then the sin is only venial. If, however, one sees a poor man in dire necessity, that is in danger of death, and if no one else is coming to his aid, one is bound under pain of mortal sin to help him with one's superfluous goods and with the goods necessary for the upkeep of one's estate, though not with one's own bare necessities, 'car je me doy mieulx amer et ma vie qu'autrui'.[172]

We are here and in much of what Gerson says about avarice very far from the gospel counsels of perfect charity and poverty. For Gerson, saving (*thesaurizare*) is not illicit but provident.[173] Christ, on the other hand, counselled His disciples not to lay up treasure on earth for themselves (Matt. 6:19ff.), and told the rich young man to sell all he had and give to the poor (Mark 10:21). Christ told His disciples to love their neighbour as themselves, whereas Gerson says one should love oneself better than others. It is true that in the sermon an ideal is set forth: 'The true riches which you ought to seek are in God. There is our whole good.'[174] Moreover in many other sermons possessions and the things of this world are portrayed as vain. But when he gets down to the details, Gerson makes a large number of concessions to the economic needs and wants of people, lay and clerical, living in the world. You may make profit by trading, though other people's rights must be respected. You may hold more than one benefice. You do not have to give generously to the poor out of the goods necessary to keep up your estate in life, except to succour someone in peril of death from starvation. The standard of justice Gerson propounds is high, but the standard of charity seems fairly low. And he is constantly stressing the rights people have to the possessions necessary for their status. We are far from monastic communism and poverty.

Sloth

Sloth is in some ways the most interesting of the seven sins because it has changed its meaning considerably since it first appeared on the list in the early days of Christianity. It began as a psychological state: *acedia*, or the state of psychic exhaustion, restlessness, tedium, depression and spiritual lukewarmness described by Cassian and caused, as he suggests, by the rigours and difficulties of life endured by the monks in the Egyptian desert.[175] As the use of the seven sins began to be extended beyond the monastic milieu, *acedia* came to mean neglect of spiritual duties. In other words the faults for which *acedia* was responsible began to be stressed more than *acedia* itself; there was a shift from the state of mind itself to external behaviour. Wenzel argues that this shift 'undoubtedly' occurred for practical reasons because the confessor and his penitent, for whom the manuals, summas and sermons were written, would be more concerned with concrete faults than with abstract states of mind.[176] From neglect of spiritual duties *acedia* was then further extended to include neglect of secular duties and responsibilities, until it finally became plain laziness. Eventually the psychological aspect of *acedia* became known as melancholy and was no longer held to be sinful. But this latter development was largely after Gerson's time.

In Gerson's writings we find all three aspects of sloth. What we do not find is a clear analysis of the mechanism of this sin. More often Gerson, like Cassian, writes as if the depressed state of mind leads to the neglect of spiritual duties, but sometimes he sees the neglect of duties leading to anguish, sadness and melancholy.[177] In other words it is not clear where the vicious circle begins.

Gerson defines sloth (*paresse* in the French works; *acedia* in the Latin ones) as 'ennuy du bien spirituel' or 'taedium interni boni'.[178] In one of his tracts he produces an almost clinical description of the psychic disorder of depression. It is the languid dejection of men about the exercise of virtues. It has six daughters:

The first is called malice, the second despair, which is diffidence about one's merits; the third is faint-heartedness, arising from a feeling of one's frailty; fourth is spite or inveterate hatred, for from anger come *acedia* and from *acedia* long-lasting anger; fifth is sluggishness with regard to the commandments and a certain insensibility; sixth wandering of mind and restlessness of body.[179]

The despair, lack of confidence, anger and lack of concentration are all there. Gerson did not invent these symptoms. They are in Gregory and are frequently listed in the moral summas.[180] Is this state of mind itself a sin? It is certainly not a mortal sin, writes Gerson, because it is not contrary to charity but only to the fervour of charity. It may not even be a venial sin, because 'weariness of spiritual good works is natural, as nature flees work' and this natural motion is not within our control.[181] The feeling of tedium may come because of one's particular temperament, or because of bad habit, or because of temptation. In these cases there is no sin. It is only when we consent to the feeling that there is sin, and then only venial sin.

However, this *ennui* can lead to mortal sin, and here we move into the area of neglect of spiritual duties. If we neglect to do anything to which we are bound, for example fulfilling the commandments of God and the regulations of the church, then there is mortal sin. Also if one lets the *ennui* get hold of one to the extent that it makes one tired of life, despairing and suicidal, one has fallen into mortal sin.[182] Gerson has, in a number of his tracts on the topic, long lists of spiritual duties that it is sinful to neglect because of sloth: thanking God for His benefits in prayer in the morning and at night, doing our duty towards the dead, saving others from sin, fulfilling vows, attending properly when we are praying, hearing mass on feast-days, thinking of death and judgement, praying for our relations and benefactors, making complete confessions, mortifying vices, acquiring virtues, perfecting our status, always doing something good. One treatise ends, after a list of the things left undone: 'And briefly I have been remiss and lukewarm in the doing of all good.'[183] Fortunately in not all of the above cases is neglect a mortal sin. Gerson is at pains to point out in one of the sermons on sloth and in two of the tracts, one in the vernacular and the other in Latin, that it is only neglect of the commandments, neglect of the regulations of the church about hearing mass on Sundays and feast-days, and not fulfilling one's vows that involve mortal sin. In the sermon he once more points out that we are not bound always to do the best we can; we are not bound to fulfil the counsels, only the precepts: 'if it is not of a commandment, the negligence is not mortal sin'.[184] Moreover, as far as the commandments go, it is more serious to neglect spiritual duties than secular ones. Of course the commandments of God could be widely interpreted and Gerson does have fairly long lists of sins in his treatise on the commandments. But he also says that the commandments are not to be interpreted more strictly or widely than God intended.[185]

Gerson is again showing his non-rigorist side. We have already seen his concern for scrupulous consciences. This is apparent also in his treatment of the sin of sloth, when he takes up the question of not paying sufficient attention at mass, or when saying prayers that have been assigned as a penance, or when saying one's hours. It is not a mortal sin when one misses only small parts by not attending properly, or even if one misses a large part, provided that there is not deliberate consent to this distraction of mind. If this is the case then the prayer must be begun again. But sometimes, Gerson admits, the prayer cannot be said over again, for instance at mass. We do not need to be anxious. 'As long as we do not will with deliberation to hold to this wandering of mind, however great it is, our habitual intention about praying as we ought remains.'[186] And it is the intention that counts.

In the sermons Gerson speaks eloquently about sloth in spiritual activities. Sloth makes it difficult for a man to begin virtuous works. If such works are begun, sloth prevents perseverance. Sloth is always putting off good works till tomorrow, but tomorrow may be too late. Sloth strangles good works, turns a man away from working for his salvation and towards wasting his time in worldly pleasures, at the tavern, in gambling, dances, great dinners. Or it turns him towards laziness in general and so to poverty, the mother of theft, to anguish, melancholy, impatience, envy, murmuring against God, langorous sadness, *ennui* with his estate and life, despair, which prevents virtuous works, and so to hell.[187]

It is also in one of the sermons that Gerson discusses the third aspect of sloth; neglect of worldly duties. In the tracts he seems generally to ignore this aspect. It is mentioned only in *Le Doctrinal aux simples gens*. Gerson makes it clear in the sermon that he is addressing the bourgeoisie. Whether his congregation on this occasion was largely made up of members of this class is difficult to tell.[188] At any rate he has some words to say to the working classes also.

The discussion of sloth in worldly duties and responsibilities occurs in the less rhetorical part of the sermon. It is not an exhaustive discussion, but merely a series of questions and answers, and unfortunately often in notes whose meaning remains obscure. First Gerson takes up the question of sleep. Seven or eight hours is enough, he argues. Sleeping longer than that may mean that good actions that could be done remain undone. Lying in bed and not sleeping can lead to evils, bad thoughts and the like. It is best for the bourgeois to get up in the morning, he concludes. Should a member of the bourgeoisie work, when he has enough wealth from other sources to live on? It depends, says Gerson. If he or she does not work in order to serve God more, this is all right. If the aim is enjoyment of the delights of the world, this too is all right, but not as a regular habit. If the bourgeois does not work for health reasons or because he knows no craft, there is no sin. But, Gerson points out, leisure can often lead to sin and so all young people should be taught a craft. And there is always the problem of poverty in old age if the bourgeois does not work. One ought, in fact, to acquire for the sake of one's children. It is more honourable, Gerson concludes, for a bourgeois to work than not to work. His next question concerns begging. Ought an able-bodied person to beg? As far as the bourgeoisie is concerned, only if it is for a good end is begging permissible; otherwise it is theft of alms that should go to the genuine poor. The sort of good end that Gerson has in mind is the showing of humility and the better service of God, possible when one is free of worldly cares. He now moves on to people who work in another's employment. If a labourer does not work as hard as he can, does he sin? The worker need work only as hard as is expected by common custom and equity, Gerson replies. If he works less than this, even for a good end, for example for the purpose of prayer, then his devotion is without discretion and he sins if he does not have the permission of his master. In this sermon on sloth Gerson also discusses the question of working too hard and the evil results of this. Over-work can lead to undesired laziness afterwards or to ill-health. Children and workers ought not to be pushed too hard, nor ought a merchant to be always thinking of his trade and profits. Too much anxiety about one's livelihood and hence too much work may be sinful, if it is caused by despair of God's providence. On the other hand, if the work is largely for prudence and the public good, then there is no sin.[189] One does not, then, have to be as 'careless' as the birds of the air or the lilies of the field.

Wenzel states that Gerson's treatment of this third aspect of sloth is the most progressive he knows in theological literature up to the fifteenth century. By 'progressive' he means moving towards the concept of sloth as plain laziness.[190] It is not that other theological writers and preachers don't castigate laziness in worldly duties. They do. Jacques de Vitry in the thirteenth century tells vineyard and other workers that they must work hard and not try to get away with doing six denarii's worth of work for their pay of twelve denarii,[191] while Antoninus in the fifteenth century complains about Florentine nobles who, to avoid work, deposit money with bankers and collect an annual return on their capital in the form of a 'free gift'.[192] And there are countless complaints about officials of all sorts who neglect the duties of their office. These criticisms, however, do not occur in connection with the sin of sloth.[193] In Gerson's case they do, in the two sermons under discussion. But, as we have seen, the chancellor has by no means left behind the two earlier concepts of *acedia*. In fact, overall he stresses these more than he does neglect of worldly work.

As a remedy against the psychological state of *acedia* Gerson suggests, as many had done before him, work and variety of work. One should also consider, he suggests, the evil of wasting time and losing salvation.[194] In one of the sermons he discusses three goads against sloth in general: honour, because God commands us to work, and to serve Him is an honour; reward, that is the feeling of sweetness (*douceur*) that accompanies good works, both religious and worldly; and fear, that is fear of hell, for we must remember that many are called but few are chosen.

In his moral teaching about the sin of sloth Gerson has, as one would expect, got beyond the monastic milieu. He is concerned for people living in the world, and the standard he sets is not too high. The ideal of always doing good and always working for God and one's salvation is there. At the same time Gerson recognises that depression and *ennui* are natural feelings, and he limits the number and type of spiritual tasks that must not be neglected on pain of mortal sin. Further he leaves room for the tasks of this world, and here his ideal seems to be a healthy moderation – neither too little work, nor too much. Work in the world is a good in itself and can be a cure for *acedia*, but one does not need to work harder than the 'union rules' ordain, nor should one work and be anxious beyond the needs of prudence. In one of the sermons Gerson raises the question about which estate is better, that of those working corporally or that of those who are occupied with the service of God directly. Unfortunately he does not answer it, but we know from elsewhere that Gerson does not exalt the monastic estate above all others and that he sees perfection as possible in all estates. One may imagine that, when he answered the question as he preached the sermon, he did not downgrade the active life of the bourgeoisie and others of the world's workers.

Gluttony

The last two sins on the list, gluttony and lust, are clearly sins of the flesh and not of the soul, though in both cases sin can occur without any outward actions. However, the sinful gluttonous or lustful desires which occur are for the satisfaction of bodily appetites, whereas this is not the case with the other sins. Considered under one of its aspects sloth's desire for sleep and bodily ease might be viewed as a sin of the flesh, and some later medieval writers did indeed view sloth in this way.[195] Gerson himself would seem to regard sloth as both a spiritual and a carnal sin.[196] Gluttony is undoubtedly a carnal sin for Gerson, and for everyone else.

He uses the traditional definition of gluttony as the immoderate or disordered desire for food and drink.[197] 'Immoderate' or 'disordered', he says, means 'more than necessity demands'.[198] *Per se* gluttony is not a mortal sin. It can even be no sin at all if the desire comes solely from nature, for men naturally desire to eat and drink when they are hungry or thirsty, and even the pleasure that comes from eating and drinking is not sinful, for it is not within our power not to take pleasure in eating and drinking. If, added to the natural desire for food and drink there is a voluntary desire and a voluntary pleasure in the delights of eating, then one has moved into the realm of sin, but only venial sin. The message here is that ideally one should not eat beyond what the body needs for sustenance, and that one should not encourage the delight one gets from eating and drinking.[199] One of the ways to discourage this delight is to read a religious book while eating. 'So ought a person when his body eats, turn Dame Reason to the loftier table of spiritual meat.'[200]

Gluttony can become a mortal sin if the pleasure in eating is so great that one puts it before the love of God and so is led to break the commandments of God and the church. The most obvious rules broken by gluttony are those of fasting and abstinence. But not everyone is bound by these rules. If fasting is harmful to one's health, for instance, then it should not be undertaken. In some of the tracts and in one of the sermons on pride, Gerson lists those who are exempt from fasting: the old, the young (under age eleven), the sick, pregnant and nursing mothers, poor beggars, those who are travelling by necessity, and 'workers who cannot make a livelihood if they do not work'.[201] Further, those who have a legitimate reason for not fasting, even if this reason is not expressly stated in the laws, may exempt themselves, though it would be safer to get an official dispensation. Thus a person who becomes physically ill or mentally disturbed because of fasting need not fast. Gerson often points out the dangers of immoderate fasting: 'Sometimes in order to avoid gluttony one can fall into the opposite vice of too great and foolish abstinence, which leads to frenzy and damages the brain so that an incurable disease results.'[202] He is a firm and vocal opponent of indiscriminate asceticism. Despite the fact that moderation in fasting had been advocated in the early days of the seven sins tradition, for example by Cassian, by no means all medieval writers and preachers are as careful as Gerson to couple their stress on the fasting rules with warnings against excessive abstinence from food.

It is not only the fasting rules that are often broken by gluttony. In one of the sermons Gerson see gluttony as capable of leading to the breaking, by sins of commission or omission, of every one of the ten commandments. The person who is a slave to gluttony cannot love God with his whole heart, for he is not the master of his heart. The glutton, and especially the drunkard, blasphemes and curses. And so Gerson goes on to describe how gluttony can lead to violence and homicide, theft, lying and especially to lust in all its forms.²⁰³ It is, of course, drunkenness rather than over-eating that is responsible for the worst of these crimes. Drunkenness, *per se*, however, is not a mortal sin. One could become drunk by accident. In this case the sin would be venial only. But if one knows that inebriation leads one to other sins, then it is a mortal sin knowingly to get drunk.²⁰⁴

Apart from leading to sins against the commandments and to the neglect of spiritual duties, gluttony can have other evil effects. It can cause one to be ill in body or mind. It can cause one to be somnolent so that one does not do those temporal things one ought to do, such as studying, manual labour or whatever one does to gain a livelihood. In all these cases there is sin, as there is if one reduces oneself and one's family to poverty by spending too much on food and drink.²⁰⁵ What counts as over-spending on food and drink depends, of course, on one's status and wealth. Clerics ought to be particularly careful in this regard because the money they spend has come from what could be said to be the alms of their subjects. Moreover, they ought to set a good example to others and help the indigent. Craftsmen with wives and families should not spend too much on food and drink.²⁰⁶ The upper classes, presumably, may be more self-indulgent.

The sermon at this point has become rather disorganised as Gerson poses a series of what seem rather haphazardly chosen questions. Is vomiting from over-eating a sin? Yes and no, Gerson replies; it depends on the manner of the eating, but it had better be confessed. Is swallowing on Friday morning the meat that became stuck between one's teeth on Thursday evening a sin? It is not. Is getting another person drunk a sin? It is if it is for a bad end, for example to make him sin, or to deceive him or to learn his secrets. Does a drunken woman who is raped sin mortally? She sins in so far as deliberate drunkenness is evil; if she could foresee the possible consequences of her inebriation, then she is additionally blameworthy. And so the sermon goes on with questions about boasting of one's capacity for eating and drinking, overfeeding servants, eating unnatural foods, giving young children wine to drink, eating food known to be stolen, stealing bread if one is starving, the permissible quantity and types of sauces, the number of permissible meals per day, the methods of killing animals for eating and so on. It seems a strange collection of trivial and important questions, no doubt partly reflecting Gerson's experience in the confessional but certainly his learning and reading in the schools.²⁰⁷ But it does seem to point to a system that has become over-concerned with sins and branches of sins, despite the fact that in every case Gerson gives what seems to be the most sensible answer. In many cases he is simply telling his congregations not to be over-scrupulous. However, the fact that he has to deal with such questions is an indication of what was happening to the confessional system.

Gluttony, then, for Gerson is a carnal sin that has a bad effect not only on the body but also on the soul. Its worst aspect is that it leads to other sins. But it is bad in itself – a venial sin – and this is because it shows that reason and will are not in control. The carnal appetites that should be submissive to reason and will have gained control whenever one eats or drinks immoderately, that is, beyond necessity, or whenever one has the desire to eat and drink immoderately or takes immoderate pleasure in so doing: 'c'est une bestialité sote at sans frain, et une servitude tres dure et vile'.[208] By contrast, man should be free, that is, his will should be free to do good, to follow right reason. This traditional view of the proper relationship between the carnal appetites and the other faculties reappears in Gerson's treatment of the last of the seven sins, the sin of lust.

Lust

Discussions of lust occur in a large number of Gerson's vernacular sermons. Seven out of the seventeen *Poenitemini* sermons are devoted to this sin and its opposing virtue, chastity, but, like pride and unlike the other sins, it also appears in a number of other sermons.[209] As far as the confessional tracts are concerned, lust is given roughly the same coverage as the other sins. But Gerson's tone when he discusses this sin is rougher than the tone he uses when writing about the other sins. He seems to reserve his strongest language for the sins of the flesh, and those who commit them receive harsh treatment and little sympathy from him. His attitude is almost Manichean. The genitals are always referred to as the *membres honteux (membra pudenda)*. Sexual functions are *turpia*. The pleasure that accompanies sexual activity is *ceste ville delectation*. Lust is hideous and abominable; her name is 'the sewer... you do not see a pig so covered in dung as she. Looking at her my hair stands on end and I shudder.'[210] On account of this sin the flood came and Sodom and Gomorrah were burned with a celestial fire and their inhabitants descended into hell alive. And by this sin which cries to heaven for vengeance come famines, wars, plagues, betrayals of kings and kingdoms and other disasters, as Scripture witnesses.[211] Sexual sins clearly form one of the most basic moral issues for Gerson and he certainly feels strongly about them. He was not alone in this attitude. The medieval church, from the time of the Fathers onwards, was very concerned – even inordinately concerned – with sexual sins, and some other late medieval moralists are as repelled as Gerson is by sins of lust and as harsh in their attitude, though for none of them is lust by any means the only grave sin.[212] A few writers state that lust is the worst of all sins. The author of the *Astesana*, a fourteenth-century confessional summa, for example, argues that gluttony and lust are the worst vices because they reduce men to the level of beasts, while the fifteenth-century *Eruditorium penitentiale* states that fornication is more detestable than homicide or plunder because one may, with justification, kill or steal in cases of necessity, but there can be no such justification for fornication.[213] The author of *Handlyng Synne* says lust is the sin 'farthest from heaven',[214] and an anonymous fifteenth-century English sermon calls it the 'moste stynkynge synne before God'.[215] These opinions are, however, exceptional, for most theologians follow Gregory and say that the sins of the flesh are less grave than the spiritual sins.[216] Nowhere does Gerson state that a particular sin of lust is the worst sin of all, but he comes close to leaving that impression, probably because, whatever his reason told him, his emotions were more strongly against sins of lust than against any other sins.

His feelings may have been further aroused because there seems to have been a fair amount of opposition on the part of the laity to the teaching that fornication is a mortal sin. In a number of places Gerson refers to people who say that fornication is not a sin at all or at least only a little one. They argue that it is impossible to live chastely, at least in youth, and that if God disapproved of sexual relationships he would not have created the sexes as they are. Fornication *is* an abominable mortal sin, Gerson replies; you *can* live chastely, for God never demands the impossible, and the sexual organs were ordained for the procreation of children in marriage.[217]

But to start with fornication is to come in in the middle of the story. There are many mortal sins before this state of affairs is reached, before even any action at all is taken. As with the other sins, the first branch of the tree of lust has hanging from it the sins of consent in thought. Medieval definitions of lust itself, unlike those of the other sins, which tend to be standardised, vary, though they are variations on the same theme. Simon of Hinton defines lust as 'incontinence of body'; Aquinas says that lust 'consists essentially in exceeding the order and mode of reason with regard to venereal acts'; while Antoninus says that it is 'an inordinate appetite for things venereal'.[218] Gerson defines it as 'an abuse or desire to abuse the shameful organs ordained for generation'.[219] It is a mortal sin *ex genere suo* whereas gluttony, which is an abuse of the nutritive faculty, is *per se* only a venial sin. This is because the generative faculty is less necessary than the nutritive. Moreover, lust is a sin against the seventh commandment, and the sexual act needs to be excused by the goods of marriage.[220] This means that any deliberate desire for lustful actions will be a mortal sin. Actually in the case of lustful desire the situation is complicated by the fact that the desire tends to be accompanied by pleasurable somatic sensations. So Gerson frequently writes about the consent to present pleasure caused by the desire for some forbidden sexual pleasure. The rule about unbidden thoughts and feelings applies or almost applies. In *Le Doctrinal aux simples gens* Gerson states, in connection with the ninth commandment, that if the thought comes to you and you neither consent nor delight in it, but rather dislike it and try to banish it, then there is no sin.[221] In one of the sermons he says that this first movement is no sin,[222] but elsewhere he says that it *is* venial sin.[223]

From this point on things become complex. If there is consent to thoughts about sexual actions which are forbidden to you and which you would perform if you got the chance, or if there is consent to the present pleasure you have by thinking about sexual sins, whether you would perform them or not, then you have committed a mortal sin of lust. But in between these cases and the case of unbidden feelings there is a very shady area. The possibilities for sins of hidden lust seem manifold. Gerson in some cases just mentions them, but in other places – including one of the sermons – he tries to work out the status of some of these sins. On the whole, given his premises, he seems to be more concerned with quieting the over-scrupulous than with proliferating mortal sins. For instance, if you give in to an unbidden feeling for a while but then your reason starts to battle with it, although there was a venial sin to begin with, once the battle commences you could be earning merit. And this would be true even if the battle goes on all day and all night, and even if nocturnal pollution occurs, provided, of course, that reason resists the pleasure of this pollution. If the pleasant thoughts are about sexual actions that are not mortal sins, for example if a woman desires her husband, then there is no mortal sin. If a person takes pleasure from thinking of a delight which is in itself only a venial sin, then the consent to the thought and the pleasure felt are only a venial sin. A fourth case occurs if one thinks of the sins of the flesh only to prepare oneself for confession, or to avoid them, or to say that if they were not against God's commandment one would commit them. Here, Gerson says, there is often no sin at all or it is only venial, but one had better be careful with such thoughts, for they may arouse one and so lead to a mortal sin. Desire for an incestuous relationship is a mortal sin, but it is not a reserved sin, so confession to one's pastor is enough to repair the damage. Presumably the same would apply to all the other reserved sexual sins, that is, whereas the action would be a reserved sin, the desire would not. One can lose one's virginity by thought alone, but it can be restored by confession and absolution. You ought to confess if you have had this *orde plaisance* in sleeping or had sexual dreams, because there may be a sin involved. It depends on what caused the dreams – gluttony, bad thoughts, temptation of the devil, disordered behaviour or too much fasting.[224] There is a certain vagueness about all this. Gerson admits as much, and obviously a lot must be left to the knowledge and skill of the individual confessor. Gerson's hearers would know that they ought to resist all lustful feelings and banish thoughts about sex. But beyond this, scrupulous persons might well be in doubt about whether they had committed a mortal sin or only a venial one. Gerson's advice seems to be that if you are in doubt you should confess.

One must never, says Gerson, nourish 'this bad carnal will' through any of the five senses.[225] Anything at all that is seen, listened to, said or done to arouse sexual feelings in oneself is sinful, mortally sinful he says in *Le Profit*. Under this heading falls a comprehensive variety of activity: looking at obscene pictures and reading obscene books; looking at a beautiful woman, though this can be done without sin, Gerson says, if the intention is not self-arousal; watching or taking part in dances; listening to or taking part in lewd conversation; hearing or singing lewd songs. Drinking too much and too strong wine and seeking dissolute company for the purpose of self-arousal are sins, and so is looking at oneself naked, though to appear naked before a doctor for medical examination is permitted. Talking about the genitals and sexual activity should be avoided, though scholars seeking truth may discuss such things.

Anything done to arouse or tempt others to illicit sexual behaviour is sinful, for example enhancing one's beauty, using perfume, dressing in a disordered manner. Also forbidden are dissolute glances and signs, love-letters, messages, promises, lies, flattery and gifts that have this purpose in view. Kissing is a dangerous activity too, though in some circumstances no sin is involved, for example when spouses or relatives kiss, or when people exchange the kiss of peace in church. Just as disordered kissing is a sin, so are lustful caresses. 'Every touching of the hands or other things which is done to move oneself to achieve carnal pleasure is forbidden outside marriage; and in marriage care must be taken to guard "honnestete."'[226] The general teaching here is clearer than it was about lustful thoughts. If the aim is sexual arousal, there is sin. And Gerson gives his hearers and readers a good idea of the sort of things that, begun innocently enough, might lead them to have and entertain a sinful intention. There is, however, a disturbing vagueness about what sort of kisses and caresses are sinless within marriage that must have bothered the more scrupulous of the married in his audience.

The question of the sins of lust that involve emission is easily answered. They are all mortal, though some are more serious than others. Nevertheless, Gerson does find some problems about these sins and he discusses them in one of the sermons; so presumably he thought that they were relevant to his congregation. One can imagine parishioners or fellow priests asking some of the questions. The least grave of these mortal sins is fornication, that is, sexual relations between a man and a woman unmarried and not related in any way to each other. The questions that arise over this sin are largely concerned with prostitutes and the keeping of concubines. Prostitutes, Gerson argues, are not in a state of salvation and ought not to be given the sacraments, though the church may receive their offerings, provided they were not acquired by theft. Should they be allowed to ply their trade? Yes, Gerson answers, lest worse befall. A man who has a concubine may 'have repentance' provided he has the intention of getting rid of her as soon as he can.[227] To the question of whether it is worse to go from one mistress to another or to keep to one, Gerson answers that in evil there can be no good. Another question that arises is whether a man who has sexual relations with a prostitute who, unbeknownst to him, is married, or a religious, or related to him, sins as much as if he knew the facts. The problem here is that adultery, sacrilege and incest were reserved sins. Gerson's answer is that the man ought to find out what the facts are and that he should confess his sin as if it were a reserved case. A confirmed *concubinaire* should not be given the Eucharist if the case is notorious, but if secrecy has been preserved the priest should give him the sacrament if he asks for it in public, though Gerson makes it clear that such a man, or indeed anyone who does not have the intention of living chastely, could not receive absolution even if he went to confession and were sorry for his sins.

Adultery is a graver mortal sin than fornication, because it involves theft. If it is publicly known it is a reserved case. Almost all the questions under this heading are, strangely enough, about sexual relations within marriage and will be dealt with later. One relevant point that Gerson does make is that he thinks it better for the injured spouse, in the case of adultery, to try to get the other to amend rather than to force the guilty party to leave home.

Sacrilege, that is, sexual relations that involve religious persons or which take place in consecrated places, is next on the list. However, Gerson thinks that a cleric or any person who has taken a vow of chastity, although he sins gravely, does not strictly break his vow by his fornication. This additional sin occurs only if he marries. To the question of whether a fornicating priest sins more than an adulterous husband Gerson replies that they are both guilty. The only way of judging between them would be to assess the effects of their sin. A priest who seduces a penitent ought to be deposed, and any penitent to whom this happens, or indeed who has any advances made to her by a confessor, ought to report the matter to the proper authorities. A priest who celebrates mass after having had sexual relations and before he confesses commits an extra and serious sin, unless there is evident necessity for him to celebrate, for example, if it were Easter Sunday and no other priest were available. This opinion must have put the priest with a concubine on the spot. It is interesting that Gerson, with his view that clerics ought not to be criticised in sermons to the laity, should discuss this at all here, but no doubt the fact that parish priests often kept concubines was no secret.

The fourth branch of this type of lust is rape and the defloration of virgins. This, says Gerson, is a very great mortal sin; it is a reserved case, and if it is publicly known it is a criminal case. Restitution and satisfaction must be rendered by the rapist. If the girl is under age, even if she is willing, the act counts as rape, if it is against the will of the parents. The raped girl loses nothing in the sight of God, but if the rape is public knowledge she ought not to be allowed to become a nun. A woman may, indeed should, defend her chastity as if she were defending her life, and more, adds Gerson. If a girl pretends she is a virgin, the assailant sins as much as if she were one.[228]

Incest is a bestial sin, for it reduces men to the level of animals, some of which copulate within the family. It is a reserved case, whether the incest is between those with a spiritual relationship, or those with a physical relationship up to the fourth degree, and it is worse the nearer the consanguinity.[229]

The last branch of lust is the sin against nature, and this sin has various sub-branches. Here an awesome silence descends. In none of the vernacular works does Gerson spell out exactly what he means. Usually he just says this is the 'abominable ordure qui ne fait a nommer', [230] or words to that effect. He gives some hints:

Every accomplishment of lust, that is to say when the pleasure is continued to the end, if it is outside the ordinance which nature has ordained between men and women for procreation, is a sin against nature. And among these filthy sins, some are more grave than others.[231]

But what the unnatural ways were and what their order of gravity was this particular congregation did not discover. Those who heard the first sermon on pride were enlightened a little further. Gerson is listing the sins that are reserved and among them is the sin against nature 'either by oneself alone, or with another of the same sex, or outside the place ordained by nature'.[232] In *Mansionem* he mentions, without any comment at all, the sins 'too filthy and abominable to be named' committed by a person (in this case a woman) alone in bed.[233] That is as far as Gerson goes in the sermons. He does not believe in being indiscreet in public. But one cannot but believe that he might have aroused some uneasiness among those who were not sure exactly what he was talking about. He is not much more explicit in the vernacular tracts. All he does here is to add to his usual list of these sins against nature a fourth: 'with another creature that is not a human person'.[234] He refuses to go any further, arguing that whoever is guilty of these sins will know what he is talking about, and he does not want to assail innocent ears.[235] The point is that he thinks these things, together with those which are 'contre l'onnestete qui appartient a mariage', are better left to be dealt with in the confessional.[236] No doubt he was right, but the 'innocent ears' could well have been tantalised or made anxious, because it is not at all clear what actions he regards as being outside 'nature's ordinance'. 'Outside the place ordained by nature' or 'outside the part of the body ordained by nature', as he sometimes puts it, is probably clear enough, but what does Gerson mean by the following, which appears in a vernacular tract?

Here as much in marriage as outside it are forbidden all types of lustful contacts in which one does not abide by the ordinance and the manner and the organs which nature wills and requires or allows for procreation.[237]

It sounds pretty comprehensive. He is clearly, along with all moralists of the period, forbidding *coitus non in debito vase*, emission outside the proper orifice.[238] But what exactly does he mean by 'manner'? Is he referring to unnatural positions in copulation, that is positions other than the 'proper' position, which was, according to the summas, many of which spell it out, with the woman beneath the man? There was controversy among the authorities about whether and why improper position was sinful. Some, because the proper position was held to be the most apt for procreation, regarded improper position as a contraceptive practice and therefore mortally sinful. Others were more concerned that unnatural position might be used to increase pleasure. This too might involve mortal sin. However, some writers regarded unnatural positions as not *per se* sinful at all, because they could be used by spouses for a rational cause, in late pregnancy, for example, to prevent harm to the foetus.[239] Gerson does not anywhere discuss improper manner, *indebitus modus*, specifically. It is not completely clear that this is what he has in mind in the passage from the vernacular *Miroir*.[240] And in the Latin *Regulae mandatorum*, in the two places where one might have expected it, it is not mentioned. It does not occur in the list of the sins against nature ('bestiality, with brutes; sodomy with the same sex or not in the proper orifice; masturbation with oneself') or among the mortal sins that can occur in marital coitus.[241]

Had Gerson written a *summa confessorum* we would no doubt be better informed about his views on improper positions. From the evidence available it seems probable that he did not regard *indebitus modus* as *per se* a sin against nature, and perhaps not even as a mortal sin *per se*. If this is the case then he stands with the more lenient of the late medieval moralists. But the general criticism remains. His vagueness about sexual sins against nature, in *Le Miroir* and in his other works intended for the laity, including his sermons, could have awkward consequences. For actions which Gerson considered innocent or only venial sins might appear to the hearer or reader to be included among the dreadful sins against nature, those most horrible sins that cry to heaven for vengeance, at which even devils grow pale and of which it is almost too shameful to speak. One hopes that confessors were well instructed.

It has been suggested that Gerson played an important role in starting a new trend of severity against the sin of masturbation.[242] It is true that he wrote a treatise specifically on the topic, but the treatise is extant in only four manuscripts.[243] In any case Gerson's concern in this treatise is not to lay any new stress on the severity of the sin, but to guide confessors in getting children to confess that they had committed it. He does say that it is a very grave sin, a sin against nature, but so do the other authorities from at least the thirteenth century onwards. Gerson draws the line between the ordinary, though still dreadful, sins of lust, on the one hand, and sins against nature, on the other, at exactly the same place as everyone else. Any sexual act where emission could not lead to insemination is a sin against nature.[244] This is why masturbation is worse than incest or adultery.

Gerson lays no particular stress on masturbation. What he does emphasise is concern for the souls of children. It was this concern that prompted him to write *De confessione mollitiei*.

In his overall teaching under the heading of lust what Gerson is demanding is total abstinence from any form of sexual desire or activity outside marriage. This doctrine, coupled with the attitude of horror that Gerson displays in the vernacular works, does seem to be monastic in both base and superstructure, with few concessions made to those living in the world.

Gerson was, however, only preaching the traditional doctrine, and the ideal of sexual behaviour remained high long after his time. We cannot accuse him of being unusually severe in his moral teaching about sex. We might be tempted to reproach him for his vagueness in certain areas, but again other medieval preachers encountered the same difficulties and coped with them no more satisfactorily than Gerson did. John Mirk in the early fifteenth century in his *Instructions for Parish Priests* says that priests should teach nothing in their sermons about the sin against nature, but merely state that it is a great sin.[245] This is what most preachers and authors of vernacular manuals do,[246] unless they say nothing at all. Perhaps to say nothing would be better, but then the preacher would be failing in his duty to inform the consciences of his congregation. Gerson is more explicit than most preachers of his time, but whether he was explicit enough is another question.

FIFTEENTH-CENTURY SIN AND SINNERS

The scheme of the seven capital sins, being a traditional one, must have directed Gerson's moral teaching to some extent at least, despite the fact that he freely chose to use that scheme far more than any of the others available to him. When he is using the scheme of the heart and the five senses, lust gets most attention, and he again reserves his greatest horror for this sin.[247] The ten commandments, used by Gerson as a framework on only two occasions in the vernacular works,[248] allow or lead him to lay more stress than does the scheme of the seven sins on idolatry, sorcery, false swearing and obedience to one's superiors. The emphasis on lust is still strong, but pride, though still there, seems less prominent when it is not treated as a separate sin, while gluttony disappears altogether. These two other schemes do not seem to enable Gerson to reproduce quite the same emphasis that he has when he is working without any scheme at all, that is an emphasis on pride, lust and worldliness. The scheme of the seven sins does enable him to do so. This is no doubt why he chose it. He has a 'seven-sins mind-set'.

This mind-set is not, however, a mental block. Gerson could escape from it, and he did especially when he wanted to castigate what he saw as particular evils of his day. One such evil was blasphemy. Blasphemy could be and often was treated under the sin of pride. Gerson sometimes mentions it there, but more often he preaches about it as a separate sin, and he wrote two vernacular treatises on it.[249] Gerson acknowledges that blasphemy which comes unbidden to one's lips in a fit of anger or because of bad habit or the disposition of the body is not a mortal sin. Nevertheless he wants to root it out, and he uses strong and emotional language about it. Blasphemy is the language of the devil and the damned, he writes. This detestable sin arouses the anger and punishment of God, and so is the cause of the pestilences, war and famines afflicting Christendom and especially France.[250] Gerson thinks blasphemy more prevalent in his day than it was formerly, and what he wants is an all-out effort by the ecclesiastical and secular authorities and heads of households to eradicate it. He wants the existing laws against blasphemy to be fully executed or new ones promulgated. He thinks that because this diabolical sin is so widespread and so deep-rooted it might be better for the moment to legislate and inflict light penalties so that no one guilty of it, whatever his condition or estate, is spared. This was probably a good idea. The existing punishments were lip-slitting and cutting out of tongues, punishments which were not very often enforced.[251] Gerson also advocates a widespread propaganda effort utilising the pulpit, public notices and processions, to inform people that blasphemy is a horrible sin. The trouble clearly was that people were taking the whole business of blasphemy and swearing by God, the Virgin, the saints and the gospels far too lightly.

Gerson's concern was shared by some of his contemporaries. D'Ailly has strong words to say against such swearing in one of his sermons,[252] and there were five royal edicts against the practice in Gerson's lifetime.[253] Later in the century Maillard thundered against swearing 'by the eyes of God' and 'by the belly of God' – 'dismembering God', as some English preachers called it. Maillard suggested that people change the initial consonant and say 'bieu' instead of 'Dieu'.[254]

A second group of sins that Gerson preaches about very frequently, and outside of the scheme of the seven sins, is sorcery and all manner of superstitions.[255] He leaves no doubt in the minds of his hearers that those who practise sorcery or consult sorcerers are engaged not only in a useless activity but also in a dangerous and sinful activity. In fact such persons are excommunicated from the church and subject to burning under the law.[256] Moreover, it is not only ordinary people who consult sorcerers but great seigneurs and nobles as well.[257] Among the superstitions mentioned in the sermons are belief in fortune-tellers, in the magical properties of charms, in magical cures for illness, in the magical powers of certain strange words either said or written down and carried about, and superstitious belief in astrology.[258] Generally it is sorcery that is described and superstition is associated loosely with it. The reason that Gerson associates superstition and sorcery is that he thinks any means used to produce an effect which cannot be expected from God working miraculously or from natural causes is to be suspected of involving an implicit or explicit pact with the devil.[259] In his later years Gerson wrote a series of Latin tracts against various sorts of sorcery, superstition and magic, including astrology, superstitious beliefs about the mass, about lucky and unlucky days, about unlucky cawing crows, mewing cats, crowing cocks, black dogs and snakes and about pacts with the devil. Gerson's concern with sorcery and superstition reflects the spread of the practice of sorcery. Superstition, sorcery and occultism had long been cultivated but they became more pervasive in the late Middle Ages, and by the fifteenth century witch-hunts had begun. Gerson was not the only one concerned. Courtecuisse castigates such beliefs and practices,[260] and at least four other Parisian university theologians wrote treatises in the first quarter of the fifteenth century against superstition and sorcery.[261] In England at the same period at least one preacher was blaming reliance on sorcery and witchcraft as the cause of current national misfortunes.[262] In Paris itself, in a move which Gerson as chancellor could well have spearheaded, the faculty of theology adopted twenty articles against sorcery and superstition.[263] Not that this solved the problem. Maillard at the end of the century still felt it incumbent on him to preach at length against them and their practitioners.[264]

If blasphemy and sorcery are the eighth and ninth capital sins, flattery and curiosity are the last two. It is almost exclusively in his sermons to the court, as one would expect, that Gerson condemns flattery.[265] It was a notorious practice of late medieval courtiers and their clients who wanted favours from the crown, and was no doubt particularly rife in the unfortunate reign of Charles VI. Gerson also wrote, in 1409, a vernacular tract against the practices.[266] When he is discussing flattery Gerson is not so much concerned with its damage to the soul of the flatterer as he is with its political and social effects. What he is doing in fact is repeating a cry that had echoed down the centuries – the cry for good counsel. If flatterers surround the king, Gerson exclaims, nothing can go well, for flattery is a lying traitor, the minstrel or enchantress of the devil, like the siren or the scorpion.[267] There is nothing a prince will not believe about himself if he is surrounded by flatterers. All the vain praise that flatterers bestow upon their lord make him judge that he is a marvel. In fact he is a poor miserable creature, subject to all afflictions and ultimately, like everyone else, meat for worms.[268] Gerson has a list of ancient kings who fell because they allowed themselves to be led astray by the bad advice of flatterers: Nebuchadnezzar, Alexander, Reaboam, Xerxes. And then there was Lucifer himself, who fell because of self-flattery and the vain praise of the bad angels, and Adam and Eve, who were led astray by the flattery of the devil, who told them that they could be like God.[269] Gerson's counter example is St Louis, who advised his son: 'Conduct yourself so that people dare tell the truth to you, so that they know they do not need to use dissimulation.'[270]

What particular political and social evils does Gerson see flattery in court circles causing in his day? One thing he has in mind is the encouragement given to sorcery and the magic arts by the king's courtiers.[271] But more often he speaks in more general terms and his basic complaint is that flatterers encourage the king to think that he can rule wilfully, that he can use his subjects and their possessions as he wills without regard to public necessity and the common good.[272] All flatterers should be banished from princely courts, he says, and good counsellors installed. A good counsellor for Gerson is one who fears God and his conscience, who puts the common good before his own and who speaks the truth fearlessly.[273]

Vain curiosity is another sin that Gerson sees as besetting the France of his day. He sometimes refers to it as an aspect of pride, but he more frequently discusses it as a sin in its own right.[274] Most often these discussions occur in doctrinal sermons. One of the dangers of curiosity, according to Gerson, is that it can easily lead to heresy and unbelief about the Eucharist, for instance, or the Trinity or the Incarnation. 'Non plus sapere quam oportet' is his catchphrase.[275] In fact he goes so far in one place as to state that the desire for knowledge is an evil hunger.[276] But he is not as anti-intellectualist as he sounds. What he has in mind, as he elsewhere makes clear, is not all desire for knowledge, but the desire to know by reason what we cannot know in this life, and in fact do not need to know. In this life we must just believe, as children at first must just believe what their teachers tell them. After all there are many natural occurrences that we do not understand: how snow and ice are formed, what causes waves, thunder and wind, how an egg turns into an ostrich or a peacock, how swallows know how to build nests, how a magnet attracts iron.[277] How then can we expect to understand the supernatural Trinity? We do not know how the natural digestive process works, how what we eat becomes bones, flesh and blood, so it is not surprising if we cannot understand the supernatural mutation that takes place in the Eucharist.[278] God would be too little if we could understand everything about him.

No doubt Gerson's strong feelings about vain and proud curiosity had their roots in his experience as a university teacher. He saw what he regarded as vain speculation occupying too much of the students' attention and diverting them from more fruitful pursuits. But the fact that he refers to this sin in a number of the vernacular sermons suggests that some of the laity too were afflicted with a lively curiosity that Gerson found baleful. Their curiosity was not only about the great mysteries, if one is to take it that some of the 'curious' questions Gerson raises in his sermons were questions that intrigued the laity: Why does the New Testament speak of Jesus' brothers when His mother was a virgin? Why does God let men sin?

Why are there no miracles now? In what language did the devil tempt Jesus? Why did the Jews think that the Apostles were drunk when they spoke in many tongues? There must be well over a hundred such questions in the sermons. Some of them Gerson tries to answer. Others he dismisses, not necessarily as stupid questions but as questions which his congregations would do better to ignore. Rather, they should concentrate on acquiring a devout love of God, for often, he says, an unlearned person who is devout and loves God has a truer knowledge of the Divinity than many a philosopher.[279] Gerson no doubt believed with Aristotle that 'All men by nature desire to know', but for the chancellor the desire should definitely be curbed.

Of these last four sins, only flattery applies to one specific social group – courtiers of the king and princes. Gerson sees blasphemy, sorcery and curiosity prevalent in all classes. He does not, of course, tend to write in terms of social classes. He thinks in terms of états, either the traditional three estates of the realm, or specific états which usually have some religious connection: parish priests, religious, the married, virgins, for example. From time to time, as we have seen, he mentions particular secular occupations and the sins he associates with them. Trading is one obvious example. Merchants and others engaged in trade and in financial and industrial activities he, like all moralists of the time, regards as especially prone to the sins associated with avarice. The same applies to lawyers, notaries and judges. In his writings on magic, superstition and astrology Gerson criticises medical doctors who make use of superstitious curing devices such as talismans.[280] University teachers and students are, in Gerson's opinion, too given to vain speculation. Tavern-keepers are singled out in one place. They sin by allowing gambling, blasphemy and procuring on their premises and by defrauding customers by mixing water with their wine. Hotel-keepers are also warned not to give accommodation to bad men, not to allow fornication in their establishments and not to charge unjust prices. In the same work soldiers are told not to strike non-combatants, to be content with their pay and to use their swords only to defend the motherland.[281] Prostitutes, apothecaries, farmers, artisans, schoolmasters and wet-nurses also occasionally pass through Gerson's pages. So one gets some glimpses of the varied society of the time, as one does from other sermon collections, and from some confessional manuals and summas.[282] But when he is analysing society as a whole Gerson does so in traditional terms.

For Gerson, as for Aristotle, man is a social animal.[283] He lives in polities and 'a polity is a society of mortal men ordained so that they can, by means of good rule and obedience, live in peace and sufficiency'.[284] Before the fall there was no need for coercive political power, but because of the fall coercive authority is now an essential attribute of any polity.[285] Gerson, following Aristotle, divides polities into three types: kingdoms, where one good man rules; aristocracies, where a few good men rule; polities, where many good men rule. Their opposites are tyrannies, oligarchies and democracies.[286] Rulers are given their power by God, to whom they are subject, and this power is given for edification, not destruction.[287] The best form of polity, according to Gerson, is the kingdom. Gerson was a convinced believer in monarchy: 'The kingdom is the best, most long-lasting, suitable and rational polity or form of government, following as it does the example of the world which is governed by a single sovereign God.'[288] And he thought hereditary monarchy, where the king thinks of the kingdom as belonging to his family, to be better than elective monarchy.[289] In other words, in theory fifteenth-century France had the best form of government. Monarchy does not, however, argues Gerson, have to be institutionally absolute. In his long discourse of 1405 for the reform of the kingdom, Gerson speaks, though rather vaguely, about limited power. It would be better, he argues, if kings had less lordship, if there were some restraints 'so that the head does not draw the blood from the other members'. This would help rather than harm the ruler, as is the case when the king submits to the decisions of the *parlement*.[290] Later on in the same work he suggests the calling of the Estates-general so that the miserable condition of the various *pays* of France can be exposed and remedial steps taken.[291] And always he speaks of good counsellors: 'Many eyes see better than one... act always with counsel and you will never repent.'[292]

Beneath the royal authority is a hierarchical society, generally described by Gerson in terms of the old and inadequate division of the three estates: clergy, nobility and bourgeoisie or *peuple*. We get no details of the complex social structure of fifteenth-century France, no details of the client relationships among the nobles, of the power structures in the towns, of the divisions among the peasantry. Gerson, like other preachers of his time, simply gives us the old clichés. The clergy provide knowledge, the nobility provides defence, and the bourgeoisie work. The clergy are the eyes of the body politic, the nobles the heart or stomach, the bourgeoisie the hands, and all estates are necessary.[293] Alternatively, if one considers the polity as a soul, the clergy represent reason, the nobility free will, and the bourgeoisie sensuality. Reason ought to advise about what is to be done, free will ought to listen to and accept this advice, and sensuality ought to obey in everything.[294] It is an inadequate picture, but Gerson's point is clear. Society is hierarchical and inferiors must obey superiors. Peace and unity will prevail in a polity made up of diverse groups only 'when each has the things that belong to him and when each is in his right place'.[295] And everyone must be visibly in his right place. Status should determine standard of living: what clothes are worn; what food is eaten; what vessels are used. The nobility, like the major prelates, should keep up a decent standard. They should have 'eminent and honourable estate above the others'.[296] It is not at all surprising that Gerson, even with his peasant background, should have this hierarchical view of society. Most people held it in his day and long after. He does, however, temper his opinion. In the temporal order there is and must be hierarchy; there are superiors and inferiors, rulers and ruled. But ultimately there is equality. On a number of occasions Gerson reminds the ruling class of this fact. They should not despise others who are not so rich and powerful as they are, for all men are of the same nature, all are disciples, all are ordained for salvation, all are made in the image of God. Subjects are not dogs but brothers, and all men are equal in that all, even kings, will come to dust.[297]

The way in which the king, the princes, the nobility and the people sin, according to Gerson, is by not fulfilling the duties of their station. His view of the duties of the ruling classes comes across much more strongly than does his view of the duties of the people, because it is largely when he is preaching to the court that he speaks of political affairs. In fact, as in the case of his contemporaries, d'Ailly and Courtecuisse, there is hardly a court sermon in which he does not speak of political conduct. There is nothing unexpected in Gerson's vision of the ideal ruling class. It is reminiscent of the medieval mirror of princes' literature and medieval coronation oaths. 'All things', he says, 'belong to the prince, but not by proprietary right and not for himself, but for the needs of the commonwealth.'[298] And what is true of princely power is true of all lordship. Ruling for the common good, in Gerson's terms, means defending and sustaining the church, protecting the people and governing them well and without oppression, preserving internal unity and peace, promulgating just laws and executing them with justice tempered by mercy. It also involves a determined attack on all evil and sin in the kingdom. Moreover, the ruling classes must live exemplary lives in order to set a good example to lesser men. To carry out this ideal programme kings and seigneurs need power, wisdom and benevolence; they also need faith in God and a willingness to follow the advice of clerics, particularly that of the theologians of the University of Paris. They need, in fact, all seven of the Christian virtues: faith, hope, charity, prudence, temperance, justice and fortitude.[299]

This ideal of good government was not being put into practice in fifteenth-century France. The ruling classes, in Gerson's opinion, were failing in their duties and consequently guilty of sin. Frequently Gerson assimilates political sins to one or more of the seven capital sins, to pride and avarice particularly, but also to sloth, lust and gluttony. But at other times he treats types of political misconduct as sins in their own right. Basically what he saw happening in France was, on the one hand, monarchy, indeed all political leadership, degenerating into tyranny and, on the other hand, the frequent occurrence of grave sins of negligence. Either lordship was being exercised solely in the interests of the lord, be he king, prince or seigneur, or it was not being exercised sufficiently. Some of his court sermons, and particularly *Vivat rex* of 1405, contain serious and bitter indictments of the governing classes. The sin Gerson sees as worst is the oppression of the people by their masters. He paints a very pitiful picture of a poor man having to pay numerous taxes: 'sa taille, sa gabelle, son imposicion, son fouage, son quatrieme, les esperons du roy, la ceinture de la royne, les truages des chaussees et passaigez'. Little remains to him; then another *taille* is imposed. He is unable to pay; officials come to take away his goods and chattels. Meanwhile his children are crying for hunger. Soldiers come; and there follow beatings, arson and rape. 'Believe me, my lords, it is as certain as death that there are more than 10,000 in the kingdom in a worse state than this.'[300] The governing classes should not oppress the people by heavy taxation, imposed not for the common good, but to sustain high living, lavish building, pomp, and expensive law-suits on the part of the nobility. They should not oppress subjects by *prises*, and they should pay their soldiers decent and regular wages so that the latter are not driven to pillage.[301] The ruling classes, including the king, should keep all their officials in order, making sure that they do not oppress the people, show favouritism or accept bribes, and that they mete out justice for all, for justice must never be sold.[302] In short, princes and seigneurs should not govern their people by fear and oppression, but by love and compassion as a father governs his children.[303]

Apart from oppressing the poor, the ruling classes are sinning by not living in unity and peace among themselves. Thus they do not set a good example to the lesser subjects of the king.[304] Nor do they set a good example by their personal behaviour, for they are voluptuous and rapacious, ambitious and extravagant. Further they are not training their sons adequately so that they grow up hardy in body and learned in the arts needed for their status.[305] Nor are they, including the king, taking the necessary steps to help end the schism in the church. One of the steps needed for this is to bring the war with the English to an end. In a sermon of 1392, Gerson argues at length for peace with England, pointing out all the evils brought by this war with its inconclusive battles, ravaging soldiery and heavy taxation. He argues that even if it meant the surrender of part of the territory of France, peace would be better than war.[306]

The king and the nobility are not being firm enough, Gerson states, in punishing practices such as sorcery and blasphemy, in rooting out evil customs in their villages and towns, or in taking action against usurers and other criminals. The secular establishment is not fulfilling its God-given duties, and the governing classes will have to answer to God for this failure of trust. This type of complaint is of course very familiar in late medieval political comment, but it does seem to be particularly relevant to the situation of early-fifteenth-century France beset by the difficulties of a mad king, quarrelling princes, civil and foreign war. The French court seems to have been prepared to listen to these indictments, but Gerson went too far for his own safety in his attack on the tyrannicide perpetrated by the Duke of Burgundy.

Tyrannicide and sedition were not the solutions Gerson urged on the people against this oppression and failure of duty on the part of the governing classes. He was far from being a revolutionary. On the contrary, he says that the duty of the people is to obey their superiors, to suffer patiently and to be content with their lot. Just as a seigneur owes loyalty, protection and defence to his subjects, so do subjects owe loyalty, subsidies and service to their seigneur.[307] And we must obey our seigneurs even if they are bad,[308] for sedition, that is, popular rebellion, is often worse than tyranny itself. It is not that Gerson thinks that nothing at all should be done about a tyrannical king or prince, but that whatever is done should be done on the advice of wise, good and experienced men and by non-violent means. The king should be urged not to be tyrannical and, if necessary, he should be persuaded to allow some limitations on his power.[309]

Meanwhile the people must be content in their estate, and in the first place this estate is one of subjection. The people must be content, he says, to be led by the king and by the two sovereign estates; otherwise the order of the political body will be completely overturned, 'as if the feet wished to usurp the office of the head or arms or stomach, and so destroy not only the body but also themselves'.[310] If their estate is one of poverty, the people must endure this too. 'This poverty may be sent to humble you, to make you chaste, to turn you to God, or to take away the danger of sin.' If you suffer it patiently 'God will reward you well either here or elsewhere as He does all His friends.'[311]

One does not get the impression from Gerson's works that the third estate was particularly sinful in respect of this ideal of keeping in their place, however lowly. He is not preaching to or about potential political insurgents contemplating class war. Rather, the social sins committed by the lower classes seem, in his eyes, to have been relatively petty, for example, not doing a proper day's work, wasting their master's goods, theft, not paying tithes, not fulfilling religious duties properly, overcharging in business transactions, drunkenness and dishonesty. No doubt there were plenty of 'private' sins – of lust particularly – and indifference in religious matters, on the one hand, and devotion run wild, on the other, if one takes account of Gerson's discussion (not usually in sermons, it is true) of religious deviancy. But Gerson is not nearly so good a source for the sins of the lower classes as he is for those of the governing classes. However, his ideal for both rulers and ruled is clear and is summed up well in his *De modo vivendi omnium fidelium*. Any superiors, be they nobles, prelates, husbands, fathers or masters should rule their subordinates justly and with kindness, while any inferiors, be they poor, monks, wives, children or servants should obey and serve their superiors well. And all should fulfil their religious duties and obey the commandments of God and the church.[312]

What we have here is undoubtedly a conservative and defensive, though by no means *passé*, view of the existing hierarchical society.[313] Gerson does not advocate any fundamental social, economic or political changes to bring society more into line with the teachings of the gospel. The existing structure is perfectly adequate in his view, provided that all fulfil the duties of their status. And all estates and callings, unless sinful *per se*, for example prostitution or usury, are necessary and have worth, though not necessarily equal worth.

A MONASTIC MORALITY?

In its broad generalisations Gerson's moral teaching sounds monastic. His countless statements about turning one's back on the world and concentrating instead on the things of God and his often expressed sentiment that the things of the world and the flesh are all vain while the things of the spirit are of over-riding importance reveal an ideal that sounds as if it could be best carried out within the confines of a monastic order. But when he comes down to discussing specific sins we find that Gerson has in some respects moved far away from the monastic morality. In the first place the monastic ideal of poverty has disappeared for those living in the world, be they laity or clergy. We have encountered the 'decent status rule' in many places. One is entitled to all those things necessary for living in a style commensurate with one's status. One is even entitled to acquire and keep superfluous things if the purpose is good. One ought to save for future contingencies. One ought to acquire for the sake of one's children. Further, one may acquire in numerous ways, by living off or working on the land, by practising a craft or profession, by trade, by being a sleeping partner in a business enterprise. All these activities are legitimate provided that sinful methods and intentions are avoided. If someone steals or defrauds one of what one has acquired then one has not only a right but a duty to seek, by lawful means, the restoration of those possessions. It is certainly possible, in Gerson's view, for a rich man, be he prince, bishop, seigneur or merchant, to enter the kingdom of heaven.

The other two monastic vows have not been so clearly abandoned. There is a strong stress in Gerson on the duty of inferiors to be obedient to superiors, though any given person living in the world could have a number of superiors: his parish priest, his bishop, his father, his school-teacher, his employer, his prince. But the obedience due is not absolute. It stretches only so far as the superior has legitimate authority. No seigneur, bishop or father, for example, may order a young person, or indeed any person, to enter a monastery or to take vows of any kind. But obedience is still an ideal, though clearly Gerson does not envisage a person living in the world as being as confined by his superiors as a monk by his abbot. A person may, for instance, within limits decide for himself whether he should fast or not. Gerson's stress on obedience to superiors does not, of course, have only a monastic base. He cannot envisage society functioning in any other way than as a hierarchy with downward responsibility and upward obedience.

The monastic ideal of chastity has left more than a trace on Gerson's moral teaching. Men and women may of course marry, but, as we shall see, marriage is an inferior status to virginity, and even within marriage a rigorous ideal of marital chastity is demanded. Outside of marriage Gerson's moral code requires total chastity, in thought, word and action. No concessions are made here. For the unmarried lay person, as for the secular and religious clergy, the monastic ideal of chastity still stands. The sexual appetites must be kept under the strict control of reason and will, and this means that they must be allowed no outlet whatsoever outside marriage.

Although Gerson shows no leniency to man's sexual drive, he does not advocate monastic asceticism in all its aspects to the laity. He is careful to point out those who are exempt from the fasting rules; he frequently warns against the dangers of excessive fasting and he strongly disapproves of individuals' prescribing for themselves any acts of rigorous asceticism. He advises that light penances, within the capacity and with the consent of the penitent, be imposed. It is really only with respect to sexuality that Gerson urges monastic asceticism on the laity.

Have the remnants of monastic morality and piety left in his teaching for the laity caused Gerson to set the goal too high? As far as the seven capital sins go, with their monastic origin, the answer has to be a qualified one. If we regard the sins as all stemming from natural human appetites or tendencies, then we can say that with some of these tendencies Gerson has sympathy and understanding and consequently keeps the goal within reasonable limits. This is true of what he says of anger particularly, but also to some extent of what he says of envy, avarice, sloth and even gluttony. Indeed he shows not only sympathy but also psychological astuteness, especially in his discussions of anger, envy and sloth. But when he writes of pride and lust his sympathy and astuteness are not so evident. His ideals of total humility and total chastity seem to run counter to fundamental human physiological and psychological needs and drives. This is not to deny that the ideals are possible of fulfilment by some. But that they can be fulfilled by all seems doubtful. Of course there is a way out of total chastity – 'chaste' marriage. But there is no way out of the ideal of humility. One cannot help wondering, however, whether Gerson's frequent references to keeping up a decent status do not run counter to what he says elsewhere about pride. Some sort of self-respect seem inevitably bound up with, if not actually demanded by, the hierarchical society.

It might be that the ideals set forth by Gerson are very lofty but are meant as models to aim at rather than as laws that must be fulfilled under pain of damnation. This certainly seems to be true of what Gerson has to say about the ideal of charity. Turning the other cheek and giving one's cloak as well as one's coat are counsels of perfection, but one does not have to despair if one cannot live up to this standard. God does not demand the impossible; one is not bound to do all the good one is moved to; it is sufficient to keep the commandments.[314] Gerson's basic argument is that the evangelical counsels, taken in the narrow sense of poverty, chastity and obedience, or in the wider sense of perfect charity (loving not only one's friends, but strangers and enemies also, and being prepared to lay down one's life for one's neighbour) are works of supererogation as far as salvation is concerned.[315]

Nor should we forget Gerson's often repeated distinction between mortal and venial sin. 'There is no commandment so strict', he writes, 'that it cannot be broken without mortal sin', for it is full consent which makes a sin mortal. And the seven sins should not be called the 'deadly' sins, 'because not all pride or anger, and so with the others, is mortal sin, but often only venial'.[316] This doctrine must have afforded a comforting and genuine way out for some, but certainly not for all, judging from Gerson's concern for the over-scrupulous who, for example, wondered whether they had fully consented to a sinful thought or not.

Frequently Gerson refers to human frailty. 'Pechier c'est fragilité humaine.'[317] It is as if, despite what he says about God's not demanding the impossible, he expects most people to sin, as if he himself really thinks that the goal, not of perfection, but of keeping the commandments and avoiding mortal sin is too high, is impossible of attainment for the ordinary run of men.[318] This does not mean that men must despair, and it does not mean that Gerson's moral teaching has a fatal flaw. For there is a way out. One can repent, confess and receive absolution and so be in a state of grace again. Consolation lies not in attaining the goal of never committing a mortal sin, but in the forgiveness of the confessional. So even if the goal is too high, and this seems to be the case in some areas, this does not necessarily mean that Gerson's moral teaching was psychologically unhealthy. One falls but one can, by means of the confessional and the grace and mercy of God, pick oneself up again.

The psychological repercussions of Gerson's teaching about sin would no doubt be affected by the general tone in which he spoke and wrote about the subject. On balance it is gentleness that predominates, especially in the vernacular tracts, and indeed even in the sermons he is more the consoler than the condemner. It is in the sermons that he speaks of human frailty. In both sermons and tracts he is at pains to state that unbidden feelings and thoughts are not sinful, that physiological states can excuse thoughts, words and actions that would otherwise be sinful. But he can be harsh. He threatens damnation to those who put off repentance, to usurers and their associates and to those who commit sins of lust, particularly the sins against nature. He was certainly capable of leaving members of his congregations feeling uneasy, uncomfortable and even terrified, if they took their preacher's words seriously.

It is very difficult to assess the psychological effects of Gerson's moral teaching. One cannot help but feel that his doctrines about pride and lust must have been very difficult to live with for people concerned about doing their best so that they would acquire grace and salvation. Some would no doubt be consoled by the thought that sins could be repented of and forgiven. But, on the other hand, this thought could have led some to sin with abandon for the time being. That this happened is clear from the number of times Gerson warns people who put off repentance. Obviously much would depend on the temperament and background of the *viator*, and on how sensitive or religiously minded he was. There can be no doubt that the stress on sin, as well as the stress on doing one's best, led some people to be afflicted by the neurosis of over-scrupulosity. There were so many sins to avoid, so much self-scrutiny to undergo before confession. The fact that Gerson was very concerned to quiet and console the over-scrupulous does not exonerate him from the charge of helping to create the disease he sought to cure. He may not have proliferated sins as much as some did, but his list is far from short.

Gerson's sermons and tracts for the laity certainly stress, if not over-stress, sin. But there is also a positive side to his pastoral theology. For one thing there is the stress on the wondrous results of repentance, confession and absolution. There are other things. Gerson speaks of the virtues which his congregations should pursue; of the help they can receive from God in this process; of the value of prayer and of the joys of heaven. He holds up saintly men and women as *exempla* for his congregations to try to follow. And above all in his sermons there is Christ, seen on the one hand as the human Jesus, 'humble, gentle, compassionate and kind', our brother to be emulated.[319] On the other hand, Christ is portrayed as the risen Saviour, ushering in the age of grace and mercy, revealing the love of God and making possible our salvation.[320] Frequently in his exposition of the gospel for the day Gerson relates some episode in Christ's life, so that his congregations over the years must have become familiar with both the human and divine sides of their Saviour. The work of the Holy Spirit in the world is another recurring theme of the sermons, with the stress on the help and comfort He brings. Gerson's 'affective' mystical theology, one of the most positive aspects of his teaching, is not particularly evident in his sermons, but he did not think it too high a matter for the laity and he wrote two long vernacular works on the subject for them. This positive side of Gerson's pastoral theology with its ideals to pursue, its *exempla* to be imitated, its hopes and promises of peace and joy, provides a counter-weight to what might be considered negative in his discussions of sin.

6

THE MYSTICAL WAY

Gerson was a professor of theology who researched, taught and published on many religious themes, among them on what today would be called mysticism. Gerson called his subject 'speculative mystical theology'. His extra-curricular lectures on this topic, given during the academic year 1402–3, were, in fact, part of his plan for the regeneration of the faculty of theology at Paris.[1] He also published and probably taught on another aspect of the topic. We might call his treatise on this aspect 'A guide to the mystical life'; he called it 'practical mystical theology'.[2] The term 'mystica theologia' by itself almost always for Gerson denotes the actual mystical experience which man can have of God, the state of mystical union with God, not the study of this experience, which is what the term suggests to us. The word 'mysticism' – and Latin and French equivalents for it – did not exist in the fifteenth century. The more usual term for what Gerson called 'mystical theology' was 'contemplation', a word Gerson uses himself, sometimes as a synonym for mystical theology, as in *La Montaigne de contemplation*, but sometimes as meaning the activity of the highest of man's intellectual powers, and thus different from mystical theology, which he chiefly connects with man's highest affective power, the synderesis.[3]

Gerson's use of the term 'mystica theologia' is not, however, peculiar to him. It was used by Hugh of Balma, writing around 1300, and by Vincent of Aggsbach in the mid fifteenth century. Both Gerson and Vincent were influenced by Hugh of Balma's teaching, and this is probably why they adopt the term.[4] Other theologians, such as Aquinas and Bonaventure, employ the term only rarely, preferring the more traditional 'contemplation'. That 'mystical theology' was used at all is because of the increasing influence from about the twelfth century of the Latin translations of the Dionysian corpus, particularly of the short treatise entitled *De mystica theologia*.

Gerson's interest in mysticism was by no means purely academic. Certainly he occupied himself with the theoretical side and tried to define and describe the mystical experience, despite its basic ineffability, a fact recognised by all mystics and theologians of mysticism. In this connection Gerson is fond of quoting from the Apocalypse. This is an experience, he writes, which no one can know unless he receives it.[5] But this did not prevent him from trying to elucidate certain aspects of the experience, and to distinguish *theologia mystica* from other types of theology. This was only part of his interest. He wanted the students of the theology faculty not only to know about mysticism but also to embrace it, to follow the mystical way in their own lives. Beyond that he wanted them to be able to teach and preach about it and so lead the laity to the full spiritual life, to the slopes and perhaps even the heights of the mountain of contemplation.[6] Gerson also addressed the laity directly in his two vernacular tracts about mysticism and the way to reach it: *La Montaigne de contemplation* and *La Mendicité spirituelle* of 1400–1, and again in a sermon of 1402.[7]

The chancellor may have been one of the first to preach and write in French on the topic of mysticism, but there were many others who were doing the same in other vernaculars. Eckhardt and Tauler preached about mysticism in German, Suso wrote mystical tracts in German, Ruysbroeck wrote in Flemish and Walter Hilton and the anonymous author of *The Cloud of Unknowing* wrote in English, to mention only the most notable of the fourteenth-century mystics.[8] There must have been a demand for instruction in the spiritual and mystical life among those ignorant of Latin and the subtleties of scholastic theology, for example nuns and laity. Alternatively, the increasing use of the vernaculars as written languages in general could have automatically opened up new religious avenues for the non-academic, *les simples*. Whatever the cause the fourteenth-century mystics and Gerson took advantage of the situation. In Gerson's case, it is clear that he was prompted by a sincere pastoral concern and zeal to get the laity to practise an interior religion and to come as close to God as possible, under proper guidance, of course – hence his lectures and treatises for theologians.

What is the interior religion and this mystical experience that Gerson and others write about? In the first place it should be made clear that what is being discussed, defined and described by them bears little, if any, resemblance to occultism, 'spiritualism', charismatic movements, visions, voices and the like. Most of these modern phenomena had their fifteenth-century equivalents. There were some people in the period, for example, who thought that they were experiencing God or getting messages from Him or from other spiritual beings when in all probability this was not the case. Gerson was fully aware of the problem and tackled it on a broad front, first in his lectures to students in the winter of 1401 on how to distinguish between true and false revelations, then in 1416 in his treatise on the testing of spirits and again in a tract of 1423 on the examination of doctrine.[9]

It was not that Gerson thought that all visions and voices should be dismissed out of hand; rather they should be assessed by sober judgement. Some theologians, he tells us, indignantly reject any new revelations, but this is as mistaken as naively accepting as divine revelations all the dreams and fantasies of neurotics. Every experience of this sort should be carefully assessed.[10] Gerson provides a series of norms by which the spirits can be tested 'to see whether they are of God' (I John 4:1), though he admits that it is difficult to arrive at an infallible judgement. He uses the metaphor of true and counterfeit coins: the coin of the revelation must be tested to see if it has the weight of humility, the flexibility of discretion, the durability of patience, the perfect image of truth and the sparkling and genuine colour of divine charity.[11] All but the fourth are characteristics of the recipient of the revelation. If he boasts about his experience, then that experience is suspect. A lack of docility to direction and counsel is another sign of the falsity of the revelation. Under this heading of discretion Gerson discusses the dangers of excessive asceticism, especially fasting, which can lead to visual, auditory or tactile hallucinations. The charity required is the theological virtue and not a love that appears chaste but which is ultimately based on sensual desire. Truth is a characteristic of the revelation itself. If the revelation contains even one small piece of misinformation, that is, information that is not in accord with Scripture, faith and good morals, then the revelation is not divine, but diabolical, morbid or feigned.[12]

These tests and Gerson's advice in general on this topic seem practical and sound.[13] He is drawing on a well-established tradition for some of his material, as well as on his own experience of 'visionaries' and the like. He cites Cassian in the section on discretion, and Gregory, Richard of St Victor, and Bonaventure elsewhere. Some of the other mystical writers of the later Middle Ages touched on the subject of visions and the testing of spirits, but not with the thoroughness of Gerson.[14] The chancellor's pastoral concern is evident again here. Theologians and future pastors must be taught how to deal with members of the laity, and others, who thought they were in touch with supernatural beings. But in any case visions and voices were certainly not of the essence of mysticism for Gerson. Joan of Arc may, as Gerson himself thought, have heard voices from heaven but that did not, by itself, make her a mystic.

In his first lecture on speculative mystical theology Gerson makes a commonplace but useful medieval distinction between mystical and two other types of theology: symbolic and proper.[15] These two terms are reasonably near equivalents of what were later called natural theology, the knowledge that can be acquired about God from a study of the created world, and dogmatic theology, knowledge of God acquired by a study of His revelation of Himself in Scripture. Taken together symbolic and proper theology constitute scholastic theology or, as Gerson frequently – and confusingly in this context – says, speculative theology. Mystical theology, he argues, in contrast to the other two, which draw on external material, draws its material from within the human heart, and while scholastic theologians strive to know God as the highest truth by reason, mystical theologians – mystics – try to embrace Him as the highest good by love.[16] This is one of the many ways in which Gerson characterises mysticism and in what it asserts it remains true for him in all his writings, though it by no means tells the whole story, as we shall see. For the moment all that need be noted is that Gerson has shown, and most people would not quarrel with him on this, that *theologia mystica* is fundamentally different from scholastic theology.

Beyond this point the ways divide and definitions of mysticism proliferate, conditioned to some extent by the time periods in which the definers live, their religious persuasion, their religious order (if any) and current topics of debate. As far as time periods go, one of the crucial eras is the sixteenth century, the century of the great Spanish mystics, Ignatius, St John of the Cross and St Theresa. Their descriptions and analyses of their experiences tended to become the norm, at least for Catholic historians and theologians. Thus Connolly, writing in 1928, in order to show the soundness of Gerson's mysticism, is anxious to link him up with the Spanish school.[17] The same bias appears in Knowles' book on the English mystics, written in 1961. Nevertheless in that book Knowles produces a definition of mysticism which appears to have been accepted as at least very useful by English-speaking historians, writing of the late medieval and Reformation periods. It will be useful here to set the scene, though its quotation is not meant to provide an absolute standard by which to measure the value of what Gerson says about mysticism.

Apart from the two kinds of knowledge acquired by natural and dogmatic theology, Knowles writes,

there is a third by which God and the truths of Christianity can not only be believed and acted upon, but can in varying degrees be directly known and experienced... This knowledge, this experience, which is never entirely separate from an equally immediate and experimental union with God by love, has three main characteristics. It is recognized by the person concerned as something utterly different from and more real and adequate than all his previous knowledge and love of God. It is experienced as something at once immanent and received, something moving and filling the powers of the mind and soul. It is felt as taking place at a deeper level of the personality and soul than that on which the normal processes of thought and will take place, and the mystic is aware, both in himself and in others, of the soul, its qualities and of the divine presence and action within it, as something wholly distinct from the reasoning mind with its powers. Finally this experience is wholly incommunicable, save as a bare statement, and in this respect all the utterances of the mystics are entirely inadequate as representative of the mystical experience, but it brings absolute certainty to the mind of the recipient.[18]

One should note here that mysticism is being viewed as the actual mystical experience detached from any preparatory steps that might be necessary. This is not an unusual way of viewing mysticism.[19] Indeed it seems to be the way Gerson sees it. It is the mystical experience, the union with God, that he is trying to define in his 1402 lectures. Nevertheless, the great majority of writers on mysticism, whether they are theologians presenting learned treatises on the subject, spiritual directors producing guides, or mystics describing their experiences, or a mixture of all three, expend as much energy, if not more, in describing the preparatory steps as they do in describing the final, truly mystical stage.[20] Gerson, it should be remembered, appended a *practica* to his *speculativa*. It seems plausible, therefore, to use the phrase 'the mystical way' to denote the whole process: the preparatory steps together with the culminating mystical experience, not, of course, that the latter necessarily follows the former. Moreover, the mystical way should be seen as flowing from the ordinary life of Christian perfection, whose essence is keeping the commandments. This life is enough for salvation, but the mystical way can purify one further, make one more like God and increase one's capacity to know and love Him. It is only in its culmination that the mystical way is mysterious. Gerson does not write about a *via mystica*, but what has been said here of the mystical way applies to what he calls 'the contemplative life'.[21]

TWO TRADITIONS OF MYSTICISM?

If Knowles has produced a characterisation of mysticism that seems satisfactory, it should not be thought that he has said everything that needs saying.[22] His definition does, as he no doubt would be the first to admit, leave a lot of unanswered questions. Who is eligible for this kind of experience, everybody or only an elite? Is it something one can strive for, and if so, how should one strive and for how much of the time? The experience is said to involve knowledge of God, but what kind of knowledge? What exactly is the relation between God's grace and man's effort, if the latter does indeed play a part? Gerson tackled these four questions and for all but the third he produced straightforward and consistent answers throughout his career.[23] It was the third question, about the type of knowledge involved in the mystical experience, that exercised him most. Man's volitional, affective powers were involved in both the preparatory stages and in the union, but he kept coming back to analyse further the role of the intellect. Even after he had written the *De elucidatione* in 1424, there is evidence in letters and Latin devotional writings that this question was still of concern to him. What was probably one of his very last works was an unfinished commentary on Dionysius' *De mystica theologia*.[24]

A number of historians during this century have dealt with medieval mysticism by distinguishing between two major strands, and the distinction is based on this very question of the relative roles of intellect and will or love. On the one side a Cistercian and Franciscan tradition is identified which is seen as stressing will and love and traditional monastic piety in the approach to God, and as understanding the mystical union as a loving conformity between the human and divine wills. The Cistercian Bernard and the Franciscan Bonaventure are usually selected as the best exponents of this tradition. The Dominicans Eckhardt and Tauler are seen as the prime examples of a second tradition, the Germanic. Here, the argument goes, stress is laid on the intellect both in the approach to God and in the union, which is conceived as an intellectual vision of God, the ultimate truth, and a merging of the human essence with God. The soul, as it were, loses its being in the divine abyss as a drop of water in a barrel of wine. One of the more recent advocates of this division of traditions is Oberman, who characterises the two traditions as, respectively, affective/penitential and intellective/essentialist (or transformationalist).[25]

This classification has not been without its critics, largely German, though in the last decade criticism has been voiced in the English-speaking world, notably by Ozment in an important paper published in 1974.[26] Briefly, what this criticism, usually based on the works of particular mystics, amounts to is that the distinction is much too sharp. A mystic who is supposed to belong to the affective tradition is found to have not slight but strong intellective elements, and vice versa. My own reading of a number of the medieval mystical authors confirms the main lines of this criticism. They all, even Eckhardt, stress the importance of will and love in the soul seeking union. St Thomas, for whom contemplation 'as regards the very essence of its activity belongs to the intellect', in answer to the question whether contemplation has nothing to do with the will, but is entirely the province of the intellect, responds with a firm negative. The will moves the intellect out of love in the first place and 'the contemplative life terminates in delight, which is in the will, and this in turn intensifies love'.[27] Eckhardt asks what possession of God depends upon. 'The real possession of God depends on the heart, and on a sincere spiritual approach and striving for God...' And he goes on to compare this possession and striving to the activities of someone with a passionate love for something, who longs for that alone and sees its image in everything. Effort and love, he says, and a careful cultivation of the inner life are necessary for a man to be able to perceive all things as divine.[28] In this search for union with God, writes Tauler, 'a man must ascend with all his faculties and affections into the high places of eternity...This ascent is led by the will, for it has the right of command over all the faculties...' A man needs a burning, consuming, melting, suffering love for God. No one can come to this union except along the way of love.[29] The *Theologia Germanica*, written by an anonymous fourteenth-century author who is influenced by Tauler – indeed Tauler is mentioned in the text – gives weight to both the intellect and the affective power.[30] Meanwhile the English mystics, Hilton and the author of *The Cloud of Unknowing*, both of whom show affinities to the German Dominicans in other respects, are alike in giving love and will a large role in the quest for union with God and indeed in its achievement. The reader of *The Cloud* is told to put down subtle thought and cover it with a thick cloud of forgetting, however holy and helpful the thought may seem to be.

And the reason is that 'only love may reach to God in this life, but not knowing'.[31] Hilton states firmly that the 'third degree of contemplation – which is the highest that can be reached in this life – consists of both knowledge and love; in knowing God and the perfect love of him'.[32]

On the other wing, some of the so-called affective mystics leave a fair bit of room for the intellect. It seems obvious, as Gerson, echoing Augustine, remarks more than once, that you cannot love what you do not in some sense know.[33] Moreover, anyone influenced by Neo-Platonism, whether coming indirectly through Augustine or directly from the Latin translations of Proclus and Plotinus that were available from the latter half of the thirteenth century, would find it rather difficult to leave intellectual activity out of contemplation altogether. And there cannot have been many medieval mystical writers who were not influenced by Augustine.[34]

The dominant theme of Bernard's mystical sermons on the Song of Songs is undoubtedly love, but he makes the same observation as Gerson that you cannot love what you do not know, so 'know God and you will also love Him'. Although the analogy Bernard uses to describe the mystical encounter is the union between the bridegroom (Christ) and the bride (the soul), he does not conceive that union as simply an affectionate embrace. The bridegroom's kiss brings a two-fold gift, the light of knowledge and the fervour of devotion, so the bride must prepare her two lips, namely her intellect for understanding and her will for wisdom. Excluded from the kiss are not only those who know the truth without loving it, but also those who love it without understanding it.[35] The other famous twelfth-century monastic mystic, William of St Thierry, has an even stronger intellectual element than Bernard. His aspiring mystic is first an animal man, then a rational man and finally a spiritual man who 'gazes upon the laws of unchangeable truth...by means of the understanding that comes from love'.[36] And who could deny that the first six stages of Bonaventure's journey of the soul to God are intellectual, though not purely intellectual, even if in the seventh all intellectual operations should be abandoned?[37] The two-fold classification that divides affective from intellective mysticism is, as Ozment neatly puts it, a 'gross' one.[38] Some refinement seems necessary.

The other part of the classification that opposes the 'transformationalism' or 'essentialism' of intellective mysticism to the mere conformity of wills of affective mysticism also appears to have flaws. It is true that some of the propositions of the German Eckhardt were condemned in 1329 because they smacked of a heretical pantheism. However well he defended himself at his trial, it remains true that Eckhardt did write passages that suggested that in mystical union the soul is totally absorbed into God. There is a mingling of substances, of essences and the distinction between creature and Creator disappears. Never was there so close a union, he writes, as that between the mystic and God. The soul is much more closely united with

God than body and soul which form one man. This union is much closer than that of a drop of water poured into a vat of wine, for that would still be water and wine; but here one is so transformed into the other that no creature could discover the difference.[39] It is also true that Ruysbroeck, some of whose statements were thought by Gerson and others before him to be dangerous because of their pantheistic overtones, belongs to the fourteenth-century 'German school'.[40] Gerson accuses Ruysbroeck of stating that a soul at the height of contemplation loses itself and its creaturely being and receives true divine being; it becomes one with the divine brightness, becomes that brightness itself.[41] Gerson does not link Ruysbroeck's teaching with the Cologne condemnations of Eckhardt in 1329. In his letter of 1402 to the Carthusian Bartholomew Clantier, he links it with the condemnation of the heresies of the Beghards in 1312 by the Council of Vienne, and in the lectures with the condemnation of the teaching of Amaury of Bène in 1210.[42] Amaury was not a mystical writer but a Parisian professor of logic and theology who had apparently argued that St Paul's 'God will be all in all' meant that the being of God is essentially the same as the being of things.[43]

Gerson, however, does not connect the pantheistic heresy with the so-called intellective mystics particularly. In a Latin sermon of March 1402 in the same breath as he again criticises Ruysbroeck he warns that the second book of the *Epistola ad fratres de Monte Dei*, which he identifies as Bernard's, should be read with caution.[44] The offending passage is interesting. William of St Thierry, whose work the treatise is, is describing unity of spirit with God. The soul has reached the point where it is perfect in its love for God and can will only what God wills.

Now to will what God wills is already to be like God, to be able to will only what God wills is to be what God is; for Him to will and to be are the same thing. Therefore it is well said that we shall see Him fully as He is when we are like Him, that is when we are what He is.[45]

The jumping-off point for this conception which has pantheistic overtones – at least for Gerson – seems to be a volitional, affective mysticism.[46] One wonders whether Gerson might not have been more severe about this passage of the *Epistola* had he not thought that it was written by a twelfth-century saint, whose works he often recommends to his readers as among the best available mystical writings. Ruysbroeck was, for Gerson, a rash newcomer and his bold statements were to be totally repudiated. Bernard's treatise was simply to be read with caution.[47]

Aside from what Gerson says, it is clear that for many of the so-called affective mystical writers the mystical experience was more than a conformity of wills. They, too, write of becoming like God, of the reformation of the image of God within the soul, of union, of being transformed into God, of deification, or of 'mixed liquids'.[48] They, too, are 'transformationalists' in some sense. The trick was to avoid slipping into the essentialist heresy when trying to describe the closeness of the union with God in figurative or any other language. The drop of water in wine image seems, in fact, to have originated in the West with Bernard. In his *De diligendo deo*, Bernard writes

It is deifying to go through such an experience [*sic affici, deificari est*]. As a drop of water seems to disappear completely in a big quantity of wine, even assuming the wine's taste and colour...so it is necessary for the saints that all human feelings melt in a mysterious way and flow into the will of God. Otherwise, how will God be all in all if something human survives in man?[49]

Bernard goes on at once to say that no doubt the substance of the soul remains, though under another form. Bonaventure's seventh and final stage in the journey to God involves union, when the 'highest peak of our affections is transferred and transformed totally into God'.[50] And this culmination follows an earlier stage where the image of God in man has been reformed and the soul made the daughter, spouse and friend of God, the sister and fellow heir of Christ.[51] There is no heresy here, but there is more than a conformity of wills, or perhaps it would be nearer the mark to say that true conformity of wills is impossible without transformation.[52]

From this discussion of the flaws in the crude two-fold classification of medieval mysticism it can be assumed that it is unlikely that Gerson will conceive of mysticism as either wholly intellective or wholly affective. However, he does sometimes indicate that he himself sees a division between mystical writers, but it is not the same division that modern historians have drawn.

In 1407 in the treatise on practical theology he says it would be worth considering whether the knowledge which is involved in the highest affective union with God through love is experiential only or whether it can be called intellectual, not indeed intuitive, but abstractive knowledge.[53] Both sides, he goes on, have most notable defenders. The commentators on Dionysius, by whom he probably means the Victorine Thomas Gallus and the Carthusian Hugh of Balma, hold the first opinion. As far as the second goes he thinks Augustine leans towards it, and also Bonaventure in the sixth chapter of his *Itinerarium*. What Gerson appears to be saying here is that both groups hold that the mystical union is an affective union with God through love, which involves experiential knowledge of God, but that the second group is prepared to go further and say that an abstractive, intellectual knowledge is also involved.

In 1424, in his *Elucidation of Mystical Theology*, Gerson states that there is both the affective knowledge of mystical theology and the other mode of contemplation which is said to be a pure and clear contemplation of divine truth. There are, he says, various commentators on each kind of contemplation and each has been expressed by different symbols: the affective by Mary (sister of Martha) seated and by the bride abounding in delights who leans on her beloved, and the intellectual by Israel and Rachel and the bride ascending as the dawn, the moon and the sun. But, he argues, it is necessary for the intelligence to be borne up to God, without any sense of time and without any phantasms. This, however, is very difficult, as Augustine says, agreeing with Plato and his followers, because the pure truth can be known only in a sort of ecstasy, in the manner of a flash of light and only rarely and by few.[54]

Gerson is here apparently distinguishing between mystical theology, which he classifies as an affective form of contemplation, and what might be called contemplation proper or intellectual contemplation. However, it is again clear that mystical theology is not purely affective; it involves knowledge of some sort. Moreover, the fact that the figure of the bride is said to be used by both 'schools' suggests that there is an element of affectivity in intellectual contemplation. Augustine, along with Plato and his followers (the Neo-Platonists?), seems to have been placed in the intellective group. The reference to Rachel suggests that Gerson is probably putting Richard of St Victor also in this group.[55] No names are mentioned for the first group.[56]

A third occasion when Gerson makes a distinction between mysticisms is in a letter of 1425, probably to his brother Jean the Celestine.[57] The letter is largely a warning against a book by Ubertino of Casale which in Gerson's opinion contains serious errors, some about the mystical union. In the course of the letter he states that *theologia mystica* consists in the union with God. Many, he says, have written and said much about mystical theology, some placing it in the knowledge of the first truth, this knowledge being either abstractive, or in some way intuitive and experiential in the feelings (*in sentimentis*).[58] Others place it in the love of the synderesis alone with the cessation of all intellectual activity. In the latter group Gerson places the Dionysian commentators and Bonaventure. He gives no names for those holding the first view, which is itself subdivided. Among those believing that the knowledge is abstractive could well be those mentioned in *De mystica theologia practica*, Augustine and Bonaventure and probably Richard of St Victor.[59] This, however, has the unfortunate effect of putting Bonaventure on both sides of the fence.[60] Those holding that the knowledge is experiential *in sentimentis* sound like the first group of mystics of the *Practica*, except that the knowledge they now have may be in some way also intuitive. In other words, Gerson is shifting his categories and his people. Moreover, a new category seems to be there from at least 1424 onwards made up of those who hold that 'the peak of the soul is carried into God by ecstatic love without previous or concomitant knowledge'. The prime example here is Hugh of Balma.[61]

In 1427 after one of the passages where he states that one cannot love the unknown, Gerson notes that some people not only say that one can love the unknown but try to prove it.[62] He does not mention whom he has in mind here, but it could well be Hugh of Balma who, in his *De mystica theologia*, does attempt to argue against Augustine's 'We can love the unseen, but never the unknown.' Hugh uses Dionysius and Thomas Gallus as his authorities and concludes that the affection is carried to God without previous knowledge in the intellect. The knowledge rather follows.[63] What Hugh seems to be arguing is that the ascent to mystical union is purely affective, and the union itself is purely affective, but then God grants 'a knowledge of Himself which is greater than any that is achieved by the intelligence and reason'. It is a knowledge by ignorance (*cognitio per ignorantiam*).[64] Bonaventure, in the seventh chapter of the *Itinerarium*, decides that at this point in the journey the affective power (and God) must take over completely so that the soul is borne 'naked of knowledge' (*inscius*) to God. He quotes two passages from Dionysius' *Mystical Theology* about the divine darkness and the 'unknowing' ascent as evidence.

This gives an indication of why some mystical writers are leaping into an apparently blind affectivity. Dionysius' radical spelling out of the ultimate incomprehensibility of God has left them thinking that the only way to God is by the affective power, by will and love. 'Only love may reach to God in this life, but not knowing', as the author of *The Cloud*, himself very much influenced by Dionysius' theme of the divine darkness, puts it. Dionysius, of course, had to be taken notice of. He was the disciple of St Paul, or so they all believed, and hence he was 'the prince of mystics' for Bonaventure, 'the divine Dionysius' for Gerson. His words were perilously close to being considered the Word of God, and in this light they must be susceptible of an orthodox Christian interpretation – no easy task, considering his Neo-Platonic views.[65] Eckhardt is a witness to the fact that not all mystical writers succeeded here. The 'blindness' of purely affective mysticism is also, according to Gerson, coming a little close to heresy. There are some, he writes, who say that we can know nothing about God except by negation; but this doctrine was one of the condemned Parisian articles.[66]

Another exponent of the 'blind' affectivity position was Vincent of Aggsbach, writing about twenty-five years after Gerson's death. Vincent is interesting on two counts. He attacked Gerson for injecting a cognitive element into the mystical experience and therefore not being true to Dionysius, and he made a clear distinction between *theologia mystica* as he conceived it and contemplation. Contemplation for Vincent was the raising of the soul to God with previous and concomitant activity by the intellect, though even this sometimes ends in darkness. Mystical theology, on the other hand, was the hidden raising of the soul to God without any previous or concomitant knowledge. Vincent goes on to reveal his preference by saying that contemplation is the servile work of the six days, while mystical theology is the rest (*quies*) of the seventh. Moreover, the two can never be in the same man at the same time. In sum 'in contemplation love and knowledge accompany each other; in mystical theology never'.[67]

If we want to divide medieval mystical writers into two groups, as Gerson and Vincent are apparently trying to do, then it might be a good idea to accept the categorisation that Vincent expresses clearly and Gerson rather confusedly: there is the mysticism that involves love and knowledge, the affect and the intellect, on the one hand, and the mysticism that involves only love, on the other. The first category, as Gerson tells us, can be subdivided according to the type of knowledge involved: experiential, abstractive, intuitive. This category, according to the evidence presented in this chapter, would seem to include most medieval mystical writers, at least most of the well-known ones. Not only do Eckhardt and the German school fit here, but also Gregory, Augustine, Bernard, William of St Thierry, Hugh and Richard of St Victor, Walter Hilton and even Bonaventure.[68] The second category turns out to embrace rather a small group: the 'pure' Dionysians, who have been carried into what is perhaps rather a curious view by Dionysius' unknowable God, who is beyond all positive and negative distinctions, beyond all things, exceeding all Being, Deity and Goodness.[69]

Gerson did not, however, expend most of his energies in trying to classify people, though the question was certainly not without interest and importance to him, for apart from anything else he was trying to clarify his own position. Sometimes he lists various definitions of *theologia mystica*,[70] but he does not invariably make a two-fold classification. In his treatise on the Magnificat he enumerates six views that people have put forward when writing about the words of Dionysius and the divine wisdom of Christians:

Some said that this theology consisted in denying all things of God; some that it consisted in affection and love; others that it lay in the purity of the intelligence; some that it was the gathering of the soul [*mentis*] to God, or union; some that it consisted in devotion, or the elevation of the soul [*mentis*]; others that it was rapture or ecstasy or alienation of spirit [*mentis*].[71]

Although some of these definitions would fit into a two-fold classification, others do not. In other words the division in terms of powers of the soul is not the only division that is interesting people, including Gerson. That Gerson *was* interested in it has not a little to do with his pastoral concern. If the mystical way was to be open to educated and uneducated alike then it could not demand exacting intellectual activity. The mystical experience must not be exclusively the culmination of a love-directed but speculative type of contemplation. For Gerson the fundamental distinction between scholastic (or speculative) theology, which was exclusive to academics, and mystical theology, which was the heritage of all Christians,[72] was not unconnected with the question of the relative roles of intellect and will or love within mystical theology itself.

MYSTICISM FOR ALL

In 1400, while at Bruges and before he gave his lectures on speculative mystical theology to the Parisian theologians, Gerson made his contribution to opening the mystical way to the *simples*. *The Mountain of Contemplation* is basically a well-organised treatise, though it has its share of medieval digression and diffusiveness. The first nine chapters form an introduction in which Gerson answers the objection that might be raised to his writing about such a lofty subject in the vernacular for the uneducated. He then defines the contemplative life; in its root and in its goal it is the love of God, and it presupposes the suppression of worldly love, which is far from easy. It has three principal stages (chs. 10–16). The first stage is humble penitence, a stage of mortification of worldly love and the things of the flesh (chs. 17–19). In chapter twenty Gerson gives a brief glimpse of the ultimate goal, the perfection of the contemplative life, where one has perfect love of God. All one's senses are closed to the world, as if one were in a dark cloud, but open to the joys of the saints. One is united to God and ravished in spirit.[73]

The second stage is one of solitude and silence, where the soul obtains simplicity and unity and thinks only of God and loves only God, asleep to everything else (chs. 21–32). This discussion is interrupted in the middle by a defence of the contemplative life against the objections that it is selfish, a sign of pride and can lead to madness or melancholy.[74] The third stage is called not union, as one would expect, but perseverance. One must persevere in humble penitence and in trying to attain a state of solitude and silence. And this is very difficult. There are many obstacles to be overcome (chs. 33–6). Gerson next examines methods for attaining contemplation that have been recommended or suggested by experts. Different methods will suit different people, but Gerson himself prefers a method suggested by William of Auvergne: the method of spiritual begging (*mendicité spirituelle*), where the soul prays to God and the saints, begging for pardon and grace (chs. 37–43).[75] In the last two chapters we encounter what seems to be another mountain, which is a rock on the shores of a turbulent sea – the world – where many ships perish. This rock has three levels: faith, hope and charity, which the soul should climb. At the top the soul attains God, but Gerson declines to say very much about this. We must not be too curious. He does say that there will be no clear vision of God, because God is not corporeal. As to union Gerson says he does not feel worthy to open his mouth on the subject; he leaves that to the experts.[76]

Such is the bare outline of the treatise. It is full of vivid and telling examples, usually from everyday life, and of wise advice. It is a pity there is so little on the culmination, on the mystical encounter itself. One can only conjecture about the reason for this. It cannot have been that Gerson thought it dangerous to tell the laity about mystical union, for he does precisely this in a sermon to the parishioners of Saint-Jean-en-Grève two years later. Combes argues that in 1400 Gerson had not formulated his ideas on mysticism sufficiently to write about the subject, but by 1402 he had. This may well be the case.[77]

La Mendicité spirituelle is basically a spelling-out of the method of contemplation mentioned in *La Montaigne*. The first part takes the form of a dialogue between a man and his soul. Gerson, like many medieval writers, found the dialogue a vivid and useful way of expounding his teaching. This, though, is more in the nature of a soliloquy, taking place within one person. The soul is disturbed, feeble, ignorant, the learner; the man is strong and wise, the teacher. Gerson did not invent this type of soliloquy between the man and the soul. Hugh of St Victor used it in his *De arrha animae*, a work Gerson knew and recommended, and so did Bonaventure in his *Soliloquium*.[78] But if the form is the same, the content is very different. What Gerson does in this first part is to tackle the basic problems about prayer: If God knows everything, He knows our needs and desires, so why ask Him? If He is immutable and everything is predestined, how can prayer alter His will? Why are our prayers often not answered? How should one pray, where, when and in what position? Is it good to use mediators? What sort of things should one ask for?

These questions were not new, and nor are Gerson's answers, but the latter are fully, clearly and convincingly expressed, more so, for instance, than Hilton's or Eckhardt's.[79] Gerson has taken the trouble to elaborate the stock answers in a way that could satisfy the unschooled but enquiring mind. The point of prayer is not to inform or change God, he writes, but to change ourselves, to make us more devout, and he goes on at some length to explain how our prayers are part of God's plan and how praying to God is in some ways like asking people for things, but in other ways different.[80] Prayers are not answered at once for various reasons: what we are asking for may not be good for our salvation; we may still have bad desires, not be truly pure in heart; God may wish to try us in perseverance.[81] For suitable times, places and positions for prayer Gerson seems to be relying, as he acknowledges, on William of Auvergne's *Rhetorica divina*. Gerson is not dogmatic here; everyone must discover what is most helpful to him, but the matter is thoroughly discussed, as is the question of what to pray for: spiritual gifts and blessings. Basically prayer is defined as a humble and devout affection directed towards God, the same definition which Gerson gives in his lectures, where he also states that love, mystical theology and perfect prayer are the same thing.[82] In the *Mendicité*, however, Gerson does not leave it at that. He spells out twenty different ways in which one can have this affection. He evidently realises that 'affection' by itself is too vague and perhaps even misleading and so he wisely describes different psychological and mental states that can express this affection. They range from fear, humility, anxiety, languor of heart and hatred of self to admiration and reverence for God, confidence and hope, joy and sober pleasure, jubilation and exaltation and finally pure love of God, when one receives the kiss on the mouth from the bridegroom.

This whole discussion about prayer takes place in the context of an allegory in which the soul in prayer is perceived as a beggar with open sack, going from saint to saint, from angel to angel, to the Virgin, to Christ, to God, begging alms. The second part of the tract largely consists of a series of long prayers and meditations, diffuse and emotional, full of metaphors, yet with a basic order and sometimes rising to a poetic beauty.[83] This series of prayers is sometimes interrupted by further debates and dialogues, for example with the devil, with Pride, with Justice. The prayers and meditations themselves provide a whole theology of sin, grace and salvation. The idea of prayer as begging is a familiar one.[84] Gerson, however, pushes the analogy to great lengths and from time to time realises that it will not work. The soul asks some very awkward questions, pointing out, for example, that the rich usually prefer to give alms to the poor who are ashamed to beg, rather than to those who are importunate in their demands. The man has to point out that God is different; his largesse is inexhaustible and he prefers that one acknowledges one's spiritual poverty.[85] Although the *Mendicité* stresses the need for complete self-abasement, despair is avoided because in the prayers the soul points out its right to be succoured. The saints are so full of charity and mercy that they ought not to refuse help; moreover God has instructed them to help.[86] God must forgive our sins; we have His own letters signed by His secretaries, the Evangelists, saying that if we forgive those who have done wrong to us, we, too, will be forgiven by Him.[87]

A note of optimism is also struck in the prayer of thanksgiving, where God's blessings are described: the goods of nature all given for man's use, the goods of grace, the Incarnation and Passion, the sacraments.[88] This prayer is followed by a meditation on death and the need to fear God. Throughout this last part of the tract Gerson is steering his readers through the narrow channel between over-confidence and despair. He gives some glimpses of the soul in a state of perfect prayer, in the presence of God and His grace. Everything is changed. Vices are uprooted and virtues firmly planted. The soul sees its faults, sins and frailty in the very light of truth. Its beauty, the image of the Trinity, is recovered and it feels a glorious peace. The true light of justice is born in its heart. But the moment is fleeting.[89]

This description of the mystical encounter, like the one in chapter twenty of *The Mountain*, is untechnical and unanalytical, as one would expect in a vernacular work. But Gerson does undertake some analysis of the mystical way in the vernacular when he explains at the beginning of *The Mountain* why it is open to all Christians.[90] The chief burden of his argument is that you do not need a training in theology, nor do you need to be living in a religious order in order to follow the mystical way. A training in theology could be helpful to someone who wishes to reach the heights, but frequently it is a hindrance, because it can lead to pride. Knowledge 'puffs up', as Paul says. Clerics who go around with their heads held high because of their great reputations for intelligence and knowledge have no hope of following the mystical way, which demands above all humility, becoming as a little child or a young girl. There *is* a type of contemplation followed by good theologians, based in knowledge (*science*) which uses reason founded in faith to seek the nature of God and His being and works. But it is the other type, based in affection, which is open to the *simples*. This seeks chiefly to love God and savour His goodness without wanting clearer knowledge than that given by faith. It is this that Dionysius taught about in his books on mystical theology and it is the highest wisdom we can have here below. Gerson makes a clear-cut distinction between science and wisdom. The former belongs to the understanding and the latter to the affection, whose powers he here spells out as desire, appetite and will. The wisdom the affection can have is a sort of knowledge, a savoury knowledge (*savoureuse science*). He illustrates the difference between the two sorts of knowledge with two examples: one can discover the nature of honey by studying books, but one can know its savour only by tasting it; doctors can understand the nature of a malady, but the sick know it better, not by reason but by experience. Obviously discursive knowledge can exist without wisdom and vice versa, and Gerson takes pains to point out that knowledgeable philosophers and theologians ought not to be called wise unless they also have ardent affection for God. In fact, though, the only previous knowledge of God necessary to reach wisdom is that provided by faith, about God's power and goodness, His commandments, our redemption, and heaven and hell. And so it is that a simple person can, when God visits him, know God better by loving Him than can any cleric or philosopher by reason alone. Love itself is knowledge, a direct awareness of God, acquired through the spiritual senses.[91]

In these few pages Gerson has given to his unlettered readers his basic teaching about mysticism in a nutshell. For the moment all that concerns us is his anti-elitism. Although he admits that there is nothing wrong with scholastic theology *per se*, the impression left by these chapters is that one is really better off without it, especially if one wishes to attain the height of Christian wisdom. There is a good deal of criticism of 'puffed-up' clerics who think themselves wise. Any layman reading this could not be faulted if he considered that he could rise as high as any cleric, however well educated, and probably even higher than some.

Gerson is not simply flattering the laity. He makes the same points, sometimes even more strongly, in Latin works. His two lectures of 1402 on the curiosity of students are an indictment of scholastic theology that is devoid of wisdom. He criticises theologians for pursuing useless (*curiosa*) questions and always seeking novelty (*singularitas*), and showing disdain for clear, sound and established teachings. He sees such theologians as seeking only to enhance their self-esteem and reputation, when they should be humbly trying to elucidate Scripture.[92] In his discussion of the differences between scholastic and mystical theology, Gerson again shows that the mystical way is more democratic. It can be followed even by a young girl or simple person (*muliercula vel idiota*). Moreover, it is a better way; the spirit fired by love can rise where rational contemplation alone can never reach; mystical theology can exist by itself without the help of speculative theology, while the latter can never be perfect without the former, for contemplation without love does not really deserve the name. Scholastic theology can become the servant of vices, and can leave one restless, but mystical theology holds to its objective firmly.[93] One of the twelve considerations of the *Elucidation* is devoted to showing why simple uneducated people (*simplices idiotae*) reach *theologia mystica* more quickly and sublimely than those learned in scholastic or discursive theology. It is because their faith is not disturbed by contrary opinions which they have not heard and therefore do not think about. Further, they are more humble and pay more heed to their salvation in fear and trembling.[94]

It is clear that Gerson is not merely paying lip-service to the idea that the mystical way is the heritage of all Christians. The idea was not new; in fact it was commonly held, as one would expect in a religion founded on the New Testament. Gregory holds that no class of persons among the faithful is excluded from the gift of contemplation. It often comes to those who hold the lesser places in the church, rather than the higher; it can come to the least of people, even to those who are married. But it can come only to those who love.[95] Gregory, too, has his criticisms of the quick-witted. They are like birds flying on the wings of their intelligence, but it is the lizard, the simple person, who has no wings, but who practises what he has learned, who is able to get into the king's palace.[96] 'We are all', writes Bernard in the context of the coming of the bridegroom, 'universally and without distinction called to possess the blessings of our heritage.'[97] Nearer Gerson's own time Tauler, Ruysbroeck and others expressed the same democratic doctrine. Tauler, like Gerson, is of the opinion that simple people often progress much faster in the mystical way than people who try to get along by their great intellectual abilities.[98] If there is doubt about the seriousness with which some mystical writers took this doctrine, there can be no doubt with Gerson. The mystical way was open to all.

Gerson did not, of course, want to abolish scholastic theology, nor did he want to substitute speculative mystical theology for dogmatic theology. The latter had an important role to play in the life of the church, but it must be reformed so that it was firmly based on faith and pursued in a spirit of humility and love. Bonaventure's theology should be the model, for he 'both inflames the affections and enlightens the intellect'.[99] To use one of

Gerson's favourite similes, Bonaventure provides both the honey and the honeycomb, both devotion and the learning needed to structure and regulate devotion so that it does not flow away, perhaps into heresy.[100] For the *simples* the honeycomb is the knowledge given by faith, but the guardians of faith are the theologians. In other words there is, as Gerson writes in one of his last works, a knowledge which does not 'puff up'.[101] Moreover, and in this one place Gerson appears to contradict what he had frequently written earlier, the rational spirit can, by theological and philosophical activity with the help of faith, hope and charity, be raised to the peak of mystical theology, higher than can unlearned, simple Christians.[102] So, despite his insistence that the mystical way is the best way and that it is open to the unlearned, Gerson is not engaged in a flight from reason.[103]

He is not engaged in a flight into the cloister either. One can follow the mystical way, he tells the readers of *The Mountain*, without taking vows. One can find inner solitude without entering a cell or a hermitage in the desert. There are, however, some people whose temperaments are such that they are not capable of sustaining a life of contemplation; these ought to occupy themselves in the active life. Others, who are quiet, peaceable and thoughtful by nature and who find the active life irksome, ought to follow the contemplative life. Some people are lucky and can move easily from one life to the other, as prelates ought to do. The distinction by temperament, Gerson argues, by no means follows the distinction between clerics and laity. Some lay people are far more fitted for a contemplative life than are some clerics.[104]

This passage and more particularly the first four considerations of the *Practica*, which elaborate on what Gerson says here, have caused controversy among commentators.[105] It does seem at first sight that Gerson is barring the mystical way to people who are restless or extrovert by temperament. And not only to these, but also to those who are not given the necessary grace, and to those whose worldly duties are very onerous.[106] But there is not really a problem. Gerson is not only showing his usual psychological astuteness here but he is also following Gregory, and Gregory's meaning is quite clear. Not everyone can sustain a life *totally* devoted to contemplation, because not everyone has the right temperament or enough freedom from worldly duties. Indeed no one should follow such a life if there are works of fraternal charity, preaching or duties to be done. Like Gerson, Gregory thinks that, though the contemplative life is superior to the active (Mary chose the better part), the mixed life is best. As for those for whom a life of contemplation is difficult, they can and should engage in some contemplation. 'Frequently love impels indolent spirits [*pigras mentes*] to labour and fear holds the restless in contemplation.'[107] In other words Gregory and Gerson are not making a stark opposition between the contemplative and active lives; everyone should follow both, or rather there should be aspects of both in each person's life. There is no one, says Gerson, who should be so taken up with the active life that he never contemplates, and no one so involved in the contemplative life that he never does any work.

Si est tousiours en une personne Marthe necessaire avecq Marie, et Marie avecq Marthe, ou plus ou moins comme dit est; mais on nomme la personne d'une vie selonc ce que plus souvent elle s'y donne.[108]

But we are all held to seek perfection and so we should all follow the contemplative life as much as we can, within the limits of our temperaments and external responsibilities.[109] To do this is not a sign of pride, for contemplation pleases God more than activity. The contemplative is not selfish, for he is giving a good example and his prayers are of more value to the whole church than the prayers of a hundred purely active people. To the charge that contemplatives often become mad or melancholy, Gerson answers that there is plenty of madness and melancholy among people who never contemplate, and, in any case, if contemplatives use discretion, if they season their contemplation with activity, they will not be afflicted.[110]

The mystical way therefore remains open to all Christians, educated and uneducated, cloistered and uncloistered. This does not mean that all will reach the top of the mountain or even get very far in the foothills. Mystical union comes only to a few, and to them but rarely. One's progress depends not only on one's efforts but on God's grace, and that is given where He wills. The mystical way is open to all only in the sense that salvation is open to all. Not all will be saved, and even fewer will become mystics. So when Gerson's mysticism is termed 'democratic', it must be understood in this limited sense, that is, that from the human point of view there are no statable exceptions. Status in society, academic ability and achievement provide no automatic advantages, for God can choose His mystics from the cottage as well as from the cell or study, and He does not choose all.[111] Nevertheless we should all aspire to the mystical way just as we should all aspire to salvation.

However, the first thing that strikes one about the mystical way as Gerson describes it is that it is very difficult. Gerson wants the *simples* to embark on it but he does not disguise the fact that they will feel down-hearted, bereft and even tormented many times during the journey. Moreover, it is not a straightforward journey or ascent. It is not a case of first achieving humble penitence and then achieving inner solitude and then achieving union. One can lose any or all of these at any time and be back where one started. But from at latest Gregory onwards mystical writers used allegories about mountains, stairways, ladders or journeys and pilgrimages to describe the mystical way, and Gerson's analogy works well enough as he does not overplay it. Complicating everything, though also making it all possible, is God's grace. It, too, can be withdrawn at any time or work in mysterious or psychologically disturbing ways.

As the goal is to love God perfectly and so to know Him, the first task is to empty one's heart of love for anything else. One must detach oneself from the world. Love of worldly things, says Gerson, is like glue which prevents the soul from spreading its spiritual wings. Like the bird which does not realise it is caught until it tries to fly away, people do not know how hard it is to cast off this love until they wish to love God perfectly. This theme of detachment from the world is a common one in mystical writing, and it implies more than abandoning inordinate love of worldly things. It means taking no pleasure even in worldly things considered good in themselves. Gerson does not elaborate on this theme apart from saying that the soul who has escaped is not held back by anything, 'ni richesse, ne deliz charnelz, ne plaisir de boire ou de mengier ou de joer'.[112] Other authors are more forthright. Thomas à Kempis, for example, tells his readers to desire to be familiar with God alone and His angels, and to avoid the acquaintance of men. We should esteem as vain all comfort that we receive from people and if we truly love God, we will despise all things that are inferior to Him.[113] For Hilton, a man who has achieved detachment considers all worldly joy and honour as nothing. He considers all creatures, himself included, as nothing. He has no pleasure in great position or in any skills he may have in learning or handicrafts. He has 'no more taste for these than for gnawing on a dry stick'.[114]

The only way, Gerson says, that one can become released from the glue of worldly love is by means of God's grace. God must let us get the scent of Him, as it were. Here Gerson uses the analogy of hunting dogs who, once they scent their prey, pursue it relentlessly, taking all obstacles in their stride, while other dogs do not run and think that the hounds are running in vain.[115] God can attract us in many different ways. He can work directly, by making us have feelings of sweetness, sober joy, peace, or by giving us an enlargement of thought, a taste, a sound without sound.[116] He can attract us indirectly by means of Scripture, good books, sermons, or by severe tribulations.[117]

It is at this point in *The Mountain* that Gerson says he is going to speak about the three stages of the ladder of contemplation, though one would have thought that one or two rungs had already been climbed. He uses two memorable images, which he recalls from time to time in the rest of the treatise, to show that one cannot reach the goal in one leap. The first could have been borrowed from Hugh of St Victor: when a fire is lit, there is at first only smoke, then there is flame and smoke and finally pure flame.[118] The second image may be Gerson's own: when a seedling is replanted, it wilts, becomes as if dead, then it recovers and finally blossoms.[119] The first stage of the ascent, humble penitence, consists in mortifying the flesh so that it is perfectly subject to the soul. This is achieved by fasting, vigils, abstinence, afflictions, tears and groanings, by the bodily labour of one's estate. In other words the active life comes first as a preparation for the contemplative life, just as Jacob had to serve with Leah first before he married Rachel.[120] Gerson points out the wisdom of this and how in religious orders the novices engage in more activity (manual work, singing, for example) than do the older members. Gerson does not stress humility at this point, but there is no doubt that he thought it essential. It is the basis of his recommended method for seeking God: spiritual begging. In the *Mendicité* the man teaches the soul that it is nothing, has nothing, knows nothing and can do nothing. It must realise its utter spiritual poverty and its peril. The soul learns the lesson and when it prays it can say: 'I am the most vile, the most indigent, the most unfortunate of all men. I have forfeited everything.'[121] Self-abasement or spiritual poverty, to put it in medieval terms, is another common theme of mystical writers. Gregory says that one must make oneself worthless in one's own eyes.[122] For Tauler the first virtue to be practised in the search for God is a profound and abject humility.[123] The corollary to the soul's abjection is, of course, the great power and goodness of God, which can turn this vile creature into a bride fit for the bridegroom. As the soul in the *Mendicité* says, the Trinity can 'cleanse me, enlighten me and make me beautiful and pleasing'.[124]

To reach the level of silence and solitude is difficult. At this point the soul is like the uprooted seedling. It has been torn away from worldly love, and takes no more pleasure in the world, but it has as yet no spiritual pleasure. It is in a state of languor and can fall into despair. It will have fierce assaults from the flesh to overcome, but little or no spiritual consolation. It may fall back to worldly things, then feel remorse. Gerson paints a vivid picture of this tormented, divided soul, agitated and despondent by turns.[125] But it must be still and find inner solitude. Usually this comes more easily if there is outer solitude and silence. But the latter does not guarantee the former. One can be all by oneself and yet be turbulent within.[126] Each person must find the places that suit him best: the woods, fields, the church, his home, his own room. Here he must, with the help of grace, achieve unity and simplicity of heart, have his thought and love fixed on God alone. And so he will be with God, for 'l'ame est plus vraiment ou elle aime que ou elle anime, c'est a dire que ou elle donne vie au corps'.[127] This elevation of the soul out of the world and to God is brought about by strong and holy thought, by ardent love. This thought or this love is so strong that it can make all other operations of the soul, all phantasms cease. To illustrate this Gerson produces examples of students, mathematicians and craftsmen so absorbed in their work that they see and hear nothing that is going on around them. So the soul can, though it is more difficult, think and live only in God, who is its place, its end and its love. The soul now lives by love. It receives the consolation of divine love without feeling the tribulations of the flesh and the world. It wants only to serve, love, think of, speak about God. The flame burns purely now, the seedling has blossomed.[128]

It is when Gerson writes about perseverance that the difficulties of the mystical way are most prominent. There is hardly a mystical writer who does not speak of difficulties, tribulations, afflictions. They are very evident in Gregory's *Moralia*, as one might expect in a commentary on the Book of Job.[129] But medieval writers vary in the amount of emphasis they put on difficulties, and in the type of difficulties they describe. Gerson seems to be among those who place a good deal of emphasis upon obstacles. He discusses twenty-four *empeschemens*, by which he means ways in which people go wrong. He may well be wise to do this. They are all things that one can easily imagine happening, and to warn people of what to expect seems a sound policy.

There is, for instance, the question of pace. Some try to go too fast, not heeding God's grace. They get ahead of grace, as it were, and so stumble. Others want to rest for a while, but to stop is to fall back. Some are trying to climb for the wrong motive, for curiosity or to be able to say 'I have been there', and to mock those below them. The only motive must be to please God and serve Him. If you have any other motive you are on the wrong mountain – the devil's. Then there is the problem of what to do with temptations, of which there will be many, for the devil works harder the closer one gets to God. Some pay too much attention to these and try to fight too hard against them. What they should do is to take no notice, but flick them away as bothersome flies.[130] There will be many tribulations, for God wants to try us. Some people attempt to run away from tribulations rather than bearing them with patience. Some souls have worn out their bodies because of lack of discretion in asceticism and so do not have the strength to climb; others are carrying too heavy a burden, for they have not sufficiently rid themselves of worldly desires and anxieties. Sometimes people feel such a strong spiritual hunger to hear the Word of God that they read and reflect too much and so forget to climb. Some neglect to ask the advice of the wise and rely on themselves alone; they will lose their way. Others are so busy asking about the way and studying about it in books that they never set out.[131]

Frequently Gerson reminds his readers that they must not expect to have pleasant feelings very often. Feelings of devotion and consolation are rare. More often they will feel arid. But they should continue on the way. They should not desire consolations for their own pleasure but only in so far as pleasant feelings help them to love God more diligently. If it pleases God that we should serve Him without consolations, then it ought to please us too. Accept this and say

Sire tout puissant, bien me souffist que vous me gardes en paradis mon loyer et ma remuneration sans m'en bailer riens a present,...que...vostre volunte soit faite.[132]

The two vernacular tracts together form Gerson's most extensive treatment of the mystical way as a whole. The *Practica* adds little that is new except on the union itself. The most interesting and comprehensive vernacular discussion of mystical union is in the 1402 sermon on the Trinity. It is quite brief – at least in its written form – and comes at the end of the sermon after a passage on the soul as a mirror or image of the Trinity.[133] Up to this point the sermon has taken the form of a dialogue between the Soul and Reason, but now a new character appears, Devotion or loving Contemplation. Devotion, says Gerson, can learn the secrets of the Trinity more perfectly, profoundly and intimately than can reason. 'Love enters where knowledge stays outside.'[134] With the help of grace, the soul has to do two things: it has to put forward its foot of understanding, believing that God is, as reason enlightened by faith has shown, all good, all loving and all desirable. Then it must put forward its other foot of affection by loving devotion

et passe tout et perse tout fiablement, car amour ne doubte riens, jusques a tant que elle se joingne a Dieu son amour, sa doulceur et plaisant desir et que elle soit si une avec luy que ce soit d'eulz deuz ung esperit: qui adheret Deo unus spiritus est; et amor transformat in amatum.[135]

Gerson makes it clear that this is a transforming union. The soul is so changed in the cinders of humility and the fierce furnace of charity that it becomes like a beautiful, clear, clean and pure glass and takes the image which the Holy Spirit wishes to give it, the image of God, to whom the soul is joined. The soul is now a beautiful mirror, clear and polished to reflect (*representer*) the Deity. For this hour the soul forgets everything else. This oblivion is like the lead which forms the other side of the mirror, for otherwise the soul could see terrestrial things and thereby be prevented from seeing heavenly things. This oblivion is the shadow, obscurity and darkness in which God is seen.

To make it quite clear that the resemblance between the soul and God should be conceived as being as close as possible, Gerson uses another analogy, that of a sculptor (*tailleur*) making an image of himself. The image could have all the *condicions* of the sculptor, that is

estre tel, vie telle, figure telle, entendement tel, sans differance de nature, ceste ymaige lors seroit proprement l'imaige du tailleur et seroit une mesme chose avec le tailleur en distinction personnelle...[136]

The creature, then, though truly like the Creator, remains distinct from Him; it does not lose its essence in the divinity. Yet the union is a close one. In this union, says Gerson now employing bridal imagery, the holy soul is made pregnant by the Holy Spirit and spiritually conceives the Son of God.[137]

But it is not just a union of love; knowledge is involved. 'Icy cognoist l'ame dieu...' A limiting clause follows this: 'and if not as He is in Himself, the soul knows Him as He is to the soul, that is good, sweet, delectable, saving, loving, helping'. Nevertheless, a simple person who is devout and loves God will have a higher and better knowledge of God, of His power, wisdom, goodness, sweetness and kindness than will philosophers or clerics, theologians and others, who are without love and devotion. 'Happy is the soul who receives this grace of union...and to this end tears and devout sighs are more profitable than intelligence or any kind of study.'[138]

LOVING AND KNOWING

From the vernacular writings we can see that, though Gerson gives love and will the larger role in the mystical way, he does not exclude the intellect and knowledge. In the Latin works he analyses and tries to make more precise both the respective roles of loving and knowing, and the nature of the knowledge involved in the mystical experience.

Mystical theology is the clear and savoury understanding [*clara et sapida intelligentia*] of those things which are believed in the gospel, and it is to be attained more by penitence than by human investigation alone.[139]

This is the first definition of *mystica theologia* that Gerson gives to his students in 1402. He goes on to say that he will discuss the question whether God can be known better in this life through penitential affection or through intellectual investigation. The goal here is expressed in terms of knowledge, but the method, whatever else it involves, involves the affective power. Later, when he is fully launched into his subject, he elaborates the definition and says that mystical theology can be described as an extension of the soul (*animi*) to God through the desire of love; or as a transcendental movement (*motio anagogica*) leading to God (*in deum*) through fervent and pure love; or as an experiential knowledge (*cognitio experimentalis*) of God attained through the embrace of unitive love; or as wisdom, that is savoury knowledge (*sapida notitia*) of God when the peak of the affective power is joined and united to Him by love, or, following Dionysius, as irrational, mindless and foolish wisdom (*irrationalis et amens et stulta sapientia*).[140] In these statements, all of which Gerson accepts at least in what they affirm, love is conceived as the way to God. In the last three the mystical encounter is conceived in cognitive terms; one achieves an experiential or savoury knowledge of God. It is not, however, a case of love ceasing and knowledge beginning.

In order to explain exactly what he means Gerson analyses the human psyche, the intellective and affective powers of the soul, their activities and the relationship between them. Gerson does not think that these powers are really distinct in the soul. The soul itself is a unity, but we may distinguish between its different activities.[141] The intellective powers are identified, in descending order, as pure or simple intelligence, the power which receives light directly from God and by which first principles are known to be true; reason, which deduces conclusions from premises and abstracts essences (*quidditates*); and sensuality, which is basically the perception, imagination and memory of sensible objects. The affective powers are the synderesis, which is the natural inclination to follow the good as presented by the pure intelligence; rational appetite, often called will, which is moved by reason; and sensual appetite, which is moved by sensory apprehension alone.[142]

There is a close relationship between the intellective and affective powers; in each case an affective power is moved by the prior activity of and the information presented by an intellective power. However, as Ozment points out, Gerson really sees the relationship as 'correlative and reciprocal'.[143] Every effect produced by man, writes Gerson, acquires some light, either because of clarity in the cognitive powers or because of heat in the affective powers, or because of both at the same time.

For it is difficult to find a cognition which is not formally or virtually a certain affect, just as it seems quite impossible to find an affect which is not a certain experiential knowledge. Indeed, neither power causes its effect without the other, since an affective power concurs in the emergence of a cognition just as a cognitive power concurs in the generation of an affect.[144]

To make the point quite clear Gerson draws the conclusion from the analogy he is using: in the sensible world light cannot exist without heat and heat always produces light.[145]

Adam's fall caused the defilement of these powers. However, it is the corruption of the intellective powers on which Gerson dwells. The pure intelligence, the eye of contemplation, for instance, is now almost totally extinct.[146] Gerson describes the proper modes of activity of the affective powers: desire for the sensual appetite; devotion or contrition for the rational appetite; and ecstatic and transcendental love for the synderesis. But he does not go on to discuss the effects of original sin on the affective powers. Instead, he says that this ecstatic love of the synderesis is the wisdom of God, hidden in mystery: it is mystical theology.[147]

Because of the reciprocal relationship between the two sets of powers, one would expect the corruption of the intellective powers to have an adverse effect on the affective. Gerson does not discuss this. However, it seems correct to conclude, as Ozment does, that what Gerson wants to stress is the reverse side of the coin – the beneficial effect of the less corrupted synderesis on the intellective powers. Gerson makes it clear that rapture, the lifting of the soul to God, has its origin in love alone and is therefore the work of the affective rather than the cognitive powers. Nevertheless, it has its effects on the latter and he goes on to describe the rapture of the imagination, of the reason and of the intelligence. Briefly, what occurs is that the intelligence is so elevated and immovable in its own act that the lower intellective powers cease performing their normal activities. Instead of a mind that is constantly busy with sense perceptions and phantasms there is a mind that is held in contemplation.[148] This leads us back to the pre-fall condition of the cognitive powers, when the eye of contemplation was 'most lively, pure and efficacious', and the soul was able to stay, when it wished, in the peak of the intelligence without falling into the activities of the inferior powers.[149] This rapture of the mind, brought about 'through the peak of affection, which is related to and appropriated by the mind, is called ecstatic love or the ascension of the mind'.[150]

Thus, both in this description of the comprehensive nature of rapture and in his definitions of mystical theology Gerson has illustrated the reciprocal relationship between the two powers. This relationship helps to explain what Gerson means by the sentence we have seen him use in *The Mountain*: 'Love itself is a knowing.'[151] Love involves concomitant knowledge because 'neither power [intellective or affective] causes its effect without the other'. We might go further than Gerson does here, but in accord with what he has written elsewhere, and say that love must involve previous knowledge, in this case, the knowledge of faith, while the acquisition of this last must involve will and desire. The same would be true of any kind of knowledge. One cannot know Pythagoras' theorem without at the same time exerting one's will to study it. With mystical theology, however, we are on a higher level than discursive reasoning. As Gerson says at the end of the lecture, when he has equated love, mystical theology and perfect prayer, the mind in affective prayer and above itself through understanding never turns back, never synthesises or analyses. Perfect prayer is the highest mental and intellectual affection.[152]

Another oft-quoted expression in Gerson's writings, 'Love enters where knowledge stays outside', at first sight seems not to fit his discussion of the reciprocal relationship between the powers of the soul. If love opens the door, surely knowledge must enter too. But the stress is on the fact that only love can open the door. Intellectual activity, if not pursued with love, never can. In a work of 1429 Gerson discusses this very question. How can love enter, he asks, and remain without knowledge? If knowledge stayed outside, love would perceive nothing, and indeed delight cannot arise without the perception of the harmony between love and its object. The powers of the soul, cognition and will or love, are distinct, but not so distinct that they do not coinhere. There is a mutual indwelling (*circumincidant se mutuo*). And so we can say that love is cognitive and that cognition, when it is ordained to love and does not remain in bare speculation of truth, is loving.[153] Gerson, then, holds the same position about the respective roles of loving and knowing in mystical theology in 1429 as he did in 1400, 1402 and 1407.[154]

We have already had some clues about the type of knowledge which Gerson thinks is involved in the mystical experience. It is a knowledge that does not involve sense perception or phantasms or discursive reason. It is more like a direct awareness, an acquaintance. The concept which Gerson

uses most frequently to explain this awareness is that of the spiritual senses
of the intellect, which he could have borrowed from a number of sources.
It appears prominently in Bonaventure, for instance.[155] The knowledge
involved in mystical union, says Gerson, is certainly experiential and is
analogous to that acquired through the physical senses.[156] Unlike Bonaventure, however, Gerson makes a distinction between the spiritual senses
and sees three of them – spiritual touch, taste and smell – as more important
in mystical theology than spiritual sight and hearing. He argues that people
who say that love is blind are correct in a way, for the knowledge
accompanying love is not luminous or declarative, is not like a clear vision
of the eyes and ears that can be shown or described to others. It is more
like savour and sweetness that cannot be so shown or described.[157] But the
knowledge of God brought by spiritual touch, taste and smell is more
intimate and so more powerful, penetrating and pure than that brought by
spiritual sight or hearing.[158] Gerson gives the example of an infant at its
mother's breast, who generally sees and hears nothing, being totally
occupied in lactation. The child is engaged in a pleasant experiential
operation, but one which is not reflexive or declarative.[159] 'Happy is the
child who can remain for a hundred years under wisdom his mother, such
as was the splendid King David, a child in his own eyes and less than all
the rest before God.'[160] Gerson recalls here his theme of mysticism for the
simples, as he does in his second example. He envisages two men, one strong
in spiritual sight and hearing but with his other three senses dull; this is
the learned philosopher or theologian who lacks love. The other man is, as
it were, blind and deaf in the perception of scholastic philosophy, but is
strong in the other senses, the smell, taste and touch of spiritual things. It
is the latter, the simple and uneducated man, who is blind and deaf except
in so far as faith resounds within him, who will have delight in God and
perceive the things of God in their savour, fragrance and consolation.[161] In
other words, knowing God in mystical theology does not involve concep-
tualising; it is a direct, immediate awareness and ultimately ineffable.
Nevertheless, it *is* a knowledge, the best that can be had of God in this life – a
knowledge born of love. 'The will, joined to God, orders the intellect, as
if saying: come and see, taste and feel how sweet is the Lord.'[162]

Gerson will not accommodate himself to those who say that mystical
theology involves no knowledge of God of any sort whatsoever or that we
can know nothing of God except what He is not. In the *Elucidatione* he
examines the thesis of the 'pure' Dionysian, Hugh of Balma, from a
number of points of view.[163] He accepts Hugh's teaching up to a point, for
instance he agrees that mystical theology consists in love and that love is
supernaturally bestowed upon those who desire wisdom. The whole of
Scripture, Gerson argues, bears witness to this. Infused love is not caused
by human knowing. It is the little ones, the pure in heart, the men of desire
whom God satisfies with eternal wisdom from the breasts of His

consolation.[164] However, although he concedes a number of points to Hugh, Gerson finally rejects the doctrine that the love which is mystical theology is not accompanied by knowledge. There *is* knowledge, not demonstrative but experiential knowledge.[165]

In a number of places Gerson tackles the problems related to the interpretation of Dionysius' negative way and divine darkness. In the *Collectorium super magnificat* he reproduces Dionysius' analogy of the sculptor who is carving a statue out of stone. The sculptor removes all the impediments that hinder the eye from seeing, and in that very removal displays the hidden form. This, says Gerson, is what happens in knowledge by negation. The sculptor adds nothing to the stone to make the statue; he only takes away, 'but he leaves something when the taking away is done, namely a beautiful image'.[166] In other words, for Gerson, Dionysius' negative way is positive. He goes on to say that Augustine agrees with Dionysius when he (Augustine) says 'When you hear "this good" and "that good" take away this good and that good and see, if you can, the good itself, good with nothing else; then you will see God. So with the true, the beautiful and above all with being, and with every divine attribute.'[167]

As for the divine darkness, in the same treatise Gerson admits that there are in fact two darknesses. The first we have already met: the obscure cloud in which all creatures, all created things, must be hidden by the soul seeking mystical union with God. But in addition there is that darkness wherein dwells God who has made the shadows His hiding-place (Ps. 17:12). Thus, says Gerson, the experiential perception of God does not terminate in a clear and untrammelled vision of God but rests in a certain darkness above itself. And yet 'this experiential perception of God through darkness does not occur without the clearest illumination'.[168] He admits that this is difficult to explain, and indeed his explanation by means of complex analogies is not particularly successful. He calls upon Augustine, Dionysius, Richard of St Victor and John Damascene to help him. The gist of his argument seems to be that in order to see darkness the eye must be between two darknesses, behind and before, but if it is to see the darkness before it, the medium must be illuminated. Moreover, he goes on, when we say there is darkness in God, we do not mean that God is strictly darkness, but that He is not light, in the sense that He is above light.[169] This seems to be in accord with Dionysius when he writes of the 'superluminous, super-manifest and super-resplendent darkness' and calls on his disciple to ascend to the 'superessential rays of divine shadows'.[170]

In his brief commentary on chapter 1 of Dionysius' *Mystical Theology*, written in 1429, Gerson asks if God in mystical union can be loved immediately, though not known. He answers in the affirmative and then adds: 'but even in such an act there is concomitant and subsequent knowledge, that is, perceptual and practical, though not speculative, knowledge'.[171]

Gerson was not, then, a 'pure' Dionysian in the sense that Hugh of Balma was. This reading of Gerson accords with the opinion of Vincent of Aggsbach, cited earlier. In the mid fifteenth century Vincent was involved in a quarrel with the cardinal, Nicholas of Cusa, about the nature of Dionysian mysticism, and by attacking the deceased chancellor he was able to cast some barbs at the living cardinal, whose doctrine on the subject was close to Gerson's. Vincent began his attack on Gerson with an objection to Gerson's identifying mystical theology with prayer and defining the latter as 'the highest mental and intellectual affection'.[172] For Vincent, if mystical theology could be called prayer, it was not an intellectual but a trans-intellectual prayer, because the peak of affection could enter the holy of holies only if it had left understanding outside.[173] Vincent objected also to Gerson's *Elucidatione* where he found his own position opposed in Gerson's discussion of Hugh of Balma, and he also blamed Gerson for knowing the true opinion but not accepting it.[174] In Vincent's eyes Gerson was a traitor to Dionysius, and he cited, among others, Hugh of Balma and Thomas Gallus to prove it.[175]

That there is an important cognitive element in Gerson's mysticism is also the opinion of Connolly and Ozment. The latter has shown that this cognitive element was present from the beginning,[176] thereby challenging Oberman's categorisation of Gerson's mysticism as 'affective and penitential', and Combes' opinion that there is a change from the mysticism of the *Speculativa* of 1402, which is 'exclusively affective' for Combes, to the more cognitive mysticism of the *Practica* in 1407.[177] The vernacular sermon of 1402, *Videmus nunc*, confirms Ozment's conclusion. Moreover, Gerson's later writings on mystical theology, as we have seen, provide evidence that in the last five years of his life he continued to hold that knowledge accompanied love in the mystical union.[178]

Is Gerson's mystical teaching then consistent from beginning to end? There are nuances, of course, and Gerson adapts his material to his audience and to circumstances. He can be hortatory, devotional, analytical, philosophical or polemical. There are definite developments. For instance, the doctrine of the spiritual senses is mentioned in *The Mountain* but not elaborated until the *Elucidation*. But in its broad lines, as described here, there is consistency. Mysticism is always for all, love always leads the way, and there is always concomitant knowledge in mystical union.[179] This is true of Gerson's formal works, academic and vernacular, sermons, treatises and tracts. Those who see Gerson as wavering in his views on mysticism are relying overmuch on Combes' interpretation, which itself places a great deal of emphasis on one letter.[180] Ozment, however, has made a very good case against Combes for consistency not only between the *Speculativa* and the *Practica* but also up to 1416 in a sermon, *Spiritus Domini*, which Gerson preached at Constance, a sermon which Combes sees as revealing a rather different, more Spirit-centred, mysticism.[181] It should be pointed out that what Combes, the most formidable and knowledgeable of twentieth-century Gerson scholars, sees in Gerson is not so much wavering as healthy development towards a fully mystical doctrine, reached on 1 October 1425, and revealed in the letter of that date.[182] For Combes the major question is not whether Gerson's concept of mysticism is affective or intellective, but whether it is essentialist, in an orthodox sense, of course. He sees Gerson in this letter, probably having had a mystical experience, reaching a concept of mysticism reminiscent of that described by Knowles. For Knowles, as we have seen, the mystical experience takes place at a deeper level of the soul than that at which the normal processes of thought take place and the mystic is aware of his soul and the divine presence and action within it as something wholly distinct from the reasoning mind with its powers. In the letter in question, Gerson states that it now seems to him that 'mystical theology, which is the union of the soul with God, consists neither in the work of the intellect nor in that of the affect, though both are necessary as preliminary dispositions'. Rather, he continues, when the soul has been purified, simplified and freed from all solicitude, all desire and all imagining, then mystical theology exists, and it consists, as Dionysius says, in the soul being united in an ineffable and unknown manner to the ineffable God. He goes on to state that just as sanctifying grace does not unite the intellect alone or draw the will alone to God, but rather acts on the essence of the soul, so it is with mystical theology, which is the union of the essence of the spirit or mind with God. Later in the letter Gerson states that our spirit, through this union with the divine and eternal, becomes deiform.[183]

Combes sees Gerson here repudiating the notion that the mystical experience is the work of either or both faculties of the soul culminating in a union primarily of love, and embracing instead the doctrine that it is the work of grace culminating in a union of essences where God becomes, as it were ('toutes précautions prises'), the form of the soul.[184] If this is indeed a 'conversion' one would expect Gerson to have retracted his earlier works. Combes acknowledges this, and indeed goes further, expecting Gerson to have retracted his criticisms of Ruysbroeck as well. In fact, Gerson did neither of these things. Instead he produced a fourth edition of the 1408 treatise with only very minor alterations. Moreover, as we have seen, he went on writing about the affective and intellective powers in connection with mystical theology.[185]

If the position of 1425 was not a 'conversion' it might nevertheless represent a temporary change of mind. But the placing of the stress on the essence of the soul rather than on the affective and intellective powers need not be interpreted as a radical alteration. Gerson had long ago stated that the distinction between the powers of the soul was not a real distinction. Perhaps in 1425 he thought that he had previously over-emphasised it and now wished to stress the transformation of the soul's very being in mystical union.

The statement in the letter that the soul is made deiform (*deiformis*) should not be cause for surprise. In *Videmus nunc* Gerson had already spoken of a transforming union in which the soul's relation to God was like that of the sculptor's image of himself to the sculptor. The image was distinct from the sculptor but 'sans différence de nature'.[186] Moreover in the *Speculativa* Gerson had made this observation:

Before the reception of form matter is imperfect, lacks beauty, power and activity. If form is given to it, it immediately attains perfection in accord with the nature of the form. In like manner, the soul... when it is united with God, receives a certain divine life.

He adds a qualifying clause to the effect that God does not actually become the form of the soul in mystical union. But the 'influx of divine life is very intimate and excludes every possibility of imperfection'.[187] There does not seem to be any radical difference between this description and the *deiformis* of the letter of 1425.

Combes is certainly mistaken if he thinks that Gerson held that mystical theology was chiefly the work of the powers of the soul before 1425 – or at least before 1416 – and solely the work of grace after 1425. Gerson never held the former position. The mystical way was always traversed in the context of grace.[188] Certainly Gerson tells his readers that they must strive, and there are passages in both the Latin and vernacular works which, if read in isolation, might lead the aspiring mystic to think he was on his own. This is true of the writings of a number of mystics. But Gerson inserts enough reminders to make it clear that human effort, though necessary, is not enough. God and the soul are co-workers. In *The Mountain*, it will be remembered, Gerson says that the difficulty of discarding worldly love is so great that it cannot be accomplished unless God provides the grace.[189] Chapter 30 of the same work is entitled 'Of the necessity of grace', this time in the achieving of solitude and silence.[190] Moreover, if it were not for God's prevenient grace we would not even start out on the mystical way. As the soul says in the prayer to the saints, they must give help because it is God's wish and command. 'If it were the will of God to condemn me, He would not have granted me the desire to repent and to ask for His aid.'[191] The importance of divine grace is stressed in the *Practica*. The twelve activities of the mystical way can be carried out successfully only if God first grants aid.[192] Even in the *Speculativa*, where the long discussion of the powers of the soul occurs, Gerson points out that human preparation does not suffice for the achievement of mystical, transforming union.[193]

Other mystical writers leave a similar impression. The reader is told what he must do to achieve the goal, but he is reminded with varying degrees of frequency that in the last resort it all depends on God. Bonaventure, for instance, describes the transforming union as 'something mystical and very secret and no one knows it except him who receives it, and no one receives it except him who desires it, and no one desires it unless the fire of the Holy Spirit inflames him to the very marrow'.[194] Tauler tells his hearers in one sermon to 'do all that you can, more than you can...', but in another he states that not only is it the Holy Spirit who fills us, but it is the Holy Spirit who must prepare the place for Himself by emptying us of everything creaturely.[195]

In the last resort, then, for medieval mystical writers, including Gerson, mystical theology is not a matter of love and/or knowledge and a third factor, God's grace. The love and the knowledge *are* divine graces. And, for Gerson at least, one might put it another way: God works with and in the soul's loving and knowing powers. Whatever he said about the essence of the soul in the letter of 1 October 1425, this statement accords with the teaching of his academic and vernacular mystical writings.

THE FEAR OF HERESY

Almost always when he writes about mystical union Gerson takes the precaution of stating that the created soul remains distinct from God. We have seen him do this in the sermon *Videmus nunc*. He takes the same precaution in the *Speculativa*, and in his treatise on the Magnificat he states that the expression 'the mind is abandoned' (*deseritur mens*) does not mean that the mind loses its own being in God. This would be the heresy of Amaury. Rather, the mind remains essentially in itself. Later in the same work when he says that the mind is transformed into God, he insists that the essence of the mind remains, although it acquires new attributes (*accidentia nova*), which are not material but deiform.[196] Gerson also distances himself from heretical views about man's pre-created state. His own view is that before creation the creature was in the divine mind as the picture that is painted is in the mind of the artist. There was not a real and essential identity between the soul that was to be created and the Creator, as the Manichees blasphemed.[197] The doctrine of the pre-created state of the soul which Gerson is opposing is, of course, connected with pantheistic interpretations of mystical union where the soul, having originally been one with the essence of God, is held to return to its source by being reabsorbed into the divine essence.

Not only does Gerson frequently underline his own orthodox position, but he also frequently warns against heretical doctrines about mystical union. We have seen that he criticised some of Ruysbroeck's statements and was concerned about possible misinterpretations of the *Epistola ad fratres Monte Dei*. He did not like the 'mixed liquids' metaphor or other images of a similar type. In the *Speculativa* he lists these: a drop of water that loses its essence in a bottle of wine; food that is converted into bodily nourishment by digestion; burning coal or iron that seems to be totally fire; solar illumination of the air, where the air and light seem to become one;

Eucharistic transformation; magnetised iron; and vaporised air.[198] Although he acknowledges that these analogies are used in an attempt to make the mystical union more understandable, he thinks they are not suitable for the purpose because they suggest a loss of identity and a total absorption of the soul into God. In the letter of 1 October 1425 he criticises Ubertino of Casale's *Arbor vitae crucifixae Jesu* for containing, among other things, an error about the law or spirit of liberty perpetrated by the Beghards and Beguines. This erroneous teaching, he writes, states that the perfected soul, returned to God, loses its will so that it has no will except the divine will which it had from eternity in the ideal divine essence (*in esse ideali divino*). From this premise, Gerson tells us, the heretics deduce that they can do, without sin, whatever carnal desire prompts them to do.[199]

This criticism of Ubertino's book provides a clue to the motive behind Gerson's frequent references to heretical teaching about mysticism. As an orthodox cleric naturally he was concerned that he and others should avoid any doctrines officially condemned as heretical, for example, Amaury's pantheism. But this was far from being merely an academic matter for Gerson. Heretical mystical teaching was having very unfortunate effects outside the university. Many times Gerson refers to the heresies of the Beghards and Beguines or Turpulins, as the Beghards and Beguines were styled in France. In the *Speculativa*, for instance, he makes the same complaint about them as he does in the 1425 letter: they teach that when a man has achieved tranquil peace of spirit he is freed from all divine laws.[200] Gerson says that he has read of this antinomianism being defended on the grounds that it accords with the apostle's words: 'Have charity and do what you will.'[201] He thinks that some of the Turpulins mistake the derangement of their minds for mystical experience of God, and he berates others, who think that God acts in them only in so far as they remain passive, for their quietism.[202] He recognises that many of them are genuinely devout. The trouble is that their devotion is not guided by knowledge (*secundum scientiam*) and so they are very prone to error, often even more so than people lacking devotion. They need guidance and this is why it is necessary, Gerson says, that students in theology should be well versed in sound mystical teaching.[203]

Gerson was not imagining these dangers. The Beguines were devout women who, although they did not belong to monastic orders, undertook to pursue a communal life of piety and celibacy, while continuing to work in the world. The Beghards, far fewer in number, were their male counterparts. The majority of these devout men and women of the later Middle Ages were perfectly orthodox, but some, generally known as the Free Spirits, were accused of embracing heretical beliefs of the pantheistic, antinomian and quietist nature described by Gerson. It was these beliefs that were condemned at the Council of Vienne in 1312.[204]

The chancellor singles out Marie of Valenciennes and her 'incredibly subtle book' for particular censure.[205] Marie de Valenciennes has been identified as Margaret Porrette, whose book was publicly burned at Valenciennes. She herself was burned at the stake in Paris in 1310. Her book, *Le Miroir des simples âmes*, does contain statements of a pantheistic and antinomian nature.[206]

Gerson has been accused of being 'obsessed with the dangers of unregulated mysticism'.[207] If Gerson was obsessed then so were a number of other people. Lerner discusses the writings of the fourteenth-century German Augustinian Jordan of Quedlinburg, who attacked Free Spirit pantheistic heresies.[208] Jordan was an Inquisitor, so his 'obsession' is perhaps understandable. But we do not even need to explain Gerson's concern on the grounds that he was always conscious of his responsibilities as Chancellor of the University of Paris. Far less influential personages than he in the later Middle Ages were concerned about heresy developing out of mystical teaching. There are at least six of Tauler's sermons in which the topic of pseudo-mysticism is discussed.[209] Tauler attacks particularly the errors of the Free Spirits. Their notion of the 'freedom of spirit' he calls a false freedom because it simply means that they follow whatever their natural inclinations may be. Their quietism, too, comes under censure. 'They are filled with love for their own false passivity, false because it is not combined with an active charity, interior or exterior.'[210] Tauler finds these self-styled mystics bold, obstinate, contentious, violent, proud and quarrelsome, full of self-love and self-esteem. 'They will listen to people preaching utter rubbish, with neither life-giving doctrine nor moral teaching in it, and imagine that they have been imbibing the purest truth.'[211] Suso is equally out-spoken. Chapter VI of his *Little Book of Truth* is a dialogue in which the Disciple points out the errors of the Wild Man's antinomianism.[212]

One of the longest single discussions of pseudo-mysticism occurs in Ruysbroeck himself.[213] The Flemish mystic makes a careful distinction between the state of the true mystic who has stripped his mind of images and activity and yet is alert because of the inward touch of God's grace, on the one hand, and the mere vacancy of mind of the pseudo-mystic who has simply sunk down into himself into a state of idleness, on the other. Because of this 'bare vacancy' the latter believes himself 'to be free, and to be united with God without means, and to be above all the customs of Holy Church, and above the commandments of God and above the law and above every work of virtue'.[214] Ruysbroeck goes on to discuss the familiar charge against the Free Spirits: their belief that they can do no sin. Chapters 23 and 38 of the *German Theology* are devoted to a discussion of false, lawless freedom and the pseudo-mystics who pay no heed to Scripture or to the rules, orders, laws and sacraments of the church, who fancy themselves to be God.[215] Even in England, not a centre of the Free Spirit heresy, we find Hilton warning against those so blinded by the false light that they think their own will is freedom of spirit, and so 'errors and heresies come from them like rain from black clouds'.[216]

Gerson is not, then, peculiar in his warnings against the heretical potentialities of mystical teaching. In fact, his two vernacular treatises and his vernacular sermon about the mystical way do not contain such warnings. It is largely in his lectures for theology students – future pastors – and in a few sermons, letters and treatises for clerics that his strictures against erroneous or carelessly worded mystical writings and his fear about pseudo-mysticism are expressed. And he – and the others – were right to be concerned. Mysticism could be very heady stuff, particularly for untutored minds or the emotionally unbalanced. This is why Gerson, though he holds that mysticism is open to all and that the way is chiefly a way of love and not of intellectual exercise, insists that devotion must be firmly grounded in faith and be *secundum scientiam*, that there must always be a honeycomb to contain the honey. He will have nothing to do with unanchored affectivity. Had he been 'obsessed with the dangers of unregulated mysticism' he would have done better to teach a restricted mysticism, confined to an elite of academics or monastic contemplatives. But his own convictions and the biblically based traditions he inherited were against this. The risks must be taken, but it was only wise to warn against them.

One would very much like to know if Gerson had had mystical experiences himself. He never says he has been so favoured. In fact he sometimes says that he is not qualified to write about mystical experiences because of lack of experience.[217] Then there is what might be interpreted as a plaintive remark in his work on the Magnificat. Mystical union, he writes, is the hidden mystery which no one knows unless he receives it, and 'yet it can be known by teaching founded on authority...or else blessed Dionysius and the rest would have laboured in vain by writing books on the subject'.[218] The lack of reference to any personal mystical experience could, of course, be the result of humble reticence. But there was no tradition enforcing such reticence. Bernard, one of Gerson's most admired authors, makes frequent reference to his own mystical experiences.[219] Neither the German Suso nor the English Rolle is reticent. On the other hand, both Eckhardt and Tauler are, or at least they do not write of any mystical experiences they might have had. Combes suggests that Gerson probably did have a mystical experience on 1 October 1425, from which followed his 'conversion'.[220] If so, Gerson does not, in the letter of 1 October, try to describe this experience in the way that Bernard, Suso and Rolle do. Rather, he writes as the speculative mystical theologian, analysing union in scholastic fashion (*scolastico more*), as he himself says.

Gerson's discussions of mystical union in his academic works appear 'bookish'; he is analysing what others have said, attempting to work out and explain his own doctrine. The vernacular tracts are better sources if one wishes to learn something of his own spiritual experiences, though even in these tracts there is much that is borrowed. Gerson, however, does write more freely here and one can gain some impression about his spiritual life. In his descriptions of the mystical way with its moments of sweetness, joy and consolation and its periods of langour, tribulation and difficulty, one does get the impression that although he has experienced the heights, if not the peak, he is more familiar with the depths. We do not seem to be dealing with a great ecstatic mystic, though we are dealing with a very good pastoral director.

For people apparently familiar with the heights and full of joy and confidence we have to look elsewhere. Despite the fact that Gerson knew, liked and recommended Bernard's sermons on the Songs of Songs, William of St Thierry's *Epistola* and Hugh of St Victor's *De arrha animae*, there could hardly be a greater contrast between the general tone of his mystical writings and theirs. The twelfth-century mystics write in a much more polished style[221] and with far more optimism than Gerson. Hugh's book, for instance, whose particular dialogue form Gerson borrowed for the *Mendicité*, does describe the ugliness of the soul befouled by sin, but this discussion is very short and the bulk of the treatise is about the beauty of the soul. 'Love yourself', says Hugh, because the bridegroom loves you. 'One so fair, so handsome, so graceful, so unique would not have been taken with your appearance had He not been attracted by comeliness, eminent and admirable beyond the rest.'[222] He urges the soul to take delight in worldly things because they are gifts of the bridegroom. 'Love them for His sake.' Hugh enumerates and discusses the betrothal gifts, from all the things in the universe, which were created for man's use, the soul's own intellectual gifts and virtues of character, to the Redemption and the sacraments. 'Happy fall', interjects the soul in the discussion of the Redemption, 'because man can rise the happier from his falling.'[223] The treatise ends with a beautifully written description of the sweetness and delight of the bridegroom's embrace.

Bernard, in the Sermons, is aglow with joy and delight, and William of St Thierry, though in quieter vein, betrays a similar confidence and assurance. These are men who seem sure they will arrive. Bernard discusses predestination in one of his sermons. His attitude to this apparently knotty and anxiety-producing problem is characteristic of the man. He simply expresses joy that the elect were predestined even before they were born; the bride was prepared from all eternity.[224] For William the monk's cell is an almost sure way to heaven. 'It is scarcely ever that anyone goes down from his cell into hell when he dies, because scarcely ever does anyone who is not predestined to heaven persevere in a cell until death.'[225] It is not that these three writers ignore the need for humility and asceticism, ignore the difficulties, but the stress is on joy.

One might argue that these are monks writing in the peaceful security of monasteries for other monks – not that Bernard's life was spent peacefully within walls, devoid of ecclesiastical problems. Moreover, they are writing in the heyday of a monastic revival. Gerson, on the other hand, is a secular priest and academic writing for the laity, and thus one would expect a difference. The spirit of twelfth-century mysticism, however, spilled over into the thirteenth-century Franciscan Bonaventure, an academic like Gerson. Bonaventure's *Soliloquium* is very reminiscent of Hugh and Bernard. A number of passages are clearly borrowed from the former's *De arrha*. There is more in Bonaventure than in Hugh on the defilement by sin of the soul's image so that it becomes like a harlot, but again the overall impression is of the beautiful, intelligent, graced bride. One would expect to find a more optimistic and joyful picture in authors working with the image of the bride than in one, like Gerson in *La Mendicité*, working with the image of a beggar, but it is perhaps significant that Gerson chose the latter rather than the former image.[226] Gerson did write a vernacular piece based on the bridal image, *Le Jardin amoureux de l'âme*.[227] The bride hears the call of the bridegroom, but the way to Him is difficult, with prickly hedges, high walls, stern guards. When the bride finally enters the garden she finds it full of the fragrance of beautiful herbs and flowers. But then she comes upon the bridegroom, dead on the cross, and is told that she must wait till after her own death to receive the kiss. Perhaps this is how Gerson conceived of his own spiritual life.

One should be tentative about concluding from limited evidence that something of the spark had gone out of mystical writing between the thirteenth and the fifteenth century. But this is the impression left from a reading of Bernard, Hugh, William and Bonaventure on the one hand, and of Gerson and some of the late medieval mystics on the other, and this despite the fact that a number of the latter were monks or friars themselves. Not that there is total homogeneity among the later writers. They are working within the same rich tradition, and one meets the same authorities, the same examples and even the same phrases many times as one reads them. Yet the mix is always different and the overall flavour varies from writer to writer. There are some like Gerson who deliberately raise puzzling questions in the course of their mystical writings, for example Hilton, who raises the problem of grace and free will,[228] and the author of the *German Theology*, who asks why God created the world and man in the first place.[229] Some are more repetitious and disorderly than Gerson, some less so. None write in such a polished style as the twelfth-century mystics or Bonaventure, perhaps because most of them are writing in the vernacular.[230] There is still some exuberance, for instance in Rolle, and mystics still write of the joy of union itself, but whatever the cause – and no doubt part of the cause is that these later medieval mystics were generally writing for a wider audience – the overall impression is that the mystical way has somehow become more difficult, and in some ways more dangerous.[231] But for Gerson the advantages far outweighed the difficulties and the dangers. We all, religious, academics and laity alike, are called to attempt, with grace, the mystical journey, and if we reach the end we shall have received the highest Christian wisdom possible for the pilgrim in this life.

7

WOMEN, MARRIAGE AND CHILDREN

It has been assumed so far that Gerson's parishioners and the laity in general who had contact, direct or indirect, with his pastoral writings formed a homogeneous group. But half – in fact probably more than half – of these people would be women. Remarks made by some medieval preachers suggest that then, as now, women were more assiduous in their attendance at church and sermons than men.[1] It cannot be taken for granted, however, that a late medieval pastor's attitude to and beliefs and teachings about the female members of his flock would be identical with those he held towards and about the male members. One would be nearer the truth if one assumed that he viewed women as inferior to men in some respects at least. Is this the position maintained by Gerson? What are his opinions and teachings on the 'woman-question' – a question which, in its literary form, became quite prominent in his lifetime with the outbreak of the controversy over the *Roman de la rose* around the turn of the century, and the *querelle des dames* during the following decades?

Gerson's position on women was not developed in a vacuum. It was strongly influenced by the theological tradition which he inherited: scriptural texts, the writings of the Fathers, the work of earlier theologians and canonists. The actual position of women in the society of his day and the attitudes taken to women in the literature of the medieval period no doubt coloured his thought, while his own experience of women possibly played its part. It would be unwise, though, to push an autobiographical explanation too far, for we know the course of his life only in general terms, with few personal details.

Whatever the promise of freedom and equality offered to women by the gospel, Western Europe in the late Middle Ages remained an androcentric society.[2] The picture of the actual role played by women during this period is not yet completely clear. What is clear is that women were not 'privatised', relegated to a purely domestic sphere. As long ago as 1926 Eileen Power argued that in everyday life women 'played an active and dignified part in society'.[3] She describes them as abbesses using their powers of organisation and spiritual leadership; as managers of large estates during the absence of their husbands, or when they were widows or dowagers. In urban society women not only shared in the work of their husbands' crafts and businesses, but often carried on crafts and businesses of their own, while in the peasant classes they formed a vital part of the family economy by working for wages or on the family's land. In fact, the lower the class to which they belonged the closer women came to being on equal terms with their husbands.[4] Power goes on to argue that in daily life a 'rough and ready equality between the sexes in all classes prevailed and that women had more scope in this period than in the eighteenth and early nineteenth centuries'.[5] More recent work has generally confirmed Power's conclusions. Studies of manorial records have revealed peasant women as landholders in their own right, inheriting, selling and bequeathing property; as producers doing some of the same outside work as men; as farm labourers often getting equal pay for equal work; as suitors to manorial courts and pleading their own cases there.[6] Women, in England at least, are also to be found bringing suits before the king's court,[7] and it would be difficult to see Margaret Paston in fifteenth-century Norfolk as anything but an equal partner with her husband in managing and defending the family estates.[8] The position of women in medieval society was not, however, static. There is reason to believe that it had declined by the thirteenth century from what it had been in the frontier situation of the early medieval period, and that further deterioration occurred by the sixteenth century.[9]

Despite the 'rough and ready equality' in late medieval daily life women had no real place in the formal organisation of power. Here the male dominated. Apart from the special case of royal minorities when queens might act as regents, women had no public duties: they were called neither to the army, nor to royal councils, nor to parliament or estates, and they could not be jurors or judges. Peasant and urban women did not become reeves, constables, heads of tithings or hold high office in guilds.[10] Further, in law, in many places, they suffered from serious incapacities. This was true in the civil law areas in France where, from the end of the fourteenth century, the incapacity of women was aggravated under the growing influence of Roman law and to some extent of theologians and canonists. Wives were no longer able to act juridically on behalf of their absent husbands. They were considered incapable and their legal status became like that of minors.[11] Even in the customary areas of France, the juridical inferiority of women was quite marked. They were regarded as under paternal authority until they married or entered religion. Once they were under a husband's tutelage the duty of cohabitation weighed more heavily on them than on their spouses. In some customary areas in the later Middle Ages, however, women could perform some juridical acts without the assistance of their husbands, and here it was not till the sixteenth century that husbands acquired complete control over the juridical acts of their wives.[12]

In canon law women were placed 'in an astonishing state of inferiority'.[13]

For Gratian, writing in the first half of the twelfth century, woman was in such a state of servitude that she had to be under the subjection of a man in everything.[14] All her juridical incapacities could be explained by this state of subjection. And her incapacities were many. In the first place, she was excluded from the priesthood. As Thomas expresses it: 'since it is not possible in the female sex to signify eminence of degree, for a woman is in the state of subjection, it follows that she cannot receive the sacrament of order'.[15] She was also excluded from the exercise of any jurisdiction in the church, except for the maternal right of government exercised over other women, as in the case of abbesses. Female religious superiors, however, as other women, were not allowed to hear confessions, or to confer the veil on their subordinates, nor could they read the gospel or preach in public, though they could, with permission, give instruction in faith and morals in private. A woman could not, according to canon law, be a judge or arbitrator; she could not bring a criminal accusation or be a witness in a criminal case. Finally, women were not permitted to serve at mass, or to touch the vessels and sacred linens of the altar; in other words, they were excluded from all participation in liturgical functions.[16]

On the other hand, canon law proclaimed a considerable equality between men and women in questions related to marriage. The conditions for the formation of a marriage were exactly the same for both sexes: both were to have complete liberty of consent and no difference was made between the intending spouses on the question of impediments. Husband and wife had equal rights as far as conjugal duties were concerned and neither could make a vow of continence or enter a religious order without the consent of the other, while the grounds for separation were the same for the wife as for the husband.[17] Adultery was one such ground. In Roman law adultery had been an offence of wives only, but medieval canonists treated it as criminal whether committed by a man or a woman.[18] There was no double standard for them, whatever may have been the popular view.[19] In marriage cases involving sexual rights women were as fully empowered as men to sue in a church court.[20] However, in aspects of married life other than the sexual, the husband was seen by the canonists as having authority over his wife; as in the secular law, he had the right to correct and chastise her.[21]

In justification of his statement about the servitude of women, Gratian cities the authority of St Paul, of Roman law and above all of St Augustine. Western thinking about women was, in fact, given its shape chiefly by the latter.[22] For Augustine woman's status was definitely one of subordination. This position corresponded to the actual social and juridical conditions of his time, which he accepted as part of the nature of things and never questioned. He regarded it as God's will that the relation between man and wife, even in Eden, should be hierarchical, 'the one ruling and the other obeying'.[23] The fall made conditions more burdensome for woman, for as a result of it her subordination in the order of creation could degenerate into servitude. The strength of Augustine's feeling about the inferiority of women may be seen in his remark that woman's role and only purpose is to help man in the work of procreation, for in all other matters a male friend is a more efficient helper and better companion than a woman,[24] a view repeated by St Thomas.[25] In fact, the influence of Aristotle, seen in the writings of Thomas, while it may have produced a more enlightened view of the sexual relationship in marriage, tended only to reinforce the Augustinian teaching of feminine inferiority.

As regards the individual nature, woman is defective and misbegotten, for the active force in the male semen tends to the production of a perfect likeness in the masculine sex; while the generation of women comes from defect in the active force or from some indisposition of the matter, or even from some external influence, for example that of the moist south wind, as the Philosopher observes in his book (*De generat. animal.* IV. 2).[26]

Thomas goes on to argue that some subordination, 'domestic or civil', is necessary for the proper government of the human family and that therefore, even before the fall, 'woman is naturally subject to man, because in man, by nature, the discretion of reason is more abundant'.[27] The doctrine of woman's inferiority and subordination to her husband persisted among theologians and canonists throughout the Middle Ages and was still to be found in Luther and Calvin.[28] The view of man as the more rational of the species was equally ubiquitous.

Despite this clear inferiority in the order of creation, women in a very real sense, according to Augustine and other theologians, and canonists, enjoyed perfect equality with men. Christ died to redeem male and female alike; sanctity was open to all; the sermon on the mount applied to all; all were called to share heaven. Whenever Augustine writes of the faith and of salvation he makes no distinction between men and women. Who is there, he writes, who would exclude women from the renovation by which we are made sons of God? 'Faithful women are renewed in the image of God in that part of their being where there is no sex, just as the human being [*homo*] was created in the image of God in that part where there is no sex, namely in his spiritual soul.'[29] At the Resurrection, Augustine argues, the subordination of women to men in the order of creation will be at an end, and a perfect equality will prevail. Similar ideas leading to the same basic doctrine of equality between the sexes in the order of salvation and grace are found in Thomas. The end of woman, Thomas states, is the same as the end of man and, because of this individual finality, women, as men, may receive baptism and the other sacraments, except of course that of orders, which pertains to the visible church in the order of creation.[30]

Moreover, there was one woman who was idealised and exalted above all other human beings by Catholic theologians: the mother of Christ. The cult of the Virgin, which was widespread among the faithful by the eleventh century and remained so in the later medieval period, was echoed by preachers in devotional sermons, by theologians and in secular writing. Jerome's 'mors per Evam, vita per Mariam' indicates one of the principal themes of this Mariology, expressed by Augustine in terms of encouragement to women, who need not despair, he wrote, despite Eve's role in the fall. God honoured both sexes in the Incarnation and thus showed that women were saved as well as men.[31] Thomas repeated this theme: Mary introduced the feminine elements in the work of redemption to show that the female sex was also freed from sin.[32] In countless sermons Mary was praised for her humility, her virginity, for being the embodiment of all the virtues, as an example for all – men as well as women.

It would seem, then, that theologians and canonists had created a paradoxical situation for woman. She was a member of the invisible church equally with man, with the same individual finality, the same call to and possibility of salvation, with one member of her sex specially singled out for a unique role in the process of redemption. Yet in the visible church, in secular society and in the family she was, by God's will, an inferior being, subordinate to man, suffering from numerous juridical incapacities. With this tradition behind and around him, Gerson can hardly be expected to produce egalitarian views about the status of women, but it should be possible to discern whether, within the given context, his position leans more towards or away from the 'enlightened' end of the spectrum.

Much of the secular literature of his time also tends to betray an androcentric and even misogynist view. Medieval literary works that discussed the 'woman-question' were far more likely to be attacks on women than defences.[33] In these satires against women, as in those of the classical period, the female sex is accused of pride, obstinacy, lasciviousness, jealousy, garrulity, vanity, greed, extravagance, caprice, infidelity, physical and moral inferiority, of being the very 'gateway of the devil', and in general making men's and especially husbands' lives miserable.[34] Dunbar's lines are not untypical.

> The beistlie lust, the furious appatite,
> The haistie wo, the verrie grit defame,
> The blind discretioun, and the foul delyte
> Off woman-kynde that dreidis for na schame.[35]

Women, indeed, figure more prominently than any other non-professional group in attacks levelled by medieval English writers.[36]

The same harsh attitude appears in French literature of the later medieval period. Woman is depicted as the temptress, the chief obstacle to the salvation of men, as an impure and inferior being, with little or no moral sense, and sometimes as not created in the image of God.[37] The anonymous late medieval satire, *Les Quinze Joyes de mariage*, enumerates fifteen ways in which the bad-tempered wife of a respectable citizen makes her husband's life very difficult, wasting his money, making irrational demands, endlessly complaining, seeking lovers and in general being perverse and cussed. Each 'joy' ends with the refrain 'And so he will spend his life in torment and end his days in misery.'[38] The *Roman de la rose* contains numerous passages of invective against women: they are fickle, avid and gluttonous, mercenary, quarrelsome, flirtatious, have no honour or sense of right and wrong; they swear and lie and continually chatter, and are full of guile and malice.[39] The *Roman* is not alone in its diatribes; and during the 100 or so years before Gerson became involved in the controversy over Jean de Meung, satiric expression against women had been growing in bulk in both France and England, while the cause of women had few defenders.[40] It is to the later fourteenth century that the French version of the *Lamentations of Matheolus* and Deschamps's *Le Miroir de mariage* belong, with their condemnations of the wiles of women and descriptions of the miseries of marriage. However, although complaint and satire against women was to continue for long after the Middle Ages, the first steps in the turning of the tide may be said to have begun during Gerson's lifetime with the strong defence of women made by Christine de Pisan in numerous works written between 1399 and 1430,[41] and initially occasioned by the debate over Jean de Meung's portion of the *Roman de la rose*.[42] Thereafter works in defence of women began to appear in France and elsewhere more frequently, though it was not until the sixteenth century that such literary defences began to approach the number of the misogynist attacks and a continued effort was made to review and even demolish the opinion that women were morally inferior to men.[43]

Gerson's lifetime, then, coincided with the beginning of a period of transition in attitudes to women in secular literature. The same cannot be said about the situation in theology and law. The theologians and canonists remained conservative in this regard, while secular law about the status and rights of women became positively reactionary in some areas.

Gerson's personal history would lead one to expect that he would have a fairly high regard and sympathy for women, or at least that he would not tend to condemn the entire sex as lacking in virtue and spirituality. Such evidence as there is indicates that his relationship with his mother and six sisters, as with his father and three brothers, was excellent.[44] The Charlier family was a pious and close-knit one. The fact that, of the ten children who reached adulthood, one became a secular priest, three entered religious orders, and six[45] embraced a life of piety and virginity at home bears witness to the religious zeal and spiritual devotion of the household. Long after he had left home Gerson maintained contact with his family by letter, and during the period from about 1395 to 1407 he sent a series of tracts to his sisters to guide them in their communal spiritual life – a life which he had himself proposed to them in his *Discours sur l'excellence de la virginité*.[46] Some of these tracts are short lists of practical instructions about communal living; others are lengthy works on meditation and the contemplative life. For his mother Gerson must have had a very high regard and affection, for in a letter to his brother Nicholas he likens her to St Monica, Augustine's mother. He reminds his brother of the longing of their mother for another child and of the tears and care with which she had borne and reared him.[47]

There is no evidence of personal relationships between Gerson and any other women, though he frequently writes of women whom he had encountered in the course of his pastoral work. Some of these were devout and spiritual persons whom he admired and held up as examples but more of them were, in his opinion, deviants or cranks. It is clearly impossible to psychoanalyse the chancellor from this distance, but there is no indication in the material available that his judgement of women was likely to be warped by unfortunate personal experience.

In *Le Miroir de l'âme*, a French treatise initially sent to his sisters but enjoying widespread popularity, Gerson stated with no equivocation that women like men have souls created in the image of God:

God governs human creatures, men and women, to whom He has given and gives immortal souls created in His likeness to know, love, serve and honour Him so that, by living well in this world, they may come to the eternal glory of paradise.[48]

There is nothing remarkable here. The doctrine, though sometimes expressed with qualifications, that woman, as man, was created in the image of God, was dominant from the early Fathers onwards. Occasionally negative opinions were voiced, but only by a small minority.[49] The great authority of Augustine stood behind the dominant doctrine. He taught that the souls of both men and women were made in the image of God, because souls were asexual. Augustine's Neo-Platonic anthropology enabled him to posit two creations: *informatio*, the simultaneous creation of the souls of male and female as depicted in Genesis 1:27, and *conformatio*, the creation of the bodies of Adam and Eve, the latter derived from the former, as depicted in Genesis 2:7, 22. Sexual differences and therefore the inferiority of women were seen by Augustine as only in the body.[50] Thomas, following Aristotle, saw a close, in fact essential relation between the soul and the body and he therefore posited, against Augustine, their simultaneous creation.[51] Despite this, for Thomas, as for Augustine, the imperfection of woman springs from her bodily, not her spiritual nature.[52] However, although Thomas agrees with Augustine that because woman possesses an intellectual soul she possesses the image of God 'in its principal signification', in the same way and degree as man, there is a secondary aspect, he argues, in which man bears the image of God and she does not, 'for man is the beginning and end of woman; as God is the beginning and end of every creature'.[53] Gerson does not appear to have voiced any such qualifications.

The quotation from *Le Miroir de l'âme* also makes it clear that Gerson followed the orthodox tradition in holding that there was equality between the sexes in the order of redemption. His French sermons and treatises contain many references to women who were obviously, because of their piety, on the way to salvation. In his long sermon on the Passion he mentions more than once the role played by the devout women on the way to Calvary. At the halt when people were asking who would carry the cross, for instance, Gerson suggests that the 'holy and devout women' moved closer to Jesus, who then turned His face towards them and spoke to them.[54] Early in his Easter sermon of 1402 he describes Mary Magdalene, the other Marys, and other devout women preparing precious ointments to anoint the body of Christ.[55] Female saints are praised in another sermon of 1402: 'the holy martyrs, the little maids, Saint Agnes, Saint Agatha, Saint Cecile, Saint Katherine, who battled against sin to the death'.[56] There are, however, as one would expect, more references to male disciples and saints, and whole French sermons are devoted to some of them. Occasionally Gerson refers to pious women of his own day, as in the *Dialogue spirituel*, written for his sisters, where he writes of a devout woman named Agnes living in Aussoire, who constantly and ardently prayed for grace for herself and others, spending her time going from one saint to another.[57] Several times he remarks that simple women often show a deeper spirituality and a more ardent devotion or a more perfect love of God than do learned men.[58] The stress here is on the simple as opposed to the learned rather than on women as opposed to men and reflects the lack of education afforded women at the time, but probably also the opinion that women are by nature less well endowed with reason than men. However, with respect to salvation and mystical experience this is no handicap in Gerson's view. Indeed it may be a positive advantage.

The chancellor, then, leaves with his audience a firm impression that equality between the sexes prevails in the realm of grace and redemption. But his hearers and readers would acquire a very different impression about the situation in society, in the order of creation. During the course of a sermon on justice preached before the king, Gerson describes, in orthodox Augustinian terms, the situation before the fall. Man in the state of innocence, he writes, would have had no need of laws or coercive justice to make him behave well. There would have been no need for political rule, only for the rule 'of father over son, of man over woman, of the more wise over the less wise, of reason over the non-rational'.[59] It follows that in everyday life it is God's will that women be subject to their husbands.[60] Even the Virgin Mary, the mother of God, was subject to this divine ordinance, and she is frequently portrayed by Gerson as an example of the ideally submissive wife. Joseph, he writes, was the head of Our Lady, according to the rule of marriage given by God and promulgated by St Paul. And 'there is no doubt that her humility was so great that she rendered herself as much, or more, subject to her loyal spouse Joseph as other women should and can be to their spouses'.[61]

The subordinate role of women in marriage is made quite clear in the *Considérations sur St Joseph*. During the course of an argument against the opinion (*frivole objection*) that there could be a valid marriage between two men, if it is held that consent alone constitutes marriage, Gerson writes, quoting Hugh of St Victor (and all orthodox theologians would have agreed with him):

> Between two men or two women there cannot be a sacrament of marriage...for in a marriage there must be in one of the parties a perfect and active virtue (*vertus*), which is in the man, and he represents God; and in the other party there must be weakness and passive virtue, which is in the woman, and she represents holy church and the soul.[62]

Wives, however, do not have to obey their husbands on every occasion. If, for instance, they are ordered to do something that is against God, they, as servants so ordered by their masters or subjects by their rulers, are not held to obedience. They are advised to seek counsel of their confessors if such a situation arises.[63] Further, wives, as husbands, have rights as well as duties in marriage, and these rights and duties are fairly fully discussed in the two sermons on conjugal chastity. Women may not make vows of chastity, go on pilgrimages, or give alms without the consent of their husbands, but the same prohibition applies to men. On the other hand, Gerson forbids a woman to fast to such an extent that she renders herself 'weak and ugly and displeasing' to her husband without his consent.[64] Nor may she go to church except on Sundays and holy days of obligation, if her husband thinks her domestic duties make it necessary for her to remain at home. But no similar admonitions are made to husbands. Gerson's teaching is standard here. Moralists of the time, though they insist that vows of chastity by either spouse require the consent of the other, always appear to be more concerned about wives than husbands over-indulging in works of religious supererogation. Antoninus, for instance, in the rule of life he drew up for Lucrezia, wife of Piero de Medici, tells this Italian noblewoman that married women cannot fast, give alms, get up during the night to say prayers, or decline invitations to banquets, without the consent of their husbands.[65]

In one of his sermons on conjugal chastity Gerson tells women that they must suffer patiently the faults of their husbands for 'irritable and angry wives make angry husbands'.[66] They should choose carefully a suitable time for criticism, avoiding occasions when their husband is already angry. On the other hand, men 'ought to lend support to the fragility of their wives. If the wife is young, the husband may chastise her, first gently with words, then with rods.'[67] A man must protect his wife but not have her on too tight a rein, for a good wife does not need a rein and a bad one can always find some way to escape. There should be division of labour, the traditional division: 'The man ought to look after the important outside affairs...and the woman ought to take care of the household in sobriety and honesty.'[68] The woman must be submissive to her husband before guests: 'Speaking little, being humble, sober and chaste are the works which make a wife pleasing to her husband.' Though the stress throughout is on the woman as subject to the authority of her husband, Gerson insists that this authority must be wielded in a spirit of love: 'One must not use one's wife as a servant or chambermaid, but in all honour.'[69] Gerson echoes Paul, Augustine and Aquinas: a wife, though subject, is not a slave, but a companion deserving of respect and love.[70] Husbands should love their wives, Gerson tells his congregation, more than their mothers and their children, as wives should obey their husbands more than their parents.

The chancellor's discussion of the sexual relationship within marriage, in the second sermon on conjugal chastity, is concerned only with occasions when a wife may or may not refuse the conjugal debt to her husband; there is no mention of the husband's duty in this regard. Similarly in the discussion of adultery, Gerson concerns himself only with the right of a husband to put away his adulterous wife, and not with the right of a wife who has an adulterous husband.[71] Admittedly his advice is that the husband should stay with his wife if there is any hope of her amendment, and he disavows the civil law that allowed the injured husband to kill his wife, but in this sermon Gerson does leave the impression that there is a certain inequality in marital sexual matters, that a double standard prevails. However, his discussion in the Latin *Regulae mandatorum* shows that he followed the theological and canonical tradition upholding sexual equality in marriage. His remarks in this work about rendering the marriage debt apply to both spouses, and he states that fornication by either party can render a betrothal void.[72] Elsewhere he makes it clear that adultery is a grave sin in either partner.[73] So, despite the impression left by the written version of this sermon on chastity, Gerson was not less liberal in his attitude to women in this respect than his clerical predecessors and contemporaries.

Outside of the marriage situation, women, Gerson teaches, are still in a position of subordination and inferiority. In a Christmas Day sermon he discusses three questions that could be raised about the Incarnation. The third of these is 'why God preferred to become incarnate as a man and not a woman?'. In reply he quotes an opinion he attributes to Durandus: because God came as governor, doctor and combatter of the devil, and these offices do not belong to woman; 'in particular women should not preach or teach in public, as the apostle says'.[74] Gerson adds another traditional reason: that God could have wanted to honour man in taking on humanity, and woman in being born from her. He then elaborates on his distaste for women who pretend to a knowledge of theology.

They wish to speak and dispute about theology more than many a great theologian, and wishing to judge sermons and reprove preachers, they say of one that he has told a story from the Bible badly, and of another that he is teaching heresy; and when they have an opinion fixed in their heads, nothing will get rid of it.[75]

This has the ring of personal experience. His *Considérations sur St Joseph* contains a speculative passage about Mary, after her betrothal to Joseph, going to live in his parents' house and there speaking to them about Scripture. He imagines her talking about the coming of the Messiah in a quiet and familiar way in the domestic circle.[76] This clearly meets with Gerson's approval and no doubt he remembers his own mother teaching within her family; but any public display of learning in a woman he feels to be both wrong and distasteful.

In general he approved of women learning to read and write in the vernacular; he urged his sisters to do so in order that they could benefit from the treatises he wrote for them. But he saw some disadvantages. Women could then read and write love letters and this might lead to sin.[77] There are other scattered remarks in Gerson's writings that show he shared the prejudices of his culture about female inferiority. More than once he notes, for instance, as if it were part of the very nature of things, that the wages women earn are lower than those of men.[78]

Nevertheless, although it is clear that in Gerson's opinion women are in a subordinate position in the family and in society and are inferior to men in the order of creation, there is never any doubt that there is equality in the realm of salvation. Gerson, as pastor, shows as much concern for the female members of the faithful as for the male, if not more, and his statements about woman's subordinate role and inferiority are written as simple statements of fact that he expected no one to question. He does not write in the hectoring tone of one on the defensive, and it is highly improbable that any woman in his contemporary audience would have taken offence at his teaching on this aspect of the 'woman-question'.

May the same be said for his opinion of the character of women? Did he see woman as the temptress, as 'the gateway of the devil' as many theologians and preachers did? The spread of the ascetic ideal and monasticism in the early church was probably the chief factor leading to the concept of woman as the supreme temptress, the most dangerous of all obstacles in the way of salvation. Disparagement of sexuality tended to lead to disparagement of woman, the sexual object, and guilt feelings about desire could be projected as female lust and seductiveness. This dread of female seduction, together with guilt about sexuality, insistence on female subjection and stress on Eve's responsibility for the fall, is already found in the Pauline Epistles,[79] and in the early Fathers, being especially striking in Tertullian.[80] Thereafter the view of woman as being sexually insatiable and morally (as well as mentally) frail appears with monotonous regularity in the writings of medieval moralists.[81]

There is something of this attitude in Gerson's sermons and vernacular writings, but it is expressed in a comparatively mild manner. As far as Eve goes, on the two occasions when Gerson discusses the fall, he apportions no more blame to her than to Adam, merely stating that our first parents by their sin of disobedience closed the entry of paradise to all humanity.[82] In his Easter sermon of 1402 he does remark in passing that woman was the first cause of death, and so it is fitting that women should have been the first to bear the news of Christ's Resurrection.[83] But nowhere in his works for the laity does he belabour the point. He appears less harsh in his attitude to the first woman than, for example, Aquinas. The latter argues that the devil employed woman as an instrument of temptation to bring about the downfall of man, because 'the woman was weaker than the man, and therefore more liable to be deceived'.[84] But this does not excuse Eve, for she was also puffed up with pride. Adam, on the other hand, was not really deceived, and, although he was guilty of pride, his was a lesser pride than Eve's, and his sin was diminished because he was also motivated by love for his wife. 'It is therefore evident that the woman's sin was more grievous than the man's.'[85] Gerson may well have believed this, but if so, he did not express it in his vernacular writings. Nor did d'Ailly in his extant vernacular sermons: when he is discussing the fall, he never singles out Eve; he either writes of the sin of Adam, or the sin of our first parents.[86] Not all preachers were quite as sensitive to their audiences.[87]

Gerson is aware that woman is a temptress in the sexual sense. He points out, in the vernacular *Dialogue spirituel*, that hearing the confessions of young women can be a perilous occupation for priests, but he does not apportion blame on one side or the other.[88] In one of his university lectures, he discusses the dangers involved in the cohabitation of holy men and holy women. What begins as spiritual love, he says, can easily turn into carnal desire, for even 'iron minds' can become consumed with lust by living with women.[89] But even here, in a lecture given to an audience of male students, throughout the whole of his lengthy discussion Gerson never blames one sex or the other. He merely describes the difficulties of the situation. There is no ranting against women here or in the *Dialogue spirituel*. Nor is there in the vernacular sermons. He sees corporeal beauty as often being the enemy of chastity and the cause of abominable sins and eternal damnation,[90] but again, in this passage on the superior value of beauty of soul over beauty of body, where there was an obvious opportunity to criticise female coquetry, Gerson exhibits no harshness towards women. Rather, the examples he uses are of effeminate men despised by others because of their appearance of lack of vigour. His list of great people of the past who have fallen because of their voluptuousness contains an equal number of men and women,[91] and his discussion of the remedies for lust seems only slightly more directed toward lustful women than towards lustful men.[92] It is true that there is a passage in one of his vernacular tracts where he states that a woman who knows that 'by her dress, or speech, or by showing off her beauty, or dancing well' she is enticing others to lust, and who does not desist, has committed a sin.[93] Here there is no equivalent condemnation of men who entice women, but this can be explained by the fact that this tract was initially written by Gerson for his sisters. To balance this there is, in one of his sermons on lust, a statement of the doctrine that the adulterous man sins more than the adulterous woman because of his greater power of resistance, with the rider that the woman could be said to sin more because of the danger to the purity of her husband's lineage.[94]

Gerson's few references to extravagant fashions, a favourite target of medieval preachers, are more critical of men than women. During his pleas for the reform of the chivalric order, he pours scorn on robes that drag two feet along the ground, wide sleeves and long furs. 'What use is all this for vigorously pursuing the enemy?'[95] There are similar criticisms of other extravagant male practices, but when he asks whether a woman should adorn herself, he replies that sobriety in clothes would be better, but one has to look at the intention of the woman and he personally would not condemn every woman who dresses richly according to her estate and the custom of the country, and for her own consolation.[96]

Women, then, are not singled out by Gerson as the prime cause of all sexual sins. If woman is a temptress, man is also a tempter. This comparatively equitable attitude on this aspect of the relation between the sexes is somewhat surprising in the light of the tirades against woman, the enticer to sin, that had echoed down the centuries and that were still heard in the sermons of other preachers of the late medieval period and beyond. Olivier Maillard, for instance, in the mid fifteenth century, frequently levelled blasts against women for their extravagant clothes and coiffures, worn with the intention of attracting men and enticing them to immorality, and for their indecent behaviour in churches, which they turned into places of prostitution.[97] The Italian Bernardine was equally persistent in his condemnation of the vanity and coquetry of women revealed in superfluous adornment.[98] Many preachers made use of the following passage: 'Who was stronger than Sampson, wiser than Solomon, holier than David? And yet they were all overcome by the cunning and wiles of women.'[99] The English Dominican Bromyard was one of the most vehement of late medieval preachers in his attacks on women.

In the woman wantonly adorned to capture souls the garland upon her head is as a single coal or firebrand of hell to kindle men with that fire; so too the horns of another, so the bare neck...in a single day, by her dancing or perambulation through the town, she inflames with the fire of lust – it may be – twenty of those who behold her, damning the souls whom God has created...For this very purpose the Devil thus adorns these females, sending them through the town as his apostles, replete with every iniquity, malice, fornication and the like...[100]

The whole tone of those passages where Gerson discusses women in connection with lust is entirely different from this satirical and bitter spirit. In fact, Gerson singles out women for criticism of any sort remarkably rarely in his vernacular sermons and tracts compared with what seems to be the case with many other preachers of the period.

Women were frequently criticised in sermons for their foolishness and the ease with which they fell into the traps of the devil, for their garrulity and love of gossip, for their desire to be always wandering abroad, and for disobedience to their husbands.[101] There are only two passages in his French sermons where Gerson might be accused of making this sort of criticism. With reference to the devout women who came 'diligemment' to the sepulchre and then hurried to tell the disciples of Christ's Resurrection, he remarks: 'Femmez parlent legierement quant ilz veulent.'[102] And in a sermon of 1402, during a discussion of the benefits of tribulation, he argues that it might be profitable for some persons if they became deaf and dumb for a time so that they could avoid the great sins they commit in hearing and speaking. People often say, he continues, 'comme par moquerie' that it is not a miracle to get a woman to talk, but it is a miracle to get her to keep silent, 'for women are too inclined to talk and often sin by doing so. The ornament of woman is chastity and silence.'[103] But these are very mild criticisms, given briefly and in passing. There is, in a vernacular tract, one further instance where women are singled out for criticism. Women sin against the sixth commandment, he writes, if they allow bastards to succeed to the heritage of their legitimate children, and if they waste their husband's goods. There is no similar stricture against men.[104]

The charge of misogyny, it seems, cannot be brought against Gerson. Certainly he did not express any bitterness against women in those works intended for the eyes and ears of the laity. However, some of his Latin works do betray a critical attitude towards the female sex. The criticisms he makes in these works seem to have grown out of his own experience; here he does not merely repeat commonplaces. Almost all the strictures occur in his writings about visionaries and the discernment of spirits. After reading these works one has the impression that Gerson had encountered a number of visionaries, that a majority of them were women, and that most of them were deluded and therefore a source of possible harm to the church. Women, in his opinion, were especially prone to this sort of delusion, whether caused by the devil or self-deception or by physical disability. If the visionary is a woman, he writes, it is especially necessary to consider how she acts towards her confessors or instructors. Is she prone to continual talking, either under the pretext of frequent confession or in relating lengthy accounts of her visions, or by any other kind of discussion? Women, he continues, are especially prone to restless curiosity and garrulity and easily accept fables and so are turned away from the truth.[105] They are also inclined to be over-enthusiastic: 'The ardour of adolescents and women is too great, too eager, unstable, unbridled and therefore suspect.'[106]

Gerson's strongest criticisms of women occur in a late work, *De examinatione doctrinarum* of 1423, in which he offers practical advice on determining whether a given doctrine is authentic or not, starting out from the text 'Do not be led away by diverse and strange teachings' (Heb. 13:9). Among many other considerations, it is necessary to take into account, he writes, the condition of the one teaching the doctrine: whether the person is an expert in the field, old or young, man or woman, of obedient or dissolute character, of sound judgement or imprudent. He writes more on the man/woman distinction than on the other four put together, and makes it clear that he considers it much more likely that authentic doctrine will be forthcoming from a man than from a woman. The female sex, he notes, is prohibited by apostolic authority from teaching publicly in words or in writing – a point he had already made in sermons. Women are especially forbidden to teach men more learned than themselves, 'to call priests of God their sons, and to teach them their profession in which they have been carefully trained'. He goes on to describe some of these self-proclaimed teachers. One will tell you that she was annihilated for an instant; another that God was united to her in a miraculous union, 'and countless other stories which could not be told in great volumes'.[107] He reminds his readers of the apostle's warning that curious, verbose women, led by diverse desires, are to be avoided, and he casts a side criticism at Eve for what he sees as her lying to the serpent about God's prohibition. Therefore, he argues,

every teaching of women, especially that expressed in solemn word or writing, is to be held suspect, unless it has been diligently examined, and much more than the teaching of men. Why? The reason is clear; because not only ordinary but divine law forbids such things. Why? Because women are too easily seduced, because they are too obstinately seducers, because it is not fitting that they should be knowers of divine wisdom.[108]

The specific examples of deluded visionaries and religious deviants that Gerson chooses to use as illustrations are far more frequently female than male, though he does not deny that men can be similarly afflicted.[109] In a lecture of 1401 he recounts the story of his encounter with a married woman of Arras who persisted, against advice and with a certain arrogance, in excessive fasting. In the same lecture there is mention of Marie de Valenciennes and her antinomian preaching.[110] An example is appended to *De examinatione doctrinarum* of a woman who, for the sake of money, pretended that she could redeem souls from hell.[111] This work also mentions Erminia, an anchoress of Rheims, by whom Gerson confesses he was almost led astray,[112] and contains an oblique reference to Catherine of Siena who, Gerson says, Gregory XI correctly blamed for the papal return to Rome and the beginning of the schism.[113]

Gerson did not, however, think all female visionaries were deluded and there was one whose visions he was prepared, after careful consideration, to regard as almost certainly authentic. In May of 1429, a week after the relief of Orleans, Gerson issued a treatise, *De puella aurelianensi*, on the subject of Joan of Arc, perhaps at the request of the king for advice, or perhaps on his own initiative.[114] In his usual careful fashion, Gerson argues that it is pious and salutary, though not necessary, to believe in Joan's mission, principally on the grounds that the enterprise to which she had been urged – the restoration of the king in his kingdom – is very just. Further, she does not resort to superstitious practices forbidden by the church, she is not trying to further her own interests, the king's council and soldiers and the people believe in her, the enemies of France fear her, and the Maid constantly urges men to righteousness. Gerson adds an argument to justify Joan's wearing of male attire.

There is no doubt some prejudice involved in Gerson's judgement of these last two women. He is suspicious of Catherine of Siena because her counsels apparently were a step towards the schism, an appalling episode, while he is prepared to approve of Joan because her counsels tended towards the restoration of France to her rightful king, a situation which Gerson considered eminently just. It would be unfair merely to say that in Joan's case his political convictions overcame his prejudice against female visionaries, though this is probably part of the truth.

The conclusion that Gerson was more equitable in his attitude to women than one might expect of a fifteenth-century theologian is reinforced by the attitude he took in the controversy over the *Roman de la rose*.[115] He did not, it is true, exhibit the same vigorous feminism as Christine de Pisan, who produced a barrage of arguments against Jean de Meung's poem and in defence of women in her letters and treatises during and after the debate. She argues that men who, as Jean de Meung, attack women are guilty of ingratitude, for they owe women everything; that men are wrong when they assail the entire female sex and accuse women of sins of which only a few are guilty; that women are really nobler than men, for they were created of finer material and in a better place than men, and God chose a woman to be the mother of His son; that from many illustrations drawn from sacred and secular history women may be seen to possess many desirable qualities, such as constancy, fidelity, intelligence, skill as inventors, the ability to govern and to fight; that education is necessary to women and that to a virtuous woman learning can never be harmful.[116] In her *Epistle to the God of Love* she points to the compassionate nature of women and to the fact that women are guilty of far fewer crimes than men. 'They murder no one, nor wound, nor harm...They do not set houses on fire, or poison, or steal...They do not make false contracts, or destroy kingdoms, duchies, empires...'[117]

Gerson's attack on the *Roman* is much more that of the moralist than the feminist, for he is moved more by his antagonism towards the naturalism and libertinism of Jean de Meung than by his consideration for women. Nevertheless, he does defend women, in his allegory of 1402, against some of Jean's charges, and he earned high praise from Christine for this work.

tresvaillant docteur, et maistre en theologie, souffisant, digne, louable, clerc solempnel, esleu entre les eleus, compila une oeuvre en brief, conduicte moult notablement par pur theologie.[118]

What concerns Gerson most about Jean's attitude to women is the latter's blanket condemnations. Ovid, writes Gerson, expressly stated that he did not wish to speak about good matrons and married women, or about those who were not free to love. But 'your book blames all women, despises all, without any exception'. Since the book professes to be Christian and speaks of heavenly as well as earthly things, why, asks Gerson, does it not at least make an exception of the female saints and the countless other women who suffered torment and even martyrdom defending their chastity?[119] He compares the sneers of Jean de Meung against women to the edifying verses of Guillaume de Lorris, who wrote the first part of the romance, and points out the unchivalric nature of these sneers that show no respect for women. However, it is in fact only against the basic charge of general lasciviousness that Gerson defends women, and he can by no means be put in the same category as Christine as a 'champion des dames'.

Gerson was, though, a champion of that exceptional woman, the Virgin Mary, but here he was quite in line with the developing theological tradition. However, the fact that Gerson believed the Virgin to have been immaculately conceived and therefore quite exceptional renders his opinion about and attitude to her almost irrelevant to his opinions about and attitudes to women in general. He does, nevertheless, hold her up as an example to all the faithful and especially to women. As well as being the ideal servant of God in her humility, she was the ideal wife in her submissiveness, and the ideal mother in her tenderness and firmness. Her beauty was such that it excited chastity and purity, not concupiscence,[120] and she taught others about her knowledge of God privately in the home, not publicly. The virtues of the Virgin are praised in many sermons of the period,[121] but Gerson's devotion to her comes across with particular fervour. This fervour and the frequency with which he mentions Mary in his sermons and vernacular writings perhaps indicates his strong feeling about the equality of the sexes in the realm of salvation and should have moved his audiences to this belief.

As a pastor Gerson must have appeared to the women in his congregations and to those who read his French tracts as fair-minded towards their sex. Most of them no doubt accepted their subordinate role in society as part of the divine ordinance, and they would find no satirical sneers or ranting attacks against them in his vernacular works. Provided that they did not attempt to preach publicly or to teach their pastor his theology or allow themselves to be deluded by visions and voices, they must have felt themselves treated on an equal level with men.

MARRIAGE

In praise of virginity

Any belief system that disparages the body and especially its sexual nature is going to encounter difficulties in accepting marriage as an ideal state. Augustine's treatise *On the Good of Marriage*, despite its title, reads more like a defence of celibacy in face of the evidence of the married patriarchs of the Old Testament than a eulogy of marriage. Augustine set the tone for the western medieval church and the clerical bias against marriage persisted among theologians till the Reformation, although some shifts in emphasis are discernible.

Gerson looked upon marriage as a third best; virginity and widowhood were preferable. 'You, virginity, as St Cyprian said, are the most beautiful part of holy church, and merit the hundredfold fruit, while widowhood merits only sixty, and marriage thirty.'[122] This argument from the parable of the sower (Matt. 13:3–8) was a commonplace and had been heard with frequency from the Fathers onwards.[123] Gerson refers to it only very rarely in his vernacular works, but there are many passages where he makes it clear that virginity is a higher state than marriage. In the *Dialogue spirituel*, when praising his sisters for their decision to embrace the virginal life, he states that they have followed not only his advice but that of St Paul, 'who says it is better for a girl to stay in the estate of virginity than to give herself in marriage'.[124] Almost all his references to Mary underline her perpetual virginity, and in arguing for the virginity of Joseph also, he states that Christ so loved virginity that he did not want to become incarnate except through a virgin mother, 'so it is good to believe that He did not want to be protected, nourished, kissed, carried and ruled, except by one in whom shone pure virginity'.[125] There is no service that pleases God more, there is no life that He loves more than that of virginity in body and thought.[126] But there are other reasons than God's pleasure for preferring a life of celibacy to one of marriage. In a sermon on chastity, Gerson lists the twelve dignities that attach to virginity.

You, virginity, were raised to be the mother of God. You enable people to die without pain. You make the soul the close friend of God. More divine secrets are revealed to you. You are powerful in miracles. You make the soul a martyr in that it dies to all carnal desires and foolish worldly pleasure. You are the cousin of the angels and already begin to partake in heavenly life. You sing a new song. You will be singled out and crowned with a divine crown in paradise. You can be consecrated in holy church, and wear the gold ring as a sign of your excellences and incorruption. You are the most beautiful part of holy church and merit the hundredfold fruit... You are queen of the earth and heaven by the ardent song of contemplation.[127]

Further, the virgin lives longer: 'It is certain that by chaste living, life is not shortened but lengthened.'[128]

Gerson has here collected together a number of traditional beliefs about the blessings of virginity and perhaps added some of his own. That a virgin will receive more glory and joy in heaven than others is a very common teaching. Bonaventure, for instance, states that virgins will receive the *aureola*, the reward due to works done over and above the basic requirement of keeping the commandments, on account of the special *decor*, the integrity of mind and body, that is peculiar to virginity. Thomas held a similar opinion.[129]

In this same sermon on chastity, Gerson answers certain objections made by 'mondaine charnalite' to this doctrine of the superiority of the virginal state. To the argument that if all men and women were celibate the world would come to an end, he replies that there is nothing to fear in this, for the world will end sometime anyhow, and in any case there is no chance whatsoever that all men and women will remain virgins. It is true, he continues, that under the old law God commanded the Jews to procreate, for then it was necessary to increase the Jewish population, but now the number of Christians can be augmented from other peoples. Thus, after the Incarnation, the duty of fecundity is no longer valid, for there is an adequate number of people now and the need is to regenerate these. But 'marriage produces only offspring of the flesh; it is virginity that engenders spiritual children in itself and by prayer'. Therefore the fecundity of good works performed by the virgin is preferable to the fecundity of generation performed by the married.[130] In his *Discours sur l'excellence de la virginité* Gerson shows more concern for the propagation of the human race. It is fitting, he writes, and even necessary that some women should marry, in order to have offspring or to avoid the vile sin of the flesh to which they are too much inclined, or to have an heir to succeed to their great estates. But such women 'have chosen the less good part'.[131] There is no need, however, he tells his sisters, for them to enter upon this less good estate. In his concern, muted though it is, for the continuation of the species Gerson has moved away from Augustine, who wished that everyone were willing to refrain from sexual intercourse, for then 'much more quickly would the city of God be filled and the end of time be hastened'.[132] Gerson is closer to Thomas, who argues that the command of Genesis, 'Increase and multiply', is binding on mankind as a whole but not on any given individual. The precept is sufficiently fulfilled if some perform the task of procreation. But, for Thomas, as for Gerson, to undertake this task is a 'lesser good'.[133] Both believe that in a world where it can be assumed that some will marry and have children, virginity is the better course to follow for those who wish to lead the more perfect life.

To the objection that a life of celibacy is very difficult and almost impossible, Gerson presents a firm, if brief, denial in the sermons on chastity and a more elaborated reply in the discourse on virginity.[134] At first a life of virginity is difficult, he says, but afterwards it is easier than marriage, for fewer occasions of sin arise. There is less temptation to lust, avarice, anger and jealousy, sins which often reign in marriages. Clearly a life of virginity is not impossible, as the conduct of many saints bears witness, and it has its own aids and remedies: spiritual consolation, good habits, the feeling of shame, regular prayer.[135] The married sometimes have to endure abstinence from sexual intercourse, he argues in the discourse, if one of them is ill for a month or half a year, or if the husband is away on business or is in prison or becomes impotent. If the married can suffer abstinence for half a year, then they can endure it for a whole year and more, and how much easier for the unmarried, who have fewer temptations. Gerson then describes in detail the difficulties involved in marriage: the financial problems and the labours involved in maintaining a household; the possibility of having a drunkard, a gambler, a spendthrift, a miser, a bully or an invalid for a husband; the anxiety and pain of bearing, nourishing and rearing children. The temptations to sin and the perils to the spiritual life entailed by marriage are detailed. Marriage tends to make wives covetous out of consideration for their children, to make them proud of their fine clothes or to envy those of others; two persons living in close proximity are bound to become angry and impatient with each other at times. Further, marriage is a distraction from the higher spiritual life, for married women are too busy to serve God properly. The married have more temptations to lust than virgins, for the more desire is satisfied the more ardent it becomes and 'wants more and more new ways to find pleasures and inordinate delights', and the less the restraint of shame remains.[136] All these difficulties and temptations the celibate escapes. The number of times Gerson refers to and tries to answer this objection that a life of celibacy puts too much of a burden on human nature suggests that there was frequent criticism of the church's ideal. In the sixteenth century Luther voiced the same objection, arguing that it was impossible, except in very rare cases, for people to win the battle to suppress their sexual nature. 'A woman', he wrote, 'is not created to be a virgin, but to conceive and bear children.'[137] The reformers repudiated the church's ideal, closed monasteries, and allowed clerical marriage. Gerson, however, firmly and consistently upheld the traditional belief.

If virginity is superior to marriage, clearly widowhood is to be preferred to a second marriage. This is an opinion stated in a number of places in Gerson's French works and in one of the sermons on conjugal chastity he elaborates his reasons: a widow or widower can serve God better, think of Him more often than one who remarries; the love and memory of the first spouse should act as a restraining influence, for 'either he was good and it would be foolish to risk getting a bad one, or he was bad and the second could be worse'. Further, it is better for children that their parent does not marry again, for it is a burden to have a step-father or step-mother.[138]

Gerson's position on the remarriage of the widowed is traditional; 'Conjugal chastity is good, but the continence of widowhood is better', wrote Augustine, and the theologians of the patristic age in general, apart from Tertullian, who would have had such remarriages forbidden, tolerated without fully approving the practice.[139] The same attitude was upheld by later theologians and canonists.[140] Many of the reasons Gerson gives for preferring widowhood to remarriage and virginity to matrimony are what might be termed practical ones: spiritual advancement and reward for both oneself and Christendom; better service of God; longer life and domestic ease. The same description can be applied to some of the reasons that Gerson gives in answer to the question he raises about why priests do not marry. If they were married, he argues, they would be tempted to pillage the church for the sustenance and gratification of their wives and children; they would tend to fear the great and flatter the middle classes, who could benefit or harm their families materially; they would have less time to study and explain Scripture. Here he makes a reference, often used by defenders of celibacy, to Cicero's argument that 'no one can attend to both a wife and philosophy'.[141] However, there is no doubt that he also conveys the suggestion here, as elsewhere, that physical sexuality involves uncleanliness and defilement. Priests do not marry, he says, 'in order that they may serve God cleanly. Note that the priests of the old law during the time of their ministry used to cease from intercourse with their wives.'[142]

Medieval theological doctrines on marriage

Those among Gerson's congregation who were married would acquire the impression from his sermons that they had chosen a second-class status. But they would not have felt that their status was thereby condemned. If virginity is better, nevertheless, says Gerson on numerous occasions, marriage is good. Moreover, virginity is not for everyone. 'I do not want here or ever to criticise marriage.' One should advise one's child or friend to think about which estate is best for his or her salvation, 'for different people are saved in different ways'.[143] Both estates are praiseworthy and for some people and in some situations marriage is better, for example where the peace of a kingdom can be gained by a marriage. In both estates there are saved and damned; 'who serves God better is the more perfect in whatever estate he is'.[144]

The doctrine that marriage is essentially good, despite the fact that virginity is a higher estate, had been generally accepted from at least the time of Augustine. The latter had tried to steer a middle course between the Manichean dualists, who saw coitus and marriage as evils, and the Pelagians, who viewed them as good and uncontaminated, and held virginity to be no better than marriage. For Augustine, marriage and coitus in themselves are good, being ordained by God, but every act of coitus in the postlapsarian order is intrinsically evil and tainted with sin. This is because of the lack of control of the will over the genitals resulting from original sin.[145] Nevertheless, when intercourse takes place within marriage for the purpose of procreation, the sinfulness is excused. A kind of dignity prevails, writes Augustine, when a husband and wife uniting in the marriage act think of themselves as father and mother.[146] Augustine's view remained as the basis of the theology of marriage throughout the Middle Ages, though various modifications appeared from time to time. In the twelfth century, for instance, Peter Lombard in his influential *Sentences* affirmed the goodness of marriage as a duty before the fall, as a remedy against concupiscence after the fall, and as a symbol of the union of Christ and the church. The (Augustinian) goods of marriage – fidelity, offspring, sacrament – excuse, he argued, the use of marriage, which is always tainted by concupiscence and which would otherwise be sinful. However, at one point he went so far as to say that even within marriage coitus nearly always involves venial sin because of the sensual pleasure and the 'absorption' of reason involved.[147] The twelfth-century canonist Huguccio went further and stated firmly that sexual intercourse can never take place without sin, because of the pleasure that inevitably accompanies it.[148] Though echoes of Huguccio's profound distrust of sexual pleasure were still heard in the late Middle Ages – and beyond – his harsh and extreme doctrine did not prevail. Already in the twelfth century the pendulum had swung the other way in Abelard's *Ethics*. Although, in one of his letters to Heloise, Abelard argues that the use of marriage is intermediate between good and evil and in fact is not wholly free from sin,[149] in the *Ethics* he takes a different position. Marital sex and the carnal pleasure that accompanies it, he states, are sinless, free of all offence against God. It is no use arguing that the act is sinless while the pleasure is not, for it is impossible to perform the act without feeling pleasure. Thus if God allows the one, He must allow the other.[150] The influence of Aristotle led to a similar positive attitude towards sexual pleasure in the writings of Albert the Great, Thomas and some other theologians of the Dominican school. Both Albert and Thomas teach that such pleasure would have accompanied coitus even before the fall; 'indeed', says Thomas, 'sensuous delight would have been the greater in proportion to the greater purity of nature and the greater sensitivity of the body'.[151] Even after the fall the pleasure remains natural and good in itself. Both repudiate the notion that the married should shun and detest this pleasure, if they wish their carnal union to be without sin. On the contrary, if the action is good, the pleasure involved in it is good, 'as Aristotle says'.[152] Further, if coitus is for procreation or to render the marital debt, it is not merely sinless, but actually meritorious.[153] Only when the act is performed solely under the impulse of desire, of concupiscence, is any sin involved, venial if the motive is the avoidance of fornication in oneself, mortal if the motive is inordinate pleasure.[154]

The Dominican Pierre de la Palude, in the early fourteenth century, went beyond Albert and Thomas. He expressed the opinion that not only do the motives of procreation and rendering the debt make the marital act perfectly licit, but the motive of avoiding fornication in oneself, if there are no other means, has the same effect. His fellow Dominican Durand de Saint-Pourçain regarded the avoidance of fornication in oneself, even if there are other means of so doing, as a legitimate motive.[155] After Gerson's time, in the latter part of the fifteenth century, a Parisian theologian, Martin le Maistre, made a reasoned defence of the sinlessness of seeking only pleasure in the marriage act.[156] His views were followed by Jean Major, another Parisian theologian, who, at the beginning of the sixteenth century, stated his opinion that coitus within marriage is without sin even if performed for the sake of one's own physical or mental health, or solely for pleasure, provided of course that no steps are taken to frustrate the end of procreation.[157] This opinion, however, remained outside the main tradition and Major himself thought it should not be preached but only borne in mind by confessors.[158]

Medieval theologians have been accused of neglecting the element of love between spouses in their evaluation of marriage and more especially in their evaluation of sexual relations. Foster, for example, suggests that the courtly love literature arose because it was felt that something was lacking in the existing situation. Thus courtly love, he argues, was in part an assertion of personal values against established opinions on sex and marriage that were felt to be inhuman; it was an attempt to vindicate for the sexual impulse an intrinsic value, a potential moral worth, apart from its procreative purpose, against a theology that was unsympathetic to the personal side of sexuality, to its connection with love.[159] This judgement is too harsh. Augustine, for instance, does write about conjugal love and companionship, though admittedly not in connection with sexuality.[160] Aquinas is more positive. Like Augustine he sees marriage ordained for mutual aid and companionship as well as for the procreation of children, and he stresses the affection and friendship (*amicitia*) that should exist between and unite the spouses. But Thomas sees this affection as being based not only on mutual service in domestic life but also on delight in the act of generation.[161] In fact 'a man loves his wife principally by reason of the carnal meeting'.[162] For Thomas there is no rupture between marriage, sexuality and love. Even Bonaventure, whose attitude to the pleasures of marital sex is much less positive than that of Thomas, states that there are two types of love necessary in marriage: a 'social love' directed to domestic living, and a 'conjugal love' directed to the procreation of children.[163] However, in the writings of Pierre de la Palude, Durand de Saint-Pourçain and Major, mentioned above, there is no reference to conjugal love in their discussions of the motivation of the sexual act. The record among medieval theologians on this point, as on other aspects of marriage is, then, mixed.

Gerson's teaching on marriage

Many of Gerson's discussions on marriage occur in sermons and tracts centred on the Virgin and St Joseph, for their marriage could be held up as an example to be followed, as an ideal union, despite its virginal nature. In his sermons of 31 December 1402 and 7 January 1403, he takes advantage of the gospels of the day, each of which narrates an incident in the life of the holy family, to launch discussions on chastity in general and conjugal chastity in particular. He makes it quite clear in the first of these sermons that by conjugal chastity he does not mean complete sexual continence, but rather 'an abstinence from intercourse except in so far as the rules of marriage allow or require it'.[164] His congregation, then, need not feel guilty because their marriages involved a sexual relationship; they could still claim to be living chastely.

In all the gospel stories about the holy family, says Gerson, 'it seems to me that the institution of marriage is highly praised'.[165] The story of the loss of the child Jesus in Jerusalem leads Gerson to list twelve excellences of marriage that match the twelve years of the young boy listening to the doctors in the temple. They form rather a mixed collection. Five of them may be grouped as direct evidence of God's approval of matrimony: the fact that He ordained it in paradise (3), that He wished His mother to be married (1), that He wished to be born in marriage (2), that He performed His first miracle at a wedding feast (6), and that He wished to save from the flood only those who were married (12). The rest present some of the other traditional reasons for praising marriage: carnal pleasure 'which would be vicious and mortal is excused by marriage' (7), it produces children who pray for their parents (8), it is a remedy for fornication and its resulting evils (9), it is one of the seven sacraments (10), and there is a solemn benediction at every marriage ceremony (11). Possible happy results of marriage are seen in the fact that virgins are born therefrom (4), and that often marriages lead to peace and friendship between whole lineages (5).[166]

There is nothing here to show that Gerson approved of the newer trends in Dominican theology. Rather the reverse seems true, for he sees carnal pleasure as sinful and needing excuse, and the only essential positive reason he gives for the ordination of marriage is the procreation of children; otherwise it is a remedy for sin and not apparently an institution to further mutual affection and companionship. He leaves the same impression in other places, for example in some of his statements about the three goods of marriage. In his sermon of 31 December on chastity, in answer to the Manichean argument that procreation cannot be accomplished without mortal sin and damnation, he states that the beauty of the sacrament of marriage excuses the sin, as does the purpose of producing children to serve God, and the faithfulness of the spouses to each other.[167] A slightly different version, but even closer to Augustine's meaning, occurs in the *Considérations sur St Joseph*. In the marriage of Mary and Joseph were

the three goods of marriage, loyalty, offspring and sacrament. There was fidelity, without violation or fornication; there was offspring, by legitimate generation; there was sacrament, without dissolution or separation. And so there was a perfect and complete marriage, although there was no carnal mingling or corruption.[168]

However, Gerson has another interpretation of the three goods, and here he reveals a more positive attitude towards love in marriage. He uses it in the sermons on conjugal chastity. The good of *sacramentum*, he tells his congregation, shows that the spouses owe faith and religious obedience to God; *fides* implies that they must have 'loving loyalty' to each other, while *proles* shows that they must be careful of their children and exhibit 'gracious discipline' towards them.[169] When he elaborates on the 'loving loyalty' that should prevail between husband and wife he lists the duties of each that should be fulfilled in order to bring about this happy relationship, stressing that wives should be obedient and long-suffering and husbands protective and loving. Gerson's attitude, then, towards marriage and towards love in marriage, as seen in his sermons as a whole, is a moderately positive one. In the two sermons specifically on marriage – or rather on conjugal chastity – his attitude appears as definitely positive. The preacher adapts his teaching to his topic and his audience.

A positive attitude to marriage, if not to sexuality, is also displayed in the French tracts on St Joseph. Gerson was one of those who gave a decisive impulse to the cult of St Joseph, which had been virtually unknown in western Europe till the early fifteenth century,[170] and he wrote a number of letters, tracts and poems on the subject to further his aim of the establishment of a feast in honour of the husband of the Virgin.[171] One of the opinions he presses in these works in order to show the worthiness of Joseph for special honour is that of his sanctification in the womb and his consequent birth without the stain of original sin. In the course of his discussions he makes several points that are relevant to the subject of marriage and sexuality. His circular letter 'à sainte eglise' of 1413, which is an exhortation for the establishing of a feast of the betrothal of Mary, for the purpose of honouring St Joseph, contains a list of reasons in favour of such a move. The feast, he writes, would honour the sacrament of marriage, which was the first sacrament, instituted as it was in paradise;

it would encourage wives to model themselves on Mary, who loved, honoured, cherished and obeyed her seigneur, Joseph, and husbands to follow the example of Joseph, who protected, nourished and loved his wife; it would enable spouses to take inspiration from the happiness of Mary and Joseph. The finality of every person, he concludes, is that he be joined to God as spouse, 'and there is no other example which shows more the tender love and loving kindness of God towards the soul than the love of a loyal husband to his loyal wife'.[172]

At about the same time as he wrote this letter, Gerson composed his long treatise *Considérations sur St Joseph*, where, among other things, he argues for the existence of Joseph's special privileges. In the course of his argument he makes some remarks that can only be interpreted as betraying the traditional prejudice against sexuality. The marriage of Mary and Joseph was perpetually virginal, he writes, and 'without vile corruption and carnal concupiscence was this beautiful and blessed infant born'. Mary and Joseph were 'one flesh and one body in a sacramental union though there was no shameful mingling'. They married 'out of obedience, not concupiscence'.[173] This work and the letters noted above were probably not, it is true, intended directly for the general public, but, as we have seen, this negative attitude towards sexuality in marriage also appears in Gerson's sermons and sometimes very similar phraseology is used, for example: 'Our Lady...never lost her virginity and never once experienced this vile delight, either in or outside marriage...'[174]

Gerson, as could be expected from the foregoing, saw consent, not coitus, as the essence of marriage, and this is one of the grounds on which he argues that the virginal relationship of Mary and Joseph was a true marriage. Actually concern among theologians about the nature of the relationship between Mary and Joseph was one of the major influences in the acceptance of the doctrine of Roman law that the essence of marriage was consent, and coitus consequently merely an accessory and not an intrinsic element. There had been conflicting views among theologians right up to the twelfth century, and between theologians and canonists after that; but by the end of the thirteenth century a consensus had emerged.[175] So Gerson's doctrine, revealed in the statements which he makes in the sermon on chastity, in answer to the objection of 'fol outrage' that the marriage of Mary and Joseph was not a true marriage because of Mary's vow of chastity, is in line with accepted and established opinion.[176]

The consent that makes a marriage, argues Gerson in his *Considérations sur St Joseph*, is a consent to give power over one's body to one's spouse, but 'God can will that...neither spouse ever ask for the carnal use of the other's body.'[177] The power need not be used; and in fact some of Gerson's passages on virginity and marriage leave the impression that an ideal marriage in his eyes may well be one in which this power is rarely or never used. He does not say this directly, however, as some earlier theologians had done. 'Matrimony is holier without carnal intercourse', Lombard had written.[178] Similarly Hugh of St Victor had argued that marriage exists 'more truly and more sacredly' if there is no sexual activity.[179] This opinion is not repeated by Thomas or, explicitly, by Gerson.

Given that there is a sexual drive, Gerson agrees with St Paul that 'it is better to marry than to burn'. He strongly defends marriage in his works that attack the *Roman de la rose*, stating firmly, along with Aristotle and his medieval followers, that marriage is natural to man.[180] But here he is defending marriage against the promiscuity that Jean de Meung apparently advocates, and not against virginity. Virginity remains the ideal state, even if it is not possible for all men and women.

It is also a safer state, for marriage involves grave dangers for the individual soul. The temptations to sins of lust are manifold. It is often easier, he says, to abstain from all sexual activity as in the case of virgins and other continent persons than to exercise marital coitus modestly.[181] Unfortunately 'modestly' is just as vague as the other expressions we have seen Gerson use in this connection: 'honourably', 'within nature's ordinance', 'within the limits of matrimony'. As any marital kisses and embraces must also be 'modest', indulged in 'pour honneste plaisance', but not to arouse 'honteuse playsance',[182] we can only say that Gerson seems to be an advocate of very restrained lovemaking.

The 'too ardent lover of his wife' was a target of all the medieval moralists, but it was difficult to define him with any exactitude.[183] Alain de Lille simply equates him with the spouse who has let his reason 'be seduced by the very allurement of the flesh'.[184] More precise definitions were attempted. Angelus de Clavasio cites, but does not endorse, the opinion that too ardent love means deliberately inciting desire so that one can copulate more frequently.[185] The second and most popular opinion held that a man was guilty of too ardent love of his wife if he would have performed the act even if she were not his wife. This, says Thomas, who endorses the opinion, shows that the husband is treating his wife not as a wife but as a woman.[186] Gerson uses neither of these definitions, though there are echoes of the first in his remarks to the laity about marital embraces. However, in the *Regulae mandatorum*, a widely used handbook for students and pastors, he makes a statement which indicates that he supports the third medieval opinion about too ardent marital love. It is a mortal sin if, while you are having intercourse with your spouse, you think of someone else as the object of the act.[187] Gerson's definition was not original. It had been used by Peter of Tarentaise, a thirteenth-century Dominican contemporary of Aquinas,[188] and incorporated into John of Freiburg's *Summa confessorum*.[189] It was no doubt in his copy of the latter work that Gerson found the opinion. Perhaps he chose it because 'thinking of someone else as the object of the act' seems to be a more identifiable circumstance than that envisaged by the second definition. A confessor could base a question on it and expect a straightforward answer from his penitent.

There were other opportunities for sexual sins in marriage. Apart from the very grave sin of using contraceptive practices in intercourse, there were times and places where the performance of the act might be sinful. As far as holy seasons and holy places are concerned, Gerson stands with those of his predecessors and contemporaries who held the milder opinion. He advises his readers to abstain from sexual activity on feast-days, before communicating and before going on a pilgrimage. However, though he leaves the impressions that a stigma attaches to sexual activity on such occasions, he does not label it as sinful as some writers did.[190] Jacques de Vitry, for instance, states that it is a sin to demand the marriage debt 'during great feasts and fasts'; for Aquinas, although it is not a mortal sin to demand the debt at a holy time, it is unlawful; while for the author of *The Book of Vices and Virtues* sexual activity in a holy place is sinful.[191] As time went on, however, the milder opinion expressed by Gerson gained ground.[192] There was also among late medieval writers an increasing toleration of intercourse during menstruation. But here Gerson holds the older, stricter view. The sexual act is mortally sinful, he writes, when it can lead to harm to offspring. Hence it is forbidden during menstruation, because of the danger of engendering defective offspring.[193] On intercourse during pregnancy Gerson holds the up-to-date opinion. It is without sin, despite the fact that it cannot be procreative, provided there is no danger to the foetus; but he gives no indication on how to judge whether there is danger to the foetus or not.[194]

Another area of possible sin in marriage lay in the obligation to render the marital debt. A spouse who refuses the other's request, unless in certain circumstances, Gerson judges guilty of sin.[195] Here he is following a long-established and firmly held tradition. Marriage, after all, had been established not only for the procreation of children but also (after the fall) as a remedy for fornication. It would be useless as a remedy if one spouse could deny the other at will.[196] The circumstances that, in Gerson's opinion, render refusal sinless are illness and when there is notable and certain danger to one's own body or that of a foetus. In the *Regulae mandatorum* he lists such circumstances: leprosy, pregnancy, menstruation, fever, epidemics 'and similar cases'.[197] Holy times and holy places, however, are not circumstances that provide a valid excuse for refusing the debt, though, says Gerson, friendly remarks beforehand about not asking for it on such occasions and in such places are permissible.[198]

The last aspect of marriage in which there was the possibility of sin was in the motivation behind the sexual act. Four motives for intercourse had been listed in the thirteenth century in the influential summa of Raymond of Penaforte: procreation, rendering the marital debt, avoiding fornication in oneself, pleasure.[199] Raymond himself thought the first two motives were sinless, the third venial and the fourth mortal. By the later Middle Ages some authors, we have seen, were arguing that the motive of avoiding fornication in oneself was also licit. Very few saw the desire for pleasure alone as a permissible motive. But Gerson was among them. 'Does a married person who seeks only pleasure in the sexual act without any other motive commit a mortal sin?', he asks in one of his sermons on lust. 'No' is his answer.[200] He goes further in the *Regulae mandatorum*. The first three motives for the sexual act are best, he writes, and if only pleasure is sought, 'provided it remains within the limits of the bond of marriage so that it would not be sought outside of it, and provided no circumstances prohibited for other reasons are transgressed, then it is either no sin or only a venial sin'.[201] For once Gerson is in the forefront of theological opinion, expressing a view that was not fully expounded and defended until some decades after his death. He was not, however, by any means enthusiastic about the seeking of sexual pleasure. It is one of those things, like sexual acts in holy places and on holy days, from which it is good to abstain.[202] There is still a hesitancy to accept sexual pleasure as good, as there is still a hesitancy in Gerson's whole teaching about marriage to accept sexuality in general as good.

Nevertheless, Gerson presents an overall picture of marriage as a praiseworthy institution, ordained by and pleasing to God. The discourse on virginity is the only place where a really bleak picture of marriage emerges. But this work was initially intended for his unmarried sisters who had determined on a life of virginity. And even here he asks pardon of virtuous wives and especially his mother, for, he writes, 'I have no intention whatsoever of criticising or dishonouring good and staunch wives who conduct themselves faithfully and chastely in marriage, as many do.'[203]

Compared with some late medieval preachers Gerson in his sermons to the laity exhibits a positive and optimistic attitude to marriage. 'In no sphere', writes Owst of medieval English sermons, 'does the sheer, overwhelming pessimism of the pulpit show itself more clearly than in its treatment of marriage.'[204] He finds far more emphasis laid on the discomforts, anxieties and perils of married life than on its dignity and worth. Owst's judgement should not, however, be applied to all medieval sermons. Bernardine, for instance, certainly describes some of the discomforts and perils of married life: unpleasant mothers-in-law and step-children, jealousy in one's spouse, unrestrained passion run rampant. But there are also passages in his vernacular sermons where he lauds marriage and points to its advantages: the equal partnership and division of labour, the comfort of being cared for.[205] In at least some of the medieval sermons specifically on marriage or for the married an optimistic note is struck, with emphasis on love between spouses, companionship and partnership.[206] The same is true of the Catholic Bishop Tunstall's (d. 1559) sermon on matrimony, where he not only praises the spiritual aspect of marriage but also stresses the joys of parenthood and the solace of a wife and children in sickness and old age.[207] The Protestants were not, then, the first to view marriage positively. The fact that virginity was no longer regarded as an ideal did mean that marriage was raised from its third-class status, so that Luther could write 'What is more desirable...than a happy and tranquil marriage, where there is mutual love and the most delightful union of souls?'[208] Yet there was still a lingering doubt about sexuality. Although he thought that marital intercourse was not unchaste and could be enjoyed with a good conscience, Luther seems to have believed that it still remained sinful to some degree.[209] And Calvin warned spouses not to pollute their marriages with 'uncontrolled and dissolute lust. For even if the honourableness of matrimony covers the baseness of incontinence, it ought not for that reason to be a provocation thereto.'[210] The concept of the too ardent lover of his wife was still abroad. Sixteenth-century Protestants certainly praised marriage more frequently than their Catholic predecessors, but Gerson is a good example of one of those predecessors who had a high opinion of marriage and said so.

CHILDREN

On a number of occasions in his sermons Gerson states that marriage was ordained not only for the procreation of children but for their education too. Children must be taught sound morals, and parents who neglect this duty 'will be held more accountable than if they let their offspring die of hunger'.[211] He holds the traditional opinion that the training of children to become spiritual sons and daughters of God is more important than their mere procreation. This was one of the points made in his discussion of the excellence of virginity; and within marriage, it seems, the spiritual and physical welfare of the individual child is to be preferred to the propagation of many offspring. In order to safeguard the health of the as yet unconceived child he counsels spouses not to weaken their bodies by overindulgence in sexual activity, or to have intercourse in time of sickness or if either is leprous.[212] This view – that there is no virtue in mere numbers – also lies behind one of Gerson's arguments against fornication, where the harm done to the child born out of wedlock without two parents to nourish and teach him is stressed. This harm is clearly not erased by any merit of the act of having generated a human being.[213]

Having told parents that they must give their children a sound religious education, Gerson does not leave them in ignorance of what this entails and the means whereby it can be accomplished. The education of youth, in fact, was one of the chancellor's chief concerns, for he believed that the reform of the church and society must begin here.[214] The amount of work to be done in this direction was vast. In both French and Latin sermons Gerson voices his opinion about the evils of the times. He finds the majority of people given over from their youth 'to all sins, to all vices, to every sort of vile filthiness'.[215] The defects in the upbringing of infants and children are 'horrifying'; it is as if 'they imbibed with the very milk, the pus of all the sins, by words and examples'.[216] In these circumstances Gerson puts the initial responsibility for reform on to parents. 'The reformation of the church must be accomplished by them.'[217] But teachers also have a very important role to play, both those who teach children (*parvuli*) and those who teach university students (*adolescentes*),[218] and among Gerson's works are to be found, apart from passages in the vernacular writings, a number of Latin tracts, letters and sermons that offer comparatively detailed instructions about the education of the young.

The chancellor's ideas on this subject have led more than one commentator to see him as an innovator, for instance as a precursor of the Jesuits and other educationalists who founded and taught in the sixteenth- and seventeenth-century colleges.[219] Certainly Gerson shows an awareness of childhood, a realisation that children are different from adults, more malleable and educable, an awareness that Ariès – probably incorrectly – sees as generally absent in the medieval period.[220] It is not that Gerson has the thoroughgoing belief in the innocence of children, a belief that Ariès thinks is part of the fully fledged awareness of childhood.[221] He does make some statements in his sermons that seem to mirror this belief. In *Beati qui lugent*, for instance, he makes the point that one ought to entrust one's delivery from purgatory to persons in a state of grace, for only their good works are efficacious. 'And here one can speak of innocent children through whom good ought to come; but where can they be found in our cities? They have been corrupted by servants and others.'[222] In a sermon for the feast of St Michael, he rails against those who lead children astray, children 'who ought to have the purity of an angel'.[223] But these remarks have to be balanced against passages in some of his Latin works where he makes it clear that the effects of original sin are manifest in small children. In his letter to Pierre Col during the controversy over the *Roman de la rose* Gerson reprimands Col for saying that a boy of two or three is in a state of innocence. 'This is the heresy of Pelagius and anyone obstinately asserting it is to be judged heretical.' If by 'innocent' Col means that the child is either ignorant or not yet guilty of actual sin, he ought to remember that 'the original corruption of morbid concupiscence' ruins everything.[224] This opinion is stated as clearly in a tract for confessors, where Gerson notes that sexual sin – in this case, masturbation – is apparent in boys of ten or twelve, and has its beginnings in the practice of even younger boys.

For we see that because of the corruption of nature even boys of three or five have an inclination to such things, because during an erection they feel a certain unknown itch, and they think it licit to touch and rub there and treat it as they do an itch in another part of the body...And so it happens that from habit delight grows with age and next they fall into masturbation or sodomy proper.[225]

Nevertheless, whether he stresses the innocence of children, as in his sermons to the laity, or their tendency to sin, as in these remarks to clerics, he is always concerned to point out that parents and teachers have a responsibility to mould children so that either their innocence and purity are preserved or their tendency to sin is counteracted. For he believes that children can be moulded, in a way that adults cannot, and that if positive steps are not taken to move them in the right direction, then, because of the general corruption of society, they will slide in the wrong direction. Children are like young plants, 'which follow easily where the hand of the gardener trains them. It is otherwise with the old, full of evil days, whom you can more quickly break than bend.'[226]

Almost every time that Gerson refers to the malleability of children he cites the authority of some previous author. Usually these are classical writers, such as Virgil, Horace, Juvenal, Seneca, Aristotle and Quintilian; but occasionally he refers to medieval theologians: 'All the philosophers and poets agree with the theologians that it is of no little importance that young people should acquire this or that habit.'[227] Augustine and Averroes are mentioned as among those writers who stress the dangers of perverse habits, but these are the only medievals he singles out by name and it is clearly the classical authors who come most readily to his mind when he writes on this topic.[228]

Home

What must parents do to help children develop in the right direction, which for Gerson means to come to Christ, to become good Christians? In his sermons and writings for the laity Gerson stresses more the need to prevent children from acquiring bad habits than the need to inculcate good ones. The avoidance of sin looms larger than the pursuit of virtue, though the latter is not ignored. There is no sermon specifically on the topic of bringing up children, but in many of his sermons on the seven capital sins Gerson states that parents and others should avoid corrupting children and leading them to indulge in the sin under consideration. In the sermon on gluttony, for instance, Gerson reprimands parents who indulge their children by giving them 'the tastiest morsels', or rich food and drink that incite lust. The children will come to expect these delicacies and this will lead to trouble later on.[229] The sermon on sloth stresses the importance of bourgeois parents' seeing that their children learn a trade so that they are not reduced to begging, which under certain circumstances can be a sin,[230] while the tract against blasphemy insists that heads of households, by teaching and good example, accustom children not to swear by God or the saints; the acquisition of good habits in youth will mean that mortal sins of blasphemy can be easily avoided for life.[231]

It is above all when Gerson is writing about the sin of lust that the importance of not corrupting children concerns him. It may be that the controversy over the *Roman de la rose* provided the stimulus, for it is from the period around 1401-2 that this concern is manifested. Although in his treatise against the *Roman* it appears that it is the corrupting effect of the book on mature men and women that he fears, in his sermons and other writings of this period and afterwards he often expresses strongly his feeling that books such as the *Roman*, together with lascivious pictures and certain family practices, are a grave danger for the souls of the young. 'Remove these books, good people, from your daughters and children, for they will take the bad from them and leave the good.'[232] One of Gerson's strongest statements on this subject is his *Expostulatio adversus corruptionem juventutis*[233] of 1402, where he urges the secular and ecclesiastical powers to promulgate, and enforce with punishments, laws against the public exhibition and sale of obscene pictures. Here again is the argument that children are malleable and easily led into vice. Gerson sees daily, he writes,

the filthy corruption of boys and adolescents by shameful and nude pictures offered for sale in the very temples and sacred places...Christian boys – Oh, horror – are here initiated by impious mothers or wayward nurses, and by fathers, full of perdition and laughing crazily, into the world of obscene songs, gestures and habits...and into many other abominations, most shameful to write or even think about, for they exceed Sodom and Gomorrah themselves.[234]

Hence the need to stop the rot at one of its sources. Similarly, Gerson would have all copies of the *Roman* burned.[235] But it is not only obscene books and pictures that can corrupt the young. Parents must see that their children are brought up in a completely pure environment. Nothing must be said or done in front of children that could arouse them to 'vile temptations'. Thus parents must never have or discuss sexual intercourse in the presence of their children, and they should not keep domestic pets. Watching and touching animals, says Gerson, makes children think of and do many vile and filthy things.[236] Parents must be careful about kissing and fondling children. No one should ever kiss or fondle the naked body of a child, especially its genitals. In fact, says Gerson, a child should refuse to be so fondled.[237] To prevent children from fondling each other it would be better if they slept alone in little beds 'as is the custom in Flanders'.[238]

Gerson's remarks on this topic of guarding children from the corruption of lust point to two things: his own sensitivity to sexuality in children, and an apparent lack of such sensitivity in contemporary society. Ariès and others have argued that, at this period and later, children under the age of puberty were generally regarded as lacking in any sexuality, and consequently were not shielded from sexual activity, ribaldry and obscenities.[239] Gerson's remarks seem to bear out this conclusion and it may well be that he is a precursor of a new awareness of sexuality in children, an awareness that was to become widespread, among educators at least, in the early modern period.[240]

The task of parents is not finished when they have provided guards against the invasion of vice. They have positive work to do also. The sermon on conjugal chastity built around the gospel text telling of the young Jesus' stay in the temple at Jerusalem gives Gerson the opportunity to speak at length on the duties of parents towards their children. There is the usual warning about guarding children from people who by example or words encourage vice.[241] But then Gerson speaks of the need to look after children's physical health, especially that of infants. And here he warns against drunken, stupid or lecherous nurses. Elsewhere he urges mothers to nurse their own infants if they can, 'for nourishment has an effect on nature and infants are usually better morally formed this way'.[242] The spiritual formation of children must be undertaken too: 'Parents ought to teach their children holily, in good religion and good habits.'[243] Gerson spells out the sort of thing this involves. They must see that their children go to church at the appointed times,[244] and above all that they go to confession and tell all their sins.

And if anyone says: 'what sins can little children, eight or ten years old, have committed? God wishes that nothing evil is done by them or others': I think that we teach them more evils than we think. Someone will say, 'what evils and who teaches them?' I say nothing about that here. I leave fathers and mothers and others to their consciences.[245]

It seems probable from what Gerson says here that the confession of children was not usual in his day. The canonical age at which yearly confession was compulsory was fourteen. However, during the course of the fifteenth and sixteenth centuries there is some evidence that the age was being lowered in some dioceses to ten or even seven.[246] A few of the writers on sin and confession of this later period also suggested that the age be lowered.[247] Gerson, then, may be a precursor of this movement to encourage the confession of children. He certainly believes that confession is the best way of giving children a Christian formation. There are other ways, he says: public preaching, private admonitions, school discipline. But confession is by far the most important.[248]

Gerson, then, does not think that the Christian formation and spiritual welfare of children can be left to parents alone; the assistance of clerics, especially confessors, is absolutely essential. It is the confessor who uncovers the hidden sins of children and roots out the poison from their souls. This purging process is essential, for if the poison remains the child's soul will never grow in Christ, but will languish, even 'be dead and buried, in the sewer of sins'.[249] Further, it is in confession that children can be given the most efficacious advice and so be helped against future temptations. It is of course difficult, Gerson continues, even to ensure that a child makes one good confession a year, for the Easter season is short and there are not enough confessors to question each child in depth and at length. But it is necessary that every child should have the opportunity at least once in his childhood to go over all his sins, without haste and 'with a wise and prudent confessor'.[250] In this way, children, many of whom commit serious sins which they do not know how to or dare not speak about, can be questioned and led to a feeling of horror at such sins so that they are fortified against future temptations and made pure again. They can be instructed in such a session on how to make a good confession in the future, by being shown how necessary it is to be quite frank and to hide nothing. Children who have had the benefit of this experience will have peaceful consciences, being happy in the thought that they will not, in adulthood, have to suffer the humiliation of having to confess their childhood sins. Fear of such humiliation prevents many adults from making a good confession, so it is very important that children should have the satisfaction of knowing all their sins have been properly and fully confessed.

Gerson is aware of a difficulty facing confessors of children; their job is to root out sin and to prevent future sin, but they might, in the process of questioning their penitents, teach them about sins of which the children were before totally ignorant and so actually lead them into new sins. But the risk must be taken. The strength of Gerson's conviction on this point is very apparent in his tract *De confessione mollitiei*, where he urges confessors to use what amounts to trickery to get their penitents to confess to masturbation.[251] He clearly thinks it vitally important that a sense of guilt be aroused in children for practices and actions that the church thinks objectively sinful, but which the child may have thought innocent and harmless. For Gerson such practices are far from harmless, whatever the state of mind of the sinner, for they bring poison into the soul and prevent the child from coming to Christ. Masturbation is a very grave sin. Confessors, and parents and teachers, must warn children of the gravity of the sin and how 'they can lose their virginity by it and suffer eternal damnation'. They must be told that if they do sin in this way, they must confess as soon as possible.[252]

Another way in which parents can help give their children a Christian formation is to teach them about their guardian angel. An early sermon on St Michael affords Gerson the opportunity of speaking on this topic. He stresses the importance of teaching children to honour and fear their good angel who sees all that they do. Parents and teachers are not always present, but the guardian angel is always watching. Children who firmly believe this will be further fortified against falling into bad habits and sinful practices.[253]

Parents who are concerned about the upbringing of their children – and all should be so concerned – can do no better than to follow the example of Joseph and Mary, portrayed by Gerson in a number of vernacular works as the perfect parents. Joseph nourished Jesus, took him each year to the temple, taught and disciplined him in accord with paternal authority, gave him all the care that a good, loyal and wise father can and should.[254] Mary and Joseph both disciplined Jesus, but in a gentle manner, and all parents should follow their example. They must exert a 'caring discipline that chastises gently, holily, prudently'. They must be neither too harsh nor too soft, though it is better, 'as Anselm and Quintilian teach', to err on the side of gentleness than of rigour.[255]

It is not that Gerson is against all physical chastisement, for in one of his Latin tracts for teachers he says beating schoolboys is sometimes necessary. But in his sermons to the laity it is always gentle discipline that he emphasises. Children must be led into virtuous ways, but this can be done by shielding them from the occasions of sin, by good example, by using the help of a good confessor and by sound teaching. Harshness is not generally necessary and indeed the young are more easily trained by kindness.[256] Is Gerson's insistence on gentleness in the treatment of children meant to curb generally harsh contemporary practices? It is not easy to tell from his writings to what extent the battered child was a common phenomenon in this period. Clearly there must have been some harshness, or Gerson would not have felt the need to insist on gentleness, but he does not seem to rail against persons who batter children in the way he rails against those who blaspheme, who commit sexual sins, who rob the poor. It is unfortunate that the examples which he notes about disciplining children in the sermons on conjugal chastity are not more explicit. As they stand they are not very revealing. Other evidence about the treatment of children in this period is not very plentiful. There is more evidence for the sixteenth and seventeenth centuries when, some historians argue, breaking the will by harshness was the key element in child-rearing.[257] However, historians who present this argument generally see severity and repression as a new phenomenon of the early modern period, perhaps caused by the puritanical fear of sin and the devil.[258] Whatever Gerson says of birching boys in school, it does not seem correct to regard him, as Ariès does, as a precursor of the idea of breaking the child's will by harshness, when he shows himself so concerned for gentleness in discipline in his sermons.

If, in Gerson's writings, there is no conclusive evidence about the prevalence of harshness towards children in the fourteenth and fifteenth centuries, it can at least be said that he himself is less concerned about it than he is about indifference towards and neglect of children. It is on this subject that he rails against offenders. They allow children to drift into sinful ways; parents do not care about the physical or spiritual health of their offspring; the clergy do not pay sufficient attention to the spiritual needs of children.[259] A similar concern appears in other preachers and moralists of the period. Bernardine, for example, is particularly critical of mothers who give too much freedom to their daughters, and who neglect to instruct them about sexual sins; and he tells mothers of young infants – in some detail – how to take care of their swaddled offspring.[260] Other moralists speak in more general terms, though with the same general message: if parents do not correct and train their children when young, they can expect only trouble later.[261] Gerson's concern, however, is particularly strong. He sees it as vital that neglect and indifference in the treatment of children come to an end, for the sake not only of the children themselves and their parents, but also of society, the church and Christendom.

School

The work that most clearly shows Gerson's deep concern for children is his tract *De parvulis trahendis ad Christum*, which is basically a defence of his work with Parisian schoolchildren. As chancellor, Gerson had under his general supervision a number of grammar schools. For some of them – those attached to the cathedral – he had the responsibility of selecting competent masters as well as overseeing their teaching. He took his responsibilities seriously, as an examination of the registers of the cathedral chapter shows. Scarcely a year passed without Gerson or others raising questions about the schools before the chapter.[262] Moreover, he involved himself directly with the schoolboys by hearing their confessions.[263] He also wrote, as examples of how the masters could instruct the boys while entertaining them, some short French moral plays, which the boys could perform.[264]

These activities led him to come under attack, he says in *De parvulis trahendis ad Christum*, from those who consider it beneath the dignity of one of his learning and position to stoop to instruct children and hear their confessions. He ought to be occupied with more important matters, they say, and not give scandal by such unusual activity. Gerson's defence is built around the text: 'Let the children come to me, and do not hinder them, for to such belongs the kingdom of heaven' (Math. 19:14). No work is more important, Gerson writes, than to snatch the souls of children from the gates of hell and, as it were, to plant and water them, 'flowers of no little worth in the garden of the church'.[265] The best way of doing this, he continues, is by hearing their confessions, not by preaching, which some would think more in keeping with his position.

Gerson agrees with his detractors that there is a great disparity in life-style (*mores*) between him and the children, but this can be overcome. And here Gerson discusses at some length his way of bringing children to Christ, by love, gentleness, friendliness, kindness, by coming down to their level and winning their confidence. If it is unusual for a chancellor to concern himself with schoolboys, what does this matter? Let each do things his own way. 'If no one is allowed to try anything new, the state will not prosper [*male iret respublica*].'[266] The whole tract gives the impression that Gerson is battling against contemporary lethargy for a cause which he thinks vitally important, and that he sees the classical authors and Christ as his allies.

Some of the schoolboys who occasioned *De parvulis* were also the concern behind Gerson's *Doctrina pro pueris Ecclesiae parisiensis.*[267] This is a set of regulations for the grammar school of Notre-Dame and it provides a good indication of how Gerson thinks his ideal of the Christian education of children can be achieved in a boarding-school environment. Of the nineteen regulations less than a quarter deal with academic and doctrinal instruction. In these he simply states that there must be sufficient time – the usual time, he says, runs from dawn until lunch, and from vespers until dinner – for the teaching of grammar, logic, poetry and the New Testament, and that the latter should be expounded in the vernacular. The boys must learn and observe the rituals of divine service, commit to memory words of praise about the love of God and be taught 'in the old way [*more antiquo*]' to say daily the hours of the Virgin and the seven psalms, so that their minds are filled with devotion. The rest of the regulations are largely concerned with the moral formation of the boys, and here Gerson's concern for a pure environment is very apparent. The master and the grammar master must each be men of good character (*incorruptissimi*) and must always set a good example to the boys, taking care never to say or do anything in front of them that is indecent; there must be no foul and obscene words, no wayward and dissolute gestures, no wanton and evil deeds.[268] The boys are to be preserved from familiarity and even contact with undesirable outsiders: no one is to be allowed to spend time with them or to share their lessons, unless special permission is given by the superiors, 'so that our boys do not acquire bad habits from intimacy with others'.[269] Adult outsiders too (*clerici et servitores capellani*) are not to be allowed to come in and converse with the boys unless one of the masters is present, while household servants must not be allowed any familiarity with the pupils. Moreover, a master must accompany the boys whenever they go out. It is clear that Gerson feels very strongly about the need to keep the boys isolated from harmful influences, for familiarity with outsiders is one of the things for which pupils may be whipped. This concern for a pure environment is manifested also in Gerson's regulations about songs, books and games. No immoral works are to be read, no dissolute songs to be sung and all games 'which lead to avarice, immodesty, undignified noise, anger or malice' are to be prohibited.[270]

Positive action too must be taken to prevent the boys from sinning. In the first place Gerson wants to set up a mechanism of internal control in each boy. They must therefore be instructed that they should at all times refrain from those actions for which they know they would be whipped if the master found out, by being told that God sees all, and that they each have a guardian angel, 'and a tempter devil, who would strangle them as soon as they commit a mortal sin', unless God and the good angel are merciful.[271] Gerson's 'obsession' with purity is again revealed by his singling out immodesty in thought, word and deed as the type of sin that must be especially guarded against. Secondly, the boys are to be encouraged, on pain of punishment for negligence, to inform against their companions who speak French, swear, lie, strike others, speak or behave immodestly, dawdle in bed in the morning, miss the recitation of the hours or chatter in church, no doubt so that the masters can have as much control – indirect in this case – as possible over every moment of their charges' lives. The boys are not to be allowed to form cliques (*societates ad partem extra alios*) and they must never change beds in the night, but stay with the companion assigned to them in the dormitory where 'more antiquo' a lamp must be kept burning all night. Such are the formidable ramparts Gerson constructs against the invasion of vice. But the children will still sin and so they must be sent to confession four or six times a year, having been instructed beforehand on how to make a good confession. The confessor must be a suitable one, wise, prudent and skilled in questioning. Those who are old enough, that is twelve or thirteen, should receive the Eucharist once a year.

Though Gerson, when addressing the laity, stresses the need for gentleness in the discipline of children, he allows whipping in the school under his care. However, he intends whipping to be the punishment for grave offences only, and it is not to be administered in a harsh manner or spirit.

But let punishments with birches be temperate, without the use of rods or other very harmful beating instruments. And let such punishment be administered without reproachful or abusive words, so that the boys feel themselves loved rather than mocked, so that they are led to the good by kindness, not severity, and so that they do not become faint-hearted.[272]

Gerson does not want to mould children by breaking their wills, and it seems from this text that he is regulating a system of corporal punishment already in existence and trying to moderate its rigour, rather than introducing something new.[273] Further, he shows a particular care for the health and well-being of the children who must have, he writes, enough, but not too much, food, together with clean rooms, beds and linen, and adequate recreation.

Gerson's general belief that it is better to lead the young gently rather than drive them rigorously appears in a Latin sermon of 1401, preached to the members of the College of Navarre.[274] Here Gerson summarises some of Quintilian's educational principles, which he fully approves. Masters should show anger as little as possible; they should be patient, answer questions willingly, give praise where it is due and not be too harsh in correcting mistakes. They should steer a course between austerity and friendliness in demeanour, but it is better to be too friendly than too austere. In short, they should behave in such a way that their pupils 'love their teachers no less than their studies, and think of them as parents, not of the body, but of the mind'. And, says Gerson 'it is Quintilian's conclusion that boys ought not to be hurt with whips'.[275]

Towards the end of his life Gerson again became directly involved with the education of children, as he had been in Paris in the first decade of the fifteenth century. This was from 1425, when the Archbishop of Lyons gave him the responsibility of the choir school attached to the College of St Paul.[276] One may presume that there he endeavoured to put his precepts into practice. But during the course of his life he also tried to get others to do the same. For instance we find him at the Synod of Rheims in 1408 urging that special attention be given, in each parish, to the instruction of children, especially to their moral and religious instruction. Suitable teachers should be appointed for these parish schools, and provided with adequate financial means for their support. Those drawn from the secular clergy should receive benefices while those from the Mendicant orders should have their needs directly provided by the bishop or local pastor.[277] Gerson shows his concern for the quality of teaching in a letter to a newly appointed bishop, whom he urges to care for the education of the young in his diocese. 'So that human plants grow into good men', the bishop should appoint teachers who are 'outstanding in knowledge' and of the highest moral integrity.[278] It is in fact the bishops, according to Gerson, who bear the major overall responsibility for the education of the young. In their visitations they should go to all schools personally and enquire into the quality of education provided; and they should ensure that new schools are established in parishes which lack them.[279] Gerson appears to be aiming at a system of universal elementary education – for boys – or at least at a nationwide system of available parochial schools. Failing that, or reinforcing school instruction where it existed, Gerson relies on the home. In a sermon to religious in 1402, he tells his hearers, whenever they preach to the people, to exhort mothers to train their children in the love and practice of religion.[280]

It was not only the children of the people that Gerson was interested in. There are extant among his Latin works two letters that he wrote to tutors of the royal princes of France on the subject of the education of their charges. The first was probably written in 1417 to the tutor of the Dauphin Charles, aged fifteen, and the second probably in 1429 to the tutor of the Dauphin Louis, aged five.[281] The former is not especially relevant here for it is more in the nature of a treatise on how a Christian ruler should behave than a dissertation on the education of children.[282] It does, however, contain a list of books that Gerson thinks suitable reading for a young prince. Although a number of classical authors are recommended,[283] these are outnumbered by authors of religious and moral works, among which Gerson includes a number of his own vernacular writings.[284]

Of more concern is the second letter, in which Gerson offers his advice on the methods to be used in educating the five-year-old Louis. The directions are rather general but serve to confirm what has already been concluded about Gerson's views on the instruction and formation of children. Religious and moral education are stressed more than academic learning; the boy should be taught about the saints, first by pictures and then by stories; he should be encouraged to have a special devotion to some particular saint of his own choosing and to his guardian angel; the ten commandments should be expounded to him at a level he can understand; and he should be shown what is the true end of man and how all men, poor, rich and kings are born in the same condition, 'for nothing is better in the great than humanity, clemency and humility towards those who, with regard to future beatitude, are their brothers and co-equals'.[285] Here also Gerson emphasises the need for gentleness in teaching and disciplining the child. The teacher must at all costs, he writes, avoid doing anything that makes his pupil hate him and so come to hate all learning. 'Even if he learns only a few things in many days, whatever he learns spontaneously should be counted as gain.'[286] Displays of anger by the tutor must be avoided and the child should not be beaten, nor should he be severely criticised for every childish fault, whatever the views of the household on strict discipline, for 'a noble nature prefers to be led than dragged, and to be fed sweetly with praise rather than dragged by a stern tyranny'.[287] But Gerson thought this of youthful human nature in general.

Innovations?

How original were Gerson's ideas about childen and their education? As far as his regulations for the school of Notre-Dame are concerned, which Ariès and others have seen as bearing the stamp of an innovator and precursor of later developments, a good case can be made for his lack of originality. There were other Parisian grammar schools, founded in the late thirteenth and early fourteenth centuries, whose statutes he could have known, and his regulations for the school of Notre-Dame bear a resemblance to those of Ave Maria College, an institution for six boys aged eight to sixteen, founded in 1339 and situated very near to the College of Navarre. These statutes lay the same stress on isolation from outside influences and on the need for masters of good character, and they contain similar regulations about academic learning, communal life, food, cleanliness and sleeping arrangements. However, at Ave Maria College a boy was to be severely whipped (*graviter verberatus*) if he lost or damaged library books, but for other breaches of the regulations he was to be reported to the governors and perhaps expelled. Gerson's regulations about moral behaviour are more detailed, and the founder of Ave Maria College did not suggest a 'sneak' system, but he did advocate weekly confession for the boys.[288] In 1386–7 d'Ailly reformed the financial aspects of the statutes of Ave Maria College and it seems very likely that Gerson had read these statutes.[289]

As far as Gerson's ideas about children and their upbringing in general go, a large part of what he has to say is to be found in some of the books he recommended, in his letter of 1417, that the dauphin should read.[290] The

De regimine principum of Giles of Rome, the *Speculum historiale* of Vincent
de Beauvais, and *La Somme le roy* of Lawrence of Orleans, all thirteenth-
century works, contain between them nearly all the ideas expounded by
Gerson: for example, the malleability of children, the characteristics of the
perfect master, the need to avoid corrupting influences, the benefits of
breast-feeding by mothers, the stress on gentleness in discipline.[291] If one
adds to these Vincent de Beauvais' *De eruditione filiorum nobilium*, where
there occur both the argument that schoolchildren should be allowed to
learn at their own pace without any forcing, and the admonition that if there
has to be any physical chastisement, it must be administered with
temperance and from a motive of love,[292] then Gerson's lack of originality
seems manifest.

Although the French – and classical – influences are no doubt paramount
for Gerson, concern for the proper formation of children and awareness of
their malleability is to be found in contemporary writings from other
countries. The Brothers of the Common Life, for instance, were firm
believers in the importance, for the individual and for the church as a
whole, of the inculcation of good habits and Christian virtue and religion
early in life.[293] A Middle English poem, *Ratis Raving*,[294] which takes the
form of advice given by a father to his son, and which deals, among other
things, with the seven ages of man, shows an awareness of how children
can be moulded. The son is told to study his father's words while he is still
young and innocent and able to be trained as a young tree. The third age
of man, from the seventh to the fifteenth year, is considered especially
important by this author, for it is then that reason develops, whose roots
must be carefully tended 'so that they be kept fair and clean'. People, then,
have a duty to teach their children and bring them up to be chaste and
charitable.[295] Mirk's *Instructions for Parish Priests* shows a concern similar
to Gerson's about the need for guarding children from impurity. Children
over the age of seven should not, writes Mirk, sleep together in the same
bed, and they must be taught God's laws.[296]

Despite the fact that most of Gerson's ideas about children and their
education are not new phenomena, his contribution should not be under-
estimated. The depth of his concern, the thoroughness of his approach, his
attempt to systematise some of his ideas in school regulations, catechetical
writings and instructions for confessors, together with his expressed
awareness of sexuality in children, and his bringing of the concept of the
gentle parent to the laity directly in vernacular sermons do perhaps add up
to something new and important. They certainly reveal a strong desire and
a concentrated effort to renovate Christendom by means of the education
of children. Gerson's views are in many ways similar to those of the
humanist educators. They, too, had a predilection for Quintilian, and
postulated the malleability of the child and his need for firm but kindly
training. 'The master must not be prone to flogging as an inducement to

learning. It is an indignity to a free-born youth, and its infliction renders learning repulsive...The habitual instrument of the teacher must be kindness.' So writes Battista Guarino of Verona (1434–60), son of one of the most influential of the Renaissance schoolmasters.[297] It would be wrong, though, to equate Gerson's views with those of the Italian humanist educators. There is emphasis in both on moral and religious formation and on early home training, but the Italians stress the study of the classics more than Gerson does, while his pedagogical ideas have a stronger religious orientation than theirs. Though Gerson wants his schoolboys to study Latin grammar, poetry and history, he is much less insistent than the humanists on the importance of classical style in composition, while their emphasis on the need for physical training is virtually absent from his educational writings. Here Gerson stands closer to the thirteenth-century Vincent de Beauvais, though he sees more value in the study of classical rhetoric at the university level than does Vincent.[298] One strong thread linking Gerson with the humanists is their shared belief that the sound education of children and adolescents is necessary for general reform. This same conviction is echoed by sixteenth-century reformers. 'The hope of our commonwealth rests on our youth' say Bucer, Capito and Hedio to the City Council of Strassburg, urging its members to undertake the reform of the entire school system...'[299] The major influence which gave Gerson the impetus to combine earlier ideas into a broad programme was no doubt his perception of the state of Christendom around the turn of the fifteenth century. The fruitless attempts to end the schism and the lack of a vigorous reform movement seem to have made him almost despair of adults and so pin his hopes on the malleable young who would form the next generation.

The reformation of the church, as someone said, must begin with children, since its corruption came from those whose upbringing was perverse and useless.[300]

8

DOCTOR CHRISTIANISSIMUS ET CONSOLATORIUS

One could detach from Gerson's thought as a whole a number of views and then label him – illicitly – a 'forerunner' of the Protestant Reformation. The views one chose to select would, of course, depend on what one saw as the essential features of the Reformation – a matter by no means settled yet.[1] Gerson certainly did present a number of opinions that would find echoes in one or another of the sixteenth-century Protestant movements. He spoke out against papal absolutism; he was a critic of speculative scholastic theology and of clerical corruption. He attacked monastic elitism and was firm in his belief that the life of Christian perfection was possible in all estates. He not only wrote works of spiritual guidance for the laity, but opened the mystical way to them. He praised marriage and he exalted family life. If his doctrine of justification, involving as it did human co-operation with divine grace and the pursuit of holiness, was not Lutheran, it nevertheless resembled that held by some of the Anabaptists. Despite the revolutionary nature of sixteenth-century Protestantism, many of the components that went into its making were already present in the rich complexity of late medieval religious life. Gerson's teaching was part of that rich complexity, so it is not at all surprising that he expressed some views that became part of the Protestant tradition.

Gerson's pastoral teaching taken as a whole leaves a different impression. If the essence of the Reformation, at least in its early stages, is viewed as a 'revolt against the Roman clergy as an entrenched estate' – and this is the view now gaining currency[2] – then Gerson's position seems essentially traditional. He upheld the papacy, if not papal absolutism. He exalted the role of pastors, both bishops and parish clergy and affirmed their sacramental powers. He never questioned clerical celibacy, and for him virginity always remained a higher estate than matrimony. He did advocate thorough-going reforms with respect to the ecclesiastical hierarchy, but the nature of these reforms would make it more licit to call him a 'forerunner' of the Catholic Counter-Reformation, which also had roots in the rich complexity of late medieval religious life, than of the Protestant Reformation.

Gerson's contribution, though, is best assessed with respect to his own time and in relation to his predecessors and contemporaries, rather than in terms of what happened a century after his death. And here, as this study has shown, Gerson's teaching has a basic conformity to existing traditions of thought. Nevertheless, he cannot be accused of following any single thinker slavishly. He can send his readers to the *Summa Theologiae* for confirmation of his views, but he can also disagree with Aquinas, for example about the status of minor prelates. If he agrees with Scotus that attrition can become contrition in confession, he insists against Scotus on the need for penitents to have the firm purpose of not sinning in the future. In theology Gerson followed a voluntarist position like that of d'Ailly, but he had a disagreement with his former teacher over the question of episcopal wealth and high-living.[3] In this sense Gerson is a man who knows his own mind. Moreover, he is not slavishly bound to traditional forms and concepts. He uses such traditional tools as the form of the medieval sermon, the concept of hierarchy and hierarchical functions, the various categories of sins, and Augustine's goods of marriage, but he can move freely within them, discard them or add to them when it suits his purpose. One might call him an eclectic theologian. But if 'eclecticism' connotes a somewhat piecemeal synthesis of acceptable opinions, then Gerson is not a mere eclectic. His synthesis is coherently organised around certain dominant motifs.

In the first place, the notion of hierarchy and paternalism is present in every aspect of his pastoral teaching. In this sense he is *doctor Christianissimus*, if one defines 'most Christian' as upholding, in broad outline at least, the traditional order in Christendom, in the church above all, but also in state and society. Moreover, in his pastoral theory and practice he says nothing to rock the boat in any fundamental way. Because Christian tradition was not monolithic he is, of course, to be found taking sides, for example for the minor prelates against the Mendicants, for the doctrine of the Immaculate Conception against the Dominican opposition. He was also in favour of reform in church and state but never in the direction of undermining hierarchy. For Gerson there is a proper hierarchical order everywhere and in everything. In the soul of man the sensual appetites should be in subjection to the will, which in its turn should obey the dictates of right reason. In the church the laity is in subjection to the clergy and can move along the road to perfection only by means of clerical and sacramental assistance. Even when he is writing about mysticism for the laity Gerson insists on the need for clerical counsel. In the secular world, too, there is hierarchy which must be preserved. And above everything is God, the seigneur of seigneurs.

Gerson saw the hierarchical order not being properly observed. In the souls of men sensual appetites were often in revolt against the other faculties, and in church and state people were not carrying out their hierarchical functions in the proper manner. This is why the notion of sin is so prominent in Gerson's pastoral works, for he views sin in terms of disorder.

This brings us to the second thread that binds Gerson's teaching into a coherent whole. He wishes above all to help move the laity along the road to repentance and salvation. Given the existing systems of beliefs, about justification and predestination, for instance, and the existing sacramental structure, especially the penitential system, this was a delicate task. He had to avoid making people too presumptuous and self-confident, on the one hand, and too despairing, on the other. He walked the tight-rope with no little skill in his teaching about justification and predestination, but above all in his teaching about confession. There are warnings and strictures to bestir hardened sinners, and there are techniques, which the twentieth century would probably not approve of, to awaken a sense of guilt. The trickery to make people confess to certain sins and the guardian angel who is the policeman in the conscience of the child come to mind here. But one must remember that Gerson was working within a system that demanded an awareness of all sins and complete confession of them. It is, however, the over-scrupulous and despairing, created no doubt by the system, who concerned Gerson most. Here he is truly *doctor consolatorius*. He is very aware of the problem of what he sees as the psychologically sick penitent, afflicted by doubts and uncertainties, and he does all he can to make the process of confession a reasonably comfortable experience, given that all sins must be uncovered and confessed. He urges priests to make sure that absolution brings psychological relief as well as sacramental grace, by insisting on an unqualified statement of absolution and a light and feasible penance. He wants the number of reserved cases reduced so that it is easier for penitents to confess. He tries to bring consolation to sinners not only by insisting on the healing powers of absolution, but also by insisting on gentleness on the part of the confessor, and by his numerous references in his sermons to the mercy of God.[4] His ability to bring consolation was helped by his psychological astuteness. His insight into the human psyche is apparent in a number of places in his writings, both in works for clerics and in vernacular works for the laity, and his advice always seems psychologically sound. Moreover, he is very aware of the psychological differences between people.

The diversity in human character and mood is beyond belief; diversity not only among the mass of men, but in the same man; and in that man not only in different years or months or weeks, but also from day to day, hour to hour and even moment to moment.[5]

He urges all pastors to realise this complexity and always to be aware of it when they are hearing confessions. In this aspect of pastoral care, the bringing of consolation to penitents, Gerson probably did make an original contribution.

He also made a contribution by distilling a large amount of previous theological and moral thought and making it available not only to pastors, in his Latin tracts, but also to the laity who were literate in their own language. His sermons served a similar end, as of course did the sermons of countless other well-educated preachers. Other people, too, wrote manuals for confessors and handbooks for the laity, but Gerson is one of the most articulate authors of this genre. His tracts are models of clarity.

From Gerson's writings one gains some impression, though not a clear picture, of popular religious mentality at the time. To Gerson it was a sinful generation to whom he preached. People behaved with a lack of decorum in church, and feast-days tended to lead to sinful activities rather than to devotion. People put off repentance. Superstition, sorcery and blasphemy flourished. False visionaries were abroad. There was some misunderstanding of basic doctrines, some doubts and even some unbelief. People frequently grumbled and murmured against God when they were afflicted by troubles. Some were puzzled about the existence of evil in the world, about the process of justification, about predestination, about purgatory and how the treasury of merit system worked and about numerous other questions to which they wanted answers. If all the questions that Gerson poses in his sermons, and answers or does not answer, came from the laity, then it was a generation with a lively curiosity. Gerson's own congregations would have a knowledge of the Bible, particularly of the gospels, but it seems unlikely that this would be true of all congregations, for Gerson, as has been seen, thought it enough if a parish priest taught about the commandments. This was his minimum requirement, but when he added anything it was such things as the creed, the seven sins, the works of mercy, the sacraments, heaven, hell and purgatory, and not the Bible. He himself wrote a montessaron[6] and a very brief summary of the chief events and teachings in the gospels with chapter references.[7] It was probably because he thought preaching on the Bible to be beyond the competence of most parish priests that he did not include it in his list, rather than that he thought it not important.

Aside from this sinful and sometimes ill-informed group, there was clearly a spiritual elite among the laity, to whom Gerson catered especially in his vernacular tracts. It was no doubt members of this elite who were sometimes afflicted with the sickness of over-scrupulosity, and therefore to whom Gerson was concerned to bring consolation. They would also form part of the audience for whom Gerson wrote his vernacular tracts on examination of conscience, temptations, the art of dying, Christian doctrine, and his other works on the spiritual life. That there was an audience for these works seems clear from the number of extant manuscripts of most of them. What proportion of the population belonged to the spiritual elite is impossible to say. The other group was without doubt the larger, but it would not be a homogeneous group and would comprise not only those who did not even fulfil their Sunday obligations regularly and who did not care about excommunication, but also those who, in varying degrees, tried to carry out the minimum requirements that Gerson laid down.

This is perhaps of some help on the question of whether the later Middle Ages was a period of flowering devotion or one of religious decadence as far as the population at large was concerned. Ozment has briefly delineated the problem[8] and the conclusion he suggests is that there was a blossoming of lay piety on the eve of the Reformation, but that it was a flawed and unsatisfying piety. This, he argues, was because the late medieval ecclesiastical authority, far from being indifferent and acting as a 'permissive, overindulgent mother' and allowing laymen too much freedom, was in fact 'mothering' the laity to death with religious expectations that were far too high, especially as regards confession. From the evidence of Gerson's writings we can agree that there was at least some blossoming of lay piety in the century before the Reformation. We can also agree that Gerson himself was not indifferent or permissive towards the laity. He was very concerned about the religiously devout and, with his paternalistic attitude, anxious to keep them on the right path. He was also concerned with the erring and wanted to bring them to repentance. For some, it is clear from Gerson's writings, the goals seemed to be too high, and they became afflicted with a neurotic over-scrupulosity, as, it has been argued, Luther did. But it would be wrong to generalise Luther's experience and to minimise the consolatory effects of a confessional system, when it operated as Gerson wished it to operate. Gerson's methods of consolation must have worked for many. Not all of the religiously devout and sensitive became Lutheran a century later.

NOTES

Introduction

1. Among the important books recently produced in English on late medieval theology are the following: F. Oakley, *The Political Thought of Pierre d'Ailly: The Voluntarist Tradition* (New Haven, 1964) (hereinafter *D'Ailly*); H. A. Oberman, *The Harvest of Medieval Theology: Gabriel Biel and Late Medieval Nominalism* (Revised edn, Grand Rapids, Michigan, 1967) (hereinafter *Harvest*); E. J. D. Douglass, *Justification in Late Medieval Preaching: A Study of John Geiler of Keisersberg* (Leiden, 1966) (hereinafter *Geiler*); D. C. Steinmetz, *Misericordia Dei: The Theology of Johannes Von Staupitz in its Late Medieval Setting* (Leiden, 1968) (hereinafter *Staupitz*); S. E. Ozment, *Homo Spiritualis: A Comparative Study of the Anthropology of Johannes Tauler, Jean Gerson and Martin Luther (1509–1516) in the Context of Their Theological Thought* (Leiden, 1969) (hereinafter *Homo Spiritualis*).

Among works covering lay medieval piety are the following: S. E. Ozment, *The Reformation in the Cities: The Appeal of Protestantism to Sixteenth-Century Germany and Switzerland* (New Haven, 1975) (hereinafter *The Reformation in the Cities*); F. Oakley, *The Western Church in the Later Middle Ages* (Ithaca, 1979) (hereinafter *Western Church*); S. E. Ozment, *The Age of Reform, 1250–1550: An Intellectual and Religious History of Late Medieval and Reformation Europe* (New Haven, 1980) (hereinafter *Age of Reform*).

2. The phrase *les simples gens* is frequently used by Gerson, but by it he does not mean merely poor, simple, illiterate people. The term includes members of the laity of all classes who are literate but not academically learned. He also refers to *les simples prestres*, where again it is the absence of academic learning and theological training that is indicated.

3. L. Mourin, *Jean Gerson, prédicateur français* (Bruges, 1952) (hereinafter *Gerson*), p. 429. Cf. Guillebert de Metz, 'Description de la ville de Paris au XVe siècle', published by Le Roux de Lincy-Tisserand in *Paris et ses historiens* (Paris, 1862), cited by E. Beltrán, 'Jacques Legrand, prédicateur', *Analecta Augustiniana*, 30 (1967), p. 148: 'It was a great thing in Paris when master Eustace de Pavilly, master Jean Gerson, brother Jacques Legrand and other doctors and clerics used to preach such excellent sermons.'

4. See G.7, pp. x–xxii, where the known manuscripts of these vernacular tracts are listed.

5. The *Opus tripartitum*, originally three vernacular tracts (*Le Miroir de l'âme, L'Examen de conscience*, and *La Science de bien mourir*) was the work cited most often (P.1, pp. clxxxi–clxxxii).

6. None of these editions was, in fact, complete. The details of these editions can be found in G.1, pp. 71–103, together with the manuscript tradition.

7. It was not until 1521 that a 'complete' edition was produced in France.

8. Douglass, *Geiler*, p. 40.

9. Oberman, *Harvest, passim.*

10. Steinmetz, *Staupitz, passim,* and 'Libertas Christiana: Studies in the theology of John Pupper of Goch', *HTR* 65 (1972) (hereinafter 'Pupper'), pp. 191–230.

11. J. Nève, ed., *Sermons choisis de Michel Menot* (Paris, 1924).

12. T. N. Tentler, *Sin and Confession on the Eve of the Reformation* (Princeton, 1977) (hereinafter *Sin and Confession*), p. 30.

13. *Jean Gerson: Oeuvres complètes,* ed. P. Glorieux, 10 vols. (Paris, 1960–73).

14. For a criticism of du Pin's edition see A. Combes' preface to L. Mourin, *Six sermons français inédits de Jean Gerson: Etude doctrinale et littéraire, suivie de l'édition critique* (Paris, 1946) (hereinafter *Six sermons*).

15. E.g., L. Mourin, E. Vansteenberghe, M. Lieberman, A. Combes, G. Ouy, P. Glorieux.

16. Not all parts of Glorieux's edition are equally trustworthy. One is safer with the vernacular sermons and tracts than some of the other works because of the editing of some of the former previously done by Mourin and others. Already editorial weaknesses elsewhere have been pointed out, e.g., by G. H. M. P. Meyjes in his *Jean Gerson et l'assemblée de Vincennes* (1329) (Leiden, 1978). Meyjes shows that in his editing of Gerson's treatise *De jurisdictione spirituali et temporali* Glorieux has for the most part simply copied du Pin's errors – and the number of errors is quite large. Meanwhile E. Colledge and J. C. Marler have found and edited a hitherto unknown work by Gerson which Glorieux had missed: '*Tractatus magistri Johannis Gerson de mistica theologia*: St. Pölten, Diözesanarchiv Ms. 25', *MS*, 41 (1979), pp. 354–86. Further, Glorieux's edition has a large number of typographical errors, his scriptural references are often wrong, and his punctuation is sometimes very misleading.

However, although much editorial work will have to be done before definitive versions of all Gerson's works are available, Glorieux's 'working' edition was worth producing; it will no doubt be many decades before a fully critical edition appears.

There is dispute about the dating of some of Gerson's writings. Where arguments for the dates of works have been published, either before or after Glorieux's edition, and if such arguments differ in their conclusions from Glorieux, this fact has been indicated in the notes. Otherwise Glorieux's dates have been accepted.

17. E.g., on ecclesiology: J. B. Morrall, *Gerson and the Great Schism* (Manchester, 1960); G. H. M. P. Meyjes, *Jean Gerson, Zijn Kerkpolitiek en Ecclesiologie* (The Hague, 1963), and *Jean Gerson et l'assemblée de Vincennes* (1329). The most prolific writer on Gerson's mysticism is A. Combes, *Essai sur la critique de Ruysbroeck par Gerson,* 3 vols. (Paris, 1945–59); *Jean Gerson, commentateur dionysien: Pour l'histoire des courants doctrinaux à l'université de Paris à la fin du XIVe siècle* (Paris, 1940); *La Théologie mystique de Gerson: Profil de son évolution,* 2 vols. (Paris, 1963–4) (hereinafter *Profil*).

18. Louvain, 1928.

19. A. Lambon, *Jean Gerson, sa réforme de l'enseignement théologique et de l'éducation populaire* (Paris, 1892) is an example of an older Protestant comment.

Connolly expends much energy in arguing that Gerson is much closer to Aquinas than to Occam. Since Connolly's day late medieval nominalism has been made respectable and is now generally viewed as having been orthodox, so there is no need for tortuous argument to safeguard Gerson's orthodoxy, which in any case was never, as far as I know, questioned in his lifetime.

20. 'Le Sermon français inédit de Jean Gerson pour la Noel: Puer natus est nobis', *Lettres romanes,* 2 (1948), pp. 315–24, 3 (1949), pp. 31–43, 105–45; 'Les Sermons français inédits de Jean Gerson pour les fêtes de l'Annonciation et de la Purification', *Scriptorium,* 2 (1948), pp. 221–40, 3 (1949), pp. 59–68; 'Jean Gerson prédicateur

français pour la fête de l'Annonciation', *Revue belge de philologie et d'histoire*, 27 (1949), pp. 561–98; 'Un sermon français inédit de Jean Gerson sur les anges et les tentations: Factum est proelium', *RTAM*, 16 (1949), pp. 99–154.
21. Leiden, 1973 (hereinafter *Gerson*).

1 Gerson's life

1. This sketch of Gerson's life is based on H. Jadart, *Jean Gerson*, 1363–1429: *Recherches sur son origine, son village natale et sa famille* (Rheims, 1882); on the biographical essay by Glorieux in G.1, pp. 105–35, and on the earlier and longer version of this essay, 'La Vie et les oeuvres de Gerson', *AHDLMA*, 18 (1950–1), pp. 149–92. Biographical sketches are also to be found in Morrall, pp. 1–16; in Connolly, pp. 16–60; and in Pascoe, *Gerson*, pp. 4–15. Cf. J. B. Schwab, *Johann Gerson, Professor der Theologie und Kanzler der Universität Paris* (Würzburg, 1858); L. Salembier, 'Gerson', *DTC*, VI, pp. 1313–30; P. Glorieux, 'Gerson', *NCE*, VI, pp. 449–50.
2. Gerson refers to financial sacrifices made by his parents in the *Dialogue spirituel* (1407), written initially for his sisters (G.7, p. 158).
3. E.g., *Puer natus*, G.7, p. 964; *Dialogue spirituel*, G.7, p. 158; *Pars animae Gerarde meae*, G.4, p. 147; *Tardiores ad te*, G.2, p. 47; *Discours sur l'excellence de la virginité*, P.3, p. 839.
4. G.2, pp. 6–8. This letter was written around 1396–7 when Jean and Nicholas were residing in Paris.
5. One of Gerson's brothers became a monk of this abbey.
6. Founded by the wife of Philip IV, Jeanne de Navarre, in 1304, the College of Navarre was the earliest effectively residential college in the university. Cf. C. E. Bulaeus, *Historia Universitatis Parisiensis*, IV (Paris, 1668), pp. 74–6; H. Rashdall, *The Universities of Europe in the Middle Ages* (Revised edn, by F. M. Powicke and A. B. Emden, Oxford, 1936) I, p. 510. In 1315, the executors of the queen's will issued new regulations, one of which stated that the masters and at least fifteen of the seventy students were to come from Champagne (the queen had been Countess of Champagne and most of the financial support for the college came from her property there) (Bulaeus, p. 90).
7. Gerson's earliest extant piece of writing is a letter he wrote to d'Ailly in 1385 asking the latter to use his influence to procure a benefice for him. Gerson refers to all the help his correspondent has already given him (G.2, pp. 1–4). Cf. G. Ouy, 'Une lettre de jeunesse de Jean Gerson', *Romania*, 80 (1959), pp. 461–72.
8. G.10, pp. 7–24. Cf. G. Ouy, 'La Plus Ancienne Oeuvre retrouvée de Jean Gerson', *Romania*, 83 (1962), pp. 433–92.
9. G.7, pp. 969–78.
10. More than a dozen university sermons in Latin are extant from these years. G.5, nos. 211, 217, 219, 223, 227, 228, 229, 233, 240, 245, 246, 249, 250, 251, 252.

For an account of how d'Ailly led the university in its movement to depose its corrupt chancellor, Blanchard, d'Ailly's predecessor, see A. E. Bernstein, *Pierre d'Ailly and the Blanchard Affair: University and Chancellor at the Beginning of the Great Schism* (Leiden, 1978).
11. The revenue of the benefice at Bruges was 200 francs a year (Connolly, p. 72). Gerson was in Bruges for a short time in 1396, when he took possession of his office in person on 12 October. He was there again in 1398 for two or three months, and for a more lengthy period in 1399–1400. There is evidence that Gerson was at Bruges again for a short time in 1405 and for a month in 1409 (G.1, pp. 112–13,

120, 124). These last two visits were rendered necessary because of manoeuvres at Bruges to oust him from his benefice. In 1411, probably as a result of his criticism of Jean Petit's defence of the murder of Orleans by Burgundy, Gerson lost his benefice.

12. Cf. G. Ouy, 'Gerson et l'Angleterre', in *Humanism in France*, ed. A. H. T. Levi (Manchester, 1970), pp. 43–81. In another article, Ouy argues that d'Ailly had intended, from at least the time he became chancellor, that Gerson should succeed him in a comparatively short time, while he himself moved on to more prestigious offices. If this was his plan, he certainly succeeded. He became Bishop of Puy, then Bishop of Cambrai and finally a cardinal ('La Plus Ancienne Oeuvre retrouvée de Jean Gerson', pp. 454–62).

13. Cf. *De substractione obedientiae* (1395), G.6, pp. 22–4.

14. *Ista est pars*, G.2, pp. 17–23. It is not clear to whom this letter was sent: perhaps to d'Ailly or to the College of Navarre. Gerson's official request to be relieved of the chancellorship was sent to the faculty of theology and was received by the chapter of Notre-Dame on 11 March 1400 (G.1, p. 113).

15. G.2, pp. 23–42.

16. His lectures of 1402, *Contra curiositatem studentium* (G.3, pp. 224–49), and his sermon to the members of the College of Navarre, *Considerate lilia* (G.5, pp. 151–68), are also devoted to criticism of existing practices in the faculty of theology and to proposals for reform. Glorieux is doubtful about the date of the sermon (G.5, p. 7). Lieberman, in *Romania*, 83 (1962), p. 70, argues convincingly for 1401. For detailed discussion of Gerson's proposals, see P. Glorieux, 'Le Chancelier Gerson et la réforme de l'enseignment', in *Mélanges offerts à Etienne Gilson* (Toronto, 1959), pp. 285–98; Connolly, pp. 71–89; Pascoe, *Gerson*, pp. 80–109.

17. G.7, pp. 16–55, 220–80. The *Piteuse complainte* (G.7, pp. 213–16) was also probably written during this period at Bruges. Gerson had already written before 1400 other vernacular pieces, chiefly for his sisters, e.g., *Neuf considérations* (G.7, pp. 1–3), *Discours sur l'excellence de la virginité* (G.7, pp. 416–21).

18. G.7, nos. 293, 298, 302, 303, 306, 310, 312, 324, 328, 330, 336.

19. Cf. P. Glorieux, 'L'Enseignment universitaire de Gerson', *RTAM*, 23 (1956), pp. 88–113.

20. Ten Latin sermons also date from the years 1400–4, eight of them preached to clerical audiences in Paris, two before the pope. G.5, nos. 207, 208, 212, 213, 214, 230, 236, 239, 242, 253.

21. Benedict XIII granted by a bull of November 1403 that the cure of Saint-Jean-en-Grève should be annexed in perpetuity to the chancellorship. However, Gerson does not seem to have gained a clear title until March 1409, as a result of an award in the *Parlement* of Paris that settled the dispute between Gerson and the former patron of the parish, the Abbot of Bec. Nevertheless, he preached frequently in this parish before 1409, and indeed before 1403. Cf. G.1, pp. 118, 124; Connolly, pp. 129–30. It was in 1403 also that Gerson became a canon of the cathedral chapter of Notre-Dame.

22. As chancellor Gerson had responsibility for the schools of seven parishes in Paris, including those of these three parishes. His connection with the schools is probably one of the reasons he preached in these churches occasionally, but no doubt his reputation for eloquence played a part too.

23. Mourin, *Six sermons*, p. 93. Mourin cites a document of the period (actually the complaints of the parishioners against the union of the cure of Saint-Jean and the chancellorship) that states that there were 'many great seigneurs, counsellors, officials and great and powerful bourgeois in this parish'.

24. Of the nine vernacular sermons of these years, seven were clearly preached before the court (G.7, nos. 348, 356, 359, 365, 389, 396, 398). The other two, no. 395 (1407), on the unity of the church, with a plea for the way of resignation, and no. 387 (1410), on the Mendicant orders, although they address the congregations as 'devot peuple', are clearly not ordinary parish sermons.

25. *Quae est ista* (probably 1419), G.5, pp. 481–6, and *Redde quod debes* (1421), G.5, pp. 487–93.

26. G.7, pp. 404–7.

27. Cf. Morrall, pp. 76–93.

28. G.5, pp. 39–50. Cf. Morrall, pp. 94–111 and Pascoe, *Gerson*, pp. 10–13.

29. Morrall, p. 95; Pascoe, *Gerson*, p. 13. Gerson was not, however, content about what he regarded as the excessive amount of centralisation that existed in the church. In *De potestate ecclesiastica* (1417) (G.6, p. 239), he argued that the pope needed enough sustenance and power for his estate, but not so much that he crushed the rest of the ecclesiastical hierarchy. Gerson goes on to complain about papal collation of benefices, the odious multiplication of exemptions and excommunications, excessive reservation of sins, and the removal of judicial cases from local episcopal courts.

30. G.7, pp. 1100–23. In his Latin work *De auferibilitate sponsi*, G.3, pp. 294–313, Gerson attacks the doctrine of tyrannicide, without, however, mentioning Petit by name. This work was originally a lecture given in 1409, but reworked for presentation at the Council of Constance, April 1415 (G.3, p. xiii).

31. *Rex in sempiternum vive*, G.7, pp. 1005–30.

32. G.5, nos. 216, 218, 222, 231, 238.

33. *Estote misericordes* (1404), G.7, pp. 326–40, about the Savoisy affair. Servants of Charles de Savoisy, after a fracas during a university procession, had wounded some students as they attended an official university mass in the church of St Catherine. *Diligite justitiam* (1408 or 1405), G.7, pp. 598–615. The general opinion used to be that this was a discourse to the *Parlement* of Paris against the action of Guillaume de Tignonville, the Provost of Paris, who had had two students executed for theft and murder. Recently, G. H. M. P. Meyjes, in *Jean Gerson et l'assemblée de Vincennes* (1329), has argued that the discourse had nothing to do with the de Tignonville affair of 1404–8, but was delivered to the *Parlement* in November 1405, in connection with some illegal appropriation of ecclesiastical goods (pp. 34–53).

34. *Miserere nostri*, G.7, pp. 714–17.

35. *Redde quod debes* (1421), G.5, pp. 487–93, is another sermon on reform, this time preached to the synod of Lyons.

36. G.10, nos. 501, 502, 503, 505, 506, 508, 509. Cf. W. H. Principe, *Gerson's Attitude towards the Occult Sciences* (Dissertation for the Licentiate in Medieval Studies, Toronto, 1951).

37. *De puella aurelianensi* (1429), G.9, pp. 661–5.

2 The art of the preacher

1. Ch. 6, in T.-M. Charland, *Artes praedicandi: Contribution à l'histoire de la rhétorique au moyen âge* (Ottawa, 1936), p. 243.

2. For a discussion of the aids that become available from the thirteenth century, see R. H. Rouse and M. A. Rouse, *Preachers, Florilegia and Sermons: Studies on the Manipulus Florum of Thomas of Ireland* (Toronto, 1979).

The most comprehensive works on the *Artes praedicandi* are Charland, *op. cit.*, and J. J. Murphy, *Rhetoric in the Middle Ages: A History of Rhetorical Theory from Saint Augustine to the Renaissance* (Berkeley, California, 1974). See also H. Caplan, *Of Eloquence: Studies in Ancient and Medieval Rhetoric* (Ithaca, 1970).

3. D'Ailly's and Gerson's sermons on this theme stand next to each other in one manuscript sermon collection. Cf. E. Brayer, *Notice du ms. 574 de la Bibliothèque Municipale de Cambrai, suivie d'une édition des sermons français de Pierre d'Ailly* (Paris, 1965). MS 574 contains over 100 sermons, arranged in the order of the liturgical year. Many of the sermons are by unidentified authors; five are Gerson's and eleven d'Ailly's. Maillard's sermon is edited by A. de la Borderie, *Olivier Maillard, Oeuvres françaises: Sermons et Poésies* (Nantes, 1877), pp. 25–30.

4. Preaching requirements had been formally incorporated into the theology curriculum of the University of Paris in the thirteenth century. Cf. H. Denifle and E. Chatelain, *Chartularium universitatis Parisiensis*, II (Paris, 1891), pp. 697–703. For a discussion of the late-twelfth- and thirteenth-century movement to increase and upgrade preaching in the vernacular, see P. Roberts, 'Master Stephen Langton preaches to the people and clergy: sermon texts from twelfth-century Paris', *Traditio*, 36 (1980), pp. 237–68; and the same author's edition of *Selected Sermons of Stephen Langton* (Toronto, 1980). The tenth canon of the Lateran Council of 1215 stressed the importance of preaching to the laity. Cf. Lat. IV, c. 10, *Conciliorum oecumenicorum decreta* (Freiburg, 1964), p. 215.

5. Cf. the author of the tract attributed to Aquinas, ed. Caplan, *op. cit.*, p. 76.

6. British Museum MS Royal 18.B xxiii, ed. by W. O. Ross in *Middle English Sermons*, EETS, OS, 209 (London, 1940). H. Spencer in *English Vernacular Sunday Preaching in the late Fourteenth and Fifteenth Century, with Illustrative Texts* (D.Phil. dissertation, Oxford, 1982) has recently shown that there was a revival of preaching in the ancient mode in late medieval England.

7. Ross, pp. 135–7.

8. T. Arnold, ed., *Select English Works of John Wyclif*, 3 vols. (Oxford, 1869–71). Vols. I and II contain the sermons. A new critical edition of these 294 sermons is currently being produced by A. Hudson. The first volume, containing the sermons on the Sunday gospels and epistles, has already appeared: *English Wycliffite Sermons*, I (Oxford, 1983) (hereinafter *English Wycliffite Sermons*).

9. Hudson, *English Wycliffite Sermons*, pp. 264–7; Arnold, I, pp. 27–9. The biblical commentary in the sermons in this Wycliffite collection is sometimes sophisticated, even academic.

10. Text printed in A. Hudson, *Selections from Wycliffite Writings* (Cambridge, 1978) (hereinafter Hudson), pp. 52–6.

11. Ross, pp. 143–6.

12. Cf. Voltaire's criticisms of Menot's sermons, in *Dictionnaire philosophique* under 'Allegories' (Vol. 26, p. 184), and 'Biens d'eglise' (Vol. 27, p. 369), cited in Nève, *op. cit.*, pp. v–vi. Cf. Murphy, *Rhetoric in the Middle Ages*, pp. 229–300; and Caplan, p. 51.

13. For a list with MS locations, see Charland, pp. 21–106. Cf. Murphy, *Rhetoric in the Middle Ages*, ch. 6, pp. 269–355. Charland sees the scholastic method of the universities as the prime influence on the development of the modern sermon; Caplan and Murphy argue for the influence of ancient rhetoric. Murphy makes a convincing case for the appearance of the modern sermon in the twelfth century, and therefore before the establishment of the universities. Cf. also P. Tibber, *The Origins of the Scholastic Sermon, c. 1130–c. 1210* (D.Phil. dissertation, Oxford, 1983).

14. 'Assumitur autem prothema, ut per ipsum fiat quedam via ad divinum auxilium impetrandum...et ne videatur occasionaliter sumptum, debet in aliquo vocabulo cum themate concordare.' (John of Wales (d. 1300), *De arte praedicandi*, MS Mazarin, 569, f. 82r and v). This passage is cited in E. Gilson, 'Michel Menot et la technique du sermon médiéval', *Revue d'histoire franciscaine*, 2 (1925), p. 310. Gilson incorrectly attributes the treatise to Thomas Waleys (Charland, p. 56).

However, Thomas Waleys in the mid fourteenth century also wrote a treatise on preaching, *De modo componendi sermones*, in which he says basically the same thing about the use of the protheme (Charland, p. 350).

15. *Forma praedicandi*, ch. 31, in Charland, pp. 268–72.

16. Caplan, pp. 58–9.

17. Ch. 1, in Charland, p. 239. Presumably then a sermon should take between half an hour and an hour to preach.

18. Ed. by M. F. Boynton in 'Simon Alcock on expanding the sermon', *HTR*, 33 (1941), pp. 201–16.

19. For Jean de Chalons see Charland, pp. 53, 211. Richard of Thetford's treatise is published as Part III of the *Ars concionandi* attributed to Bonaventure, in *Bonaventurae Opera omnia* (Florence: Quaracchi, 1882–1902), Vol. IX, pp. 16–21; Basevorn, *Forma praedicandi*, ch. 39, Charland, pp. 291–4; 'Aquinas', Caplan, pp. 60–72.

20. E.g. Alexander of Ashby, *De modo praedicandi* (*c.* 1200). This treatise survives in two manuscripts: Oxford Magdalen College MS 168, ff. 128v–130r, and Cambridge University Library MS Ii.1.24, ff. 169–73. Cf. Murphy, *Rhetoric in the Middle Ages*, pp. 312–17. Basevorn also writes about the conclusion in chapter 47, Charland, pp. 307–30.

21. Cambridge Corpus Christi College MS 455, ff. 1–96. The work is discussed in Murphy, *Rhetoric in the Middle Ages*, pp. 317–26.

22. *Treatise on Preaching*, trans. by the Dominican students, Province of St Joseph (London, 1955), pp. 32–5.

23. Edited by Caplan, *op. cit.*, pp. 143–57. Caplan is of the opinion that the tract is *not* the work of the well-known Henry of Hesse, more commonly called Henry of Langenstein.

24. '...auditus allectio' (ch. 24, Charland, p. 260). Rendering the audience 'attentive, well-disposed and receptive' was the purpose of the *exordium* in the classical oration. Cf. Cicero, *De inventione* (London, 1960), I, 15.

25. f. 76, cited in Murphy, *Rhetoric in the Middle Ages*, p. 323.

26. Caplan, pp. 57–8.

27. *De modo componendi sermones*, Charland, p. 356.

28. Tract attributed to Henry of Hesse, Caplan, p. 151.

29. Ross, pp. 220–8.

30. Basevorn thought that beginning a sermon with a prayer was permissible (ch. 25, Charland, pp. 262–4).

31. Dividing a theme by means of questions is fairly common. Very often the questions are variations on the commonplaces of scriptural explication: *quis, quibus, ubi, quando, quomodo* and *quid*.

32. Edited by D. M. Grisdale, in *Three Middle English Sermons from the Worcester Chapter Manuscript f.* 10 (Leeds, 1939).

33. N. Marzac, *Edition critique du sermon 'Qui manducat me' de Robert Ciboule* (1403–1458) (Cambridge, 1971). The sermon is very long and was probably preached in two halves, one in the morning and the other in the afternoon or evening.

34. The sermon occurs in seven MSS. In all cases the sermon is complete (*ibid.*, pp. 4, 7, 37–8).

35. There was a custom at Paris of employing special writers to report the university sermons. Cf. A. L. de la Marche, *La Chaire française au moyen âge* (Paris, 1886), p. 326.

36. St Thomas Aquinas, for instance, had a very good contemporary reputation as a preacher (Caplan, p. 48), but some of the extant outlines for sermons, as produced in the Vivès edition (*Opera omnia*, Vol. XXIX, e.g. pp. 208–9) make this hard to

believe. Perhaps the new Leonine edition currently being prepared by L. J. Bataillon will include some complete sermons that reveal Thomas' skill.

37. All are reproduced in G.7. The du Pin edition has Latin versions only.

38. G.7, nos. 376 (avarice), 379 (anger), 380 (envy), 367, 368 (gluttony), 377, 378 (sloth), 381, 382, 383 (pride), 369, 370, 371, 372, 373, 374, 375 (lust).

39. G.7, nos. 385, 351 (Christmas), 386, 346 (Ash Wednesday), 366, 353 (Easter Sunday), 459, 352 (Palm Sunday), 340–55 (Pentecost), 351, 391, 397 (Trinity), 344, 390, 356 (All souls), 342 (Epiphany), 341 (Good Friday), 388 (All Saints).

40. G.7, nos. 384, 345, 347 (St Anthony), 361 (St Peter and St Paul), 350 (St Michael), 360 (John the Baptist), 392 (Purification), 343 (Annunciation), 393 (Immaculate Conception).

41. G.7, pp. 748–52. *Misereor* (G.7, pp. 709–13) and *Multi* (G.7, pp. 717–20) also deteriorate in this way.

42. Cf. Mourin, *Gerson*, pp. 19–28, 427–8. Mourin bases this conclusion on his own close study of the manuscripts, not on any statements made by Gerson or the scribes who wrote the manuscripts. His arguments are persuasive.

43. E.g., *Hoc sentite* (1402?), G.7, p. 651.

44. Caplan, p. 53.

45. *Forma praedicandi*, Ch. 1, Charland, p. 238.

46. Humbert of Romans is an exception among the theorists in that he discusses all these questions in detail.

47. *Quomodo stabit* (1410), G.7, p. 982.

48. *Non in solo pane* (1402?), G.7, p. 746. Cf. 'Et pourquoy Jhesu Cristi ne monstra tantost sa gloire a tout le monde. Il souffisoit que par ses messaigers et par luy aussi il se monstra a tous par predicacion.' *Gloria* (1402), G.7, p. 643.

49. *Non in solo pane* (1402?), G.7, p. 739.

50. *Omne regnum* (1402?), G.7, p. 762. Cf. *Tota pulchra es* (1401), G.7, p. 1080.

51. *Bonus pastor* (1408), G.5, p. 128.

52. Caplan, p. 53.

53. Bernardine of Siena, *Sermons*, ed. D. N. Orlandi, trans. H. J. Robins (Siena, 1920), pp. 5–6. Cf. L. McAodha, 'The nature and efficacy of preaching according to St. Bernardine of Siena', *Franciscan Studies*, 27 (1967), pp. 221–47.

54. Arnold, Vol. II, pp. 339–41. Cf. the sermon by Brother Clement, O.P., on the theme 'Bonum est audire verbum Dei' (Br. Mus. Egerton 655, f. 142, cited in J. Sweet, 'Some thirteenth-century sermons and their authors', *JEH*, 4 (1953), pp. 27–36).

55. *Mansionem* (1401), G.7, p. 685. Cf. The 'Aquinas'-tract, Caplan, p. 53. The author, citing Cicero, Augustine and Gregory as references, says that the way something is said is as important as what is said. The preacher should penetrate the hearts of his audience and kindle and inflame them.

56. Sermon for the sixth day after Ash Wednesday, in Nève, p. 299. Menot's sermons, though preached in French, were printed in Latin.

57. *Adversus superstitionem in audiendo missam* (c. 1429), G.10, pp. 142–3.

58. *Non in solo pane* (1402?), G.7, p. 741. Cf. *Bonus pastor* (1408), G.5, p. 127.

59. *Redde quod debes* (1421), G.5, p. 492. Cf. *Puer natus est* (1402), G.7, pp. 958–9.

60. *Redde quod debes* (1421), G.5, p. 487. His clerical audience would hardly have been surprised by this advice. It was commonplace and occurs in many of the treatises on preaching. Gregory, in fact, has thirty-six pairs of opposed types, some relating to social position, some to personal habits, some to level of education, and others to age and sex (*Regula pastoralis MPL*, 77 : 12–126). Jacques de Vitry has 120 categories of hearers (Caplan, p. 151).

61. *Scriptum est melius* (1408?), G.2, p. 111.

62. *Bonus pastor* (1408), G.5, p. 131, Cf. *Quomodo* (1410), where Gerson says that parish priests are not called upon to preach subtly to their parishioners. It suffices and is more profitable if they speak broadly (*grossement*) on the ten commandments, the seven mortal sins, etc. (G.7, p. 985).

63. *Bonus pastor* (1408), G.5, p. 128. The example of opposing vices that he gives is avarice/prodigality.

64. *Ibid.*, p. 129.

65. A. de Poorter, 'Un manuel de prédication médiévale', *Revue néo-scolastique de philosophie*, 25 (1939), p. 202.

66. *Summa de arte praedicatoria*, MPL, 210:112.

67. *Ibid.*, p. 114.

68. E. Delaruelle *et al.*, *L'Eglise au temps du Grand Schisme et de la crise conciliare*, II (Paris, 1964) (hereinafter Delaruelle, *L'Eglise*), pp. 629-56. Cf. Francis Rapp, *L'Eglise et la vie religieuse en Occident à la fin du moyen âge* (Paris, 1971) (hereinafter Rapp, *L'Eglise*), pp. 130-6.

Lewis W. Spitz argues that this moral emphasis is apparent also in late medieval confessional and catechetical instructional materials which leave the impression of a Christianity which 'was 80 percent morals, 15 percent dogma, and 5 percent sacraments'. ('Further lines of inquiry for the study of "Reformation and Pedagogy"', in *The Pursuit of Holiness in Late Medieval and Renaissance Religion: Papers from the University of Michigan Conference*, ed. C. Trinkaus and H. O. Oberman (Leiden, 1974) (hereinafter *Pursuit of Holiness*), p. 300.)

69. De la Borderie, pp. 90-134, 161.

70. Ch. 4, Charland, p. 241.

71. *Treatise on Preaching*, pp. 38-41.

72. Cf. T. F. Crane, *The Exempla or Illustrative Stories from the Sermones Vulgares of Jacques de Vitry* (London, 1890).

73. The author of the 'Aquinas'-tract would no doubt have been of one mind with Gerson about this. He writes in connection with sermons *ad populum*: 'The preacher should conduct himself and speak with as great a gravity as he should maintain in speaking of Christ in His presence' (Caplan, p. 73).

74. E.g., in sermons in the Lollard cycle, as *Designavit Dominus Jesus*, in Hudson, *Selections from English Wycliffite Writings*, pp. 119-22.

75. Crane, p. lxix.

76. Ed. by T. Erbe, EETS, ES, 96 (London, 1905).

77. *Ibid.*, pp. 191-4.

78. E.g., Richard of Thetford, *op. cit.*, and the author of the 'Aquinas'-tract (Caplan, pp. 72-3). Warnings against excessive intellectualism occur also in other sermons of the period; e.g., MS 48, Bayeux, Sermon 57, f. 179v, where intellectual subtlety in a preacher is characterised as a seeking after vainglory. Cited by H. Martin, 'Les Procédés didactiques en usage dans la prédication en France du nord au XVe siècle', *La Religion populaire* (Colloques Internationaux du Centre National de la Recherche Scientifique, no. 576, Paris, 1977), p. 66.

79. *Edition critique*, pp. 54-6.

80. E.g., sermon, *Sit civitas Jherico anathema*, in de la Borderie, pp. 8-13. After the protheme and prayer in this sermon, Maillard says to his audience that he will begin in his usual way by taking up a theological question.

81. Nève, pp. 22-4.

82. The vernacular sermon that Menot actually preached may well have been different from the edited, Latin version that survives.

83. *Non in solo pane* (1402?), G.7, p. 741.

84. Jean de Montreuil, *Opera*, Vol. I, ed. E. Ornato (Turin, 1963), p. 195. Jean

Courtecuisse attended the same college as Gerson – the College of Navarre. In 1408 he became almoner to the king. He was acting chancellor of the university from 1419 to 1421, Bishop of Paris, 1420–2, and Bishop of Geneva, 1422–3. Cf. G. di Stefano, *L'Œuvre oratoire française de Jean Courtecuisse* (Turin, 1969), pp. 3–4.

85. A. Combes, *Jean de Montreuil et le chancelier Gerson* (Paris, 1942), p. 592.

86. *Chronique du religieux de Saint-Denys*, ed. M. L. Bellaguet (Paris, 1839–52), Vol. III, p. 604.

87. Enguerrand de Monstrelet, *Chronique* (6 vols.), ed. L. Douët-d'Arcq (Paris, 1857–62), Vol. III, ch. CXXXIII, p. 55. The Duke of Orleans had been assassinated in 1407, but, because of the political situation, the official funeral ceremony was delayed till 1415. The text of this vernacular sermon is lost.

88. Thomas Waleys, in the first chapter of his *De modo componendi sermones*, on the qualities of a good preacher (Charland, pp. 328–41), stresses the importance of variety in style, especially in vocal delivery.

89. Di Stefano, pp. 155–71.

90. Cf. B. Smalley, in a paper given to the Medieval Sermon Studies Symposium in 1979: 'The doctrinal contents of sermons, apart from University sermons, is too banal to be worth study.' An abstract of this paper, including the sentence cited, appears in *Medieval Sermon Studies Newsletter* (1979), pp. 2–3.

91. G.7, pp. 449–519. This is a very long sermon and was delivered in two parts. It survives in more manuscripts – about twenty – than any other of Gerson's vernacular sermons.

92. MS 48, Bayeux, sermon 43, f. 123v., cited in Martin, *op. cit.*, p. 66.

93. Di Stefano, pp. 337–419.

94. *O Vos*, lines 2099–2170; *Ad deum vadit*, G.7, pp. 505–6. One preacher must have copied from the other, unless both are copying from another French source (Courtecuisse's sermon is undated). There are Latin works that find echoes in both sermons, e.g., *Meditationes vitae Christi*, attributed to Bonaventure; *Liber de Passione Christi*, attributed to Bernard; *Liber Jesu Christi* by Ludolph of Saxony. Cf. di Stefano, pp. 27–8.

95. C. Brunel, ed., 'Le Sermon en langue vulgaire prononcé à Toulouse par Saint Vincent Ferrier le vendredi saint, 1416', *Bibliothèque de l'Ecole de Chartes*, CXI (1953), pp. 5–53. Vincent does not interrupt his narrative with questions.

Both Olivier Maillard and Michel Menot acknowledge their debt to Gerson's *Ad deum vadit* in their Passion sermons. Cf. M. Peignot, ed., *Histoire de la Passion de Jésus-Christ, par R. P. Olivier Maillard* (Paris, 1828), especially pp. 34, 37, 53, 68. Maillard is, if anything, more dramatic than Gerson. Menot's Passion sermon is in Nève, pp. 177–98; the reference to Gerson is on p. 179.

96. G.7, p. 549 (1401).

97. E.g., *Sancta* (1404?), G.7, p. 1031.

98. *Poenitemini...Repentez vous car penitence* (1396 or 1403), G.7, p. 935.

99. G.7, pp. 717–18 (1403?).

100. G.7, p. 959 (1396).

101. E.g., *Ecce rex* (1395 or, according to Lieberman, *Romania*, 78 (1957), p. 34, 1414), G.7, pp. 615–22; *Hoc sentite* (1402), G.7, pp. 651–9; *Omne regnum* (1402), G.7, pp. 753–62; *Vade in pace* (1407), G.7, pp. 1093–1100. Many of the *Poenitemini* series on the seven capital sins also begin in this way.

102. Only rarely does Gerson not use the *Ave*, e.g., in *Vivat rex* (1405), G.7, pp. 1137–85. Here the prayer 'Dieu doint bonne vie au roy; vivat rex, vive le roy' takes its place. Courtecuisse, d'Ailly and Maillard all use the *Ave*. The English practice seems to be to end the protheme with the *Pater* and the *Ave*. The Germans Biel and Geiler use the *Ave* alone (Douglass, p. 31).

NOTES TO PAGES 25–7 267

103. In *Multi* (1403?), G.7, pp. 717–20, *Suscepimus* (1396), G.7, pp. 1048–57, and *Factum* (1393), G.7, pp. 622–39 there is nothing between the protheme and the division. The same is true for some of the discourses of circumstance.

104. *Memoriam* (1402?), G.7, pp. 698–709.

105. G.7, pp. 978–92 (1410).

106. *Sancta* (1404?), G.7, pp. 1031–40.

107. *Dedit* (1403), G.7, pp. 585–98.

108. D'Ailly and Courtecuisse, although they often employ both a protheme and an introduction, sometimes make the latter very brief. E.g., Courtecuisse's *Tamquam sponsum* (di Stefano, pp. 175–89).

109. Cf. Part I of *Ars Concionandi* in *Bonaventurae Opera omnia* (Florence: Quaracchi, 1901), Vol. IX, pp. 8–15. Part I is an anonymous treatise. Part III is the tract by Richard of Thetford. Part II is simply a paragraph of transition. Cf. Charland, pp. 30–3; Murphy, *Rhetoric in the Middle Ages*, p. 327.

The sermon attributed to Hugo Legat had an intrinsic (*intra*) division, following the order of the words.

110. *Gloria* (1402), G.7, pp. 639–50.

111. *Suscepimus* (1396), G.7, pp. 1048–57. The text of this sermon is one of the few taken from the Introit of the mass.

112. Here Gerson is following the theorists who advised this method for sermons *ad populum*.

113. G.7, pp. 615–22 (1395 or 1414).

114. G.7, pp. 753–62 (1402).

115. G.7, p. 551 (1401).

116. E.g., Thomas Waleys, *op. cit.*, Charland, pp. 372–6.

117. G.7, pp. 1123–37 (1402).

118. *Memoriam* (1402?), G.7, pp. 698–709.

119. G.7, pp. 822–32, 833–41.

120. *Hoc sentite* (1402), G.7, pp. 651–9. For other examples see Mourin, *Gerson*, pp. 314–15.

121. E.g., *Ecce nunc dies salutatis* (Brayer, pp. 126–38). This is not to say that d'Ailly's sermons are ineffective. He can be eloquent and lyrical, as, for example, in the sermon on the Resurrection: *Maria Magdalene* (Brayer, pp. 139–43). Statements of intent and summaries at the end of sections were undoubtedly meant to help the congregations follow the sermon. But d'Ailly overuses them.

122. Di Stefano, pp. 211–25. Eleven of Courtecuisse's vernacular sermons have been discovered, one – *O vos* – in Bibl. Arsenal, MS 2674, the other ten, together with ten Latin sermons, in BN. lat. 3546. The French sermons are not all complete, but it is di Stefano's opinion that they are in Courtecuisse's own hand (pp. 4–5).

123. There is no confirmation of the parts in *Certamen* (1402?), G.7, pp. 561–72; *Suscepimus* (1396), G.7, pp. 1048–57; *Vade* (1407), G.7, pp. 1093–1101.

124. Cf. the anonymous English sermon for the third Sunday after the Epiphany octave in an early-fifteenth-century collection (Lambeth MS 392, ff. 148–218). In 200 lines the author accumulates almost forty quotations from the Bible and the Fathers (ff. 171–4). I should like to thank Ms Ruth Evans for drawing my attention to this collection of twenty-one sermons.

At the other pole is Olivier Maillard, whose far longer sermon for the fifth Sunday in Lent has only eleven quotations: ed. J. Labouderie (Paris, 1826). Cf. Martin, *op. cit.*, p. 69. Gerson's practice falls somewhere between these two.

125. *Factum* (1393), G.7. pp. 622–39; *Gloria* (1402), G.7, pp. 639–50; *Memento* (1406), G.7, pp. 690–8.

126. *Beati*, (1401), G.7, pp. 549–60; *Veniat pax* (1408?), G.7, pp. 1100–23.

Enumeration is very common in late medieval sermons. Its purpose is clearly pedagogical.

127. *Certamen* (1402), G.7, pp. 561–72.

128. G.7, pp. 1057–80 (1401). Cf. the sermon on the Trinity, *Si terrena* (1401), G.7, pp. 1040–7.

129. G.7, pp. 714–17 (1406).

130. G.7, pp. 720–39 (1392?).

131. G.7, pp. 679–89 (1401).

132. E.g., *Ave* (1397?), G.7, pp. 538–49; *Gloria* (1402), G.7, pp. 639–50. The French court was criticised to its face by other preachers of the time. Cf. passages in Courtecuisse's *Replevit totam* and *Gloria et* (di Stefano, pp. 229–47, 273–90). The most vehement criticism of the period comes in a sermon of 1396 attributed to Jacques Legrand, edited by J. Beltrán in *Romania*, 93 (1972), pp. 460–78.

133. *Videmus nunc* (1402), G.7, pp. 1123–37.

134. *Puer natus est* (1402), G.7, pp. 948–65; *Ad deum vadit* (1403), G.7, pp. 449–519; *Pax vobis* (1394), G.7, pp. 779–93.

135. *Memoriam* (1402), G.7, pp. 698–709.

136. *Si terrena* (1401), G.7, pp. 1040–7.

137. Courtecuisse and d'Ailly, for example, cite Pseudo-Dionysius only once each in their extant sermons (di Stefano, p. 49; Brayer, p. 142).

138. Cf. *infra*, chs. 2 and 6.

139. E.g., Aquinas and Bonaventure are quoted only twice each (G.7, pp. 613, 919; 867, 987).

140. Whereas Gerson appears to know Aristotle, Cicero, Seneca, Virgil and Ovid directly, he may know most of the other classical writers only at second hand, either via Augustine or Cicero or in *florilegia* (medieval equivalents of *The Oxford Book of Quotations*). Cf. Mourin, *Gerson*, pp. 362–77.

Courtecuisse cites from the same classical authors as Gerson, though he adds Plautus to his repertoire. The proportion of classical authors to Christian authors cited in Courtecuisse's sermons is higher than in Gerson's. For example, Courtecuisse cites Gregory only five times, while there are twenty-two references to Cicero. This may, however, be because a greater proportion of Courtecuisse's eleven extant sermons were delivered before the court. Di Stefano suggests that Courtecuisse had a first-hand familiarity with a number of the classical writers he cites, including Terence and Plautus (p. xi).

D'Ailly, by contrast, in his eleven French sermons, uses classical quotations very sparingly. A rough count yields only three from Seneca, two from Aristotle and one each from Livy and Virgil.

141. G.7. pp. 784 and 974. Di Stefano (p. 83) has identified four quotations in Courtecuisse as coming from Petrarch.

142. *Poenitemini, de la chasteté* (1403), G.7, p. 860.

143. *Convertimini* (1402?), G.7, p. 579.

144. *Poenitemini, de la chasteté* (1402), G.7, p. 860.

145. *Ecce Rex* (1395 or 1414), G.7, p. 617.

146. In *Adorabunt* (1391), G.7, p. 526; *Certamen* (1402?), G.7, p. 566; *Vivat rex* (1405), G.7, p. 1167.

147. In *Adorabunt* (1391), G.7, p. 525; *Ave Maria* (1397?), G.7, p. 544; *Gloria* (1402), G.7, p. 645.

148. In *Certamen* (1402?), G.7, p. 570; *Vivat rex* (1405), G.7, p. 1159; *Diligite justitiam* (1408), G.7, p. 612; *Rex in sempiternum* (1413), G.7, p. 1017.

149. *Ave Maria* (1397?), G.7, p. 548.

150. In *Adorabunt* (1391), G.7, p. 530; *Regnum coelorum* (1391?), G.7, p. 1001; *Ecce rex* (1395 or 1414), G.7, p. 621.

151. *Ave Maria* (1397?), G.7, p. 548.

152. *Veniat pax* (1408?), G.7, p. 1114. *Exempla* and similitudes about schools are very common in sermons. Cf. d'Ailly's *Ille vos*, where the school of the Holy Spirit is contrasted with the school of the devil (Brayer, pp. 168–72).

153. G.7, pp. 519–38 (1391).

154. *Suscepimus* (1396), G.7, p. 1052.

155. E.g., *Ad deum vadit* (1403), G.7, p. 471; *Quomodo* (1410), G.7, p. 979. This is a very common similitude. Cf. Aquinas, *Opera omnia*, Vol. xxix (*Sermones*) (Paris, Vivès, 1876), pp. 208–9; Ross, *Middle English Sermons*, pp. 188–9; Courtecuisse in di Stefano, pp. 195–203. It probably goes back at least to Augustine; e.g., *De civitate dei*, xx, 15, *CCSL*, 48, p. 725.

156. G.7, pp. 1057–80 (1401). Courtecuisse also constructs heavenly debates when he wishes to explain doctrine; e.g., the debate between Mercy and Truth about the Incarnation in *Bonum est* (di Stefano, pp. 162–6). Cf. d'Ailly's debate on the same subject in *Verbum caro factum est* (Brayer, pp. 114–18).

157. Cf. d'Ailly's 'Oyseus la fole, Pechiet le villain' (Brayer, p. 169).

158. Many of Gerson's similes are, of course, commonplaces. The comparisons of the sinner with the leper and of sin with physical sickness are particularly well-worn. The sermon in Lambeth MS 392, ff. 171–4 is entirely constructed around the former, and d'Ailly's Ash Wednesday sermon, *Ecce nunc*, around the latter (Brayer, pp. 126–38).

159. G.7, pp. 805 and 807.

160. *Sancta et salubris* (1404, or 1401, according to Lieberman, *Romania*, 70 (1948), pp. 61–6), G.7, pp. 1031–40.

161. *Puer natus est* (1402), G.7, pp. 958–9.

162. *Poenitemini, contre la luxure* (1402), G.7, p. 815.

163. E.g., Sermon xix, in *Sermones*, pp. 109–18.

164. De la Borderie, p. 11.

165. *Tamquam sponsus* (di Stefano, pp. 175–89).

166. D'Ailly: two each for the Nativity and Pentecost; one each for the Circumcision, Ash Wednesday, the Resurrection, the Rogation before Ascension, the Ascension and All Saints. This last is a sermon for peace. Courtecuisse: one each for the Nativity, Good Friday, the Resurrection, Pentecost, Trinity, the Eucharist, All Saints. Of the remaining four, *Bonum michi* is a plea to the court for the maintenance of the Cabochien ordinances; *Justum adiutorium* (1416) is on the evils of the schism and contains a bitter attack on Benedict XIII; *Testamentum suum* (1406) was preached during the ceremonies attending the presentation of a relic by Louis II of Anjou to the cathedral at Mans; *Bonum est* (1406) is a sermon for the first Sunday in Advent preached in the same cathedral.

167. Letter *Qui tam multa* (to Guillaume Fillastre) in Combes, *Jean de Montreuil et le chancelier Gerson*, p. 592.

168. Cf. Gilbert Ouy, 'La Plus Ancienne Oeuvre retrouvée de Jean Gerson', *Romania*, 83 (1962), pp. 433–92; 'Gerson et l'Angleterre', in A. H. T. Levi, *Humanism in France*, pp. 43–81. Cf. E. Ornato, *Jean Muret et ses amis Nicholas de Clamanges et Jean de Montreuil* (Paris, 1969), pp. 148ff.

169. *Factum est…Draconi*, G.5, p. 321. The particular authors Gerson mentions in this passage are Seneca, Cicero (*Paradoxa, De Officiis, De Senectute, De Amicitia, Hortensius, De Republica*), Boethius (*Consolationes*), Aristotle (*Ethica*) and Plato (Ethica [sic]).

170. The letters were written 1378–9, and are translated in *Humanism and Tyranny*, ed. E. Emerton (Cambridge, Mass., 1925), pp. 290–311.

171. G.10, pp. 7–24.

172. *De duplici logica*, G.3, pp. 58–63.

173. A number of classical treatises on rhetoric were available in the Middle Ages, among them Aristotle's *Rhetoric*, Cicero's *De inventione*, the Pseudo-Ciceronian *Rhetorica ad Herennium* and a mutilated text of Quintilian's *Institutio oratoria*. Cf. Murphy, *Rhetoric in the Middle Ages*, pp. 89–132; J. J. Murphy, *Three Medieval Rhetorical Arts* (Berkeley, 1971), pp. viii–xi.

174. Book IV, *MPL*, 34:89–122.

175. *Summa de arte praedicandi*, f. 75r, cited in Murphy, *Rhetoric in the Middle Ages*, p. 322.

176. Delivery is discussed at some length in the *Rhetorica ad Herennium* (Murphy, *op. cit.*, p. 14).

177. Caplan, pp. 56–7, 73.

178. Cf. the English scene. J. W. Blench states of the period between 1450 and 1547: 'There is no English sermon of this period, however, which I have seen, which is built on the full scheme of the classical oration' (*Preaching in England in the late Fifteenth and Sixteenth Centuries: A Study of English Sermons, 1450–1600* (Oxford, 1964) (hereinafter *Preaching*), pp. 85–6).

179. Murphy, *Rhetoric in the Middle Ages*, pp. 457–60.

180. D. Erasmus, *De ratione concionandi libri quattuor*, ed. F. A. Klein (Leipzig, 1820), pp. 210–43. Treatises on preaching were also written by Reuchlin and Melanchthon. Cf. Caplan, p. 133.

181. For examples of sixteenth-century sermons in the classical style, see Blench, *Preaching*, pp. 102–12.

182. Cf. Blench, *Preaching*, pp. 94, 101–2.

183. G.7, pp. 326–40.

184. The chief parts of the classical oration were the exordium, narration, proposition and confirmation (i.e. argumentation and proof of the proposition), refutation and peroration. Cf. Cicero, *De inventione* I.15–55.

185. His house in Paris was destroyed, he had to pay compensation to the University, and he had to establish a foundation for the church of St Catherine, where the original incident (during a procession) had occurred (Connolly, p. 127).

3 The role of the pastor

1. J. Wirth, *Luther, Etude d'histoire religieuse* (Geneva, 1981), p. 24.

2. In a sermon of 1512 Luther violently attacks priests for their pursuit of temporal goods (*WA*, 1, pp. 10ff.). Cf. *Commentary on Romans*, where he accuses priests of being proud, lustful, adulterers and thieves (*WA*, 56, p. 189).

3. Ross, p. 282.

4. *Contra sectam flagellantium*, G.10, p. 48. Cf. *De perfectione cordis*, G.8, p. 132.

5. Book I, ch. 9.

6. *Traité de la vie spirituelle*, in B. H. Vanderberghe, *Saint Vincent Ferrier: Textes choisis et présentés* (Namur, 1956), pp. 43–4.

7. *De examinatione doctrinae*, G.9, p. 473. The milk/solid food metaphor is a commonplace.

8. *Contra curiositatem studentium*, G.3, p. 249. The first French translation of the Bible was produced in 1280. By Gerson's time there were also available French versions of separate books or segments of the Bible. This translation of Scripture in France was neither licensed nor prohibited by diocesan authority. It appears to have been a stationers' venture. Cf. C. A. Robson, 'Vernacular Scriptures in France', in *The Cambridge History of the Bible*, Vol. II, ed. G. W. H. Lampe (Cambridge, 1969), pp. 436–52.

9. *Puer natus est*, G.7, p. 952.

10. *Peregrinus* (Strasburg, 1513), XI B, cited in Douglass, p. 76. There were a number of German translations of the Bible and parts of the Bible in circulation in the fifteenth century. In Germany, in contrast to France, some steps were taken to censor the translations, for example, the Censor's Edict of 1486 issued by the Archbishop of Mainz. Cf. W. B. Lockwood, 'Vernacular Scriptures in Germany and the Low Countries before 1500', in *The Cambridge History of the Bible*, Vol. II, pp. 415–36.

11. Cf. *Contra curiositatem studentium*, G.3, pp. 224–49, and two letters to the members of the College of Navarre, *Ecce pareo* and *Bene actum esset*, G.2, pp. 36–42.

12. See below, chs. 6 and 7.

13. Cf. especially the treatise in G.10, pp. 77–143. For accounts of the deviant beliefs and practices of the period, see P. Adam, *La Vie paroissiale en France au XIVe siècle* (Paris, 1964), ch. III, and Rapp, *L'Eglise*, ch. VI.

14. *De libris teutonicalibus*, ed. A. Hyma, *Nederlands Archief Voor Kergeschiedenis*, N.S., 17 (1924), p. 48. Cited in G. Gerrits, *Inter Timorem et Spem: A Study of the Theological Thought of Gerard Zerbolt of Zutphen* (Ph.D. dissertation, Queen's University, Kingston, Canada, 1978), p. 401.

15. In 1407 in England the possession of vernacular bibles was prohibited unless the owner had prior permission from his bishop and unless the translation dated from before the time of Wyclif. Cf. D. Wilkins, ed., *Concilia Magnae Britanniae et Hiberniae*, Vol. III (London, 1937), p. 317. For a Lollard tract defending biblical translations see Hudson, *Selections from English Wycliffite Writings*, pp. 189–91.

16. *Bonus pastor*, G.5, p. 131. Cf. *Redde quod debes*, G.5, p. 492; *De orationibus privatis fidelium*, G.10, p. 137.

17. *Sermo de vita clericorum*, preached to a synod in Paris in 1404, G.5, pp. 447–58; *Bonus pastor*, a sermon to the synod of Rheims in 1408, G.5, pp. 123–44; *De visitatione praelatorum*, a supplementary document for the same synod, G.8, pp. 47–55; *Scriptum est melius*, a letter of 1408 to the new bishop of Coutances, G.2, pp. 108–16; *Redde quod debes*, preached to the synod of Lyons in 1421, G.5, pp. 487–93. There is also a university lecture of 1402 on the subject: *Super victu et pompa praelatorum*, G.3, pp. 95–103.

18. *Quomodo stabit*, G.7, pp. 978–92.

19. E.g., *Gratia vobis*, G.2, p. 234: 'Church principally signifies the universal congregation of the faithful and hence is called catholic, that is, universal.'

20. E.g., Aquinas: 'Church means congregation and Holy Church is the congregation of believers of which each Christian is a member.' *Exposition of the Apostles' Creed*, in T. Gilby, ed., *St. Thomas Aquinas: Theological Texts* (Oxford, 1955), p. 340. Cf. Ciboule: 'Holy church, which is the mystical body of Christ, is the congregation of people bound together by the tie of love and charity they have to Christ and to each other.' *Qui manducat me*, p. 47.

21. William of Occam, *Dialogus inter magistrum et discipulum*, ed. M. Goldast (Frankfurt, 1688), Part I, Book II, 26. This view is partly based on the tradition that, at the time of the Crucifixion, the Virgin alone remained steadfast in faith. Hence the whole church rested in her while Christ was in the sepulchre. The story is told in a number of late medieval sermons, e.g., Ross, p. 322.

22. *De auferibilitate sponsi*, G.3, p. 298. Cf. *Propositio facta coram Anglicis*, G.6, p. 132.

23. Cf. *The Confession of Hawisia Moone of London*, 1430 (Hudson, p. 35): 'Every man and every woman being of good life out of sin is as good priest and hath as much power of God in all things as any priest, be he pope or bishop.'

24. *De orationibus privatis fidelium*, G.10, pp. 134–8. The letter to Guillaume de Chalançon, Bishop of Puy-en-Velais, that accompanied Gerson's tract is in G.2, p. 335.

25. He was a late-fifth- or early-sixth-century writer who attempted to widen the

common ground between the Neo-Platonism of his day and Christianity. By Gerson's time there had been four Latin translations of his works. Greek texts of his four major works, together with a Latin translation, are in *MPG*, 3: *The Celestial Hierarchy*, 119–369; *The Ecclesiastical Hierarchy*, 370–584; *The Divine Names*, 585–996; *Mystical Theology*, 997–1064. For studies of Dionysius' thought, see R. Roques, *L'Univers dionysien* (Paris, 1954); R. F. Hathaway, *Hierarchy and the Definition of Order in the Letters of Pseudo-Dionysius* (The Hague, 1969). Y. M.-J. Congar discusses some of the ways in which Dionysian concepts were adapted by theologians of the thirteenth and fourteenth centuries in 'Aspects ecclésiologiques de la querelle entre mendiants et séculiers dans la seconde moitié du XIIIe siècle et le début du XIVe siècle', *AHDLMA* 28 (1961), pp. 35–151. For a comprehensive discussion of Gerson's view of the nature of the church, see Pascoe, *Gerson*, ch. 1. Cf. Meyjes, *Jean Gerson Zijn Kerkpolitiek en Ecclesiologie*.

26. *Celestial Hierarchy*, chs. 6, 7, 8, 9. Cf. Roques, chs. 2, 5.

27. *Celestial Hierarchy*, ch. 3, and *passim*. Cf. Roques, ch. 3.

28. *Ecclesiastical Hierarchy*, chs. 5, 6. Cf. Roques, ch. 6.

29. Congar, pp. 115–51.

30. *De orationibus privatis fidelium*, G.10, p. 135.

31. *Ibid.* The same doctrine occurs in the vernacular sermon *Quomodo stabit*: 'If anyone asks how the kingdom of Christianity here below can have stability, the answer is by keeping the order and pattern of the kingdom above.' G.7, p. 980.

32. *La Mendicité spirituelle*, G.7, pp. 250–1. Medieval theologians generally followed Dionysius' scheme for the celestial hierarchy. E.g., Aquinas, *Summa contra gentiles* (hereinafter *Cont. G.*), III, ch. 80; *The Disputed Questions on Truth*, q.9. Needless to say, what Gerson states as a bald fact, Thomas discusses in detail, raising numerous 'curious' questions.

33. *De postestate ecclesiastica*, G.6, p. 227. Cf. *Quomodo stabit*, G.7, p. 981.

34. *De consiliis evangelicis*, G.3, p. 25. Cf. *Quomodo stabit*: 'The pope cannot destroy or annul the estate of parish clergy, because the estate comes not from positive ordinance but by the direct authority of God.' G.7, p. 984. Cf. *De statu papae et minorum praelatorum*, G.9, pp. 28, 31; *De potestate ecclesiastica*, G.6, p. 241. The idea that parish priests were the successors of the seventy-two disciples is a commonplace in medieval theology. E.g., Hugh of St Victor, *De sacramentis*, II, 3, *MPL*, 176:428; Aquinas, *Summa Theologiae* (hereinafter *S.Th.*), II–II, q.184, a.6, ad 1; Wycliffite sermon *Designavit Dominus Jesus*, in Hudson, p. 119. The idea, however, yielded different conclusions in different theologians about the current status of parish priests.

35. *De consiliis evangelicis*, G.3, p. 35.

36. *De statu papae et minorum praelatorum*, G.9, p. 29.

37. *Regulae mandatorum*, G.9, p. 130.

38. *Contra bullam Regnans in excelsis*, G.10, p. 30. Cf. *Quomodo stabit*, G.7, pp. 982ff.

39. Hugh of St Victor, *De sacramentis*, Book II, 10; Aquinas, *S.Th.*, Supp., q.19, a.5.

40. Cf. *Twelve Conclusions of the Lollards*, Hudson, p. 25; Hus, *On the Church*, in H. A. Oberman, *Forerunners of the Reformation* (London, 1967), pp. 225–9.

41. Letter to Conrad de Vechte, Archbishop of Prague (1414), G.2, p. 162.

42. *De potestate ecclesiastica*, G.6, p. 212, Cf. *De orationibus privatis fidelium*, G.10, p. 139, and *De statu papae et minorum praelatorum*, G.9, p. 30.

43. *De morte virtuali sive gratie*, in *Sermones prestantissimi* (Strasburg, 1515), II, 210rl, cited in Douglass, p. 99.

44. For comprehensive treatments of the developments of Gerson's thought about papal power and general councils see J. B. Morrall, *Gerson and the Great Schism*;

Meyes, *op. cit.*; Pascoe, *Gerson*. Translations of the important documents relating to the conciliar movement are in C. M. D. Crowder, *Unity, Heresy and Reform,* 1378–1460: *The Conciliar Response to the Great Schism* (London, 1977).

45. *De auferibilitate*, G.3, pp. 298–9. Cf. Marsilius, *Defender of Peace : The Defensor Pacis*, Trans. A. Gerwith (New York, 1967), Book II, ch. 21, sect. 9, pp. 293–4.

46. *De auferibilitate*, G.3, p. 298.

47. *De ecclesiastica potestate*, ed. R. Scholz (Weimar, 1929), Book III, ch. 12, pp. 208–9.

48. *De vita spirituali*, G.3, pp. 152–3.

49. These were both at the University of Paris when they put forward their proposals that a general council should meet and make a decision on the legitimacy of the two papal claimants. Conrad's *Epistola concordiae* was published in 1380, and Henry's *Epistola concilii pacis* in 1381. The latter is translated in M. Spinka, ed., *Advocates of Reform* (London, 1953), pp. 106–39.

50. G.5, pp. 44–5; G.6, pp. 226–40. Gerson's position as set forth in these works found its embodiment in two of the most important decrees of the Council of Constance: *Haec sancta* (1415) and *Frequens* (1417), translated in Crowder, pp. 83, 128–9.

51. G.9, pp. 459–60.

52. The Council of Basle was called in 1431. It lasted till 1449, but became schismatic when it continued to meet after being dissolved by Pope Eugenius in 1437.

53. *Propositio facta coram anglicis*, G.6, p. 133. Cf. *De potestate ecclesiastica* G.6, p. 224.

54. E.g., Bonaventure, *De triplici via*, in *The Works of Bonaventure, Cardinal, Seraphic Doctor and Saint*, Vol. I, *Mystical Opuscula*, trans. J. de Vinck (Patterson, New Jersey, 1960), pp. 59–94, where the three successive stages towards mystical union are purgation, illumination and perfection.

55. *Quomodo stabit*, G.7, p. 982.

56. *De potestate ecclesiastica*, G.6, pp. 218–19, 241.

57. *De orationibus privatis fidelium*, G.10, p. 135.

58. 'Ecclesia consistit principalius in ordine primo et secundo quam in tertio qui est ordo laicorum, et maxime feminarum,...' *Ibid.*

59. *Domine si in tempore*, G.5, pp. 211–12.

60. 'Omnium animarum et rerum salus et directio manibus praelatorum commissa est', *Scriptum est melius*, G.2, p. 115.

61. 'Infima reducuntur ad summa per media.' E.g., *Contra bullam Regnans in excelsis*, G.10, p. 34; *De potestate ecclesiastica*, G.6, p. 219; *Quomodo stabit*, G.7, p. 981; *Nimis*, 'les choses basses se ramenent aux haultes par les moyennes', G.7, p. 728. Cf. Aquinas with reference to angels in *The Disputed Questions on Truth*, q.9, a.2.

62. *Nimis*, G.7, p. 728.

63. *Bonus pastor*, G.5, p. 129.

64. *Quomodo stabit*, G.7, p. 980. Cf. *Ecce pareo*, G.2, p. 36. For Gerson's views on how theologians must aid in the work of reform, see Pascoe, *Gerson*, pp. 80–109.

65. *An liceat in causis fidei a papa appellare*, G.6, p. 24. Cf. *De vita spirituali*, G.3, p. 162; *Tractatus pro unione ecclesiae*, G.6, p. 14. This latter tract is anonymous but it may be attributable to Gerson (G.6, p. ix).

66. *De fide et ecclesia*, in Oberman, *Forerunners*, pp. 87–89. The Latin text is in P.1, pp. 805–903.

67. *Quaestiones quodlibetales*, ed. R. Spiazzi (Rome, 1956) (hereinafter *Quodl.*), I, q.7, a.2.

68. *WA*, 7, p. 162.

69. *Collatio XXII in Hexaemeron*, in *Opera omnia*, Vol. V, pp. 440–1.

70. *Redde quod debes*, G.5, p. 491.

71. *Domine si in tempore*, G.5, p. 212. Aquinas too posits immediate contact between God and man. Cf. *Cont. G.*, III, ch. 57; *S.Th.*, I q.12, a.1, a.5.

72. *Lumen gentium*, 40, in A. Flannery, ed., *Vatican Council II: The Conciliar and Post-Conciliar Documents* (New York, 1975), p. 397.

73. E.g., *La Montagne de contemplation*, G.7, pp. 16–55. Gerson also saw the mystical way as open to all. See below, ch. 6.

74. *De consiliis evangelicis*, G.3, pp. 10–13.

75. *S.Th.*, II–II, q.184, a.3; *Quodl.* IV, q.12, a.1, a.2.

76. *De consiliis evangelicis*, G.3, p. 14.

77. *Ibid.*, pp. 16–18. E.g., 'If voluntary poverty were essential to the perfection of the Christian life, it would follow that the possession of wealth and riches necessarily renders a man imperfect.'

78. *Ibid.*, p. 14. Aquinas, *S.Th.*, II–II, q.185, a.6, ad 1, also uses the example of Abraham to bolster his argument against the elitist view.

79. *Contra conclusiones Matthaei Graben*, G.10, p. 70.

80. *De consiliis evangelicis*, G.3, p. 22. Cf. the Dominican mystic Tauler, *Spiritual Conferences*, ed. E. Colledge (St Louis, 1961), p. 134: 'I believe that there are some people living in the world who far surpass some religious and put them completely in the shade.'

81. *Lumen gentium*, 42 (Flannery, p. 401).

82. *De conciliis evangelicis*, G.3, p. 20: 'It is clear that, although the evangelical counsels are a great help [*plurimum expediant et valeant*] in acquiring perfection, yet they are not necessarily required for this end.'

83. E.g., sermon in Lambeth MS 392, f. 171v.

84. *The Colloquies of Erasmus*, trans. C. R. Thompson (Chicago, 1965), pp. 500–16.

85. *Ibid.*, p. 514.

86. *De consiliis evangelicis*, G.3, p. 20.

87. E.g., *Bonus pastor*, G.5, p. 133. This, naturally, was a favourite metaphor for preachers criticising bishops and parish clergy, for example the Wycliffite sermon *Ego sum pastor bonus* in Hudson, pp. 64–6; and a fourteenth-century sermon by bishop Brunton, in MS Harl. 3760, f. 191, cited in G. R. Owst, *Preaching in Medieval England* (Cambridge, 1926), p. 253. For a discussion of the mediocrity and failings of the bishops and parish clergy of the period, see Adam, pp. 140–252. His evidence is based partly on the writings of Gerson and other reformers, but also on the records of episcopal visitations and synodal statutes. It seems that the situation had not improved a century later; French reformers of the early sixteenth century were still attacking, in their sermons, the same faults of pastors. Cf. M. Piton, 'L'idéal épiscopal selon les prédicateurs français de la fin du XVe siècle et du début du XVIe', *RHE*, 61 (1966), pp. 77–118, 393–433.

88. G.6, pp. 218–19. Gerson was of the opinion that excommunication was used far too frequently and in illicit ways, so that it had fallen into disrepute. Cf. *Rememoratio agendorum durante subtractione*, G.6, p. 108; *Bonus pastor*, G.5, pp. 136–7. The over-frequent use of excommunication is discussed by Adam, pp. 179–206.

89. G.5, p. 489.

90. G.5, pp. 125, 139. Cf. *De consiliis evangelicis*, G.3, p. 22.

91. The office of preaching 'est de necessitate annexum pastorali dignitati'. *Bonus pastor*, G.5, p. 125. Cf. Basevorn, *Forma praedicandi*, chs. II and III.

92. *Bonus pastor*, p. 126. Cf. *Redde quod debes*, G.5, p. 489.

93. *S.Th.*, III, q.67, a.2, ad 1.

94. *Forma praedicandi*, Charland, pp. 238–42.

95. He does not go quite as far as the Lollard glossed gospel commentary on John 10:11-16, in Hudson, p. 62: 'If curates preach not the word of God they should be damned. If any curate cannot preach, the proper remedy is to resign his benefice.'

96. *De vita spirituali*, G.3, pp. 137-8.

97. *Redde quod debes*, G.5, p. 489. Cf. Aquinas, *S.Th.*, III, q.71, a.4, ad 3: 'Instruction is manifold...Another type is that by which a man is taught the rudiments of faith and about how to comport himself in receiving the sacraments: this belongs...primarily to priests...A fourth is the instruction in the profound mysteries of faith, and on the perfection of Christian life: this belongs to bishops *ex officio*.' Cf. Basevorn, *Forma praedicandi*, Charland, p. 242.

98. *Replevit totam*, di Stefano, p. 237.

99. G.5, p. 127.

100. *Scriptum est melius*, G.2, pp. 110, 112. The 'recent tracts' are probably Gerson's own.

101. *Ibid.*, p. 111. Cf. Hugh Legat's advice to parish priests that they should not try to preach about things they have not mastered, but should confine themselves to the five virtues, the seven sins and the ten commandments (Grisdale, p. 8).

102. *De statu papae et minorum praelatorum*, G.9, p. 32.

103. *S.Th.*, Supp., q.36, a.2 ad 1, ad 2. Aquinas leaves the understanding of difficult legal points to the bishop.

104. Cited in L. E. Boyle, 'Aspects of clerical education in fourteenth-century England', in *The Fourteenth Century*, *Acta IV* (Center for Medieval and Early Renaissance Studies, SUNY, Binghamton, NY, 1977), p. 19.

105. Dominican priories, where the ordinary brothers (*fratres communes*) were trained in pastoral theology by a teacher or *lector* formed a type of seminary system for the order. Probably some of the urban secular clergy were able to attend these local Dominican (and Franciscan) theological schools. Cf. L. E. Boyle, 'Notes on the education of the *Fratres communes* in the Dominican order in the thirteenth century', *Xenia Medii Aevi Historiam Illustrantia oblata Thomae Kaeppeli, O.P.* (Rome, 1978), pp. 246-67. For the training or rather lack of training of many parish priests, see Adam, pp. 141-51; H. Jedin and J. Dolan, eds., *Handbook of Church History* (London, 1970), IV, ch. 58.

106. Bayeux MS 48, sermon 37, f. 187v, cited in Martin, p. 66. Cf. Maillard, in de la Borderie, p. 108.

107. *Bonus pastor*, G.8, p. 131. Cf. *Rememoratio agendorum durante substractione*, G.6, p. 112. D'Ailly, Dietrich of Niem and Henry of Langenstein made the same type of suggestion (M. Mollat, *La Vie et la pratique religieuse au XIVe et dans la Ire partie du XVe siècle, principalement en France* (Paris, 1965), ch. XI).

108. *Regulae mandatorum*, G.9, p. 434. It seems likely that Gerson has Boniface VIII's constitution 'Cum ex eo' in mind here. Boniface allowed parochial clergy up to seven years' absence for study if certain conditions were fulfilled – the same conditions listed by Gerson. For a discussion of 'Cum ex eo' and the liberal use made of it, in England at least, see L. E. Boyle, 'The constitution "Cum ex eo" of Boniface VIII: education of parochial clergy', *MS*, 24 (1962), pp. 263-302.

109. *Bonus pastor*, G.5, pp. 131-3. Cf. *Rememoratio agendorum durante subtractione*, G.6, p. 113; *Scriptum est melius*, G.2, p. 116.

110. *Doctrinal aux simples curés*, G.10, pp. 366-9.

111. G.10, pp. 295-321. It should be noted in this context of the education of the clergy that the *Compendium theologiae* attributed to Gerson by du Pin (P.1, pp. 233-422) is actually the *Summa iuniorum* of the English Dominican Simon of Hinton, composed some time between 1250 and 1260. Cf. A. Dondaine, 'La Somme de Simon de Hinton', *RTAM*, 9 (1937), pp. 5-22, 205-18.

112. *Bonus pastor*, G.5, pp. 127–8.

113. Book I, ch. 2. Behind Gregory there lies, apart from the New Testament, the Roman rhetorical tradition with its insistence that the orator be a good man. Cf. Cicero, *De oratore*, I, 118.

114. Bernadine, *Sermons*, p. 15: 'The priest does more grievous wrong by giving bad example by a wicked life, than if a layman were to go out to rob in the highway...the one takes from the man his money, his horse and his garments, but the other with his evil example makes away with both the soul and body of the man.'

115. This is true of other critics too. Of all the sins, it is covetousness for which clerics are most often castigated in this period. The criticism occurs even in vernacular sermons, for example in Courtecuisse, Menot, Maillard, Savonarola, Geiler and, of course, Lollard sermons and writings.

116. *De concilio unius obedientiae*, G.6, p. 54.

117. *Conversi estis*, G.5, p. 173. For a full discussion of Gerson's beliefs about the Donation of Constantine, see L. B. Pascoe, 'Gerson and the Donation of Constantine: Growth and development within the church', *Viator*, 5 (1974), pp. 469–85. Mollat, part III, ch. VI, has a discussion of the quarrel of the fourteenth and fifteenth centuries over the question of apostolic poverty, spearheaded on one side by the Spiritual Franciscans.

118. *De concilio unius obedientiae*, G.6, pp. 54–5.

119. *Si de temporali*, G.2, p. 127.

120. *Quomodo stabit*, G.7, p. 992.

121. *Bonus pastor*, G.5, p. 133. Cf. Courtecuisse, *Justum adiutorium* (di Stefano, pp. 199–200). Courtecuisse here also attacks the unworthy ambitions of clerics. For a discussion of the 'frantic pursuit of benefices', and clerical rapacity in general in the fourteenth and fifteenth centuries, see Mollat, part I, ch. VI.

122. *Bonus pastor*, G.5, pp. 134, 136. Cf. *De visitatione praelatorum*, G.8, p. 53.

123. *Rememoratio agendorum durante subtractione*, G.6, p. 109.

124. *Mansionem*, Brayer, p. 171.

125. Lenten sermon at Nantes (de la Borderie, pp. 108–9). Cf. Menot's attack on simony and pluralism in a Lenten sermon at Paris (Nève, p. 234).

126. *De visitatione praelatorum*, G.8, p. 54. Cf. *Bonus pastor*, G.5, p. 137; *Rememoratio agendorum durante subtractione*, G.6, p. 109.

127. *Ad reformationem contra simoniam*, G.6, pp. 179–81.

128. *Bonus pastor*, G.5, pp. 137–8. Cf. Savonarola, who tells the priests and prelates of Florence to renounce their pomp, parties and banquets. He also tells them to renounce their multiple benefices, their concubines and their boys. Sermon on the text: 'Repent for the kingdom of heaven is at hand', *Prediche e scritti*, ed. M. Ferrara (Milan, 1930), pp. 99–114.

129. *Super victu et pompa praelatorum*, G.3, pp. 95–103. Cf. *Sermo de vita clericorum*, G.5, p. 452.

130. *Bonus pastor*, G.5, p. 135. Cf. *Super victu et pompa praelatorum*, G.3, p. 101. Gerson is here stating, though not very technically, what was by his time the standard doctrine. Cf. Aquinas, *S.Th.*, II–II, q.187, a.7.

131. *Scriptum est melius*, G.2, p. 109. Cf. *Bonus pastor*, G.5, pp. 134–5.

132. *Bonus pastor*, G.5, pp. 135–6. Cf. *De statu papae et minorum praelatorum*, G.9, pp. 31–2; *Redde quod debes*, G.5, p. 491. For the financial position of the parish clergy of this period, see Adam, pp. 13–14, 134–7.

133. *Domine si in tempore*, G.5, p. 214; *Rememoratio agendorum durante subtractione*, G.6, p. 108.

134. *Scriptum est melius*, G.2, p. 110. Cf. Ciboule, *Qui manducat me*, p. 51: 'Priests must be chaste, flee all lasciviousness and not frequent taverns or dissolute people.'

135. Adam, pp. 151–63, thinks Gerson and others did exaggerate the problem. Mollat, part I, ch. II, also thinks the reformers of the time, such as Gerson, tended to paint things blacker than they were. His evidence is based largely on visitation records.

136. *Rememoratio agendorum durante subtractione*, G.6, pp. 112–13.

137. *De orationibus privatis fidelium*, G.10, p. 136.

138. *Bonus pastor*, G.5, p. 139. A great deal of hard theological thinking and debate, during the two centuries or so before Gerson's time, had gone into the production of this doctrine which Gerson states here about the role of the minister and the working of the sacraments. Cf. Aquinas, *S.Th.*, III, qq.60–4. Particularly relevant here are q.63, a.4, ad 3; q.64, a.1, R and a.8. Gerson specifically mentions Thomas as his authority in *De forma absolvendi* when he is discussing the instrumental role of the priest in the sacrament of penance. (G.9, p. 174).

139. 'One who lies in confession or secretly places an obstacle is never absolved.' *De potestate ecclesiastica*, G.6, p. 221.

140. *Bonus pastor*, G.5, p. 140. Cf. *Rememoratio agendorum durante subtractione*, G.6, p. 111. Bernadine adverts to the same fault in one of his sermons, as an example of culpable ignorance (*Sermons*, p. 84).

141. *Redde quod debes*, G.5, p. 490.

142. *Bonus pastor*, G.5, pp. 140–2. D'Ailly objected as much as Gerson to the ever-increasing number of feast-days (*De reformatione*, P. II, p. 911). Cf. Nicholas of Clamanges's treatise, *De novis festivitatibus non instituendis*, in which the author points out the apocryphal nature of some of these new festivals. Cited in J. Huizinga, *The Waning of the Middle Ages* (New York, 1954), p. 153.

143. *Bonus pastor*, G.5, p. 139.

144. Cf. P. Michaud-Quantin, *Sommes de casuistique et manuels de confession au moyen âge* (Louvain, 1962) (hereinafter *Sommes de casuistique*); Tentler, 'The Summa for confessors as an instrument of social control' (hereinafter 'Summa for confessors'), in *Pursuit of Holiness*, pp. 103–30, and *Sin and Confession*.

145. *De modo confessionis sacramentalis*, G.9, p. 646. The authority he quotes is the traditional one: 'Whatsoever you shall bind on earth, etc.'. Cf. *Regulae mandatorum*, G.9, p. 126.

146. *Doctrinal aux simples gens*, G.10, p. 314. Cf. *Regulae mandatorum*, G.9, p. 128.

147. *De parvulis ad Christum trahendis* (hereinafter *De parvulis*), G.9, pp. 675–6.

148. *Contra sectam flagellantium*, G.10, p. 47. This tract was written at Constance in 1417. Gerson hoped that the council would act on it, but nothing was done. The movement had in fact already been condemned by Clement VI in 1349. Gerson was also concerned about the Flagellants who collected around the preacher Vincent Ferrier, and he and d'Ailly sent a letter to Vincent, advising him to be on his guard in case his own reputation suffered as a result of the excesses of his followers (G.2, pp. 200–2). By contrast, Bernardine speaks of the movement, at least as it manifested itself among Third Order Franciscans at Crema in Italy, with approval (*Sermons*, pp. 75–6).

149. G.10, p. 317.

150. Cf. P. E. McKeever, 'Penance', *NCE*, XI, pp. 75–83; P. DeLetter, 'Contrition', *NCE*, IV, pp. 278–83; Aquinas, *S.Th.*, Supp., q.6, a.1, R; *Cont. G.*, Book IV, ch. 72, 12.

151. *Bonus pastor*, G.5, p. 141.

152. E.g. *Bonus pastor*, G.5, p. 144; *Quomodo stabit*, G.7, p. 990. Gerson, like other writers of the period on the subject, advocates confession in the open, i.e. in view of others ('coram oculis omnium') to avoid any shameful activity that might occur if penitents confessed privately to priests (*Bonus pastor*, G.5, p. 141). If, however, the penitent is finding himself (or herself) embarrassed at confessing certain sins, the confessor should avert his eyes from the penitent's face. The Middle English handbook by John Mirk, *Instructions for Parish Priests*, ed. by E. Peacock, EETS, OS, 31 (London, 1868), p. 27, advises the priest to pull his hood over his eyes when he is hearing confessions and never to look at the face of a female penitent. This work is based on the influential *Oculus sacerdotis*, written by William of Pagula between 1320 and 1326. Cf. L. E. Boyle, 'The *Oculus sacerdotis* and some other works of William of Pagula', *TRHS* (5th ser.), 5 (1955), pp. 81–100.

Although Gerson, like everybody else, often uses medical metaphors to describe the confessor's skills ('cutting out the twisted serpent of sin', 'curing the diseases of the breast', 'removing the pestilential poison from the heart', *De parvulis*, G.9, p. 676), the techniques he advocates more closely resemble those of the psychotherapist, who is, arguably, though governed by general rules and practices, more concerned with individual differences and situations.

153. *Le Profit de savoir quel est péché mortel et véniel* (hereinafter *Le Profit*), G.7, p. 383. Cf. Aquinas, *Quodl.*, I, q.6, a.2; Antoninus of Florence, *Summa Theologica* (Verona, 1740), Vol. III, p. 765, writing in the later fifteenth century and citing Thomas, Peter of Palude, Bonaventure and Durandus as his authorities.

There were some writers, however, who answered differently. 'Go hastily', says the author of the fourteenth-century Middle English tract *Handlyng Synne*, EETS, OS, 119 (London, 1901), p. 353. 'Go as soon as you are befouled with any filth of sin', says Hugh Legat (Grisdale, p. 19). 'Go hastily and soon', says Lorens d'Orléans (c. 1220–1300), in *Somme le roi*. This latter work was translated into English in the fourteenth century as *The Book of Vices and Virtues*, EETS, OS, 217 (London, 1942), p. 174.

154. For a study of how the doctrine that it was a mortal sin to communicate without prior confession of mortal sin became established during the thirteenth century, see L. Braeckmans, *Confession et communion au moyen-âge et au concile de Trent* (Gembloux, 1971).

Gerson does allow one exception to the rule. If a person is unable, because of the absence of a penitentiary or bishop, to confess his reserved sins, he may nevertheless be given permission by his ordinary confessor to communicate at Easter, provided that he has the intention to confess those sins when opportunity arises. If, however, he is under public excommunication or has committed public, reserved sins, he may not communicate until actually released. *Poenitemini, contre l'orgueil*, G.7, p. 923.

155. *Le Profit*, G.7, p. 382. Cf. *L'Examen de conscience selon les péchés capitaux* (hereinafter *L'Examen*), G.7, p. 398; *Poenitemini, contre l'orgueil*, G.7, p. 923.

156. *L'Examen*, G.7, pp. 393, 398; *De parvulis*, G.9, p. 676. The other late medieval writers on sin and confession also recommended more frequent recourse to the sacrament than once a year (Tentler, *Sin and Confession*, pp. 73–82). The statutes of the diocese of Paris for 1429 recommend four or five confessions a year (Delaruelle, *L'Eglise*, p. 854).

157. *Le Profit*, G.7, p. 383. Cf. Gerson's advice to over-scrupulous religious about how often they should confess in *De remediis contra pusillanimitatem* (hereinafter *De remediis*), G.10, p. 397.

158. *Poenitemini, contre l'orgueil*, G.7, p. 921.

159. C. J. Hefele and H. Leclerq, *Histoire des conciles*, 8 vols. (Paris, 1907–16), V, pp. 1350–1.

160. *Notes sur la confession*, G.7, p. 411; *De statu papae et minorum praelatorum*, G.9, p. 312.

161. Bernardine, *Sermons*, p. 96; Maillard, de la Borderie, p. 119; Cf. Sermon 42 in Ross, p. 278.
162. E.g., *The Book of Vices and Virtues*, p. 174.
163. *Treatise on Preaching*, p. 153.
164. 'Confessio' in *Summa de casibus conscientiae cum additionibus noviter additis* (Lyon, 1500) (hereinafter *Angelica*).
165. Aquinas, *S.Th.*, III, q.84, a.3, R.
166. E.g., *Confession of Hawisia Moone*, Hudson, p. 34; 'Absolucion' in *The Middle English Translation of the Rosarium Theologie*, ed. C. von Nolcken (Heidelberg, 1979), pp. 55–9, where it is stated that binding and loosing is by God alone, the priest's action being merely declarative. This contrasts with Gerson's orthodox teaching that the priest's action is instrumental.
167. A critical view along these lines occurs in J. C. Payen, 'La Pénitence dans le contexte culturel des XIIe et XIIIe siècles', *Revue des sciences philosophiques et théologiques*, 61 (1977), pp. 399–428. Payen sees sacramental confession eventually tending to become a mere formality, except among the spiritual elite.
168. *Peter Abelard's Ethics*, ed. D. E. Luscombe (Oxford, 1971), pp. 89–127.
169 *Sent.* IV, 18, 1–7, *MPL*, 192:887.
170. *S.Th.*, Supp., q.18, a.1, R. Cf. Bonaventure, *In IV Sent.*, 17, 2.
171. *In IV Sent.*, 14–16. In *Quaestiones in librum quartum sententiarum*, 2 vols. (Antwerp, 1620).
172. *Ibid.*, 14.4; 16.1.
173. E.g., 'entiere contriction, c'est assavoir du pechié passé desplaisir, propos ferme de non y rechoir et de soy confesser en temps at en lieu ordonné par l'Eglise' (*Tota*, G.7, p. 1072). Cf. *Convertimini*, G.7, p. 574; *Doctrinal aux simples gens*, G.10, p. 314; *Memento*, G.7, p. 694.
174. *In IV Sent.*, 14.4, 7.
175. G.9, p. 128.
176. The author of the *Angelica* is an example ('Confessio sacramentalis').
177. Tentler, *Sin and Confession*, p. 122.
178. 'tu demanderas: faut il que je croye certes que jamais je ne pecheray? Je di que non, mais propos souffist.' *Omne regnum*, G.7, p. 762.
179. 'Fit etiam ut attritio minus sufficiens fiat in confessione contritio.' *Regulae mandatorum*, G.9, p. 128. Aquinas (*S.Th.*, Supp., q.1, a.3; q.18, a.1, R) makes a distinction on this point. He argues that things caused by diverse principles, as attrition and contrition are, cannot be changed one into the other. An attrite man, however, can with the help of divine grace be made contrite. Other theologians are content to write less accurately about attrition becoming contrition.
180. *The Disputed Questions on Truth*, q.28, a.8.
181. E.g., Antoninus, *Summa Theologica*, III, p. 763. Cf. *Angelica*, 'Contritio'.
182. *Doctrinal aux simples gens*, G.10, p. 314.
183. *Convertimini*, G.7, p. 574.
184. G.9, p. 174.
185. *Poenitemini, contre l'orgueil*, G.7, pp. 927–8.
186. P. DeLetter, 'Contrition', *NCE*, IV, p. 280.
187. *Ibid.*; Oberman, *Harvest*, pp. 147, 460, 464; Douglass, pp. 148–9.
188. E.g., *Le Profit*, G.7, p. 389.
189. Tentler, *Sin and Confession*, pp. 150–73.
190. In one tract he defines contrition simply as 'the intention and desire of abstaining from sins'. *Le Profit*, G.7, p. 383.
191. E.g., *Quaerite*, G.7, p. 975.
192. *Poenitemini, contre l'orgueil*, G.7, p. 921. Cf. *Omne regnum*, G.7, p. 762.

193. Aquinas, *S.Th.*, Supp., q.1, a.2; q.3, a.1; Antoninus, *Summa Theologica*, III, p. 766; *Angelica*, 'Contritio'.

194. E.g., *The Book of Vices and Virtues*, p. 172; *Handlyng Synne*, p. 360; d'Ailly, *Ecce nunc*, Brayer, pp. 134–5.

195. *Le Miroir de l'âme*, G.7, p. 204.

196. *Convertimini*, G.7, p. 579.

197. *Beati qui lugent*, G.7, p. 555.

198. *De forma absolvendi*, G.9, p. 174.

199. *Ibid.*, pp. 173–4. Cf. Gerson's letter to his brother Nicholas on sacramental absolution, G.2, pp. 134–5.

200. Cf. Tentler, *Sin and Confession*, pp. 281–94.

201. E.g., *Angelica*, 'Interrogationes'.

202. E.g., Johann Nider, *Manuale confessorum. De lepra morali* (U. Gering, Paris, 1479), II, 6; *Confessionale ad usum Albiensis diocesis* (Lyon, 1499), G5b. Cited in Tentler, *Sin and Confession*, pp. 289–90.

203. Such a characterisation also occasionally occurs in authors writing in genres other than the practical literature for confessors, for example, the fourteenth-century English mystic Walter Hilton, who holds an almost Lombardian position. Cf. *The Scale of Perfection*, ed. G. Sitwell (London, 1953) (hereinafter *Scale*), Book II, ch. 7, pp. 156–60.

204. E.g., Hermannus de Schildis, *Speculum sacerdotum de tribus sacramentis principalibus* (Speier, *c.* 1479); J. P. Foresti, *Confessionale seu interrogatorium* (Venice, 1497), f. 67. Cited in Tentler, *Sin and Confession*, pp. 286–7.

205. E.g., Aquinas, *S.Th.*, I-II, q.88, a.1, a.2; Antoninus, *Summa Theologica*, III, pp. 971–3.

206. *Le Profit*, G.7, pp. 370, 386–7.

207. *De peccato veniali duplici*, G.9, p. 170.

208. *Le Profit*, G.7, p. 371.

209. *De primis motibus et consensu*, G.9, p. 167.

210. Cf. C. Vogel, *Le Pécheur et la pénitence au moyen âge* (Paris, 1969); Jacques le Goff, 'Métier et profession d'après les manuels de confesseurs au moyen âge', *Miscellanea Mediaevalia*, III (1964) (hereinafter 'Métier et profession'), pp. 40–60; M.-D. Chenu, *L'Eveil de la conscience dans la civilisation médiévale* (Paris, 1969).

211. For a discussion of this, see below, ch. 5.

212. *Brève manière de confession pour les jeunes*, G.7, p. 408.

213. Robert of Flamborough in the early thirteenth century recommends using the seven capital sins as a guide. *Liber poenitentialis*, ed. J. J. F. Firth (Toronto, 1971), p. 62. *The Book of Vices and Virtues* recommends using the seven capital sins and the five senses (pp. 177–80).

214. Tentler, *Sin and Confession*, pp. 135–7.

215. *L'Examen*, p. 398.

216. E.g., 'Omnis agens contra conscientiam aedificat ad gehennam...', *Regulae mandatorum*, G.9, p. 96. This sentence is almost identical with Gratian's 'qui facit contra conscientiam aedificat ad gehennam', cited in P. Michaud-Quantin, 'La Conscience individuelle et ses droits chez les moralistes de la fin du moyen âge', *Miscellanea Mediaevalia*, VI (1968) (hereinafter 'La Conscience individuelle'), p. 50. Cf. *Le Profit*, G.7, p. 382; *De remediis*, G.10, p. 393.

217. *De remediis*, G.10, p. 393.

218. Cf. Aquinas, *The Disputed Questions on Truth*, q.19, a.4; *Angelica*, 'Conscientia'.

219. *Regulae mandatorum*, G.9, p. 95. Cf. *Le Profit*, G.7, p. 382: 'Ignorance can come from negligence, from not taking pains to learn what one ought to know...and such ignorance does not excuse one's sins.' Cf. *Poenitemini, contre la paresse*, G.7, p. 892, where Gerson states that ignorance – in this case of the commandments – stemming from laziness does not excuse. The preacher Bernardine also emphasises the fact that ignorance does not excuse. In one sermon he urges mothers to instruct their daughters about the sinful practices that can occur in the marital act, and to bring their children to sermons so that they can learn about sin (*Sermons*, p. 83; cf. p. 145).

220. *Le Profit*, G.7, p. 382. Cf. *Regulae mandatorum*, G.9, p. 95. Cf. Aquinas, *S.Th.*, Supp., q.10, a.5, ad 4. Aquinas' example is of a man having sexual intercourse with another's wife, thinking her his own. Gerson's example seems more plausible.

221. *De confessione mollitiei*, G.8, p. 73. Cf. *Mansionem*, G.7, p. 684.

222. Cf. Michaud-Quantin, 'La Conscience individuelle'; M. G. Baylor, *Action and Person: Conscience in Late Scholasticism and the Young Luther* (Leiden, 1977) (hereinafter *Action and Person*). Baylor examines the doctrines of Aquinas, Occam and Biel.

223. Aquinas' discussion about conscience is also clear, if complex, but it takes care of every possible difficulty, as befits an academic work. *The Disputed Questions on Truth*, q.17.

224. *De arte audiendi confessiones*, G.8, p. 11.

225. *Ibid.*, pp. 10–12.

226. *Ad deum vadit*, G.7, p. 482.

227. E.g., *Angelica*, 'Confessio': 'Be benign and consoling'; *Handlyng Synne*, p. 338: 'Show as much charity to the penitent as you would that God show to you'; Vincent Ferrier, *Traité de la vie spirituelle* (Vanderberghe), pp. 71–2: 'Be like a mother... show profound charity for timid souls and hard hearts alike.'

228. *Doctrinal aux simples gens*, G.10, pp. 314–15; *L'Examen*, G.7, p. 399; *Memento*, G.7, p. 694.

229. *Quaestiones 4*, G.9, p. 70.

230. *De forma absolvendi*, G.9, p. 174. Cf. *De modo confessionis sacramentalis*, G.9, p. 648.

231. Contrast the *Angelica* with its exceedingly long article 'Interrogationes', containing vast detail.

232. *De arte audiendi confessiones*, G.8, pp. 10–17.

233. *Poenitemini, contre l'orgueil*, G.7, p. 924; *Factum est*, G.7, p. 634; *Poenitemini, contre l'avarice*, G.7, p. 882.

234. *Doctrinal aux simples gens*, G.10, p. 316.

235. *De arte audiendi confessiones*, G.8, p. 17.

236. *De potestate absolvendi*, G.9, p. 422. Cf. *De potestate confessorum*, G.9, p. 649. The William of Paris referred to by Gerson was probably the Dominican who, between 1300 and 1314, compiled the very popular *Dialogus de administratione sacramentorum*, principally from the writings of St Thomas (L. E. Boyle, 'The *Summa Confessorum* of John of Freiburg and the popularization of the moral teaching of St. Thomas and his contemporaries', in *St. Thomas Aquinas, 1274–1974: Commemorative Studies*, ed. by A. A. Maurer *et al.* (Toronto, 1974), II, p. 267).

237. *Angelica*, 'Confessio sacramentalis'. On the older penitential system, see Tentler, *Sin and confession*, pp. 3–18.

238. *Doctrinal aux simples gens*, G.10, p. 317.

239. Antoninus, *Summa Theologica*, I, pp. 193–204.

240. *De praeparatione ad missam*, G.9, p. 36.

241. *Ibid.*, p. 37.

242. *Qui manducat me*, p. 55.

243. *De praeparatione ad missam*, G.9, pp. 37–8.

244. *Ibid.*, p. 38.

245. *De remediis*, G.10, p. 387. This work is found in both a French and a Latin version and Glorieux is not sure which is the original (G.10, pp. 385–6).

246. *Ibid.*

247. 'Decipiantur in hoc multi ex simplicibus distinguere nescientes inter ea quae portio animae superior agit per consensum et ea quae portio animae inferior patitur absque superioris assensu.' *De praeparatione ad missam*, G.9, p. 38.

248. *Ibid.*, p. 39.

249. *De remediis*, G.10, pp. 393–4. It is clearly necessary to warn people against religious complacency. However, in this passage, written for the scrupulous, Gerson may be laying ground for further anxiety by saying that a sense of spiritual well-being could be dangerous.

250. *Contre conscience trop scrupuleuse*, G.7, p. 140.

251. *De remediis*, G.10, pp. 393–4.

252. *De praeparatione ad missam*, G.9, pp. 46–7.

253. *De remediis*, G.10, pp. 389, 392.

254. *Ibid.*, p. 394.

255. *Ibid.*, p. 397. Contrast Luther's 'semper justus, semper peccator'.

256. *De praeparatione ad missam*, G.9, pp. 47–8.

257. *Ibid.*, p. 46.

258. *De remediis*, G.10, pp. 338–9; *De praeparatione ad missam*, G.9, p. 50.

259. *Contre conscience trop scrupuleuse*, G.7, pp. 140–1. In some of his sermons, when he is concerned with the unrepentant rather than with the scrupulous, Gerson advises his hearers to think of hell and death, especially sudden death.

260. 'Aussi doibvent noter les pusillanimes scrupuleux que non pas tousiours sommes tenus faire meilleurs ouevres et en la meilleure manière que nous pouons...', *De remediis*, G.10, p. 398.

261. *De potestate absolvendi*, G.9, pp. 421–2; *De visitatione praelatorum*, G.8, pp. 52–3; *Bonus pastor*, G.5, pp. 141–2; *L'Examen*, G.7, pp. 398–9; *Super moderatione casuum reservandorum in foro* (a letter to a bishop), G.2, pp. 90–3.

262. *De potestate absolvendi*, G.9, p. 422.

263. *Confessionale* (Antwerp, 1518), 20, 9 and 23–4, cited in Tentler, *Sin and Confession*, p. 316.

264. *Summa summarum, que Sylvestrina dicitur* (Bologna, 1515), 'Confessor 3', q.1, cited in Tentler, *Sin and Confession*, pp. 316–18.

265. *Modus confitendi* (Nuremberg, 1508), E3b-E4b, cited in Tentler, *Sin and Confession*, pp. 306–7.

266. *Summula confessionis* (Strasburg, 1499), 3.

267. *Bonus pastor*, G.5, p. 142.

268. Connolly, pp. 95–8.

269. *Rememoratio agendorum durante subtractione*, G.6, p. 110.

270. *De visitatione praelatorum*, G.8, pp. 48–51.

271. *Rememoratio agendorum durante subtractione*, G.6, pp. 113–14.

272. The original mission was a preaching one, but less than a decade after their founding the pope added the hearing of confessions to their functions. Cf. L. E. Boyle, 'The Summa for Confessors and its religious intent', in *Pursuit of Holiness*, p. 127. Father Boyle is here writing of the Dominicans.

273. For details about the earlier phases of, and the arguments used in, this conflict, see Congar, *passim*.

274. *Erreurs de Jean Gorel*, G.10, pp. 32–3.

275. *Ibid.*, p. 33.

276. E.g., by the German preacher John Pupper of Goch (Steinmetz, 'Pupper', pp. 215–30).

277. *De statu papae et minorum praelatorum*, G.9, p. 33.

278. *Quomodo stabit*, G.7, p. 988. Gerson uses the adjective 'factitius' quite frequently of the religious orders, indicating their human, not divine, institution: e.g., 'religiones (quas Anselmus nominat factitias, quia factae videntur post institutionem legis evangelicae), *De perfectione cordis*, G.8, p. 121. Cf. *Gratia vobis*, G.2, p. 234.

279. *Quomodo stabit*, G.7, pp. 984–5. Cf. *De statu papae et minorum praelatorum*, G.9, pp. 33–4.

280. *De statu papae et minorum praelatorum*, G.9, p. 29. Cf. *Quomodo stabit*, G.7, p. 984.

281. *S.Th.*, II–II, q.184, a.6, ad 2.

282. Aquinas, *Contra impugnantes dei cultum et religionem*, C.4, section 8: 'It is clear that commissions can be given both for preaching and confessions without any need for a licence from parish priests.' This was written in 1256. Thomas may have changed his mind later, for in *S.Th.*, II–II, q.188, a.4, ad 2, he states: 'Certain religious orders are established for preaching and hearing confessions, not indeed by their own authority, but by the authority of the superior and inferior prelates, to whom these things belong by virtue of their office.' It is possible that by 'inferior prelates' Thomas means parish priests. In q.184, a.6, ad 1, he distinguishes between bishops and priests by calling the former *maiores* and the latter *minores*, though he does not use the term 'prelate' in this connection.

283. *Breviloquium*, in *The Works of Bonaventure, Cardinal, Seraphic Doctor and Saint*, Vol. II (hereinafter *Brevil.*), VI, 12.

284. *Quomodo stabit*, G.7, p. 983.

285. *De statu papae et minorum praelatorum*, G.9, pp. 29–30.

286. *De consiliis evangelicis*, G.3, p. 22. On p. 24, he cites Aquinas, *S.Th.*, II–II, q.186, a.1, ad 3 and 4, in support of the opinion that religious are in a state of acquiring perfection only. Cf. *Contra conclusiones Matthaei Graben*, G.10, pp. 70–1.

287. *De consiliis evangelicis*, G.3, pp. 22–3.

288. *S.Th.*, II–II, q.184, a.7, R, and a.6, R. Cf. *Quodl.*, I, q.7, a.2; III, q.6, a.3. One of Thomas' arguments for this opinion is based on the authority of Pseudo-Dionysius, that is, that of the three ranks – bishops, priests and ministers – only the bishops perform the hierarchical activity of perfecting.

289. Cf. Thomas' negative but measured and cautious response to the question 'Whether parish priests and archdeacons are more perfect than religious' (*S.Th.*, II–II, q. 184, a.8).

290. *De comparatione vitae contemplativae ad activam*, G.3, p. 71. Actually Gerson states that there are two views on this subject. One assigns all external activities, whether ministering to the spiritual welfare of others (for example, preaching, administering the sacraments) or to their temporal need, to the active life. The second view assigns only ministering to temporal needs to the active life. Gerson here – and generally – opts for the second view. In *De mystica theologia practica*, however (G.8, p. 24), he includes preaching in the active life.

291. *De comparatione vitae contemplativae ad activam*, G.3, p. 73.

292. *Spiritus Domini*, G.5, p. 525. For a full discussion of this sermon, see L. B. Pascoe, 'Jean Gerson: mysticism, conciliarism and reform', *Annuarium historiae conciliorum*, 6 (1974), pp. 143–53.

293. *Quomodo stabit*, G.7, p. 983: 'If this bull, *Regnans in excelsis*, is put into effect it will disturb the whole hierarchical order of prelates of holy church: great, median and small, who are the parish priests.'

294. *Contra bullam Regnans in excelsis*, G.10, p. 37.

295. *Ibid.*, p. 38.

296. *Quomodo stabit*, G.7, pp. 984–92. Cf. *De consiliis evangelicis*, G.3, p. 26; *De statu papae et minorum praelatorum*, G.9, pp. 31–5, especially the ninth consideration on burials and the tenth on preaching.

297 E.g., William of Saint-Amour, *Collectiones catholicae et canonicae scripturae* (1265–6) in *Opera* (Constance, 1632), pp. 146–50, cited in Congar, pp. 54–5.

298. *Frater secundum* (letter to his brother Nicholas), G.2, p. 45.

299. *Dedit illis*, G.7, pp. 587–8: 'We are in this world as wayfarers or pilgrims who all ought to try to arrive in the noble city of paradise; and because the better, the surest and most fair way to get there is a religious order, Saint Anthony, thinking about his goal, became a monk.'

300. He probably also saw the Mendicants as useful in university teaching, for he seems to have been a moving force in the return of the Dominicans to the University of Paris in 1403, after their exclusion in 1388.

301. *De statu papae et minorum praelatorum*, G.9, p. 33.

302. *Ibid.*

303. *Quomodo stabit*, G.7, pp. 985–6, 991. The German theologian Staupitz wrote a tract on this subject citing Gerson and reaching the conclusion that the parish church was the proper place to hear mass on Sundays and feast-days, unless there were just cause for going elsewhere. *Decisio questionis de audiencia misse in parrochiali ecclesia dominicis et festivis diebus*, cited in Steinmetz, *Staupitz*, p. 5.

304. *De statu papae et minorum praelatorum*, G.9, pp. 33–4.

305. *Ibid.*, p. 35. For an account of the wrangles between seculars and Mendicants, see Adam, pp. 220–45.

306. *Domine si in tempore* (June, 1409), G.5, pp. 212–13, 216.

4 The means of salvation

1. For a more thorough characterisation of the traditional view of nominalism, see Courtenay, 'Nominalism and late medieval religion', in *Pursuit of Holiness*, pp. 26–31 (hereinafter 'Nominalism').

2. Oberman, *Harvest*. Some of Oberman's other relevant works are the following: 'Some notes on the theology of nominalism', *HTR*, 53 (1960), pp. 46–76 (hereinafter 'Notes'); 'Gabriel Biel and late medieval mysticism', *CH*, 30 (1961), pp. 259–87; '*Facientibus quod in se est, deus non denegat gratiam*: Robert Holcot, O.P., and the beginnings of Luther's theology', *HTR*, 55 (1962), pp. 317–42 (hereinafter 'Holcot').

3. E.g., 'The shape of late medieval thought: the birthpangs of the modern era', in *Pursuit of Holiness*, pp. 3–25 (hereinafter 'Shape'); 'Fourteenth-century religious thought: a premature profile', *Speculum*, 53 (1978), pp. 80–93 (hereinafter 'Fourteenth-century thought').

4. Douglass, *Geiler*; Steinmetz, *Staupitz*; Steinmetz, 'Pupper'.

5. Oakley, *D'Ailly; The Medieval Experience: Foundations of Western Cultural Singularity* (New York, 1974); *Western Church*.

6. Oberman, 'Notes', p. 49. Cf. Oakley, for whom the central core of nominalism is not to be located in philosophy, 'for that would be to put the philosophical cart before the theological horse' (*D'Ailly*, p. 16).

7. 'Contingency is perhaps the best one-word summary of the nominalist program.' Oberman, 'Shape', p. 13. Cf. Steinmetz, *Staupitz*, pp. 27–8; Baylor, *Action and Person*, p. 79.

8. Oberman, *Harvest*, pp. 30–46. Cf. Oberman, 'Shape', pp. 13–14; Steinmetz, 'Pupper', p. 196: 'because God is a covenant-keeping God, his *potentia ordinata* has taken captive his *potentia absoluta*'.

9. Oberman, *Harvest*, p. 99. Cf. Steinmetz, *Staupitz*, p. 42; Baylor, *Action and Person*, p. 80; Oakley, *D'Ailly*, pp. 17–29.

10. Oberman, *Harvest*, pp. 361–408; Douglass, p. 104; Steinmetz, 'Pupper', pp. 195–205.

11. Oberman, *Harvest*, pp. 78–81; Douglass, p. 69; Oakley, *D'Ailly*, p. 31.

12. Oberman, *Harvest*, pp. 146–96. Cf. Douglass, pp. 126–8; Steinmetz, *Staupitz*, pp. 21, 80.

13. There are some complicating factors. For example, in 1960 Oberman saw four different schools of nominalism ('Notes', pp. 54–5). Two of these, 'the radical left wing school' that included the Englishmen Holcot and Woodham, and the Frenchmen Autrecourt and Mirecourt, and 'the Parisian syncretistic school' of John of Ripa and Peter of Candia, who combined Occamism and Scotism, have since disappeared. The latter school has been dropped altogether, while members of the former, such as Holcot, have been incorporated into the main-line school of Occam and Biel (Oberman, 'Holcot', pp. 119–41). Oberman's works of the 1970s indicate that he now sees only the two major nominalist schools described above.

14. E.g., P. Boehner, *Collected Articles on Ockham* (New York, 1958); D. Trapp, 'Augustinian theology of the fourteenth century', *Augustiniana*, 6 (1956), pp. 146–274. For other examples of this approach, see Courtenay, 'Nominalism', pp. 31–2.

15. 'Nominalism', p. 36. Courtenay mentions specifically the work of Hochstetter, Vignaux, Moody and Oberman.

16. *Ibid.*, p. 26.

17. 'Anti-Occamist' by Fr. Ehrle, *Der Sentenzenkommentar Peters von Candia*, cited by Connolly, p. 85; 'realist' by Connolly, p. 236; 'voluntarist' by F. Clark, 'A new appraisal of late medieval theology', *Gregorianum*, 40 (1965), p. 739; 'Bonaventurian' by A. Combes, *Essai sur la critique de Ruysbroeck par Gerson* (Paris, 1959), III, p. 217; 'Augustinian' by Oberman, 'Notes', p. 64; 'Thomistically inclined' by Georges de Lagarde, *Recherches sur l'esprit politique de la Reforme* (Douai, 1926), p. 30, cited in Oberman, *Harvest*, p. 96; 'eclectic' by Jedin, IV, p. 368; 'Gersonism' by Combes, *op. cit.*, p. 217.

18. Connolly, pp. 85–6, 236. In 1437, argues Connolly, the teaching of nominalism in philosophy was resumed.

19. E. Gilson, *History of Christian Philosophy in the Middle Ages* (New York, 1955), pp. 528–33.

20. S. E. Ozment, 'Mysticism, nominalism and dissent' (hereinafter 'Mysticism'), in *Pursuit of Holiness*, pp. 71–2. Combes expressed the view that Ozment cites in *Essai sur la critique de Ruysbroeck par Gerson*, III, pp. 219–33.

21. Oakley, *D'Ailly*, p. 16.

22. Courtenay, 'Nominalism', p. 56.

23. Steinmetz, *Staupitz*, p. 156.

24. Douglass, pp. 43–4; Baylor, *Action and Person*, p. 92.

25. This is clear, for instance, from the manner in which certain Parisian masters, who had been labelled nominalists and attacked in a royal decree of 1474, defined themselves in their defence. They were, they said, teachers who refused to multiply things according to the multiplication of terms, and who were concerned with the analysis of terms and the fundamentals of dialectic argumentation. They acknowledged that Occam, who along with Gregory of Rimini, Buridan and d'Ailly had been among the authors proscribed in the royal decree, was one of their leaders, and that he shared their approach to logic. They also cited Gerson as one who saw the advantages of knowing logic. Gerson had not been among the proscribed group of authors. Cf. C. E. Bulaeus, *Historia Universitatis Parisiensis*, Vol. V (Paris, 1670), pp. 708ff.; N. W. Gilbert, 'Ockham, Wyclif and the "via moderna"', *Miscellanea*

Medievalia, IX (1974), pp. 93–6; H. Hermelink, *Die theologische Fakultät in Tübingen vor der Reformation* (Tübingen, 1906), pp. 133–45, 151.

26. Courtenay, 'Nominalism', pp. 52–3. Cf. P. O. Kristeller, 'The validity of the term: "nominalism"', in *Pursuit of Holiness*, p. 66. Oberman himself in 1974 acknowledged that 'nominalism' is a problematic term for what he sees as the dominant movement in late medieval theology, that it is simply a convenient label imposed by historians. Nevertheless he has decided to continue to use 'nominalism' in the wider sense ('Shape', p. 12).

27. G. Leff, *The Dissolution of the Medieval Outlook: An Essay on Intellectual and Spiritual Change in the Fourteenth Century* (New York, 1976), pp. 12–13. Cf. pp. 14–18. Leff explicitly criticises Oberman's restatement of the thesis of a nominalist theology: 'The label of Nominalism lies like a pall – recently renewed – across the philosophy and theology of the fourteenth century' (p. 13).

28. *Du péril qui est de cellui qui pèche mortelement*, G.10, p. 321. Cf. *La Mendicité spirituelle*, G.7, p. 270.

29. *Doctrinal aux simples gens*, G.10, p. 299.

30. *Factum est*, G.7, p. 625.

31. *Ad deum vadit*, G.7, p. 407. Cf. *Poenitemini, contre l'orgueil*, G.7, p. 917; *Doctrinal aux simples gens*, G.10, pp. 308–9.

32. E.g., Brayer, pp. 106, 116, 117, 119, 146, 197. The image of God as king is more prevalent in other vernacular sermons, e.g., Hugh Legat's sermon in Grisdale, pp. 8ff.; Biel's sermon on the Circumcision in Oberman, *Forerunners*, p. 173.

33. *Poenitemini...Repentez vous, car penitence donne*, G.7, p. 938.

34. E.g., *Ibid.*, p. 938; *Tota*, G.7, p. 1069; *Le Miroir de l'âme*, G.7, p. 195.

35. *Videmus nunc*, G.7, p. 1130.

36. *Contra curiositatem studentium*, G.3, p. 232.

37. The Parisian articles Gerson refers to are the Condemnations promulgated by Bishop Tempier of Paris in 1277.

38. 'God acts, not out of natural necessity, but by His own will' (*Cont. G.*, II, 23). Cf. I, 81, 87; II, 26, 27. 'God can do other things by His absolute power than those He has foreknown and preordained He would do' (*S.Th.*, I, q.25, a.5, ad 1); cf. q.19, a.3, a.4, a.5.

39. *De vita spirituali*, G.3, pp. 125–6.

40. In 1 *Sent.*, d.35, q.5, in *Opera Philosophica et Theologica*, Vol. I (*Opera Theologica*), Part IV (New York, 1979).

41. *S.Th.*, I, q.15, a.1.

42. *Princ. in* 1 *Sent.*, E.F. 21v, cited in Oakley, *D'Ailly*, pp. 22–4. D'Ailly, like Gerson, refers to Occam's discussion of the divine ideas, which he describes as done 'very beautifully' (*valde pulchre*). (*Sent.* 1, q.6, a.3).

43. *Poenitemini, contre la luxure*, G.7, p. 835.

44. *Poenitemini, contre l'orgueil*, G.7, p. 929.

45. *Convertimini*, G.7, p. 578. This is reminiscent of d'Ailly's frequent attacks on 'ignorant jurists' who, he says, show their ignorance of Scripture by imagining that God is limited or bound by 'created laws'. E.g., *Sent.*, 1, q.12, a.2, cited in Oakley, *D'Ailly*, pp. 22–3.

46. *Gloria*, G.7, p. 640.

47. *La Mendicité spirituelle*, G.7, p. 223.

48. *S.Th.*, I–II, q.109, a.1, R.

49. Occam, *Quodl.*, IV, q.22, in *Opera Philosophica et Theologica*, Vol. I (*Opera Theologica*), Part IX (New York, 1980). Cf. D'Ailly, *Princ. in* 1 *Sent.*, K, cited in Oakley, *D'Ailly*, p. 26.

50. *Quodl.*, VI, q.1; q.4; In 4 *Sent.*, q.14, D, in *Opera Plurima* (Lyon, 1494–6). Leff argues that this last example – of God as the cause of hate – seems to be out of character with anything else Occam said on the matter. G. Leff, *William of Ockham: The Metamorphosis of Scholastic Discourse* (Manchester, 1975), p. 498.

51. Occam, *In 4 Sent.*, q.3, Q.
52. Cf. the discussion in *Cont. G.*, I, 95 on the proposition that God cannot cause evil.
53. *Memoriam*, G.7, p. 701.
54. *Ibid.*
55. *Tota*, G.7, p. 1066.
56. *Sent.*, I, q.13, a.1, D, cited in Oakley, *D'Ailly*, p. 27.
57. 4 *Sent.*, d.1, q.1, a.3, K, in *Collectorium circa quattuor libros Sententiarum* (Tübingen, 1973–84).
58. Occam, *Quodl.*, VI, q.1.
59. *Tota*, G.7, p. 1069.
60. *Poenitemini, contre la luxure*, G.7, p. 835.
61. *Poenitemini, contre l'orgueil*, G.7, p. 929.
62. *De vita spirituali*, G.3, p. 124.
63. Staupitz uses the same terms in his sermon on Job, in *Staupitz, Tübinger Predigten, Quellen und Forschungen zur Reformationsgeschichte*, Vol. III, ed. G. Buchwald and E. Wolf (Leipzig, 1927), 23, 186, 27ff., cited in Steinmetz, *Staupitz*, pp. 53–4. Cf. Biel, 3 *Sent.*, d.37, q.1, a.1; Occam, *Dialogus*, III, Book II, I, 10.
64. *De vita spirituali*, G.3, p. 124.
65. *Ibid.*
66. *Ibid.* Cf. D'Ailly, *Sent.*, I, q.9, a.2, R; q.14, a.1, B; *Princ. in* I *Sent.*, E and H, cited in Oakley, *D'Ailly*, pp. 184–5. Cf. Occam, *In 2 Sent.*, q.5, q.19; *Quodl.*, III, q.14. Cf. Biel, I *Sent.*, d.43, q.1, a.4.
67. *De vita spirituali*, G.3, p. 131.
68. *Dedit illi gloriam*, G.5, p. 184. Cf. Aquinas, *S.Th.*, I–II, qq.90–108, where Thomas discusses law at length. See especially q.90, a.1; q.93, a.1.
69. *Factum est*, G.7, pp. 623–4.
70. *Memoriam*, G.7, pp. 700–1. Cf. *Diligite justiciam*, G.7, p. 602.
71. *Videmus nunc*, G.7, p. 1132.
72. E.g., G.7, pp. 456, 602, 640, 1047.
73. E.g., *Enchiridion ad Laurentium de fide et spe et caritate*, XI, *CCSL*, 46, pp. 64–7.
74. E.g., *Brevil.*, II, 2 and 4; *Itinerarium mentis in deum*, in *The Works of Bonaventure, Cardinal, Seraphic Doctor and Saint*, Vol. II (hereinafter *Itin.*), I, 9–14.
75. 'God is simple and one, and one ought to seek Him in simplicity and unity of heart', *La Montaigne de contemplation*, G.7, p. 38.
76. *In* I *Sent.*, d.45, a.1.
77. *Princ. in 2 Sent.*, F and R, cited in Oakley, *D'Ailly*, pp. 23, 183.
78. I *Sent.*, d.38, q.1, a.3; d.45, q.1, a.2.
79. *The Disputed Questions on Truth*, 23, a.6, Cf. *S.Th.*, I, q.3, a.3, a.7; q.13, a.12, R: 'God, however, as considered in Himself is one and simple, yet our intellect knows Him according to diverse conceptions, because it cannot see Him as He is in Himself.'
80. *De potentia*, in *Quaestiones disputatae*, ed. R. Spiazzi (Rome, 1949), Vol. II (hereinafter *De pot.*), q.7, a.6: 'Whence if there were nothing in God according to Him or His effects, which corresponded to our concepts, the intellect would be false when it made propositions signifying attributes of this type; which is incongruous (*inconveniens*)...And so it is to be said that all these many and diverse concepts have something corresponding in God, to which these concepts of the intellect are likenesses.'
81. *Cont. G.*, I, 35.

82. *Quodl.*, III, q.2.

83. *De vita spirituali*, G.3, p. 125.

84. *Ecce rex*, G.7, p. 617. Gerson has in mind here not only the ecclesiastical schism but also the political divisions in France caused by the illness of the king.

85. *Poenitemini...Repentez vous, car penitence donne*, G.7, p. 942.

86. *Certamen*, G.7, p. 568.

87. *Convertimini*, G.7, p. 578; *Poenitemini, contre l'orgueil*, G.7, p. 928.

88. Di Stefano, pp. 193–207. His arguments apparently convince the preacher himself, for he feels it necessary to tell his congregation that they should not ask God specifically to send them adversities.

89. E.g., *Ad deum vadit*, G.7, p. 482.

90. E.g., G.7, pp. 2, 25, 436, 571, 576–8, 596, 648, 757, 841.

91. *Misereor*, G.7, p. 712.

92. *Mansionem*, G.7, p. 684.

93. *Rex in sempiternum*, G.7, p. 1009.

94. *Factum est*, G.7, pp. 629–31; *Ad deum vadit*, G.7, pp. 459, 467. In the latter passage Gerson gives some statistics about angels.

95. *Regnum coelorum*, G.7, pp. 992–1005, a sermon for the feast of All Saints. Cf. G.7, pp. 721, 739, 941, 947–8.

96. *Beati qui lugent*, G.7, pp. 549–60; *Sancta et salubris*, G.7, pp. 1031–40. Both sermons are for the feast of All Souls.

97. *Certamen*, G.7, p. 568.

98. *Contre les tentations de blasphème*, G.7, p. 414.

99. *Omne regnum*, G.7, p. 756. Cf. G.7, pp. 576, 943. This is traditional teaching. Although the devil appears rarely in academic works, except in connection with the fall of Lucifer and the fall of man, when he does this doctrine is stated or it is made clear that God could restrain the devil if He wished. E.g., Aquinas, *S.Th.*, I–II, q.80, a.2, R; a.3, R; Bonaventure, *Brevil.*, II, 7.

100. *Factum est*, G.7, pp. 622ff.

101. Brayer, p. 193; di Stefano, p. 196; Grisdale, p. 4.

102. *Factum est*, G.7, p. 629. Pride and envy were traditionally held to be the sins of the fallen angels. Cf. Augustine, *De civitate dei*, XIV, *CCSL*, 48, p. 417. 'The devil is not a fornicator or a drunkard, or carnally vicious in any way; yet he is proud and envious.' Cf. Aquinas, *S.Th.*, I, q.63, a.2.

103. *Poenitemini...Repentez vous, car penitence donne*, G.7, p. 943: 'The enemies have free will and cannot be constrained by others, except by God.'

104. *Regnum coelorum*, G.7, pp. 995–1003.

105. *Accipietis*, G.7, p. 432. This metaphor is quite common. Cf. Maillard: 'The enemy of human nature makes cruel assaults against the citadel of our soul and wants to enter and drive out all the virtues' (de la Borderie, p. 25).

106. *Pax vobis*, G.7, p. 790.

107. *Veniat pax*, G.7, p. 1103. This sermon was delivered in 1408.

108. *Poenitemini, contre la luxure*, G.7, p. 825. Cf. pp. 435, 1054, 1150.

109. For example, in a sermon in which he is complaining about the political factions in Siena, Bernardine says that the devil 'has had these symbols made, these images, these banners, which are adored even in churches'. And with reference to working on Sundays he says: 'Whoever gathers in grapes tomorrow for the vintage, the devil will carry him away' (*Sermons*, pp. 56, 229).

110. Cited by Oberman, '*Simul gemitus et raptus*: Luther and mysticism', in S. E. Ozment, ed., *The Reformation in Medieval Perspective* (Chicago, 1971), p. 227. Cf. Luther's statement: 'Gerson is the first who came to grips with the issue which concerns theology: he too experienced many temptations' (*ibid.*).

111. E.g., Tauler's sermon for the twelfth Sunday after Trinity, in W. Elliot, trans., *The Sermons and Conferences of John Tauler of the Order of Preachers* (Washington, 1910), pp. 494–7; and Courtecuisse's sermon *Bonum est* (di Stefano, pp. 155–71).

112. *Traité des diverse tentations de l'ennemi*, G.7, pp. 343–60.

113. *Ibid.*, p. 344.

114. *Ibid.*, p. 347.

115. For examples of Gerson's teachings about temptation in his sermons, see G.7, pp. 544, 569, 628, 741, 937, 1043.

116. *Factum est*, G.7, p. 629.

117. *Ibid.* Cf. *Poenitemini...Repentez vous, car penitence donne*, G.7, p. 942.

118. *Poenitemini...Repentez vous, car penitence donne*, G.7, p. 943. Cf. G.7, pp. 569, 678.

119. *Omne regnum*, G.7, p. 762. Cf. G.7, pp. 943, 956.

120. Etienne de Bourbon (*fl.* 1250), *Anecdotes historiques*, ed. A. L. de la Marche (Paris, 1877), pp. 155–7, cited in an unpublished paper by A. E. Bernstein, 'Theology and popular belief: confession in the later thirteenth century'. Cf. *Handlyng Synne*, pp. 375–6, where the fourth result of confession is said to be the confounding of the fiend of hell, here because confession shames the fiend, showing that he has failed in his task and 'evermore he is more coward for to tempt you afterwards'. The seventh result is the blinding of the devil, and there follows an *exemplum* about how by confession a man 'made himself invisible to the fiend who before used to lead him about chained'.

121. *Dialogue spirituel*, G.7, p. 164. For other examples of Gerson's remedies against temptation, see G.7, pp. 543, 627, 678, 937, 1043. Hilton, in his much shorter treatment of remedies against temptations of the devil, urges a similar combination of self-help ('distract your mind and occupy it with something else') and turning to God (*Scale*, I, ch. 38).

122. *Non in solo pane*, G.7, p. 742.

123. *Le Miroir de l'âme*, G.7, p. 193.

124. *In nomine patris*, G.7, p. 678. Cf. *Videmus nunc*, G.7, pp. 1132–3.

125. *Apparuit gratia*, G.5, p. 9. Cf. *Consideranti mihi*, G.5, p. 145.

126. *Pax hominibus*, G.7, p. 767.

127. *Si terrena*, G.7, p. 1046.

128. Plato, *The Republic*, ch. 13. Plato's three elements are discussed by Thomas in *S.Th.*, I, q.82, a.5. Augustine, *De trinitate*, XII, 15; XIV, 3, *CCSL*, 50, pp. 377–80, 50A, pp. 426–8. Bonaventure, *Brevil.*, II, 9; *Itin.*, I, 14. Hugh of St Victor, *De sacramentis*, I, 3, *MPL*, 176:227–31.

129. Aquinas does, however, try to reconcile this division with the Augustinian position by subsuming memory under the intellective faculty (*S.Th.*, I q.79, a.7).

130. E.g., *De theologia mystica*, G.3, pp. 257–62.

131. *Tota*, G.7, p. 1063. Cf. *Diligite justiciam*, G.7, pp. 606–7.

132. *Diligite justiciam*, G.7, p. 605.

133. *Omne regnum*, G.7, pp. 753–4.

134. *Cont. G.*, IV, 52. Aquinas sees prelapsarian man as being endowed with the natural faculties, with original justice and with an inclination to virtue (*S.Th.*, I–II, q.85, a.1, R). Earlier Thomas had indicated that the inclination to virtue is, properly speaking, not natural. The conflict among man's faculties was involved from the beginning, because of their very multiplicity (*In II Sent.*, d.33, q.2, a.1). Bonaventure in explaining why the fall was possible states that the creature 'made from nothing and defective was capable of deficiency in acting according to God' (*Brevil.*, III, 1).

135. *Tota*, G.7, pp. 1063–4. Cf. *Suscepimus*, G.7, p. 1050. D'Ailly also speaks of lese-majesty in this connection (Brayer, p. 113).

136. *Tota*, G.7, p. 1066.

137. *Suscepimus*, G.7, p. 1050. Cf. *La Mendicité spirituelle*, G.7, p. 221.
138. Connolly, p. 364, n. 1.
139. *Le Miroir de l'âme*, G.7, p. 194.
140. *Autres considérations sur Saint Joseph*, G.7, p. 97.
141. *Dialogue spirituel*, G.7, p. 160.
142. *Ibid.*, p. 179.
143. *Diligite justiciam*, G.7, p. 606.
144. *Definitiones terminorum theologiae moralis*, G.9, p. 140.
145. Biel, 2 *Sent.*, d.30, q.2, a.1; Aquinas, *S.Th.*, I–II, q.82.
146. E.g., Oberman, *Harvest*, pp. 120–31; Steinmetz, *Staupitz*, pp. 64–5; A. Harnack, *History of Dogma*, VI, trans. W. McGilchrist (London, 1899), pp. 275–317.
147. *Retractationes*, I, 15, *MPL*, 32, p. 608, and cited by Thomas, *S.Th.*, I–II, q.82, a.3. Thomas defines concupiscence here as 'the inordinateness of the powers of the soul, that is their turning inordinately to mutable good'.
148. Lombard, *II Sent.*, d.30, c.10: 'And from this we can understand what original sin is, that is, the vice of concupiscence, because into all born from concupiscence, it enters, through Adam, and vitiates them.' Gregory of Rimini, *II Sent.*, d.30–3, q.1, a.2: 'I do not deny that man is lacking original justice...But I do not hold that this is original sin but rather the effect of original sin' (cited in Oberman, *Harvest*, p. 124).
149. Anselm, *De conceptu virginali*, *MPL*, 158:434: 'Original sin is the absence of original justice.' Cited by Thomas, *S.Th.*, I–II, q.82, a.1.
150. 'There are two ways of speaking about original sin: *de facto* and *de possibili*. Now *de facto*, I hold that original sin, as Anselm says, is not anything positive in the soul, but rather it consists in the absence of original justice which should be in the soul' (*Quodl.*, III, q.10).
151. *S.Th.*, I–II, q.82, a.3, R.
152. 2 *Sent.*, d.30, q.2, a.2.
153. Brayer, p. 106. Cf. pp. 119–20. Courtecuisse refers to the fall only once, in passing. He mentions the loss of spiritual gifts and the ignorance that followed (di Stefano, p. 294).
154. *Obsecro vos*, G.7, p. 749. Cf. *Memoriam*, G.7, p. 708, where the Eucharist is described as the manna that sustains us 'ou desert horrible de ce monde'. Cf. *La Mendicité spirituelle*, G.7, p. 221. The image of the present life as a time of exile and of the world as a desert is a very common one. Cf. Courtecuisse, *Bonus est*, di Stefano, p. 156.
155. *Videmus nunc*, G.7, pp. 1130–1.
156. *Puer natus est*, G.7, p. 964.
157. *Ad deum vadit*, G.7, pp. 463–4.
158. *Poenitemini, contre la gourmandise*, G.7, p. 799.
159. *Regnum coelorum*, G.7, p. 997. Cf. *Adorabunt*, G.7, p. 525.
160. *Nimis*, G.7, p. 739.
161. *De spiritu et littera*, III, 5, *CSEL*, 60, p. 157.
162. Cited in Steinmetz, *Staupitz*, pp. 70–1. Cf. Gregory of Rimini, who states that 'no one, before having grace, can perform any act of free will that is not culpable' (*II Sent.*, d.26–8, q.1, a.1, cited in Steinmetz, *Staupitz*, p. 70). Thomas Bradwardine states that 'grace...is the efficient cause of every good and meritorious act', *De causa dei contra Pelagium* (London, 1618), I, ch. 40.
163. *S.Th.*, I–II, q.109, a.2, R; q.85, a.1, R; a.3, R.
164. *S.Th.*, II–II, q.10, a.4, R. Cf. I–II, q.63, a.2.
165. *De vita spirituali*, G.3, p. 117. Luther: 'After the fall free will is something

in name only and when it does what is in it [*facit quod in se est*], it sins mortally.'
Cited in Ozment, *The Age of Reform*, p. 294.

166. *De vita spirituali*, G.3, p. 117. The rejection of doctrine on the grounds of its
harmful psychological or spiritual effects has a respectable ancestry. Cf. Aquinas'
discussion of the opinion that a man who sins after receiving the sacraments cannot
return to a state of grace. This doctrine would cast men into the sin of despair, he
argues, and make it dangerous to receive the sacraments. The teaching is absurd
(*inconveniens*) and therefore it must be wrong (*Cont. G.*, IV, 71).

167. *De vita spirituali*, G.3, pp. 117–18. In late medieval theology man's own moral
efforts are said by some to have congruity, because they are graciously regarded by
God as merits in a metaphorical sense (*de congruo*), rewarded with grace by a liberal
God who gives so much for so little. By contrast, man's moral efforts aided by grace
are held by some to be fully worthy (*de condigno*) of divine acceptation.

168. *S.Th.*, I–II, q.109, a.6, R and ad 2.

169. *In 4 Sent.*, q.9, Y. Occam goes on to say that infused grace is necessary before
man's acts can merit *de condigno* 'grace and glory', that is eternal blessedness.

170. Biel, *2 Sent.*, d.28, q.1, a.3; d.40, q.1, a.2; d.27, q.1, a.2. For Geiler, who
quotes Gerson's *De vita spirituali animae* quite often on this question, see Douglass,
pp. 112–18.

171. *De vita spirituali*, G.3, p. 116.

172. Oakley, *Western Church*, p. 133; Ozment, *The Age of Reform*, p. 29; cf.
Oberman, 'Shape', p. 22.

173. Cf. the sermons of d'Ailly and Courtecuisse.

174. *Nimis*, G.7, p. 728.

175. For Augustine's arguments against Pelagianism and what has come to be
known as the 'semi-Pelagian' position, see especially his *De spiritu et littera* (412),
CSEL, 60, pp. 155–229; and *De gratia et libero arbitrio* (426c), *MPL*, 44:881–912.
The position of his opponents can also be discerned in these works. Pelagius
(*c.* 354–*c.* 418) did not teach that man, unaided by God, can work his own salvation.
But he did minimise the role of grace, holding that Adam's sin left no permanent
disability in man's nature, that even fallen man was fitted by nature for a holy and
perfect life. The semi-Pelagian position gives a much greater role to grace, but
argues that the granting of grace can in some cases depend on man's meriting it,
not fully, but to some extent. Cf. Cassian's (*fl.* 400) reply to Augustine in *John
Cassian: Conferences*, *NPNF*, 2nd Series, Vol. XI (New York, 1894), pp. 293–545.

176. *Le Profit*, G.7, p. 370.

177. *Convertimini*, G.7, p. 576.

178. *Ibid.*, p. 583. Cf. *Tu discipulus*, G.7, pp. 1091–2.

179. Di Stefano, pp. 169, 199, 221, 245. Cf. d'Ailly, who says that God gives grace
to the humble and to those who ask reasonably and discreetly (Brayer, pp. 148, 150).

180. *Sermons*, p. 98.

181. The same analysis of the causes of tardy repentance occurs in the *Raymundina*,
an early summa written by Raymond of Penafort between 1220 and 1245. *Summa
sancti Raymundi de Penafort de poenitentia et matrimonio* (Rome, 1603; reprint,
Farnborough, England, 1967), III, pp. 498ff.

182. *Hoc sentite*, G.7, pp. 657–9. Much of this sermon is in the form of notes and
Gerson lists under each remedy examples which he no doubt spelled out when he
delivered the sermon.

183. *Beati qui lugent*, G.7, pp. 551–2. There are many other places in his sermons
where Gerson lays great stress on man's moral efforts, but enough examples have
been given to show the drift of this aspect of his preaching.

184. *Tota*, G.7, pp. 1070–2.

185. *Le Miroir de l'âme*, G.7, p. 195.

186. *Mansionem*, G.7, p. 687. Cf. G.7, pp. 370, 892.

187. This problem afflicted clerics also, especially religious, for Gerson makes the same point in a number of his Latin works, for example in *De perfectione cordis*, G.8, pp. 124–9.

188. *Poenitemini, de la chasteté*, G.7, p. 842.

189. *Convertimini*, G.7, p. 581.

190. *De vita spirituali*, G.3, p. 188. Cf. *Definitiones terminorum theologiae moralis*, G.9, p. 138.

191. E.g., G.7, pp. 432, 945, 1140.

192. *De vita spirituali*, G.3, p. 118. Cf. *Definitiones terminorum theologiae moralis*, G.9, p. 138.

193. *Poenitemini, contre l'orgueil*, G.7, p. 925. As this is a sermon against pride, it is not surprising that Gerson puts the stress on God's grace rather than on man's efforts.

194. *Poenitemini…Repentez vous, car penitence donne*, G.7, p. 935.

195. *Gloria*, G.7, p. 650.

196. *La Mendicité spirituelle*, G.7, p. 268.

197. *Mansionem*, G.7, p. 683.

198. *Poenitemini, contre la gourmandise*, G.7, p. 799. Cf. G.7, pp. 651, 699, 740, 762.

199. *Douze considérations*, G.7, p. 102.

200. *Convertimini*, G.7, p. 589.

201. *Accipietis*, G.7, p. 431.

202. *Ibid.*, p. 436. Cf. G.7, p. 563.

203. *Sermons*, p. 59.

204. Di Stefano, pp. 169, 235, 304.

205. *Dedit illis*, G.7, p. 589.

206. *Pax hominibus*, G.7, p. 774.

207. *La Montaigne de contemplation*, G.7, p. 36. Gerson defines 'special grace' as spiritually infused grace, distinct on the one hand from God's general providence, and on the other from vivifying or sanctifying grace (*Definitiones terminorum theologiae moralis*, G.9, p. 138).

208. *In 4 Sent.*, Dubitationes addititie, AA. Cf. 4, q.9 Y.

209. *2 Sent.*, d.28, q.1, a.3. That Biel thinks it more likely for this to occur with the infusion of grace is clear from a passage in his sermon on the Circumcision: 'And although, according to some doctors, man can love God above everything else with his natural powers alone, this applied particularly to man before the fall; but man can never love God as perfectly and easily a with grace.' *De circumcisione domini*, in Oberman, *Forerunners*, p. 170.

210. *S.Th.*, q.109, a.2, a.3.

211. G.7, p. 640.

212. *Poenitemini, contre la paresse*, G.7, p. 885.

213. *Ad deum vadit*, G.7, p. 471.

214. *De circumcisione domini*, pp. 165–74.

215. 'nam habito isto acto deus statim infundit gratiam, et de potentia dei ordinata non potest non infundere' (*In 4 Sent.*, q.9 Y).

216. *Super libros sapientiae*, lecture 145, in Oberman, *Forerunners*, pp. 148–50.

217. G.9, p. 106.

218. *De vita spirituali*, G.3, pp. 114–15.

219. E.g., by Oberman, *Harvest*, p. 206.

220. *S.Th.*, I–II, q.112, a.3.

221. *Ibid.*, q.112, a.2. In his younger days Thomas seems to have argued that man could prepare himself for grace by the use of his natural powers alone (*II Sent.*, d.28, q.1, a.4). But his mature position is the one described.

222. It is true that Gerson also defines 'to do what is in one' as 'facere quod homo potest secundum vires quas actualiter habet' (*De vita spirituali*, G.3, p. 188). This is a definition that seems to put him in the same camp as Occam and Biel. However, what he says about prevenient grace (see below) indicates that he is nearer to Thomas on this question than Occam and Biel are.

223. *Brevil.*, 5, ch. 2.

224. *Convertimini*, G.7, p. 576.

225. *Ibid.*, p. 577.

226. G.7, p. 164.

227. Some theologians sometimes use the term *gratia gratis data* to indicate supernatural gifts given principally for the benefit of others, that is charisms, for example, the gift of prophecy.

228. *Dialogue spirituel*, G.7, pp. 164–6. The simile of the rider and the horse is a common one. It is used, for example, by Biel in his sermon on the Circumcision (Oberman, *Forerunners*, p. 170).

229. The same question that Gerson is addressing in this part of the dialogue is discussed with subtlety and clarity by Aquinas (*S.Th.*, I–II, q.109, a.6). His answer is in essence the same as Gerson's.

230. *Spiritus domini*, G.5, pp. 527–8.

231. 'Our works cannot bring us to this state, since man's nature is incapable of knowing or wanting or doing good.' *Libellus de executione eterne praedestinationis*, VI, in Oberman, *Forerunners*, p. 182. Cf. Steinmetz, *Staupitz*, pp. 93–7.

232. *WA*, I, pp. 224–6; II, p. 394. Cf. Oberman, '*Justitia Christi* and *Justitia Dei*: Luther and the scholastic doctrine of justification', *HTR*, 59 (1966), pp. 1–26.

233. Cf. *De vita spirituali*, G.3, p. 116, where Gerson describes those things which cause the death of the soul's four lives, that is, the lives of nature, of grace, of meritorious action derived from grace, and of stability in grace: 'Any perverse action or ceasing from work that is owed is contrary to the third life.' Cf. *Neuf considérations*, G.7, p. 1.

234. R. F. Evans, *Pelagius: Inquiries and Reappraisals* (London, 1968). Cf. H. Bettenson, *Documents of the Christian Church* (Oxford, 1943), pp. 73–88.

235. Cf. Canon 4 of the Council of Orange, in Bettenson, p. 86. Neither Occam nor Biel is a semi-Pelagian in this sense, for they do not hold that God has to wait till man takes the initiative, even in the ordained order. Occam himself argued that he was not Pelagian, for whereas the Pelagians, according to Occam, taught that man could, *de potentia dei ordinata*, win merit *de condigno* by the exercise of his natural powers alone, he himself taught that this would be possible only *de potentia dei absoluta* (*Quodl.*, VI, 1).

236. *Contra curiositatem studentium*, G.3, pp. 225–6.

237. E.g.: 'St Paul knew about the secret judgements of God, how of his free will He gave some grace and glory and others He left and reprobated; about which Paul wrote: O the majesty of the riches of the wisdom and knowledge of God, how incomprehensible are His judgements and unsearchable and unknown His ways.' *Nimis*, G.7, pp. 732–3. Cf. *Videmus nunc*, G.7, p. 1131.

238. He is unusual in this. I have found very few discussions of or even references to predestination in other vernacular sermons of the period.

239. *De civitate dei*, XII, 27, *CCSL*, 48, p. 385.

240. *Cont. G.*, III, 163.

241. *S.Th.*, I, q.23, a.3. Cf. *The Disputed Questions on Truth*, q.6, a.1: 'God does not will sin as He wills grace. Yet reprobation is said to be a preparation of the punishment which God wills consequent to sin.'

242. *S.Th.*, I, q.23, a.3, ad 3. Cf. q.19, a.3; *The Disputed Questions on Truth*, q.6, a.3.

243. Aquinas, *The Disputed Questions on Truth*, q.6, a.2, difficulties 1–14; Bradwardine, *De causa dei contra Pelagium*, in Oberman, *Forerunners*, pp. 151–2.

244. *De praedestinatione*, q.4. Occam allows some exceptions. The cause of predestination in the case of baptised infants and the Virgin, he says, does not lie in their earned merits.

245. I *Sent.*, d.41, q.1, a.3, dub. 3: 'God has ordained to damn no one except for personal guilt nor ordinarily [*regulariter*] to save any adult without personal merit.' Biel's exceptions are the Virgin and St Paul.

246. *WA*, 2, p. 394.

247. I *Sent.*, d.41, q.1, a.2, cited in P. Vignaux, *Justification et prédestination au XIVe siècle* (Paris, 1934), pp. 166ff.

248. Bradwardine, *De causa dei contra Pelagium*, I, ch. 47, in Oberman, *Forerunners*, pp. 161–2: 'He punishes no man with eternal damnation unless such a man deserves it, that is to say, unless through his sins he deservedly and justly requires eternal damnation.' Staupitz, *Libellus de executione eterne praedestinationis*, in Oberman, *Forerunners*, pp. 175–200.

249. *De consolatione theologiae*, G.9, p. 194.

250. *Convertimini*, G.7, p. 578.

251. *Poenitemini, contre la colère*, G.7, p. 899.

252. *Puer natus*, G.7, p. 964. The same doctrine of predestination based on God's foreknowledge is propounded in *Le Miroir de l'âme*, G.7, p. 195, and in *Traité des diverses tentations*, G.7, p. 359. Both works date from 1400–1.

253. *Convertimini*, G.7, pp. 577–9.

254. *Ibid.*, pp. 580–4.

255. *Videmus nunc* (1402), G.7, p. 1131.

256. *Poenitemini, contre la paresse* (1403), G.7, p. 886.

257. *Ibid.*, p. 885.

258. *Poenitemini, contre la colère* (1403), G.7, p. 898.

259. *Dialogue spirituel*, G.7, pp. 169–70.

260. G.9, pp. 193–4.

261. Bradwardine, in Oberman, *Forerunners*, pp. 161–2. Cf. Romans 9:22–3: 'What if God, desiring to show His wrath and to make known His power, has endured with much patience the vessels of wrath made for destruction, in order to make known the riches of His glory for the vessels of mercy, which he has prepared beforehand for glory.' Thomas quotes the same passage, glossing 'wrath' as 'the vengeance of His justice', and 'endured' as 'permitted' (*S.Th.*, I, q.23, a.5, ad 3).

262. *Super libros sapientiae*, Lecture 145, in Oberman, *Forerunners*, pp. 149–50.

263. *A Diatribe or Sermon Concerning Free Will* in *Erasmus–Luther: Discourse on Free Will*, trans. and ed. E. F. Winter (New York, 1961), p. 93.

264. G.9, p. 193.

265. *Ibid.*, p. 197.

266. *Ibid.*, p. 196. Cf. Aquinas, *S.Th.*, I, q.23, a.8, R: 'The predestined must strive after good works and prayer, because through these means predestination is most certainly fulfilled.' This is why, Thomas continues, there are so many passages in Scripture exhorting us to prayer and other good works.

267. *ABC des simples gens*, G.7, p. 157, where he lists the joys and pains. Cf. *Doctrinal aux simples gens*, G.10, pp. 317–21, where he describes at greater length the fires of purgatory, the pains of hell, the last judgement and the joys of paradise.

268. *Memento*, G.7, pp. 692–4. For other passages stressing judgement, heaven, purgatory and hell, see G.7, pp. 550, 558, 663, 669, 690, 717, 813–16, 994–9, 1004, 1034, 1113, 1118.

269. On hope and the mercy of God, see G.7, pp. 482, 508, 583, 746, 1051, 1091. On the justice of God, see G.7, pp. 551, 599, 602, 663, 999.

5 The analysis of sin

1. Tentler, *Sin and Confession*. Cf. S. E. Ozment, *The Reformation in the Cities; The Age of Reform.*

2. P. Michaud-Quantin, *Sommes de casuistique*, pp. 80–2.

3. Glorieux lists the known MSS of each of these works in the introductions to each of the volumes in which the works are printed (G.7, 8, 9, 10).

4. *Sin and Confession*, p. 46.

5. Cf. A. Dondaine, 'Guillaume Peyraut: Vie et oeuvres', *Archivum Fratrum Praedicatorum*, 18 (1948), pp. 162–236.

6. *Dialogue spirituel*, G.9, pp. 158–61; *Claro eruditori*, G.2, p. 211.

7. M. W. Bloomfield, *The Seven Deadly Sins: An Introduction to the History of a Religious Concept with Special Reference to Medieval English Literature* (East Lansing, Michigan, 1952), pp. 123–5.

8. *Gratia tibi*, G.2, pp. 133, 136.

9. L. E. Boyle, 'The *Summa Confessorum* of John of Freiburg and the popularization of the moral teaching of St. Thomas and of some of his contemporaries', pp. 245–68.

10. *Scriptum est melius*, G.2, pp. 110, 112. The IIa-IIae, that part of the *S.Th.* devoted to moral theology, often circulated as a separate work in the later Middle Ages. Cf. L. E. Boyle, *The Setting of the Summa Theologiae of Saint Thomas* (Toronto, 1982), pp. 23–6.

11. G.9, pp. 158–61.

12. E.g., *ibid.*, p. 159: 'Envy, according to Augustine, is hatred of the happiness of another. It has five daughters, according to Gregory...' References to Gregory abound in the literature on sin, in sermons as well as manuals.

13. S. Wenzel, *The Sin of Sloth: Acedia in Medieval Thought and Literature* (Chapel Hill, N. Carolina, 1967), p. 133, n. 119; J.-L. Flandrin, 'Mariage tardif et vie sexuelle', *Annales E.S.C.*, 27 (1972), pp. 1356–61.

14. E.g., Ozment, *Age of Reform*, pp. 220, 222.

15. *Le Profit*, G.7, p. 370.

16. *Convertimini*, G.7, p. 575. Cf. G.7, p. 754.

17. E.g., G.7, pp. 174, 700, 1046.

18. *Poenitemini, contre la paresse*, G.7, p. 863; *A Deo exivit*, G.5, p. 15. Animal similes are frequently used by medieval preachers to describe man in a state of sin.

19. *Mansionem*, G.7, p. 689.

20. *Hoc sentite*, G.7, p. 655.

21. *Dialogue spirituel*, G.7, p. 174.

22. *Mansionem*, G.7, p. 689.

23. *Dialogue spirituel*, G.7, p. 174. Cf. G.7, p. 655.

24. E.g., G.7, pp. 174, 584, 793, 795, 1054.

25. *Poenitemini, contre la gourmandise*, G.7, p. 793. Cf. G.7, p. 462.

26. *Dialogue spirituel*, G.7, p. 174. Cf. G.7, pp. 584, 654, 928.

27. *Poenitemini, contre la gourmandise*, G.7, p. 795.

28. *Hoc sentite*, G.7, pp. 654–5. Cf. G.7, pp. 174, 928.

29. *Hoc sentite*, G.7, p. 655. Cf. G.7, pp. 174, 576, 795; G.10, p. 321.

30. E.g., *Veniat pax*, G.7, p. 1104.

31. Cf. J. Walter and K. Wrightson, 'Dearth and the social order in early modern England', *Past and Present*, 71 (1976), pp. 22–44.

32. Maillard, de la Borderie, p. 103; Bernardine, *Sermons*, p. 163.

33. *Summa Theologica*, I, 532–8. Cf. R. M. Haines, 'Church, society and politics in the early fifteenth century as viewed from an English pulpit', in *Church, Society and Politics*, ed. D. Baker (Oxford, 1975), p. 156. The anonymous fifteenth-century sermon described here argues that sin arouses God's anger and brings retribution in the form of poverty and ill-fortune. Walsingham saw the Peasants' Revolt of 1381 as caused by the same mechanism. *Chronicon Anglicana*, ed. H. T. Riley (Rolls Series, 1863–4), II, pp. 8–13.

34. *Veniat pax*, G.7, pp. 1100–23.

35. *Ibid.*, p. 1103.

36. *Poenitemini, contre l'envie*, G.7, p. 912.

37. *Poenitemini, contre la luxure*, G.7, p. 835.

38. There is no more confusion in Gerson's answer to this question than in the answers produced by twentieth-century psychiatry to what is virtually the same question, that is, why people behave in aggressive, self-destructive, socially unacceptable, deviant ways.

39. Cf. Aquinas, *S.Th.*, I-II, q.74, a.1, R; Antoninus, *Summa Theologica*, I, 521: 'The efficient cause of sin is the will.'

40. *Accipietis*, G.7, p. 432. Cf. G.7, p. 754, where pride becomes 'le desdaigneux', envy 'la maleureuse', avarice 'convoiteuse', and lust 'la traiteuze'.

41. *Poenitemini, contre la gourmandise*, G.7, p. 794.

42. E.g., *Vivat rex*, G.7, p. 1150.

43. *Poenitemini, contre l'orgueil*, G.7, p. 933. Cf. G.7, p. 755.

44. E.g., G.7, pp. 343–60, 628, 633, 754, 827.

45. *Factum est*, G.7, pp. 628ff.

46. *Dialogue spirituel*, G.7, p. 179.

47. In *A New Language for Psychoanalysis* (New Haven, 1976), Roy Schafer argues for a psychoanalytical language that enables the person to be viewed as an agent who does things for reasons rather than as a being acted upon by forces. E.g., instead of such locations as 'the impulse seized me', 'one part of me says "yes" while the other part says "no"', one should use expressions that convey control by the speaker, e.g., 'I doubt', 'I choose to do or not to do.' Gerson, as has been seen, frequently uses language that conveys the idea that the person is being acted upon by forces, though his forces are different from Freud's. Nevertheless there are enough locutions conveying the idea of the sinner as agent not to leave his audience paralysed and quietist.

48. Aquinas, *S.Th.*, II-II; Antoninus, *Summa Theologica*. Despite its title this latter work is essentially a *Summa moralium*.

49. The large confessional summas of the period make more use of Aristotelian notions. The devil, however, is still seen as an external force that man has to contend with (cf. Antoninus, *Summa Theologica*, I, 503–16).

50. *S.Th.*, I-II, q.71, aa.1, 2, 6.

51. *Dialogue spirituel*, G.7, p. 180.

52. *Convertimini*, G.7, p. 976.

53. *Nimis*, G.7, p. 726.

54. *Poenitemini, contre l'orgueil*, G.7, p. 916. Cf. G.7, pp. 592, 641, 691, 697.

55. *La Montaigne de contemplation*, G.7, p. 22. Cf. G.7, p. 10.

56. *Dedit illis*, G.7, pp. 593–4.

57. *Convertimini*, G.7, p. 976. Cf. G.7, pp. 665, 915.

58. *Douze degrés d'humilité*, G.7, p. 100.

59. *John Cassian: Institutes*, NPNF, 2nd Series, Vol. XI (New York, 1894), p. 290.

60. Pp. 131–43. Cf. Sermon 20 in Ross, p. 115.

61. Cf. Bloomfield, *passim*. Bloomfield details the entire history of the seven sins

in all types of literature up to the fifteenth century. Cf. Wenzel, *The Sin of Sloth*, p. 70.

62. Ozment, *The Reformation in the Cities*, p. 17. Ozment goes on to state: 'The Reformation came as a vigorous protest against all this.'

63. 'Further lines of inquiry for the study of "Reformation and pedagogy"', in *Pursuit of Holiness*, p. 295. He goes on to state that Luther did not allow any space for the seven deadly sins in either his prayer book or his catechism (p. 296).

64. Cf. *Handlyng Synne*. *The Book of Vices and Virtues* has boughs, branches and twigs for most of the sins. Even Thomas, Antoninus and Angelus de Clavasio always at least mention the Gregorian daughters when they are discussing the capital sins.

65. *Institutes*, pp. 201–90.

66. Bloomfield, p. 72.

67. *Ibid.*, p. xiv. Cf. S. Wenzel, 'The seven deadly sins: some problems of research', *Speculum*, 43 (1968), pp. 1–22. L. K. Little in 'Pride goes before avarice: social change and vices in Latin Christendom', *American Historical Review*, 76 (1971), pp. 16–49, argues, largely from the evidence of the visual arts, that avarice rose to pre-eminence from the eleventh century.

68. He devotes 402 columns to avarice, 126 columns to pride. Antoninus' order is the following: avarice, pride, vainglory, lust, gluttony, anger, envy, *acedia* (*Summa Theologica*, II, 1–1042).

69. This conclusion is based on twenty passages in the sermons and tracts, where Gerson lists or discusses at length the capital sins. The following table shows the number of times a sin occurs in first, second, third etc. place.

	1st	2nd	3rd	4th	5th	6th	7th	Not mentioned
Pride	15	1	0	0	0	0	1	3
Envy	0	10	4	2	0	2	0	2
Anger	1	4	7	4	2	1	0	1
Avarice	2	3	2	7	4	0	1	1
Sloth	0	0	3	5	6	0	2	4
Gluttony	1	0	0	2	3	8	3	3
Lust	1	2	3	1	0	5	7	1

Source: G.7, pp. 524, 432, 725, 637, 779, 1054, 681, 754, 1150, 155, 174, 282–4, 394–6, 371–81, the *Poenitemini* series of sermons on the seven sins (pp. 793–934); G.9, pp. 84–6, 102–18, 159–60; G.10, pp. 302–6.

70. Pp. 10–53.

71. Ross, pp. 46–55. Hilton, writing for religious, devotes eight chapters to pride, seven to anger and envy together, one to gluttony and sloth taken together, and one each to avarice and lust (I, chs. 55–60, 62–73).

72. G.7, pp. 172, 179–80.

73. Augustine, *De civitate dei*, XIV, 13, *CCSL*, 48, p. 434; Aquinas, *S.Th.*, II–II, q.162, a.1 ad 2; Antoninus, *Summa Theologica*, II, 418; *Angelica*, 'Superbia'. Cf. Ross, p. 49: 'Pride is a wicked love of a man's highness.'

74. *Le profit*, G.7, pp. 372–3. Cf. *Enumeratio*, G.9, p. 159; *Modus brevis*, G.9, p. 84; *Regulae mandatorum*, G.9, p. 102. The same manifestations of pride are described more rhetorically in some of the sermons, e.g., G.7, pp. 471, 971.

75. Gregory, *Moralia in Job* (hereinafter *Moral.*), XXIII, 6, *MPL*, 76:258; Antoninus, *Summa Theologica*, II, 418.

76. *Poenitemini, contre l'orgueil*, G.7, pp. 917, 921. All three of the sermons on pride are based on the theme that pride prevents penitence. Cf. *Enumeratio*, G.9, p. 102; *Doctrinal aux simples gens*, G.10, p. 303.

77. *L'examen*, G.7, p. 394. Cf. *Enumeratio*, G.9, p. 159.

78. *Ad Deum vadit*, G.7, p. 497. Cf. *Gloria*, G.7, p. 645; *Enumeratio*, G.9, p. 159. Lucifer and Adam and Eve are stock examples in sermons or discussions of the sin of pride.

79. *Quaerite*, G.7, p. 970.

80. *Ibid.*, pp. 972–5. Cf. *Modus brevis*, G.9, p. 84; *Enumeratio*, G.9, p. 159; *Doctrinal aux simples gens*, G.10, p. 302.

81. *Regulae mandatorum*, G.9, p. 103: 'Presumption, arrogance, boasting and hypocrisy have less sin and danger when they are about the goods of nature or fortune than when they are about the goods of grace.' The spiritual manifestations of a sin are always worse for Gerson, as for the scholastics, than the material manifestations. This is the case, for instance, with the sins of envy and sloth.

82. *La Mendicité spirituelle*, G.7, p. 272. Cf. *La Montaigne*, G.7, p. 43.

83. *Regulae mandatorum*, G.9, p. 103. Gerson's insistence on relying on the opinions, advice and orders of superiors is apparent here as elsewhere.

84. *Ibid.*, p. 106. Cf. *Enumeratio*, G.9, p. 159.

85. Gerson occasionally (e.g. in the sermon *Non in solo pane* and in the vernacular tract *Le Profit*) discusses vainglory as a separate sin. Here he is following Gregory and Thomas, who treated them separately. Generally, though, he, as most late medieval writers, treats vainglory as a daughter of pride. Cf. Antoninus, whose example of the link between pride and vainglory is the building of the Tower of Babel, where the builders want to raise a tower with its top in the heavens (pride) and so make a name for themselves (vainglory) (*Summa Theologica*, II, 543).

86. *Non in solo pane*, G.7, p. 745. Cf. G.7, p. 1071.

87. *Le Profit*, G.7, pp. 371–2.

88. *Ibid.*, p. 372.

89. Bernardine, *Sermons*, pp. 168, 186–8; Maillard, de la Borderie, p. 98.

90. *L'Examen*, G.7, p. 394; *Doctrinal aux simples gens*, G.10, p. 302.

91. G.9, p. 84.

92. *Le Profit*, G.7, p. 373.

93. *Regulae mandatorum*, G.9, p. 105.

94. *Ibid.*

95. *Ibid.*

96. *Quaerite*, G.7, p. 971. All the branches of pride Gerson discusses come from the traditional stock. He is fairly moderate in the number of branches and twigs he uses compared with some writers. He could have added as separate categories contention, discord, rebellion, ingratitude, schism, withholding tithes, singularity, prodigality, foolish undertaking, ambition.

97. *Le Profit*, G.7, p. 374.

98. *Regulae mandatorum*, G.9, p. 103.

99. *Ibid.* In the same work Gerson is at pains to point out that prelates and others in positions of authority are not to abuse their power by interpreting the law of God more strictly and widely than He intended, thereby making the burdens of the faithful too heavy (pp. 97, 99).

100. *L'Examen*, G.7, p. 394; *Doctrinal aux simples gens*, G.10, p. 302.

101. *Poenitemini, contre l'orgueil*, G.7, p. 919.

102. G.7, p. 272.

103. *Nimis*, G.7, pp. 730–1.

104. Peraldus' *Summa de vitiis et virtutibus* has separate sections on the virtues, the gifts, the beatitudes and the seven capital sins. *The Book of Vices and Virtues* has sections on the ten commandments, the articles of faith, the seven sins, the virtues, the Paternoster, and the seven gifts. Antoninus' massive *Summa Theologica* is divided into four chief parts: the soul and its powers, the seven sins, the rights, duties and sins of people of different statuses, and the virtues.

105. *S.Th.*, II–II, q.162, a.1, R.

106. *Ibid.*, q.162, a.4, ad 2.

107. *Ibid.*, qq.129, 130.

108. *Ibid.*, qq.131–2.

109. *Summa Theologica*, II, 419. Bloomfield, pp. 209–10, discusses a fifteenth-century verse sermon in which the sinless aspects of each of the seven sins are listed. The sinless aspect of pride is self-respect.

110. Gerson's teaching about pride could be contrasted with this twentieth-century view expressed by Pope Pius XII: 'Protection, respect, love and service of oneself are not only justified but are direct requirements of both psychology and moral law. That is at once a self-evident fact of nature and an article of Christian faith. The Lord taught, "Thou shalt love thy neighbour as thyself" (Mark, 12:31). Christ therefore considered love of oneself to be the criterion of neighbourly love and not the reverse...We should fail to do justice to this reality, if we dismissed all regard for the ego as psychological imprisonment...' *Acta Apostolica Sedis*, Annus XXXXV, Series II (1953), p. 283, cited by J. Rudin, 'A Catholic view of conscience', in *Conscience : Theological and Psychological Perspectives*, ed. C. E. Nelson (New York, 1973), pp. 99–100.

111. *Enumeratio*, G.9, p. 159. Cf. G.9, pp. 84, 107; G.7, pp. 375, 395, 432; G.10, p. 303.

112. *Poenitemini, contre l'envie*, G.7, p. 912.

113. *Le Profit*, G.7, p. 375. Cf. *Regulae mandatorum*, G.9, p. 107; *Poenitemini, contre l'envie*, G.7, p. 912.

114. *Le Profit*, G.7, p. 375; *Regulae mandatorum*, G.9, p. 107. It is the conclusion of Aquinas (*S.Th.*, II–II, q.36, a.2, R), Antoninus (*Summa Theologica*, II, 871) and Angelus de Clavasio (*Angelica*, 'Invidia').

115. *Poenitemini, contre l'envie*, G.7, p. 912.

116. *Summa Theologica*, II, 827. Cf. Aquinas, *S.Th.*, II–II, q.36, a.1, R; *Angelica*, 'Invidia'.

117. *Regulae mandatorum*, G.9, p. 107.

118. *Ibid.* Cf. *Le Profit*, G.7, p. 375.

119. *Poenitemini, contre l'envie*, G.7, pp. 908–12.

120. *Ibid.*, pp. 914–15.

121. *Poenitemini, contre la colère*, G.7, p. 904.

122. *Regulae mandatorum*, G.9, p. 107. Cf. *Le Profit*, G.7, pp. 375–6.

123. *Le Profit*, G.7, p. 376.

124. *Ibid.* Cf. *Regulae mandatorum*, G.9, p. 107.

125. Thomas treats anger under temperance, but he connects it with justice, and argues that if one desires revenge to be taken in accordance with right reason and by due process and for a due end, namely the maintaining of justice, then the desire of anger is praiseworthy (*S.Th.*, II–II, q.158, a.2, R). He treats vengeance in the context of the virtue of justice and argues that taking vengeance may be lawful provided 'due circumstances be observed' (*S.Th.*, q.108, a.1, R).

126. *Le Profit*, G.7, p. 376. Cf. *Regulae mandatorum*, G.9, p. 107.

127. Cf. Gregory's description of the angry person: 'The heart goaded by the prick of anger is convulsed, the body trembles, the tongue entangles itself, the face is inflamed, the eyes are enraged and fail utterly to recognize those whom they know; the tongue makes sounds indeed, but there is no sense in its utterance' (*Moral.*, V, 45, *MPL*, 75:724).

128. *Poenitemini, contre la colère*, G.7, p. 900.

129. *Ibid.*, pp. 901–2. Cf. *L'Examen*, G.7, p. 395.

130. *Doctrinal aux simples gens*, G.10, p. 303. Cf. *Le Profit*, G.7, p. 376; *Enumeratio*, G.9, p. 159; *Poenitemini, contre la colère*, G.7, p. 900.

131. *Poenitemini, contre la colère*, G.7, p. 906.

132. *Traité des tentations*, G.7, p. 350, where Gerson warns of the danger of bottling up things like suspicions that others are mocking one, for example, or plotting to harm one.

133. Aquinas, *S.Th.*, II–II, q.58; Antoninus, *Summa Theologica*, II, 801–13; *Angelica*, 'Ira'. On turning the other cheek see Aquinas' discussion of reviling (*S.Th.*, q.72, a.3).

134. E.g., Bernardine, *Sermons*, pp. 51–3; *The Book of Vices and Virtues*, p. 25 (very brief); Ross, pp. 51, 306 (very brief indeed).

135. *Institutes*, pp. 260, 263.

136. Cf. J. T. Noonan, *The Scholastic Analysis of Usury* (Cambridge, Mass., 1957) (hereinafter, *Usury*), and J. Gilchrist, *The Church and Economic Activity in the Middle Ages* (London, 1969).

137. *Poenitemini, contre l'avarice*, G.7, pp. 871–2. Cf. *Enumeratio*, G.9, p. 160; *Le Profit*, G.7, p. 377; *Regulae mandatorum*, G.9, p. 109.

138. This was standard teaching. Cf. Bonaventure, *In IV Sent.*, d.20, a.2, q.3 (*Opera Omnia*, Vol. IV, p. 535). Aquinas argues that private property is not contrary to natural law but 'an addition to it devised by human reason', and necessary to human life to prevent neglect ('every man is more careful to look after what is for himself alone than that which is common to many or to all'), confusion and quarrels (*S.Th.*, II–II, q.66, a.2, R and ad 2). Bernardine makes the same point in a Latin sermon, *De evangelio aeterno* (*Opera omnia*, Vol. IV, p. 120), cited in R. de Roover, *San Bernardino of Siena and Sant'Antonino of Florence: The Two Great Economic Thinkers of the Middle Ages* (Cambridge, Mass., 1967), p. 8.

139. *Poenitemini, contre l'avarice*, G.7, p. 874. Statements about the insatiability of avarice and the anxieties it causes are ubiquitous in the literature.

140. *Ibid.*, pp. 869–77. Some theologians try to reconcile pride's being the beginning of all sin and avarice's being the root of all evil by distinguishing between origins and roots: e.g., Antoninus, *Summa Theologica*, I, 527–8.

141. Gerson uses this pattern for a number of his sermons in the *Poenitemini* series. The rhetorical passages were no doubt meant to move people to repentance, and the analytical ones to inform them about the church's doctrines and/or Gerson's opinions about particular actions and their status as sinless, venial or mortal.

142. *Le Profit*, G.7, pp. 377–8. Cf. *Regulae mandatorum*, G.9, p. 109; *L'Examen*, G.7, p. 396; *Doctrinal aux simples gens*, G.10, p. 303.

143. Foolish talking, jocularity, unseemly joy, levity and scurrility were usually treated as some of the daughters of gluttony. Cf. Gregory, *Moral.*, XXXI, 45, *MPL*, 76:621; Aquinas, *S.Th.*, II–II, q.148, a.6.

144. *Poenitemini, contre l'avarice*, G.7, p. 880. Cf. *Doctrinal aux simples gens*, G.10, p. 303; *Enumeratio*, G.9, p. 160; *L'Examen*, G.7, p. 379.

145. Gerson is in line with tradition here. Long before his time usury and sins in trade had come to be regarded as sins against justice rather than against charity. The significance of this is that, for the sacrament of penance, a sin against justice required restitution of the loss caused, whereas a sin against charity did not.

Aquinas treats avarice, cheating in trade and usury in the context of justice; almsgiving he treats under charity. Cf. Noonan, *Usury*, pp. 12–37.

146. *Regulae mandatorum*, G.9, p. 109.

147. *Ibid.*, p. 113. The other illicit practices mentioned occur scattered throughout this tract and the others already cited. All are standard cases.

148. G.9, p. 110.

149. *Ibid.*, pp. 110–11.

150. *Poenitemini, contre l'avarice*, G.7, p. 878. Cf. *Regulae mandatorum*, G.9, p. 112: 'Usury proper, which is contrary to divine and natural law and which is *de se* mortal sin, is to receive from a loan contract anything beyond the capital.' Cf. Antoninus, *Summa theologica*, II, 74: 'Usury is gain from a loan contract [*lucrum ex mutuo*], the gain being the principal intention; as when you lend 100 florins or a certain amount of grain, wine or oil etc., with the principal intention of receiving back more than the 100 florins or the grain etc. you originally lent.'

151. *Poenitemini, contre l'avarice*, G.7, p. 878. Cf. *Regulae mandatorum*, G.9, p. 112. One can, by contrast, legitimately charge for 'lending' land or a house. The contract here would be a lease, not a loan. Cf. Aquinas, *S.Th.*, II–II, q.78, a.1, R: 'The principal use of money is its consumption or alienation.' In such things as money, grain or wine, 'the use of the thing must not be reckoned apart from the thing itself, and whoever is granted the use of the thing, is granted the thing itself; and for this reason, to lend things of this kind is to transfer ownership'.

152. *Regulae mandatorum*, G.9, p. 112.

153. De Roover, p. 31.

154. Antoninus, *Summa Theologica*, II, 100–1. For Bernardine, see Noonan, *Usury*, pp. 126–8.

155. *Regulae mandatorum*, G.9, p. 112.

156. *S.Th.*, II–II, q.78, a.4, ad 1, ad 3.

157. *Poenitemini, contre l'avarice*, G.7, pp. 878–9.

158. Cf. Noonan, *Usury*, pp. 90–5.

159. The central section of Glorieux's edition of this sermon on avarice is rather cryptic. Part of it is in note form and some of the sentences are ungrammatical. The Latin translation in du Pin is somewhat more comprehensible.

The practice of forestalling, if that is what Gerson is talking about, was generally condemned outright by moralists.

160. p. 32.

161. Noonan, *Usury, passim*. The authors of the late medieval summas, for example Antoninus and Angelus de Clavasio, discuss more cases of possible hidden usury (e.g., government bonds, deposit banking) and at much greater length than Gerson does.

162. Aquinas' example of this type of fraud is the selling of alchemical gold and saying it is real gold. If, however, he continues, 'real gold were to be produced by alchemy, it would not be unlawful to sell it for the genuine article' (*S.Th.*, II–II, q.77, a.3, ad 1).

163. The same example about manuscripts occurs in *The Book of Vices and Virtues*, pp. 40–1.

164. *Summa Theologica*, II, 255. According to De Roover this last characteristic (*complacibilitas*), which De Roover glosses as subjective utility, was first introduced by the Franciscan Pierre Olivi (1248–98), and then taken up by Bernardine (pp. 18–20). The first two determinants of value appear in a number of writers. Cf. Aquinas, *S.Th.*, II–II, q.77, a.2 ad 3 (usefulness); ad 2 (scarcity).

165. *Poenitemini, contre l'avarice*, G.7, pp. 879–80. Cf. *Regulae mandatorum*, G.9, p. 114.

166. Cf. Bernardine, *Sermons*, pp. 198–200, where these and other examples of fraudulent practices occur.

167. *Le Miroir*, G.7, p. 197. Cf. *Le Profit*, G.7, p. 376.

168. Cited by Raymond of Penaforte, *Summa*, p. 248, and attributed to Pope Leo.

169. *S.Th.*, II–II, q.77, a.4, R: trading for profit 'is justly deserving of blame, because, considered in itself, it satisfies the greed for gain, which knows no limits and tends to infinity'.

170. *Ibid.*, a.1, R.

171. De la Borderie, p. 122. Cf. Bernardine in a Latin sermon cited by De Roover, p. 11. Maillard sees the practice of law as providing more opportunities for sin than the practice of trade or industry.

172. *Le Profit*, G.7, p. 379. Cf. *Regulae mandatorum*, G.9, p. 114. Cf. Aquinas, *S.Th.*, II–II, q.32, a.5, R; Antoninus, *Summa Theologica*, II, 334.

173. *Regulae mandatorum*, G.9, p. 114. Cf. Thomas' qualified approval of moderate solicitude for the future (*S.Th.*, II–II, q.55, a.7, ad 3), and Antoninus' whole-hearted approval of the rational laying up of treasure by fathers with families to provide for, educate and marry (*Summa Theologica*, II, 117).

174. *Poenitemini, contre l'avarice*, G.7, p. 877.

175. *Institutes*, pp. 266–75.

176. Wenzel, *The Sin of Sloth*, p. 177.

177. *Poenitemini, contre la paresse*, G.7, p. 981. The second interpretation is the more common in other preachers of the period, the first in the summas.

178. *Le Profit*, G.7, p. 376; *Regulae mandatorum*, G.9, p. 107.

179. *Enumeratio*, G.9, p. 160.

180. Gregory, *Moral.*, XXXI, 45, *MPL*, 76:621. Cf. Aquinas, *S.Th.*, II–II, q.35, a.4; *Angelica*, 'Acedia'; Simon of Hinton, *Ad instructionem iuniorum*, cited in A. Dondaine, 'La Somme de Simon de Hinton', p. 218. The sixth daughter is generally called 'wandering of the mind after unlawful things'.

181. *Le Profit*, G.7, p. 376.

182. *Ibid.*, pp. 376–7.

183. *Modus brevis*, G.9, p. 85. Cf. *Doctrinal aux simples gens*, G.10, pp. 305–6; *L'Examen*, G.7, pp. 396–7.

184. *Poenitemini, contre la paresse*, G.7, pp. 892–3. Cf. *Le Profit*, G.7, p. 377; *Regulae mandatorum*, G.9, p. 97.

185. *Regulae mandatorum*, G.9, p. 97.

186. *Ibid.*, p. 108.

187. *Poenitemini, contre la paresse*, G.7, p. 891. A similar chain of disasters is described in *Handlyng Synne*, pp. 143–52.

188. Glorieux does not indicate where each sermon in the *Poenitemini* series was preached. He says only that the series was preached to the people. One of the sermons on gluttony was preached at Saint-Germain, and one of those on lust at Saint-Jean-en-Grève (G.1, p. 117). It seems likely that the other sermons were preached at one or other of these churches, as Gerson sometimes makes references backwards and forwards to other sermons in the series.

189. *Poenitemini, contre la paresse*, G.7, pp. 893–6. Cf. *Doctrinal aux simples gens*, G.10, p. 305. The question about whether a wealthy bourgeois ought to work appears in Peraldus' treatment of sloth in his *Summa de vitiis et virtutibus* (Antwerp, 1587), f. 18, cited in Wenzel, *The Sin of Sloth*, p. 250.

190. *The Sin of Sloth*, p. 233. Wenzel says also (p. 141) that in theological literature begging is not usually seen as a symptom of *acedia*. It is only Gerson who discusses the question of able-bodied beggars. Wenzel finds examples of begging seen as a sin of sloth in some secular literature of the period, e.g., in *Piers Plowman* (Prol. I, 45).

191. J. T. Welter, *L'Exemplum dans la littérature religieuse et didactique du moyen âge* (Paris, 1927), p. 465.

192. *Summa Theologica*, II, 80. The chief complaint is, of course, against the hidden usury involved in deposit banking, but the idleness of the nobles concerns the archbishop too.

193. John Mirk is an exception. In his *Instructions for Parish Priests*, p. 37, he tells the penitent, when examining his conscience about the sin of sloth, to ask himself among other things if he has helped his wife when necessary. If the penitent is a servant, he should ask if he has worked hard enough to deserve his pay and food.

194. *Dialogue spirituel*, G.7, p. 192. Cf. *Contre le Roman de la rose*, G.7, p. 314.

195. E.g., Hilton, *Scale*, I, ch. 72; Ross, p. 32. Cf. Wenzel, *The Sin of Sloth*, pp. 164–8.

196. In *Obsecro*, G.7, p. 750, Gerson includes sloth with gluttony and lust as sins that seek carnal pleasure.

197. *Le Profit*, G.7, p. 379. Cf. *Enumeratio*, G.9, p. 160; *Regulae mandatorum*, G.9, p. 115.

198. *Modus brevis*, G.9, p. 84. Cf. *Doctrinal aux simples gens*, G.10, p. 304.

199. *Poenitemini, contre la gourmandise*, G.7, p. 804.

200. *Dialogue spirituel*, G.7, p. 189.

201. *Doctrinal aux simples gens*, G.10, p. 304. Cf. *Regulae mandatorum*, G.9, p. 116; *Poenitemini, contre l'orgueil*, G.7, p. 919.

202. *Poenitemini, contre la gourmandise*, G.7, p. 803.

203. *Ibid.*, pp. 801–2. The path from gluttony through lust, theft, homicide and despair to hell is described in a fifteenth-century English sermon (Haines, 'Church, society and politics', p. 152). Cf. Grisdale, p. 31.

204. *Poenitemini, contre la gourmandise*, G.7. p. 805. Cf. *Le Profit*, G.7, pp. 379–80.

205. *L'Examen*, G.7, p. 398.

206. *Poenitemini, contre la gourmandise*, G.7, p. 807.

207. *The Book of Vices and Virtues* concerns itself with eating too early in the day, too late in the evening, too much, too often, too eagerly, too richly, and with too many elaborate dishes (pp. 46–53). Mirk sees vomiting as a sign of the sin of gluttony (p. 40).

208. *Dialogue spirituel*, G.7, p. 191.

209. E.g., *Regnum*, G.7, pp. 1002ff., *Ave Maria*, G.7, pp. 545ff., *Certamen*, G.7, pp. 564ff., *Tu discipulus*, G.7, p. 1091, *Dedit illis*, G.7, p. 594.

210. *Poenitemini, contre la luxure*, G.7, p. 811.

211. *Le Miroir*, G.7, p. 201. This sequence of disasters caused by sins of lust is frequently used in the sermons too. Cf. *Certamen*, G.7, p. 566, where the falls of Troy, the Tarquins, Alexander, Julius Caesar, Antony, David, Solomon and Samson are added to the list. Cf. *Ave Maria*, G.7, p. 546; *Poenitemini, contre la luxure*, G.7, p. 812.

212. V. L. Bullough argues that only 10 % of canon law was concerned with sexual topics in the period from the twelfth to the fourteenth century, and that the proportion falls off towards the end of the period. 'Sex and canon law', in *Sexual Practices and the Medieval Church*, ed. V. L. Bullough and J. Brundage (Buffalo, 1982), pp. 89–101.

213. Cited in Tentler, *Sin and Confession*, p. 229.

214. P. 234.

215. Lambeth MS 392, f. 173v.

216. *Moral.*, XXXIII, 12, *MPL*, 76:688. Cf. Aquinas, *S.Th.*, II–II, q.154, a.3, R and ad 1, 2, 3; Hilton, *Scale*, I, ch. 74.

217. E.g., *Certamen*, G.7, pp. 564–6; *Regnum*, G.7, p. 1002; *Memento*, G.7, p. 697; *Poenitemini, contre l'orgueil*, G.7, pp. 834–5. Other theologians also feel it necessary to insist on the sinfulness of fornication because 'some deny this'. E.g., Maillard, de la Borderie, p. 115; Aquinas, *Cont. G.*, III, 122.

218. Dondaine, 'La Somme de Simon de Hinton', p. 218; Aquinas, *S.Th.*, II–II, q.153, a.3, R; Antoninus, *Summa Theologica*, II, 635.

219. *Poenitemini, contre la luxure*, G.7, p. 826.

220. *Regulae mandatorum*, G.9, p. 117. Cf. *Poenitemini, contre la luxure*, G.7, p. 826. Gerson's teaching about marriage and sexual activity in marriage will be discussed in ch. 7.

221. G.10, p. 301.

222. *Poenitemini, contre la luxure*, G.7, p. 826.

223. *Le Profit*, G.7, p. 380.

224. Most of this discussion occurs in the sermon *Poenitemini, contre la luxure*, G.7, pp. 826–32, and *Le Profit*, G.7, pp. 380–1. But cf. *L'Examen*, G.7, p. 397; *Modus brevis*, G.9, p. 85; *Doctrinal aux simples gens*, G.10, pp. 301, 304–5; *Le Miroir*, G.7, p. 202.

225. *Le Profit*, G.7, p. 380. Cf. *Poenitemini, contre la luxure*, G.7, pp. 837–8.

226. *Poenitemini, contre la luxure*, G.7, p. 840. Discussion of kisses and touches almost invariably occurs in any extended medieval treatment of lust. E.g., *Angelica*, 'Luxuria'; Aquinas, *S.Th.*, II–II, q.154, a.4; Ross, p. 235; *Handlyng Synne*, pp. 240–62; *The Book of Vices and Virtues*, p. 44.

227. *Poenitemini, contre la luxure*, G.7, p. 818.

228. *Ibid.*, p. 820. Gerson could have been clearer here. The summas generally distinguish between seduction (intercourse with an under-age virgin) and rape (intercourse with an unwilling woman, virgin or not). As Thomas says, 'Sometimes rape coincides with seduction, sometimes there is rape without seduction, and sometimes seduction without rape' (*S.Th.*, II–II, q.154, a.7, R).

229. *Poenitemini, contre la luxure*, G.7, pp. 817–21.

230. *Ibid.*, p. 811.

231. *Ibid.*, p. 821.

232. *Poenitemini, contre l'orgueil*, G.7, p. 922.

233. G.7, p. 683. The context here is a discussion of ways in which the Holy Spirit 'knocks on our door'. The woman mentioned heard a voice which so filled her with the fear of hell that she went to confession and amended. The incident, Gerson says, was reported by a Dominican, a penitentiary in the diocese of Cambrai, in a book Gerson had read recently.

234. *L'Examen*, G.7, p. 398. Cf. *Le Miroir*, G.7, p. 201.

235. *Le Miroir*, G.7, p. 201.

236. *L'Examen*, G.7, p. 397. For how Gerson thought one of these sins – masturbation – could be dealt with in confession, see ch. 7 *infra*.

237. *Le Miroir*, G.7, p. 201. The French reads as follows: 'Icy tant en mariage comme dehors est deffendue toute maniere de atouchemens luxurieux es quels on ne garde l'ordonnance et la maniere et les parties que nature veult et requiert ou souffre pour avoir lignie.'

238. Cf. Antoninus, *Summa Theologica*, III, 82. About *coitus non in debito vase* Antoninus says, 'This is always a mortal sin according to all the doctors because it prevents procreation, and the whole intention of nature is frustrated.'

239. *Ibid.*, 82–3. Antoninus lists a number of authorities holding each of these views. He himself holds that *indebitus modus* is not a mortal sin *per se*, but that spouses are to be reprimanded and told to abstain from it unless they have just cause. Cf. *Angelica*, 'Debitum conjugale'. Cf. J. T. Noonan, *Contraception: A History of its Treatment by the Catholic Theologians and Canonists* (Toronto, 1965) (hereinafter *Contraception*), pp. 389–99; Tentler, *Sin and Confession*, pp. 186–208.

240. Noonan, *Contraception*, p. 290, argues that Gerson is referring to *indebitus modus* here; Tentler, *Sin and Confession*, p. 195, argues that he is not. Both are working from the Latin translation of *Le Miroir* (P. I, p. 431): 'Prohibetur etiam Praecepto hoc tam in matrimonialiter conjunctis quam in solutis omnis luxuriosus attactus membrorum genitalium, quo non servatur naturalis ordo inditus a natura, vel non rite copulantur partes ad generationem a natura deputatae.' The French original seems more susceptible to an interpretation that includes *indebitus modus* as well as *non in debito vase*.

241. G.9, pp. 117–18.

242. Flandrin, *op. cit.*, pp. 1356–61. Cf. J. Bossy, 'The social history of confession in the age of Reformation', *TRHS* (5th ser.), 25 (1975), p. 36.

243. *De confessione mollitiei*, G.8, pp. 71–5. Cf. p. xv for MSS.

244. Except of course *per accidens*, e.g., if the woman were barren.

245. Pp. 7–8.

246. E.g., *Handlyng Synne*, pp. 241, 257, 265; *The Book of Vices and Virtues*, p. 46; Grisdale, p. 7.

247. Cf. *Tu discipulus*, G.7, pp. 1088–9; *Brève manière*. G.7, pp. 408–9.

248. *Le Miroir*, G.7, pp. 195–203; *Le Doctrinal aux simples gens*, G.10, pp. 300–2.

249. *Contre le péché de blasphème*, G.7, pp. 3–5; *Contre les tentations de blasphème*, G.7, pp. 412–16.

250. *Contre le péché de blasphème*, G.7, pp. 4–5. Here is another example of the doctrine of judgements.

251. M. Lieberman, 'Chronologie gersonienne', *Romania*, 83 (1962), pp. 52–89. Cf. J. Huizinga, *The Waning of the Middle Ages*, pp. 163–5.

252. Brayer, p. 180.

253. In 1397, 1405, 1409, 1420 and 1425. The last such edict was promulgated in 1660 (Lieberman, *op. cit.*).

254. De la Borderie, pp. 99–103; Ross, pp. 99, 109.

255. E.g., G.7, pp. 544, 567, 596, 619, 628, 647, 678, 711, 759, 775, 790, 955, 1001, 1055, 1147, 1183.

256. *Suscepimus*, G.7, p. 1055.

257. *Regnum*, G.7, p. 1001.

258. *Puer natus*, G.7, p. 955.

259. '...as Augustine and all the holy doctors say' (*De erroribus circa artem magicam*, G.10, p. 79).

260. Di Stefano, p. 305.

261. Nicolas de Jauer, *Tractatus de superstitionibus* (1405); Jean de Francfort, *Quaestio utrum cohercendi demones* (1412); Henri de Gorkum, *Tractatus de super-stitionibus quibusdam casibus* (1425); and the anonymous *Tractatus de daemonibus* (1415). These are discussed in F. Bonney, 'Autour de Jean Gerson. Opinions de théologiens sur les superstitions et la sorcellerie au début du XVe siècle', *Le Moyen Age*, 77 (1971), pp. 85–98. Bonney thinks Gerson's works show the most sophistication and take the firmest stand. Cf. Principe, *op. cit.*, p. 42.

262. Haines, 'Church, society and politics', p. 152.

263. Bonney, *op. cit.*

264. De la Borderie, pp. 95–8. Maillard preaches against sorcerers, charmers, diviners, chiromancers (who inspect hands and nails and claim to predict the future), and interpreters of dreams.

265. E.g., G.7, pp. 473, 525, 544, 617, 646, 944, 1162–6.

266. *Contre les fausses assertions des flatteurs*, G.7, pp. 360–3.

267. *Ave Maria*, G.7, p. 544.

268. *Vivat rex*, G.7, pp. 1162–3.

269. *Ibid.*, p. 1161.

270. *Gloria*, G.7, p. 648. D'Ailly (Brayer, pp. 110–11) and Courtecuisse (di Stefano, p. 262), who also deplore the evil effects of flattery at court, cite Seneca and Cicero to bolster their cases.

271. *Ave Maria*, G.7, p. 544.

272. *Contre les fausses assertions des flatteurs*, G.7, pp. 360–1.

273. *Vivat rex*, G.7, p. 1165. A number of Gerson's strictures against flatterers occur as prefaces to sermons in which he himself fearlessly preaches about reforms and policies that he thinks urgently need to be put into effect in France.

274. E.g., G.7, pp. 656, 673, 698, 703–4, 711, 954, 1000, 1041, 1135. Curiosity is treated by most theologians as a branch of pride. Antoninus, after quoting Aristotle's 'All men desire to know', defines curiosity as a vice opposed by excess to the virtue of desiring and seeking knowledge; the vice by deficiency is negligence (not seeking to know what we should) (*Summa Theologica*, II, 418). Cf. Aquinas, *S.Th.*, II–II, q.167, a.1, a.2.

275. Romans 12:3, cited, for example, in *Regnum*, G.7, p. 1000. 'Do not seek to know more than you need' is probably a fair rendering of what Gerson takes the Latin Vulgate to mean here.

276. '...note five evil hungers, in general, for glory and power, for understanding and knowledge [*de savoir et cognoissance*], for delight and pleasure' (*Misereor*, G.7, p. 711).

277. *Si terrena*, G.7, p. 1041.

278. *Memoriam*, G.7, p. 704.

279. *Videmus*, G.7, pp. 1135–6.

280. *De erroribus circa artem magicam* (an excerpt from a speech given to the licentiates in medicine at the University of Paris), G.10, pp. 77–90.

281. *De modo vivendi fidelium*, G.8, p. 4. This is a Latin work of 1404, extant in a large number of MSS. The occasion of Gerson's writing it is not known but it reads as if it were meant indirectly for popular consumption via pastors. The complete list of 'faithful' mentioned is as follows: nobles, soldiers, the simple, bishops and prelates, clerics, religious, rich, poor, virgins, widows, married women, women, husbands, parents, sons, masters, servants, merchants, tavern-keepers, hotel-keepers, the old. This is a grand mixture of categories.

In his poem, *La Danse macabre*, G.7, pp. 286–301, Gerson divides the lay participants in traditional fashion into emperor, king, constable, knight, squire, bailiff, bourgeois, merchant, sergeant, usurer, poor man, doctor, lover, lawyer, minstrel, worker, child.

282. E.g., the sermons of Bernardine and Maillard. Antoninus devotes almost the whole of the third part of his *Summa* to different statuses: the married, virgins, widows, temporal lords (royal, feudal and civic), soldiers, doctors, and scholars, lawyers, merchants and artisans, judges, the dying. After this follow the various ecclesiastical estates, and the volume ends with the state of the blessed (various ranks) and of those in purgatory. Cf. J. Le Goff, 'Métier et profession', pp. 44–60; P. Michaud-Quantin, 'Aspects de la vie sociale chez les moralistes', *Miscellanea Mediaevalia*, III (1964), pp. 30–43.

283. 'Homo enim natura animal civile est.' *De vita spirituali*, G.3, p. 135.

284. *Diligite justiciam*, G.7, p. 605.

285. *De vita spirituali*, G.3, p. 144.

286. *Diligite justiciam*, G.7, p. 605.

287. *Adorabunt*, G.7, p. 519; *Accipietis*, G.7, p. 436.

288. *Vivat rex*, G.7, p. 1139. Cf. *Rex in sempiternum*, G.7, p. 1010. Aquinas too used this as one of his arguments in favour of monarchy (*De regimine principum*, ch.

12, in *Aquinas: Selected Political Writings*, trans. J. G. Dawson (Oxford, 1954), p. 67).

289. *Rex in sempiternum*, G.7, p. 1011. Cf. *Vivat rex*, G.7, p. 1148. Contrast Bonaventure who, 150 years earlier, had stated that a kingdom where the ruler is elected is better governed. Bonaventure points to the example of the Romans who, he says, when they elected their rulers chose the wisest men and so were governed well, but when the rulership became hereditary total destruction followed. *In Hex.*, v. 19 (*Opera omnia*, v, p. 357).

290. *Vivat rex*, G.7, p. 1159. For a full discussion of Gerson's conception of political authority, see M. C. Batts, *The Political Ideas of Jean Gerson* (Ph.D. dissertation, University of Ottawa, 1976).

291. *Vivat rex*, G.7, pp. 1165–6.

292. *Ibid.*, p. 1164.

293. *Poenitemini, contre l'envie*, G.7, pp. 910–11. Cf. d'Ailly (Brayer, pp. 124–5), where the clergy are likened to the eyes which enlighten the whole body, the nobles to the hands which defend the body, and the people to the feet that sustain and carry the body. An English preacher of the early fifteenth century was more original. He compares the human race to a field, with the magnates bearing the corn of honour, the merchants bearing the barley of riches, and the poor left fallow in this world (P. J. Horner, 'A sermon on the anniversary of the death of Thomas Beauchamp, Earl of Warwick', *Traditio*, 34 (1978), pp. 381–401). Another English preacher of the same period describes the ship of state: the forecastle is the clergy, the hindcastle is the baronage (king and nobles), the body of the ship is the commonalty (merchants, artisans and farm workers), and the topcastle is the saints of the realm (R. M. Haines, '"Our master mariner, our sovereign lord": a contemporary preacher's view of King Henry V', *MS*, 38 (1976), pp. 85–96).

294. *Omne regnum*, G.7, p. 753.

295. *Vivat rex*, G.7, p. 1149. Here once more Gerson refers to Dionysius and his hierarchical orders.

296. *Ibid.*, pp. 1177–8. Cf. G.7, pp. 806, 831.

297. E.g., G.7, pp. 436–7, 667, 970, 998.

298. *Regulae mandatorum*, G.9, p. 113.

299. This ideal, in whole or in part, is expressed in a number of sermons, e.g., G.7, pp. 520, 547, 621, 678, 700, 1155, 1175. The same ideal is expressed by d'Ailly and Courtecuisse in their sermons to the French court. D'Ailly too speaks of the need for princes to be endowed like God with power, wisdom and benevolence, but it is benevolence and love that he emphasises most (e.g., Brayer, p. 124). Courtecuisse bolsters his arguments for the ideal by citing Cicero's *De officiis*, offering glorious renown to a ruler who is loved by his people, governs with justice and prudence and excels in virtuous deeds performed for the common good, not just for his own profit (di Stefano, pp. 186–7). The power/wisdom/benevolence triad occurs also in some of the thirteenth-century sermons of Guibert of Tournai to the upper bourgeoisie in cities. Guibert here applies the traditional ideals of royal and noble governmental authority to the power elites of cities (D. L. d'Avray, 'Sermons to the upper bourgeoisie by a thirteenth-century Francisan', *Studies in Church History*, 16 (1979), pp. 187–99).

300. *Vivat rex*, G.7, pp. 1170–1.

301. *Ibid.*, p. 1170. Cf. G.7, pp. 440, 545–7, 648, 867.

302. *Ecce rex*, G.7, pp. 615–17. Cf. *Vivat rex*, G.7, p. 1172; *De modo vivendi*, G.8, p. 1. Courtecuisse (di Stefano, pp. 240–1) attacks the covetousness of temporal princes who use their officials like sponges to soak up the sustenance of the poor; Legrand (Beltrán, pp. 472–7) attacks heavy taxation that destroys the poor, wastage of public funds and maladministration of justice.

303. *Adorabunt*, G.7, p. 527. Cf. *Ave Maria,* G.7, p. 547. These sermons date from 1391 and 1397 respectively. In other words, Gerson viewed the government of France under Charles VI as oppressive from the 1390s onwards. *Accipietis*, of 1392, also refers to injustice and financial oppression.

Gerson's stress on compassion is echoed by d'Ailly (Brayer, p. 195): 'The prince should be the father of the fatherland and show that not by fear, but by love, he wishes to govern his people as a father his children.'

304. Criticism of the factions within the ruling elites of the Italian cities is a recurring theme in the sermons of Bernardine (e.g., *Sermons*, pp. 35, 54, 98).

305. *Rex in sempiternum*, G.7, p. 1010; *Vivat rex*, G.7, p. 1168. Cf. Courtecuisse's criticism of the 'chevaliers dorés' (di Stefano, pp. 243-4).

306. *Accipietis*, G.7, pp. 442-7. Cf. J. Verger, 'The University of Paris at the end of the hundred years war', in *Universities in Politics*, ed. J. W. Baldwin and R. A. Goldthwaite (Maryland, 1972), pp. 47-78. Verger analyses the 'peace at any price' policy of the university in the period 1418-50. Cf. *Society at War: The Experience of England and France during the Hundred Years War*, ed. C. T. Allmand (Edinburgh, 1973), pp. 37-43, where the complaints of other clerics about the Anglo-French war and its evil effects are documented.

307. *Vivat rex*, G.7, p. 1155.

308. *Puer natus*, G.7, p. 958.

309. *Vivat rex*, G.7, p. 1159.

310. *Rex in sempiternum*, G.7, p. 1030. Courtecuisse (di Stefano, p. 239) states that the correct attitude of the *menu peuple* is 'loving fear'.

311. *Poenitemini, contre l'avarice*, G.7, p. 882.

312. G.8, pp. 1-5.

313. The same view was expressed in the following century by Archbishop Cranmer in England: 'every degree of people, in their vocation, calling and office, has appointed to them their duty and order. Some are in high degree, some in low; some kings and princes, some inferiors and subjects, priests and laymen, masters and servants, fathers and children, husbands and wives, rich and poor...Where there is no right order, there reigneth all abuse, carnal liberty, enormity, sin and babylonical confusion.' *Works of Archbishop Cranmer* (Parker Society), I, 392, cited in C. Russell, *The Crisis of Parliaments: English History 1509-1660* (Oxford, 1971), pp. 105-6.

314. Cf. G.7, pp. 687, 976, 1070, 1072.

315. Cf. Aquinas, *S.Th.*, II-II, q.184, a.2, ad 3.

316. *Le Profit*, G.7, p. 371.

317. *Mansionem*, G.7, p. 687, Cf. G.7, pp. 416, 634, 932, 1032.

318. His view that prostitution and concubinage must be tolerated is evidence that he thought the goal of chastity too high for many people.

319. *Ecce rex*, G.7, p. 616. Cf. *Puer natus*, G.7, pp. 960, 965; *Hoc sentite*, G.7, p. 652.

320. E.g., *Puer natus*, G.7, p. 965. Cf. *Ibi eum videbitis*, G.7, p. 668.

6 The mystical way

1. *De mystica theologia speculativa* (hereinafter *M.T. spec.*), G.3, pp. 250-92. The two lectures *Contra curiositatem studentium* (hereinafter *Contra curiositatem*), G.3, pp. 224-49 were also part of this plan.

2. *De mystica theologia practica* (hereinafter *M.T. prac.*), G.8, pp. 18-47. This was written in 1407, and in 1408 it was combined with *M.T. spec.* and published in Paris as a single treatise. The treatise was revised three times, though not extensively, at

Lyons, probably in 1422, 1423, 1429 (G.3, p. xii). In 1424 he published a further treatise, the *De elucidatione scholastica mysticae theologiae* (hereinafter *Eluc.*), G.8, pp. 154–61.

3. *M.T. spec.*, G.3, p. 273. The synderesis is defined by Gerson as an appetitive or affective power of the soul which receives directly from God a certain natural inclination to good (p. 260), and its activity is ecstatic, transcendent love (*extatica et anagogica*) (p. 272). The synderesis was more usually located by medieval theologians on the intellectual side, for example by St Thomas in *S.Th.*, I, q.79, a.12. Bonaventure, however, is like Gerson in placing it among the affective powers, defining it as that which prompts the will towards good. Cf. *Brevil.*, II, 11.

4. Hugh of Balma, *De mystica theologia*. This work used to be attributed to Bonaventure and is found in Vol. VIII, pp. 1–53, of his *Opera*, ed. A. C. Peltier (Paris, 1866). Gerson, however, knew it was Hugh's. He usually refers to it by its *incipit*, *Viae Sion lugent*. It often went under another name: *De triplici via*. For Vincent of Aggsbach see E. Vansteenberghe, *Autour de la docte ignorance: une controverse sur la théologie mystique au XVe siècle* (Münster, 1915) (hereinafter *Docte ignorance*).

5. Apoc. 2:17 'quod nemo scit nisi qui accipit'. Gerson quotes this, for example, in *De probatione spirituum* (hereinafter *De prob.*) (1415), G.9, p. 178, and in *Collectorium super Magnificat* (hereinafter *Magnificat*) (1428), G.8, p. 310. Bonaventure uses the same quotation. Cf. *Itin.*, IV, 3.

6. *M.T. spec.*, G.3, p. 255.

7. *Videmus nunc*, G.7, pp. 1123–37. This seems, perhaps, rather a meagre vernacular corpus. But it should be remembered that Gerson's popular vernacular sermons peter out after 1403 and that it was only from about 1400 that he began to develop his interest and expertise in the study of mysticism. Cf. A. Combes, *Essai sur la critique de Ruysbroeck par Gerson* (hereinafter *Essai*), Vol. III, pp. 34–174.

8. In 1907, L. Salembier, in *Les Oeuvres françaises de Cardinal Pierre d'Ailly* (Paris), edited four French works on the spiritual life which he thought were written by d'Ailly. In fact two of these are Gerson's: *Le Jardin amoureux de l'âme* (G.7, pp. 144–54); *Pitieuse complainte* (G.7, pp. 213–16). The other two are poems, one of which is very short and about the perils of a life of opulence and sensual pleasure. The other, *Le Livre du rossignolet*, is longer (350 lines) and is of a more mystical nature, being basically a meditation on the life and Passion of Christ. It is, in fact, a translation of a work attributed to Bonaventure (in Vol. VIII of the Quaracchi edition, 1898). The later Chancellor of the University of Paris, Robert Ciboule (1403–58), wrote a tract in the vernacular entitled *Livre de saincte meditacion en cognoissance de soy*, in which he describes a technique of meditation and a theory of contemplation. Cf. A. Combes, 'Un témoin du socratisme chrétien au XVe siècle, Robert Ciboule', *AHDLMA*, 8 (1933), pp. 93–259.

9. *De distinctione verarum revelationum a falsis* (hereinafter *De distinctione*), G.3, pp. 36–56; *De prob.*, G.9, pp. 177–85; *De examinatione doctrinarum* (hereinafter *De exam.*), G.9, pp. 458–75.

10. *De distinctione*, G.3, pp. 39, 55–6.

11. *Ibid.*, p. 56. The coin metaphor was often used with reference to the soul as the true or 'worn down' image of God. It appears in Augustine, Bede, Bernard, Tauler and Ruysbroeck. Cf. E. Colledge, *The Medieval Mystics of England* (New York, 1961), p. 21.

12. *De distinctione*, G.3, pp. 39–55.

13. A tribute was paid to Gerson in this century when the two earlier treatises were translated into English, commented upon and schematised for current use by Catholic pastors, in P. Boland, *The Concept of Discretio Spirituum in John Gerson's*

'*De probatione spirituum*' and '*De distinctione verarum visionum a falsis*' (Washington, 1959).

14. E.g., Walter Hilton, *Scale*, Book I, chs. 10 & 11, pp. 14–18; *The Cloud of Unknowing by an English Mystic of the Fourteenth Century*, ed. J. McCann (London, 1943) (hereinafter *Cloud*), ch. 48, pp. 61–3.

15. *M.T. spec.*, G.3, p. 252. Cf. Bonaventure, *Itin.*, I, 7.

16. *M.T. spec.*, G.3, pp. 252, 274ff.

17. Connolly, pp. 176–80. There is indeed a link between some of Gerson's mystical writings and the Spanish school: via the *Spiritual Exercises* of Garcia de Cisneroa to Ignatius, and via the *Tercer Abecedario* of Francis of Osura to St Theresa. By the sixteenth century a number of Gerson's spiritual works, including *La Montaigne* and the combined treatise on mystical theology, had been translated into Spanish.

18. D. Knowles, *The English Mystical Tradition* (London, 1961), pp. 2–3. The passage is used by others, e.g., by S. E. Ozment, *Mysticism and Dissent: Religious Ideology and Social Protest in the Sixteenth Century* (New Haven, 1973) (hereinafter *Mysticism and Dissent*), pp. 3–4. Cf. F. Oakley, *Western Church*, p. 90.

19. Cf. St Thomas who, following Richard of St Victor, defines contemplation as 'a simple gaze upon truth' (*S.Th.*, II–II, q.180, a.3, ad I).

20. William of St Thierry's *Epistola ad fratres de Monte Dei*, trans. T. Berkeley (Spencer, Mass., 1971) (hereinafter *Epistola*) is a good example from the twelfth century of a treatise that combines all three types of writing on mysticism. It was frequently recommended by Gerson to his students and readers, though he thought that the author was Bernard.

21. Cf. *Videmus nunc*, G.7, pp. 1123–37; *Factum est*, G.7, p. 623; *In nomine patris*, G.7, p. 678; *La Mendicité*, G.7, pp. 279–80. Hilton's *Scale* portrays the same sort of flowing from the good Christian life through various degrees of contemplation culminating in the full 'reform in faith and feeling', i.e. the mystical experience.

22. Father Jean Leclercq, writing the introduction to a collection of papers originally given at a conference on spirituality, applauds the authors for defining their terms, particularly 'mysticism', and reports that 'In all instances mysticism was a complex blend of knowledge, reasoning, wisdom, love, intuition, poetry, contemplation of divine truth and its service among men.' The statement occurs in E. R. Elder, ed., *The Spirituality of Western Christendom* (Kalamazoo, Michigan, 1976), p. xxx.

23. To be fair to Knowles, one must acknowledge that he does discuss the questions about elites and grace later in the chapter.

24. Edited by E. Colledge and J. C. Marler, '*Tractatus magistri Johannis Gerson de mistica theologia*: St. Pölten, Diözesanarchiv MS. 25', *MS*, 41 (1979) (hereinafter 'Tractatus'), pp. 362–70.

25. *Harvest*, pp. 323–40. Actually Oberman uses 'speculative', not 'intellective', but it seems best here to reserve 'speculative' for mystical meta-theology and for scholastic theology, setting them both apart from the practical aspects of mystical theology. For references to other historians who use the two-fold distinction see Ozment, *Age of Reform*, p. 116, n. 110.

26. 'Mysticism', pp. 67–92. On p. 68, n. 1, Ozment briefly discusses the German criticisms. Oakley, *Western Church*, pp. 95–100, succinctly summarises them and Ozment's and adds evidence of his own.

27. *S.Th.*, II–II, q.180, a.1, R.

28. *Talks of Instruction*, no. 6, in *Meister Eckhardt: Selected Treatises and Sermons*, trans. J. M. Clark and J. V. Skinner (London, 1958) (hereinafter *Meister Eckhardt*), pp. 68–71. Cf. the sermon on eternal birth in R. B. Blakney, *Meister Eckhardt: A*

Modern Translation (New York, 1941), pp. 118–24. Both these pieces were originally in the vernacular.

29. *John Tauler, Spiritual Conferences*, ed. Colledge, Sermons XXII, p. 66; XXXVII, p. 76; XLIV, pp. 121–4.

30. *The Theologia Germanica of Martin Luther*, trans. B. Hoffman (London, 1980).

31. *Cloud*, ch. 8, p. 17.

32. *Scale*, Book I, ch. 8, p. 11.

33. *Eluc.*, G.8, p. 158; *Magnificat*, G.8, p. 308. The idea is found in Augustine, *De trinitate*, x, 1 and 2. Cf. Suso's *Horologium sapientiae*, ed. P. Kunzle (Freiburg, 1977), p. 383. It was, in fact, a commonplace among late medieval religious writers.

34. Augustine also, of course, carries the message that love is very important. This message stems not only from the New Testament, but also from Neo-Platonism, in fact from Plato himself, for whom one cannot know the unchangeable good without loving it.

35. *Bernard of Clairvaux, On the Song of Songs*, trans. K. Walsh *et al.*, 4 vols. (Spencer, Mass., and Kalamazoo, Michigan, 1971–80), Sermon 37:1, Vol. II, p. 181; Sermon 8:6, Vol. I, pp. 49–50.

36. *Epistola*, Book II, p. 99.

37. *Itin., passim.*

38. *Age of Reform*, p. 116.

39. Clark and Skinner, *Meister Eckhardt*, pp. 92–3.

40. For Gerson's criticisms of Ruysbroeck see his two letters to the Carthusian Bartholomew Clantier, written in 1402 and 1408 respectively, G.2, pp. 55–62, 97–103. Cf. *M.T. spec.*, G.3, p. 286. Cf. Combes, *Essai*, where the criticism is thoroughly discussed.

41. Cf. John of Ruysbroeck, *The Adornment of Spiritual Marriage*, Book III, ch. 3, in C. A. Wynschenk, trans., *The Adornment of Spiritual Marriage; The Sparkling Stone; The Book of Supreme Truth* (London, 1951), p. 174.

42. G.2, p. 60; G.3, p. 286.

43. E. Gilson, *History of Christian Philosophy in the Middle Ages*, p. 240.

44. *A Deo exivit*, G.5, p. 14.

45. *Epistola*, Book II, p. 94.

46. There is no necessary connection between heretical essentialism and intellective mysticism. The crude two–fold classification leaves one with the impression that if a theologian sees mysticism as a penetration of the divine intelligence by the human intellect and at the same time sees God's intellect as identical with His being, then he must see the union as a union of essences in which the distinction between Creator and creature is lost (cf. Oakley, *Western Church*, pp. 94–5; Ozment, *Age of Reform*, p. 116). But in the quoted passage, William is taking up a voluntarist position – 'for God to will and to be are the same thing' – and is seeing mysticism as based on the soul's will and love, and yet he, too, is tending toward the essentialist heresy.

Eckhardt certainly stressed the unity of God's intellect with his essence (cf. Clark and Skinner, *Meister Eckhardt*, pp. 208–12; Gilson, *History of Christian Philosophy*, pp. 439–40). But the fact that it was he and other members of his 'intellective school' who strayed furthest into pantheism was not because they were intellective mystics or Thomists, but because they were very strongly influenced by the Plotinian doctrine of emanation and return as found in the Dionysian corpus. Although Dionysius influenced just about all medieval mystical writers, the majority were too firmly rooted in the Christian doctrine of creation to take up Plotinian emanationism.

47. In *M.T. spec.* also Gerson links Ruysbroeck and Bernard.

48. Cf. R. E. Lerner, 'The image of mixed liquids in late medieval mystical thought', *CH*, 40 (1971) (hereinafter 'Mixed liquids'), pp. 397–410.

49. *Bernard of Clairvaux, Treatises II*, trans. A. Conway and T. Walton (Washington, 1974), p. 120. Cf. *On the Song of Songs*, Vol. IV, Sermon 71:5, p. 52.

50. *Itin.*, VII, 4.

51. *Itin.*, IV, 8. Cf. *Brevil.*, V, ch. 1.

52. It should be noted that both Eckhardt and Ruysbroeck drew back from their more extreme statements when criticised. Cf. J. M. Clark, *Meister Eckhardt: An Introduction to the Study of His Works* (London, 1957), pp. 21–5; Ruysbroeck, *The Sparkling Stone*, ch. 10, in Wynschenk, *op. cit.*, pp. 208–12.

53. G.8, p. 45. By 'abstractive' knowledge of God, Gerson means, as his next paragraph makes clear, that just as we can gain a general conception of man as such by abstracting from accidents of shape, place, motion etc., so we can form a proper concept of God by abstracting Being from all potentiality, privation, dependence and any other imperfections. By 'intuitive' knowledge Gerson presumably means a penetrating grasp of God's true nature.

54. G.8, pp. 160–1. Rachel is the figure most often used by Richard of St Victor to represent the contemplative life (in opposition to Leah, the representative of the active life).

55. Cf. A. Combes, *Profil*, Vol. II, pp. 451ff.

56. The reference to Mary seated is no help, because nearly all mystical writers mention Mary and Martha at some point or other as representatives of the contemplative and active lives respectively. Whether Mary was seated at Jesus' feet loving and experiencing or loving and experiencing and thinking is not a question generally discussed. The bride leaning on her beloved suggests Bernard, but this is a figure also used by Richard and Hugh of St Victor and many others.

57. G.2, pp. 259–63.

58. G.2, pp. 261–2.

59. Cf. Combes, *Profil*, Vol. II, pp. 532–3.

60. There seem to be only two occasions when Bonaventure is named as a purely affective mystical writer: here and at the beginning of the *Elucidation* (G.8, p. 155), where Gerson again links him with Hugh of Balma, the latter being actually named on this occasion. The reference is to the seventh chapter of the *Itinerarium*. In *M.T. prac.*, where Bonaventure is put with those who hold that abstractive knowledge is involved in mysticism, the reference is to the sixth chapter.

61. *Eluc.*, G.8, p. 155. Cf. a letter to Oswald (1428), G.2, p. 320, where Gerson says that Hugh asks 'si affectus possit fieri in deum sine cognitione praevia vel comite, et determinat quod sic,...'.

62. *Magnificat*, G.8, pp. 308–9.

63. 'Ergo primo affectus movetur in deum sine cogitatione praevia intellectus, sed potius ipsum sequitur.' In A. C. Peltier (ed.), *S. Bonaventurae Opera Omnia*, Vol. VIII, p. 49.

64. *Ibid.*, p. 50.

65. Luther, though, thought Dionysius 'more Platonising than Christianising' (*plus Platonisans quam Christianisans*) (*De captivitate Babylonica, WA*, 6, p. 562).

66. *Eluc.*, G.8, p. 159. The article in question was one of the errors of Avicenna, who had argued that nothing positive could be known or said about God. Cf. Combes, *Profil*, Vol. II, p. 432. In *M.T. spec.*, G.3, p. 252, also, Gerson is critical of this position. 'Who', he asks, 'would say that mystical theology follows only a negative way, leaving no positive knowledge or experience of God?'

67. *Treatise against Gerson* in Vansteenberghe, *Docte ignorance*, p. 200. On Vincent's definitions, Bonaventure's journey would consist of six stages of contemplation and then a final one of *theologia mystica*. Whether Vincent is correct in seeing himself and Hugh of Balma and others holding the same position as the only 'pure' Dionysians is another question.

68. In *De triplici via* Bonaventure, having traversed various levels of contemplation, arrives at Dionysius' negative way, by which it is understood that God is above all concepts. He goes on: 'Then the vision of truth, having experienced the night of the intellect, rises higher and penetrates deeper, because it exceeds the intellect itself as well as every created thing. This is the most noble manner of elevation. To be perfect, however, it postulates the affirmative manner, as perfection supposes illumination, and as negation supposes affirmation.' In *The Works of Bonaventure*, Vol. 1, *Mystical opuscula*, p. 93. This would seem to indicate that the mystical experience, for Bonaventure, does at least involve previous knowledge (Hugh of Balma's *cognitio praevia*).

69. *The Mystical Theology*, ch. 1, in *Dionysius the Areopagite : The Divine Names and The Mystical Theology*, trans. C. E. Rolt (London, 1940), pp. 191–4.

70. E.g., *M.T. spec.*, G.3, p. 274.

71. *Magnificat*, G.8, p. 308. The word 'mens' for Gerson and other medieval writers usually means the spiritual soul as a whole, 'heart and mind', as we might say, rather than the intellect alone. Cf. Bonaventure's *Itinerarium mentis*.

72. *De libris legendis a monacho* (1426), G.9, p. 613: 'debet tamen omnis christianus ad illos aspirare quoniam theologia haec mystica proprie est christianorum'.

73. G.7, pp. 29–30. Cf. *Magnificat*, G.8, p. 310: 'The spirit [*mens*] must desist from all cognitive and affective activity about any creature, even about itself, and be in the most utter silence and finally die to every creature in order to live alone to God.'

The idea of being asleep to the world but awake to eternity occurs in Gregory, *Moral.*, VI, 56, *MPL*, 75:760. The dark cloud is reminiscent of Dionysius, though, like Richard of St Victor, Gerson has the cloud obscuring the world, rather than being the superessential God, which it is for Dionysius.

74. Cf. *Cloud*, chs. 18 and 19, pp. 29–30, where the author discusses the complaints of actives against contemplatives.

75. William of Auvergne (1191–1249), a professor at the University of Paris, and later Bishop of Paris, wrote the *Rhetorica divina seu Ars oratoria eloquentiae divinae*, in *Opera omnia* (Orléans–Paris, 1674), Vol. 1, pp. 336–405.

76. For *M.T. prac.* Gerson borrowed much from *La Montaigne*, but in the Latin treatise he writes much more about union.

77. *Essai*, Vol. III, pp. 130–74. Combes argues that the two vernacular tracts are about asceticism, not mysticism. This, I think, is incorrect. The goal Gerson sets before his readers is the mystical encounter, and he does write something about it, while the ascent, which of course involves asceticism, is similar to that described by other medieval mystical writers, e.g. William of St Thierry, Hilton, Tauler, the author of *Theologia Germanica*. There is a common denominator of themes in all.

78. Hugh of St Victor, *De arrha animae*, *MPL*, 176:951–70. Bonaventure, *Soliloquium de quattuor mentalibus exercitiis* in *The Works of Bonaventure*, trans. J. de Vinck, Vol. III (Patterson, New Jersey, 1966), pp. 33–129.

79. Hilton, *Scale*, Book 1, chs. 24 and 25, pp. 36–7. Eckhardt, *On Detachment*, in Clark and Skinner, *Meister Eckhardt*, pp. 164–5.

80. The basic answer here Gerson could have found in Hugh of St Victor's *De modo orandi deum*, *MPL*, 176:977–81. This is another of the books that Gerson frequently recommends.

81. Cf. Bonaventure, *Soliloquium*, p. 105; Gregory, *Moral.*, XX, 61, *MPL*, 76:173–4.

82. *Mendicité*, G.7, p. 238; *M.T. spec.*, G.3, pp. 289–90: 'Oratio...est elevatio mentis in deum per pium at humilem affectum.' Cf. William of St Thierry, *Epistola*, p. 71: 'Prayer is the affection of a man who clings to God.'

83. Contrast the Latin prayers composed by Nicholas de Clamanges, Gerson's friend and contemporary. These are more restrained and polished and less diffuse than Gerson's prayers, and they have a sustained poetic beauty. But the basic tone is similar. Cf. J. Leclercq, 'Les Prières inédites de Nicholas de Clamanges', *Revue d'ascetique et mystique*, 23 (1947), pp. 171-83.

84. Cf. Bonaventure, *De triplici via*, p. 74; Tauler, Sermon XVII, in Colledge, *Spiritual Conferences*, p. 340.

85. G.7, pp. 232-3.

86. *Ibid.*, p. 253.

87. *Ibid.*, p. 248. The same insistence on the soul's rights is a major feature of William of Auvergne's *Rhetorica divina*. William models the art of prayer on the classical art of pleading in court, where the advocate must make the best case he can for his client. William, too, writes of the soul in all humility holding out its large bag to receive divine gifts (ch. 31). Gerson has used material from this treatise but adapted it for a different audience.

88. G.7, pp. 265-7. This passage does bear some resemblance to parts of Hugh of St Victor's *De arrha animae*.

89. G.7, pp. 276-80. The mystical encounter is always fleeting. There is hardly a mystical writer who fails to say this.

90. Before he launches into his argument, Gerson gives one of his lists of sound authors: Gregory (*Moral.*), Bernard (Song of Songs), and Richard of St Victor. Later in the tract he refers to Dionysius, Augustine, Hugh of St Victor, William of Auvergne and the *Horologium sapientiae* (Suso).

The longest of Gerson's list of mystical writers is the bibliography appended to *M.T. spec.* In first place is Dionysius, followed by Richard, Hugh, Augustine, Cassian, Gregory (especially Book VI of *Moral.*), Bernard, Bonaventure. He then lists a few 'new' works, among them *De ornatu spiritualium nuptiarum* 'cuius tertia pars suspecta est'. This is Ruysbroeck's. The only author named in this short section is Hugh of Balma (G.3, p. 293). Often when he is recommending mystical writers Gerson singles out Bonaventure as especially good, and he advises particularly the *Itinerarium* and the *Breviloquium*, e.g. in *De libris legendis a monacho*, G.9, pp. 612-13.

Book VI of Gregory's *Moralia* was obviously a quarry which Gerson mined thoroughly for a number of chapters of *The Mountain*.

91. G.7, pp. 16-22. Cf. Hilton, *Scale*, Book I, ch. 4, pp. 6-7. Hilton here describes what he calls the first degree of contemplation but which is really another type of contemplation, for intellectuals, attained by reason. It is, however, only a shadow of true contemplation, Hilton writes, as it involves no inward experience. Moreover, both bad and good men can have it. However, if intellectuals are also humble and have charity they are pursuing something which will dispose them for true contemplation. Unfortunately knowledge more often leads to pride. This is very similar to the view Gerson holds.

92. *Contra curiositatem*, G.3, pp. 233-49. Gerson was not the first to attack *curiositas*, which had for Christian writers the sense of an inordinate desire to know. The biblical source is probably I John 2:16, where the phrase is 'the lust of the eyes' (*concupiscentia oculorum*). Augustine in *Confessiones*, X, 35, *CSEL*, 33, p. 267 interprets this as *curiosa cupiditas* and discusses many kinds of what we should call 'idle curiosity'. Bernard in *The Steps of Humility and Pride*, in *Bernard of Clairvaux, Treatises II* (Washington, 1974), pp. 57, 70, lists curiosity as the first step of pride and singularity as the fifth. Cf. Gregory, *Moral.*, VI, 19, *MPL*, 75, pp. 739-40; Thomas à Kempis, *Of the Imitation of Christ*, Book I, ch. 5. At times it has been thought that Gerson was the author of *The Imitation*. The consensus now is that he was not. Cf. A. Ampe, *L'Imitation de Jésus-Christ et son autour* (Rome, 1973). The Latin style is quite different from Gerson's and it is clearly a work written by a monk for religious. Moreover, the author is more anti-intellectualist than Gerson.

93. *M.T. spec.*, G.3, pp. 274-9. For a full discussion of this work see Ozment, *Homo Spiritualis*, pp. 49-83.

94. *Eluc.*, G.8, pp. 158-9. Cf. *M.T. spec.*, G.3, p. 277; *Letter on Bernard* (1402), G.2, p. 55; *Tractatus de oculo* (1424), G.8, p. 153.

95. *Homiliae in Ezechielem prophetam*, Book II, Hom. 5:19, 20, *MPL*, 76:996.

96. *Moral.*, VI, 12, *MPL*, 75:735-6. Cf. Augustine, *Confessiones*, VIII, 8, *CSEL*, 33, p. 186.

97. Sermon 52:2, Vol. III, p. 97. Cf. Sermon 83:1, Vol. IV, p. 180.

98. Sermon III, p. 84, *Spiritual Conferences*, ed. Colledge. Cf. Sermon x, p. 61; Sermon XXIII, p. 204. Cf. Ruysbroeck, *The Sparkling Stone*, v, p. 198: 'The first work which God works in all men in common consists in His calling and inviting them all, without exception, to union with Himself.'

99. *Letter to a Franciscan* (1426), G.2, p. 280. The *Breviloquium*, Bonaventure's small *summa theologiae*, has blended together perfectly spirituality and theology. However, because the work is so concise, the intellect, though enlightened, is left with a number of puzzles. Contrast Thomas' *Summa*, where all possible difficulties seem to be dealt with. Gerson himself, though he admires Bonaventure above all, does not write like him. Gerson tends to punctuate much of his writing with the discussion of awkward questions.

Bonaventure has set out Gerson's ideal of a blend between devotion and learning in *Itin.*, Prologue: 'We must not believe that it is enough to read without unction, to speculate without devotion, to investigate without admiration, to observe without joy, to act without piety, to know without love, to understand without humility, to study without divine grace.' Cf. *Itin.*, IV, 8, where the message is 'love that you might understand'.

100. E.g. *Benedic haereditati*, G.5, p. 119; *First Letter to Clantier*, G.2, p. 62. The source of the comparison is Ecclesiasticus 24:27. The comparison is used also by Bernard in the same way as Gerson, e.g. Sermon 8:6, Vol. I, p. 49, and by Bonaventure, *In Hexam.*, I, 8 (*Opera omnia*, Vol. 5, p. 330).

101. *Magnificat*, G.8, p. 303. Most of the writers who attack idle curiosity state that the knowledge of useful things that does not 'puff up' is good. E.g., Bernard, Sermon 36:2, Vol. II, pp. 174-5. Bernard recalls Paul, who did not forbid thinking, only inordinate thinking (Rom. 12:3).

102. '...sublimius quam rudis et simplex christianus'. *Anagogicum de verbo et hymno gloriae* (hereinafter *Anag.*) (1428), G.8, p. 553.

103. Gerson probably did meet with some scorn in his attempt to turn back the theological clock to the thirteenth century. In *Magnificat*, G.8, p. 303, he bemoans the times in which he lives when such doctors as Gregory, Bernard, Augustine and Bonaventure are derided as naive and old-fashioned (*idiotas et vetulas*), and their teaching regarded as good only for preaching and devotion, as if, Gerson says, devotion and learning could not go together.

104. G.7, pp. 17-18.

105. For details of this controversy see Combes, *Profil.*, Vol. I, pp. 121-36.

106. *La Montaigne*, G.7, pp. 27-8; *M.T. prac.*, G.8, pp. 19-23.

107. *Moral.*, VI, 56-61, *MPL*, 75:760-5. Cf. Thomas, *S.Th.*, II-II, q.182, a.4. Thomas uses Gregory extensively in qq.179-82 on the active and contemplative lives.

108. *La Montaigne*, G.7, p. 28. The preference for a mixed life, though by no means necessarily a half-and-half mixture, is found in many mystical writers. Few would deny the need for even cloistered contemplatives to undertake works of fraternal charity when desirable. Plato himself wanted his philosophers to come down to the market place in turns to help govern the republic. Cf. Augustine, *De civitate dei*, XIX, 19; Bernard, Sermon 23:1, 2, Vol. II, pp. 25–7; William of St Thierry, *Epistola*, Book II, p. 76; Eckhardt, Fragment 14, in Blakney, *Meister Eckhardt*, p. 238; Ruysbroeck, *The Sparkling Stone*, ch. XIV, pp. 220–1. Cf. R. Petry, 'Social responsibility and the late medieval mystics', *CH*, 21 (1952), pp. 3–19.

109. *M.T. prac.*, G.8, p. 24.

110. *La Montaigne*, G.7, pp. 35–8.

111. *Ibid.*, p. 30. Cf. *De libris legendis a monacho*, G.9, p. 673. Gerson's democratic mysticism is analogous to the sixteenth-century Zwingli's universalism. For Zwingli salvation was universal in the sense that it *could* be granted by God to those living in the era before Christ's Redemption as well as to those living afterwards. But this did not mean that all would be saved. Cf. M. Schuler and J. Schulthess (eds.), *Huldreich Zwinglis Werke* (Zurich, 1828), Vol. IV, p. 115. Cf. G. W. Locher, *Zwingli's Thought: New Perspectives* (Leiden, 1981), pp. 121–41. Zwingli's universalism is therefore different from that of Hans Denck (*c.* 1500–1527) which apparently did involve the ultimate salvation of all. Cf. G. Baring and W. Fellman (eds.) *Hans Denck: Schriften*, Part II (Gütersloh, 1960), pp. 27–47.

Gerson's democratic mysticism should, on the other hand, be contrasted with the doctrine of Thomas Müntzer. For the latter 'mystical faith' appears to have been a pre-requisite for salvation. Cf. H.-J. Goertz, *Innere und äussere Ordnung in der Theologie Thomas Müntzers* (Leiden, 1967). For Gerson, salvation was entirely possible without mystical achievement.

112. *La Montaigne*, G.7, pp. 21–4.

113. *Imitation*, Book I, chs. 8, 10; Book II, ch. 5.

114. *Scale*, Book II, ch. 37, pp. 261–2.

115. This analogy is also used by Tauler, Sermon XX, *Spiritual Conferences*, ed. Colledge, pp. 90–1.

116. Cf. Rolle's feelings of fire, song, and sweetness (*calor, canor, dulcor*), *The Fire of Love*, trans. C. Wolters (London, 1972), ch. 14, pp. 88–9.

The origin of the 'son sans son' is perhaps the prayer for priests in preparation for mass, found in missals as early as the twelfth century: 'Summe Sacerdos: Intret spiritus tuus bonus in cor meum, qui sonet ibi sine sono.' Cf. A. Wilmar, *Auteurs spirituels et textes dévots du moyen âge latin* (Paris, 1932), pp. 101ff.

117. *La Montaigne*, G.7, p. 26.

118. Hugh of St Victor, *In Ecclesiasten*, MPL, 175:117.

119. *La Montaigne*, G.7, p. 26.

120. Like Mary and Martha, Rachel and Leah were frequently used to represent the contemplative and active lives. Gerson is following Gregory (*Moral.*, VI, 59–61, MPL, 75:763–5) quite closely here.

121. *La Mendicité*, G.7, p. 252.

122. *Moral.*, IX, 26, MPL, 75:874.

123. Sermon VIII, *Spiritual Conferences*, ed. Colledge, p. 53. Cf. Bonaventure, *Soliloquium*, ch. 3, pp. 56–60.

124. G.7, p. 280.

125. *La Montaigne*, G.7, pp. 30–1.

126. Bernard distinguishes between these two solitudes in Sermon 40:5, Vol. II, pp. 202–3.

127. *La Montaigne*, G.7, p. 39. This is a commonplace. Cf. Bernard, *De praecepto et dispensatione*, ch. 20:60, MPL, 182:943; Bonaventure, *Soliloquium*, ch. 4, p. 109.

128. *La Montaigne*, G.7, pp. 39–41. In this passage Gerson uses both 'thought' and 'love', sometimes interchangeably, sometimes not.

Most medieval mystical writers describe a state of 'recollection', where one retires into oneself, shutting out everything else. Often this is the state where one seeks to know oneself, to realise that one is nothing. Gerson's state of solitude and silence seems to be a stage beyond this. However, there are infinite variations of the same themes: penitence, detachment, recollection, humility or 'self-stripping', extinction of phantasms from the mind, union. Ruysbroeck, for instance, sees three main stages. The faithful servants of God are those who pursue external works of virtue and mortification (works of the active life). The secret friends of God have achieved a loving and inward cleaving to God; they are wholly turned to God, but they still keep something of their own selfhood. It is only the hidden sons of God who have died to self and who go forth into God, free from images, lifted up by love, above reason and without reason (*The Sparkling Stone*, chs. VII, VIII, IX, pp. 194–207).

129. E.g. VI, 14, 39, 40, 41, 46, *MPL*, 75:737, 750–2, 754.

130. Cf. Hilton, *Scale*, ch. 38, pp. 54–5, where similar advice is given about dealing with temptations.

131. *La Montaigne*, G.7, pp. 41–6. One theme that is not very prominent in Gerson's two vernacular tracts is that of the imitation of Christ's suffering. This is a theme that a number of other late medieval mystics develop, e.g. Suso, Tauler, Thomas à Kempis, Julian of Norwich, Margery Kempe. It appears strongly in the sixteenth-century radical reformer Thomas Müntzer. In *La Montaigne* (G.7, p. 47), when he is discussing various methods of meditation and prayer, Gerson does refer to Bernard's sermon on the sufferings of Christ, but he does not develop the theme (Bernard, Sermon 43, Vol. II, pp. 220–4).

132. *La Montaigne*, G.7, pp. 52–3.

133. *Videmus nunc*, G.7, pp. 1134–7.

134. 'Amor intrat ubi cognitio foris stat.' Gerson gives his source: Hugh of St Victor. But the statement is a commonplace.

135. G.7, p. 1136. Gerson uses the image of the two feet quite often, e.g., *Ad deum vadit*, G.5, p. 7; *Le Jardin amoureux*, G.7, p. 145. Combes thinks that Gerson owes this image to Bertrand de Alen's *De novo saeculo*, a work Gerson knew (*Essai*, III, p. 151). 'Amor transformat in amatum' is reminiscent of Bonaventure, *Itin.*, VIII, 5: 'apex affectus totus transferatur et transformetur in deum'.

136. G.7, p. 1136.

137. In the Latin sermon *Fulcite me* (probably 1402), for the feast of St Bernard, Gerson, in his explication of the mysticism of Bernard's sermons on the Song of Songs, uses the same image: 'Illic ipsa concipit et fit verbigena' (G.5, p. 336). Bernard does not say this. For him, Christ, the Word, is the bridegroom. Bernard does write of the bride's children, but these are the works of fraternal charity performed by the bride after she has enjoyed the bridegroom (Sermon 85, Vol. IV, p. 209). The theme of the birth of the Word in the soul occurs frequently in Eckhardt, e.g., Sermon 3 in Blakney, *Meister Eckhardt*, pp. 109–17, and in Tauler, e.g., Sermon 1 in Colledge, *Spiritual Conferences*, pp. 153–8.

138. *Videmus nunc*, G.7, pp. 1135–7.

139. *Contra curiositatem*, G.3, p. 249.

140. *M.T. spec.*, G.3, p. 274. By 'foolish wisdom' Gerson and Dionysius (*Divine Names*, ch. 7, pp. 146–54) mean wisdom that seems foolish in the eyes of the world. Cf. I Cor. 1:25: 'The foolishness of God is wiser than men.' 'Irrational and mindless' refers to the fact that this wisdom, as Gerson states later in the lectures, 'transcends reason and mind, leaping up in an affection, not just any affection, but a pure one which is congruent with mental understanding and by which God is seen by the pure in heart' (*M.T. spec.*, G.3, p. 290).

141. *M.T. spec.*, G.3, p. 257. The distinctions are 'non re sed nomine'.

142. *Ibid.*, pp. 252–62. For a full discussion of Gerson's analysis see Ozment, *Homo Spiritualis*, pp. 59–91. Gerson owes something to Richard of St Victor's *Mystical Ark* and to Bonaventure's *Itinerarium* for his description of the powers of the soul and their activities. But it is not a slavish copying. There are notable differences in the analyses. All three writers are relying on St Augustine.

143. *Homo Spiritualis*, p. 64.

144. *M.T. spec.*, p. 262 (Ozment's translation, *Homo Spiritualis*, pp. 64–5).

145. Cf. *Videmus nunc*, where both the foot of intelligence and the foot of affection had to be advanced (G.7, p. 1136).

146. *M.T. spec.*, G.3, p. 270.

147. *Ibid.*, p. 273.

148. *Ibid.*, pp. 283–4.

149. *Ibid.*, p. 270.

150. *Ibid.*, p. 284.

151. G.7, p. 22. Gerson uses this sentence often. Cf. *M.T. spec.*, G.3, p. 290; *De simplificatione cordis*, G.8, p. 92. The biblical source is I John 4:8. In *La Montaigne* Gerson gives Augustine as his source. 'Amor ipse notitia est' is also found in Gregory, e.g., *Homiliae in Evangelia*, hom. 27, *MPL* 76:1207. Cf. Bernard, *De diversis*, Sermon 29:1; *MPL* 183:620; William of St Thierry, *Epistola*, Book I, ch. 68, where the words are 'Amor ipse intellectus est.'

152. *M.T. spec.*, G.3, p. 290. Cf. *M.T. prac.*, G.8, p. 44: 'Mystical theology is ecstatic love which accompanies the understanding of man, an understanding which is completely free of clouds of phantasms.'

153. *Super cant.* (1429), G.8, pp. 582–3. One might wonder how there can be 'bare speculation [*nuda speculatio*] of the truth' if there is a mutual indwelling of the powers. Gerson does not seem to hold with Plato that if one knows the truth by reason one automatically loves it. Gerson makes two points that are relevant to this question: love can enable the intellect to rise beyond itself; the mind heated by love may boil over and ascend where rational contemplation alone cannot take it (*M.T. spec.*, G.3, p. 275). Secondly, the speculative theologian does not necessarily conform to what he knows; he may lack practice or be still caught up in carnal and worldly desires (*ibid.*, p. 279). This reinforces Gerson's consistent position that in mystical theology love must lead the way.

154. *La Montaigne*, *M.T. spec.*, *M.T. prac.*

155. E.g., *Itin.*, IV, 3. Gerson gives William of Auxerre and Bonaventure as his sources when he uses the concept in *Notulae*, G.3, p. 215, and Aristotle and Basil as his sources in *Eluc.*, G.8, p. 159. Many mystical authors write about tasting and feeling God, e.g. *Theologia Germanica*, ch. 1, p. 60.

156. *De simplificatione cordis*, G.8, p. 92.

157. *Ibid.*

158. *Eluc.*, G.8, p. 159.

159. 'et fit mulcebris quaedam operatio experimentativa non reflexa nec declarativa vel enuntiativa' (*Eluc.*, G.8, p. 160).

160. *Ibid.*

161. *Ibid.*

162. *Super cant.*, G.8, p. 584. The biblical source is Ps. 34:8.

163. For a full discussion of this work see Combes, *Profil*, II, pp. 395–465.

164. *Eluc.*, G.8, pp. 156–7.

165. *Ibid.*, p. 157.

166. G.8, p. 313. The analogy is in Dionysius' *Mystical Theology*, ch. 2, p. 195. Gerson's reproduction is faithful, though expanded.

167. Gerson uses the same Dionysian image in his vernacular sermon *Videmus nunc*

(G.7, p. 1134) to illustrate one of the ways by which we can gain knowledge of God. Gerson may well be correct in his positive interpretation of Dionysius' negative way. Cf. Rolt (p. 195, n. 1), who argues that 'if Dionysius were open to the charge of pure negativity so often brought against him, he would have wanted to destroy his block of marble instead of carving it'.

168. *Magnificat*, G.8, p. 311.

169. *Ibid.*, pp. 311–12.

170. Dionysius, *Mystical Theology*, ch. 1 (from the passage quoted by Bonaventure and translated by G. Boas, *The Mind's Road to God* (New York, 1953), p. 45). Gregory writes of chinks in the obscure clouds through which divine rays can penetrate, e.g., *Moral*, V, 52, MPL, 75:707. Cf. Richard of St Victor who, like Gerson, has two darknesses. The upper one for him, the cloud of unknowing in God, could be pierced to emit rays of light (Knowles, *The English Mystical Tradition*, p. 32). Cf. Bernard (Sermon 57:8, Vol. III, p. 103): 'this ray of intense brightness will pour itself in not through open doors but through chinks and crevices'.

171. 'Sed eciam in actu tali semper cognicio perceptive et practica comictatur et sequitur' (Colledge and Marler, 'Tractatus', p. 365).

172. *M.T. spec.*, G.3, p. 290. For the quarrel between Cusa and Vincent see Vansteenberghe, *Docte ignorance*, pp. 19–36.

173. *Treatise against Gerson*, in Vansteenberghe, *Docte ignorance*, p. 197.

174. *Ibid.*, p. 198.

175. 'The venerable doctor does not always agree with the text of Dionysius, or with the expositors of Dionysius, or with the practitioners of the art of mystical theology…' (*Treatise against Gerson*, p. 189). Cusa came to Gerson's defence, arguing that it was Vincent, not Gerson, who misunderstood Dionysius.

176. *Homo Spiritualis*, pp. 50–83.

177. Combes, *Profil*, I, pp. 175–9.

178. *Eluc.* (1424), *Magnificat* (1428), *Super cant.* (1429), *Commentary on Dionysius' Mystical Theology* (1429).

179. Gerson may not, as Combes suggests, have fully worked out this last doctrine by 1400 when he wrote *The Mountain*. But he says nothing there to preclude it. The fact that he re-edited his combined treatise on speculative and practical mystical theology with only minor alterations in 1422, 1423 and 1429 is an indication of a basic consistency of position. There would be nothing wrong, of course, in inconsistency over a lifetime.

180. This is true of F. Scalvini, 'Lo scrittore mistico Giovanni Gersone, 1363–1429', *Rivista di ascetica e mistico*, 8 (1963), pp. 40–60. Colledge and Marler ('Tractatus'), although their article contains an attack on both Combes and Gerson, appear to rely on Combes for the 'wavering' up to 1425. For the 'wavering' after 1425 they rely on the MS they have discovered of Gerson's commentary on Dionysius' *Mystical Theology*, and on a brief letter written by Gerson in 1428 to Oswald of Corda, a Carthusian, about Hugh of Balma's *Viae Sion lugent* (G.2, p. 320). The commentary, as we have seen, restates Gerson's earlier position on concomitant knowledge in mystical union. In the letter Gerson states firmly that Hugh of Balma's insistence that the affect can be carried to God without previous or concomitant knowledge is contradicted by the nature of things and by 'every doctor, philosophical and theological, learned in mystical theology'.

181. S. E. Ozment, 'The university and the church: patterns of reform in Jean Gerson', *Medievalia et Humanistica*, N.S. 1 (1970), pp. 111–26. Combes, *Profil*, II, pp. 229–49.

182. G.2, pp. 259–63. Apart from editing Gerson's major mystical works, Combes has produced three books, comprising six very long volumes, on Gerson's mysticism.

183. G.2, p. 262. Cf. Combes, *Profil*, II, pp. 468–568.

184. *Profil*, II, p. 650.

185. Combes does find some evidence of the 'conversion' position in later works, but this is more than balanced by evidence of the 'pre-conversion' position, if indeed there are two positions.

186. G.7, p. 1136.

187. G.3, p. 287.

188. For other and more detailed criticism of Combes' 'conversion' thesis see A. Ampe, *Ruusbroec: Traditie en Werkelijkheid* (Antwerp, 1975), pp. 196–209, and Colledge and Marler, 'Tractatus', pp. 377–86. The latter, though their basic argument against Combes seems sound, have misunderstood Combes in one respect. They argue that it is part of Combes' thesis that after Gerson's 'conversion' Hugh of Balma and his *Viae Sion lugent* became the chancellor's guiding lights. In fact, Combes states precisely the reverse; he argues that after the 'conversion' Gerson abandoned Hugh of Balma and the Dionysian commentators. Cf. *Profil*, II, pp. 583, n. 49; 604ff.; 667, n. 417; 671.

189. G.7, pp. 23–6.

190. G.7, p. 38.

191. *La Mendicité*, G.7, p. 258.

192. G.8, p. 18.

193. G.3, p. 287.

194. *Itin.*, VII, 4.

195. Sermons X and XXV, *Spiritual Conferences*, ed. Colledge, pp. 63, 179. Not all mystical writers, of course, are working with exactly the same doctrine of the relation between grace and human effort. Hardly any, in their mystical writings, attempt to define the relationship with any precision.

196. G.8, pp. 318, 435.

197. *A deo exivit*, G.5, pp. 13–14.

198. G.3, pp. 286–7. Cf. G.2, p. 99, where, in the second letter to Clantier about Ruysbroeck, Gerson criticises the 'mixed liquids' metaphor even more strongly: 'It is to be repudiated without qualification.' Cf. *Spiritus domini* (1416), G.5, p. 531.

199. G.2, p. 260. Colledge and Marler, 'Tractatus', pp. 378–83, argue that Gerson is misinterpreting Ubertino and that therefore his attack is unfair.

200. G.3, p. 51.

201. *De distinctione*, G.3, p. 51. The words are Augustine's (*Tractatus in epistolam Joannis ad Parthos*, VII, 8, *MPL*, 35:2033), not Paul's.

202. *De consolatione theologiae*, G.9, p. 234.

203. *M.T. spec.*, G.3, pp. 255–6.

204. Cf. R. E. Lerner, *The Heresy of the Free Spirit in the Later Middle Ages* (Berkeley, California, 1972).

205. *De distinctione*, G.3, pp. 51–2.

206. Ed. R. Guarnieri, 'Il movimento del libero spirito', *Archivio italiano per la storia della pieta*, 4 (1965), pp. 501–635. For evidence of other Free Spirit writings containing pantheistic doctrines, see Lerner, 'Mixed liquids', pp. 403–6, 410–11. Lerner is of the opinion that Eckhardt's sermons influenced others to go further in a pantheistic direction than he did himself (p. 403).

207. Lerner, 'Mixed liquids', p. 408. This appears to be the opinion of Colledge and Marler also ('Tractatus', p. 586). Lerner argues that it was Gerson's influence that barred the use of the 'mixed liquids' image for the duration of the fifteenth century.

208. Lerner, 'Mixed liquids', pp. 404–5.
209. *Spiritual Conferences*, ed. Colledge, pp. 208–33.
210. *Ibid.*, p. 230.
211. *Ibid.*, p. 232.
212. Henry Suso, *The Little Book of Eternal Wisdom and the Little Book of Truth*, trans. J. M. Clark (New York, 1953), pp. 201–5.
213. *The Adornment of Spiritual Marriage*, Book II, chs. 66 and 67, pp. 154–66.
214. *Ibid.*, p. 159.
215. *The Theologia Germanica of Martin Luther*, pp. 90–2, 114–20.
216. *Scale*, Book II, ch. 26, p. 213.
217. E.g., *La Montaigne*, G.7, p. 55.
218. *Magnificat*, G.8, p. 310.
219. E.g., Sermon 74:5, 6, 7, Vol. IV, pp. 89–92.
220. *Profil*, II, pp. 537–9.
221. Bernard's sermons were written compositions, using the form of sermons, produced over a number of years. Cf. Jean Leclercq, introduction to Vol. II of the sermons, pp. vii–xxx.
222. Trans. F. Sherwood Taylor, *The Soul's Betrothal Gift* (Westminster, 1945), p. 11.
223. *Ibid.*, p. 25.
224. Sermon 78:3, Vol. IV, pp. 131–2.
225. *Epistola*, Book I, p. 21.
226. Bonaventure's *Soliloquium* is not entirely based on the bridal image. He, too, writes of the soul humbly begging for help.
227. G.7, pp. 144–54.
228. *Scale*, Book II, ch. 20, p. 191.
229. Ch. 29, pp. 100–2. The 'souls' in both Hugh of St Victor's *De arrha animae* and Bonaventure's *Soliloquium* ask questions, but they are much more easily led than is Gerson's 'soul' in the *Mendicité*. The latter persists in his awkward questioning.
230. The *Imitation* was written in Latin but despite its popularity and the praise it receives for being well-written, parts of Books I and II do not flow well at all, and there is a fair amount of repetition.
231. That mysticism is, by definition, dangerous to established churches and their institutional means for salvation has been argued by Ozment in *Mysticism and Dissent*. He shows the influence of medieval mysticism on sixteenth-century Protestant radicals who dissented from the established Lutheran and Calvinist churches. Cf. W. O. Packull, *Mysticism and the Early South German–Austrian Anabaptist Movement*, 1525–1531 (Scottdale, Pennsylvania, 1977).

7 Women, marriage and children

1. E.g., Bernardine, *Sermons*, p. 8, when the women in the congregation are urged to wake up their husbands, sons and brothers and bring them to hear sermons. Cf. Berthold of Regensburg (1220–72) in R. C. Petry, *No Uncertain Sound: Sermons that Shaped the Pulpit Tradition* (Philadelphia, 1948), p. 211: 'Ye women,...ye go to church more readily than men, and ye pray more readily than men, and come to hear preachers and to earn indulgences more readily than men.'
2. For discussions of New Testament doctrines on women, see G. H. Tavard, *Woman in Christian Tradition* (Notre Dame, Indiana, 1973), ch. 2; D. S. Bailey, *The Man–Woman Relation in Christian Thought* (London, 1959), ch. 2.
At least two factors seem to have combined to prevent the early Christian spirit

of feminine freedom and equality from permanently changing attitudes towards women or their actual status: the influence of existing Jewish and Gentile andro-centric customs and assumptions, and the spread of an ascetical spirit with consequent disparagement of sexuality and hence of women.

3. E. Power, 'The position of women', in *The Legacy of the Middle Ages*, ed. C. G. Crump and E. F. Jacob (Oxford, 1926), p. 433.

4. E. Power, *Medieval Women*, ed. M. M. Postan (Cambridge, 1975), *passim*.

5. 'The position of women', p. 410.

6. R. H. Hilton, *The English Peasantry in the Later Middle Ages* (Oxford, 1975), pp. 95–110. Hilton notes, however, that women's wages in France in the late Middle Ages were lower than men's, probably because of a different economic situation in this plague-ridden era from that prevailing in England, i.e., in England, population fell more than productive capacity and so the market was in the labourer's favour and higher wages (for males and females) could be obtained, whereas in France, because of the destructive wars fought on her soil, population fell less than pro-ductive capacity and so there was no 'golden age' for labourers (p. 102). Cf. F. & J. Gies, *Women in the Middle Ages* (New York, 1978), pp. 143–64. B. A. Hanawalt, 'Childrearing among the lower classes in late medieval England', *Journal of Interdisciplinary History* 8 (1977), p. 8, finds evidence from fourteenth-century coroners' rolls of women as well as men reaping, stacking hay and straw and taking grain to the mill.

7. R. C. Palmer, 'Contexts of marriage in medieval England: evidence from the king's court circa 1300', *Speculum*, 59 (1984), pp. 42–67.

8. *The Paston Letters*, ed. by J. Warrington, 2 vols. (London, 1956), *passim*.

9. J. McNamara and S. F. Wemple, 'Sanctity and power: the dual pursuit of medieval women', in *Becoming Visible: Women in European History*, ed. by R. Bridenthal and C. Koonz (Boston, 1977). Cf. D. Herlihy, 'The medieval marriage market', *Medieval and Renaissance Studies: Proceedings of the Southeastern Institute of Medieval and Renaissance Studies*, 1974, 6 (1976), pp. 3–27; K. Casey, 'The Cheshire cat: reconstructing the experience of medieval women', in *Liberating Women's History*, ed. by B. A. Carrol (Illinois, 1976), pp. 224–45.

10. D. M. Stenton, *The English Woman in History* (London, 1957), ch. 2; Hilton, *op. cit.*, p. 105; Casey, *op. cit.*, p. 233.

11. F. Olivier-Martin, *Histoire du droit français, des origines à la Révolution* (Paris, 1951), p. 654.

12. P. Petot, 'Le Statut de la femme dans les pays coutumiers français du XIIIe au XVIIIe siècle', in *Recueils de la Société Jean Bodin*, 12 (1962), pp. 243ff. Cf. J. R. Hale, *Renaissance Europe*, 1480–1520 (London, 1971), pp. 124–36. Hale argues that during this period the Roman notion that *in femina minus est rationis* was gaining ground, and that there is some indication that laws entitling widows to a proportion of their husband's effects at his death were being set aside. Casey, *op. cit.*, pp. 235–6, also notes a hardening position towards women in legal thought and the courts, beginning in Italy in the later Middle Ages and spreading from there to northern Europe by the sixteenth century. The trend was particularly evident in property law.

13. R. Metz, 'Le Statut de la femme en droit canonique médiéval', in *Recueils de la Société Jean Bodin*, 12 (1962), p. 59.

14. 'Propter conditionem servitutis, qua [mulier] viro in omnibus debet subesse', c. 33, q.5, *dictum post* c.11, ed. Friedberg, *Corpus juris can.*, I, col. 1254, cited in Metz, *op. cit.*, p. 74.

15. *S.Th.*, Supp., q.39, a.1, R. A male slave, however, Thomas continues, despite his state of servitude, can receive the sacrament of order validly, though not lawfully, because whereas 'a woman is subject by her nature, a slave is not' (*ibid.*, a.3, ad 4).

16. Metz, *op. cit.*, pp. 97–108. The exclusion of women from all liturgical functions owes more to the belief, inherited from Judaism, that women are 'unclean' than to the doctrine of the subjection of women.

17. *Ibid.*, pp. 83–6. Cf. J. T. Noonan, 'Power to choose', *Viator*, 4 (1973), pp. 419–34.

18. J. A. Brundage, 'Adultery and fornication: a study in legal theology', in V. L. Bullough and J. Brundage, eds., *Sexual Practices and the Medieval Church* (Buffalo, 1982), p. 131.

19. K. Thomas, 'The double standard', *Journal of the History of Ideas*, 20 (1959), pp. 195–216, argues that despite the opposition of Christian writers the double standard operated extensively in law and opinion in medieval as well as modern times.

20. E. M. Makowski, 'The conjugal debt and medieval canon law', *Journal of Medieval History*, 3 (1977), p. 111.

21. Metz, *op. cit.*, pp. 86–91. Cf. F. & J. Gies, *op. cit.*, p. 46.

22. For a full discussion of Augustine's position, together with the doctrines of major early and medieval theologians and Luther and Calvin, see the following: F. X. Arnold, *La Femme dans l'église* (Paris, 1955); Bailey, *op. cit.*; K. E. Borresen, *Subordination et équivalence: Nature et rôle de la femme d'après Augustin et Thomas d'Aquin* (Oslo, 1968); W. G. Cole, *Sex in Christianity and Psychoanalysis* (Oxford, 1955); R. R. Ruether, ed., *Religion and Sexism: Images of Women in the Jewish and Christian Traditions* (New York, 1974); Tavard, *op. cit.*

23. *De bono conjugali*, I, 1, CSEL, 41, p. 188. Cf. *De civitate dei*, XIX, 14, CCSL, 48, p. 681; Borresen, pp. 8off.

24. *De Gen. ad litt.*, IX, 5, CSEL, 28, p. 273.

25. 'It was necessary for woman to be made, as the Scripture says, as a helper to man; not indeed as a helpmate in other works, as some say, since man can be more efficiently helped by another man in other works, but as a helper in the work of generation.' *S.Th.*, I, q.92, a.1, R.

26. *S.Th.*, I, q.92, a.1, ad 1. Thomas explains that with regard to human nature in general woman is not misbegotten, but is included in nature's and therefore God's intention for the work of generation. For a discussion of the contribution of ancient and medieval medical opinion to the conception of the inferiority of women, see V. L. Bullough, 'Medieval medical and scientific views of women', *Viator*, 4 (1973), pp. 485–501.

27. *S.Th.*, I, q.92, a.1, ad 2. Thomas explains the difference between domestic or civil subjection and servile subjection. In the former the superior governs for the benefit of the inferior; in the latter only the interests of the superior are considered.

28. Tavard, *op. cit.*, pp. 172–4. Cf. S. E. Ozment, *When Fathers Ruled: Family Life in Reformation Europe* (Cambridge, Mass., 1983), pp. 50–72; L. Stone, *The Family, Sex and Marriage in England*, 1500–1800 (London, 1979), pp. 136–42. The doctrine is still found in Puritan writers of the seventeenth century. Cf. K. M. Davies, 'The sacred condition of equality – how original were Puritan doctrines of marriage?', *Social History*, 5 (1977), pp. 566–7.

29. *De trinitate*, XII, 7, CCSL, 50, p. 367.

30. *S.Th.*, III, q.70, a.2, ad 4; q.72, a.8, ad 3; q.72, a.10, ad 4.

31. Borressen, pp. 67–73.

32. *S.Th.*, III, q.31, a.4, R.

33. F. L. Utley, *The Crooked Rib* (Columbus, Ohio, 1944), p. 50. Utley discovered 403 works on women written in English between the thirteenth and sixteenth centuries, of which only 85 were in defence of women, and most of these defences came from the last 150 years of the period (1450–1600).

34. For discussions of attitudes to women in Latin, French and English literature, see the following: B. H. Dow, *The Varying Attitudes toward Women in French Literature of the Fifteenth Century* (New York, 1936); L. M. Richardson, *The Forerunners of Feminism in French Literature of the Renaissance* (Oxford, 1929); R. Rigaud, *Les Idées féministes de Christine de Pisan* (Neuchâtel, 1911); J. Peter, *Complaint and Satire in Early English Literature* (Oxford, 1956); K. M. Rogers, *The Troublesome Helpmate: A History of Misogyny in Literature* (Washington, 1956); Utley, *op. cit.*

35. Cited in Rogers, *op. cit.*, p. 64. Cf. Antoninus, *Summa Theologica*, III, 116–23. Antoninus ends his discussion of the sins that can occur in marriage with an alphabetical list, with comments, of the vices of women. One can only suppose that the list is meant as a joke. It goes from 'Avidum animal', through 'Bestiale baratrum', 'Garralum guttur' and 'Regnorum ruina' to 'Zelus zelotypus'.

36. Peter, *op. cit.*, p. 86. His impression of the proportion of defences of women to the attacks corresponds to Utley's statistics: 'There are...occasional exceptions who decline to hunt with the pack, but by and large the complaints are very nearly unanimous in their condemnation of women' (pp. 90–1).

37. Rigaud, *op. cit.*, ch. 3.

38. *Les Quinze Joyes de mariage*, ed. J. Crow (Oxford, 1969). The inspiration for the title comes from a prayer that lists the fifteen joys of the life of the Virgin Mary.

39. *The Romance of the Rose*, trans. by H. W. Robins (New York, 1962), especially pp. 97, 176, 179, 185. The later courtly love literature in general began to betray elements of misogyny (Rogers, *op. cit.*, pp. 58–61). Some critics argue that courtly love literature does not in fact exalt women, but rather love itself, of which woman is simply the tool. Cf. K. Foster, *Courtly Love and Christianity* (London, 1963); J. F. Benton, 'Clio and Venus: an historical view of medieval love', in *The Meaning of Courtly Love*, ed. F. X. Newman (New York, 1968), pp. 19–42.

40. Dow, *op. cit.*, p. 51.

41. Notably *L'Epistre au Dieu d'amour* (1399), *Epistre sur la Roman de la rose* (1402), *Le Livre de la cité des dames* (1404–5), *Le livre des trois vertus* (1405).

42. The second part of the *Roman* was written around 1277.

43. Richardson, *op. cit.*; Rogers, *op. cit.*, ch. 3.

44. The evidence consists chiefly of letters between Gerson and members of his family, and the treatises he wrote for his sisters. For the letters, see G.2, pp. 6–8, 9, 14–17, 45–8, 133–42, 192–8, 224–6. For the treatises, see G.7, pp. 1–3, 16–55, 55–7, 158–93, 193–206, 220–80, 343–60, 370–89, 416–21.

45. Gerson's eldest sister, Marion, had married, but by 1395 or 1396 was a widow and rejoined the family, where she shared the spiritual life of her five sisters, until she remarried around 1401 (G.1, p. 115). Sometime after the death of their mother (1401) and father (1404), Gerson's other sisters left the family home and went to Rheims, where they probably entered a convent (Connolly, pp. 26–7).

46. G.7, p. 419. Gerson suggests that they live at home rather than enter a convent, that they subsist on their labour and the inheritance they will receive from their parents (the brothers, he says, will not take any of this inheritance), and that they 'ask for no other husband than God'.

47. *Frater secundum*, G.2, p. 47. For further evidence of the religious and moral training given to Gerson and his siblings by their parents, see *Magnificat*, G. 8, pp. 369–70; *De simplificatione cordis*, G.8, p. 93; *Puer natus*, G.7, pp. 964–5. In all three places Gerson relates incidents from his childhood bearing witness to his parents' concern for his religious education.

48. G.7, p. 193.

49. In the fourth century, for instance, Theodoret of Cyr declared that only man was created in the image of God; woman was only the image of an image (M. Bardèche, *Histoire des femmes*, I (Paris, 1968), p. 273). Gregory of Tours reported that at the Council of Mâcon in 585 a bishop put forward the view that a woman could not be called *homo* in the full sense of the word (Richardson, *op. cit.*, p. 143). Echoes of this were heard in the sixteenth century: e.g., in 1595 at Wittenberg one of the fifty-one theses that doctoral candidates had to discuss was one which asked whether woman was a human creature (Metz, *op. cit.*, p. 80). In the same year a book was published entitled *Dissertation paradoxale, où l'on essaye de prouver que les femmes ne sont pas des créatures humaines*, wherein the author set out to prove that woman does not have an immortal soul (Richardson, *op. cit.*, pp. 143–5).

50. *De Gen. ad litt.*, XI, 34, *CSEL*, 28, p. 368.

51. *S.Th.*, I, q.90, a.4, R.

52. *S.Th.*, II–II, q.156, a.1, ad 1.

53. *S.Th.*, I q.93, a.4, ad 1. Thomas is here answering an objection based on I Cor. 11:7–10: 'Man is the image of God, but woman is the image of man. For man was not made from woman, but woman from man; and man was not created for woman, but woman for man.' He attempts to counter the objection while saving Paul, and so introduces a qualification.

54. *Ad deum vadit*, G.7, p. 498.

55. *Ibi eum videbitis*, G.7, p. 661. This reference was a common one in Easter sermons, being demanded by the gospel text. Cf. D'Ailly's sermon on the Resurrection (Brayer, pp. 140–1).

56. *Hoc sentite*, G.7, p. 654.

57. G.7, p. 172.

58. E.g., *Omne regum*, G.7, p. 761; *La Montaigne*, G.7, p. 18.

59. *Diligite justiciam*, G.7, pp. 605–6. Cf. Augustine, *Quaest. in Hept.* (cited in Borresen, p. 39): 'For the natural order in mankind is that woman should serve man, and children their parents, for it is just that the mind weaker in reason should serve the mind stronger in reason.'

60. *Dialogue spirituel*, G.7, p. 174.

61. *Considérations sur St Joseph*, G.7, p. 66. Cf. *Poenitemini, de la chasteté conjugale*, G.7, p. 843; *Jacob autem genuit*, G.5, p. 344.

62. G.7, p. 82. Cf. *Regulae mandatorum*, G.9, p. 130. Cf. Bonaventure, *Brevil.*, VI, 3: 'Matrimony consists in the conjunction of two parties, one active and influencing and the other passive and receiving...therefore matrimony must be the conjunction of two persons who differ as agent and patient, that is, as male and female, their union proceeding from the consent of the will alone.'

63. *Poenitemini, de la chasteté conjugale*, G.7, pp. 860–1.

64. *Ibid.*, p. 861.

65. *Saint Antonin: Une règle de vie au XVe siècle*, trans. Mme Thiérard-Baudrillart (Paris, 1921), pp. 148–53, 165. Cf. Raymond of Penaforte, *Summa*, II, 8, pp. 251–3. This thirteenth-century Dominican, like Gerson, is concerned that women do not do anything to displease their husbands, for 'the husband is the lord and head of the wife'.

66. *Poenitemini, de la chasteté conjugale*, G.7, p. 862.

67. *Ibid.*

68. *Ibid.*, p. 863. This sentiment is commonplace among theologians. It is found as far back as Chrysostom (Tavard, *op. cit.*, pp. 87–8). Leon Battista Alberti, the Italian artist and man of letters, in *I Libri della Famiglia*, written 1434–7, makes the same division: 'The woman, as she remains locked up at home, should watch over things by staying at her post, by diligent care and watchfulness. The man should guard the woman, the house, and his family and country, but not by sitting still.' Rather he should be 'engaged outside with other men in arranging matters of wider consequence'. *The Family in Renaissance Florence*, trans. R. N. Watkins (Columbia, S. Carolina, 1969), pp. 207–8.

69. *Poenitemini, de la chasteté conjugale*, G.7, p. 863.

70. Augustine, *De bono conjugali*, I, 1; XII, 14, *CSEL*, 41, pp. 187, 206; Paul, Eph. 5:22–5; Aquinas, *S.Th.*, I, q.92, a.1, ad 2. The doctrine was a commonplace and was often accompanied by the (equally commonplace) statement that Eve was created from Adam's rib, not his feet. Cf. Bonaventure, *II Sent.*, d.44, a.2, q.2, cited by E. T. Healy, *Woman according to Saint Bonaventure* (New York, 1956), p. 15; Bernardine, *Sermons*, p. 65; Jacques de Vitry and Guibert de Tournai in some of their marriage sermons, discussed by D. L. d'Avray and M. Tausche, 'Marriage sermons in *Ad status* collections of the central middle ages', *AHDLMA*, 47 (1981), pp. 106–8; M.-T. d'Alverny, 'Comment les théologiens et les philosophes voient la femme', *Cahiers de civilisation médiévale*, 20 (1977), pp. 105–28.

71. *Poenitemini, de la chasteté conjugale*, G.7, p. 863.

72. G.9, pp. 130–2.

73. *Poenitemini, contre la luxure*, G.7, p. 819.

74. *Puer natus est*, G.7, p. 959. There is disagreement over the date of this sermon. Glorieux gives 1402, while Mourin (*Gerson*, pp. 60–2) argues that it is of the early 1390s. Cf. Basevorn (Charland, p. 242): 'No woman, however learned and saintly, ought to preach.'

75. *Puer natus est*, G.7, p. 959.

76. G.7, p. 83.

77. *Poentemini, contre la luxure*, G.7, p. 831. Other late medieval French writers voiced this same fear of women's learning to read and write, e.g., Phillippe de Navarre, author of *Les Quatres Ages de l'homme*, and the Knight of La Tour Landry, author of *Livre pour l'éducation de mes filles* (Power, *Medieval Women*, p. 80).

78. E.g., *Poenitemini, de la chasteté*, G.7, p. 849.

79. Cf. I Cor. 7:1, 7–9, 14:34–6; Eph. 5:22–4; I Tim. 2:11–14.

80. Tavard, *op. cit.*, p. 59; Rogers, *op. cit.*, p. 15.

81. Aquinas, for instance, regards it as a matter of medical fact that women are more prone to sexual concupiscence than men, because 'the humours are more abundant in them' and 'in women there is not sufficient strength of mind to resist concupiscence' (*S.Th.*, II–II, q.149, a.4, R. Cf. Supp., q.62, a.4, ad 5).

82. *Le Miroir*, G.7, p. 194; *Tota*, G.7, p. 1063.

83. *Ibi eum videbitis*, G.7, p. 667. Cf. *Ad deum vadis*, G. 7, p. 491.

84. *S.Th.*, II–II, q.165, a.2, ad 1.

85. *S.Th.*, II–II, q.163, a.4, R; q.165, a.2, ad 1. Cf. I Tim. 2:14: 'And Adam was not deceived, but the woman being deceived was in the transgression.'

86. E.g., Brayer, pp. 106–7, 113, 119–20.

87. E.g., Ross, pp. 137, 333.

88. *Dialogue spirituel*, G.7, p. 185.

89. *De distinctione*, G.3, p. 51.

90. *Tota*, G.7, p. 1074.

91. *Vivat rex*, G.7, p. 1107.

92. *Ave Maria*, G.7, p. 546.

93. *Le Profit*, G.7, p. 372.

94. *Poenitemini, contre la luxure*, G.7, p. 819. Cf. Aquinas, *S.Th.*, Supp., q.62, a.4, ad 2, 3, 5. The doctrine has some support in canon law and appears in some of the

authors of manuals for confessors. Cf. Brundage, *op. cit.*, p. 132; Tentler, *Sin and Confession*, p. 151. Similar arguments are found in seventeenth-century Puritan writers (Davies, *op. cit.*, p. 576).

95. *Vivat rex*, G.7, p. 1169.
96. *Poenitemini, contre la luxure*, G.7, p. 831.
97. De la Borderie, pp. 97–9; A. Samouillan, *Etude sur la chaire et la société française au XVe siècle: Olivier Maillard, sa prédication et son temps* (Toulouse, 1891) (hereinafter *Olivier Maillard*), pp. 309ff.
98. *Sermons*, pp. 7, 48, 74, 168, 177, 186.
99. G. R. Owst, *Literature and the Pulpit in Medieval England* (Cambridge, 1933), (hereinafter *Literature*), p. 385. Cited with reference to sermons by seven different English preachers.
100. *Ibid.*, p. 395. The sinfulness of superfluous adornment is often noted in manuals for confessors, e.g., *Handlyng Synne*, p. 112; *The Book of Vices and Virtues*, pp. 179–80. D'Alverny's conclusions about the scholastics is as follows: 'Dans presque tous les textes des moralistes, on retrouve cette même finale. Certes, la femme est dangereuse, faible et astucieuse à la fois, querelleuse et coquette, souvent inconstante et infidèle...' (d'Alverny, *op. cit.*, p. 128).
101. Owst, *Literature*, pp. 368–404; Samouillon, *Olivier Maillard*, pp. 309–27. The chattering of women is a favourite target for Bernardine (*Sermons*, pp. 30, 74, 145), and for Alberti, who notes the incapacity of women to keep secrets and their tendency to ask silly questions (*The Family in Renaissance Florence*, pp. 207–10).
102. *Ibi eum videbitis*, G.7, p. 667.
103. *Omne regnum*, G.7, p. 757.
104. *Le Miroir*, G.7, p. 201. Cf. *L'Examen*, G.7, p. 396.
105. *De prob.*, G.9, p. 184.
106. *Ibid.*, p. 180.
107. *De exam.*, G.9, pp. 467–8.
108. *Ibid.*, p. 468. Cf. *Bonus pastor*, G.5, p. 130; *De orationibus*, G.10, pp. 137–8.
109. Bernardine too, in one of his vernacular sermons, points the finger at women when he is pouring scorn on those who say they have seen visions (*Sermons*, p. 136).
110. *De distinctione*, G.3, pp. 43, 51–2.
111. *De exam.*, P. I, pp. 19–20. This passage is omitted, without explanation, by Glorieux in his edition.
112. *De exam.*, G.9, p. 474. In a letter of 1408, Gerson had approved the publication of a book about the marvels of the life of Erminia (*Religioso et bono viro*, G.2, pp. 93–6).
113. *De exam.*, G.9, p. 469.
114. The authenticity of this work is accepted by Lieberman, 'Chronologie Gersonienne', *Romania*, 78 (1957), p. 147, by Glorieux, and by H. G. Francq, 'Jean Gerson's theological treatises and other memoirs in defence of Joan of Arc', *Revue de l'Université d'Ottawa*, 41 (1971), pp. 58–80, as against D. G. Wayman, 'The chancellor and Jeanne d'Arc', *Franciscan Studies*, 17 (1957), pp. 2–35. The treatise is published in G.9, pp. 661–5.
115. The documents involved in the controversy were published by C. F. Ward, *The Epistles on the Romance of the Rose and other Documents in the Debate* (Chicago, 1911). The defence of Jean de Meung and the *Roman* was undertaken by Jean de Montreuil, provost of Lille, Gontier Col, councillor of the king, and Pierre Col, canon of Paris and Tournai.
116. Cf. Dow, *op. cit.*, pp. 127–224; Richardson, *op. cit.*, pp. 12–34; Rigaud, *op. cit.*, *passim*.
117. *Oeuvres poétiques*, ed. M. Roy (Paris, 1965), II, p. 21.

118. *Letter to Pierre Col*, in Ward, *op. cit.*, p. 86.

119. *Contre le Roman de la rose*, G.7, p. 310.

120. *Tota*, G.7, pp. 1077–9.

121. E.g., Courtecuisse, di Stefano, p. 184; d'Ailly, Brayer, pp. 108–10; Ross, pp. 244–9, 318–22, 327–8; Vincent de Ferrier, *In vigilia nativitatis Christi*, in B. H. Vanderberghe, *Saint Vincent Ferrier*, pp. 129–33.

122. *Poenitemini, de la chasteté*, G.7, p. 846.

123. Metz, *op. cit.*, p. 95. Cf. Augustine, *De bono conjugali*, XIX, 22, *CSEL*, 41, p. 216; *De sancta virginitate*, 45, *CSEL*, 41, p. 289; Aquinas, *S.Th.*, II–II, q.152, a.5, ad 2: *The Book of Vices and Virtues*, p. 259.

124. G.7, p. 158. The Pauline text is I Cor. 7:38 – another favourite text for praises of virginity.

125. *Considérations sur St Joseph*, G.7, p. 67.

126. *Discours sur l'excellence de la virginité*, G.7, p. 418. Cf. *Le Miroir*, G.7, p. 196; *Ad deum vadit*, G.7, p. 459.

127. *Poenitemini, de la chasteté*, G.7, pp. 845–7.

128. *Dedit illis*, G.7, p. 595. Opinion on this point seems to have been undergoing change, or at least to have been under discussion in the later Middle Ages. According to Bardèche, *op. cit.*, II, pp. 53–4, chastity was regarded throughout the Middle Ages as very harmful to health. However, by at least the fifteenth century the opposite opinion was frequently voiced by secular, medical and clerical writers. Cf. Hale, *op. cit.*, pp. 129–30; Tentler, *Sin and Confession*, pp. 225–8.

129. P. G. Reilly à Brooklyn, *Ideals of Matrimony and Virginity in the Writings of St. Bonaventure* (Rome, 1964), pp. 49–58. Cf. Augustine, who also writes of 'singing a new song', and the 'foretaste of the heavenly and angelic life' (*De sancta virginitate*, 24–7, *CSEL*, 41, pp. 258–65). Cf. *The Book of Vices and Virtues*, pp. 259–60.

130. *Poenitemini, de la chasteté*, G.7, p. 847.

131. P. 3, p. 831. Glorieux omits a large part of du Pin's version of this discourse. The reason, I suspect, is that he has used as his text E. Vansteenberghe's edition, published in *RSR*, 14 (1934), pp. 205–11, and entitled 'Sept enseignements et autres extraits du *Traité sur l'excellence de la virginité*', and failed to notice the work 'extraits'. The MSS used by Vansteenberghe are the same as those used by du Pin. In *Dedit illis*, Gerson makes reference to his tract on virginity in such a way as to make it clear that the passage omitted by Glorieux was part of the original work (G.7, p. 594).

132. *De bono conjugali*, X, 10, *CSEL*, 41, p. 201.

133. *S.Th.*, II–II, q.152, a.2, ad 1.

134. Parts of the sermons are in note form and no doubt Gerson was not so brief when he preached them.

135. *Poenitemini, de la chasteté*, G.7, pp. 847, 856. Cf. *Dedit illis*, G.7, pp. 594–6.

136. P.3, p. 836. Preaching on the discomforts, anxieties and perils of married life was fairly common in the later Middle Ages (Owst, *Literature*, pp. 378–9).

137. Luther, *Why Nuns may Leave Cloisters with God's Blessing* (1523), cited in Ozment, *When Fathers Ruled*, p. 17.

138. *Poenitemini, de la chasteté conjugale*, G.7, pp. 866–7.

139. Augustine, *De bono viduitatis*, 5, *CSEL*, 41, p. 308. Cf. Tavard, *op. cit.*, pp. 61, 116; Bailey, *op. cit.*, pp. 31–3.

140. E.g., Aquinas, *S.Th.*, Supp., q.63, a.1, ad 3, who argues that priests are debarred from being present at second marriages (Lombard, *IV Sent.*, D. 42) not because such marriages are unlawful, but because they 'lack the decorum which was in a first marriage'. Cf. Bernardine, *Sermons*, pp. 92–7; I. Origo, *The World of San*

Bernardino (New York, 1962), pp. 67–9; *The Book of Vices and Virtues*, pp. 249–51.
141. *Poenitemini, de la chasteté conjugale*, G.7, p. 867. Cf. Abelard (1079–1142), *Historia calamitatum*, ed. J. Monfrin (Paris, 1967), p. 76, where Heloise is made to argue that she and Abelard, the cleric and philosopher, ought not to marry because married life is full of worries, worldly responsibilities, noise and confusion. Cicero, Seneca, Theophrastus and Jerome are all quoted in support of the argument that it is impossible to attend to a wife and family and at the same time to attend to philosophy and the life of the spirit. The same argument backed by the same authorities appears in Abelard's *Theologia christiana* (*MPL*, 178:1197–1201).
142. *Poenitemini, de la chasteté conjugale*, G.7, p. 867.
143. *Poenitemini, de la chasteté*, G.7, pp. 847–8.
144. *Ibid.*, p. 854.
145. 'Far be it from us to think that in marriages which would have taken place in paradise, the genitals would have been excited by the ardour of lust and not by the bidding of the will' (*De grat. Chr. et de pecc. orig.*, ii, 41, cited and trans. by Bailey, *op. cit.*, p. 58).
146. *De bono conjugali*, III, 3, *CSEL*, 41, p. 191.
147. *Sentences*, II, 39.8 (*MPL*, 192:725–6). Cf. S. Pinckaers, 'Ce que le moyen âge pensait du mariage', *La Vie spirituelle*, Supplément, 82 (1967), pp. 414–21; P. Delhaye, 'Fixation dogmatique de la théologie dogmatique du mariage', *Concilium*, 55 (1970), pp. 78–9.
148. E. M. Makowski, *op. cit.*, pp. 102–3.
149. Ed. T. P. McLaughlin, 'Abelard's rule for religious women', *MS*, 18 (1956), p. 278.
150. Pp. 18–23.
151. *S.Th.*, I, q.98, a.2, ad 3. For Albert, see Pinckaers, *op. cit.*, pp. 424–5; L. Brandl, *Die Sexualethik des heiligen Albertus Magnus* (Regensburg, 1955).
152. Aquinas, *S.Th.*, Supp., q.49, a.6, R. Cf. II–II, q.142, a.1, R: 'To fly in the face of nature is wicked, and in the natural order of things pleasure goes with the operations necessary for human life. And so a person is expected to enjoy them in so far as they are bound up with human well-being and with the preservation of the individual and the race.' Cf. Aristotle, *Ethica Nicomachea*, X, 5.
153. *S.Th.*, Supp., q.41, a.4, R. Cf. Pinckaers, *op. cit.*, p. 425.
154. *S.Th.*, Supp. q.49, a.6, ad 2; q.41, a.4, R. For Albert, see Noonan, *Contraception*, p. 346.
155. L. Vereecke, 'Mariage et sexualité au déclin du moyen âge', *La Vie spirituelle*, Supplément, 57 (1961), pp. 199–225.
156. Noonan, *Contraception*, pp. 368–72.
157. 'For if anyone eats a pear or a beautiful apple for the sake of pleasure, he does not sin, therefore neither does he by knowing his own wife for the sake of pleasure' (Jean Major, *In IV Sent.*, d.31, cited by Vereecke, *op. cit.*, p. 223).
158. Noonan, *Contraception*, p. 375.
159. Foster, *Courtly Love and Christianity*, pp. 20–3.
160. E.g., *De bono conjugali*, III, 3, *CSEL*, 41, p. 190. Cf. Borresen, pp. 101–3.
161. *C. Gent.*, III, 123: 'Now, there seems to be the greatest friendship [*amicitia*] between husband and wife, for they are united not only in the act of fleshly union, which produces a certain gentle association even among beasts, but also in the partnership of the whole range of domestic activities' (Trans. by V. J. Bourke, *On the Truth of the Catholic Faith* (New York, 1956), III, part 2, p. 148).
162. *S.Th.*, II–II, q.26, a.11, ad 3.
163. *I Sent.*, d.10, a.2, q.1, cited in M. M. De Benedictis, *The Social Thought of Saint Bonaventure: A Study in Social Philosophy* (Washington, 1946), p. 136. For

a thorough treatment of medieval marriage doctrines, see M. Müller, *Die Lehre von Paradiesesehe* (Regensburg, 1954).

164. *Poenitemini, de la chasteté*, G.7, p. 842.

165. *Poenitemini, de la chasteté conjugale*, G.7, p. 858.

166. *Ibid.*, p. 859. Twelve is higher than the number of 'excellences' usually listed by medieval writers. Numbers, 3, 6, 7, 9 and 10 occur frequently; e.g., Alain de Lille uses four of these five, omitting the miracle at Cana, but adding some other facts that show the great worth of marriage, e.g., marriage was the state of life of the patriarchs and of some of the apostles; it maintains between the spouses an undivided life together (*MPL*, 172:869, trans. in d'Avray and Tausche, *op. cit.*, p. 79).

167. *Poenitemini, de la chasteté*, G.7, p. 853. Cf. G.7, p. 835.

168. G.7, p. 64. Cf. Augustine, *De Gen. ad litt.*, IX, 7, *CSEL*, 28, pp. 275–6: 'In fidelity, the main concern is that there be no relations with another man or woman outside the marriage bond; in offspring, that they be received with love, raised with kindness, educated to religion; in the sacred pledge, that the marriage be not severed and the banished husband or wife united to another for the sake of the children' (trans. by J. E. Kerns, *The Theology of Marriage: The Historical Development of Christian Attitudes towards Sex and Sanctity in Marriage* (New York, 1964), p. 56).

169. *Poenitemini, de la chasteté conjugale*, G.7, p. 858. There were various interpretations of the two goods, *fides* and *sacramentum*, current in the Middle Ages. Jacques de Vitry, for example, includes the duty of paying the marital debt under *fides*, and sees *sacramentum* as indicating that marriage is a symbol of the union of Christ and the church, or Christ and the soul (d'Avray and Tausche, *op. cit.*, pp. 92–3).

170. P. Glorieux, 'S. Joseph dans l'oeuvre de Gerson', *Cahiers de Joséphologie*, 19 (1971), p. 414.

171. He also preached two sermons at Constance to this end: *Jacob autem genuit*, G.5, pp. 344–62; *Suscepimus deus*, G.5, pp. 538–46.

172. *Exhortation générale pour la fête de la desponsation Notre Dame*, G.7, p. 14. Gerson wrote three other letters presenting similar arguments: *Ecclesiis universis*, G.8, pp. 61–6, written 17 August 1413, to all churches and especially those dedicated to the Virgin; *En considerant moult*, G.2, pp. 155–7, written on 23 November 1413, to the Duke of Berry; *Reverendo patri, domino ac magistro*, G.2, p. 167–9, written from Constance on 7 September 1416, to Dominique Petit, Vice-Chancellor of the University of Paris.

173. G.7, pp. 64, 80.

174. *Poenitemini, de la chasteté*, G.7, p. 852.

175. Bailey, *op. cit.*, pp. 120–33. Cf. J. A. Brundage, 'Concubinage and marriage in medieval canon law', *Journal of Medieval History*, 1 (1975), pp. 1–17.

176. *Poenitemini, de la chasteté*, G.7, p. 852. Cf. Aquinas, *S.Th.*, III, q.29, a.2, R.

177. G.7, p. 81. Cf. Aquinas, *S.Th.*, Supp., q.58, a.1, ad 1: 'Although the act of carnal intercourse is not essential to marriage, ability to fulfil the act is essential, because marriage gives each of the spouses power over the other's body, in relation to marital intercourse.'

178. *IV Sent.*, D. 26, cited, but not endorsed by Aquinas, *S.Th.*, Supp., q.42, a.1, Sed contra.

179. *De sacramentis*, II, 11. Cf. P. S. Gold, 'The marriage of Mary and Joseph in the twelfth-century ideology of marriage', in Bullough and Brundage, *op. cit.*, pp. 102–17.

180. E.g., *Talia de me scribis*, G.2, p. 62. Cf. Aquinas, *S.Th.*, Supp., q.41, a.1, R.
181. *Regulae mandatorum*, G.9, p. 118. Cf. *Dedit illis*, G.7, p. 594.
182. *Poenitemini, contre la luxure*, G.7, p. 838; *Le Miroir*, G.7, p. 207. Gerson does not explain to the audiences of these works how 'honteuse' and 'honneste' pleasure are to be distinguished.
183. The dictum 'The too ardent lover of his wife is an adulterer' was ascribed to Sextus the Pythagorean, used by Jerome and Augustine, then by Gratian and Lombard, and from there found its way into the works of many medieval canonists, theologians and moralists. Cf. H. A. Kelly, *Love and Marriage in the Age of Chaucer* (Ithaca, 1975), p. 245.
184. D'Avray and Tausche, *op. cit.*, p. 79.
185. *Angelica*, 'Debitum conjugale'. This view was upheld in a number of late medieval confessional summas and manuals (Tentler, *Sin and Confession*, pp. 174–84).
186. *S.Th.*, Supp., q.49, a.6, R.
187. G.9, pp. 117–18.
188. L. E. Boyle, Review of *Sin and Confession*, by T. N. Tentler, in *The Canadian Journal of History*, 13 (1978), p. 272.
189. 4.2.27. The definition is also used in the fifteenth-century summa, the *Sylvestrina* (Tentler, *Sin and Confession*, p. 184).
190. *Doctrinal aux simples gens*, G.10, p. 312.
191. D'Avray and Tausche, *op. cit.*, p. 97; Aquinas, *S.Th.*, Supp., q.64, a.7, a.8; *The Book of Vices and Virtues*, p. 249.
192. Tentler, *Sin and Confession*, pp. 213–20.
193. *Doctrinal aux simples gens*, G.10, p. 312; *Regulae mandatorum*, G.9, p. 117. Cf. Aquinas, *S.Th.*, Supp., q.64, a.3. Gerson's opting for the older view here is probably a sign of his concern for children rather than a sign of narrowness about sexuality. The opinion that the offspring resulting from intercourse with a menstruating woman would most probably be defective was a very common one, held even by those authors who allowed such intercourse (Tentler, *Sin and Confession*, pp. 208–11).
194. *Poenitemini, contre la luxure*, G.7, p. 819. According to Tentler (*Sin and Confession*, p. 212) no indication was given by any of the writers he has studied either. Some of the early penitentials (of the sixth to the twelfth centuries) did, by contrast, specify that intercourse should not take place during the last three months or the last forty days of pregnancy, presumably because it was felt to be more dangerous to the foetus then. Cf. J.-L. Flandrin, 'L'Attitude à l'égard du petit enfant et les conduites sexuelles dans la civilisation occidentale', *Annales de démographie historique* (Paris, 1973), p. 189.
195. *Doctrinal aux simples gens*, G.10, p. 312.
196. Cf. Aquinas, *S.Th.*, Supp., q.64, a.1; Antoninus, *Summa Theologica*, III, 87: 'To deny the debt is a mortal sin, if there is no rational cause, because the spouses are in each other's power.' The biblical foundation for the doctrine is I Cor. 7:1–5.
197. G.9, p. 132. Cf. *Doctrinal aux simples gens*, G.10, p. 312. Lists of 'rational causes' for refusing the debt vary. Danger to health or to a foetus generally appear, but opinions with regard to leprosy, pregnancy and menstruation vary. Aquinas, for instance, does not regard either leprosy or menstruation as valid excuses (*S.Th.*, Supp., q.64, a.1, ad 6; a.4, R). Gerson omits two circumstances considered valid by Antoninus (*Summa Theologica*, III, 91) and the *Angelica* ('Debitum conjugale'): temporary impotence and an adulterous spouse.
198. *Poenitemini, de la chasteté conjugale*, G.7, p. 863; *Regulae mandatorum*, G.9, p. 132. Even those writers who thought it sinful for a spouse to demand the debt

at holy times or in holy places agreed that the other spouse could not refuse without sin. This is the opinion of, for example, Jacques de Vitry (d'Avray and Tausche, *op. cit.*, p. 97).

199. Book IV, p. 519. Some authors conflate the last two motives – not surprisingly, for it would seem to be difficult to distinguish between them.

200. *Poenitemini, contre la luxure*, G.7, p. 819.

201. G.9, p. 117.

202. *Doctrinal aux simples gens*, G.10, p. 312.

203. P.3, p. 836.

204. Owst, *Literature*, p. 378.

205. E.g., *Sermons*, pp. 52, 65, 79–80, 87–8, 224.

206. D'Avray and Tausche, *op. cit.*, with particular reference to the thirteenth-century *ad status* sermons of Jacques de Vitry and Guibert de Tournai.

207. Blench, p. 260. One of the most positive and optimistic pre-Reformation appreciations of marriage occurs not in a sermon but in Alberti's dialogue (*The Family in Renaissance Florence*, p. 98).

208. *WA.*, 43, 313, cited in E. J. D. Douglass, 'Women in the continental Reformation', in Ruether, *op. cit.*, p. 301.

209. Ozment, *When Fathers Ruled*, p. 11.

210. *Institutes*, IV, xix, 36, cited in Douglass, 'Women in the continental Reformation', p. 299.

211. *Hoc sentite*, G.7, p. 656. Cf. *Claro eruditori*, G.2, p. 215.

212. *Poenitemini, de la chasteté conjugale*, G.7, p. 865.

213. *Poenitemini, contre la luxure*, G.7, p. 835. Gerson's opinion here is traditional. Cf. Noonan, *Contraception*, pp. 338–42.

214. *De parvulis*, G.9, p. 671. Glorieux dates this work 1406. F. Bonney, *Jean Gerson et l'enfance* (Thèse de troisième cycle, University of Bordeaux III, 1972), pp. 3–5, suggests 1402–3. Cf. *Bonus Pastor*, G.5, p. 132.

215. *Videmus*, G.7, p. 1125.

216. *Fulcite me floribus*, G.5, p. 338. Cf. *Considerate lilia*, G.5, p. 161. Glorieux dates this latter sermon, preached to the members of the College of Navarre, as probably of 1393. Lieberman argues for 1401 ('Chronologie gersonienne', *Romania*, 63 (1962), p. 70).

217. *Notes sur la confession*, G.7, p. 412. Mourin thinks this work formed the last part of the sermon, *Tota* (*Six sermons*, p. 374).

218. In *Poenitemini, contre la paresse*, G.7, pp. 885–6, Gerson lists the seven ages of man. Some, he says, obey the call of God 'in infancy, as St Nicholas, and infancy lasts till 7 years; others obey the call during puberty [*pucellage*] and this lasts till 14 years; others during adolescence, which lasts till 21 years; others in youth [*jeunesse*], which lasts till 28 years or 30...'. He has a variation on this scheme in *Considérations sur St Joseph*, G.7, p. 75: 'for the first age is infancy, which lasts till 7 years, then there is adolescence, which lasts till 28 years; then there is youth [*jouvence*]...'. Generally, however, Gerson seems to conflate infancy and puberty, and, though he might use the term 'adolescents' for children below the age of 14, when he uses the terms 'parvulus', 'puer' or 'infans' he means a child of less than 14.

219. Connolly, p. 89; Delaruelle, *L'Eglise*, p. 846; P. Ariès, *Centuries of Childhood: A Social History of Family Life* (trans. R. Baldick, New York, 1962), p. 108.

220. Ariès, pp. 411–12. For criticisms of Ariès on this point see M. M. McLaughlin, 'Survivors and surrogates: children and parents from the ninth to the thirteenth centuries', in L. deMause, ed., *The History of Childhood* (New York, 1974), pp. 101–81; J. B. Ross, 'The middle-class child in urban Italy, fourteenth to early sixteenth century' (in *Ibid.*, pp. 183–228); L. Demaitre, 'The idea of childhood and child care in medical writings of the middle ages', *Journal of Psychohistory*, 4 (1976–7), pp. 461–90.

221. Ariès, p. 110.

222. G.7; p. 556. Cf. *De parvulis*, G.9, p. 670.

223. *Factum est*, G.7, pp. 631–2. Cf. *Exsultabunt*, G.5, p. 274.

224. *Talia de me scribis*, G.2, p. 66. Cf. *De cognitione castitatis*, G.9, p. 54: 'No one is without sin, even an infant of one day.'

225. *De confessione mollitiei*, G.8, pp. 72–3.

226. *De parvulis*, G.9, pp. 671–2.

227. *Ibid.*, p. 670.

228. Had he known of the work he could have cited Peter Damian's (d. 1072) *On the Perfection of Monks*. Addressing the young, Peter remarks, 'You are at the pliant age; if the clay suffers any injury in the potter's hands, this, if not corrected at once, becomes hard as stone', just as the twig, once bent, can never be straightened (cited in M. M. McLaughlin, *op. cit.*, p. 173). Cf. Anselm (d. 1109), who uses the simile of the tree-shoot (*The Life of Anselm, Archbishop of Canterbury, by Eadmer*, pp. 37–8, cited in *ibid.*).

229. *Poenitemini, contre la gourmandise*, G.7, pp. 803–4.

230. *Poenitemini, contre la paresse*, G.7, p. 893.

231. *Contre la péché de blasphème*, G.7, pp. 4–5.

232. *Poenitemini, contre la luxure*, G.7, p. 839.

233. G.10, pp. 27–8. Despite the word 'juventutis' in the title of the work used by Glorieux, it is clear from the text that Gerson is concerned with the corruption of children and adolescents.

234. *Ibid.*, p. 28.

235. *Talia de me scribis*, G.2, p. 69; *Poenitemini, contre la luxure*, G.7, p. 839.

236. *Contre les tentations de blasphème*, G.7, pp. 415–16. Cf. *Poenitemini, contre la luxure*, G.7, p. 829.

237. *Poenitemini, contre la luxure*, G.7, p. 838.

238. *Ibid.*, p. 831. Cf. *Bonus pastor*, G.5, p. 139.

239. Ariès, pp. 100–6; J. Bossy, 'Holiness and society', *Past and Present*, 75 (1977), p. 126; F. Bonney, 'Jean Gerson: un nouveau regard sur l'enfance', *Annales de démographie historique* (1973), pp. 137–42.

240. Ariès, pp. 108–10. In the early sixteenth century, Robertus Caracciolus in one of his sermons lamented that children were now guilty of lust before the age of puberty (*De quadragesima: de penitentia*, 28, ch. 1, q.3, cited in Tentler, *Sin and Confession*, p. 70, n. 1).

241. *Poenitemini, de la chasteté conjugale*, G.7, p. 865.

242. *Puer natus*, G.7, p. 953. A number of medieval moralists and doctors inveighed against the use of wet-nurses, though it would be only the wealthy who could afford them. It was a general belief that the milk the infant imbibed affected not only his physical constitution but also his character (M. M. McLaughlin, *op. cit.*, p. 116). Cf. Bernardine (*Sermons*, pp. 89–90), who finds a mother who gives her infant to a nurse to be suckled, solely to procure pleasure for herself, guilty of mortal sin. If the infant is given to a 'dirty drab', from her 'the child doth acquire certain of those customs she hath who doth suckle him'.

243. *Poenitemini, de la chasteté conjugale*, G.7, pp. 864–5. Cf. *Jacob autem genuit*, G.5, p. 350.

244. *Exhortation générale pour la fête de la desponsation Notre Dame*, G.7, p. 13.

245. *Notes sur la confession*, G.7, pp. 411–12.

246. J. Toussaert, *Le Sentiment religieux en Flandre à la fin du moyen-âge* (Paris, 1963), pp. 107–9.

247. Tentler, *Sin and Confession*, p. 70, n. 1.

248. *De parvulis*, G.9, pp. 675–6.

249. *Ibid.*, p. 676.

250. *Ibid.*

251. G.8, p. 71: 'What did you do to stop the erection? And this should be said with a tranquil expression, so that it appears that what is being asked about is not something shameful that cannot be talked about, but rather as if it were a remedy sought in good faith against the erection of the penis. If the boy will not reply, then say: my friend, did you not stroke and rub your penis, as boys often do?...And this should all be said as if the confessor did not think this activity unusual or a sin.'

252. *Ibid.*, p. 72.

253. *Factum est*, G.7, p. 631.

254. *Considérations sur St Joseph*, G.7, p. 66. Gerson draws some pictures of Mary and Joseph caring for the infant Jesus in his poem *Josephina*, G.4, pp. 44–5.

255. *Poenitemini, de la chasteté conjugale*, G.7, p. 865. Much of this sermon is in note form, and in this passage Gerson mentions seven examples about disciplining children. No doubt he spoke about these in detail when he delivered the sermon.

256. *Considerate lilia*, G.5, p. 162.

257. D. Hunt, *Parents and Children in History: The Psychology of Family Life in Early Modern France* (New York, 1970), pp. 133–9; Ariès, pp. 241–68; L. Stone, *Family, Sex and Marriage*, pp. 115–27. For criticism of this opinion see Ozment, *When Fathers Ruled*, pp. 132–72.

258. Ariès, pp. 241–68; L. Stone, 'The massacre of the innocents', *New York Review of Books*, 14 November 1974, p. 30.

259. *De parvulis*, G.9, p. 673.

260. *Sermons*, pp. 83, 92, 122.

261. E.g., Maillard (de la Borderie, pp. 106–8); Ross, p. 20; *Handlyng Synne*, p. 161. Cf. Owst, *Literature*, pp. 460–8. Owst finds, in the medieval English sermons he has examined, fairly frequent manifestation of a concern for the proper upbringing of children, coupled with complaint at parents who should be inculcating virtue in the growing child, but who more often provide bad examples themselves.

262. P. Glorieux, 'Quatre dialogues de Gerson en vers français', *Mélanges de science religieuse*, 7 (1950), p. 216. For the period from June 1404 to November 1405, Glorieux notes seventeen such occasions.

263. D. E. Adams-Smith, *Some French Works of Jean Gerson: An Introduction and Translation* (Ph.D. dissertation, University of South Carolina, 1976), p. 15, states that Gerson taught the boys Latin pronunciation, music and Scripture. She gives no source for this information.

264. *L'Ecole de la raison*, G.7, pp. 103–8; *Complainte de la conscience*, G.7, pp. 109–11; *L'Ecole de la conscience*, G.7, pp. 5–10. All these present dramatic conflict between reason and conscience, on the one hand, and the unruly heart and five senses, on the other. There is also *Livret-proverbes pour écoliers*, G.7, pp. 367–9, a rhymed collection of thirty-seven 'improving' proverbs. For a discussion of these see Glorieux, 'Quatre dialogues de Gerson en vers francais', and Adams-Smith, *op. cit.* Gerson also wrote, perhaps at this period (the first few years of the fifteenth century), the *Donatus spiritualis* (G.9, pp. 689–700), a Latin work for grammar students. The framework is provided by the parts of speech, but the material is of a moral and religious nature. In other words it is a form of catechism. Other works of a catechical nature for children are his *ABC des simple gens* (G.7, pp. 154–7), of 1401–2, and the *Brève manière de confession pour les jeunes* (G.7, pp. 408–9), undated by Glorieux, but suggested by Bonney (*Jean Gerson et l'enfance*, p. 7), to have been written 1401–2.

265. *De parvulis*, G.9, p. 681.

266. *Ibid.*, p. 682.

267. G.9, pp. 686–9. The school in question took about ten students. It was one of a number of such preparatory schools, some of them attached to the Parisian colleges. Cf. A. L. Gabriel, 'Preparatory teaching in the Parisian colleges during the fourteenth century', *Revue de L'Université d'Ottawa*, 21 (1951), pp. 449–83.

268. *Doctrina pro pueris Ecclesiae parisiensis*, G.9, p. 686. Descriptions of the ideal master occur also in *Exsultabunt*, G.5, p. 275 (*bonus, sanctus, pudicus, incorruptus*), and in *Considerate lilia*, G.5, pp. 162–4.

269. *Doctrina pro pueris Ecclesiae parisiensis*, G.9, p. 688.

270. *Ibid.*

271. *Ibid.*, p. 687.

272. *Ibid.*, p. 689.

273. The whole text, in fact, suggests that Gerson is revising rather than innovating: e.g., he uses the term 'more antiquo' or its equivalent in some of the regulations, as indicated.

274. *Considerate lilia*, G.5, pp. 151–68.

275. *Ibid.*, pp. 162–4. Cf. Quintilian, *Institutio oratoria*, Book I, chs. 2–3.

276. G.1, p. 136.

277. *Bonus pastor*, G.5, p. 132.

278. *Scriptum est melius*, G.2, p. 111.

279. *De visitatione praelatorum*, G.8, p. 50.

280. *Fulcite me floribus*, G.5, p. 338.

281. There is dispute over these dates. A. Thomas, *Gerson et l'éducation des deux dauphins de France* (Paris, 1930), argues for 1408–10 for the first letter, and 1417 for the second. M. Lieberman, 'Chronologie gersonienne', *Romania*, 73 (1952), pp. 480–96 and 74 (1953), pp. 289–337, argues convincingly for 1417 and 1429. Glorieux accepts Lieberman's dates. More recently, however, Bonney has opted for Thomas' dates, but with no fresh evidence (*Jean Gerson et l'enfance*, pp. 6–7).

282. The Dauphin Charles had just recently become lieutenant-general and taken up the reins of government, his father being once more incapacitated.

283. *Claro eruditori*, G.2, pp. 212–13: Aristotle, Valerius Maximus, Sallust, Vegetius, Seneca, Cato, Aesop, Livy, Suetonius. Where Gerson specifies which works of these authors should be read, they are largely of a political or military nature.

284. *Ibid.*: Le Miroir, L'Examen, La Science de bien mourir, La Montaigne de contemplation, La Mendicité spirituelle; the sermons and discourses Ad deum vadit, Sancta et salubris, Vivat rex, Veniat pax, Diligite justitiam, a poem, De scala mystica, and 'quaedam alia'.

285. *Erunt omnes docibiles*, G.2, p. 338.

286. *Ibid.*, p. 337.

287. *Ibid.*

288. A. L. Gabriel, *Student Life in Ave Maria College, Medieval Paris* (Notre Dame, Indiana, 1955). The statutes of Ave Maria College are much longer than Gerson's regulations, being also concerned with all the financial arrangements of the college.

289. A. L. Gabriel, 'Pierre d'Ailly and the new statutes of Ave Maria College' in *Recueil des travaux offerts à Clovis Brunel* (Paris, 1955), Vol. I, pp. 476–89. Cf. Bonney, *Jean Gerson et l'enfance*, pp. 85–90.

290. *Claro eruditori*, G.2, pp. 212–13.

291. Bonney, *Jean Gerson et l'enfance*, pp. 90–107.

292. Ed. by A. Steiner (Cambridge, Mass., 1938: reprint, New York, 1970), pp.

88–103. Cf. J. M. McCarthy, *Humanistic Emphases in the Educational Thought of Vincent de Beauvais* (Leiden, 1976).

293. A. Willot, *Éducateurs chrétiens à travers de l'histoire* (Paris, 1969), pp. 67–8.

294. Ed. by J. R. Lumby, EETS, OS, 43 (London, 1870), pp. 26–103.

295. *Ibid.*, pp. 60, 109–11.

296. P.7.

297. *De ordine docendi et studendi*, trans. W. H. Woodward, *Vittorino da Feltre and other Humanist Educators* (Cambridge, 1897; reprint, New York, 1963), p. 63. The same opinion is expressed by Vergerio (1370–1444), in his *De ingenuis moribus*, and by Piccolomini (d. 1471) in his *De liberorum educatione* (*ibid.*, pp. 103, 137).

298. *De duplici logica*, G.3, pp. 58–63; *Gallia que viris semper*, G.10, pp. 7–10. Cf. McCarthy, *op. cit.*, pp. 89–90.

299. G. Strauss, 'Reformation and pedagogy: educational thought and practice in the Lutheran Reformation', in *Pursuit of Holiness*, p. 273. The belief that it was necessary to ensure the proper religious and moral formation of the young, if reform of the Christian community was to take place, was also one of the motives behind the creation of adolescent confraternities in fifteenth-century Florence (R. C. Trexler, 'Ritual in Florence: adolescence and salvation in the Renaissance', in *Pursuit of Holiness*, pp. 200–64).

300. *Bonus pastor*, G.5, p. 132. Cf. Otto Brunfel, a pro-Reformation preacher, then schoolmaster of Strasburg from 1524 to 1534, citing 'words I once read by a man of God: "If one wants to reform the world and make it Christian, one must begin with children"' (cited in Ozment, *When Fathers Ruled*, p. 136).

8 Doctor Christianissimus et consolatorius

1. J. M. Stayer, 'Luther studies and Reformation studies', *Canadian Journal of History*, 17 (1982), pp. 499–505. Stayer argues that Reformation scholarship since about 1960 has been increasingly 'between paradigms' (p. 499).

2. *Ibid.*, p. 504.

3. *Si de temporali* (Letter from Gerson to d'Ailly), G.2, pp. 125–8. Cf. F. Oakley, 'Gerson and d'Ailly: an admonition', *Speculum*, 40 (1965), pp. 74–83, where the independence of Gerson from d'Ailly in various aspects of his thought is discussed, e.g., in mystical theology and in philosophy.

4. At least one of Gerson's lay congregations would have known that the chancellor thought that confessors should be gentle and bring consolation. In *Ad deum vadit* (G.7, p. 482), he says 'This is an *exemplum* for confessors and clergy reminding them that they should not be harsh in replying or speaking to penitents; and at least that they should not let penitents go without giving them good comfort and good consolation.'

5. *De perfectione cordis*, G.8, p. 129.

6. A single narrative based on the four gospels, G.9, pp. 245–373.

7. *L'Evangile à grands traits*, G.9, pp. 373–85.

8. *The Reformation in the Cities*, pp. 15–22.

BIBLIOGRAPHY OF WORKS CITED

Primary sources

Abelard, Peter. 'Abelard's rule for religious women'. Ed. T. P. McLaughlin. *MS*, 18 (1956), pp. 241–92.
Historia calamitatum. Ed. J. Monfrin. Paris, 1967.
Peter Abelard's Ethics. Ed. D. E. Luscombe. Oxford, 1971.
Theologia Christiana. *MPL*, 178:1113–30.
Aegidius Romanus. *De ecclesiastica potestate*. Ed. R. Scholz. Weimar, 1929.
Ailly, Pierre d'. *Sermons français*. Ed. E. Brayer. *Notice du ms. 574 de la Bibliothèque Municipale de Cambrai, suivie d'une édition des sermons français de Pierre d'Ailly*. Paris, 1965.
Alain de Lille. *Summa de arte praedicatoria*. *MPL*, 210:111–98.
Alberti, Leon Battista. *I Libri della famiglia*. Trans. R. N. Watkins. *The Family in Renaissance Florence*. Columbia, S. Carolina, 1969.
Alcock, Simon. 'Simon Alcock on expanding the sermon'. Ed. M. F. Boynton. *HTR*, 33 (1941), pp. 210–16.
Angelus de Clavasio. *Summa de casibus conscientiae cum additionibus noviter additis*. Lyons, 1500.
Anon. Twenty-one Middle English sermons. Lambeth MS 392, ff. 148–218.
Antoninus of Florence. *Saint Antonin: une règle de vie au XVe siècle*. Trans. Mme Thiérard-Baudrillart. Paris, 1921.
Summula confessionis. Strasburg, 1499.
Summa Theologica. 4 vols. Graz, 1959 (reprint of the Verona edition, 1740).
Aquinas, Thomas. *Contra impugnantes dei cultum et religionem*. In *Opera omnia iussu impensaque Leonis XIII P.M. edita*. Vol. XLI, Part A. Rome, 1970.
The Disputed Questions on Truth. Trans. R. W. Schmidt. 3 vols. Chicago, 1954.
Opera omnia. 34 vols. Paris: Vivès, 1871–80.
Opera omnia iussu impensaque Leonis XIII P.M. edita. Rome, 1882–
Quaestiones disputatae. Ed. R. Spiazzi. Rome, 1949.
Quaestiones quodlibetales. Ed. R. Spiazzi. Rome, 1956.
Scriptum super libros sententiarum magistri Petri Lombardi episcopi Parisiensis. 3 vols. Ed. R. P. Mandonnet. Paris, 1929.
Selected Political Writings. Trans. J. G. Dawson. Oxford, 1954.
Summa contra gentiles. Editio Leonina Manualis. Rome, 1934.
Summa theologiae. 5 vols. Madrid, 1955–8.
Theological Texts. Trans. T. Gilby. Oxford, 1955.
Aristotle. *Ethica Nicomachea*. Trans. W. D. Ross. Oxford, 1925.
Augustine. *Confessiones*. *CSEL*, 33.
De bono conjugali. *CSEL*, 41, pp. 185–231 (trans. *FC*, 27).
De bono viduitatis. *CSEL*, 41, pp. 303–43 (trans. *FC*, 16).
De civitate dei. *CCSL*, 48.
De Genesi ad litteram. *CSEL*, 28, pp. 1–435.

337

De gratia et libero arbitrio. MPL, 44: 881–912 (trans. *FC*, 59).
De sancta virginitate. CSEL, 41, pp. 233–302 (trans. *FC*, 27).
De spiritu et littera. CSEL, 60, pp. 155–229.
De trinitate. CCSL, 50, 50A (trans. *FC*, 45).
Enchiridion ad Laurentium de fide et spe et caritate. CCSL, 46, pp. 21–114 (trans. *FC*, 4).
In epistolam Joannis ad Parthos. MPL, 35: 1977–2062.
Bernard of Clairvaux. *On the Song of Songs*. Trans. K. Walsh *et al.* 4 vols. Spencer, Mass. and Kalamazoo, Michigan, 1971–80.
Treatises II. Trans. A. Conway and T. Walton. Washington, 1974.
Bernardine of Siena. *Sermons*. Ed. D. N. Orlandi. Trans. H. J. Robins. Siena, 1920.
Bettenson, H. *Documents of the Christian Church*. Oxford, 1943.
Biel, Gabriel. *Collectorium circa quattuor libros sententiarum*. Ed. W. Werbeck and U. Hofmann. Vols. I, II, IV. Tübingen, 1973–84.
Bonaventure. *The Mind's Road to God*. Trans. G. Boas. New York, 1953.
Opera omnia. 10 vols. Florence: Quaracchi, 1882–1902.
The Works of Bonaventure, Cardinal, Seraphic Doctor and Saint. Trans. J. de Vinck. 5 vols. Patterson, New Jersey, 1960–6.
The Book of Vices and Virtues: A Fourteenth-Century English Translation of the Somme le Roi. Ed. W. N. Francis. EETS, OS, 217. London, 1942.
Bradwardine, Thomas. *De causa dei contra Pelagium et de virtute causarum ad suos Mertonenses, libri tres*. Ed. H. Saville. London, 1618.
Cassian, John. *Conferences*. Trans. E. C. S. Gibson. *NPNF*, 2nd Series, Vol. XI. New York, 1894.
Institutes. Trans. E. C. S. Gibson. *NPNF*, 2nd Series, Vol. XI. New York, 1894.
Chartularium universitatis Parisiensis. 4 vols. Ed. H. Denifle and E. Chatelain. Paris, 1889–97.
Christine de Pisan. *Oeuvres poétiques*. 3 vols. Ed. M. Roy. Paris, 1965 (reprint of the edition of 1891).
Chronique du religieux de Saint-Denys. 6 vols. Ed. M. L. Bellaguet. Paris, 1839–52.
Ciboule, Robert. *Edition critique du sermon 'Qui manducat me' de Robert Ciboule (1403–1458) par Nicole Marzac*. Cambridge, 1971.
Cicero, Marcus Tullius. *De inventione*. London, 1960.
De oratore. 2 vols. London, 1967–8.
The Cloud of Unknowing and Other Treatises by an English Mystic of the Fourteenth Century. Ed. J. McCann. London, 1943.
Concilia Magnae Britanniae et Hiberniae. Vol. III. Ed. D. Wilkins. London, 1937.
Courtecuisse, Jean. *L'Oeuvre oratoire française*. Ed. G. di Stefano. Turin, 1969.
Denck, Hans. *Schriften*. Ed. G. Baring and W. Fellman. Gütersloh, 1960.
Duns Scotus, John. *Quaestiones in librum quartum sententiarum*. 2 vols. Antwerp, 1620.
Eckhart, Meister. *A Modern Translation: Sermons and Fragments*. Trans. R. B. Blakney. New York, 1941.
Selected Treatises and Sermons. Trans. J. M. Clark and J. V. Skinner. London, 1958.
Erasmus, Desiderius. *The Colloquies of Erasmus*. Trans. C. R. Thompson. Chicago, 1965.
A Diatribe or Sermon Concerning Free Will. In *Erasmus–Luther: Discourse on Free Will*. Ed. and trans. E. F. Winter. New York, 1961.
De ratione concionandi libri quattuor. Ed. F. A. Klein. Leipzig, 1820.
Ferrier, Vincent. *Saint Vincent Ferrier: Textes choisis et présentés*. Ed. B. H. Vanderberghe. Namur, 1956.

'Le Sermon en langue vulgaire prononcé à Toulouse par Saint Vincent Ferrier le vendredi saint, 1416'. Ed. C. Brunel. *Bibliothèque de l'Ecole de Chartes*, CXI (1953), pp. 5–53.

Gerson, Jean. 'Jean Gerson prédicateur français pour la fête de l'Annonciation'. Ed. L. Mourin. *Revue belge de philologie et d'histoire*, 27 (1949), pp. 561–98.

Oeuvres complètes. 10 vols. Ed. P. Glorieux. Paris, 1960–73.

Opera omnia. 4 vols. Ed. L. Ellies du Pin. Antwerp, 1706.

'Le Sermon français inédit de Jean Gerson pour la Noël: Puer natus est nobis'. Ed. L. Mourin. *Lettres romanes*, 2 (1948), pp. 315–24; 3 (1949), pp. 31–43, 105–145.

'Un Sermon français inédit de Jean Gerson sur les anges et les tentations: Factum est proelium'. Ed. L. Mourin. *RTAM*, 16 (1949), pp. 99–154.

'Les Sermons français inédits de Jean Gerson pour les fêtes de l'Annonciation et de la Purification'. Ed. L. Mourin. *Scriptorium*, 2 (1948), pp. 221–40; 3 (1949), pp. 59–68.

Six Sermons français inédits de Jean Gerson: Etude doctrinale et littéraire, suivie de l'édition critique. Ed. L. Mourin. Paris, 1946.

'*Tractatus magistri Johannis Gerson de mistica theologia*: St. Pölten, Diözesanarchiv MS. 25.' Ed. E. Colledge and J. C. Marler. *MS*, 41 (1979), pp. 354–86.

'Trois règlements de vie de Gerson pour ses soeurs'. Ed. E. Vansteenberghe. *RSR*, 14 (1934), pp. 191–218.

Gregory the Great. *Homiliae in Evangelia. MPL*, 76: 1075–1314.

Homiliae in Ezechielem prophetam. MPL, 76: 786–1072.

Moralia in Job. MPL, 75: 540–1162; 76: 9–786. *CCSL*, 143, 143A (libri I–XXII).

Regula pastoralis. MPL, 77: 12–126.

Grisdale, D. M. *Three Middle English Sermons from the Worcester Chapter Manuscript f*. 10. Leeds, 1339.

Hilton, Walter. *The Scale of Perfection*. Ed. G. Sitwell. London, 1953.

Horner, P. J. 'A sermon on the anniversary of the death of Thomas Beauchamp, Earl of Warwick'. *Traditio*, 34 (1978), pp. 381–401.

Hudson, A. ed. *English Wycliffite Sermons*. Vol. I. Oxford, 1983.

Selections from English Wycliffite Writings. Cambridge, 1978.

Hugh of Balma. *De mystica theologia*. In Bonaventure, *Opera omnia*, Vol. VIII, pp. 1–53. Paris: Vivès, 1866.

Hugh of St Victor. *De arrha animae. MPL*, 176: 951–70 (trans. F. Sherwood Taylor, *The Soul's Betrothal Gift*. Westminster, 1945).

De modo orandi deum. MPL, 176: 977–81.

De sacramentis christianae fidei. MPL, 176: 173–618.

In Ecclesiasten. MPL, 175: 113–256.

Humbert of Romans. *Treatise on Preaching*. Trans. the Dominican Students, Province of St Joseph. London, 1955.

Jacques de Vitry. *The Exempla or Illustrative Stories from the Sermones Vulgares of Jacques de Vitry*. Ed. T. F. Crane. London, 1890.

Jean de Montreuil. *Opera*. Vol. I. Ed. E. Ornato. Turin, 1963.

John of Freiburg. *Summa confessorum*. Lyon, 1518.

Langton, Stephen. *Selected Sermons*. Ed. P. Roberts. Toronto, 1980.

Legrand, Jacques. 'Un sermon français inédit attribuable à Jacques Legrand'. Ed. J. Beltrán. *Romania*, 93 (1972), pp. 460–78.

Lombard, Peter. *Libri quattuor sententiarum. MPL*, 192: 519–962.

Lorris, Guillaume de, and Jean de Meung. *The Romance of the Rose*. Trans. H. W. Robins. New York, 1962.

Luther, Martin. *D. Martin Luthers Werke: Kritische Gesamtausgabe*. Weimar, 1883–

Maillard, Olivier. *Histoire de la Passion de Jésus-Christ*. Ed. M. Peignot. Paris, 1828.
Oeuvres françaises: Sermons et Poésies. Ed. A de la Borderie. Geneva, 1968 (reprint of the Nantes edition, 1877).
Mannying of Brunne, Robert. *Handlyng Synne*. Ed. F. J. Furnival. EETS, OS, 119 and 123. London, 1901–3.
Marsilius of Padua. *The Defender of Peace: The Defensor Pacis*. Trans. A. Gerwith. New York, 1967.
Menot, Michel. *Sermons choisis de Michel Menot*. Ed. J. Nève. Paris, 1924.
Mirk, John. *Festial*. Ed. T. Erbe. EETS, ES, 96. London, 1905.
Instructions for Parish Priests. Ed. E. Peacock. EETS. OS, 31. London, 1868; rev. 1902.
Monstrelet, Enguerrand de. *Chronique*. 6 vols. Ed. L. Douët-d'Arcq. Paris, 1857–62.
Nicholas de Clamanges. 'Les Prières inédites de Nicholas de Clamanges'. Ed. J. Leclercq. *Revue d'ascetique et mystique*, 23 (1947), pp. 171–83.
Occam, William of. *Dialogus inter magistrum et discipulum*. Ed. M. Goldast. In *Monarchiae S. Romani imperii sive Tractatuum de iurisdictione imperiali, regia, et pontificia seu sacerdotali*. II. Frankfurt, 1688.
Opera Philosophica et Theologica. Vol. I (Opera Theologica), Parts I–VI, and IX. New York, 1967–82.
Opera plurima. Lyon, 1494–6 (reprint, London, 1962).
Predestination, God's Knowledge, and Future Contingents. Trans. and ed. M. M. Adams and N. Kretzmann. New York, 1969.
The Paston Letters. 2 vols. Ed. J. Warrington. London, 1956.
Peraldus, William. *Summa de vitiis et virtutibus*. Antwerp, 1587.
Petry, R. C. *No Uncertain Sound: Sermons that Shaped the Pulpit Tradition*. Philadelphia, 1948.
Plato. *The Republic of Plato*. Trans. F. M. Cornford. Oxford, 1941.
Pseudo-Dionysius the Areopagite. *The Divine Names and the Mystical Theology*. Trans. C. E. Rolt. London, 1940.
Opera. MPG, 3.
Quintilianus, Marcus Fabius. *Institutio oratoria*. 2 vols. Trans. J. S. Watson. London, 1899.
Les Quinze Joyes de mariage. Ed. J. Crow. Oxford, 1969.
Ratis Raving. Ed. J. R. Lumby. EETS, OS, 43. London, 1870.
Raymond de Penafort. *Summa sancti Raymundi de Penafort de poenitentia et matrimonio*. Rome, 1603 (reprint Farnborough, England, 1967).
Richard of St Victor. *The Twelve Patriarchs, the Mystical Ark, the Trinity*. Trans. G. A. Zinn. New York, 1979.
Richard of Thetford. *Ars concionandi*. In *Bonaventurae Opera omnia*, Vol. IX, pp. 16–21. Florence: Quaracchi, 1901.
Robert of Flamborough. *Liber poenitentialis*. Ed. J. J. F. Firth. Toronto, 1971.
Rolle, Richard. *The Fire of Love*. Ed. C. Wolters. London, 1972.
Ross, W. O. *Middle English Sermons from B.M. MS Royal* 18.B xxiii. EETS, OS, 209. London, 1940.
Rosarium theologiae. The Middle English Translation of the Rosarium Theologie. Ed. C. von Nolcken. Heidelberg, 1979.
Ruysbroeck, John of. *The Adornment of Spiritual Marriage; The Sparkling Stone; The Book of Supreme Truth*. Trans. C. A. Wynschenk. London, 1951.
Salutati, Coluccio. *Letters to the Chancellor of Bologna*. In E. Emerton, ed., *Humanism and Tyranny*, pp. 290–311. Cambridge, Mass., 1925.
Savonarola, Girolamo. *Prediche e scritti*. Ed. M. Ferrara. Milan, 1930.

Suso, Henry. *Horologium sapientiae.* Ed. P. Kunzle. Freiburg, 1977.
  The Little Book of Eternal Wisdom and the Little Book of Truth. Trans. J. M. Clark.
  New York, 1953.
Tauler, John. *The Sermons and Conferences of John Tauler of the Order of Preachers.*
  Trans. W. Elliot. Washington, 1910.
  Spiritual Conferences. Trans. E. Colledge. St Louis, 1961.
Theologia Germanica. The Theologia Germanica of Martin Luther. Trans. B. Hoffman.
  London, 1980.
Thomas à Kempis. *Of the Imitation of Christ.* Trans. A. Hoskins. Oxford, 1940.
Vatican Council II: The Conciliar and Post-Conciliar Documents. Ed. A. Flannery.
  New York, 1975.
Vincent of Aggsbach. *Treatise against Gerson.* In E. Vansteenberghe, *Autour de la
  docte ignorance: Une controverse sur la théologie mystique au XVe siècle.*
  Münster, 1915.
Vincent of Beauvais. *De eruditione filiorum nobilium.* Ed. A. Steiner. Cambridge,
  Mass., 1938 (reprint, New York, 1970).
Vittorino da Feltre. *De ordine docendi et studendi.* In W. H. Woodward, ed.,
  Vittorino da Feltre and Other Humanist Educators. Cambridge, 1897 (reprint,
  New York, 1963).
Walsingham, Thomas. *Chronicon Anglicana.* 2 vols. Ed. H. T. Riley. Rolls Series,
  London, 1863–4.
William of Auvergne. 'Un manuel de prédication médiévale'. Ed. A. de Poorter.
  Revue néo-scolastique de philosophie, 25 (1939), pp. 196–206.
  Rhetorica divina seu ars oratoria eloquentiae divinae. In *Opera omnia,* Vol. I, pp.
  336–405. Orléans–Paris, 1674.
William of St Thierry. *Epistola ad fratres de Monte Dei.* Trans. T. Berkeley.
  Spencer, Mass., 1971.
Wyclif, John. *Select English Works of John Wyclif.* 3 vols. Ed. T. Arnold. Oxford,
  1869–71.
Zwingli, Huldreich. *Huldreich Zwinglis Werke.* Ed. M. Schuler and J. Schulthess.
  Zurich, 1828.

Secondary sources

Adam, P. *La Vie paroissiale en France au XIVe siècle.* Paris, 1964.
Adams-Smith, D. E. *Some French Works of Jean Gerson: An Introduction and
  Translation.* Ph.D dissertation, University of South Carolina, 1976.
Allmand, C. T., ed. *Society at War: The Experience of England and France During
  the Hundred Years War.* Edinburgh, 1973.
Alverny, M.-T. d'. 'Comment les théologiens et les philosophes voient la femme'.
  Cahiers de Civilisation Médiévale, 20 (1977), pp. 105–28.
Ampe, A. *L'Imitation de Jésus-Christ et son auteur: Reflexions critiques.* Rome, 1973.
  Ruusbroec: Traditie en Werkelijkeid. Antwerp, 1975.
Ariès, P. *Centuries of Childhood: A Social History of Family Life.* Trans. R. Baldick.
  New York, 1962.
Arnold, F. X. *La Femme dans l'église.* Paris, 1955.
Avray, D. L. d'. 'Sermons to the upper bourgeoisie by a thirteenth-century
  Franciscan'. *Studies in Church History,* 16 (1979), pp. 187–99.
Avray, D. L. d' and M. Tausche. 'Marriage sermons in *Ad status* collections of the
  central middle ages'. *AHDLMA,* 47 (1981), pp. 71–119.
Bailey, D. S. *The Man–Woman Relation in Christian Thought.* London, 1959.
Bardèche, M. *Histoire des femmes.* 2 vols. Paris, 1968.

Batts, M. C. *The Political Ideas of Jean Gerson*. Ph.D dissertation, University of Ottawa, 1976.

Baylor, M. G. *Action and Person: Conscience in Late Scholasticism and the Young Luther*. Leiden, 1977.

Beltrán, E. 'Jacques Legrand, prédicaheur'. *Analecta Augustiniana*, 30 (1967), pp. 148–209.

Benton, J. F. 'Clio and Venus: an historical view of medieval love'. In *The Meaning of Courtly Love*. Ed. F. X. Newman. New York, 1968, pp. 19–42.

Bernstein, A. E. *Pierre d'Ailly and the Blanchard Affair: University and Chancellor at the Beginning of the Great Schism*. Leiden, 1978.

'Theology and popular belief: confession in the later thirteenth century'. Unpublished paper.

Blench, J. W. *Preaching in England in the Late Fifteenth and Sixteenth Centuries: A Study of English Sermons, 1450–1600*. Oxford, 1964.

Bloomfield, M. W. *The Seven Deadly Sins: An Introduction to the History of a Religious Concept with Special Reference to Medieval English Literature*. East Lansing, Michigan, 1952.

Boehner, P. *Collected Articles on Ockham*. New York, 1958.

Boland, P. *The Concept of Discretio Spirituum in John Gerson's 'De probatione spirituum' and 'De distinctione verarum visionum a falsis'*. Washington, 1959.

Bonney, F. 'Autour de Jean Gerson: opinions de théologiens sur les superstitions et la sorcellerie au début du XVe siècle'. *Le Moyen Age*, 77 (1971), pp. 85–98.

Jean Gerson et l'enfance. Thèse de troisième cycle, University of Bordeaux III, 1972.

'Jean Gerson: Un nouveau regard sur l'enfance'. *Annales de démographie historique*, 1973, pp. 137–42.

Borresen, K. D. *Subordination et équivalence: Nature et rôle de la femme d'après Augustin et Thomas d'Aquin*. Oslo, 1968.

Bossy, J. 'Holiness and Society'. *Past and Present*, 75 (1977), pp. 119–37.

'The social history of confession in the age of Reformation'. *TRHS*, (5th ser.), 25 (1975), *pp.* 21–38.

Boyle, L. E. 'Aspects of clerical education in fourteenth-century England'. *The Fourteenth Century, Acta IV*. Center for Medieval and Early Renaissance Studies, SUNY, Binghamton, NY, 1977, pp. 19–32.

'The constitution "Cum ex eo" of Boniface VIII: education of parochial clergy', *MS*, 24 (1962), pp. 263–302.

'Notes on the education of the *Fratres Communes* in the Dominican order in the thirteenth century'. *Xenia Medii Aevi Historiam Illustrantia oblata Thomae Kaeppeli, O.P.* Rome, 1978, pp. 249–67.

'The *Oculus sacerdotis* and some other works of William of Pagula'. *TRHS* (5th ser.), 5 (1955), pp. 81–110.

Pastoral Care, Clerical Education and Canon Law, 1200–1400. London, 1981.

Review of *Sin and Confession on the Eve of the Reformation*, by T. N. Tentler, *Canadian Journal of History*, 13 (1978), pp. 272–4.

The Setting of the Summa Theologiae of Saint Thomas. Toronto, 1982.

'The Summa for Confessors and its religious intent'. In *The Pursuit of Holiness in Late Medieval and Renaissance Religion*. Ed. C. Trinkaus and H. A. Oberman. Leiden, 1974, pp. 126–30.

'The *Summa Confessorum* of John of Freiburg and the popularization of the moral teaching of St. Thomas and his contemporaries'. In *St. Thomas Aquinas, 1274–1974: Commemorative Studies*. Ed. A. A. Maurer et al. Toronto, 1974. Vol. II, pp. 245–68.

Braeckmans, L. *Confession et communion au moyen âge et au concile de Trente*. Gembloux, 1971.

Brandl, L. *Die Sexualethik des heiligen Albertus Magnus*. Regensburg, 1955.

Bridenthal, R. and C. Koonz, ed. *Becoming Visible: Women in European History*. Boston, 1977.

Brundage, J. A. 'Adultery and fornication: a study in legal theology'. In *Sexual Practices and the Medieval Church*. Ed. V. L. Bullough and J. A. Brundage. Buffalo, 1982.

'Concubinage and marriage in medieval canon law'. *Journal of Medieval History*, 1 (1975), pp. 1–17.

Bulaeus, C. E. *Historia Universitatis Parisiensis*, Vols. IV & V, Paris, 1668 & 1670.

Bullough, V. L. 'Medieval medical and scientific views of women'. *Viator*, 4 (1973), pp. 473–501.

'Sex and canon law'. In *Sexual Practices and the Medieval Church*. Ed. V. L. Bullough and J. A. Brundage. Buffalo, 1982, pp. 89–101.

Bullough, V. L. and J. A. Brundage, ed. *Sexual Practices and the Medieval Church*. Buffalo, 1982.

Caplan, H. *Of Eloquence: Studies in Ancient and Medieval Eloquence*. Ithaca, 1970.

Casey, K. 'The Cheshire cat: reconstructing the experience of medieval women'. In *Liberating Women's History: Theoretical and Critical Essays*. Ed. B. A. Carrol. Illinois, 1976, pp. 224–45.

Charland, T.-M. *Artes praedicandi: Contribution à l'histoire de la rhétorique au moyen âge*. Ottawa. 1936.

Chenu, M.-D. *L'Eveil de la conscience dans la civilisation médiévale*. Paris, 1969.

Clark, F. 'A new appraisal of late medieval theology'. *Gregorianum*, 40 (1965), pp. 733–65.

Clark, J. M. *Meister Eckhardt: An Introduction to the Study of his Works*. London, 1957.

Cole, W. G. *Sex in Christianity and Psychoanalysis*. Oxford, 1955.

Colledge, E. *The Medieval Mystics of England*. New York, 1961.

Combes, A. *Essai sur la critique de Ruysbroeck par Gerson*. 3 vols. Paris, 1945–59.

Jean de Montreuil et le chancelier Gerson: Contribution à l'histoire des rapports de l'humanisme et de la théologie en France au début du XVe siècle. Paris, 1942.

Jean Gerson, commentateur dionysien: Pour l'histoire des courants doctrinaux à l'université de Paris à la fin du XIVe siècle. Paris, 1940.

'Un témoin du socratisme chrétien au XVe siècle: Robert Ciboule (1403–58)'. *AHDLMA*, 8 (1933), pp. 93–259.

La Théologie mystique de Gerson: Profil de son évolution. 2 vols. Paris, 1963–4.

Congar, Y. M.-J. 'Aspects ecclésiologiques de la querelle entre mendiants et séculiers dans la seconde moitié du XIIIe siècle et le début du XIVe siècle'. *AHDLMA*, 28 (1961), pp. 35–151.

Connolly, J. *John Gerson: Reformer and Mystic*. Louvain, 1928.

Courtenay, W. J. 'Nominalism and late medieval religion'. In *The Pursuit of Holiness in late Medieval and Renaissance Religion*. Ed. C. Trinkaus and H. A. Oberman. Leiden, 1974, pp. 26–59.

Crowder, C. M. D. *Unity, Heresy and Reform, 1378–1460: The Conciliar Response to the Great Schism*. London, 1977.

Davies, K. M. 'The sacred condition of equality – how original were Puritan doctrines of marriage?'. *Social History*, 5 (1977), pp. 563–80.

De Benedictis, M. M. *The Social Thought of Saint Bonaventure: A Study in Social Philosophy*. Washington, 1946.

Delaruelle, E. *et al. L'Eglise au temps du Grand Schisme et da la crise conciliare*. 2 vols. Paris, 1962–4.

DeLetter, P. 'Contrition'. *NCE*, IV, pp. 278–83.

Delhaye, P. 'Fixation dogmatique de la théologie dogmatique du mariage'. *Concilium*, 55 (1970), pp. 77–81.

Demaitre, L. 'The idea of childhood and child care in medical writings of the middle ages'. *Journal of Psychohistory*, 4 (1976–7), pp. 461–90.

deMause, L., ed. *The History of Childhood*. New York, 1974.

De Roover, R. *San Bernardino of Siena and Sant'Antonio of Florence: The Two Great Economic Thinkers of the Middle Ages*. Cambridge, Mass., 1967.

Dondaine, A. 'Guillaume Peyraut: Vie et oeuvres'. *Archivum Fratrum Praedicatorum*, 18 (1948), pp. 162–236.

'La Somme de Simon de Hinton'. *RTAM*, 9 (1937), pp. 5–22, 205–18.

Douglass, E. J. D. *Justification in Late Medieval Preaching: A Study of John Geiler of Keisersberg*. Leiden, 1966.

'Women in the continental Reformation'. In *Religion and Sexism: Images of Women in the Jewish and Christian Traditions*. Ed. R. R. Ruether. New York, 1974, pp. 292–318.

Dow, B. H. *The Varying Attitudes toward Women in French Literature of the Fifteenth Century*. New York, 1936.

Elder, E. R., ed. *Spirituality of Western Christendom*. Kalamazoo, Michigan, 1976.

Evans, R. F. *Pelagius: Inquiries and Reappraisals*. London, 1968.

Flandrin, J.-L. 'L'Attitude à l'égard du petit enfant et les conduites sexuelles dans la civilisation occidentale'. *Annales de démographie historique* (1973), pp. 143–210.

'Mariage tardif et vie sexuelle'. *Annales E.S.C.*, 27 (1972), pp. 1351–78.

Foster, K. *Courtly Love and Christianity*. London, 1963.

Francq, H. G. 'Jean Gerson's theological treatises and other memoirs in defence of Joan of Arc'. *Revue de l'Université d'Ottawa*, 41 (1971), pp. 58–80.

Gabriel, A. L. 'Pierre d'Ailly and the new statutes of Ave Maria College'. In *Recueil des travaux offerts à Clovis Brunel*. Paris, 1955.

'Preparatory teaching in the Parisian colleges during the fourteenth century'. *Revue de l'Université d'Ottawa*, 21 (1951), pp. 449–83.

Student Life in Ave Maria College, Medieval Paris: History and Chartulary of the College. Notre Dame, Indiana, 1955.

Gerrits, G. *Inter Timorem et Spem: A Study of the Theological Thought of Gerard Zerbolt of Zutphen*. Ph.D. dissertation, Queen's University, Kingston, Canada, 1978.

Gies, F. and J. *Women in the Middle Ages*. New York, 1978.

Gilbert, N. W. 'Ockham, Wyclif and the "via moderna"', *Miscellanea Medievalia*, IX (1974), pp. 85–125.

Gilchrist, J. *The Church and Economic Activity in the Middle Ages*. London, 1969.

Gilson, E. *History of Christian Philosophy in the Middle Ages*. New York, 1955.

'Michel Menot et la technique du sermon médiéval'. *Revue d'histoire franciscaine*, 2 (1925), pp. 301–60.

Glorieux, P. 'Le Chancelier Gerson et la réforme de l'enseignment'. In *Mélanges offerts à Etienne Gilson*. Toronto, 1959, pp. 285–98.

'L'Enseignement universitaire de Gerson'. *RTAM*, 23 (1956), pp. 83–113.

'Gerson'. *NCE*, VI, pp. 449–50.

'Quatre dialogues de Gerson en vers français'. *Mélanges de science religieuse*, 7 (1950), pp. 215–36.

'S. Joseph dans l'oeuvre de Gerson'. *Cahiers de Joséphologie*, 19 (1971), pp. 414–28.

'La Vie et les oeuvres de Gerson: Essai chronologique'. *AHDLMA*, 18 (1950–1), pp. 149–92.

Goertz, H.-J. *Innere und äussere Ordnung in der Theologie Thomas Müntzers*. Leiden, 1967.

Gold, P. S. 'The marriage of Mary and Joseph in the twelfth-century ideology of marriage'. In *Sexual Practices and the Medieval Church*. Ed. V. L. Bullough and J. A. Brundage. Buffalo, 1982, pp. 102–17.

Guarnieri, R. 'Il movimento del libero spirito'. *Archivio italiano per la storia della pietà*, 4, 1965, pp. 501–635.

Haines, R. M. 'Church, society and politics in the early fifteenth century as viewed from an English pulpit'. In *Church, Society and Politics*. Ed. D. Baker. Oxford, 1975, pp. 143–57.

'Our master mariner, "our sovereign lord"': a contemporary preacher's view of King Henry V'. *MS*, 38 (1976), pp. 85–96.

Hale, J. R. *Renaissance Europe, 1480–1520*. London, 1971.

Hanawalt, B. A. 'Childrearing among the lower classes in later medieval England'. *Journal of Interdisciplinary History*, 8 (1977), pp. 1–22.

Harnack, A. *History of Dogma*, Vol. VI. Trans. W. McGilchrist. London, 1899.

Hathaway, R. F. *Hierarchy and the Definition of Order in the Letters of Pseudo-Dionysius*. The Hague, 1969.

Healy, E. T. *Woman according to Saint Bonaventure*. New York, 1956.

Hefele, C. J. and H. Leclerq. *Histoire des conciles*. 8 vols. Paris, 1907–16.

Herlihy, D. 'The medieval marriage market'. *Medieval and Renaissance Studies: Proceedings of the Southeastern Institute of Medieval and Renaissance Studies*, 1974. 6 (1976), pp. 3–27.

Hermelink, H. *Die theologische Fakultät in Tübingen vor der Reformation*. Tübingen, 1906.

Hilton, R. H. *The English Peasantry in the Later Middle Ages*. Oxford, 1975.

Huizinga, J. *The Waning of the Middle Ages: A Study of the Forms of Life, Thought and Art in France and the Netherlands in the Fourteenth and Fifteenth Centuries*. New York, 1954.

Hunt, D. *Parents and Children in History: The Psychology of Family Life in Early Modern France*. New York, 1970.

Jadart, H. *Jean Gerson, 1363–1429: Recherches sur son origine, son village natale et sa famille*. Rheims, 1882.

Jedin, H. and J. Dolan, eds. *Handbook of Church History*. Vol. IV. London, 1970.

Kelly, H. A. *Love and Marriage in the Age of Chaucer*. Ithaca, 1975.

Kerns, J. E. *The Theology of Marriage: The Historical Development of Christian Attitudes toward Sex and Sanctity in Marriage*. New York, 1964.

Knowles, D. *The English Mystical Tradition*. London, 1961.

Kristeller, P. O. 'The validity of the term: "nominalism"'. In *The Pursuit of Holiness in Late Medieval and Renaissance Religion*. Ed. C. Trinkaus and H. A. Oberman. Leiden, 1974, pp. 65–6.

Lambon, A. *Jean Gerson, sa réforme de l'enseignement théologique et de l'éducation populaire*. Paris, 1892.

Leff, G. *The Dissolution of the Medieval Outlook: An Essay on Intellectual and Spiritual Change in the Fourteenth Century*. New York, 1976.

William of Ockham: The Metamorphosis of Scholastic Discourse. Manchester, 1975.

Le Goff, J. 'Métier et profession d'après les manuels de confesseurs au moyen âge'. *Miscellanea Mediaevalia*, III (1964), pp. 44–60.

Lerner, R. E. *The Heresy of the Free Spirit in the Later Middle Ages*. Berkeley, California, 1972.

'The image of mixed liquids in late medieval mystical thought'. *CH*, 40 (1971), pp. 397–411.

Levi, A. H. T., ed. *Humanism in France at the End of the Middle Ages and in the Early Renaissance*. Manchester, 1970.

Lieberman, M. 'Chronologie gersonienne'. *Romania*, 70 (1948–9), pp. 51–67; 73 (1952), pp. 480–96; 74 (1953), pp. 289–337; 76 (1955), pp. 289–333; 78 (1957), pp. 433–62; 79 (1958), pp. 339–75; 80 (1959), pp. 289–336; 81 (1960), pp. 43–98, 338–79.

'Gersoniana'. *Romania*, 78 (1957), pp. 1–36, 145–81; 83 (1962), pp. 52–89.

Little, L. K. 'Pride goes before avarice: social change and vices in Latin Christendom'. *American Historical Review*, 76 (1971), pp. 16–49.

Locher, G. W. *Zwingli's Thought: New Perspectives*. Leiden, 1981.

Lockwood, W. B. 'Vernacular Scriptures in Germany and the Low Countries before 1500'. In *The Cambridge History of the Bible*. Vol. II. Ed. G. W. H. Lampe. Cambridge, 1969.

MacLean, I. *The Renaissance Notion of Woman: A Study in the Fortunes of Scholasticism and Medical Science in European Intellectual Life*. Cambridge, 1980.

Makowsky, E. M. 'The conjugal debt and medieval canon law'. *Journal of Medieval History*, 3 (1977), pp. 99–114.

Marche, A. L. de la. *La Chaire française au moyen âge*. Paris, 1886.

Martin, H. 'Les Procédés didactiques en usage dans la prédication en France du nord au XVe siècle', in *La Religion populaire*. *Colloques Internationaux du Centre National de la Recherche Scientifique*. No. 576. Paris, 1977.

McAodha, L. 'The nature and efficacy of preaching according to St. Bernardine of Siena'. *Franciscan Studies*, 27 (1967), pp. 221–47.

McCarthy, J. M. *Humanistic Emphases in the Educational Thought of Vincent de Beauvais*. Leiden, 1976.

McKeever, P. E. 'Penance'. *NCE*, XI, pp. 75–83.

McLaughlin, M. M. 'Survivors and surrogates: children and parents from the ninth to the thirteenth centuries'. In *The History of Childhood*. Ed. L. deMause. New York, 1974, pp. 101–87.

McNamara, J. and S. F. Wemple. 'Sanctity and power: the dual pursuit of medieval women'. In *Becoming Visible: Women in European History*. Ed. R. Bridenthal and C. Koonz. Boston, 1977.

Metz, R. 'Le Statut de la femme en droit canonique médiévale'. *Recueils de la Société Jean Bodin*, 12 (1962), pp. 59–113.

Meyjes, G. H. M. P. *Jean Gerson et l'assemblée de Vincennes (1329)*. Leiden, 1978.

Jean Gerson: Zijn Kerkpolitiek en Ecclesiologie. The Hague, 1963.

Michaud-Quantin, P. 'Aspects de la vie sociale chez les moralistes'. *Miscellanea Mediaevalia*, III (1964), pp. 30–43.

'La Conscience individuelle et ses droits chez les moralistes de la fin du moyen âge'. *Miscellanea Mediaevalia*, VI (1968), pp. 42–55.

Sommes de casuistique et manuels de confession au moyen âge (XIIe–XVIe siècles). Louvain, 1962.

Mollat, M. *La Vie et la pratique religieuse au XIVe et dans la Ire partie du XVe siècle, principalement en France*. Paris, 1965.

Morrall, J. B. *Gerson and the Great Schism*. Manchester, 1960.

Mourin, L. *Jean Gerson prédicateur français*. Bruges, 1952.

Müller, M. *Die Lehre von Paradiesesehe*. Regensburg, 1954.

Murphy, J. J. *Rhetoric in the Middle Ages: A History of Rhetorical Theory from Saint Augustine to the Renaissance*. Berkeley, California, 1974.

Three Medieval Rhetorical Arts. Berkeley, California, 1971.

Newman, F. X., ed. *The Meaning of Courtly Love*. New York, 1968.

Noonan, J. T. *Contraception: A History of its Treatment by the Catholic Theologians and Canonists.* Toronto, 1965.
'Power to choose'. *Viator*, 4 (1973), pp. 419–34.
The Scholastic Analysis of Usury. Cambridge, Mass., 1957.
Oakley, F. 'Gerson and d'Ailly: an admonition'. *Speculum*, 40 (1965), pp. 74–83.
The Medieval Experience: Foundations of Western Cultural Singularity. New York, 1974.
The Political Thought of Pierre d'Ailly: The Voluntarist Tradition. New Haven, 1964.
The Western Church in the Later Middle Ages. Ithaca, 1979.
Oberman, H. A. '*Facientibus quod in se est, deus non denegat gratiam*: Robert Holcot, O.P. and the beginnings of Luther's theology'. *HTR*, 55 (1962), pp. 317–42.
Forerunners of the Reformation: The Shape of Late Medieval Thought. New York, 1966.
'Fourteenth-century religious thought: a premature profile'. *Speculum*, 53 (1978), pp. 80–93.
'Gabriel Biel and late medieval mysticism'. *CH*, 30 (1961), pp. 259–87.
The Harvest of Medieval Theology: Gabriel Biel and Late Medieval Nominalism. Rev. edn. Grand Rapids, Michigan, 1967.
'*Justitia Christi* and *Justitia Dei*: Luther and the scholastic doctrine of justification'. *HTR*, 59 (1966), pp. 1–26.
'The shape of late medieval thought: the birth pangs of the modern era'. In *The Pursuit of Holiness in Late Medieval and Renaissance Religion.* Ed. C. Trinkaus and H. A. Oberman. Leiden, 1974, pp. 3–25.
'*Simul gemitus et raptus*: Luther and mysticism'. In *The Reformation in Medieval Perspective.* Ed. S. E. Ozment. Chicago, 1971, pp. 219–51.
Some notes on the theology of nominalism'. *HTR*, 53 (1960), pp. 46–76.
Olivier-Martin, F. *Histoire du droit français des origines à la Révolution.* Paris, 1951.
Origo, I. *The World of San Bernardino.* New York, 1962.
Ornato, E. *Jean Muret et ses amis Nicholas de Clamanges et Jean de Montreuil.* Paris, 1969.
Ouy, G. 'Gerson et l'Angleterre'. In *Humanism in France at the End of the Middle Ages and in the Early Renaissance.* Ed. A. H. T. Levi. Manchester, 1970, pp. 43–81.
'Une lettre de jeunesse de Jean Gerson'. *Romania*, 80 (1959), pp. 461–72.
'La Plus Ancienne Oeuvre retrouvée de Jean Gerson'. *Romania*, 83 (1962), pp. 433–92.
Owst, G. R. *Literature and the Pulpit in Medieval England.* Cambridge, 1933.
Preaching in Medieval England. Cambridge, 1926.
Ozment, S. E. *The Age of Reform, 1250–1550: An Intellectual and Religious History of Late Medieval and Reformation Europe.* New Haven, 1980.
Homo Spiritualis: A Comparative Study of the Anthropology of Johannes Tauler, Jean Gerson and Martin Luther (1509–1516) in the Context of Their Theological Thought. Leiden, 1965.
Mysticism and Dissent: Religious Ideology and Social Protest in the Sixteenth Century. New Haven, 1973.
'Mysticism, nominalism and dissent'. In *The Pursuit of Holiness in Late Medieval and Renaissance Religion.* Ed. C. Trinkaus and H. A. Oberman. Leiden, 1974, pp. 67–92.
The Reformation in the Cities: The Appeal of Protestantism to Sixteenth-Century Germany and Switzerland. New Haven, 1975.
ed. *The Reformation in Medieval Perspective.* Chicago, 1971.

'The university and the church: patterns of reform in Jean Gerson'. *Medievalia et Humanistica* (N.S.), 1 (1970), pp. 111–26.

When Fathers Ruled: Family Life in Reformation Europe. Cambridge, Mass., 1983.

Packull, W. O. *Mysticism in the Early South German–Austrian Anabaptist Movement*, 1525–1531. Scottdale, Pennsylvania, 1977.

Palmer, R. C. 'Contexts of marriage in medieval England: evidence from the King's Court circa 1300'. *Speculum*, 59 (1984), pp. 42–67.

Pascoe, L. B. 'Gerson and the Donation of Constantine: growth and development within the church'. *Viator*, 5 (1974), pp. 469–85.

'Jean Gerson: the "Ecclesia primitiva" and reform'. *Traditio*, 30 (1974), pp. 379–409.

'Jean Gerson: mysticism, conciliarism and reform'. *Annuarium historiae conciliorum*, 6 (1974), pp. 135–53.

Jean Gerson: Principles of Church Reform. Leiden, 1973.

Payen, J. C. 'La Pénitence dans le contexte culturel des XIIe et XIIIe siècles'. *Revue des sciences philosophiques et théologiques*, 61 (1977), pp. 399–428.

Peter, J. *Complaint and Satire in Early English Literature*. Oxford, 1956.

Petot, P. 'Le Statut de la femme dans les pays coutumiers français du XIIIe au XVIIe siècle'. *Recueils de la Société Jean Bodin*, 12 (1962), pp. 243–54.

Petry, R. 'Social responsibility and the late medieval mystics'. *CH*, 21 (1952), pp. 3–19.

Pinckaers, S. 'Ce que le moyen âge pensait du mariage'. *La Vie spirituelle*, Supplément, 82 (1967), pp. 413–40.

Piton, M. 'L'Idéal épiscopale selon les prédicateurs français de la fin du XVe siècle et du début du XVIe'. *RHE*, 61 (1966), pp. 77–118, 393–423.

Power, E. *Medieval Women*. Ed. M. M. Postan. Cambridge, 1975.

'The position of women'. In *The Legacy of the Middle Ages*. Ed. C. G. Crump and E. F. Jacob. Oxford, 1926, pp. 401–34.

Principe, W. H. *Gerson's Attitude towards the Occult Sciences*. Dissertation for the Licenciate in Medieval Studies, Toronto, 1951.

Rapp, F. *L'Eglise et la vie religieuse en Occident à la fin du moyen âge*. Paris, 1971.

Rashdall, H. *The Universities of Europe in the Middle Ages*. Rev. edn by F. M. Powicke and A. B. Emden. Oxford, 1936.

Reilly à Brooklyn, P. G. *Ideals of Matrimony and Virginity in the Writings of St. Bonaventure*. Rome, 1964.

Richardson, L. M. *The Forerunners of Feminism in French Literature of the Renaissance*. Oxford, 1929.

Rigaud, R. *Les Idées féministes de Christine de Pisan*. Neuchâtel, 1911.

Roberts, P. 'Master Stephen Langton preaches to the people and clergy: sermon texts from twelfth-century Paris'. *Traditio*, 36 (1980), pp. 237–68.

Robson, C. A. 'Vernacular Scriptures in France'. In *The Cambridge History of the Bible*, Vol. II. Ed. G. W. H. Lampe. Cambridge, 1969, pp. 436–52.

Rogers, K. M. *The Troublesome Helpmate: A History of Mysogyny in Literature*. Washington, 1956.

Roques, R. *L'Univers dionysien*. Paris, 1954.

Ross, J. B. 'The middle-class in urban Italy, fourteenth to early sixteenth century'. In *The History of Childhood*. Ed. L. deMause. New York, 1974, pp. 183–228.

Rouse, R. and M. *Preachers, Florilegia and Sermons: Studies on the Manipulus Florum of Thomas of Ireland*. Toronto, 1979.

Rudin, J. 'A Catholic view of conscience'. In *Conscience: Theological and Psychological Perspectives*. Ed. C. Ellis Nelson. New York, 1973, pp. 95–114.

Ruether, R. R., ed. *Religion and Sexism: Images of Women in the Jewish and Christian Traditions*. New York, 1974.

Russell, C. *The Crisis of Parliaments: English History 1509–1660*. Oxford, 1971.

Salembier, L. 'Gerson'. *DTC*, VI, pp. 1313–30.

Samouillan, A. *Etude sur la chaire et la société française au XVe siècle: Olivier Maillard, sa prédication et son temps*. Toulouse, 1891.

Scalvini, F. 'Lo scrittore mistico Giovanni Gersone, 1363–1429'. *Rivista di ascetica e mistica*, 8 (1963), pp. 40–60.

Schwab, J. B. *Johann Gerson, Professor der Theologie und Kanzler der Universität Paris: Eine Monographie*. Würzburg, 1858.

Shafer, R. *A New Language for Psychoanalysis*. New Haven, 1976.

Smalley, B. 'The relevance of sermon studies to the historian'. *Medieval Sermon Studies Newsletter* (1979), pp. 2–3.

Spencer, H. *English Vernacular Sunday Preaching in the late Fourteenth and Fifteenth Century, with Illustrative Texts*. D.Phil. dissertation, Oxford, 1982.

Spinka, M. *Advocates of Reform*. London, 1953.

Spitz, L. W. 'Further lines of inquiry for the study of "Reformation and pedagogy"'. In *The Pursuit of Holiness in Late Medieval and Renaissance Religion*. Ed. C. Trinkaus and H. A. Oberman. Leiden, 1974, pp. 294–306.

Stayer, J. M. 'Luther studies and Reformation studies'. *Canadian Journal of History*, 17 (1982), pp. 499–505.

Steinmetz, D. C. 'Libertas Christiana: studies in the theology of John Pupper of Goch'. *HTR*, 65 (1972), pp. 191–230.

Misericordia Dei: The Theology of Johannes von Staupitz in its Late Medieval Setting. Leiden, 1968.

Stenton, D. M. *The English Women in History*. London, 1957.

Stone, L. *The Family, Sex and Marriage in England, 1500–1800*. London, 1979.

'The massacre of the innocents'. *New York Review of Books*, 14 November 1974, pp. 25–31.

Strauss, G. 'Reformation and pedagogy: educational thought and practice in the Lutheran Reformation'. In *The Pursuit of Holiness in Late Medieval and Renaissance Religion*. Ed. C. Trinkaus and H. A. Oberman. Leiden, 1974, pp. 272–93.

Sweet, J. 'Some thirteenth-century sermons and their authors'. *JEH*, 4 (1953), pp. 27–36.

Tavard, G. H. *Women in Christian Tradition*. Notre Dame, Indiana, 1973.

Tentler, T. N. *Sin and Confession on the Eve of the Reformation*. Princeton, 1977.

'The Summa for confessors as an instrument of social control'. In *The Pursuit of Holiness in Late Medieval and Renaissance Religion*. Ed. C. Trinkaus and H. A. Oberman. Leiden, 1974, pp. 103–30.

Thomas, A. *Gerson et l'éducation des deux dauphins de France*. Paris, 1930.

Thomas, K. 'The double standard'. *Journal of the History of Ideas*, 20 (1959), pp. 195–216.

Tibber, P. *The Origins of the Scholastic Sermon, c. 1130–c. 1210*. D.Phil. dissertation, Oxford, 1983.

Toussaert, J. *Le Sentiment religieux en Flandre à la fin du moyen âge*. Paris, 1963.

Trapp, D. 'Augustinian theology of the fourteenth century'. *Augustiniana*, 6 (1956), pp. 146–274.

Trexler, R. C. 'Ritual in Florence: adolescence and salvation in the Renaissance'. In *The Pursuit of Holiness in Late Medieval and Renaissance Religion*. Ed. C. Trinkaus and H. A. Oberman. Leiden, 1974, pp. 200–64.

Trinkaus, C. and H. A. Oberman. *The Pursuit of Holiness in Late Medieval and*

Renaissance Religion: Papers from the University of Michigan Conference. Leiden, 1974.

Utley, F. L. *The Crooked Rib.* Columbus, Ohio, 1944.

Vansteenberghe, E. *Autour de la docte ignorance: une controverse sur la théologie mystique au XVe siècle.* Münster, 1915.

Vereecke, L. 'Mariage et sexualité au déclin du moyen âge'. *La Vie spirituelle,* Supplément, 57 (1961), pp. 199–225.

Verger, J. 'The University of Paris at the end of the hundred years war'. In *Universities in Politics.* Ed. J. W. Baldwin and R. A. Goldthwaite. Maryland, 1972, pp. 47–78.

Vogel, C. *Le Pécheur et la pénitence au moyen âge.* Paris, 1969.

Walter, J. and K. Wrightson. 'Dearth and the social order in early modern England'. *Past and Present,* 71 (1976), pp. 22–44.

Ward, C. F. *The Epistle on the Romance of the Rose and Other Documents in the Debate.* Chicago, 1911.

Wayman, D. G. 'The Chancellor and Jeanne d'Arc'. *Franciscan Studies,* 17 (1957), pp. 2–35.

Welter, J. T. *L'Exemplum dans la littérature religieuse et didactique du moyen âge.* Paris, 1927.

Wenzel, S. 'Poets, preachers and the plight of literary critics'. *Speculum,* 60 (1985), *pp.* 343–63.

'The seven deadly sins: some problems of research'. *Speculum,* 43 (1968), pp. 1–22.

Carolina, 1967.

Wilmar, A. *Auteurs spirituels et textes dévots du moyen âge latin.* Paris, 1932.

Willot, A. *Educateurs chrétiens à travers de l'histoire: Dimensions spirituelles de l'éducation.* Paris, 1969.

Wirth, J. *Luther: Etude d'histoire religieuse.* Geneva, 1981.

INDEX

Abelard, Peter, 59, 64, 230, 329 n. 141
absolution, 59, 62–3, 88, 254
acedia (*see also* sloth), 117, 124, 144–5,
  147–8, 302 n. 90
active life, 46, 76–7, 188–9, 191
Adam: capabilities of, after the fall,
  99–101; faculties of, before the fall, 96–7;
  and original sin, 29, 87, 92, 97–9, 127,
  160, 220
adolescents, 222, 239, 241, 251, 333 n. 233,
  336 n 299
adultery, 72, 155, 218, 221
Aegidius Romanus, 42, 250
affective powers, 171, 175, 176, 181, 194–6,
  200–1
Ailly, Pierre d': on blasphemy and flattery,
  159, 306 n. 270; career of, 4, 5, 8,
  260 n. 14; on ecclesiastical reform, 53,
  253, 275 n. 107, 277 nn. 142, 148; on the
  fall, 99, 220; on God, 84, 86; 87–9, 253,
  286 n. 45; on grace, 105, 291 n. 179;
  mystical works of, 309 n. 8; and
  nominalism, 81, 82, 285 n. 25; on
  political order, 164, 307 nn. 293, 299;
  sermon style of, 11, 26, 27, 32–3,
  266 n. 102, 267 n. 108, 268 nn. 137, 140,
  269 nn. 156, 157, 166
Alain de Lille, 21, 235, 330 n. 166
Albert the Great, 82, 117, 230
Alberti, Leon Battista, 325–6 n. 68,
  327 n. 101, 332 n. 207
Alcock, Simon, 14
Alexander V, Pope, 8, 74, 75
Amaury of Bène, 178, 202, 203
Ampe, A., 314–15 n. 92, 320 n. 188
Anabaptists, 252
angels, 87, 89, 91, 92, 121; fallen, 92–3, 96;
  guardian, 45, 243, 246, 249, 254;
  hierarchy of, 39–40, 41
Angelus de Clavasio (*Angelica*): on
  absolution and satisfaction, 68; on
  confession, 58, 279 n. 176, 280 n. 218,
  281 nn. 227, 231; on contrition, 60, 61,
  279 n. 181; on sins, 235, 297 n. 64,
  299 nn. 114, 116, 300 n. 133, 302 n. 180,
  304 n. 239, 331 n. 197

anger, 93, 118, 120, 134–7, 168, 228
Anselm, 6, 97, 98, 244, 333 n. 228
antinomianism, 203, 204, 223
Antoninus of Florence, 299 n. 104,
  306 n. 282; on contrition, 60, 61,
  279 n. 181; on magnanimity, 132; on
  pusillanimity, 69; on sin, 72, 120, 124,
  125, 278 n. 153, 280 n. 205, 296 n. 39,
  297 n. 64, 300 n. 140, anger, 300 n. 133,
  avarice, 141, 142, 147, 301 n. 150,
  302 n. 173, curiosity, 306 n. 274, envy,
  133, 299 n. 114, lust, 152, 304 nn. 238,
  239, 331 nn. 196, 197, pride, 127,
  297 n. 73, vainglory, 298 n. 85; reliance
  on Aristotle, 121; on women, 217,
  324 n. 35
apostles, 41, 44, 48, 88
Aquinas, Thomas, 6, 50, 117, 253,
  263 n. 36; on confession, 278 n. 153,
  280 n. 218, 281 n. 220; on contemplation,
  171, 176, 309 n. 3, 310 n. 19; on
  contrition, 59, 60, 61; on ecclesiastical
  hierarchy, 41, 46, 47, 49, 75, 76,
  271 n. 20, 272 nn. 32, 34, 274 n. 78,
  275 n. 97, 283 n. 286; on the fall and
  original sin, 96, 97, 98, 100; on God, 85,
  86, 87, 89, 90, 288 n. 99; on grace, 106,
  107–8, 110, 292–3 n. 221, 293 n. 229; on
  marriage and coitus, 227, 230–2, 235,
  236, 328 nn. 123, 140, 330 n. 177,
  331 nn. 196, 197; on monarchy,
  306 n. 288; on predestination, 111–12; on
  sacraments, 59, 277 n. 138, 279 n. 175,
  291 n. 166; on sin, 121, 131–2,
  280 n. 205, 296 n. 39, 297 n. 64, *acedia*,
  302 n. 180, anger, 299 n. 125, 300 n. 133,
  avarice, 141, 143, 301 nn. 145, 151, 162,
  164, 302 n. 173, envy, 299 nn. 114, 116,
  gluttony, 300 n. 143, lust, 152,
  303 n. 216, 304 nn. 217, 228, pride,
  297 n. 73, vainglory, 298 n. 85; on
  women, 211, 212, 215, 218, 220,
  326 n. 81
'Aquinas'-tract, 13–14, 15, 19, 34,
  264 n. 55, 265 n. 73
Ariès, P., 239, 241, 244, 249, 332 n. 219

351

DATE DUE

HIGHSMITH 45-220